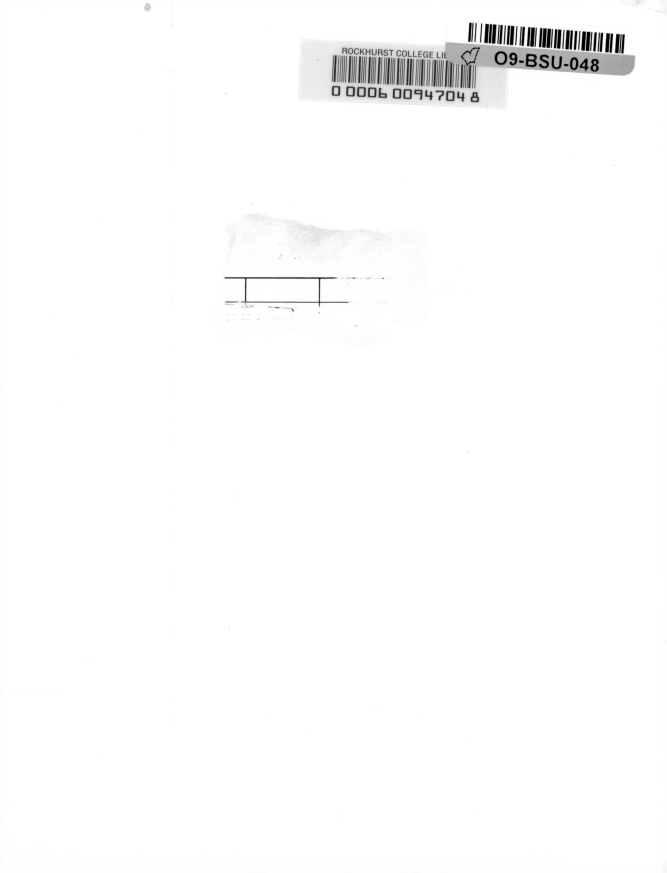

Third Edition

Strategic Advertising Campaigns

CRAIN

Third Edition

Strategic Advertising Campaigns

Don E. Schultz
Northwestern University

NTC Business Books
a division of *NTC Publishing Group* • Lincolnwood, Illinois USA

Published by NTC Business Books, a division of NTC Publishing Group,
4255 W. Touhy Avenue, Lincolnwood (Chicago), Illinois 60646-1975 U.S.A.
© 1990 by Don E. Schultz.
Library of Congress Catalog Card Number: 89-60185
Manufactured in the United States of America.

0 1 2 3 4 5 6 7 8 9 AG 9 8 7 6 5 4 3 2 1

Contents

Preface

Dramatic changes have occurred in the advertising business, advertising planning, and advertising thinking in the past five or so years. Overall the advertising business simply isn't what it was when the first edition of this text was conceived and written. Mergers and acquisitions, globalization, the development of new media systems and the decline of existing ones, and the need for integrated marketing communications have changed how we think about, plan, and execute advertising campaigns today. No doubt, there will be more changes in the future.

Part of the challenge in revising this text has been to reorient its basic planning approach from a unidimensional advertising concept to one that includes the new and growing areas of sales promotion, direct marketing, and public relations. The integration of new concepts, new methods, and new thinking, with those we know to be basic to the advertising business has been another part of the challenge. We hope you will agree that we have met the challenges well in this third edition of *Strategic Advertising Campaigns*.

Many thanks go to the people who helped make this new edition possible. First, to the students in the Advertising Division of the Medill School of Journalism at Northwestern University with whom all the concepts in this book have been tested and proven. Their willingness to listen, try, and then comment on these ideas and others has given direction to this book. Thanks should also go to the panel of advertising professors who reviewed the second edition and made helpful suggestions on the revision. Thanks also to the faculty and staff of Medill for their support and encouragement during the writing process. Thanks to Bill Brown and Ron Hoff for their excellent contributions in media and presentations. Most of all, though, thanks to Beth Barnes, presently a Ph.D. student at Northwestern, who will soon become one of the best advertising teachers in the country. Beth guided, directed, typed, chided, encouraged, and kept the process going over the too many months it took to develop this revision. I've learned as much from her as, I hope, she has from me.

So, as Ron Hoff would say, "Here's what we have done. What do you think of it?"

Introduction
Advertising and the Changing Marketplace

For the last fifty years or so, mass market consumer advertising has dominated the media and the marketplace. As national media systems were developed in the 1930s, 1940s, and 1950s, advertisers quickly took advantage of the opportunities. In some cases, media was developed not just to provide communication to consumers but simply to serve as an advertising delivery system. From the 1940s until the late 1970s, general advertising was king—the major way many marketers promoted their products and services.

Today, the marketplace in the United States is vastly different. Dramatic changes have occurred in the U.S. economy. Slow to no growth is the rule. Competition is global rather than domestic. The consumer base continues to change and evolve. Women have entered the workforce in massive numbers. Time is now a more precious commodity for many two-income families: "Baby boomers" are reaching middle age. In response to changing consumer needs and wants, the media have fragmented, broken into more and more specialized, highly targeted systems, which deliver much smaller but more closely knit groups of consumers. Concentration and consolidation in the retail area have switched marketplace power from the national manufacturer and marketer to the local chain store or mass merchandiser. In short, we have had a major marketplace revolution in the past ten years. And, that revolution, in turn, has had a dramatic impact on advertisers; the form that advertising is now taking; how consumers respond to advertising; and, most particularly, how advertising must now be planned and implemented.

THE KEY TO THE 1990s IS INTEGRATED MARKETING COMMUNICATIONS

As the marketplace has changed, it has become more and more evident to advertising and marketing managers that the key to successful product promotion in this rapidly diffusing marketplace is through integrated marketing communications. That simply means that each marketer, each advertiser, each brand, must have one clear, concise, easily understandable, and, most of all, competitive sales message to deliver to consumers. Today, advertising, public relations, sales promotion, direct marketing, packaging, personal selling, and even employee communications must be thought of as a single communications system. Each element must dovetail with the others. Each message must support the others being distributed. Each impression the consumer receives must fit with what he or she already knows or believes about the brand, the marketer, and the organization behind it.

That's a unique situation for many marketers and particularly for many advertising planners. For years, advertising has been the major tool used by marketers to build brand franchises and brand impressions. Today, a combination of promotion elements is used—advertising is only one of the many forms of communication available.

Although the need for marketing communications integration may be new, in many cases, the responsibility for orchestrating the many available communication elements will still fall on the shoulders of the advertising planner. The reason: Advertising is, for the most part, the personification of the brand and the marketer to the consumer. Because there may not be dramatic product features or benefits that will differentiate one brand from another, the advertising and the images, concepts and ideas, associated with the brand may well be the key thing which a consumer uses in making a brand choice. Advertising, as the key image-building technique, is, in general, the guiding force in the development of integrated marketing communications programs. In other words, advertising establishes the image and all other forms of communication must or should support and enhance that idea. Thus, the advertising planner is still the key player in most brand marketing situations. As the key player, the advertising planner must look beyond the advertising and envision how the public relations specialists, the sales promotion managers, the direct marketing experts, and even the sales force, can play off and support the image that is being created for the brand.

AN ADVERTISING PLAN IS MORE VITAL THAN EVER

In the first two editions of this text, we developed the premise that advertising, to succeed, must be based on a well-conceived, well-documented plan. There is little question that the advertisers, who, over the years, have seen the most reward from their advertising investment, have been those who have developed and followed a clearly designed advertising program. Advertising people in successful marketing organizations know why they are advertising and have expectations of the results they will achieve. They know to whom they are advertising, who their advertising prospects are, where they are located, their life-styles, their media usage, and so on. In short, successful advertisers use their advertising investment as a planned, business-building technique designed to build the brand or the company over time. They don't use it as a one-shot, scattergun approach to try and solve a short-term volume or distribution problem.

Successful advertisers carefully integrate their advertising into the overall promotional plan for the product or service. They develop an integrated marketing communications plan in which advertising meshes with sales promotion, public relations, direct marketing, product literature and brochures, in short, any form of persuasive communication which might influence the consumer in favor of the product or service. All these communication efforts are then carefully coordinated and integrated into the overall sales and marketing mix of the organization. Without this planning and integration, advertising, like any other business activity, cannot provide the organization with the necessary return on investment so vitally important in today's equity-driven marketplace.

ADVERTISING: A SALES MESSAGE FOR THE PRODUCT

One of the major problems we have seen develop in advertising over the past few years is the drive for so-called creativity. Advertising people, in their zeal to develop new and innovative approaches, seem to have lost sight of the true purpose of advertising: to encourage someone to make a purchase. Instead, some advertising people have decided that anything that is dramatically different from traditional approaches, that uses new or unusual camera angles, or type styles, or computer animation is, by definition, "creative." It seems that some advertising creative persons have decided that the purpose of advertising is not to sell but to entertain, and some have even said so publicly. David Ogilvy, one of the premier advertising people of this century, in an issue of *Forbes* magazine, has called this problem the "disease of entertainment." He warns that advertising is not meant just to get attention or to entertain; its purpose is to persuade someone to make a purchase, to sway his or her intention, to convince her or him to buy or try. As usual, Ogilvy couldn't be more right for today's confused and confusing marketplace.

The most persistent flaw we have seen in current advertising is the mistaken view some advertising people hold that advertising is separate and independent of the overall marketing efforts of the organization. They seem to look at advertising as somehow being "different" or "unique" or in a world of its own, divorced from the overall selling effort. In truth, however, advertising people are or should be no different from the salesperson on the floor of the retail store, or in the business office of an industrial company, or making a presentation in the office of a service company.

They are simply trying to make a sale—to convince someone to try or buy or continue using or use more of a particular product or service. The difference is that the sales presentation is being made through some form of media, not in person.

ADVERTISING: A SURROGATE FOR FACE-TO-FACE SELLING

The true purpose of advertising, any advertising, is simply to deliver a sales message for the product or service, that is, to attempt to persuade or convince the receiver of the advertising message of the value or difference or superiority of the product or service. The difference is that the salesperson (read here: *advertising* person) is delivering his or her sales message to a large number of unseen customers and prospects. In truth, most marketing executives know that face-to-face selling is far more effective than advertising—and far more costly. Thus, the only reason they use advertising rather than face-to-face selling is the efficiency of advertising. Advertising has the ability to deliver the same sales message to thousands or perhaps millions of prospects at a fraction of the cost and a corresponding savings in time as does person-to-person selling.

In a nation of 240 million people, in a land mass that covers half a continent, face-to-face selling for widely distributed and widely used consumer products isn't financially practical or physically possible. The same is becoming increasingly true of products sold business to business. The number of prospects is large, locations are widespread, the persons who influence the purchasing decision are often unknown. Therefore, advertising is used to deliver sales messages in places a salesperson cannot penetrate on a regular basis.

Most companies use advertising as a surrogate for a personal sales call. The marketer talks to the prospects through the media but the intended effect is the same as a direct sales call. One of the best examples of this approach to advertising is a television comercial developed by the Quaker Oats Company for its Aunt Jemima Pancake Mix a few years ago. Although we're sure Quaker and its advertising agency didn't have the development of an advertising teaching tool in mind when they conceived the commercial, in only thirty seconds it sums up what advertising is all about. Take a look at Exhibit I–1. The commercial shows a salesperson going door to door attempting to sell Aunt Jemima Pancake Mix—delivering sales messages for the product. That's a demonstration of what advertising is all about. That's Advertising Lesson 1. Advertising Lesson 2 is the message that the salesperson is delivering. At the first three doors, he tries to sell the attributes of the product, that is, buttermilk, the lightness of the product, and so on. In each case he fails. It's not until the fourth house that he starts to talk about the true benefit of the product, good tasting pancakes. He further demonstrates that benefit just as a good salesperson should. Adver-

Exhibit I-1 Sound Advertising: A Commercial for Aunt Jemima

1. (Natural sfx)

2. MAN: Good morning ma'am.

3. This is our Aunt Jemima Buttermilk Complete pancake mix.

4. (Sfx: slam!)

5. Ma'am, our Aunt Jemima Buttermilk Complete...

6. ...has more buttermilk.

7. Makes lighter pancakes.

8. This has more buttermilk than any other mix.

9. Any other. (Sfx: slam!)

10. How do I get to these people? I know.

11. (Sfx: tap, tap) MAN: You can't deny...

12. ...it's a great pancake. (Sfx: slam!)

13. (Natural sfx)

14. WOMAN: What kind of pancake is that?

15. (Anncr VO) Aunt Jemima Buttermilk Complete. You can't deny it's a great pancake.

SOURCE: Courtesy of Quaker Oats Company.

tising Lesson 2 is that consumers buy product benefits, not product attributes. These two lessons will be reinforced again and again in this book.

THE ADVERTISING CAMPAIGN

The most common method of planning, executing, and integrating advertising into the organization's overall sales and marketing effort is through the advertising campaign. The campaign approach, in the military sense of the word, means that the advertiser sets a measurable goal or objective for the advertising effort. In most military operations, a single thrust or maneuver will most likely not achieve the objective. Thus, several activities or efforts are needed. The same is true in advertising. Most consumers will not jump from their easy chair, rush to the store, and make a purchase based on every advertisement or commercial they see. Thus, we think of advertising in terms of multiple exposures, multiple tactics, multiple messages, perhaps even multiple offers to achieve our goal of getting some form of sales response.

As a result of this campaign approach, the advertising planner, having set the advertising goal, develops the necessary strategies to achieve the goal. He or she then prepares implementations of those strategies which will assure that the advertising messages are effectively and efficiently delivered to the selected audience. And, to make sure that the campaign works, the planner must be sure that his or her efforts mesh with all the other marketing communications activities being used by the company to influence customers and prospects. That's what is meant by integrated marketing communications programs.

This book is about only one part of the integrated marketing communications programs which are necessary for success in today's marketplace—advertising and the advertising campaign. On the following pages, we'll discuss in detail how to set advertising objectives, develop advertising strategies, and execute those strategies successfully in the marketplace. Although the emphasis of this text and the examples used are generally on consumer package goods, the same campaign approaches have worked and will continue to work, for business-to-business, services, retailers, and wholesalers, in short, any company that wishes to deliver sales messages to their customers and prospects through some form of media.

WHAT IS AN ADVERTISING CAMPAIGN?

In its simplest form, most advertising campaigns consist of

- Identification of consumer wants and needs
- Development of the right sales message to show how the product or service fills or meets those needs
- Delivery of the sales messages to the identified prospects at the proper time and place and at the most efficient cost

- Measurement of the effect or impact of the advertising sales message on the targeted prospects
- Integration of the advertising sales message with other forms of marketing communications which the company may be using in support of the product or service

Advertising itself is a rather simple business—the development and delivery of sales messages about products and services to customers and prospects. It becomes complex, however, when you start to ask such questions as: Who is the right prospect? What is the right message? What is the right timing? Which placement of the ad will have the most impact? What is a reasonable cost? And, that's what this text is designed to help you do. Answer these and numerous other questions that arise when you start to develop an advertising campaign.

THE FIRST STEP

To develop a sound advertising campaign, and integrate it not only with the other communication efforts of the company, but also with the overall marketing efforts of the organization, you must understand the organization that produces the product or service; the products or service that are produced, and the overall sales efforts. You must also have some idea of the cost and profitability of the product and the distribution system that gets it to customers. In other words, you must understand the total marketing system of which your advertising is only one part.

Understanding marketing and the marketing activities that support the product or service for which this advertising campaign is being developed is the first step. Therefore, we start with a review of the marketing organization, the structure of marketing, and the various forms of selling activities available to a marketer.

Third Edition

Strategic Advertising Campaigns

1

Marketing, the Marketing Plan, and Advertising

WHAT IS MARKETING?

In the 1980s, marketing became the ultimate "buzz word" in the business community. Today, we hear the phrase "let's market this product" or "let's market that service." It seems "marketing" is used for everything from health services to political candidates to rock 'n' roll CDs. Although the concepts and possibly even the techniques of each of these marketing programs may be the same, it's obvious that the term *marketing* is being used by different people to mean different things. So, our first question is just what is "marketing"?

There are literally scores of definitions of marketing. According to the official definition of the American Marketing Association:

> Marketing is the process of planning and executing the conception, pricing, promotion, and distribution of ideas, goods, and services to create exchanges that satisfy individual and organizational objectives.[1]

Philip Kotler, a Northwestern University marketing professor, has simplified and at the same time expanded the concept with this definition:

> Marketing is a social and managerial process by which individuals and groups obtain what they need and want through creating and exchanging products and value with others.[2]

Kotler's view is much more attuned to the managerial process and the idea of exchange that more closely relates to advertising. Therefore, we'll use it as the basis for our understanding of marketing as it is used in the development of an advertising campaign.

---

[1]"AMA Board Approves New Marketing Definition," *Marketing News* (March 1, 1985):1.
[2]Philip Kotler, *Marketing Management,* 6th ed. (Englewood Cliffs, N.J.: Prentice-Hall, 1988):3. Copyright 1983 by Prentice-Hall. All rights reserved. Reprinted by permission.

THE ORIGINS OF MARKETING

The actual process of marketing is relatively simple. Basically, it involves some form of exchange of things of value among members of a society. The exchange might be in the form of money for clothing, for example. Or, it might be trading a basket of peaches for a bushel of wheat. Or, exchanging an hour of one's time to repair a friend's broken window for assistance in repairing one's washing machine. Marketing, in its simplest terms, is an exchange in which both parties profit.

It's obvious there have been marketing activities occurring, with exchange as a base, almost as long as there have been people. Some persons had somethings that were needed or wanted by others. Therefore, they "marketed" to one another. As societies became increasingly complex, however, people moved from individual marketing activities to the collective production and distribution of goods and services. To start and maintain these new organizations, capital was needed. So, the idea of investment and return on investment was born. To support an investment, a profit had to be made. Thus, the exchange process evolved from the idea of a simple trade for equal value, to that of exchange with profit for the many parties involved.

As these social and production organizations expanded, they began to specialize; soon only certain parts or elements of the total product were produced. Rather than marketing these parts or elements directly to the ultimate consumer, they were sold to others who completed or distributed the final product or service. In this form of the mass production system, the concept of production efficiency sprang up. Companies and organizations that manufactured only parts of products or provided only peripheral services to the marketplace became much more interested in generating their profits from the efficient production of their parts or elements than in actually filling the needs and wants of consumers or even their customers. Therefore, many companies became "production oriented," that is, they became more involved in producing items or elements efficiently and profitably than in finding or identifying what their customers or prospects really wanted or needed. This production-efficiency system continued to grow until the early part of this century. At that point, some farsighted individuals and companies started to practice what they called the "marketing concept," and the emphasis on marketing was reintroduced.

Quite simply, the marketing concept that was identified and codified in the middle part of this century is just a return to the basics of the exchange system of centuries ago. It involves determining what customers or prospects might want or need and then developing and providing the satisfaction of those needs or wants through the production of goods and services at a profit. It isn't much different from the old marketplace, when the carpenter or potter or butcher made things to order for people who passed by. Today, we've adapted our activities to the new marketing environment. Obviously, there are many more customers, many more products, many more marketplaces. Yet, the concepts are still the same. Marketing works when the marketer learns what the customer wants or needs and then provides it. It doesn't work as well when the organization concentrates its efforts on what it can manufacture or distribute efficiently or profitably, with little regard for the consumer.

The marketing organization should always be oriented to the consumer or user of the final product. Although many more production- than marketing-oriented organizations actually exist in our economy, it is from the point of view of the marketing-oriented organization that this text is written.

This marketing-oriented view of advertising becomes even more important when one considers the massive changes that have occurred in the U.S. marketplace in the past few decades. Today, we live in an age of surplus. There are too many products. Too many stores. Too many brands. All compete for the same consumers in a slow-growth economic system. Our marketplace has become international and global rather than just domestic. There is an increasing emphasis by management on short-term programs and activities to obtain short-term rewards to satisfy the equity market. Thus, there is more emphasis on price cutting and sales promotion to move products rather than on advertising to build long-term brand franchises. In short, the marketplace has changed, and changed dramatically. To continue to be effective, advertising and advertising planning must change to meet these new marketing challenges. Today, well-planned, well-executed advertising campaigns, developed in support of sound, marketing-oriented programs, are needed more than ever.

MARKETING IN THE ORGANIZATION

In spite of the seemingly obvious advantages of the marketing concept, that is, determining and then filling customer or prospect needs or wants, not all organizations embrace this approach. Kotler has identified five competing concepts of marketing activity in today's business organizations. It is important for an advertising planner to know these concepts because they have a great deal to do with how advertising can be developed and the approach which can be taken in planning the campaign. According to Kotler:

1. The production concept holds that consumers will favor those products that are widely available and low in cost. Manager of production-oriented organizations concentrate on achieving high production efficiency and wide distribution coverage.
2. The product concept holds that consumers will favor those products that offer the most quality, performance, and features. Managers in

these product-oriented organizations focus their energy on making good products and improving them over time.

3. The selling concept holds that consumers, if left alone, will ordinarily not buy enough of the organization's products. The organization must therefore undertake an aggressive selling and promotion effort.

4. The marketing concept holds that the key to achieving organizational goals consists in determining the needs and wants of target markets and delivering the desired satisfactions more effectively and efficiently than competitors.

5. The societal marketing concept holds that the organization's task is to determine the needs, wants, and interests of target markets and to deliver the desired satisfactions more effectively and efficiently than competitors in a way that preserves or enhances the consumer's and the society's well-being.[3]

It is clear that these five different views about how the organization should "market" its products have a dramatic impact on the marketing and advertising methods, approaches, and even the style each organization chooses to fit its needs in the marketplace—in how each will go about "marketing" their product or service. From the view of the advertising planner, the way the organization views their marketing approach will have much to do with the type of advertising program that can or should be developed and that might be used. For example, it is unlikely a production-oriented company will be very interested in an advertising approach that stresses the company's commitment to social causes, such as the Olympics or charitable organizations.

No matter what orientation or view of marketing the organization has, in the broadest sense, each develops some form of marketing system. Although these marketing systems vary widely according to the type of organization employing them, all have four basic elements which they use to create some form of exchange. These elements are

1. A *product* or service of some sort to be offered to customers and prospects

2. A *price* at which the product or service is offered

3. A *place* or distribution system through which the product or service is made available to customers or prospects

4. Some form of *promotion* or communication by means of which prospects or customers are made aware of the product or service's availability

These are often called the "four Ps" of marketing.

The actual task of marketing consists of the mixing and refining of these various elements by the firm's management to optimize the profitable ex-

---

[3]Kotler, *Marketing Management*, 6th ed.: 13–17. Copyright 1983 by Prentice-Hall. All rights reserved. Reprinted by permission.

change of its products or services in the marketplace. In economic terms, firms in our society take scarce resources, in the form of capital, labor, and raw materials, then process or convert them into products or services that they exchange in the marketplace, it is hoped, at a profit.

This so-called marketing mix of these four basic elements, product, price, place, and promotion, is what marketing managers adapt and/or refine to meet the needs of their organization, the consumer, and the marketplace. For example, the rapidly changing personal computer market has seen several adjustments in the marketing mix in the past few years. Initially, when personal computers were first introduced, there was great emphasis on the product. As the product was improved and refined, emphasis moved to the distribution systems, that is, making PCs widely available through distributors and retailers. As competition increased, emphasis shifted to price and price promotion. Today, because products are essentially at parity and distribution has been developed, we see a mix of price, promotion, and advertising being used. As technological advances continue, we may well see a return to emphasis on the computer product in the next few years. In all areas, the marketing manager is the key player in the identification and implementation of the marketing mix for the product or service.

As important as the four Ps are to marketing success, they are not the only elements involved today. Present marketing managers also must deal with the "four Cs." These elements are becoming increasingly important in today's product and marketing mix. They are

1. The *consumer.* With the fragmentation of the marketplace, there must be much more emphasis on identifying and selecting the right consumer for any marketing program.
2. *Cost* is a big factor in any marketing plan—cost of the product or service compared to competition; cost of the marketing program to be implemented; cost of distribution; and so on.
3. *Competition.* In many cases, the marketing mix is adjusted or adapted to moves competitors make. No marketing organization exists within a vacuum. Marketing plans must be developed with competitors' actions and reactions in mind.
4. *Channels* are the various forms of distribution, such as retailers, wholesalers, distributors, and brokers, which may be used to take the product to the consumer. Today, as a result of the consolidation and concentration of the retail trade, more and more attention must be paid to how the channel members will accept and react to proposed marketing and promotion plans. This is in addition to the attention paid to the consumer's reaction.

We'll see more of the four Ps and the four Cs when we discuss the advertising campaign development process.

Because there are many customers, many firms, many products, and many markets, it quickly becomes evident that success for a product or service is unlikely to occur without some form of planning. The marketing planning process becomes even more vital when a firm's management realizes that its limited resources are in demand by other organizations in the economy and even within its own organization. The marketplace is wide, varied, and constantly shifting. The demand for a product or service is in a state of flux. And competitors are often offering the same or similar products or services in the marketplace. Without some sort of plan, management stands little chance of successfully marketing its products or services. The development of a plan or program usually involves a series of considerations, evaluations, and decisions by the management of the organization and commonly includes consideration of the four Ps and the four Cs. It's called the marketing process because it attempts to consolidate all the elements within the organization into a system that can successfully manufacture, distribute, and profitably sell the product or service the organization has or can make available.

PLANNING FOR MARKETING

In its broadest form, the marketing planning process is implemented through some form of strategic planning—in other words, the way in which the organization will use its resources to successfully bring a product or service to market. Exhibit 1–1 illustrates a common approach.

A brief review of this business strategic planning process will put the ultimate marketing plan into better perspective.

Exhibit 1–1   Strategic Planning Process

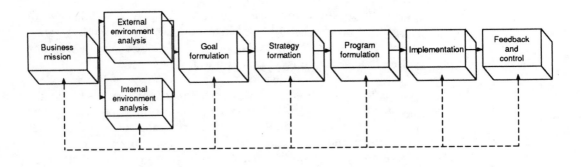

The Business Mission

The business mission is a statement of the goals and aspirations of the organization or unit. It defines the industry in which the organization will compete, identifies the target market it will serve, the geographic area it will cover, the technology it anticipates using, and the type of manufacturing and distribution system that it will use. In short, the business mission summarizes the what, why, and how the organization proposes to do in the marketplace.

Environmental Analysis

Two forms of environmental analysis are done. The first looks at the external environment in which the organization will compete. That environment includes macroenvironmental forces (such as the economy, demographic changes, political climate, legal system, and social norms) and the microenvironmental forces (such as customers, competitors, suppliers, and channel members) which will impact on the company.

In addition, a review of the internal environment must be made. This review includes such factors as the financial strengths of the company; the marketing capabilities, level, and quality of manufacturing facilities; and the management skills of the total organization.

In most cases, these external and internal environmental reviews take the form of lists of threats and opportunities that the organization faces or its significant strengths and weaknesses.

Organizational Goals

Specific goals can be determined for the organization using the mission statement and the environmental analyses. These goals, in general, take the form of a description of what the organization wants to achieve in any of several planning periods. Commonly, this description is a mix of financial, manufacturing, employee satisfaction, and market goals.

Generic Strategies

Once the unit's goals have been established, management then sets about determining strategies to accomplish those objectives. Porter has identified three generic strategies which apply to most organizations. (See Exhibit 1–2.) These three strategic alternatives are

1. Overall cost leadership. Become the lowest cost producer and distributor. Price below the competition. Achieve high market share.
2. Differentiation. Achieve superior performance in some important

Exhibit 1–2   Porter Strategies

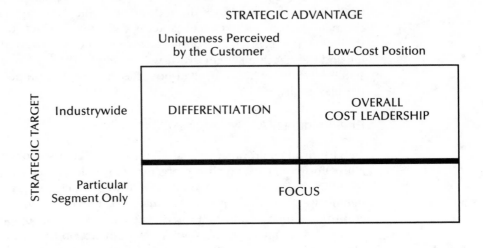

STRATEGIC ADVANTAGE

	Uniqueness Perceived by the Customer	Low-Cost Position
Industrywide	DIFFERENTIATION	OVERALL COST LEADERSHIP
Particular Segment Only	FOCUS	

STRATEGIC TARGET

SOURCE: Michael E. Porter, *Competitive Strategy: Techniques for Analyzing Industries and Competitors* (New York: Free Press, 1980):39.

consumer benefit area either through the product itself or through some form of marketing excellence.

3.   Focus. Identify and target some segment of the total market. Develop expertise, cost leadership, and/or a focused approach to serve that niche in the market.[4]

This basic business strategy which the organization has or is in the process of developing is the key element with which many advertising planners work. This strategy commonly determines the advertising approach that can be taken.

Marketing Programs

Specific marketing programs are then developed from the strategy or strategies that have been determined. These programs are generally the basis for an advertising campaign. For example, if the company's strategy focuses on developing a peanut butter that will appeal to children, then its program should include developing a product that children like, a package

---

[4]Summarized from Michael E. Porter, *Competitive Strategy: Techniques for Analyzing Industries and Competitors* (New York: Free Press, 1980): Chapter 2.

that will appeal to those children, and an advertising campaign designed to communicate the appeal of the product to that target group.

Implementation

Implementation is the form in which the program is applied. In the case of an advertising campaign for our peanut butter example, implementation might take the form of a television commercial, a comic print ad, or a package design that would appeal to children.

Feedback and Control

Feedback and control are the elements by which management evaluates and adjusts the overall business process. As the results of the program are obtained, adjustments are made. Of course, one of the most important elements of any strategic plan is control over the entire system to make sure it conforms to the original plan.

The actual marketing plan grows out of this strategic planning process.

PLANNING THE MARKETING

Although the strategic plan previously discussed guides the overall direction and efforts of the organization, a more specific program is usually needed to define and describe the marketing actions that are to be taken. The development of that plan comes about through the marketing management process illustrated in Exhibit 1–3.

Exhibit 1–3   Marketing Management Process

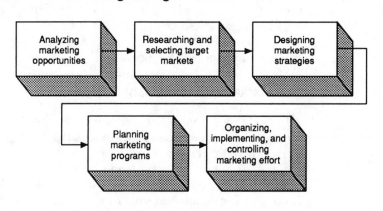

SOURCE: Philip Kotler, *Marketing Management,* 6th ed.:67.

The first step (1) in the market planning process involves analyzing marketing opportunities. In many instances, this analysis comes directly out of the strategic planning process. In other cases, it might consist of evaluating the potential of either existing or new markets to determine their potential value to the organization. The second step (2) is the researching and selecting of target markets for the product or service; that is, identifying and evaluating the persons who are currently buying or using or who are the most likely to want or need the product or service. Today, because of the increasing fragmentation of the mass market, many marketing managers consider this step to be the key element in their marketing plan. The third step (3) is to design marketing strategies to reach and influence the selected target market. The fourth (4) is the actual planning of the marketing programs. The fifth and last step (5) is the organization, implementation, and control of the marketing effort.

For most larger companies, the first three steps in the marketing process are developed and finalized by marketing managers operating within the organization. As a result, the advertising planner is often not involved in the marketing planning process until the fourth or fifth step. In smaller organizations, however, the advertising planner may be directly involved and contribute to all stages of the marketing planning process. We'll see more of how and where advertising fits in the process as we look at organizational structure of marketing organizations and advertising agencies.

MARKETING ELEMENTS OF PARTICULAR INTEREST TO THE ADVERTISING PLANNER

Depending on the organization, the organizational structure, and the importance of advertising in the marketing mix, the advertising planner may or may not be involved in determining specific marketing plans or actions. Whether involved or not, there are five areas of the marketing planning process that are of critical importance in the development of an advertising campaign. These key elements are briefly reviewed to provide background and understanding, even if the advertising planner is not involved in the entire marketing process.

The Marketing Environment Analysis

All marketing organizations operate within an environment that dictates what the firm can and cannot do. (Similarly, the environment also controls what can and cannot be done in an advertising campaign.) The environment exists at both the macro and micro levels. (See Exhibit 1–4.) At the macro level, the environment consists of all those elements, forces, situations, and restrictions external to the organization itself. These influence the type of products the organization may produce, the prices it may set for those products, the methods by which the products may be distributed, and the manner in which they may be promoted or advertised to prospective consumers. The macroenvironment generally consists of such elements as:

1. Social. These are the characteristics of the people within the society—their values, culture, social class, life-style, and goals. Given the importance of social and cultural values on advertising, these are key elements that the advertising planner must understand.
2. Natural. Natural elements encompass the physical situation in which the marketer operates, including such factors as natural resources, climate, terrain, pollution, and population density.

Exhibit 1–4   The Marketing Environment

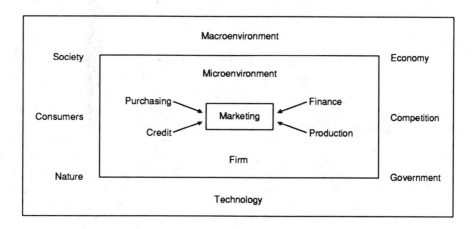

3. Economic. The economic system in which the marketing organization operates and how that system influences such things as potential growth rate, inflation, raw material availability, investment capital availability, and even interest rates, impinge on the firm and its ability to conduct marketing activities. The slow to no-growth economic rate of the U.S. in the late 1980s had a dramatic and lasting influence on how advertising was planned and used.
4. Government. Governments directly affect marketing activities as a result of the specific rules and regulations the marketer must conform to. In addition, government actions influence economic and societal conditions as well. The deregulation of major U.S. industries, such as banking, finance, and the airlines in the early to mid-1980s, had a dramatic impact not only on the amount of advertising the in-

dividual organizations used but also on the type and content of that advertising as well.

5. Technological. The increase in knowledge and ability and the application of new inventions or innovations can have either a stimulating or restraining effect on the marketing activities of the firm. These factors, of course, influence the need for and the value and impact of an advertising campaign.

6. Competitive. There may be many or few competitors depending on the economy, the type of product or service offered, the product category, and so on. In addition, there are both direct and indirect competitors for almost all products or services, as we will see later.

7. Consumer. The users or purchasers or prospective customers for the product or service have much to do with the overall marketing environment in which the organization operates. We've seen dramatic changes in consumers (two-career families, latchkey children, time as well as money pressures, etc.) in the past few decades, all of which have had an impact on how and why advertising campaigns are planned and implemented.

Most, if not all of these macro forces are totally outside the control of the marketing organization. They exist and must be considered and dealt with by the firm's managers as a vital part of any marketing activity. In addition, the macroenvironment for every firm is different. For example, although a company that develops and markets new computer measurement equipment systems and one that breeds race horses may exist side by side geographically, they have totally different macroenvironmental considerations when they start to develop their marketing programs. Nature and the physical environment have a great effect on race horses, but they have little or none on the development and marketing of computer measurement equipment. On the other hand, technology greatly affects computer equipment, but has little direct effect on the economic viability of race horses. Thus, we see that individual analyses of the macroenvironment are required to develop an effective marketing program.

The microenvironment, or the situation within the firm, also dictates the type and form of marketing actions that the organization can conduct. The microenvironment consists of such internal functions as finance, credit, production, and purchasing. The development, organization, and control the firm has over these internal functions greatly influence the final marketing activities the firm can develop and use. Although the marketer has much more control over the microenvironmental situations than over the macroenvironmental, these situations still dictate to a great extent what can and cannot be done in the firm's marketing program.

The environment in which the organization operates is one of the most basic considerations in the development of an overall marketing program.

In general, it dictates the selection and type of overall goals and objectives that management can set. It certainly influences marketing objectives and actions and, ultimately, the advertising program that can be developed and implemented.

Consumer or Business-to-Business Markets

Whether the organization has defined its potential market as consumers or business to business has a great deal to do with the type of marketing program that can or should be developed. The marketing mix for a company selling laundry detergent through supermarkets to housewives will differ greatly from that of a company that manufactures wheels and casters to sell to companies making office furniture. Obviously, the products are different, but so are the pricing structure; the type of distribution system; the forms and methods of selling; and, of most interest to us, the advertising campaign which might be employed. All of these marketing mix variables are influenced and determined by the buyer behavior or methods that potential purchasers use in evaluating and selecting products. These methods of evaluation vary dramatically between the consumer and the business-to-business market. (More on this in Chapter 3.)

Competition

The identification of competitors is another of the key elements in the marketing process. In a surplus marketplace, such as exists in the U.S. today, competitors often dictate the type, style, and even depth of marketing activities that the firm must undertake.

Generally, competitors can be viewed as being either direct or indirect. Direct competitors are those who market similar products in the same category to the same group of customers or prospects. For example, the marketing programs used by most Florida resort hotels are similar because they are in direct competition with each other for the consumer's vacation dollar. But, the marketers of fur coats in Chicago may well have dramatically different marketing programs, even though that Florida resort and the Chicago fur coat retailer are competing for the same disposable consumer dollar from the same consumer. Thus, the marketing manager must look not only at direct brand-to-brand competitors, but to indirect competitors as well; the funds for which they are competing may very well be the same.

Target Market Identification

One of the key decisions marketing managers must make is the selection of the group of consumers or prospects to whom the marketing program will be directed. In general, those initially targeted as prospects are current users of the product or category or class. Then, further information, such as demographic, psychographic, or geographic details on the selected group, may be added. This additional information helps to further clarify or identify the group to be targeted in marketing programs.

The most important aspect of target market selection is finding a group of people who are either not served or are underserved by products presently on the market. Of course, the target group must be sufficiently large initially or possess that potential to be expanded so that marketing of the brand to the group will provide a financially feasible and profitable use of the organization's limited resources.

Stage in the Product Life Cycle

Most marketing managers believe that most products in most categories go through a product life cycle, similar to that experienced by a human. That is, there is a birth or introduction stage, a growth stage, maturation, and then decline. That concept is illustrated in Exhibit 1–5.

Exhibit 1–5 Product Life Cycle

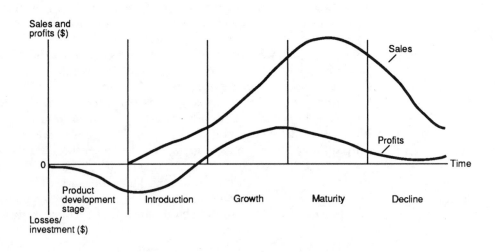

SOURCE: Philip Kotler, *Marketing Management,* 6th ed. Copyright 1983 by Prentice-Hall. All rights reserved. Reprinted by permission.

The location of the product in the product life cycle is believed to be of critical importance in the marketing process. For example, in the introductory stage, when there are few users, the goal of the marketing plan generally is to get more consumers to try the product. That goal, of course, entails using a specific set of marketing mix elements. Conversely, managers whose products are in the decline stage of the product life cycle should be more interested in keeping present customers than attempting to gain new ones. Therefore, they would use a different marketing mix. Knowing the position of the product in the life cycle determines, to a certain extent, how a marketing manager can organize and implement a marketing program.

In most instances, the goals and objectives of products in various stages of the life cycle can be summarized as:

1. Introduction. This is a period of slow sales growth while the product is being introduced. Marketing efforts are primarily designed to gain product exposure to, and trial by, prospects.
2. Growth. This is a period of rapid market acceptance of the product category. Many competitors enter. Marketing objectives, in general, are designed to increase trial and acceptance of the product and to differentiate it from other competitive brands.
3. Maturity. This is a period of slowdown in sales growth. Many competitors have entered the market. The primary goals of the marketing efforts are to hold present customers and defend against increased competitive efforts, generally of a price nature.
4. Decline. The product's sales and profits start to erode. Competitors withdraw from the market. Marketing expenditures are made to maintain or expand product usage and to hold on to present customers.[5]

As can be seen, the stage the product is at in the life cycle has much to do with the marketing program that can be developed. In each instance, the marketing plan developed directly influences what can be done with the advertising.

Marketing Mix

Earlier, we said the marketing organization had four broad elements that could be used to influence consumer purchases: the product, the price, the availability (distribution or place), and the promotional effort. In addition, the four Cs (consumers, channels, cost, and competition) play an increasingly important role in determining, planning, and selecting the proper marketing mix for the organization's products. It is the mix of these eight

---

[5]Summarized from Kotler, *Marketing Management,* 6th ed.: 350. Copyright 1983 by Prentice-Hall. All rights reserved. Reprinted by permission.

elements that truly determines the success or failure of the product in the marketplace. For example, an incorrectly priced product is not likely to succeed. Similarly, a sound product, properly priced and well promoted, will fail without sufficient or proper distribution. Furthermore, it is not likely that a marketer can succeed with a sound product, fair pricing, sound distribution, and even solid promotion if he does not pay attention to cost and competition. Thus, it is clear that a mix of the four Ps and the four Cs really determines the success of most marketing programs.

Finally, most marketers have to select between two broad strategic marketing mix alternatives for their product or service. In one, primary emphasis can be put on a mix of elements that will influence the members of the distribution channel, that is, the retailers or distributors or wholesalers. This approach is commonly called a "push" strategy because the marketing manager's primary objective is to "push" the product into the distribution channels and let the channel members move it on through the channel to the final consumer. This type of strategy is widely used by marketers of products whose consumers give a great deal of thought to the purchase, or products that require a demonstration or explanation by the sales force. In other words, when the retailer, distributor, wholesaler, or sales force is important in convincing the consumer to buy, then the marketing effort by the manufacturer is aimed at that group, assuming that they will have much to do with the final sale.

Alternatively, the "pull" strategy can be used. In this instance, the marketer advertises or promotes the product or service directly to the ultimate consumer. The assumption made by the marketing manager is that the consumer is capable of making the purchasing decision based on advertising or promotional information and does not need the product explained, demonstrated, or assembled by the retailer or sales force. Thus, the marketer assumes that his or her marketing efforts, commonly in the form of consumer advertising and sales promotion, will be strong enough to influence the ultimate consumer, with little or no help from those in the channels of distribution. In addition, in a "pull" strategy, the manufacturer assumes that these efforts will also be strong enough to influence the retailer or distributor to stock or carry the product in inventory, based on the demand created by the consumer promotion. This type of marketing strategy is widely used by package goods companies which sell their products through self-service food and drugstores and mass merchandisers.

Push and pull strategies are actually at the extremes of a marketing strategy continuum. In practice, most marketers' strategies contain elements of both push and pull. The individual marketer actually determines the exact mix which is or should be most effective for the particular product or service based on his or her understanding of the consumer. At the same time, the marketer determines how and in what way promotion, in general, and advertising, in particular, will be used to most effectively and efficiently move the product from the plant, through the distribution channels, to the ultimate consumer. Given the need for integrated marketing communications in the marketplace, we follow the rule that a mix of push and pull marketing activities are needed to maximize the marketing investment.

After all the decisions have been made, that is, after the strategic planning has been done, the macro- and microenvironments analyzed, the competition evaluated, the product or service located in the life cycle, the target market selected, and the marketing mix elements considered and coordinated, the marketing manager puts his or her thoughts, concepts, and plans into a formal document, the marketing plan. This is where all the elements are combined and coordinated. It's the "bible" by which marketing managers and advertising planners live, and from which most advertising decisions are derived.

THE MARKETING PLAN

Marketing plans can take many forms. One example of a marketing plan format, developed by the Association of National Advertisers for their members, is illustrated in Exhibit 1–6. A more extensive outline covering the background, planning, implementation, and controlling areas may use

- Company mission, scope, and goals
- Situation analysis
- Current marketing organization
- Marketing objectives
- Marketing strategies, policies, and procedures
- Marketing programs
- Schedules and assignments
- Personnel plan
- Budgets
- Pro forma profit and loss and balance sheets
- Controls and continuity

The basic structure and amount of detail of the marketing plan are determined by the management of the organization. For a small retail operation, a simple listing of the target market for the store, the general marketing objectives to be achieved, an outline of the marketing program, sales forecasts, and budgets may suffice. Because the retailer knows the details of the organization and what he or she hopes to achieve, the marketing plan can be very simple in some sections, but expanded to include more detail in others. For example, a very complete outline of the promotional calendar may be the key element in a retail plan. Other, more complex organizations may require such information as analysis, factual support, and financial justification for each section. Thus, although all marketing plans have some subjects in common, in general, they are developed to fit the needs of the organization and those who will use them.

Exhibit 1–6   Format for an Annual Marketing Plan

The annual marketing plan comes in many styles and types, with each organization typically adapting a rather basic format to meet its own particular situation and needs. The outline that follows was developed by F. Beaven Ennis for the Association of National Advertisers and is rather typical for a consumer products manufacturing company.

BRAND NAME   19__ Marketing Plan

I. Current Year Performance—How the brand has performed so far this year

II. Recommendations—Brand objective in units and sales and expenditures needed to achieve those sales

III. Profit and Loss Effect of the Recommendation—Summary of marketing effects over three-year period (last year, current year, projected year)

IV. Background
   A. Market
      1. Size—Unit sales, growth rate, and competition
      2. Consumer—Profile of consumers by geographic areas
      3. Pricing—Company and competitive pricing by unit size
      4. Competitive Spending—Media and promotional spending by six-month period
      5. Other—Any other helpful data
   B. Brand
      1. Product—Formulation, unique attributes, sizes/variety, and margins
      2. Manufacturing—Plant capacity, capital investment required, and any production/purchasing problems
      3. Product Research—Major studies relating to brand or its performance
      4. Market Research—All other pertinent research information
      5. Other—Any other helpful data

V. Opportunities and Problems
   A. Opportunities—Where sales are expected to be gained in coming year
   B. Problems—Factors that might jeopardize success of plan

VI. Strategies
   A. Marketing—Brand's basic objective and strategy planned to achieve it
   B. Spending—Investment for the coming year
   C. Copy—Brief review of advertising objectives, strategy, executions, and copy rotation plan
   D. Media—Brief review of media objectives, strategy, and comparison of sales volume to media expenditures
   E. Promotion—Brief review of objectives, strategy, and trade deals by area

VII. Tests/Research—What is planned for coming year and costs

SOURCE: Adapted and used with permission of Association of National Advertisers, Inc. Taken from F. Beaven Ennis, *Effective Marketing Management: Planning and Control Systems for Making Better and Faster Marketing Decisions* (New York: Association of National Advertisers, 1973): 1–32.

Typically, the marketing plan outlined in Exhibit 1–6 is supported by four basic financial and marketing exhibits. These are

1. The price and profit structure for the brand
2. The brand's current profit and loss statement
3. The proposed media allocation schedule
4. The proposed promotion spread sheet[6]

The most detailed part of the marketing plan usually includes those sections that describe the actual activities to be carried out to achieve the goals of the firm. These *marketing tactics* are the specific steps and programs that will be used during the life of the marketing plan and typically include sales, service, promotion, pricing, distribution, and marketing research activities. Because the implementation and coordination of these activities are crucial to the success of the overall marketing plan, they are spelled out in as much detail as is possible and practical.

Of greatest concern to the advertising campaign planner is the overall promotional plan, sometimes called the marketing communications section. This section details the specific plans, tactics, and activities that will be used in personal selling, advertising, sales promotion, and publicity, to support the sale of the product. Because advertising people are most concerned with these promotional activities, we'll look at them in greater detail in the next section.

THE PROMOTION PLAN

The Promotion Mix

The promotion plan of the marketing organization reflects how the marketing mix will rely on the promotion alternatives available. These alternatives usually include (a) personal selling, (b) advertising, (c) sales promotion, and (d) publicity and/or public relations. For each of these activities, the idea of communicating a sales message is key. For example, the salesperson delivers the message through personal contact; the advertising through various media forms; sales promotion most commonly at the point of purchase; and public relations and publicity through the delivery of information about the company or organization through news items that will help promote good feelings or understanding of what the company is trying to achieve or how it is serving its various publics. As can be seen, it is here that the coordination and integration of marketing communications becomes so important.

---

[6]F. Beaven Ennis, *Effective Marketing Management: Planning and Control Systems for Making Better and Faster Marketing Decisions* (New York: Association of National Advertisers, 1973): 32.

Both short- and long-term, marketing management can coordinate the various promotional elements, depending on the marketing goals to be achieved. In business-to-business marketing, for example, advertising, sales promotion, and public relations are used primarily to help presell or generate leads for the personal sales force. Because most industrial sales are made as a direct result of a presentation by a salesperson, the other elements are used to assist or support these personal selling situations. For consumer package goods, however, advertising is commonly the most important element in the promotion mix. The ultimate consumer is told the uses for, the benefits of, the location of, the pricing, and other important selling messages about the product, through advertising. Usually, little or no personal selling is involved in the sale of these products. In still other cases, sales promotion or publicity may well take the lead in the overall effort to generate sales. In many cases, particularly for widely available products, the most important decision a marketer can make is the correct allocation or mix of these various promotional elements.

THE NEED FOR INTEGRATED MARKETING COMMUNICATIONS PROGRAMS

In today's cluttered and confusing marketplace, the need for integrated marketing communications has never been greater. There are simply too many products, too many brands, and too many marketers for the consumer to keep straight or to understand, unless the image and benefits of the promoted product or service are clear and concise. The key in today's marketplace is to have one clear marketing program and one clear, concise promotion program in which all elements are coordinated and communicate the same message to the consumer, the retailer, and the wholesaler. Only through this coordination is it possible for the marketer to be heard and understood and have his or her messages acted upon.

In the past, the goals for the various promotional functions, such as personal selling, advertising, public relations, packaging, sales promotion, product literature and publicity, may have been set separately; that is, these may have been individual goals and communication objectives based on the plans of various functional managers. In some instances, the messages that these various promotion mix elements communicated were different; in other cases, they were in direct conflict. Given the cost of promotional communication today, such confusion is simply not allowable. All promotional and communication elements must be coordinated so that a central theme is developed and communicated to the target market. This coordination is the real responsibility of today's marketing, communication, and advertising managers.

In all cases, the basic theme for all promotional activities must come from the marketing plan that has been set for the brand. The advertising, the sales promotion, the public relations, the direct marketing, and even the sales materials and salesperson's kits must flow from that plan. The advertising planner must know the marketing plan as well as he or she knows the advertising recommendations for the advertising must fit, support, and add synergy to all the other promotional elements that are being used to support the brand.

THE ADVERTISING PLAN

In the development of an advertising campaign, the planner must first identify the specific advertising objectives that are to be achieved. Then, the available funds must be allocated in the best way to achieve those objectives. For example, a successful advertising campaign combines the proper sales message with the correct media allocation. This combination assures that all messages are presented to the target market. Likewise, the proper advertising media must be selected to optimize the results of those advertising messages. The formal development of this advertising combination and allocation process is the advertising plan.

The advertising plan is always an integral part of the overall marketing plan. Although it may be developed separately, it usually is a specific subsegment of the marketing plan. (See Chapter 4 for specific details on the development and implementation of the advertising plan.)

An advertising plan consists of the following general topic areas:

- Situation analysis
- Marketing goals
- Advertising recommendations
- Media recommendations
- Sales promotion recommendations (if not included in a separate plan)
- Direct marketing recommendations (if not included separately)
- Budget
- Evaluation methods

The development of the advertising plan marks the start of the actual advertising campaign development procedure. However, we cannot stress too greatly the importance of the analysis, development, and planning of the total marketing program which leads up to the development of the advertising plan. Unless the advertising specialist fully understands and incorporates all the previously developed marketing material and information into the advertising plan, it is likely to fail. That is why we believe advertising planners must first be marketing generalists. They must have a full and complete understanding of the marketing process before attempting to develop an advertising campaign. (More will be said about this in later chapters.)

Having completed this review of the marketing process and the steps leading up to the development of the advertising plan, we shall now take a brief look at the organization and structure of marketing and advertising organizations.

MARKETING AND ADVERTISING ORGANIZATIONS

In the development of an advertising campaign, the campaign planner should understand the various structures and functions of businesses, marketing departments, and advertising organizations. In general, five specific groups or types of organizations may be involved in the development and/ or execution of the advertising campaign. They are

1. Marketing organizations
2. Advertising or marketing communications agencies
3. Media, such as newspapers, radio, and television
4. Suppliers, such as film studios, typographers, and art studios
5. Support organizations, such as marketing and advertising research groups and audience data suppliers

Because our primary interest is the development of an advertising campaign, we will deal with the structure of the marketing organizations and advertising and marketing communications agencies. Because the media, suppliers, and support organizations sell or furnish services and facilities to the marketer and the agency, we will deal with them only in general terms.

MARKETING ORGANIZATION STRUCTURES

Marketing organizations found in those companies or firms that develop and/or market products or services to customers generally have one of four types of organizational designs: (a) functional, that is, the grouping of marketing activities into areas of specialization, such as sales, advertising, research; (b) market, that is, the emphasis in the organization is on managing markets rather than functions; (c) product, that is, specialization and management by product or product line; and (d) product-market, a hybrid system where function, market, and product approaches are combined in some manner. (See Exhibit 1–7 for illustration of the general makeup of these various organizations.)

Although new systems are currently being developed, most consumer product marketing organizations in the United States use some form of product or brand management system. Exhibit 1–8 illustrates a hypothetical marketing organization in the U.S. in the late 1980s. The figure shows the relationship between marketing and other groups. Of particular interest is the relationship of the brand manager to other service departments.[7]

---

[7]Robert Dewar and Don E. Schultz, "The Product Manager: An Idea Whose Time Has Gone? Fast Track or Dead End," *Marketing Communications* (May 1989):28–35.

Exhibit 1-7 Typical Marketing Organization Structures

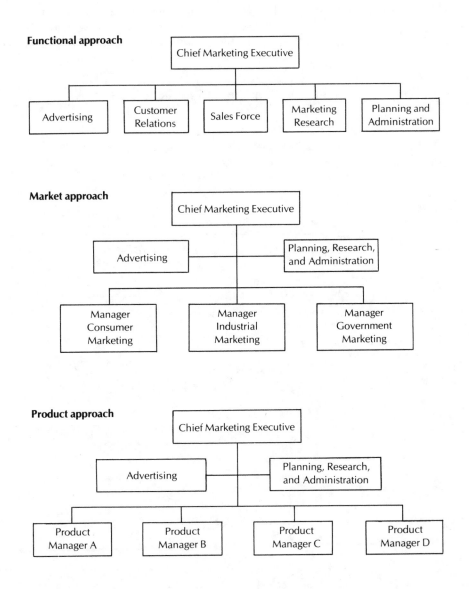

SOURCE: David W. Cravens, Gerald E. Hills, and Robert B. Woodruff, *Marekting Decision Making, Concepts and Strategy,* revised edition (Homewood, Ill. Richard D. Irwin, 1980):460.

In today's larger package goods firms, the brand manager is usually entrusted with a particular brand and functions as the responsible agent (or president) of the brand. Although a brand manager may delegate many or all of various functions in the marketing and advertising program to others, for instance, the advertising agency or the package designer, he or she is ultimately responsible for the final promotional decisions made on the

Exhibit 1–8   Traditional Product Management Design

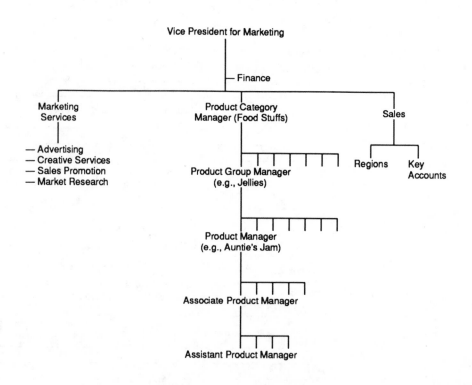

Note that in some organizations, Sales Promotion and/or Advertising are decentralized and report to the Product Manager directly.

Key Account Managers in Sales, until recently, had little or no clout relative to Product or Brand Managers for Marketing Services Support.

Sales may report to the Vice President of Marketing or directly to the next level up. In some cases, Sales is decentralized under product categories.

brand. The brand manager answers directly to the division brand manager, who in turn reports to the marketing director. Some of the management levels shown in Exhibit 1–8, for example, division brand manager, may be eliminated in smaller firms or expanded in larger ones.

As illustrated in the left-hand side of Exhibit 1–8, brand managers are separated from the marketing services personnel. Thus, each brand manager must work through his or her group managers and the vice president of marketing to get the support services to accommodate the particular needs of his or her brand. This is where the brand manager's talents and skills are put to the test; he or she must literally compete for the same support resources used by the other brand managers within the organization.

In recent years, the brand management system has come under attack by top management of the firm, the sales force, and even the retailer and distributor. The primary complaint has been that the brand manager is *too* focused on the brand, *too* short-term oriented, and *too* myopic about the brand with regard to the overall good of the entire corporation. Also, the growing strength of the retail trade has led to a restructuring of the relationship between the company and its retail customers in terms of planning and implementing advertising and sales promotion programs. Thus, the need for closer contact has increased the importance of the key ac-

Exhibit 1–9   New Marketing Designs

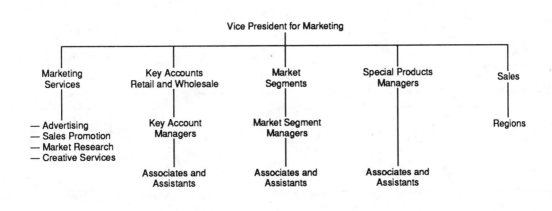

Note that Sales may still report to the Marketing Vice President or to the level above.

Special Product Managers function as traditional Product Managers, but only for products with special needs, e.g., if the product is new, or is facing new kinds of competition, etc.

count representative who works directly with larger customers to plan and sell the company's products.

Perhaps the greatest need within the marketing organization is to make sure the focus of the company is on the consumer, not on the product. Several new organizational designs have been suggested. Exhibit 1–9 illustrates one which appears to have strong possibilities in terms of assuring "consumer focus" by the management group.

THE ADVERTISING AGENCY

Because the advertising agency is often an important partner in the development and execution of the marketer's advertising campaign, a brief look at the organization of the typical agency should prove helpful.

Typically, the advertising agency operates in a functional manner; that is, there are separate managers for the various functions and activities that the agency conducts. Exhibit 1–10 illustrates the functional structure of a typical member of the American Association of Advertising Agencies (AAAA).

Exhibit 1–10   Typical AAAA Advertising Agency Structure

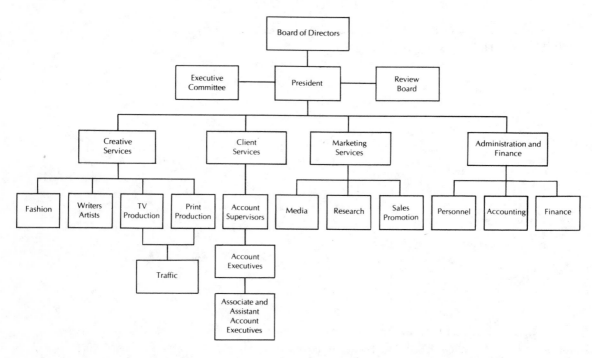

SOURCE: Adapted from material supplied by the American Association of Advertising Agencies. Used with permission.

One alternative to a functional structure is a structure based on individual accounts. In this format, client services, creative, media, and sales promotion personnel are gathered around an individual client or group of clients. The administrative, financial, and market research groups are still functionally organized.

Although the functional structure shown in Exhibit 1–10 is typical of most advertising agencies, it is perhaps a bit misleading in terms of the way in which specific advertising campaigns are actually developed. For the most part, advertising agencies are structured by account groups, that is, a group of functional experts assigned to a specific client. This group is usually coordinated by an account supervisor. Reporting to the account supervisor may be several account executives who are responsible for various portions or brands of the general client. The account supervisor and the account executives act as the leaders or coordinators of the various other service functions that the agency may provide to the marketer/client. Exhibit 1–11 illustrates this typical account group structure. Client services personnel (account supervisors, account executives, associate and assistant account executives) are the coordinating forces that bring all the agency facilities and capabilities together to plan and develop an advertising campaign for the client.

Exhibit 1–11   Agency Services to the Client

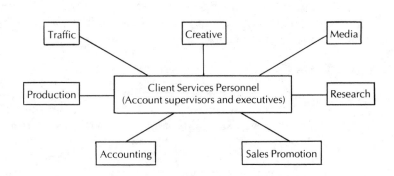

The functional structure illustrated in Exhibit 1–10 is the traditional method of agency organization. In the last few years, a new position has been formed in many agencies that will have or may have already had a major impact on how advertising campaigns are developed. The position is that of account planner. The structure of the account group under the account planner concept is illustrated in Exhibit 1–12.

Exhibit 1–12   Account Group Structure

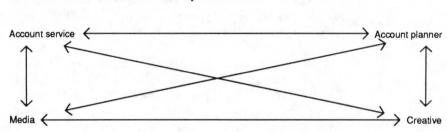

As can be seen, the account planner turns the traditional agency triangular account structure of account service, creative, and media into a rectangle. The account planner's assigned duty is to represent the consumer and his or her views to the advertising agency during the planning process. In other words, the account planner is an expert on the consumer, knowing from research how the consumer feels about the category, the product, the company, the use of the product, and so on. The account planner then helps the account service, creative, and media people develop advertising that will fill consumer's wants and needs for information about the product or service. Typically, the account planner has a research or consumer behavior background and also is well versed in marketplace operations and dynamics.

Although the account planner system is found in only a few major agencies in the U.S., at this point, it is prevalent in Europe. Those planning an advertising campaign might want to consider the addition of an account planner to make sure the consumer's view is adequately considered in the development of the advertising program.

AGENCY ALTERNATIVES

As in the case of the marketing function within the manufacturing organization, dramatic changes are taking place in the external organizations that provide advertising and marketing services to the manufacturer. For example, in the late 1970s there was a major period of advertising agency consolidation and concentration. Large agencies began to purchase the smaller, specialized agencies and groups who planned and executed sales promotion, public relations, media buying, and direct marketing. The idea was that these major agencies could then offer the full range of services needed by their clients. Then, in the early 1980s, the larger advertising agencies began to buy the smaller to midsize advertising agencies which had accounts which the larger agencies couldn't attract or serve profitably. As a result, by the late 1980s, most advertising agencies of any size were owned or controlled by one of the internationally owned and often operated mega-agencies such as Saatchi & Saatchi or Omnicom. These new mega-agencies are changing the manner and system in which traditional advertising agencies have functioned. It is not clear at this point what the final result will be.

As a by-product and result of the mega-agency trend, a number of alternatives to the traditional advertising agency have sprung up to serve marketing organizations. Many of these have taken the form of specialized boutiques in areas such as media planning, creative, or even production. Thus, the manager in a marketing organization may well have a traditional advertising agency plus a creative boutique and media buying service assisting in the development of an advertising campaign.

In addition, as manufacturing organizations have concentrated and consolidated, it has also become practical for them to start doing some of the advertising functions in house. For example, most large organizations have a media manager or a sales promotion group which provides either in-house capability or an overview facility to evaluate the work of outside agencies.

One of the results of this rethinking of the advertising agency function has been the change in advertising agency compensation. Traditionally, the 15 percent commission on media space or time was used. Today, there are many types of compensation arrangements, ranging from reduced media commissions to fee-for-services-provided to monthly retainers. It is beyond the scope of this text to describe this very fluid state that exists in agency compensation. It is clear, however, that more and more marketing organizations are involved in finding new methods of compensation, many of which are dramatically different from the traditional approach to media commission.

MEDIA, SUPPLIERS, AND SUPPORT GROUPS

The development of an advertising campaign, even for a local retailer, is often a very complex process, usually requiring a fairly large number of outside specialists in addition to the advertiser and the agency. These individuals or groups furnish the ingredients, materials, or services used by the advertiser and the advertising agency to prepare the advertising campaign. The importance of these specialists varies greatly with the type or complexity of the advertising program.

Of particular interest are the media, because they deliver advertising messages to consumers or prospects. In most instances, media are independent of the advertiser or the agency. Thus, the advertiser, often through the agency, simply purchases time, space, or facilities from the media for the campaign.

In terms of organizational structure, a group of salespersons represents the media to the advertiser or agency. These media representatives, who may be employees of the media or simply represent them on a commission basis, service the needs of the agency or advertiser by quoting rates for time or space, furnishing information on the media coverage and audience, providing proof of performance, and performing the necessary duties to assure that the advertising appears as ordered. In many cases, the only contact between the advertiser and agency and the media is through these sales or service representatives.

Almost the same pattern develops between suppliers and support groups. (Suppliers include film studios, typography houses, printers, and art studios. Support groups include legal services, talent and residual groups, and accounting firms.) As in the case of the media, these suppliers and support groups are represented to the advertiser and the advertising agency through sales or service personnel. Thus, the immediate contact is with the sales or service representative. Often, in both the media and the service and support groups, the sales representative operates within that organization, much like the account executive functions within the advertising agency. He or she marshals all the interior forces of the media, the service, or support group to fill the needs of the advertiser or advertising agency.

ADVERTISING: INVESTMENT OR EXPENSE?

Having developed this understanding of the basic marketing activities within the various organizations, we come to a final overall area that should be discussed, that is, the firm's financial view of marketing and, in particular, of advertising.

Most financial managers view any expenditure that results in rewards to the organization over a relatively long period of time as an investment. For example, the physical plant, trucks, warehouse facilities, and the like are considered investments, and their value is depreciated over time. Unfortunately, although marketing activities are typically viewed as being long term (i.e., many marketing activities do not result in immediate sales), all firms take marketing as an expense item on their profit-and-loss sheet. Thus, marketing funds spent this year are taken as an expense item, although the results of those activities may not occur until a year or even several years later. This arrangement is quite typical under most accounting systems.

With some marketing expenditures taking costs as current year expenses is quite reasonable. For example, distribution costs and warehousing, although they are a marketing function, unquestionably are expenses generated in selling the product. Likewise, current year price markdowns or discounts are also costs of selling the product at that particular time. A question arises, however, when we move into such areas as research and development costs for new products, and, particularly, when we start to consider advertising expenditures.

The question of whether advertising should be considered an investment or an expense to the firm has long been debated. Marketing people have traditionally tried to view advertising as an investment (or at least to convince financial people to do so). They stress that even though the funds may be spent in one period of time, value often will be received over the longer term. They also argue that in our diffused and complex marketplace, consumers often have little personal contact with or knowledge of the firm or its products except through the advertising they see or hear. Thus, consumers may develop their opinions and attitudes about the brands, and even the whole company, as a direct result of advertising messages they receive. For example, although most people may never purchase or even have occasion to be in the market for an IBM mainframe computer, a definite feeling about the company, its products, and its reputation has been built up through IBM's direct advertising to the consumer. This goodwill toward the firm is often cited as a direct result of advertising expenditures. And, goodwill is normally carried on the firm's balance sheet as an asset that has been built up over time.

People in the financial and accounting sections of a company usually have a different view of advertising. Because advertising funds are normally spent in one period of time, say a fiscal year, and because there may be no direct method of measuring the value or effect of advertising, they contend there is no satisfactory way to depreciate the expenditure. The financial view is, therefore, that advertising is a direct expense related to the manufacturing and selling of the product and should be charged to the operation of the firm in the period in which the funds were expended.

Presently, federal and state governments regard advertising as an expense item. That is, the money invested in advertising is taken as an expense deduction in the period in which it was used, and, for accounting purposes, is considered a cost of doing business. Some legal authorities, having taken the view of the advertising practitioner who views advertising as an investment, have suggested that if advertising truly is an investment, it should be treated as such in terms of business deductions. In other words, advertising could only be charged off as a business expense as it is used up or as the investment value declines. This question, along with the one of whether or not advertising is subject to taxation, are major legal issues on the horizon. Although the decisions may or may not have an impact on the planning of advertising campaigns in the future, the advertising planner should be aware of the concern on the part of the marketing organizations involved.

SUMMARY: HOW MARKETING AND ADVERTISING FIT TOGETHER

With this brief review of the marketing process, marketing organizations, and the financial view of advertising, it should be clear that advertising is often only a very small part of the overall marketing activities of a company or firm, although it may be a very important part. As was stressed earlier (and this theme will continue throughout this text), advertising is simply the communication of a sales message for a product or service made through various media forms. As such, it is an integral part of the marketing process, but it is totally dependent for success on the other elements in the marketing mix. No advertising campaign can succeed without a sound product—a product that is properly priced and adequately distributed.

Because advertising is simply the communication of a sales message for or about the product, the next logical step is a brief review of the communication process, which follows in Chapter 2.

Case Studies

Bossy Products

As they neared the end of the fiscal year, management at Bossy Products realized that the company was in a position similar to that of many older companies. Established in 1936, the company produced processed milk products, including powdered milk and canned condensed and evaporated milks. Its products were nationally distributed and had strong retailer support. Bossy sales accounted for 30 percent of the powdered milk and 25 percent of the canned milk market. It was the second largest seller in both of these categories.

Despite its strong showing, Bossy management was actively seeking new alternatives. Sales in both categories had declined over the past decade. As a result, profits had remained static, and there was little possibility of growth.

Powdered milk was used in approximately 14 percent of all U.S. households.* The chief buyers were one- or two-person households. Bossy studies suggested that these were people who used milk infrequently and viewed powdered milk as the most convenient form. The milk was used for drinking and baking.

Condensed and evaporated canned milks were purchased by 41.4 percent of U.S. households. The chief users were women aged 35 to 44 in higher-income households with teenage children at home. Unlike most milk products, which showed broad geographic distribution, canned milks were used principally in the South. Bossy studies revealed that canned milks were used primarily in cooking.

After a major consumer research study conducted in two years previously, Bossy had targeted women who baked as a key market for powdered and canned milks. More specifically, the target consumer was defined as

> a married woman with a teenage child living at home. She works outside the home. During the week, the family either dines out or eats convenience foods. However, she enjoys baking and prepares breads, pies, and cakes from scratch once or twice a month. She does not view liquid milks as a staple and sees Bossy products as a convenient alternative.

Bossy's advertising had targeted this woman and was viewed as successful because market share had remained steady.

---

*Unless otherwise noted, all demographic information is from the *Mediamark Research Study* (Spring 1986): Volume P-15.

Realizing that this well-defined market was somewhat limited, Bossy management was eager to find a way to expand their consumer base. A technological breakthrough late in the previous year provided new possibilities. Bossy researchers had developed a patented process for producing powdered cream, which, like powdered milk, could be reconstituted with water. The researchers also felt that with some modifications, the product could be added directly to coffee or tea as a beverage lightener.

Management explored the potential market for both scenarios. Dollar sales of fluid milk and cream had declined by 2 percent in each of the last two years. Use of canned milks was down 8 percent. However, per capita consumption of cream had increased by 4 percent since last year. And, use of a similar product, dry buttermilk, had increased by 27 percent.

Based on their knowledge of the powdered milk consumer, management believed that there was a similar market for powdered cream. There was also the probability that other homemakers would buy the product. Unlike milk, cream was not a staple in larger households. Women on a Bossy consumer panel had indicated that they were often reluctant to use recipes calling for cream. They explained that the amount of cream called for was usually so small that much of the package was left over. Because they used cream infrequently, the leftover cream had to be thrown out. Bossy could promote their powdered cream as economical and efficient.

Nondairy creamers are used by 23.1 percent of all U.S. households. Bossy felt that a substantial portion of these people would prefer a *dairy* powdered creamer to the nondairy products that were currently available. They cited as evidence the new emphasis on "natural" food products. They also felt that the strength of the Bossy name would help support the natural claim.

In order to more fully evaluate the potential of each alternative, Bossy set preliminary goals for the new products:

1. If marketed as a powdered cream for use in baking, the product should have a 10 percent share of the dairy cream market at the end of Year 1.
2. If marketed as a beverage creamer, the product should have a 15 percent share of the creamer market at the end of Year 1.
3. Distribution would represent at least 65 percent of national all-commodity volume (ACV). (Bossy powdered and canned milks had 75 percent ACV distribution.)
4. Return on investment would be 30 percent. (This was standard for all Bossy products.)

Questions

1. Looking at the elements making up the macroenvironment for a marketing company, evaluate Bossy's actions. Can you see the impact each factor has had on the situation?

2. If plotted on a business portfolio matrix, Bossy's powdered and canned milks would be labeled cash cows, because they have high market share in an industry with low growth. What would the expected matrix position be for the new product under both scenarios—baking aid and beverage cream?

3. Assume the product will be marketed as a beverage creamer. What recommendations would you make with regard to price and place?

4. How would you market the product? As a baking aid along the lines of powdered milks or as a beverage creamer? Why?

AyreGard

AyreGard, a manufacturer of business-to-business accessory equipment items, hired a marketing communications consulting firm to conduct an audit of its operations. AyreGard's marketing environment was undergoing a great deal of change. Depending on how successfully AyreGard responded to the changes, sales would either increase rapidly or the long-term viability of the product line could be severely limited. Although AyreGard had enjoyed record sales growth in the past few years, many within the company felt this was due primarily to a series of fortunate coincidences rather than any optimal strategic direction. Consequently, the decision was made to bring in an outside group to assess the company's current situation and its ability to adapt to the continuing changes in the market.

AyreGard marketed a line of air-cleaning devices for commercial use. The products were designed to remove pollutants—tobacco smoke, dust, and other particles—from indoor air. Typically, the air cleaners were installed in places where people tended to gather for fairly long periods of time, such as restaurants, bars, bowling alleys, hospital waiting rooms, and offices. The filtering device inside the air cleaner could be removed and cleaned periodically, ensuring long life for the unit. Prices started at $400 for the smaller units and ranged to over $1,000 for larger units. AyreGard's units were usually priced 15–20 percent above competitive units.

Although category market share information was not widely available, internal analyses of competitive sales suggested that AyreGard was the market leader. There were three other national competitors, as well as several other regionally distributed brands.

AyreGard sold its air cleaners through a national network of exclusive distributors. Each distributor was assigned to a regional sales manager, who counseled the distributors on selling techniques, helped out on sales calls to potentially large accounts, established the sales quota for the distributor's territory, and monitored distributor performance. Overall sales goals were set by a national sales manager.

Product decisions were the responsibility of two product managers. Wes Tedder, who reported to the national sales manager, was in charge of overseeing production-related decisions, such as product performance, new model development, and quality control. In addition, Wes often identified markets that should receive additional sales attention in order to boost sales of a particular model. He would issue memos to the distributor organization discussing the importance of these markets.

Jennifer Balber, who reported to the national marketing manager, was responsible for all marketing communications support for the product, including administration of an advertising budget supported, in part, by distributor contributions. Jennifer also established market priorities, usually based on perceived sales opportunities or consumer demand. She would then select mailing lists or place trade journal ads tailored to the targeted markets.

The market priorities of the two product managers sometimes conflicted. For example, Wes might decide to emphasize the value of the larger air-cleaner models in high dust areas, such as high school shop classrooms. At the same time, Jennifer might be emphasizing the use of smaller models in office settings. Both product managers had a line of communication to distributors through a monthly newsletter and periodic sales meetings, in addition to issuing regular memorandums.

Each product manager worked with a number of outside suppliers. Wes worked with the engineering department to identify suppliers for the materials used in constructing the air cleaners, as well as shippers, packagers, and the like. Jennifer worked with several advertising agencies, a printer, a direct marketing mailing house, and trade magazine space salespeople.

Because the air cleaner product line was technologically complex and required distributor installation, personal selling was required to close sales. Consequently, advertising was used to generate leads for the distributor network. Public relations activities, such as product publicity press releases sent to trade publications, were also used as lead-generation devices.

As noted earlier, the market situation was changing rapidly. Increasing sentiment against smoking in public places had the greatest influence. AyreGard's air cleaners were very useful in solving this problem; they could remove tobacco smoke from the air before it drifted and irritated nonsmokers. Distributors reported that the high visibility of the smoking issue had improved sales, particularly to the office and restaurant markets. Lead generation was up also.

Despite the promising sales outlook, there were some concerns that tempered management's enthusiasm. First, several competitors had recently lowered their prices, increasing the premium charged for the Ayre-Gard brand. Some distributors had reported losing sales because of price. Second, it appeared that some cities were reacting to the smoking controversy by implementing outright bans on smoking in public places. If smoking were banned entirely, the need for an air cleaner would be greatly reduced.

In terms of marketing communications, advertising costs continued to increase. Jennifer had recently stepped up the direct mail program in an attempt to more specifically target different uses for the air cleaners. For example, mailings to the office market might be subdivided based on the number of employees or the type of business. Although response rates had increased through targeting, so had costs.

Overall response rates continued to be low. Although AyreGard was the market leader, a recent research study had found that prospect awareness of the AyreGard brand (or any air-cleaner brand, for the matter) was extremely low, even in those markets with very strong AyreGard distributors. This suggested that the advertising and the sales force's efforts were missing a great many potential AyreGard customers.

Finally, the distributor organization was split on the question of which markets should take priority. Those distributors who had been with the company for a number of years tended to direct most of their attention to the bar, restaurant, and bowling alley markets. Newer distributors tended to emphasize the office market. (The two leading distributors in terms of quota attainment had been with the company for some time, but had increasingly turned their efforts to the office market. Both were located in metropolitan areas.)

In a meeting with the consulting company, management noted that it hoped to continue the current rate of sales growth without investing in major product changes or greatly increased marketing communications activity. One of the justifications given for keeping the marketing communications budget at or near the current level was that it was unlikely that distributors would agree to contribute more dollars to the program. Many distributors were becoming actively involved in local marketing activities to supplement the national program and would not want to take money away from their own activities.

Questions

1. Which of the marketing activity concepts discussed on pages 2–4 does Wes seem to be following? Jennifer? Explain your answer.

2. The AyreGard *product* seems to be of reasonable quality (based on the market leader position). *Price* is premium over the competition. *Place* (distribution) is national via exclusive, and therefore presumedly expert, distributors. *Promotion* uses a variety of marketing communications techniques. Which of the four Ps do you feel is AyreGard's weakest point? Why?

3. Evaluate AyreGard's situation in terms of any three of the environmental factors discussed on pages 10–12.

4. What would you guess AyreGard's organizational strategy to be? Why?

5. Comment on AyreGard's internal organization. What, if any, changes would you recommend? Why?

2

Advertising as Communication

In the Introduction and Chapter 1, we stressed the importance of considering advertising as only one of several methods of delivering sales messages on behalf of a product or service. All of these methods are used as part of the effort to move customers and prospects toward the ultimate purchase. This idea of advertising "delivering sales messages" is not a new one. It is why advertising was developed originally and what it continues to be today. Many companies have chosen advertising, rather than personal selling or public relations or sales promotion, to deliver their sales messages. For most consumer products, advertising is almost always a very efficient method of distributing sales messages. For a number of package goods products, it also appears to be more effective than other methods, as well.

If advertising, therefore, is a method and system of delivering sales messages, it's obvious that an advertising planner, to develop effective advertising, needs to know something about communication and communication systems. In this chapter, we'll explore the common forms of communication, such as how people process information (advertising), and some of the basic concepts of how we believe advertising works or is supposed to work. This review of the basics of communication should provide the advertising planner with a better idea of how advertising can be planned to communicate the right sales message to the right audience at the right time. Further, through this discussion of the communication process, the planner should have a better idea of how advertising messages are received by customers and prospects and how they might be acted upon in making purchasing decisions.

WAYS OF LOOKING AT COMMUNICATION

Advertising tends to be a special form of communication—that is, it is intended to persuade customers and prospects to respond in a positive way toward a product or service. This response can take several forms, such as (a) developing positive attitudes about the product or service, (b) prompting a conscious attempt by the consumer to locate and purchase the product at a retail store, (c) commenting to others or attempting to influence them to take action in favor of the product or service, or (d) reinforcing the good feelings toward the product or service that may exist now. Whatever the advertising task, a review of basic communications principles will help us understand how advertising delivers and communicates these persuasive messages.

Three basic types of communication processes are of interest to the advertising planner: (a) individual communication, (b) interpersonal communication, and (c) mass communication. Each of these forms of communication provides insight into how advertising "works" with consumers. We'll start with individual communication.

Individual Communication

To successfully communicate our sales message to a customer or prospect, the targeted person must first decide to select our message out of an increasingly cluttered media environment. In addition, that person must remember it for future use in making a purchase decision. At the individual level of communication, our primary concern is with how a person selects advertising messages to attend to and how the memory works to retain the information and impressions conveyed through that advertising.

A person's selection of messages to attend to can occur at several levels. First, our customer or prospect must decide to expose him- or herself to our message. This can occur in a planned or very unplanned way. For example, a customer or prospect may actively seek out our advertisement because they are already interested in our product or service category or even brand. Or, exposure to our ad might occur because the ad is very unique. Therefore, it breaks through the media clutter and attracts the customer or prospect to it. An example of a very unique advertisement that seeks to break the clutter and gain attention for the advertiser is the one for Reebok® shoes shown in Exhibit 2–1.

From the advertising planner's perspective, this advertisement selection process or selective exposure requires that the advertisement and the sales message (a) be of enough interest value that viewers will want to attend to it, (b) be unique or creative enough to seek out customers and prospects, and (c) be in those media vehicles where consumers would be most likely to find it.

But, exposure to the advertisement is not enough. Many people will be exposed to a message and yet decide not to attend to it or retain it in their memories. In communications research terms, they did not "process" the information made available. For example, a very unique advertisement, such as that for Calvin Klein's "Obsession" fragrance (see Exhibit 2–2),

Exhibit 2-1   Reebok Ad

REEBOKS LET U.B.U.   Reebok

might easily achieve wide exposure for the brand and category. However, before this message can be remembered (that is, retained for future reference), the customer or prospect must decide to consciously attend to the advertisement. Attention is another selective process. If the advertisement's sales message does not offer a consumer any information worth storing, it will be forgotten almost immediately.

There are many approaches to the study of memory. For practical purposes, it is important only to know that memory, or at least memory that can be accessed easily, is limited. Therefore, most people are very selective in deciding what to remember and what not to remember. Most of us simply cannot process and store in memory everything we see, read, hear, or experience. Therefore, we must make choices and select from all the available alternatives presented to us.

Exhibit 2–2   Obsession Ad

SOURCE: Used by permission of Calvin Klein Cosmetics Corporation.

Memory is the cornerstone on which the use of creative strategies in advertising are based. The basic assumption of an advertising strategy is that (a) the media environment is cluttered, (b) attention is hard to get, and (c) information processing and storing are difficult to achieve. Because processing and storage are limited, it is important that the advertising give your customers and prospects something worth processing and remembering. Otherwise, they will simply ignore or forget you and your advertising message.

Novelty advertising approaches can tease or trick viewers into watching or reading or listening or otherwise exposing themselves to the advertisements on occasion. However, once a customer or prospect realizes that there is nothing of value in the advertising for him or her, he or she generally will not waste precious time and energy in processing or storing the advertising message. It is in this approach, where advertising creativity for the sheer sake of creativity is used, that much of today's advertising falls short. Advertising that is creatively unique and offers consumers information or ideas or concepts of value to them is the most effective in today's cluttered media environment. That which doesn't, isn't.

We'll see how these individual communication concepts come together in the model of how advertising works presented later in this chapter.

Interpersonal Communication

Another way to look at communication is to study those factors that lead to successful interpersonal or person-to-person communication. (A model of this face-to-face communication can be found in Exhibit 2–3.)

Exhibit 2–3   Face-to-Face Communication

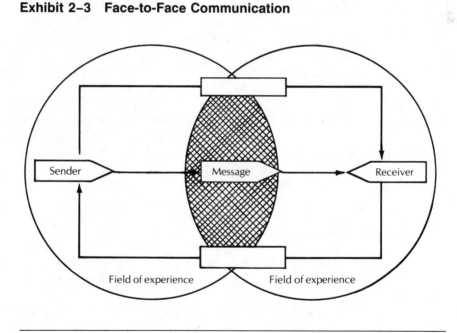

SOURCE: Adapted from Wilbur Schramm and Donald Roberts, eds., *The Process and Effects of Mass Communication* (Urbana: University of Illinois Press, 1971).

Face-to-face situations occur most frequently in personal selling. There, the seller communicates directly with the potential buyer. In most successful advertising, the same is true. It is the seller (the sender in the model in Exhibit 2–3) who attempts to communicate or persuade or sell the product to a prospective buyer (the receiver) through a chosen medium. In a face-to-face situation, the medium is conversation between the two. In advertising, it may well be a magazine advertisement or a radio commercial. The biggest difference is that in face-to-face selling there is give and take between the two parties, whereas in advertising there is only the one-way flow, from seller to buyer.

The true success of face-to-face or interpersonal communication depends on the sender's ability to elicit in the receiver thoughts and feelings that both have in common. Both sender and receiver must have some common experiences to draw on to be able to do this. (These are labeled the "field of experience" in Exhibit 2–3. The crosshatched area indicates where these experiences overlap.) The key to face-to-face communication is for the sender to be able to identify and tap into those experiences which are shared with the receiver. Two persons usually discover the common ground between them in the course of ordinary conversation or a question-and-answer dialogue.

In the case of advertising, the process of finding a shared field of experience between the advertiser and the customer (or prospect) is commonly done through consumer research. The advertiser conducts research among consumers to determine what problems they might have that a given product could solve. The advertiser also investigates the choice of language used by the consumer in discussing a solution to the problem; tries to identify those persons involved in the purchase decision process; and so on. In other words, the advertising planner must find words and pictures and concepts and ideas that truly relate to the need or want the consumer has that the advertised product or service can fill or provide.

The advertising must be able to relate to those experiences that consumers have in common. Establishing these relationships should then enable the advertiser to persuade or convince the prospect of the value of his or her particular solution to the specific need or want. In some instances, this is called empathy—the ability to understand how others feel about things. A good advertising creative person uses this empathy and shared field of experience to create advertising which is seen, processed, and acted upon.

In addition to finding common fields of experience, to develop successful advertising, the advertising planner must develop a method of overcoming the "background noise" common in most face-to-face or interpersonal communication systems. *Background noises* are all those other things that are going on at the same time communication is supposed to be taking place. For instance, imagine a typical father sitting in his easy chair reading a newspaper. The television is on. His teenage kids are upstairs playing their stereo. The dog is barking and you can hear a fire engine siren in the distance. Now, through all this noise, you can vaguely make out a commercial on TV. How successful do you think the commercial will be? It will really have to be great to get through. The problem is noise—just too much "noise" in most of today's advertising situations.

Clutter in the media is also a form of noise. Anything that can interfere with the reception and processing of the advertising message is noise. The advertising planner must constantly keep in mind the noise that is inherent in most media systems. The job of the media planner is to put the message where it can be seen or heard by the target market and where the noise level is the lowest.

Think of all the competition for the receiver's attention. Then consider the limited capacity of the consumer's memory. Combined the two give you a rather frightening picture of what an advertisement has to go through to successfully communicate its message. No wonder the average consumer remembers only about 14 percent of the advertising to which he or she is exposed.

Up to this point, we have talked as if communication is a one-way process, something a sender does to a receiver. Face-to-face communication has the important characteristic of being a two-way process. When we talk to each other, we provide "feedback" upon which future messages are based. This feedback can be something we say, a facial expression, or the way we are sitting or standing. Mass communication situations generally lack this type of feedback. Indeed, the field of direct marketing has grown and prospered as a result of having this response mechanism built into it as compared to more general advertising.

When we don't have direct access to the receiver of our advertising messages, we try to compensate through the use of research in several forms. We'll look at those methods of trying to estimate or quantify expected consumer responses to our advertising messages in Chapter 6 and 11.

The Assael Model.   Henry Assael has taken the basic structure of the face-to-face communication model and shown how the different advertising institutions must work together to effectively communicate with consumers. (See Exhibit 2–4.)

The communication process components are shown across the top row in Assael's model. Notice the similarities with the face-to-face model. The source component is the same in both models. Assael has also retained the feedback loop. The receiver component has been replaced with the response we hope the consumer will make; the message has been replaced with the term *transmission.* Transmission includes not only a message but the media through which it will be sent to the audience.

Assael has also included the processes by which messages are developed (encoding) and deciphered (decoding). *Encoding* involves all those processes writers, artists, and producers go through to translate advertising ideas or product benefits into symbols that consumers will understand and

Exhibit 2–4   Advertising Communication Process

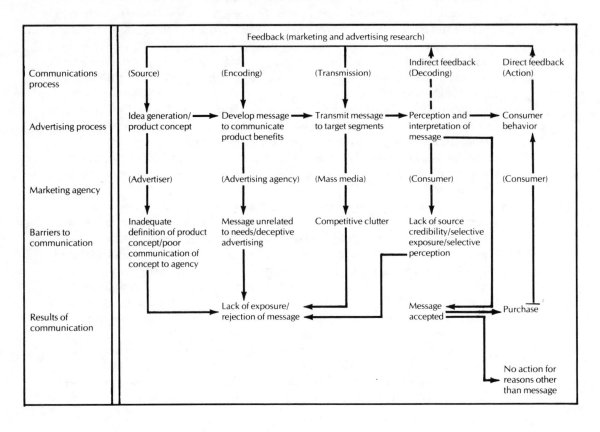

SOURCE: Henry Assael, *Consumer Behavior and Marketing Action* (Boston: Kent Publishing Co., 1981): 480.

be interested enough in to take action on and buy the product. *Decoding* involves all the previously discussed selective processes that consumers use when deciding to attend to and remember messages and their components.

Parallel to each element in basic communication process is an analogous element specific to the advertising process. The source of the message, or the advertiser, is ultimately responsible for the product concept and the package of benefits that must be communicated to consumers. This is the most important step in the advertising process. The product must be a good one for advertising to be successful. If the product is lacking in perceived merit or not wanted by consumers, then the best advertising available will not be able to sell it. This barrier to successful communication is shown in the fourth row of the model under the column headed "Source."

It is the advertising planner's job to develop messages that will successfully convey the important product benefits to the consumer. If this message incorrectly presents the product benefits or deceives the customer into trying the product, consumers either will not attend to the message or eventually will reject it. Either of these situations will not only hurt the credibility of the advertising but may influence sales as well.

The media provide channels through which advertising messages can be conveyed simultaneously to large groups of consumers. The environment provided by each vehicle can influence the receptivity of the message. Excessive clutter and noise will impede the communication process. This barrier to communication appears in the fourth row under the column labeled "Transmission."

Consumer selection of a message and interpretation for retention in memory are as important as the development of the advertisement itself. In truth, most messages, particularly advertising messages, are either rejected or misinterpreted. Consumers will defend against persuasive attempts and misinterpret messages to fit their own biases. If we are lucky enough to get our message through this difficult and complex process and into the consumer's mind as intended, we have a chance of stimulating the consumer's desire for our product.

All of the major components of the advertising process influence the likelihood of success. They are intertwined in such a way as to make planning essential to successful advertising. Haphazard or arbitrary advertising can only be successful through luck. Although planning does not guarantee success, it increases the probability of success substantially.

Mass Communication

The problems that most advertising planners are confronted with differ from those inherent in interpersonal communication in a number of important ways. First, when we advertise, we generally do not know, individually, the people we are trying to communicate with. If we are lucky, we might have some consumer research that describes our best prospects, but we do not know these people the way we know our friends and neighbors or the way a salesperson knows his or her prospect. Second, the feedback we get from our communication attempts is very indirect. Normally, it takes a long time to see if people are reacting positively to our advertising. Thus, we cannot react as quickly as we can in face-to-face communication.

In addition to these problems, we still have to deal with the communication problems already discussed. Consumers' selective processes and memory limitations, noise, and tapping common experiences are problems present in all communication situations from face-to-face to mass communications.

The communication models that best illustrate what we should know about mass communication are called "step-flow" models. These models simply and clearly describe the way messages such as advertisements travel from the media to the general population to, ultimately, the target prospect, and the steps involved in this process. For this reason they are useful to the advertising planner. Additionally, these models focus on the "transmission" of our ads. Step-flow models are concerned with the channels through which our ads must flow and how these channels can influence the ads' reception.

Exhibit 2–5   Multistep-Flow Model

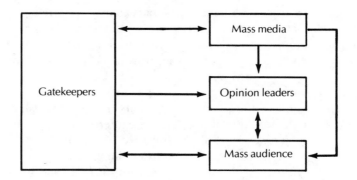

The planning and control of advertising is vital to its success. Step-flow models can be an important tool for managing the process. Among the step-flow models, the most comprehensive and useful one to the advertising planner is the multistep-flow model depicted in Exhibit 2–5. Control of the way in which a message is received is much easier to manage in face-to-face situations than it is in mass communication situations. The mass communication situation involves intermediaries who influence the ultimate reception of the messages.

When we decide to run a commercial on network television, a number of things can happen to it before it reaches its final destination—the prospective consumer. There are people in our society who, through education and interests, are more active consumers of information than are those in the average population. They tend to see new ads first. They also tend to be very active in talking to others about what they have seen. And they don't merely convey the information in the advertisements; they interpret the information too. These people have been labeled opinion leaders by mass communication scholars.[1] They are important to advertisers for two reasons. First, they help to disseminate the advertiser's message to people who might not otherwise have been exposed to it. Second, they interpret and sometimes distort the message. Thus, they influence the nature of the content of an ad that is ultimately received by consumers.

Opinion leaders are also important because they generally have more credibility than advertisers and can take advantage of the characteristics of face-to-face communication situations. Their influence is most often exerted through word-of-mouth communication. An advertiser's task is to be able to identify opinion leaders and use them to his or her advantage. Opinion leaders can act as an extension of a media campaign, but they can also impede a campaign's success. Negative opinion leaders like Ralph Nader can certainly hurt a campaign through interpretation of the campaign's content. Positive opinion leaders—doctors, teachers, and fashion leaders—can be employed to benefit an advertiser.

Notice the intense activity of many personal computer companies as they try to get educational institutions to employ computers in their instruction today. Some technologically oriented colleges now require students to own personal computers. In such situations, educators are prime opinion leaders in the dissemination of information. Advertisers actively try to reach educators with information they want spread to students and their families. In this way, the advertisers hope to use the educators' credibility to aid in the communication of their sales messages.

The opinion leader concept can also be employed in the development of advertisements themselves. The testimonial format is an attempt to use a well-known and credible personality to sell products and services. Bill Cosby, Bob Hope, Cliff Robertson, and, of course, Lee Iacocca, and many other well-known people have been used to add their credibility to products and services.

Of course, in many situations advertisers do communicate directly with the ultimate prospect. Still, there is another type of intermediary who exerts a certain degree of control over the messages we receive. These people are called gatekeepers because they are in positions where they can control the dissemination of information through the media. The gatekeeper concept is very important in the dissemination of news. Editors of newspapers and television anchors act as gatekeepers of the news we read or see because they decide what news is printed or broadcast and what is left out.

In advertising, family members can act as gatekeepers of product infor-

---

[1] Elihu Katz and Paul F. Lazarsfeld, *Personal Influence* (Glencoe, Ill.: Free Press, 1955).

mation. Different family members typically have different interests and are relied upon for certain types of information. For example, children might be considered more knowledgeable about products they use. Parents will rely on them to bring information concerning these products to the family. Knowing this, advertisers can target both the child, the gatekeeper, and the parent, the person who might ultimately purchase the product.

The flow of information in the multistep-flow model is typically from the mass media through gatekeepers and opinion leaders to the larger audience. Yet, we must also remember that gatekeepers and opinion leaders often interact with one another as well as with other people. So, the flow of information is often not as clear as described here.

Some advertisers take advantage of word-of-mouth communication and the step-flow process simply by creating excitement through their advertising. They intentionally try to get people talking. The Apple computer television commercial, "1984," of a few years ago is an example of this approach. (See Exhibit 2–6.) The introduction of new products necessitates generating this kind of excitement to break through media clutter.

The lesson to be taken from the step-flow model is the realization that advertising often does not influence consumers directly and that opinion leaders and gatekeepers can be used effectively to extend and reinforce the effort of a well-planned campaign.

YOUR AUDIENCE: ACTIVE OR PASSIVE?

An age-old axiom in the advertising business is, "Know your audience." This truism shows up again and again in communication models and theories. The focus on the individual's selective processes and memory limitations is an attempt to better understand the audience. The emphasis on the importance of shared experiences in the face-to-face model further underlines the importance of the receiver of advertisements.

Another important distinction to make in trying to better know who it is we are communicating with is whether our audience members are likely to be "active" or "passive" receivers of our message. Up to this point, we have been talking about consumers as if they were very "active" participants in advertising campaigns. In other words, they want and seek out advertising for categories and brands. In truth, the most active participants are opinion leaders and gatekeepers. They seek out advertisements and do a lot of the work in the communication process. But, these consumers are also very stubborn. They are among the most selective people who will see or hear our advertising. And, they are not easily persuaded. They are members of what has been labeled the "obstinate audience."[2]

---

[2]R.A. Bauer, "The Obstinate Audience," *American Psychologist* 19 (May 1964): 319–28.

Exhibit 2–6 Apple 1984 Commercial

SOURCE: Used by permission of Apple Computer.

How do we know if most of our prospective consumers are likely to be difficult to persuade and, what is more important, how does this possible difficulty influence the success of our advertising? To find out if your audience is made up of mostly active consumers, the advertising planner must analyze the product and its importance to the prospect. High-involvement products, such as shopping or specialty goods, tend to attract prospects who are very active participants in the search for information about those products. Specialty goods are most usually expensive items like major appliances, furniture, automobiles, cameras, sporting goods, and clothing. These items involve the active consumer because it is very important to make the right choice. If a bad choice is made, the prospect can lose a considerable amount of money or experience a great deal of negative social pressure with regard to his or her selection. To assure a good choice and thus reduce the risk of a poor choice, consumers of these products shop extensively and are difficult to persuade with most advertising.

Advertisements for high-involvement products tend to appear in very selective print media. The advertisements give the active consumer reasons for purchasing a particular brand. These advertisements strive for more than exposure and attention; they often try to get the consumer to retain information about the product or service.

Herbert Krugman, when he was with General Electric, realized that not all products and advertisements attract prospects who are highly involved in the selection and purchase process. In fact, many of the packaged goods advertised in the mass media are greeted by a big yawn from many consumers. Why? Because the products are relatively unimportant when compared to the specialty goods just discussed. These products are the everyday products found on the shelves of local supermarkets—soap, cereal, soft drinks, dish detergent, and snacks are typical. When confronted by advertising for these products on TV, most consumers are "passive."[3] Their ability to selectively view the advertising is down as is their interest in the advertising itself.

Does this mean we cannot get many of these consumers to learn something from our advertising? Not at all. In fact, in these situations, passive learning can take place. Passive learning requires interesting advertising that will gain the attention of the viewer. A simple 30-second TV spot with an intriguing creative approach like McDonald's "Big Mac" campaigns may be all that is needed to get consumers to remember the name of the product and try it the next time they buy fast food.

Unfortunately, as simple as it might seem, the clutter of advertisements trying to reach passive consumers places a premium on creativity. These

[3]Herbert E. Krugman, "The Impact of Television Advertising: Learning without Involvement," *Public Opinion Quarterly* 29 (Fall 1965): 349–56.

ads are also the most memorable of all advertising, from Alka Seltzer's "Spicy Meatball" spot to the Federal Express fast-talking man to Wendy's "Where's the Beef?" campaign. The objective of advertising in those situations was to get across the name and a very simple claim about the product. To do this, the advertising must be very, very memorable. Think of the TV spots you can remember and the ones you talk about at parties. These spots are usually advertisements written to make the brand name memorable above everything else the campaign might accomplish.

The basic differences between active and passive learning situations are listed in Table 2–1.

Table 2–1 Active versus Passive Learning

Active	Passive
The consumer is . . .	The consumer is . . .
1. A very *selective* processor of product information.	1. Exposed to product information at *random*.
2. A very *active* seeker of product information.	2. A *passive* gatherer of product information.
3. *Involved* with the purchase decision.	3. *Uninvolved* with the purchase decision.
4. A *complex* decision maker.	4. Likely to try the product due to *simple* recognition of the brand name.
The advertising should be . . .	The advertising should be . . .
1. *Informative* and of high interest value to prospective consumers.	1. *Creatively unique* to cut through the clutter.
2. *Rational*.	2. *Memorable*.
3. In *selective* media likely to attract the target prospect.	3. In *general* media, primarily television.

THEORIES OF HOW ADVERTISING WORKS

The discussion to this point has been based on a fairly important assumption regarding the way in which advertising works. The assumption is that before a prospective consumer will go out and buy a product, he or she must know something about it. The consumer must learn something from our advertising and promotional efforts. In high-involvement situations the active consumer must learn a great deal about competing brands before making a choice. In contrast, the passive consumer only has to learn the name of the product and perhaps a simple message or each purchase alternative. Yet, he or she still must learn something. Learning, therefore, is a key to how advertising works.

There are many theories about how learning takes place, but the two most important to the advertising planner are the behaviorist approach and the cognitive learning approach. In fact, as we discuss these approaches, refer to the ideas behind active and passive learning. The behaviorist tradition describes a rather simplistic learning process that has some similarities to passive learning. The cognitive approach is much more closely aligned with active learning. Therefore, both approaches provide interesting insights into how people learn from advertisements.

Behaviorist Theory

Within the behaviorist approach to learning are two dominant schools of thought. The first is called *classical conditioning* and describes what might happen from repetitious exposure to advertisements that attempt to convey a brand image. Typically, this type of advertising will attempt to get consumers to associate something unique or pleasant with a product. Through repetition of the association it is hoped that the pleasant or unique imagery will trigger a desire for the product.

An example of classical conditioning principles can be seen in the Perrier advertising. Perrier water has connected itself with purity and healthfulness; its advertising imagery revolves around the spring in France that is the water's source. Over the years, all Perrier advertising has been designed to reinforce this image of a healthful, pure drinking water. Therefore, whenever the "healthy, pure drink" emotion is triggered, Perrier hopes that the consumer will turn to their product. (See Exhibit 2–7.)

The other dominant behaviorist tradition, *instrumental conditioning,* focuses on how reward and punishment can be used to persuade people to learn a correct response. In advertising, the correct response is the purchase of an advertiser's product. The reward that should trigger the response is satisfaction with the product. Advertising is also used to further reinforce this satisfaction by telling consumers why they should be satisfied with their choice.

Instrumental conditioning principles are the cornerstone of the marketing concept. The marketing concept directs a firm to identify and fulfill consumer needs and desires. The fulfillment of these needs should reward the consumer and, in doing so, lead to repeat purchases of a product.

Advertising also offers consumers rewards other than just the product itself. Many rewards in our society are psychological and social. The promises of better looking hair, a better sex life, more comfort, and more excitement are all rewards for purchasing products. If consumers perceive that these promises are fulfilled by a product, then their behavior has been reinforced and should lead to repeat purchases until a better product with a better promise comes along.

Think of advertising for such products as cosmetics and shampoo. Physically or tangibly, many of these products are quite similar. At least most consumers cannot tell the difference through simple inspection of the contents. It is the promise of an important benefit (reward) that often attracts different groups of consumers to different brands.

Exhibit 2–7   Perrier Ad

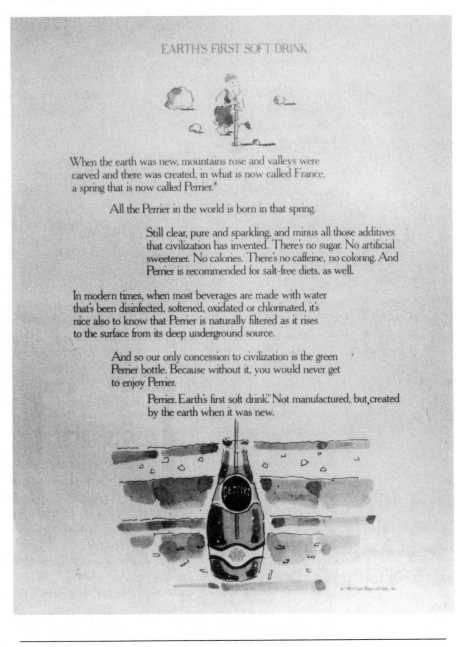

SOURCE: Used by permission of Great Waters of France.

When products do not fulfill their advertising's promises, the consumer is "punished" for the purchase and will not repurchase the product. Instrumental conditioning teaches us not to trick consumers into trying a product we know cannot live up to the things promised by advertising.

The behaviorist tradition carries with it the implication that a consumer is passive and can easily be conditioned into exhibiting a desired response. Although most purchase situations are not that simple, we can still see some of the behaviorist principles used in advertising. Repetition, pleasant associations, and reinforcement are all useful devices in many advertising campaigns.

Cognitive Learning Theory

The cognitive approach to learning is very different from the behaviorist approach. A cognitive approach assumes that people are more actively involved in the learning process. This approach sees consumers as goal-oriented people trying to fulfill their needs through the active pursuit of product information and, ultimately, through the purchase of the best product available. Consumers are seen as much more rational and complex from this perspective.

Cognitivists focus their attention on a series of intervening variables in the consumer's mind that influence how he or she will respond to advertisements and promotional activities. Perception, beliefs, attitudes, motivation, and learning are among the more frequently studied variables.

The Howard–Sheth model of consumer behavior is a good example of the cognitive tradition. This model consists of four major components that take us away from the simplistic relationships between exposure to advertising and learning supported by the behaviorists. These major components are (a) input stimuli; (b) intervening factors—perception and learning; (c) exogenous factors; and (d) a hierarchical series of responses—attention, comprehension, attitude, intention, and purchase.[4]

Input stimuli include items such as price and product advertising. Perceptual processes include the consumer's biases, attention, and search for information. Learning, according to Howard and Sheth, is far more complex than a simple conditioned response to an advertisement or other information. It involves a person's motives, criteria used to select a product, confidence in the choice, comprehension of products, attitude toward products, and satisfaction with a purchase.

Once incoming stimuli are processed, Howard and Sheth theorize, a hierarchical series of responses are possible. This hierarchy assumes that

---

[4]John A. Howard and Jagdish Sheth, *The Theory of Buyer Behavior* (New York: John Wiley & Sons, 1969).

before a purchase can be made, a consumer must pass sequentially through these responses, from attention to actual purchase. (The hierarchical concept will be discussed more thoroughly in a later section.)

Additionally, factors external to an individual's perceptual and learning processes influence the output of a decision. Culture, social class, time pressure, and financial status can influence a consumer's decision. (These will be discussed in the next chapter.)

From a learning perspective, the Howard–Sheth model depicts decision making based on learning as a very complex process. In any given situation, every variable in the model can take on a different value. Input changes from situation to situation as does the way in which we perceive the input. Motive, attitudes, levels of comprehension, confidence, and satisfaction all differ in importance from one purchase situation to another.

The Howard–Sheth model clearly illustrates the complexity of learning. More so than the behaviorist approach, this model describes an active consumer trying to make a difficult choice from among brands in an important and expensive product category.

Cognitive learning: A purchase decision.   Mr. Smith has just seen a spot on TV for a Chevy Blazer. He has a family composed of his wife and two kids. They presently own a Ford LTD which is six years old. Mr. Smith likes to go fishing and hunting and the Blazer would be ideal for this sort of activity. But he cannot afford two cars right now, so the Blazer would replace the LTD.

Mr. Smith is a factory worker and the economic slow-down has hit his firm rather hard. He is not likely to earn any large salary increases for the next two years.

Mr. Smith likes the Blazer because he feels it is large enough to carry his family and he can still use it to go ''off-roading.'' Advertising describes the Blazer as durable yet still comfortable. Mr. Smith also likes the image he associates with the vehicle. It's rough and macho.

Mr. Smith shopped around extensively and looked closely at competitive vehicles such as the Ford Bronco and Jeep Cherokee. Due to financial constraints, Mr. Smith decided not to buy the Blazer right away. He is still considering buying another family car.

Notice in this example the input and criteria Mr. Smith used to make his decision. Advertising was just a triggering device to get him thinking about the possibility of buying a new car. His financial situation was a key exogenous variable which had a very strong influence on his decision. Mr. Smith's motives and criteria for making a choice were strongly influenced by his sports interests and family considerations. What Mr. Smith learned from this process was that this was not the right time to buy the Blazer.

The complexity of Mr. Smith's situation is in stark contrast to the behaviorist principles employed in less important purchase situations. Advertising is a more influential promotional tool in situations involving simple decisions. In complex decision-making situations, many more variables enter into the learning situation.

A Cognitive Approach to How Advertising Works

In advertising, communication occurs when the consumer has accepted and internalized the information in some way. How advertising works, then, is very dependent on how the message is accepted, stored, and later used to make decisions. This storage and retrieval system is often based on what we call the *judgment system*.

It is believed that judgments about products or services are made as information from the advertising to which the person is exposed is processed. This information is then compared with information the person has previously acquired. In other words, people acquire new knowledge by relating the new information to what they already know. They make a judgment. This judgment may be to (a) reinforce present knowledge and beliefs, (b) to reject the advertising as not fitting with previous knowledge or information, or (c) to adjust current beliefs based on the new information or advertising.

Three Information Stores

Incoming information, in the form of advertising or any other sensory activity, passes through or is subject to three information store systems.

The first step is to the *sensory register* (*SR*). (See Exhibit 2–8.) It has three purposes. First, all incoming information, either auditory or sensory, is transduced so that patterns can be recognized. For example, the SR detects forms (letters such as *B* or *Z*), sounds (such as "Ah" or "Ouch"), and shapes (such as balls or circles or figures). It then holds the information for later processing. Finally, it alerts higher brain centers so they can process the information.

The second stage is the *short-term memory store* (*STS*). Information is held temporarily in STS while reasoning takes place and judgments are made. Because STS is *active* memory, it has a very limited capacity.

The third stage is the *long-term store* (*LTS*). This is the repository of all information that a person has ever processed. The LTS holds information that is currently not being used. Long-term memory is organized in two ways so it can be retrieved. First, there is a semantic organization, which is believed to be hierarchical. For example, if a person is thinking of the cookie category, the first level might be the various forms of cookies, such as hard or soft, large or small, and filled or unfilled. At the next level might be flavors of cookies, such as chocolate chip, vanilla wafers, or coconut macaroons. At the bottom might be brands of cookies, such as Keebler,

Exhibit 2–8   Family Life Cycle

1. The Bachelor Stage: young, single people
2. Newly Married Couples: young, no children
3. Full Nest I: young married couples with youngest child under 6
4. Full Nest II: young married couples with youngest child 6 or over
5. Full Nest III: older married couples with dependent children
6. Empty Nest I: older married couples with no children living with them and household head in labor force
7. Empty Nest II: older married couples with no children living with them and household head retired
8. Solitary Survivor I: older single people in labor force
9. Solitary Survivor II: older retired single people

SOURCE: William D. Wells and George Gubar, "Life Cycle Concept in Marketing Research," *Journal of Marketing Research* 3 (November 1966): 355–63.

Grandma's, or Duncan Hines. In addition, at each level, other actors, such as color, time of use, method or phrase, or even cost might be associated.

The second way information is stored is temporally. In other words, people store information in the order in which events or activities have occurred over time. Thus, people can recall their lives in the order in which they experienced events or can recall experiences with products or even advertising messages from times long past. These two forms of storage are important, as we will see later in some advertising models.

Retrieval, Storage, and Representation

Let's assume a person is watching television and sees a commercial. The information presented is in the SR. If the commercial is not processed further, there will be no recall of the message. It simply passes away.

If the commercial is processed, the person becomes aware of it and several responses are possible. One response is not to devote further processing to the commercial. If this occurs, there will be little recall of the message at a later time. If, however, the person decides to activate information previously stored in LTS, a process called *retrieval* occurs. In other words, the person decides that the new information is worthwhile or interesting enough to call up previously stored information for comparison.

When that comparison is made—that is, when the person relates the new information in the commercial to previously stored information from

LTS, the process is called *rehearsal*. Based on comparison of the new information in the commercial in STS with previously stored information from LTS, he or she makes a judgment. This judgment can be acted on immediately or may go back to LTS to be called up again and reconsidered.

As shown in Exhibit 2–8, two factors that often impact on the sensory register, signal strength and pertinence, determine whether or not sensations or patterns go to short-term memory. *Signal strength* can range from the scream of a child in pain to the hum of a bee in summer. It also can relate to the number of times the advertisement or commercial has been seen before. *Pertinence* is based on how the person's experiences have been formed and the interest the person has in the subject from which the information comes. There must be a strong signal and the messages must be pertinent enough for the receiver to go through the judgment process.

In summary, judgments are made in the following way. First, information presented in advertising is represented in the SR. The SR holds the information for further processing and interprets the characteristics of the stimulus. If the signal in the form of advertising is sufficiently strong and pertinent to the person, it calls forth information that has been held in long-term storage. This enables the new information in the advertising to be brought to short-term storage and processed and then stored again.

From this description, we can see that there are several important factors in the development of effective advertising strategies. Two come to mind immediately. First, the information contained in the advertising must be strong enough and pertinent enough to be considered for further processing. If the information is too obtuse or too irrelevant, the advertising has no chance of having an impact. Second, advertising must be consistent enough so that it will be accepted when judged against information previously processed and held in long-term storage. If, for example, the advertising says that hot coffee is a good beverage for a very hot summer day, it is likely that this message will not square with information people have stored about summer drinks or the use of coffee.

The Hierarchical Approach to How Advertising Works

Setting objectives for the advertising campaign is a key advertising planning activity. To decide in which areas objectives must be set, it is necessary to understand the relationships between various consumer responses to advertising and the ultimate purchase of a product. Otherwise, objective setting and planning become arbitrary, and we have no way of knowing if achievement of our objectives will contribute to the sale of the product.

A hierarchical scheme for setting and measuring advertising objectives was developed by Lavidge and Steiner and has become the foundation for objective setting in many companies and agencies.[5] Others have also developed hierarchical approaches similar to that of Lavidge and Steiner. The hierarchical approach to how advertising works assumes that there are a series of steps a consumer must pass through in sequential order, from initial awareness of a product to knowledge about the product to actual purchase. The typical configuration of this hierarchy is indicated at the top of the columns in Table 2–2. This text uses Lavidge and Steiner's approach because of its popularity and usefulness in describing key advertising variables measured in the industry today.

The key components of the hierarchy, regardless of labels given to them, are learning, attitude formation or feeling, and purchase or the connotative component. Table 2–2 includes some of the more popular hierarchies, including that developed by Lavidge and Steiner.

The Lavidge and Steiner hierarchy is based on the hierarchy developed by Russell Colley in his book, *Defining Advertising Goals for Measured Advertising Results* (*DAGMAR* for short).[6] A comparison of Colley's hierarchical scheme with Lavidge and Steiner's shows some minor differences. The comprehension and knowledge terms under learning are really interchangeable. Colley places conviction under feeling, a strong attitudinal response after comprehension. Lavidge and Steiner include weaker attitudinal responses before conviction. The purchase and action responses are really the same. These two hierarchies are the most popular in the industry today.

Let's use a hypothetical new product introduction to demonstrate how the hierarchy works. A new line of ice cream flavors called "vegetable flavors" is about to be introduced. The new flavors range from carrot to broccoli. Distribution has been achieved in all major supermarket chains, and a network television campaign will introduce the new flavors to homes in the top 200 TV markets. Because there is not awareness of this new line presently, an ambitious awareness objective has been set for the first year of the campaign.

The manufacturer of "vegetable flavors" expects some resistance to the idea of combining vegetable flavors with ice cream. (Remember the "judgment process" from the previous section.) Therefore, another goal of the introductory campaign is to teach (i.e., knowledge) consumers about the

---

[5]Robert J. Lavidge and Gary A. Steiner, "A Model for Predictive Measurements of Advertising Effectiveness," *Journal of Marketing* 24 (October 1961): 59–62.

[6]Russell H. Colley, *Defining Advertising Goals for Measured Advertising Results* (New York: Association of National Advertisers, 1961).

Table 2–2   Hierarchy of Effects

Terminology in the Hierarchy of Effects

Name(s) of theorist(s)	Learning (cognitive)	Feeling (affective)	Acting (conative)
Anonymous	Attention	Interest, Desire	Action
Lavidge & Steiner (1961)	Awareness Knowledge	Liking Preference	Conviction Purchase
Colley (1961)	Awareness Comprehension	Conviction	Action
Rogers (1962)	Awareness	Interest Evaluation	Trial Adoption
Mendelsohn (1962)	Rudimentary response (recall)	Emotional response (affect)	Active response
Wolfe, et al. (1962)	Awareness Acceptance	Preference Interest	Sale
Aspinwall (1964)	Acceptance	Preference	Insistence
A.R.F. (undated)	Exposure, Perception, Communication (knowledge)	Communication (attitude)	Action
M.S.I. (1968)	Awareness Knowledge	Liking Preference	Conviction Purchase
Schwartz (1969)	Exposure, Attention, Retention	Attitude change	Purchase
Howard & Sheth (1969)	Attention Comprehension	Attitude	Intention Purchase
Howard (undated)	Facts-exposed Facts-coded	Attitude	Intention Purchase
Murphy (1971)	Attitude Comprehension	Significance Differentiation	Activation
Taylor & Peterson (1972)	Attention	Interest Desire	Conviction Action
Young (1972)	Attention Communication	Persuasion	
Holbrook (1975)	Attention, Perception, Memory	Attitude	Intention

SOURCE: Charles Ramond, *Advertising Research: The State of the Art* (New York: Association of National Advertisers, Inc., 1976): 15.

nutritional value of the ice cream flavors. Due to the current health trend, the manufacturer expects the new health segment to react favorably and like the flavors. To build a preference for "vegetable flavors" an ambitious promotional campaign is planned to support the national advertising. Taste tests and nutritional programs are being planned. The taste tests will occur in all national supermarket chains (again, in an attempt to change opinions and influence judgments). The nutritional programs will be offered in booklet form with each purchase of a gallon or more of one of the new flavors.

To bring consumers to the conviction stage, nationally known authors of best selling books on health and exercise, such as Jane Fonda and Richard Simmons, are being used to extol the virtues of the new flavors on talk shows and to civic groups. The combination of all these efforts is expected to pull consumers through the hierarchy to trial and repeat purchase of vegetable-flavored ice cream.

The assumption of the hierarchical approach described is that it is necessary for a campaign to pull a consumer through all the steps before he will purchase the product. Yet, there are situations in which a consumer might buy a product after simple exposure to an ad and before developing an attitude about the product. This is exactly what happens with many of the products we buy.

The passive learning situation described previously is exactly the situation Herbert Krugman was referring to. He labeled the hierarchical sequence involved in these situations the "low-involvement" hierarchy. The low-involvement sequence takes the consumer from passive learning straight to purchase. Only after experience with the product is an attitude formed.[7]

An example of the low-involvement hierarchy in action is a new advertising campaign for a relatively unimportant product, such as a candy bar. The recent Hershey's campaign for their Skor candy bar reminds the consumer that "you can never be too rich or too thin." This is an interesting approach for a product about which you might not have thought recently. The catchy line brings you into the advertisement. As a result of this simple, yet memorable advertising approach, you might well purchase a Hershey's Skor bar instead of another brand the next time you want a candy bar. This is how the low-involvement hierarchy works.

We might summarize the hierarchical approach to how advertising works with the four-step process illustrated in Exhibit 2–9 following. Called the "buyer response sequence," this approach illustrates why the four steps are necessary for advertising to be successful.

---

[7]Herbert E. Krugman, "The Impact of Television Advertising": 349–56.

Exhibit 2–9   Buyer Response Sequence (from Rossiter and Percy)

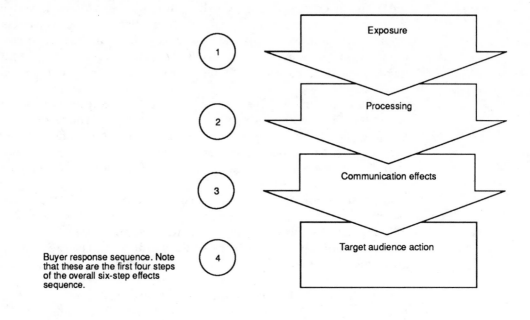

Buyer response sequence. Note that these are the first four steps of the overall six-step effects sequence.

SOURCE: John R. Rossiter and Larry Percy, *Advertising and Promotion Management*, (New York: McGraw-Hill, 1987): 17.

Exposure, processing, communication effects, and action are the steps that you yourself go through when you buy a product as a result of advertising. Rossiter and Percy describe it this way:

Think of the television campaign for Diet Coke not too long ago.

1. EXPOSURE: With regard to the first of the steps in the buyer response sequence, unless you were an absolute non-TV watcher, you were undoubtedly exposed to one or more commercials for Diet Coke. The Coca-Cola Company ran a very heavy TV media campaign for this brand.
2. PROCESSING: With regard to the second step, you probably paid attention to some parts, such as the music or visuals, of at least one of the commercials. In other words, you processed the Diet Coke advertising to some, or perhaps a considerable, degree.

3. COMMUNICATION EFFECTS: The third step is communication effects. There are usually several effects. If you learned the brand name from the advertising, "Diet Coke," and remembered what the new brand looked like, you have attained one of the communication effects (brand awareness). If you also formed an opinion for or against Diet Coke, you attained another communication effect (brand attitude). Brand awareness plus a favorable brand attitude would largely determine whether you have taken the final step intended for the target audience—action.

4. TARGET AUDIENCE ACTION: The relevant target audience action for Diet Coke is purchase. This is the fourth and final step in the buyer response sequence. If you have purchased Diet Coke, then the advertising has influenced you successfully in the four steps in the buyer response sequence.

Of course, advertising is rarely responsible, by itself, for purchase. The rest of the marketing mix contributes too: product performance, such as taste (especially important for repeat purchase following trial of the brand); price, assuming price is similar to other colas; distribution, assuming you could find the brand in stores; and other forms of promotion, such as favorable comments from your friends. But the advertising undoubtedly has played a large part. Because of all the people who purchase Diet Coke, it is now the third-largest selling soft drink in the United States.[8]

These two hierarchies—learning and low involvement—account for the majority of the situations confronted by most advertisers. However advertising and consumer purchase patterns are dynamic. Once someone has purchased a product, the sequence of events does not stop. A hierarchy that demonstrates the sequence of events following purchase is the dissonance–attribution hierarchy.

To illustrate this hierarchy, let's return to Mr. Smith's car purchase situation. Now, let's assume he did purchase the Chevy Blazer and not a Jeep or Ford. What happens next? The dissonance–attribution hierarchy says that Mr. Smith is likely to experience an uneasy feeling about his purchase. This is called *dissonance*.[9] The uneasy feeling is caused by the realization that the Chevy Blazer is not a perfect purchase. The Blazer has some negative aspects that are now recognized by Mr. Smith. Also, he now realizes that the Jeep Cherokee and Ford Bronco have positive aspects that would make them reasonable purchases. These realizations after the purchase undermine Mr. Smith's confidence in the purchase he made.

Mr. Smith does not like this dissonant feeling, so he tries to reduce the pressure by seeking out information that supports his purchase. He now notices all the Chevy Blazers on the road that he had never noticed before.

---

[8]John R. Rossiter and Larry Percy, *Advertising and Promotion Management* (New York: McGraw-Hill, 1987): 16–18.

[9]Leon Festinger, "Cognitive Dissonance," *Scientific American* (October 1962): 93–100.

He also starts to notice more and more ads for Chevy Blazers. All this information is taken in and reinforces a positive feeling in Mr. Smith for his new Blazer. The dissonance has been reduced.

Advertisers can take advantage of the dissonance–attribution hierarchy by reinforcing consumers' reasons for their purchases in advertising and promotional materials. By helping consumers reduce dissonance, purchase behavior is reinforced and the likelihood of another purchase is greatly enhanced.

Models of How Advertising Works at the Societal Level

The previous section describes how advertising affects individual consumers. Now it is necessary to describe briefly how advertising affects many people simultaneously.

Two theoretical approaches that deal with how groups of people respond to advertising are diffusion theory and agenda setting. These topics are discussed in some depth in Chapter 3, so they will be treated only briefly here.

Diffusion theory.   Diffusion theory attempts to explain how new ideas and products spread through the population. The basic theory uses the structure of the step-flow models previously discussed, but focuses more closely on how word-of-mouth communication helps to disseminate innovation through society.

The major components of diffusion theory are diffusion, adoption, communication, adoption units, innovations, and time. The diffusion model tries to explain how an innovation is tried and adopted by people, groups, organizations, or countries over time.

A prominent communications researcher, Everett Rogers, in *Diffusion of Innovations,* segmented the population into five groups based on the amount of time it takes for each group to adopt an innovation. The earliest group to try a new product are "innovators." They are considered risk takers. The second group is labeled "early adopters." Next to adopt are "early majority" members followed by the "late majority" and "laggards." These groups plus the adoption process are diagrammed in Chapter 3.[10]

Of importance to the study of advertising is the role that interpersonal communication plays in disseminating news about products and services. The diffusion model can be observed in operation in the motion picture industry where word-of-mouth communication can make or break a film. Initially, film producers try to create awareness to interest avid film goers

[10]Everett M. Rogers, *Diffusion of Innovations* (New York: Free Press, 1962): 162.

in their new picture. Next, the first group to see a film will tell friends about the film. If the word-of-mouth communication is positive, it will spread quickly, and more and more people will become involved in the communication process as they see the film and talk about it with others. This model is analogous to the spread of contagious diseases. Advertisers of new products and services hope for an epidemic of positive communication as a result of their advertising.

Advertising's role in this process is to create initial awareness and interest and give people information content to spread via word-of-mouth communication. This strategy is based on the premise that the best salesperson for your product is a satisfied customer.

The concept of opinion leadership as described previously is central to the diffusion process. Opinion leaders are both active seekers and disseminators of information. Campaigns that target opinion leaders, such as doctors and teachers, are attempting to use the influence and credibility of these persons to spread favorable word-of-mouth communication.

Agenda setting.   The major premise of agenda-setting theory is that "the mass media don't tell us what to think, but they do tell us what to think about."[11] In essence, the media set our agenda. An agenda-setting approach to understanding how advertising works would suggest that advertising focuses our attention on what products, brands, and attributes to think about as opposed to trying to persuade us what to think of them.

The agenda-setting approach dovetails nicely with low-involvement learning. It suggests that salience of a brand is important in low-involvement situations where simple recognition might induce product trial. The evoked-set concept discussed in the next chapter is a marketing application of the agenda-setting idea. An evoked set consists of those brands of a product that are serious alternatives for a consumer. The goal of many advertisers is to make sure their brand is in a consumer's evoked set. Products not in the evoked set have little chance of being purchased. The evoked set is the agenda for a product category in the consumer's mind.

SUMMARY: HOW DOES ADVERTISING WORK?

Exhibit 2–10 summarizes many of the concepts we have discussed to this point. It combines the key elements of individual, face-to-face, and mass communication. As you look at the model, notice the clutter of messages that clamor for the receiver's attention. This clutter represents the over a thousand messages a day that many of us are exposed to. To deal with the

---

[11]Max Sutherland and John Galloway, "Role of Advertising: Persuasion or Agenda Setting?" *Journal of Advertising Research* 21, 5 (October 1981): 25.

clutter, the consumer screens out or selects only those messages that interest him or her. To get through this screen, advertisers must appeal to the consumer's needs, tap common experiences, and be unique enough to gain attention.

Exhibit 2–10   How Advertising Communicates

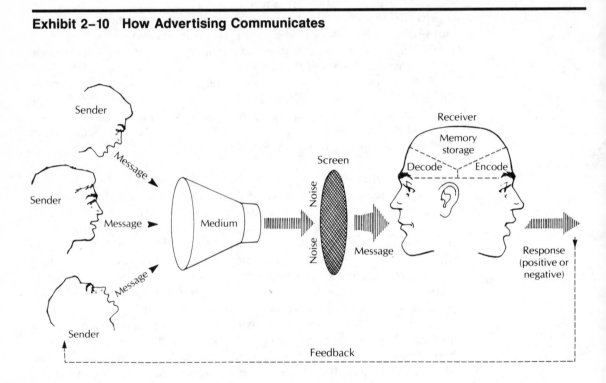

The decoding, encoding, and memory processes are also clearly indicated in Exhibit 2–10. Remember that memory is limited and will influence what information is stored. Also, some information not immediately needed will also be stored for future use.

This model generally describes high-involvement situations conceptualized by the learning hierarchy. Passive learning situations can be accommodated if we visualize the receiver in a passive model, not selecting, but merely catching messages that grab his or her attention.

The active and passive learning situations account for most of the advertising situations you are likely to encounter. Although the models described here might suffer from oversimplification, they are useful to the planner's understanding of how advertising works. And, this understanding will affect the goals the planner set for the campaign and the strategies and tactics selected to achieve these goals.

This chapter has attempted to illustrate the important factors involved in the communication of sales messages to consumers. How consumers respond to these messages is largely influenced by individual consumer characteristics and environmental factors not covered in this chapter. The next chapter will discuss those factors that influence how and why consumers react to our ads as they attempt to make purchase decisions.

Case Studies

Maverick Brewing Company

The Maverick Brewing Company is a small, regional brewer located in eastern Tennessee. Maverick is a family-owned business with a short, 20-year history of brewing and marketing beer in an area of the country not known for its beer drinking. Maverick markets its line under the Ole South and Rebel Flag labels. Until recently, Maverick sold a premium beer under the Old South label and popularly priced beer under the Rebel Flag label. Last year, a light beer was added to the line and given the name Ole South Light. This addition was made so that Maverick could compete locally in the light beer segment of the market, which had been slow to catch on in their area but was now showing signs of growth.

Although Maverick has never attempted to compete head-on against the major national brands, it has enjoyed success as a regional brewer. This success has not gone unnoticed. At least one major brewer is interested in merging with Maverick to gain easy entry into the beer market in the Southeast.

Last year, Maverick sold approximately three million barrels of beer in a six-state area from North Carolina to Mississippi (Alabama, Georgia, Mississippi, North Carolina, South Carolina, and Tennessee). Maverick's advertising budget of $500,000 has been spent primarily in local radio and outdoor in the major metropolitan markets in the six-state area. In fact, more than half the budget has been spent during the football season to support regional college and professional teams.

In a recent issue of *Southern Advertising News,* Mr. Ronald Cummings, owner and president of Maverick, described what he thinks are the reasons for Maverick's success in the region. Mr. Cummings said:

> What we really try to do is to keep the business simple. We brew three high quality beers with a formula that gives them a distinctive taste people in the Southeast like. Our market is not New York or the Midwest. We have to appeal to the South's unique taste preferences.
>
> Next, we appeal to local sporting interests and pride through our advertising. If you've never been to an Alabama or Georgia football game, then you don't know what I mean. But it's very important to our customers, and we try to associate our beer with these events.
>
> In our advertising, the beer is always the focus of the ad. It's the reason for the ad's existence. To tie in with pride in local sports, we associate ourselves with local sports heroes who have "made it" in professional sports. Joe Namath is an example. He was a quarterback at Alabama and with the New

York Jets. After he retired, we used him a lot in our ads. People like Joe Namath add a lot of impact to our ads. And on our budget, impact is important.

It's really quite simple. Start with a beer brewed specially for the region and appeal to our customers' pride in their local teams and sports heroes. It's gotten us this far. Why fool with success?

NEW COMPETITION

Maverick's line of beers has been a success in the past twenty years primarily because other brewers did not see the South as a very lucrative market. However, the Cummings family saw changes in the region that would lead to the general public's acceptance of social drinking and sale of alcoholic beverages. Now, Anheuser-Busch, Miller, and Coors are making serious promotional efforts in a market Maverick once had to itself. This worries Mr. Cummings because the promotional clout these companies bring into the region is something Maverick has not had to face in the past.

Anheuser-Busch and Miller dominate the national beer market with over a 50 percent combined share of the market. Their dominance is so great that industry experts describe the beer industry as a two-tier industry. The second tier of the industry includes smaller national brewers, such as Heileman, Coors, and Olympia, plus regional brewers, such as Lone Star, the Pittsburgh Brewing Company, and Maverick.

Even though Anheuser-Busch and Miller dominate the market, second-tier regional brewers have been able to succeed in their local markets by appealing to local pride and tastes. Olympia and Coors are very successful brewers in the West. Lone Star does well in Texas. Iron City Beer and Mustang Malt Liquor do well for the Pittsburgh Brewing Company in western Pennsylvania. In fact, it is not uncommon to find regional brands outcompeting the national brands in their regions.

The national brewers who worry Mr. Cummings the most are Anheuser-Busch, Miller, and Coors. Each has different strengths and weaknesses.

THE NATIONAL COMPETITION

Anheuser-Busch's brand list includes Budweiser, Busch, Michelob, Michelob Light, Michelob Dry, Natural Light, and Bud Light. The strength of the list is Budweiser, which continues to be the number-one premium beer in the world.

Anheuser-Busch continues to dominate the industry's advertising spending. They also have breweries in Virginia and Florida that will provide the production needed to support their serious promotional efforts in the South.

Miller has based its resurgence in the beer industry on three brands—Miller High Life, Miller Lite, and Lowenbrau. Since being taken over by

Phillip Morris in the late 70s Miller has steadily climbed toward the top of the beer industry behind the success of its Lite beer.

Coors, like Maverick, is a family-owned brewery that has achieved a reputation for brewing a smooth, light-tasting beer that could only be bought west of the Mississippi. The regional exclusivity of Coors is a thing of the past as the conservative brewer has expanded nationally. Coors markets a light beer, premium, and superpremium all under the Coors name. Coors does not have the same advertising support as Anheuser-Busch and Miller, but it does have a line of beers especially suited to the Southeast in terms of taste and reputation.

MAVERICK'S PLAN

Cummings's first step to fight the increased marketing efforts of Anheuser-Busch, Miller, and Coors will be to add a superpremium to his brand list to compete against those offered by the competition (Michelob and Lowenbrau). Additionally, a deal is being negotiated with another small regional brewer to produce the new superpremium. Although a name has not been chosen, Cummings's preference is to use a variation of one of his two existing brand names. Ole South Golden is the name Cummings prefers, but Rebel Gold is also a possibility.

Cummings plans to compete against the national brands by being aggressive, not defensive. To do this, he plans to invest $2 million in advertising to support the introduction of his new superpremium brand. The problem, as Cummings sees it, is one of gaining a fair share of the consumer's attention for his brands. He feels that he has a definite advantage in the region because he knows the people better than the national brewers. But he does not want to rest on his laurels. In fact, the new superpremium addition is really a rallying point for his new campaign. Maverick needed something "new" to help create some excitement in the marketplace.

Questions

1. Using the step-flow model, discuss how Maverick Brewing Company might expand the impact of the new campaign for its new superpremium brand.
2. Analyze Maverick's communication advantages and disadvantages in the Southeast using the individual and the face-to-face models of communication.
3. Which hierarchy of communication effects is Mr. Cummings confronted by? Describe how Maverick's new advertising campaign is likely to affect the different steps of the hierarchy.

4. Using the distinction between active and passive audience members, describe what you think Maverick's customers are like. Also, outline a brief plan for what you think the advertising should be like for the new superpremium introduction.
5. Using Assael's model of how advertising works, describe the process Mr. Cummings must go through to successfully gain a strong position for his new brand in the customer's mind.

"The Laugh's On Us" Cable Comedy Network

Jerry Hughes, president of "The Laugh's On Us," a Chicago-based chain of comedy clubs located throughout the Midwest, was reviewing some information on the current status of cable television networks. "The Laugh's On Us" was considering launching a cable comedy network as a way of enhancing its brand franchise and a means of long-term financial growth. Hughes was interested in developing some initial marketing communications ideas for such a network.

The audience for cable television in the United States has experienced tremendous growth over the past several years. Cable penetration is at over 55 percent nationally. In addition to broadcast network affiliates and local independent stations, cable subscribers receive as many as four superstations (WTBS, WGN, WWOR, WPIX) and thirty-four basic cable networks (such as ESPN, CNN, USA, MTV, Nickelodeon, and The Weather Channel). In addition, there are at least five pay cable alternatives (HBO, Showtime, Cinemax, The Disney Channel, and The Movie Channel).

Cable advertising revenues continue to grow as the cable networks show their ability to woo viewers away from the traditional broadcast networks. The appealing financial picture has encouraged the continued development of cable networks which hope to capture a larger share of the television-viewing audience for their own programming. Many of the new networks have tried to differentiate themselves through program offerings directed at particular audience segments. CNBC bills itself as an information channel. "Nick at Night," with its lineup of classic situation comedies, is programmed for the baby boomer generation. The Discovery Channel is for those viewers who fondly remember their days in science classes and who thrilled to Mr. Wizard.

Programming costs for a cable television network can be as low as $40 million annually (for an all-rerun lineup) or can escalate into the hundreds of millions (for original programming). Still, cable networks that are able to capture an audience segment with advertiser appeal make money, money that can be used to hold onto viewers through promotion, or to fund new channel alternatives.

"The Laugh's On Us" planned to use its network of comedy clubs as a source of programming. Although costs for established comedians would likely be high, up-and-coming performers would probably perform for free in exchange for the exposure the channel would give them. Consequently, Hughes believed that programming costs could be kept under $100 million annually.

Although there were no other cable networks that offered comedy programming exclusively, a number of networks programmed comedy-based shows as part of their overall program schedule. Nick at Nite offered humorous programs including "The Best of Saturday Night Live," "SCTV," and "Laugh-In," while several of the pay cable networks featured well-known comedians in both special and regular programming ("Comic Relief" on HBO; "It's Garry Shandling's Show" on Showtime). Despite the competition, Hughes felt that a purely comedy network could win an audience. He expected the network to attract two audience groups: comedy addicts, who would make a point of knowing the day's schedule and pre-plan their viewing accordingly; and comedy fans, who would include the channel as an alternative to other programming.

A typical programming day for "The Laugh's On Us" network might look something like this:

12 P.M.–3 A.M.   **Insomniac Heaven**—A collection of classic comedy films and specials, including Laurel and Hardy and Abbott and Costello films.

3–4 A.M.   **The Three Stooges Hour**

4–6 A.M.   **Cartoon Greats**—Cartoons from the 40s, 50s, and 60s.

6–9 A.M.   **The Morning Retort**—A comic alternative to the morning news shows, humorous twists on news stories, "Today's Tabloid Teaser," etc.

9–10 A.M.   **Comic's Corner**—A series of how-to lessons in stand-up comedy featuring tips from a variety of successful comedians.

10–11 A.M.   **The Three Stooges Hour**

11 A.M.–2 P.M.	**The Nooner**—Same programming as "Insomniac Heaven."
2–4 P.M.	**Cartoon Greats**
4–5 P.M.	**Who's On First?**—A review of current comedy happenings including album releases, tours, and television appearances.
5–6 P.M.	**Rolling in the Aisles**—A movie review/preview program highlighting current and upcoming comedy film releases and performers.
6–7 P.M.	**Laugh Lines**—Tips on how to get a job as a comedy writer, how to submit script ideas, etc.
7–10 P.M.	**Standup Showcase**—Live and taped performances from the stages of "The Laugh's On Us" clubs throughout the Midwest.
10–11 P.M.	**The Three Stooges Hour**
11–12 P.M.	**Comic's Corner**

Hughes was considering a number of media alternatives for promoting "The Laugh's On Us" network. Commercials on other cable television networks would reach the cable subscriber, and could be placed in comedy programming on those networks. Radio might also be used, featuring excerpts from particular programs, such as "Now appearing on 'The Laugh's On Us' Comedy Network. . . . Print ads might be effective in highlighting the network's programming schedule.

Hughes knew that most of the advertising alternatives he was considering would have a great deal of wasted exposure—that is, the ads would reach people who were not likely prospects for the network. It was difficult to define the comedy audience demographically, making highly efficient media buying almost impossible. Hughes was also unsure how cross-promotion between the network and the clubs might work. On one hand, the clubs would be an ideal place to advertise the network, because anyone visiting a comedy club was likely to be a comedy fan. On the other hand, would promoting the network cut into club attendance figures? And would regular club attendees tune into the network during the important prime-time hours to watch a stand-up routine they'd seen in person the week before?

Questions

1. Use the elements in the step-flow model on page 48 to argue in support of using the clubs as a way of promoting the network.

2. Evaluate each of the mass media alternatives Hughes is considering in terms of the clutter the comedy network's message might face.

3. Apply one of the models of how advertising works (classical conditioning, for example) to the comedy network's situation in trying to attract viewers.

4. How might the diffusion of innovation theory discussed on pages 66–67 relate to the ability of the comedy network (and all cable networks) to attract viewers?

5. Looking at the summary model of advertising communication on page 68, how would you sell an advertiser on buying time on the comedy network? Be sure to include a description of the audience you expect the network to attract and how you believe that audience will feel about the network and its programming. Argue that advertising on the comedy network will stand a better chance of getting into the audience's memory store than advertising on the other networks.

Marketing, Advertising, and the Consumer

The background material on the way in which advertising works should help in understanding how advertising communicates selling messages to customers or prospects. But to develop an advertising campaign, the planner also needs a basic understanding of consumers—that is, how they act and react to advertising messages and how they go about making their purchasing decisions. Unless the advertising planner understands the consumer, he or she really has only a partial view of how advertising affects the marketplace. With a myriad of product categories available to most consumers and with many brands actually interchangeable with one another, the primary question in developing a sound advertising campaign becomes, how do consumers make choices in the marketplace? That's called consumer behavior. We look at it in some detail in this chapter.

WHAT IS CONSUMER BEHAVIOR?

Let's start with a definition: *consumer behavior* is "the behavior that consumers display in searching for, purchasing, using, evaluating, and disposing of products, services, and ideas which they expect will satisfy their needs."[1] Obviously, to develop the most effective sales message for a product, marketers and advertisers need to know many things about the present or prospective users of the product. They first need to know what consumers and prospects buy, then why they buy what they do; how they buy the product or service; when they buy it; where they buy it; how often they buy it; and even what they are likely to do with the product when

---

[1] Leon G. Schiffman and Leslie Lazar Kanuk, *Consumer Behavior,* 3rd ed. (Englewood Cliffs, N.J.: Prentice-Hall, 1987): 6.

they are through with it (especially important in those communities where recycling is a fact of life). In addition, it is usually helpful to know how consumers feel about the product or service they have purchased or how they feel when they use it, if and how and why they might purchase it again in the future, and so on. In short, to devise an effective advertising sales message, the advertising planner needs to know as much as possible about how consumers behave, how they react or don't react, and why they do what they do. This knowledge is the basis of a sound advertising campaign. The following overview of the more important concepts of consumer behavior, particularly as they relate to advertising, will be helpful in the planning process.

TYPES OF CONSUMERS AND INFLUENCES ON CONSUMER PURCHASES

Essentially, in any marketplace in any society, there are two types of buyers: those who buy for personal use and those who buy for an organization. Those who buy for personal use have the sole or ultimate purchasing decision power, whether they plan to use the product themselves or not, as is usually the case with most consumer products. No doubt many factors, such as the influence of opinion leaders and gatekeepers (discussed in Chapter 2), come into play when people make a purchase within a particular product category or even of a particular brand. Ultimately, however, the choice is up to the individual.

On the other hand, when an organizational purchase is made, a number of people have a direct influence on the product category chosen and the brand purchased. For example, assume that there is a group of people in a large manufacturing plant considering the purchase of a new piece of metal-forming equipment to be used in constructing the outer cabinet of the company's air filter units. Although it is true that only one of these people will most likely have to sign the purchase order, many people will be involved in the purchasing decision. As shown in Exhibit 3–1, the purchasing "influencers" might include members of the operations management staff, the plant manager, the safety engineer, and even the chief financial officer and chief executive officer. Most important in this particular purchasing decision, however, would be the design engineer.

Organizational purchasers are usually found in most industrial or business-to-business sales fields. They are often termed the *buying center.* The existence of the buying center means that the various components of the promotional campaign, including advertising, may have to influence a number of people, each with different needs or objectives in the purchase situation.

Exhibit 3–1   Purchasing "Influencers"

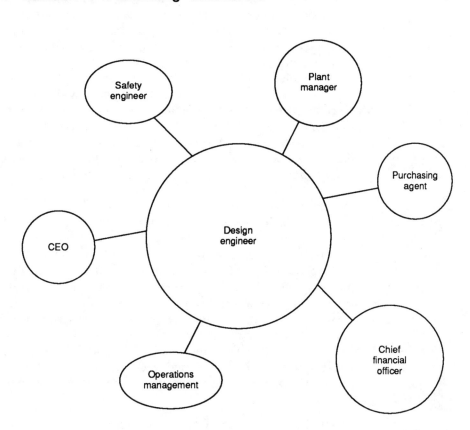

It is important for the advertising planner to understand the difference between the personal and organizational types of buyers. It can make a definite difference in the way the advertising campaign is developed, from the setting of advertising objectives to the design of the message to the advertising media selection. This text will deal primarily with individual consumers as the decision makers, but it is important to recognize the influence of others, even on individual purchase decisions.

In most cases, consumers or prospects for products or services can make the individual decision as to whether or not to purchase. Still, it is important to remember one fact: even individual purchasers come in two types, (a) those who buy for their own use or consumption, and (b) those who purchase products for use by others. In our mobile society and diffuse marketplace, the purchaser of a particular product is not always the final user. For example, Mom buys peanut butter but consumes none herself.

She's buying for the children in the family. In this situation, she may respond to the wishes of the children who will actually eat the peanut butter, or she may make the decision on her own. The husband, at the request of his wife, stops at the corner drugstore on his way home from work and purchases her shampoo and conditioner. He may or may not have had an influence on the brand purchased. The couple make up the shopping list and then allocate the purchases between them, although both may use or consume the products purchased. And, in more and more homes with two working parents, teens are taking over the family shopping responsibilities. That is why it is important to remember that the buyer is not always the user, nor the user the buyer. And that's why, often, advertising campaigns are developed to encourage the purchaser to influence the user or to encourage the user to influence the purchaser. Perhaps, at this point, it would be helpful to look briefly at what influences consumers or purchasers in their actual buying decisions.

In our society, few consumer purchasing decisions are made in a rational, unemotional, economic way. It's quite often the opposite, particularly for those consumer products that are used often. The environment, our emotions, hopes, wishes, and wants often have greater influence on our purchasing decisions than do sheer economic values. That's why sales of products such as hoola-hoops and pet rocks soar even in economic recessions. Although it is a difficult one, the basic task of the advertiser planner is to know and understand as nearly as possible what those influences are and what effect they might have on the success or failure of the advertising message being developed. Generally, the influences on consumer purchasing behavior can be separated into internal and external factors.

Internal Influences on Consumer Behavior— Needs and Wants

Factors that come from the personality or psychological makeup of the individual are considered to be *internal influences*. These are all those things that make "me" what I am, or what I think I am, or what I would like to be. Although these factors are often quite complex, researchers have classified them as needs and wants.

The basic factor that influences nearly all consumer purchases is the arousal of a need or a want. This is the most important factor in marketing and advertising; the entire idea of marketing is built around determining consumers' needs or wants and then attempting to fill them with a product or service, at a profit to the marketing organization. (See the discussion of the marketing concept in Chapter 1.)

Needs and wants are handled quite differently when it comes to using them in the development of an advertising campaign. *Needs* have been defined as "the gap or discrepancy experienced between an actual and a desired state of being. This experience may be biological or social in nature."[2] Needs vary in importance to consumers. It does appear, however, that there is a basic structure for needs among all people. One of the most widely known and accepted theories of motivation as a result of needs is the hierarchy developed by Abraham H. Maslow. (See Exhibit 3–2.)

Most researchers call needs those things that humans require for survival, such as food, clothing, and shelter. On the other hand, the methods by which we satisfy those needs are often called *wants*. For example, we all need to drink water to replenish the fluids in our bodies. However, over time, some groups of humans have decided that bottled water, especially particular "designer" waters, are a better or perhaps more socially prestigious method of getting sufficient water than drinking plain tap water. In our society of abundance, marketers try to satisfy the wants rather than the needs of consumers. Coffee may be prepared by boiling the grounds in an iron pot over an open fire. Yet, consumers want automatic drip percolators, which, when set in advance, come on at a certain time each morning, brew the coffee, then turn themselves off, and still keep the coffee warm. Consumers may "need" an iron pot, but they "want" a Mr. Coffee. Thus, most advertising campaigns are directed at consumer wants rather than human needs.

It is important to keep these concepts of needs and wants in mind when developing an advertising campaign. Because there are few unfilled consumer needs in our society, products and services are usually targeted at perceived wants. It is this exploring differences in wants that leads to market segmentation, about which more will be said later. For example, most consumers need detergent to clean their clothing, but some want Tide because it fights tough stains, while others want Cheer because it cleans in cold water.

External Influences on Consumer Behavior

Whether we are born with them or acquire them through learning, needs and wants make up our personalities. They influence our attitudes toward various products and services. More specifically, we learn or discover through experience or are told by others or by advertising that certain products and even certain brands satisfy various needs better than others. In some instances, our attitudes about various products and brands are influenced by what happens to us in society. We call these occurrences the *external influences*.

Although we normally bring our needs into a given purchasing situation—that is, we were born with these needs or they have been em-

---

[2]Gerald Zaltman and Melanie Wallendorf, *Consumer Behavior: Basic Findings and Management Implications* (New York: John Wiley & Sons, 1979): 318.

Exhibit 3–2 Maslow's Hierarchy of Needs

Maslow developed the idea or concept that all human actions are based on a hierarchy of needs (some researchers term them *motives*). He identified the basic needs as physiological, safety, love, esteem, and self-actualization. Maslow's basic concept was that as the lower needs are fulfilled, the next highest order of needs comes into play.

Thus, the most basic needs, the physiological needs of food, drink, shelter, and relief from pain, dominate behavior until they are satisfied. Once that occurs, the factors that most influence behavior are those next up the scale: safety and security. And so on up the scale.

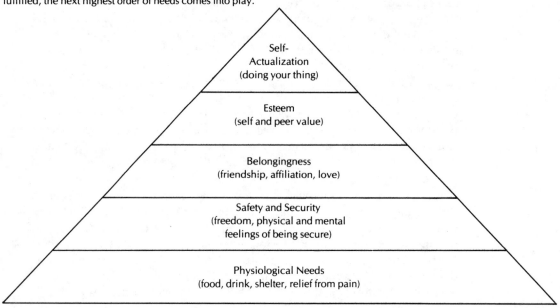

Maslow estimated that the typical adult in our society has satisfied about 85 percent of the physical needs, 70 percent of the safety and security needs, 50 percent of the need to belong and love, 40 percent of the need for esteem, and 10 percent of the self-actualization need. Obviously, every individual has a different method of satisfying his or her particular needs, and each progresses through the hierarchy at a different speed and with different solutions. Maslow's theory is helpful, however, for the advertising planner's understanding of why and how various products or services might fit into the plans, goals, and lives of prospects. One should also remember that as the individual progresses up the hierarchy, there are more and more ways of satisfying

needs. For example, food and drink are easily identified as methods of solving some of the basic needs, but there are many and varied ways in which the needs for esteem fulfillment might be satisfied. The advertising planner must always view the product or service to be advertised in terms of how it might fit into the need patterns of prospective consumers.

While Maslow theorized that all people are born with the basic needs in the hierarchy he proposed, others have argued that many human needs, particularly those at the higher levels, are learned. For example, David McClelland has proposed that many needs are learned through the childhood socialization process. Thus, McClelland and others theorize that each individual has a unique set of motivational needs.*

SOURCE: Abraham H. Maslow, *Toward a Psychology of Being,* 2nd ed. (New York: Van Nostrand, 1968): 380.
*David C. McClelland, *Personality* (New York: Holt, Rinehart & Winston, 1951).

bedded in our personalities at an early age—the same is not true of wants. Wants are largely influenced by factors outside us. These external factors may take many forms, and experts still fail to agree on a detailed listing of all of them. However, most researchers agree on the basic concept of external influences and what they consist of—for example, culture, subcultures, social classes, social groups, families, and personal influences. (See Exhibit 3–3.) David Loudon and Albert J. Della Bitta have visualized these external influences as a series of concentric circles, with the most general influences on the outside, the farthest away, and those more personal in nature located closer to the individual.

Exhibit 3–3   External Influences on Consumer Behavior

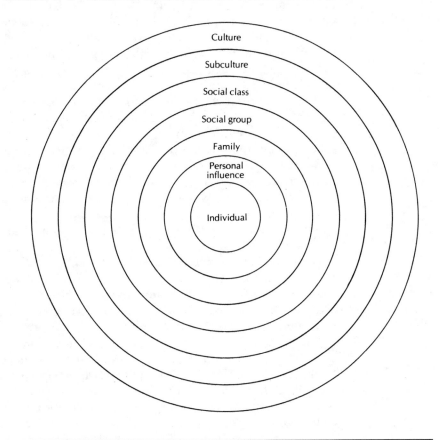

SOURCE: Adapted from David L. Loudon and Albert J. Della Bitta, *Consumer Behavior: Concepts and Applications* (New York: McGraw-Hill, 1979): 122.

Culture.   Culture is a very broad concept, although researchers, in general, agree that E.B. Taylor's 1891 definition is still appropriate: "That complex whole which includes knowledge, belief, art, law, morals, custom and any other capabilities and habits acquired by man as a member of society."[3] Culture is the broad, general framework within which many of our ideas and our behavior develops.

The aspects of world cultures are many and varied, and this is reflected in advertising. Cleanliness is a major force in our culture. Such is not the case in many other areas of the world. Thus, media in the U.S. are filled with advertising for products such as soap, detergents, shampoos, bleaches, and deodorants. These products are not nearly so important in many other countries.

Subcultures.   Within most cultures there are several subcultures. The most common of these subcultures are usually based on race, religion, or nationality. For example, in the U.S., there are large subcultures of blacks, Hispanics, and Orientals, among others. Religious subcultures in the U.S. revolve around Protestantism, Catholicism, and Judaism. Nationality subcultures include such groups as Mexican-Americans, Cuban-Americans, Latin-Americans (all three of which are Hispanic subsegments), Afro-Americans, and others not indigenous to North America.

We also find subcultures developing or having developed in the U.S. as a result of age or sex. The "over-50" market, which can be targeted through specific publications and programming, is quickly becoming a major force in America. The youth subculture, another example, has been important to many marketers in recent years. Subcultures based on sex are quite common. The traditional women's subculture, built around home and family, has changed and is continuing to change and evolve. As more and more women move into the labor force, new and different types of subcultures are developing.

There also are subcultures based on geographic location. In the U.S., the cultures of urban and rural locations are dramatically different. The same is true for specific geographic areas of the country. For example, the "laid-back," health-oriented subculture that has developed in California has devotees across the entire nation.

Finally, in addition to these basic subcultures, some researchers have classified groups that have sprung up around a specific belief or life-style as subcultures. For example, a definite subculture exists among those who use and sell drugs. Subcultures of this type can certainly be a factor in the short term. Advertising campaigns often are significantly influenced by the culture and the various subcultures that exist in the country.

---

[3]Edward B. Taylor, *Primitive Culture* (London: Murray, 1891): 1.

Social class.   Classifying or separating groups of people by social class is probably one of the world's first attempts at stratification. In general, social class is some type of hierarchy that attempts to delineate the whole society into homogeneous groups based on attitudes, values, life-styles, and perhaps other variables of the population. A recent analysis of social class in the U.S. is shown in Table 3–1.

Social class is signified in many ways in the U.S., ranging from customs, such as membership in certain clubs and organizations, to the physical lo-

Table 3–1   The Gilbert-Kahl New Synthesis Class Structure: A Situations Model from Political Theory and Sociological Analysis

Upper Americans

The capitalist class (1 percent). Their investment decisions shape the national economy; income mostly from assets, earned, inherited; prestige university connections

Upper middle class (14 percent). Upper managers, professionals, medium business people; college educated; family income ideally runs near twice the national average

Middle Americans

Middle class (33 percent). Middle-level white collar, top-level blue collar; education past high school typical; income somewhat above the national average

Working class (32 percent). Middle-level blue collar; lower-level white collar; income runs slightly below the national average; education is also slightly below

Marginal and Lower Americans

The working poor (11 to 12 percent). Below mainstream America in living standard, but above the poverty line; low-paid service workers, operatives; some high school education

The underclass (8 to 9 percent). Depend primarily on welfare system for sustenance; living standard below poverty line; not regularly employed; lack schooling

SOURCE: Richard P. Coleman, "The Continuing Significance of Social Class to Marketing," *Journal of Consumer Research*, 10 (December 1983): 267.

cation of the home. For example, some suburbs are considered more socially prestigious than others. Social class is also signified by possessions,
such as automobiles and clothing, and even the colleges or universities at-
tended by members of the group.

One of the most important features of U.S. society is great social mobil-
ity. For example, some rock music stars are touted as being part of the upper class although they may have come from very humble beginnings. In
addition, the ebbs and flows of financial status greatly influence social
class. One of the most important effects social class may have on consumers is life-style definition. Often, because of social ranking, consumers
may or may not consider themselves to be prospects for some types of
products or services.

Social groups.   The total society is made up of social groups or reference groups with which people interact. These groups are usually deline-
ated on the basis of some shared interest or some activity or action. This
shared interest can range from that of rock and roll "groupies" to those of
traditional organizations, such as civic groups, churches, colleges and universities, and country clubs.

Members of social groups are important to advertisers because their
shared interest may provide the key to developing the advertising strategy
or message. For example, the "yuppie" phenomenon has contributed to
the popularity of a number of products and brands, such as the BMW automobile and Perrier water. Such "badges" of group affiliation are used to
signify a person's belonging to, or belief in, the group. These badges are often used by members of the group to identify themselves; in many instances, they are promoted by advertisers who hope to profit from an
association with the group's identity.

Family.   The family is the basic external influence on most consumers. It
is within the context of the family that many personality traits are developed. As a result, there is little question that family influence on future
purchasing decisions is great. For example, if the family always used Crest
toothpaste and Mom further confirmed the value of Crest to the children
as a decay preventive toothpaste, there is a good chance the children will
continue to purchase and use Crest toothpaste even after they leave the
family situation. Kool-Aid powdered soft drink mix has used this family influence approach in advertising over the past few years. Their line, "You
loved it as a child, you trust it as a mother," is designed to build sales and
acceptance through family influence.

Obviously, the family life cycle is important to both marketing and advertising planners. In certain situations and in certain life cycles, people
will be much better prospects for some products than they will be for
others—for example, children's toys to members of Full Nest I or vacation

condominiums to Empty Nest I. This family life cycle concept can assist the advertising campaign planner not only in selecting the proper persons to whom the advertising message should be directed but also can assist in determining what message might be most effective. As such, it is often more useful than a simpler descriptor, such as age.

Personal influence.   The final external influence, usually the most direct on the consumer, is the result of direct involvement with others. This is the one-on-one influence that may be a result of a friendship, a business relationship, a chance meeting, or any other form of nonfamily human interaction. This is the well-known "word-of-mouth" advertising discussed in Chapter 2: One person tries a product or service and tells others about the experience. Word-of-mouth advertising is perhaps the strongest external influence on purchasing decisions and is the most difficult for the advertising campaign planner to affect or control.

DEMAND

No matter what other influences may have an impact on the consumer, the key question is still whether or not the person or organization actually purchases a product or service. Economists refer to this "purchasing effect" which all consumers have on products or services as *demand*. Advertising campaign planners should be most interested in consumer demand and how to estimate or increase it.

As consumer needs and wants develop and as the various internal and external influences activate those needs and wants, demand for products or services develops in society. Consumers are willing to exchange goods, services, and/or labor for products and services they cannot or do not produce themselves. The greater the desire by consumers for those products or services, the stronger the demand. This demand is illustrated by a series of curves usually showing the relationship of sales to such factors as availability and price. The best known demand curve illustrates the sales response to price. (See Exhibit 3–4.) The lower the price, the greater the demand. That simply means that as marketers reduce the price for a product, more and more people usually are inclined to purchase it.

Marketers and advertisers are primarily interested in two measures of demand. The first is the measurement of overall demand, that is, the amount of the product or service a certain group of consumers might purchase in a certain time period, in a certain geographic area, at a certain price, and under certain economic conditions. The second area is *demand forecasting*—the estimate of what a certain group of consumers *might* purchase in a certain time period, in a certain geographic area, at a certain price, under certain economic conditions if a particular marketing program were used. Both measures of demand are very important in the development of an advertising campaign.

Exhibit 3–4   Demand Curve

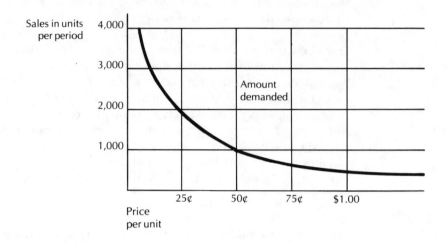

For purposes of advertising campaign planning, the market for a product is the demand or estimated demand that may exist for that product by consumers. In advertising campaign planning, three basic market measurements are used: (a) market demand, (b) market forecast, and (c) market potential. The market forecast shows the estimated demand for the product or service. The market potential is the highest possible market demand that might occur under a given set of conditions. Based on the market demand and market forecast, a planner can calculate potential market share by multiplying the demand by the population. Actual market share can be determined by taking sales of the product as a percentage of total sales in the category. Market shares are an important calculation in terms of advertising planning because they illustrate how well a product is doing in relation to its competition.

For purposes of advertising campaign planning, the total dollar potential market for a product or service is determined by the formula:

Number of buyers X quantity purchased by average buyer
X price of an average unit = total market potential

Using this simple calculation, a marketer can estimate the value of any given market. Further, it is possible to determine the desirability of various advertising and promotion efforts against that market based on the expected return from the advertising expenditure.

Types of Demand

To properly develop an effective advertising campaign, a planner needs to know two basic forms of demand for the product or service. First, there is the *generic* (total) demand for the entire product category. To develop an advertising campaign for a powdered soft drink mix, for example, a marketer needs to know how much soft drink mix will be consumed in the entire country during the year of the campaign. This is called the generic demand, or demand for the total product category.

Second, while it is important to know the total volume in a category, it is often more important to know what the demand for the brand may be, or could be. That commonly forms the basis of the development of the advertising campaign. Knowledge of the demand that a marketer believes can be created for a specific brand within a specific category is important when developing the basic advertising strategy and message. For example, should the advertising be designed to develop demand among customers and prospects for the generic product category of powdered soft drink mix? Or, should it be designed to build demand only for the specific brand among those consumers who already demand powdered soft drink mixes? Or, should the advertising concentrate efforts on getting current users of the brand to buy and use more? The concept of targeted user groups based on their experience with the product category and/or specific brand will be discussed further in Chapter 6.

The Product Life Cycle

Consumer demand for a product or service is not constant over time. Every product or service is believed to have a life cycle. This life cycle illustrates how demand for the product is small in the introductory stage, grows rapidly, eventually levels off at maturity, and then declines. Exhibit 3–5 describes the product life cycle concept and how it relates to an advertising campaign.

The concept of the product life cycle is important in the development of an advertising campaign because the life cycle stage the product is in often determines the type of advertising strategy that should be used and the advertising message that should be developed.

Estimating Market Demand

The estimated demand for the product or service to be advertised is of great interest to the campaign planner. Although the development of this forecast may not be the province of the planner, a brief look at four basic methods of estimating market demand will be helpful.

Exhibit 3–5   The Product Life Cycle

The concept of the product life cycle, on which much current marketing management theory is now based, was formalized by the consulting firm of McKinsey & Co., Inc. The description by Donald K. Clifford, Jr. illustrates this concept:

The product life cycle concept derives from the fact that a product's sales volume follows a typical pattern that can readily be charted as a four-phase cycle. Following its birth, the product passes through a low-volume introduction phase. During the subsequent growth period, volume and profit both rise. Volume stabilizes during maturity, though unit profits typically start to fall off. Eventually, in the state of obsolescence, sales volume declines.

The length of the life cycle, the duration of each phase, and the shape of the curve vary widely for different products. But in every instance, obsolescence eventually occurs for one of three reasons.

First, the need may disappear. This is what happened to the orange juice squeezer when frozen juice caught on.

Second, a better, cheaper, or more convenient product may be developed to suit the same need. Oil-based paint lost its position in the home to water-based paint; plastics have replaced wood, metal, and paper in product categories ranging from dry-cleaning bags to aircraft parts.

Third, a competitive product may, through superior marketing strategy, suddenly gain a decisive advantage. This happened to competing products when Arthur Godfrey's personal charm got behind Lipton Tea, and again when Procter & Gamble secured the American Dental Association's endorsement of its decay-prevention claims for Crest toothpaste.

The Product Life Cycle Concept

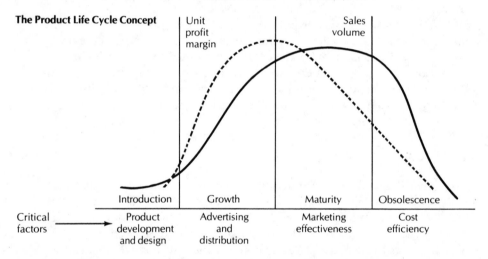

As the chart shows, a product's profit cycle is shaped quite differently from its sales cycle. During introduction, a product may not earn any profit at all because of high initial advertising and promotion costs.

In the growth period, before competition catches up, unit profits typically attain their peak. Then they start declining, though total profits may continue to rise for a time on rising sales volume. In the chemical industry, for example, rapid volume increases often more than offset the effect of price reductions early in the growth phase.

During late growth and early maturity, increasing competition cuts deeply into profit margins and ultimately into total profits. For instance, as a result of drastic price cutting, general-purpose semiconductors, once highly profitable, now return so little profit that many companies have left the business.

Finally, in the period of obsolescence, declining volume eventually pushes costs up to a level that eliminates profits entirely.

SOURCE: Donald K. Clifford, Jr., "Managing the Product Life Cycle," in *Marketing Management and Administrative Action,* 4th ed., Steuart Henderson, Britt and Harker W. Boyd, Jr. (New York: McGraw-Hill, 1978): 237–43.

Market buildup.   The market buildup approach is very simple. One simply determines, through data or estimation, the total number of purchasers for a product or service and adds up what they buy. Obtaining this total is often difficult, however. The number of buyers may not be known, or their volume of purchase may be difficult to determine.

Expert opinion.   Expert opinion is simply a forecast made by asking a panel of knowledgeable people to estimate what they believe the demand for the product will be in the marketplace in a certain time period. A summary of those opinions is then used.

Sales force opinion.   Often, companies rely on the estimates of their sales force to determine the estimated market demand. The reasoning is that the sales force is closer to the market and has a better feel for what will actually be purchased in the coming period. This approach is widely used for industrial products or services.

Market research.   Various forms of market research, ranging from surveys of buyer intentions to formal test market approaches, are used to estimate demand. Consumer market research is often used because it provides a more direct method of estimating demand by gathering the information directly from those who are likely to be purchasers rather than using surrogate measures, such as the opinions of experts or the sales force. For example, scanner panel data are beginning to show evidence of differing levels of demand at a given price among different consumer groups. These data and other consumer information are often available in syndicated research studies (discussed in more detail in Chapter 5).

No matter how the forecast of demand for the product or service is developed, it is a vital ingredient in the preparation of an advertising campaign. If demand for a product is declining, advertising's role in the promotion mix will be much different than if demand for the product is increasing rapidly. Although demand forecasting or estimating may be one of the most difficult of all marketing tasks, it is the basis for most of the decisions that influence the development of a successful advertising campaign.

Types of Purchasing Behavior

The determination of consumer demand for a product or service is often based in part on the way in which consumers purchase products. Various products are purchased in different ways by consumers. Not all consumers purchase the same product, or even brand, in the same way. Often, these purchasing patterns are related to the product life cycle. Consumers' views of alternative products within a product category (i.e., whether they are new and innovative; established and reliable; or on their way down) will determine how they make purchasing decisions. John A. Howard has identified three basic types of purchasing behavior based on the amount of information, effort, and length of time required by consumers to make their purchasing decision. He labels them as follows:

1. Extensive Problem Solving (EPS). To make these types of purchasing decisions, consumers normally need a great deal of information on simply whether to buy in the product class at all. With these products, consumers usually make up their minds rather slowly. This often occurs when a consumer is faced with a decision in an unfamiliar product class.

2. Limited Problem Solving (LPS). In these decision situations, consumers have some basis of criteria against which to judge various products—for example, a new product in a known product class. Usually consumers need less information and less time in which to make a decision in LPS than in EPS.

3. Routinized Response Behavior (RRB). In these decision situations, the product category is known, the brands are known, and in many instances the purchasing decision may be based strictly on price or some other marketing variable, such as a sales promotion event. In RRB, consumer purchasing behavior has become a habit. It is done with little thought and may even have become automatic. This type of behavior is exhibited by most consumers purchasing products or services used on a regular basis. It is the basis for the concept of "brand loyalty"—that is, consumers continue to buy what they have always bought.[4]

All these patterns of purchasing behavior must be considered in the development of an advertising campaign. They are most important in the identification of market segments toward which the advertising campaign may be targeted.

MARKET SEGMENTATION

As may have become evident, consumer behavior and motivation are extremely complex and difficult to understand. In fact, when asked why they purchase various products, consumers often cannot explain how or why they make certain market or product choices. But, although information is limited, planners must have some method of viewing or grouping consumers to develop an effective advertising approach.

---

[4]Adapted from John A. Howard, *Consumer Behavior: Application of Theory* (New York: McGraw-Hill, 1977): 1–18. See this text for a complete discussion of these concepts.

Marketers see the marketplace in terms of either market aggregation or market segmentation. *Market aggregation* assumes that all consumers are somewhat alike and that a given product or service would appeal to many of them. Although there is an understanding that not all will buy, it is assumed that a single marketing and advertising program will appeal to enough consumers to make the product successful. The alternative to this approach is *market segmentation.* Here, the marketer decides to concentrate efforts on that segment of the total market thought to have the most purchasing potential. Thus, rather than developing a broad-scale marketing and advertising program, all the marketing mix variables, particularly advertising, are included in a more specific targeted approach. The idea of a "target market" for an advertising campaign is part of this view. The *target market* is simply that segment of the market toward which advertising will be directed.

To effectively select a segment, or target market, several conditions must be met. First, the segment must be identifiable; that is, there must be some basis for determining who belongs and who doesn't belong in the chosen segment. This, of course, implies that the segment can be measured in some way to determine its value in terms of sales or market potential. Next, the segment must be large enough or have the potential to purchase enough of the product to make the advertising and marketing efforts worthwhile. It is possible, for example, to identify a very tightly organized or available group of consumers. If, however, there is not enough potential purchasing power or volume usage in the group to justify the advertising or marketing expense, the segment may not be a worthwhile target.

Furthermore, the segment or group must be accessible to marketing and advertising efforts. One of the problems with market segmentation is that media access and usage information are often limited (see Chapter 12). Unless advertising messages reach the selected segment, that group is not a practical target from a campaign standpoint. Finally, it is necessary to get some form of specific response from the chosen segment of the market population. If selected segments cannot be expected to respond better or more directly or more strongly to specific advertising messages than the general population, there is no reason to develop the segmentation program. In such cases, the market should be approached in the aggregate with a broad-scale advertising campaign.

Methods of Segmenting Markets

In general, marketers attempt to segment markets on a basis that allows the use of specific advertising media or advertising messages. Although it is often possible to identify an extremely important consumer segment, there may be no practical method of reaching that segment through the media. For example, a marketer might identify those people who use or wear only all-cotton socks as the most important segment for the advertising campaign. However, if there isn't any advertising medium that reaches the segment, or any method of contacting it, the segment becomes useless. Although direct marketers are able to reach increasingly well-defined market segments, most other market segmentation efforts follow rather broad demographic lines (discrete measurable factors about consumers that can be easily determined, such as age, sex, income, marital status, and number of children) and general geographic definitions. As a general rule, most markets are segmented on the following broad lines:

1.   Geographics. Nations, regions, states, Standard Metropolitan Statistical Areas (SMSAs), Areas of Dominant Influence (ADIs), counties, cities, zip codes, and so on.
2.   Demographics (as described earlier). Markets are also segmented on the basis of some socioeconomic characteristics, such as education, occupation, income, and willingness to purchase.
3.   Psychographics or life-style. An increasingly important method of segmentation involves the way in which people spend their time, how they view themselves, and the things with which they surround themselves. Often these are called activities, interests, and opinions, and they offer another dimension for advertising campaign planners. (See Exhibits 3–6 and 3–7). In many instances, "life-style" identifications are major factors in the consumer's purchasing decision.

Exhibit 3–6   Psychographic Research

One of the important areas of marketing and advertising research is psychographic or life-style research. Many purchases are made on the basis of satisfying the customer's inner desire or inner view. In addition, we have become a nation of "exhibitors"; that is, we try to show the type of person we are or hope to be by the type of outward appearance we present, the types of groups with which we associate, the opinions we hold, and so on. Thus, we try to differentiate ourselves by the type of life-style we have or seek.

More and more these life-style or psychographic approaches are being used by marketers and advertisers as methods of segmenting the population. For example, Joseph T. Plummer has identified several life-style dimensions among consumers.* By researching these activities, interests, and opinions, the advertiser often can develop a profile of a group of people who might be an excellent market for a specific product or service.

*Joseph T. Plummer, "The Concept and Application of Life Style Segmentation," *Journal of Marketing,* 38 (January 1974): 34.

Exhibit 3–6   Psychographic Research

Activities	Interests	Opinions	Demographics
Work	Family	Themselves	Age
Hobbies	Home	Social issues	Education
Social events	Job	Politics	Income
Vacation	Community	Business	Occupation
Entertainment	Recreation	Economics	Family size
Club membership	Fashion	Education	Dwelling
Community	Food	Products	Geography
Shopping	Media	Future	City size
Sports	Achievements	Culture	Stage in life cycle

Through this type of life-style research, advertisers and marketers have attempted to develop and define specific life-styles that might be used in advertising campaign planning. DDB Needham, Chicago, has defined ten major life-style groups, shown as follows with approximate percentage of the male or female population in each (in parentheses):

- Ben, the self-made businessman (17%)

- Scott, the successful professional (21%)

- Dale, the devoted family man (17%)

- Fred, the frustrated factory worker (19%)

- Herman, the retiring homebody (26%)

- Cathy, the contented housewife (18%)

- Candice, the chic suburbanite (20%)

- Eleanor, the elegant socialite (17%)

- Mildred, the militant mother (20%)

- Thelma, the old fashioned traditionalist (25%)**

Obviously, the groups change over time as our social values change. They do, however, illustrate the concept of life-style and how important this approach is today to the advertising campaign planner.

A widely used form of psychographic analysis is that developed by SRI International. Their VALS (Values and Lifestyle System) was first developed in 1978, and segmented consumers into three major groups and nine subgroups based on their life-styles and values. VALS 1 identified those groups as follows:

- The Need-Driven. These are "money-restricted" consumers who struggle to buy the basics. Eleven percent of the population fell into this category, which was subdivided into the older *Survivor* group and the relatively young *Sustainer* group.

- Outer-Directed Consumers. This group, over two-thirds of the adult population, has as its main concern that others think well of them. This group was subdivided into the traditionalist *Belongers*, the upwardly mobile *Emulators*, and business, professional, and governmental leaders, the *Achievers*.   *(continued)*

**Peter W. Bernstein, "Psychographics Is Still an Issue on Madison Avenue," *Fortune* (January 16, 1978): 78–84. Copyright 1978 *Time,* Inc. All rights reserved.

Exhibit 3–6   (Continued)

- Inner-Directed Consumers. These are people who buy for their own inner needs rather than responding to the opinions of others. Subdivided into the *I-am-me's,* young, impulsive narcissists; the *Experientials,* older, naturalistic, and focused on inner growth; and the *Societally conscious individuals,* supporters of conservation, consumerism, and environmentalism.

- The Integrated Group. These are people who meld the power of outer-directedness with the sensitivity of inner-directedness. Two percent of the population falls into this group.[†]

SRI has recently introduced an updated version, VALS 2. This new version moves away from values to segments developed from psy-chological foundations for consumer motivations. VALS 2 has three basic categories: *Principle Oriented, Status Oriented,* and *Action Oriented.* Consumers are further subcategorized into one of the eight groups (shown in the diagram) based on such "resources" as levels of education and income, health, energy level, self-confidence, and consumerism. Those in the *Actualizer, Fulfilled, Achiever,* and *Experiencer* segments possess high amounts of the various resources, while the *Believers, Strivers, Makers,* and *Strugglers* have fewer resources.[‡]

From this classification and identification of consumers, VALS researchers believe they can provide advertisers with a clearer picture of the purchasing and media habits of consumers in the marketplace so that the advertising plan can be more finely tuned.

The VALS 2 Network

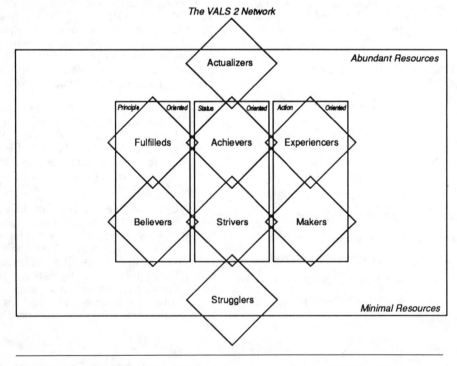

SOURCE: SRI International.

[†]Niles Howard, "A New Way to View Consumers," *Dun's Review* (August 1981): 43–46.

[‡]Judith Graham, "New VALS 2 Takes Psychological Route," *Advertising Age* (February 13, 1989): 24.

Exhibit 3–7   Buying Behavior Exhibited by Groups

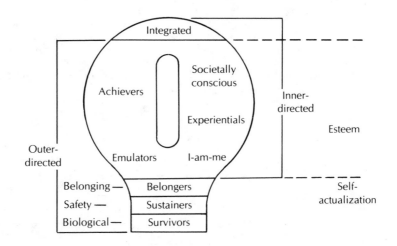

4. Media usage. Often, markets may be segmented simply by the type of media consumers use or are exposed to. For example, daytime television, which includes the well-known soap operas, has brought together groups of people with similar interests and concerns. The same is true for late night television. Specific cable television networks such as Nickelodeon, ESPN, and MTV appeal to particular groups as well. In addition, many new life-style magazines that are dedicated to individual interests, activities, and opinions have sprung up over the past few years. Thus, a marketer may segment prospective customers for products through the media vehicles they use, as well as their demographic and psychographic variables.

5. Buying and use. Perhaps, one of the most important methods of segmenting people into markets or potential markets is through their purchase or usage of products and services. Here, marketers attempt to identify customers or prospects based on what products they buy, how often they buy, how rapidly they use up the product, when and how they repurchase, and so on. For example, not all consumers use products at the same rate. In fact, there appears to be a very distinct "heavy-user" group for most product categories (see Exhibit 3–8). Scanner panel data, collected from households that agree to have their supermarket purchases monitored electronically, are providing marketers with a wealth of information on purchasing behavior. Though analysis of the data collected from scanners is still being de-

Exhibit 3–8   Market Segmentation

Often we segment markets based on volume usage of the particular product or service, employing the terms light, medium, and heavy users. This is particularly helpful to advertising campaign planners because obviously the larger the usage of the product category or brand, the more important that person is to the advertiser. Interestingly, heavy users of a product often consume an inordinately large percentage of the total in a particular product category. Dik

Warren Twedt labeled this group the "heavy half" and, through consumption data, illustrated how important they are in certain product categories.

Numbers above bars are percentages of the population categorized according to non-users, "light half," and "heavy half." Numbers within bars are the amount of total volume consumed by "light half" and "heavy half." For example, in the first bar (Lemon-lime), 42 percent of the population are

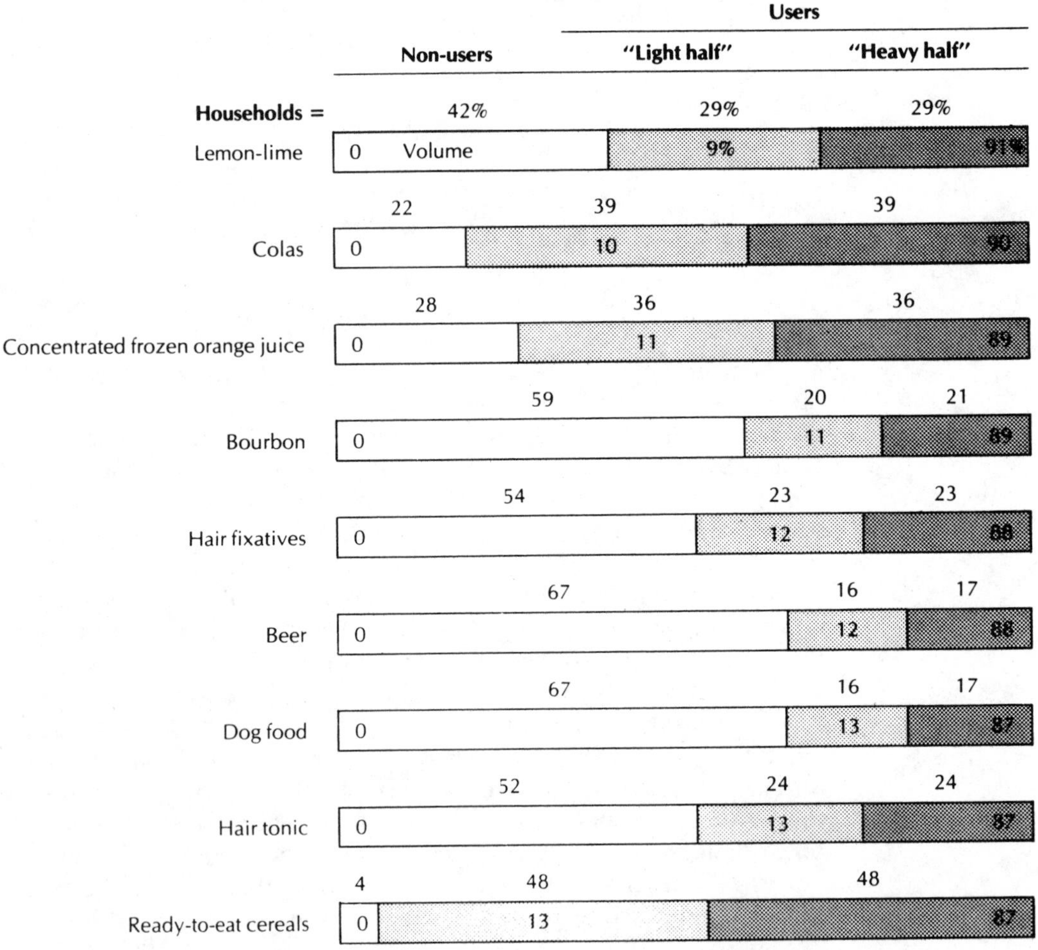

	Non-users	Users "Light half"	"Heavy half"
Households =	42%	29%	29%
Lemon-lime	0 Volume	9%	91%
	22	39	39
Colas	0	10	90
	28	36	36
Concentrated frozen orange juice	0	11	89
	59	20	21
Bourbon	0	11	89
	54	23	23
Hair fixatives	0	12	88
	67	16	17
Beer	0	12	88
	67	16	17
Dog food	0	13	87
	52	24	24
Hair tonic	0	13	87
	4	48	48
Ready-to-eat cereals	0	13	87

SOURCE: Reprinted from Dik Warren Twedt, "How Important to Marketing Strategy Is the 'Heavy User'?" *Journal of Marketing,* 28 (January 1964): 72.

Exhibit 3–8 Market Segmentation

non-users, 29 percent are "light half," and 29 percent are "heavy half." Of the 58 percent who make up the user base, 91 percent of the total consumption is by the "heavy half," while only 9 percent is consumed by the "light half."

Through use of this consumption data, advertisers try to group people who are heavy users by other factors such as demographics, psychographics, or media patterns so that they can be reached with advertising messages. For example, heavy users of beer tend to be heavy viewers of sports programming on television, thus the attempt to reach them through that medium.

Of some concern to the advertising planner, however, is the fact that the heavy user of a product tends to be the most difficult to influence. Since many exhibit RRB purchasing behavior, they are often quite difficult to change or to get to consider new brand alternatives.

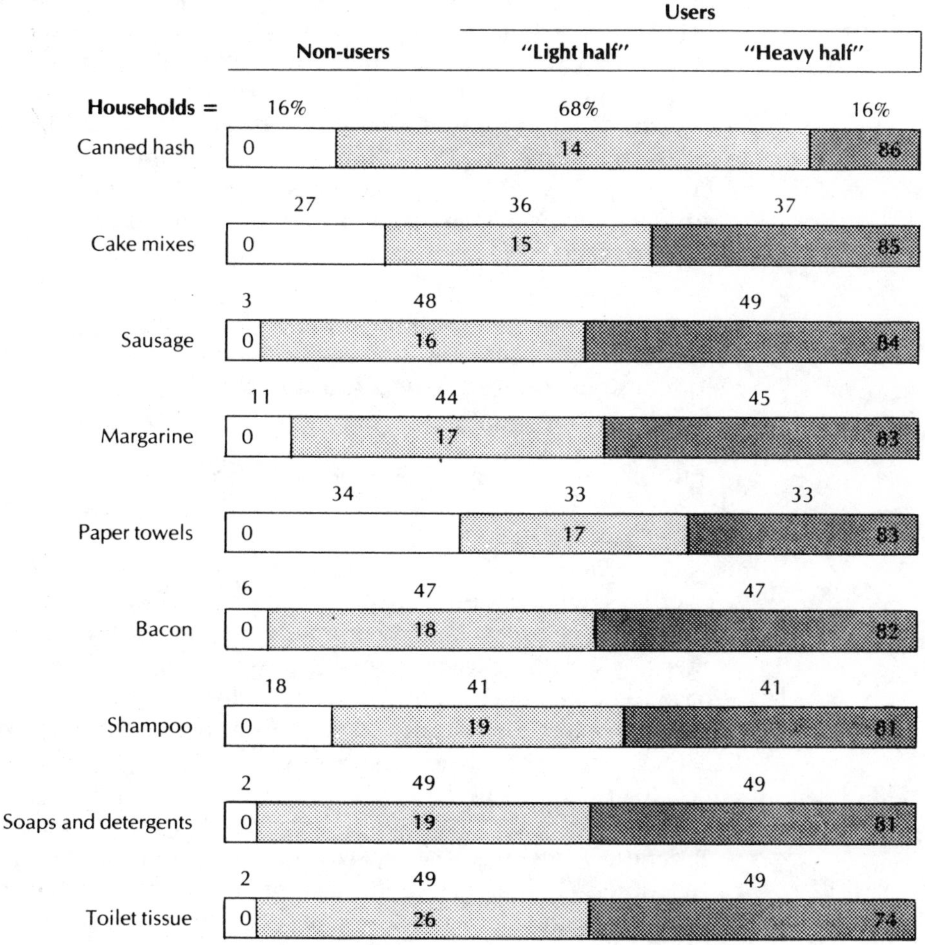

		Users	
	Non-users	"Light half"	"Heavy half"
Households =	16%	68%	16%
Canned hash	0	14	86
	27	36	37
Cake mixes	0	15	85
	3	48	49
Sausage	0	16	84
	11	44	45
Margarine	0	17	83
	34	33	33
Paper towels	0	17	83
	6	47	47
Bacon	0	18	82
	18	41	41
Shampoo	0	19	81
	2	49	49
Soaps and detergents	0	19	81
	2	49	49
Toilet tissue	0	26	74

veloped, definite user segments are beginning to emerge within many product categories. Exhibit 3–8 describes one such segmentation scheme.

With this view of market segmentation, we now look at the area where we believe our advertising campaign may have an actual effect—that is, in developing or changing attitudes of consumers toward various products or services.

ATTITUDE AND ATTITUDE CHANGE

In Chapter 2, it was stated that the primary purpose of advertising is to help people gain information of interest or benefit about the product or service in order that this information might result in a change or continuation of attitudes about the product or service. Generally, the influence of advertising on consumer behavior can be illustrated, as it is in Exhibit 3–9. Thus, an advertising planner must first know how consumers behave and how they react to various influences before he or she can influence their attitudes, which may in turn influence behavior. Attitudes must first be influenced before behavior can be changed.

Exhibit 3–9   Attitudes and Attitude Change

Attention ⟶ Learning ⟶ Attitude change ⟶ Behavior change

The general purpose of an advertising campaign is to communicate a sales message for a product or service to a previously selected group of consumers or prospects. In communicating this sales message, an advertiser hopes to trigger some sort of response in the consumer which will have some influence on his or her behavior resulting in the purchase of a product or service. Because there are many intervening marketing variables between the advertising message and the actual purchase of a product (for example, the retail price of the product and its availability), the advertiser's primary interest is to influence consumers' attitudes toward or about the product or service. Martin Fishbein and Icek Ajzen have defined an attitude as "a learned predisposition to respond in a consistently favorable or unfavorable manner with respect to a given object."[5]

---

[5]Martin Fishbein and Icek Ajzen, *Belief, Attitude, Intention and Behavior: An Introduction to Theory and Research* (Reading, Mass.: Addison-Wesley, 1975): 6.

Most researchers believe that attitudes are related to an object; that they have direction, intensity, and degree; that they have some sort of structure; and usually that they are learned. All of us have attitudes toward everything around us and everything within us. Usually, attitudes are formed and develop from our needs and wants and the values we place upon objects that will satisfy those needs and wants. Of particular interest in the development of an advertising campaign is how attitudes toward products or brands may be formed. Exhibit 3–10 illustrates a simplified model of how that attitude formation is believed to occur.

Almost all theories about attitudes and how attitudes are formed or change are based on the general idea that the human mind strives to maintain a harmony or consistency among currently perceived attitudes. Thus, individuals constantly strive to maintain some sort of consistency among what they currently believe and what is going on around them. They form new attitudes to coincide with what they already believe and events they see or perceive. They change or modify attitudes to fit with what occurs in the world around them.

Attitudes toward brands and products or services are generally thought to have three basic components: (a) the *cognitive component,* which is the individual's beliefs and knowledge about the product or service; (b) the *affective component,* or the emotional reactions toward it; and (c) the *behaviorial component,* or how the person actually reacts toward the brand or product, for instance, buying the product regularly or avoiding it at all costs. To change an attitude, all three of these components must be considered and must be affected in some way.

Advertising's task is often difficult because of attitudes and these attitude changes. Consumers are constantly trying to maintain a mental balance, yet advertising is constantly encouraging them to change in some way. Thus, there is a pull and tug going on between what consumers presently believe about products and services and what advertisers are trying to communicate to them through their advertising messages. The easiest state for the human mind is a constant state, such as one characterized by brand loyalty, or being in an RRB buying situation. However, consumers are constantly being besieged by advertising messages that attempt to create a change in their attitude toward the advertised product, service, or brand.

Influencing Attitudes

Advertising campaign planners are primarily concerned with either (a) maintaining a favorable attitude toward their brand, product, or service; or (b) changing or modifying existing consumer attitudes so they will be more in favor of their brand, product, or service. To do so, advertisers generally concentrate on the cognitive component of the attitude; that is, they hope to influence beliefs or add knowledge to the consumer's information

Exhibit 3–10   How User Attitudes Are Formed

While there are many models of consumer behavior and many explanations of how attitudes are formed, the one developed by David L. Loudon and Albert J. Della Bitta is a clear, concise explanation as illustrated in the model below.

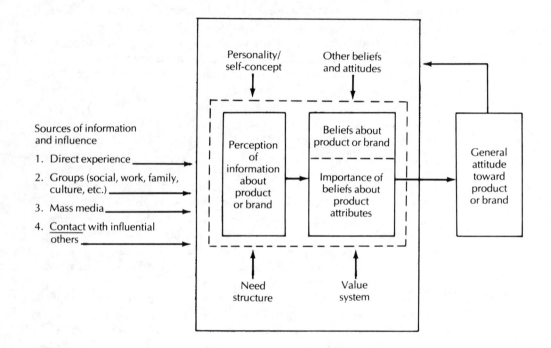

"It shows that several sources provide consumers with information and influence about products, services, retail stores, and other objects. The individual selectively perceives and distorts the information according to his individual needs, values, and personality and according to how well the information 'fits' with currently held beliefs and attitudes. This processed information initiates either development, change, or confirmation in the consumer's beliefs about the product and the importance of each of the product's attributes to him and his current needs. Out of this process is synthesized a general attitude toward a product. Admittedly, this model is an oversimplification. However, it does reflect current understanding of attitudes and presents a concise picture of the psychological and external elements involved in the process of forming attitudes toward products. Also, it should be pointed out that the process is dynamic; it continues to change over time."

SOURCE: Loudon and Della Bitta, *Consumer Behavior* (New York: McGraw-Hill, 1979): 392.

base so that the present attitude will become more favorable. There are five basic methods of changing attitudes toward a product or brand through the use of advertising and advertising appeals.

1. Affect product class linkages with goals and events. If attitudes are related to certain groups or social events, can the advertiser change the attitudes toward the brand by pointing out or linking these certain desirable social groups or events to the brand?
2. Add a salient characteristic. Can something be added to the brand that will be important to the consumer? Can what the product or service is or does be improved through a change or innovation in manufacturing process, ingredient, effect, or the like?
3. Alter the perception of existing product characterstics. Can product disadvantages be turned into advantages? Or can a relatively unimportant product benefit be made the primary decision point in the consumer's selection of a product in that class?
4. Change perceptions of the advertiser's brand. Can consumers' present beliefs about the brand be changed to something else? Can the product have "more" of something or be "better" or perhaps "improved" to change the consumers' image of the product?
5. Change the perception of competing brands. A common method of attempting to change perceptions of competitors is through comparative advertising. Is it possible to show that the competitor's product is not as good, as useful, or as inexpensive as the brand to offset what consumers now believe?[6]

Almost all advertising campaigns attempt to develop or change consumer attitudes through one or a combination of these five methods. Often, this attempt to change consumer attitudes forms the basis for the advertising message and usually is a central part of the actual advertising strategy.

The Evoked Set

When a consumer feels a need or a want for a particular product category, he or she goes through a mental process. The individual searches his or her knowledge, background, and experience to find a solution—that is, a product that might satisfy that particular need. Searching further, the individual "evokes" from his or her own experience and background a specific brand or brands that might fill that need. The *evoked set* of brands is a

---

[6]Adapted partially from Harper W. Boyd, Jr., Michael L. Ray, and Edward C. Strong, "An Attitudinal Framework for Advertising Strategy," *Journal of Marketing*, 36 (April 1972): 27–33.

result of consumer's well-developed attitudes about products and brands. For example, if a person decided to buy a new outfit for an upcoming party, first that person would recall what types of clothing might be appropriate for his or her taste and for the party; such factors as type of cloth, pattern, color, and styles would come into play. If the party-goer were a woman, this process might lead to a decision to purchase a cocktail dress. She might then recall designer brands, such as Albert Nippon, Victor Costa, Liz Claiborne, and Diane Von Furstenberg. From that group, she would then do an evaluative summary of each before making the actual purchasing decision. The brands that came immediately to mind constitute the evoked set.

People have evoked sets of brands for all types of products and services, from insurance companies to candy bars to washing machines. Usually, unless the purchase decision is a major one, say in EPS, consumers choose from among brands that exist in their evoked set. For example, when a person stops to purchase a bottle of salad dressing, the actual brand decision often is made from among brands within the evoked set; a sales promotion incentive, such as a coupon, might contribute to the final choice. Little additional search or decision making is required or involved. The consumer, through the use of the evoked set, attempts to simplify the purchase-decision process. It is here in the evoked set, or the formation of the evoked set, that advertising may have its greatest effect. By moving a brand into a consumer's evoked set, an advertiser can assure that the brand will at least be considered for purchase rather than be totally ignored in a particular purchasing situation.

Agenda Setting

As mentioned in Chapter 2, another major method of using advertising to influence consumer purchasing decisions is through the process of agenda setting. For example, an automobile battery is not purchased on a regular basis by most consumers. Other than knowing that the battery is supposed to furnish the electrical power to start and run the automobile engine, most consumers know little about the product class or the brands within the class. The manufacturer of the battery understands this situation and attempts to influence and inform consumers about the basis on which a battery should be selected. The advertising planner thus develops an advertising campaign featuring the particular brand attribute in which the product excels.

If Battery Manufacturer A's battery has superior power in cold weather, she would attempt to get consumers to consider cold-weather starting as the primary benefit to seek when making a battery purchasing decision. Manufacturer B, however, might have more cells or plates in his product. He would thus try to "set the agenda" for battery purchase selection, making it the number of cells or plates the battery contains. Manufacturer C might stress a warranty or guarantee that is superior to Brands A and B and make that the most important factor. Thus, although all products would serve essentially the same purpose, each manufacturer, through advertising, would attempt to identify the major decision factor or to set the agenda by which consumers should go about deciding on an automobile battery brand. As more and more products reach parity in the marketplace, this agenda-setting approach will likely become more and more important in the development of an advertising campaign.

Diffusion of Innovation and the Adoption Process

Although attitude development and change are important concepts, it is also important for the advertising campaign planner to understand the actual purchase behavior of consumers in the marketplace. Often, simply creating or changing an attitude toward a brand or product does not automatically result in a product purchase decision, nor does it guarantee that the brand, once tried, will be repurchased on a regular basis. Researchers have found that most consumers and most social groups go through a set of measurable steps called the *adoption process* in deciding to try a new product or brand or to change the brand they are presently using.

Of equal importance is the fact that not all consumers or social groups go through these steps at the same time or at the same speed. Thus, we find that some people adopt new ideas and new concepts more rapidly than others—the *diffusion of innovation* mentioned in Chapter 2.

In general, the adoption process consists of several steps that can be predicted and charted. Originally identified by Everett M. Rogers while studying how native tribes adopt a new idea or concept, these steps are used today to describe the stages of the adoption process:

Step 1—Awareness of the innovation

Step 2—Interest in the innovation

Step 3—Evaluation of the innovation

Step 4—Trial of the innovation

Step 5—Decision as to whether to adopt the innovation

Step 6—Confirmation of the decision to adopt the innovation[7]

---

[7]Everett M. Rogers and F.F. Shoemaker, *The Communication of Innovations: A Cross-Cultural Approach* (New York: Free Press, 1971): 23.

Although almost all members of society go through Rogers's process in the adoption of an innovation, not all people move through the steps at the same speed, nor do they adopt new innovations at the same time. Rogers and others have found the adoption process, or how the idea diffuses through the population, actually resembles a bell-shaped curve when measured over time. An example of the diffusion process based on time is illustrated in Exhibit 3–11. The curve illustrates that only a few persons actually adopt the new idea at the very beginning. Only 2.5 percent of the group can really be called innovators. Others in the group are slower to adopt the idea and are a relatively large group; the laggards are the very last to adopt the innovation. In fact, not all members of the group may actually adopt the innovation no matter what the length of time is.

Exhibit 3–11   Adopter Categorization on the Basis of Innovativeness

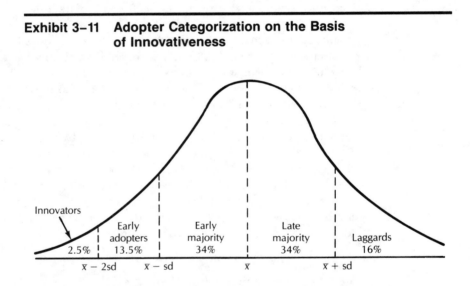

The innovativeness dimension, as measured by the time at which an individual adopts an innovation or innovations, is continuous. However, this variable may be partitioned into five adopter categories by laying off standard deviations from the average time of adoption.

SOURCE: Rogers and Shoemaker, *The Communication of Innovations:* 23.

The importance of this concept to the advertising campaign planner should be obvious. First, when developing a new advertising campaign, often consisting of relatively new information about the brand in the advertising message, the planner should remember that not all customers and prospects will become aware of the advertising message at the same time. Usually, this creation of awareness is a consequence of the media selected. In addition, a new advertising message must take the consumer through the various mental steps necessary for the receiver to accept the sales message. Further, not all persons accept the sales message at the same rate over time, even if they receive equal exposure to the message. Thus, the importance of advertising message repetition through the media plan becomes clear (see Chapter 12).

In introducing new products or new advertising ideas, sometimes it may be important for the advertising campaign planner to concentrate efforts on innovators, or those who are most likely to adopt the new idea, new concept, or new advertising message. This observation further supports the idea of selecting a specific target market for the advertising campaign message. Finally, the advertising planner should keep this concept of diffusion and adoption in mind when developing the advertising strategy and advertising messages in various product categories and for individual brands. If the product or brand is startlingly new, time will usually be required for the adoption process to occur. If, however, the product or brand is well established and only the advertising message is new, the adoption process and resulting diffusion through the marketplace will take less time. In any event, the diffusion of innovation and the adoption process clearly illustrate why it is sometimes difficult to measure the results of an advertising campaign in a short period of time.

Other Promotional Influences on Consumer Behavior

As a final note, it is important to keep in mind that advertising is not the only tool a manufacturer can use to influence consumer attitudes and purchase intent for his brand. Remember Mr. Smith and his Chevy Blazer from Chapter 2? Exhibit 3–12 illustrates many of the factors, including advertising, that might play a role in the automobile purchasing situation. Sales promotion might include the availability of rebates or free option packages offered by the manufacturer and/or the dealer. Special salesperson training on the Blazer's features might influence Mr. Smith's choice. Or, Mr. Smith might have received a direct marketing piece in the mail inviting him to test drive the Blazer. Knowledge of the area Chevrolet dealer might have brought Mr. Smith into the showroom. Personal selling will certainly play a part in whether or not Mr. Smith actually purchases. Recent newspaper or magazine articles discussing the Blazer's features would have public relations influence. Lastly, literature on the Blazer available at the dealer showroom might depict particular features Mr. Smith was not aware of. As Exhibit 3–12 shows, all of these influences are often at work on the consumer and each plays a part in convincing him or her to purchase. Because they all have an impact on the consumer, it is important that all elements communicate the same message. Although the advertising campaign planner may not be responsible for any element other than the advertising, he or she should make an effort to coordinate the advertising message with that being conveyed through sales promotion offers, public relations activities, direct marketing, and the like.

Exhibit 3–12   Factors in a Purchasing Situation

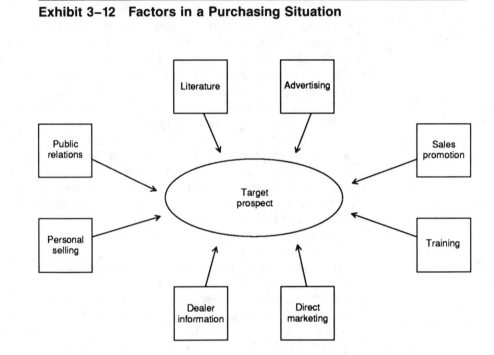

SUMMARY

Understanding your consumer—what he or she wants, doesn't want, what he or she needs or doesn't need—and what motivates a person to purchase one product instead of its competitor is a crucial part of advertising campaign planning. The planner must understand the different types of consumers and the many internal and external influences on them. In terms of campaign planning it is especially important to understand the types of needs, demand, and the product life cycle concept, and how consumers make purchasing decisions.

All of these elements determine the character of the market segment which is critical to developing the proper advertising message and choosing the proper media to get that message to the potential buyer.

Case Studies

Potato Pouches

Brigitta Tedder, a member of the new product development team at Cristel Products, had been asked to develop a preliminary consumer profile identifying possible segments that might be targeted for a new product, Potato Pouches.

The Potato Pouch product line had been developed to take advantage of the retort pouch packaging technique. Originally developed for use in the space program, retort pouches were a convenient alternative to traditional frozen food packaging. Unlike frozen foods, products packaged in retort pouches needed no refrigeration. The packaging was commonly referred to as being "shelf stable." The advantages for manufacturers and retailers were obvious. Instead of having to invest in refrigerated transport cars, manufacturers could ship through standard vehicles. The frozen food section in the supermarket is already overcrowded; stores typically resist enlarging the section because of the consumer inconvenience and cost associated with renovation.

The Potato Pouch product line was made up of four varieties of potato dishes: Potatoes Au Gratin, Garlic and Herb Potatoes, Mexican Potatoes, and Dilled Potatoes. Each variety consisted of sliced potatoes in a sauce. The products were precooked and just needed to be reheated. The consumer could prepare the product by either boiling the retort pouch in a saucepan on the stove or cooking it for a few minutes in a microwave oven. After cooking the product, the consumer simply opened the pouch and poured the product into a serving dish. There was little mess associated with serving the product, because the consumer did not have to add any ingredients or do any mixing. Potato Pouches would be competing against boxed potato dish mixes and frozen potato dishes that featured similar product lines.

Brigitta knew that several food manufacturers experimented with retort pouch packaging previously. A competitor had introduced a line of retort pouch entrées in the early 1980s, but had met with little success. Although retail acceptance was high, consumers had never really accepted the technology. Unlike the more traditional frozen boil-in-bag packaging that had been especially popular at that time, it was impossible to see the retort-pouch-packaged product until after it was cooked. The entrée line had included meat-based dishes, and consumers felt that the packaging made it impossible to know if the meat was really "done" after the recommended cooking time. With boil-in-bag packaging, it was possible to actually see the meat and check for "doneness." The entrée line had been phased out after about a year.

109

Retort pouch packaging had received some attention from the press. Early stories had focused on the "space-age" technology that made the process possible. Brigitta believed these stories had probably increased consumer uneasiness about the packaging. However, more recent stories had put more emphasis on the benefits of the packaging, highlighting the convenience and energy savings associated with retort pouches. Although Brigitta was not sure how much attention such stories had received from consumers, she figured they were a step in the right direction.

Currently, one other food manufacturer was distributing retort-pouch-packaged products nationally. Their product line was made up of five dishes including beef stew, salisbury steak, and three chicken entrées. The product was being shelved with prepared foods, next to such products as macaroni and cheese mixes and canned meats. The product had only been in stores for about three months; Brigitta was not sure how sales were going.

Cristel had a strong sales force, and preliminary talks with some major food store chains suggested that the distribution of Potato Pouches would not be a problem. Although the standard slotting allowance would have to be paid, it seemed likely that most stores would accept the product. The real question was consumer acceptance. Cristel management was enthusiastic about the potential of retort pouch packaging and believed that a solid success with Potato Pouches would position Cristel as a leader in retort packaging.

All four Potato Pouch varieties had been taste-tested with consumers against both frozen and boxed potato dishes. The majority of those tested felt that the Potato Pouch product tasted better than the boxed product and as good as the frozen product. Potato Pouches would be priced slightly below the frozen potato dish average at retail, and about 20 percent higher than boxed potato mixes.

Brigitta outlined some potential consumer reactions to Potato Pouches:

Negative/Neutral Reactions

- I usually buy boxed potato mixes because I like to have one in the pantry to use on the spur of the moment. Why should I pay 20 percent more for this product?
- I usually buy frozen potato dishes—my freezer's pretty big. Why is this better?
- How can something that's already mixed, especially something that contains a sauce, not need refrigeration?
- What does the product look like when it's cooked?
- How do I fix this?

- I've never had this before—what if my family doesn't like it? I know they like what I've been buying.

Positive Reactions

- I saw something about these pouches in my newspaper. It sounds like a pretty neat idea. Besides, you can't really mess up potatoes, can you?
- I don't like the mess and preparation involved in the boxed mixes, and my freezer's pretty small (and full of ice cream). If this tastes good, I'd probably have potato dishes more often.
- This is a little cheaper than the frozen food I usually buy.
- My kids usually complain about any kind of vegetables, even potatoes. I can tell them this is like "astronaut food." Who knows, they might even believe it!

Unfortunately, Brigitta suspected that more consumers would fall into the negative group than into the positive. It would be important to get fairly quick consumer acceptance for Potato Pouches to keep the product on supermarket shelves. She decided to go back to some consumer behavior basics and see if she could identify some potential segments that might find Potato Pouches especially appealing. Then, Cristel could conduct more testing with members of those groups to decide on the best marketing approach for the product.

Questions

1. Should Cristel focus on creating generic demand for retort-pouch-packaged products or specific demand for Potato Pouches? Why? Which marketing communications techniques would you recommend for creating generic demand? specific demand?
2. Although retort pouch packaging has been around for a number of years, it's probably still in the introductory stage of the product life cycle given consumer knowledge and perceptions. What would have to happen to push retort packaging into the growth stage? How might Potato Pouches help that process?
3. Which of the demand estimation techniques discussed in this chapter would you recommend using for Potato Pouches? Why?
4. What demographic and psychographic characteristics would you use to develop a market segment for Potato Pouches?
5. Draw a picture of the influencers who might be involved in the Potato Pouch purchasing decision, similar to that shown in Exhibit 3–1. Briefly describe what role you think each would play.

Direct Marketing Recruitment

A major Midwestern university was faced with the problem of developing a recruitment campaign for a new graduate program it was planning to offer. The school had long had a graduate program in general advertising; it was designed primarily to train people for advertising management positions in advertising agencies and client organizations. In response to growing advertiser interest in direct marketing, and the lack of qualified people to fill the available jobs in that area, the school had decided to offer an additional graduate program specializing in direct marketing. Funding for the program had been obtained from several direct marketing trade associations; a curriculum had been developed and approved; and faculty recruitment was underway. All that remained to be done was to attract applicants to the program.

Despite the growing proportion of promotional dollars being channeled into the direct marketing area, it remains a curiosity to many people, particularly people interested in beginning a career in the promotional area. Direct marketing concepts and applications typically receive only minimal attention in an undergraduate advertising or marketing curriculum; even then the focus tends to be on the media vehicle of direct mail, which is only a small part of the direct marketing area. Direct marketing also lacks the somewhat glamourous image associated with a career in advertising. And, few schools offer specialty courses or graduate programs in direct marketing.

Although direct marketing has low visibility in the academic community, the field offers attractive incentives to prospective employees. Tangible benefits include a relatively high placement rate compared to traditional advertising—rather than having many excellent candidates competing for a few select jobs, direct marketers who wish to hire usually have to search for qualified applicants. Because direct marketing is more of a seller's market, starting salaries for trained people also tend to be higher than those in general advertising. An assessment of promotional spending trends would indicate another benefit: direct marketing is likely to continue to grow at a faster pace than general advertising, suggesting continued entry-level job opportunities and the promise of advancement once hired.

The university's program had been carefully designed to provide a strong grounding in marketing basics, as well as specialty courses in direct marketing. Students would take classes in marketing management, consumer and organizational behavior, research techniques, finance and accounting, and media systems. These courses would be similar in scope and level to those taught in an MBA curriculum. Direct marketing specialty courses would include a fundamentals of direct marketing class, market segmentation, computer systems, creative strategy for direct marketing, data base management, pricing and promotion strategy, and consumer acceptance. As a capstone course, students would work in groups to develop a direct marketing campaign for a real-world client.

One facet of the curriculum that the university expected to be especially beneficial was a residency program. Each student would spend one term working as an intern at a direct marketing company. For instance, a student might analyze the company's customer retention program to identify ways the system might be improved. Or, a student interested in the creative aspect of direct marketing might help develop the copy and layout for a catalog and then analyze the results of the offer. The university had identified a number of direct marketing companies that were interested in taking on trained student interns. The students would move into the residency program after having three terms of course work. Following the residency, they would return to the university to complete the final term of the program.

This residency program, which was essentially a paid internship, would serve several purposes. It would give the students a chance to apply the theories they had learned in their course work. It would give them in-depth exposure to the workings of a direct marketing organization, helping them to focus their career interests. It might serve as a placement device (though that was not really the intention of the program); students who did well in the residency program and who liked their employer's corporate environment might end up working for that company following graduation. Finally, it might also prove to be an attractive recruiting device.

The university was trying to determine how best to recruit applicants for the program. The established advertising program did relatively little outside recruiting—as a long-running, nationally known program, it relied primarily on word of mouth and alumni referrals for applicants. Obviously, the direct marketing program could not be treated in the same way.

The faculty had suggested that a mix of students would be appropriate, that is, students with work experience in advertising or direct marketing and those without should be admitted to the program. The core curriculum courses would bring both groups "up to speed" on the basics of the industry. Because the faculty tended to focus on current issues in marketing and promotion, the basic course work would probably not be too elementary for persons with undergraduate degrees in marketing or prior work experience. The specialized courses would likely be entirely new to both groups, because those courses focused on state-of-the-art computer-based applications of theory. By including some students with work experience, in-class discussion would likely be richer and both groups would benefit from the interaction.

At a basic level, a description of the direct marketing program would be included in the university publication sent to persons interested in the advertising program. A separate brochure describing the direct marketing course offerings in more detail was also being developed, though no plans had been made to distribute that brochure. The faculty member who would direct the program had been hired and was willing to make recruiting visits. Target enrollment for the first year was twenty-five students (compared with fifty in the general advertising program).

Questions

1. Would internal or external influences likely play a greater role in the decision to enroll in a graduate program such as this? Why?
2. Who are some of the specific influencers who might play a role in this decision process? Briefly describe the role each might play.
3. a) Should the university's recruitment campaign emphasize creating generic demand or brand-specific demand? Why? b) Does the product life cycle concept play a role here? If so, how?
4. Apply the principle of the diffusion of innovations to this situation. How is this diffusion likely to affect the university's recruitment efforts?

Developing an Integrated Advertising Plan

Traditionally, advertising plans have been developed from a very narrow view; that is, the advertising planner or the advertising agency, took the basic company mission or business objectives, from which had come the marketing objectives and using that as a guide, developed the advertising plan. Commonly, the advertising plan was developed with little or no consideration of the other communication tools that might be used. Public relations, direct mail, sales promotion, sales literature, and the like, were different animals and the advertising planner either ignored them or felt they would be adjusted to fit the advertising plan. The reason for this single-minded approach to advertising was simple. In most instances, each of the communication areas was headed by a functional specialist. His or her primary concern was the success of that particular element, not the success of the overall program. When advertising was the major communication tool of the organization, the approach worked. Today, however, most companies and brands need a combination of communication approaches, techniques, and tactics. Therefore, although our interest here is primarily in the development of a successful advertising program through a solid advertising plan, the advertising planner today must give consideration to the other communication tools that can and will be used in developing a successful overall communications program, whether advertising plays a major or a minor part.

DEVELOPING AN INTEGRATED COMMUNICATIONS PLAN

Although the advertising planner often may not develop the overall communications plan, he or she needs an understanding of the basic concepts

115

and approaches that will be used to make sure the advertising is successfully integrated into the overall communications program.

The Cascade Approach

One of the concepts used by many organizations to plan and implement an overall communications program is based on the idea of the *cascade*. In other words, general strategic plans and decisions are first made at upper levels of management—for example, the products to be manufactured, the markets to be served, the financial goals to be achieved. From these basic decisions, the lower-level choices or alternatives are developed. They are said to flow out of or "cascade" from these general objectives and strategies. For example, advertising objectives generally "cascade" out of marketing plans. Media plans "cascade" out of the overall advertising objectives, and so on.

If we look at a typical U.S. organization and how marketing and advertising decisions are made, we might visualize this cascading approach to communication and advertising planning as shown in Exhibit 4–1.

The highest level of decision is made by the top level corporate managers. They develop the basic business plan for the organization. They develop the "mission statement" or "vision" that defines the total objectives of the company. From their vision comes the business plan. This determines the markets to be served, the products to be produced, the financial goals to be achieved, and so on.

From this general business plan, the specific unit's marketing plan is developed. This plan outlines how the business plan will be achieved. For example, the marketing plan usually states the sales and profit goals of various products, the market penetration desired, the geographic areas to be served, the distribution system, pricing, and so on.

The unit's overall communication plan "cascades" out of this general marketing plan. In the past, advertising was the dominant promotion strategy used by most consumer package goods organizations. Public relations, sales promotion, direct marketing, and the like, were of minor importance. Therefore, the communications plan was almost the same as the advertising plan. Today, with diffused markets, harder to reach consumers, more product specialization, and a host of other factors, many companies are now spending less and less in advertising and more and more in the other forms of communication. For this reason, many companies require a basic communications plan, to be sure that all communication approaches are using the same basic strategy.

Once the basic strategy has been chosen, in our example, that is, advertising, the objectives, strategies, and tactics cascade out of those previous decisions. This cascading approach is an important concept for it clearly shows that advertising is a result of prior decisions which must be consid-

Exhibit 4–1   The Cascade Approach

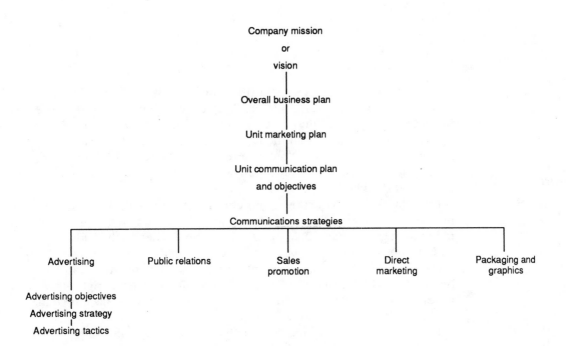

ered in developing an advertising program. It also illustrates how important it is for advertising to be integrated and coordinated with the other
communication tools of public relations, sales promotion, direct marketing, and the like.

Generally, we might conceptualize the various communications techniques as strategic approaches on a continuum, as illustrated in Exhibit
4–2.

As shown, packaging, graphics, and general advertising are considered
the broadest and least targeted of the promotional techniques. Some might
argue that public relations, in its broadest terms, also necessarily tries to
reach broad segments of the population. Today, however, with the growth
of issues management, and the identification of specific and often limited
audiences, public relations is probably more targeted than advertising, as

Exhibit 4–2 The Strategic Continuum

Packaging and graphics	Advertising	Public relations	Sales promotion	Direct marketing

Messages . . . . Targeted messages

used in the mass media. Next in the continuum is sales promotion. Because sales promotion can often be targeted against present product users by means of in-pack promotions, cross-ruffs, and the like, it does give the marketer a more clearly identified target than those activities that rely only on the mass media. At the "most targeted" end of the spectrum is direct marketing or direct communication with known users, identified prospects, and the like.

In an integrated marketing communications approach, the emphasis is put on the problem to be solved and the communication task(s) at hand, rather than using traditional or preselected approaches, such as advertising and sales promotion. This new integrated marketing communications approach focuses the planner's attention on the needs of the company or brand first. With attention focused, he or she then selects the right strategy to solve the problem, rather than trying to force fit one of the approaches to the communications task.

In addition, this integrated communications approach also suggests that a combination of activities likely will perform better than any one alone. Thus, the communications planner should think in terms of using the strengths of the various alternatives to overcome the weaknesses of others so that the communications tasks are achieved.

Finally, this concept of a targeted promotional continuum represented by the various communications approaches clearly illustrates the need to integrate the various forms of promotion so that all work together. For example, with the integrated approach, advertising and sales promotion tactics should feature the same message or concept. The same is true of direct marketing and public relations or any combination of the techniques chosen. Unquestionably, there is synergy among the various communication tools. This new integrated approach to developing marketing communications programs brings the elements into much clearer focus than the traditional method of developing functional plans in virtual isolation. An example of this integrated marketing communications approach is shown in Exhibit 4–3. This illustrates the integrated program developed by the American Cancer Society to communicate the concern about overexposure to the sun or "sunburn" to the American public.

Exhibit 4–3   American Cancer Society Integrated Marketing Strategy

	General advertising	Public relations	Sales promotion	Direct response
Health objective	To encourage the target to avoid sunburn			
Purpose	To encourage the target to protect their skin from the cancer-causing rays of the sun by using a sunscreen with a sun protection factor (SPF) of 15 + instead of other tanning lotions or oils.			
Target	Adult "sun worshippers"	*Primary* Adult "sun worshippers"	*Secondary* Cosmetic, Toiletry and Fragrance Assn. Physicians Pharmacists	
Promise	When I use a sunscreen with an SPF of 15 + , I will feel in control of my health because sunscreen with SPF 15 + helps protect me from the deadly, cancer-causing rays of the sun while allowing me to obtain an attractive "light" tan.	*Primary* Same as for advertising	*Secondary* CTF Assn.: "I will feel satisfied that I am helping to create a favorable sales environment." Physicians, pharmacists: "I will feel satisfied that I am doing the best job possible for my patients'/customers' preventive health maintenance."	
Support	Studies show that unprotected sun exposure is closely related to all types of skin cancer, including those that can kill you. Doctors advise to moderate exposure to sun and to use sunscreen. Sunscreen with SPF of 15 + gives 15 times your natural defenses against the sun's rays.			
Personality	(Warm) (Caring) (Foremost authority) (Professional) (Renowned)			

(continued)

Exhibit 4–3   (Continued)

	General advertising	Public relations	Sales promotion	Direct response
Media	National TV MTV (cooperative program) Pop radio Print magazine ads Billboards	Program w/CTF Assn. to help with visibility, reach, materials distribution, and costs Collateral materials: Educational brochure (w/coupon to purchase any SPF 15 + product) Poster (professionals only) Spokesperson	Work with CTF to develop and implement system to code (via symbols and/or colors) grades of protection for sunscreen products to include packaging and POP chart coordinated w/packaging Coupon	Direct response offer

Let's now assume the choice has been made that general advertising is indeed the proper approach to the specific problem which has been identified. The next step is the development of the advertising plan.

DEVELOPING AN ADVERTISING PLAN

Most experts agree that great advertising cannot be produced from a rigid formula. However, the campaign planner who attempts to develop an advertising program without first preparing a carefully written plan generally fails. Although a written plan isn't foolproof, it does provide the blueprint that assures that all the necessary decisions are made in, it is hoped, a logical and effective sequence. Further, it assures there are no glaring holes or exceptions in the development process.

WHAT IS AN ADVERTISING PLAN?

One way to define an advertising plan is to describe what it is *not:*

1. The advertising plan is not a marketing plan. That means it does not contain marketing objectives, such as sales or profits or return on investment. The advertising plan is part of the marketing plan and contains only that information relevant to the advertising or promotion program that will be conducted for the brand during the given time

period. The marketing information belongs in the marketing plan, not the advertising plan.

2. The advertising plan is not a sales document. Although it is important to be enthusiastic about the program that has been developed, the purpose of the advertising plan is to provide an outline of what is recommended and what is to be done. As such, the selling arguments should be restricted to the "Conclusion" section or in the formal presentation of the material.

3. The advertising plan is not a ponderous tome. The objective of the plan is not to show how much information has been gathered or how many pages the planner can prepare. The purpose of the plan is to communicate clearly and completely what is proposed for the coming advertising period and why those recommendations are being made. Keep it to that.

What the advertising plan is, specifically:

1. The advertising plan is the background, history, and past records of the advertising programs that have been conducted for the brand. It's the recommendations of what is proposed for the coming period in terms of specific advertising and, perhaps, sales promotion, and/or publicity programs. As such, it contains a record of what has gone before and provides an outline of what is to come. Therefore, the plan should contain only those elements that will be helpful in understanding what is proposed, judging the likely success of that program, and preparing future programs.

2. The advertising plan is an opportunity to explain and illustrate the logic and reasoning that has gone into the development of the advertising program. By explaining the problems and opportunities that the brand or the company face, the planner can illustrate how the proposed program solves these problems and capitalizes on the identified opportunities. The plan gives the campaign planner an opportunity to illustrate how all the parts of the plan fit together over time. Because advertising plans often cover time periods of a year or longer, it gives the planner an opportunity to illustrate how the program will unfold and build over the course of the campaign.

3. The advertising plan is an action document. Because the development and implementation of an advertising program is usually a very complex scheduling and coordinating activity, the advertising plan lists on paper all the steps that are to be taken. It can also indicate who is to implement the plan. Therefore, the advertising plan serves as a formal document used throughout the period of the campaign.

4. The advertising plan provides management with an outline of the financial commitments being made on behalf of the brand, and a general outline of when those funds will be spent. Because many advertising programs for national brands involve millions of dollars,

this outline is vital for the financial planning of the company. Further, the advertising plan provides a form of control over the approved expenditures and puts a limit on the funds that will be made available by management.

With this brief look at the advertising plan, the next step is the actual development. We'll look first at the entire planning process. Then we provide a step-by-step procedure for developing an advertising plan.

ELEMENTS OF THE ADVERTISING PLAN

The best way to develop any plan is to outline the basic decisions that need to be made. Then, put those decisions in sequence. The same is true for an advertising plan. There are a certain number of decisions that need to be made and a certain sequence exists in which those decisions can and should be made. Exhibit 4–4 illustrates one method of advertising campaign planning. It shows a very thorough step-by-step procedure which assumes that not only is the advertising program properly planned but that the other key communications tools are considered and integrated as well.

Although the model in Exhibit 4–4 is excellent for visualizing the process, the inexperienced planner may need a more detailed description of the exact steps in the process and more definition in what exactly should and should not be included. That description follows. (Note that we start at about the midpoint of the model in Exhibit 4–4. We assume that the decisions about the other communications areas have been determined as was previously discussed.)

Following this section is a working model of an advertising plan in outline form. The system we use here is suitable for most types of marketing organizations as well as for advertising agencies who have been asked by their client to prepare a proposal for review. If there are unique situations faced by the planner, the system can be easily adjusted.

I. Executive Summary

As the title suggests, this is a brief digest or abstract of the key elements of the plan. The purpose of this summary is to provide the plan's highlights in a form that management can quickly read and understand and on which a decision can be made. Top level executives often want a brief thumbnail sketch of what is proposed in advertising because they assume that the planner is expert. Further, if management personnel have a question about one or more sections of the plan, they can quickly refer to those sections for more detail. This executive summary should be one or two pages at most; it outlines what is proposed and highlights the most important areas, such as spending, advertising, creative strategy, general media schedules, and sales promotion.

Exhibit 4–4   Advertising Campaign Planning

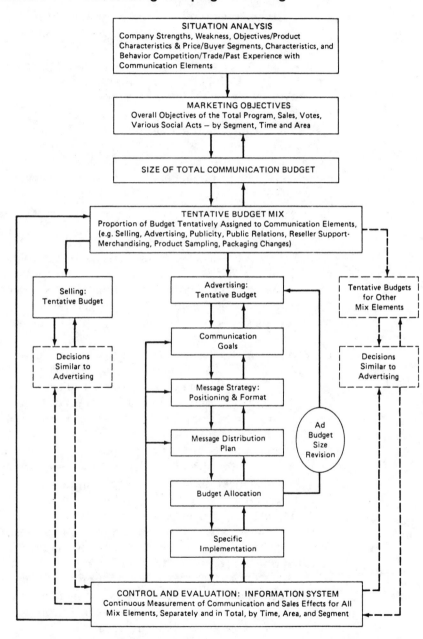

SOURCE: Michael L. Ray, *Advertising and Communication Management* (Englewood Cliffs, N.J.: Prentice-Hall, 1982): 54.

II. Situation Analysis

A. Company and product history. Traditionally, a brief history or sketch of the company is given first. Usually, a single paragraph will do. The history of the brand may need to be a bit longer, perhaps a half page or so. It should, however, stick to the key issues that face the brand today and are relevant to the brand's future success. Above all, avoid the temptation to stroke management with a verbose, yawn-producing "century-of-progress" report.

Relevant history here may relate to the sales history of the brand and perhaps key competitors. Equally important may be the historical growth of the category—if it has not been included in the marketing plan. However, this is not a marketing exercise. It is simply a review of what has happened in the market and to the brand. If possible, this information should be related to past advertising programs in a way that might indicate why the sales patterns occurred as they did.

Perhaps the most important element to include in this analysis is a brief review of the previous advertising plan and its success or failure. For example, if there was a reason the previous year's plan did not meet expectations, tell why it didn't work and what necessary changes have been made for this year. The goal is to update management on what is happening in the marketplace and set the stage for what is proposed in the plan.

B. Product evaluation. All those elements (discussed in Chapter 1) that might affect sales of the product or service should be discussed and evaluated here, including benefits offered, distribution, pricing, and so forth. This information should be in brief outline form and deal only with specifics, not guesses or estimates. It should, however, point out those areas that will impact specifically on the success of the advertising program. For example, if the brand has a distribution problem, the problem should be pointed out. You should also discuss the expected effect that distribution problems might have on the success of the advertising program. Perhaps as important is the need to point out the assumptions being made about the marketplace and marketing activities during the period of the plan. You should point out which of these assumptions will be likely to affect the program being recommended. For example, if prices are to be raised during the course of the advertising plan, some statement should be made about what effect this might have on advertising response.

This section need not be a total and complete review of the product. It should simply cover those relevant facts that might have an effect on the outcome of the proposed advertising program.

C. Consumer evaluation. This section should give an accurate picture of the target market (TM) to whom the advertising will be directed. It should be as specific as possible, including demographics, psychographics, geographics, and the like. Of key importance are statistics, such as how many purchasers there are in the category, how many purchasers the brand has, and the brand's market share. Those are all-important factors in supporting the recommendations that you are making.

All other available consumer data also should be included. Such data include information of the life-style of consumers or prospects, how they use the product now, what attitudes they have toward the brand, how they feel about competition—in short, any information that will give a better picture of the target market of proposed advertising messages. This material can be vital to management in making a positive decision about the plan. Remember, management doesn't know the prospects and customers as well as you do. So, paint a picture of whom your advertising will be expected to influence. Such data can help immeasurably in getting approval for the campaign.

D. Competitive evaluation. Most modern marketing language has been borrowed from military strategists. As any commanding officer knows, accurate intelligence on the enemy is crucial if a successful military campaign is to be launched. The same is true in advertising. You must know what your competitors are doing and what they can or might do. This information will help guide you in developing a plan that not only anticipates competitive reaction to your plan, but also gives you an opportunity to offset any programs that the competition might implement during the period your plan will be in effect.

So, start with a review of current competitive advertising campaigns. Point out to whom these campaigns are directed, give an indication of the advertising weight being used, and how this campaign might affect the target market. Further, show the timing of previous competitive programs and the strategy that this timing indicates is being used. This review can be quite helpful in illustrating how and why the creative and media recommendations will be effective. If at all possible, give some indication of the spending level being used by competition. This will help support the budget proposed in the plan and gives management a benchmark against which to measure. In brief, include any competition advertising information that will show why and how the plan was developed and how you hope to offset competitive activities with the proposed program.

III. Marketing Goals

Although the advertising plan should deal with advertising and not marketing, it is often helpful to include a brief review of marketing goals that have been set for the brand or company. Often, that review will assist management in seeing how the advertising program is designed to support and assist in the sales and profit objectives which have been set.

Typically, marketing goals are stated both short term and long term. Most short-term goals are for the coming year or coming financial period. Long-term goals are for from three to five years. Whether the goals are short or long term, they should be expressed quantitatively, that is, in numbers or figures that can be measured. (See Chapter 1.)

In addition to the marketing goals, it is a good idea to give a brief description of the basic marketing mix that will be used by the brand or company during the planning period. The marketing mix is the combination of pricing, distribution, promotion, and the like, that will be used to support the brand. If communication is only of minor importance in the overall marketing mix for the brand, it should be stated as such. Or, if advertising is the key element in the success of the brand, it should be noted. In other words, there should be some indication of how important advertising and the advertising program is felt to be in the success of the overall marketing program. This information will help those who evaluate or who are to approve the advertising plan to better understand why certain decisions, assumptions, and even budget levels have been set for the advertising program.

IV. Budget

Usually, the budget comes next. Often the question uppermost in management's mind is, "What will this advertising campaign cost?" Therefore, the best time to show the proposed spending is when marketing goals and the marketing mix elements are still fresh in management's minds. It is always easier and quicker to review the marketing goals and relate them to the proposed advertising expenditure if they are located close together.

You may want to include a brief historical note on what traditionally has been spent on the brand and what spending is proposed in this section. This notation can take many forms, such as a recap of the past five years' expenditures, the relationship of advertising to sales or distribution or number of units operated or other factors. Doing this will help tie the proposed expenditure to some other known factor.

Be sure to include all costs for the campaign here. For example, if evaluation is an advertising cost, include that. Don't forget to add, among other things, the cost of production of the materials or the research expenditures for pretesting the creative material.

Most advertising budgets can be presented on one page with a backup page or two of explanation or support for spending amounts. If competitive expenditures are to be included, be sure to include the sources of the estimates or information. Or, if you are estimating based on experience, be sure to say so. The more support given for suggestions and recommendations, the better their chances of approval.

V. Advertising Recommendations

As you can see, we have been moving from the general to the specific or "cascading" from the general marketing objectives down to the specifics of the proposed advertising program. In your recommendations you will describe the creative elements, the media plan, and so on, which make up the proposal.

If your descriptions and explanations of what is happening in the market, how the consumer is reacting, what the competition is doing or expected to do, and so on, have been complete in previous sections, the first statements in this section should know how this advertising plan is designed to either take advantage of or offset those situations. If the first sections are carefully and completely planned and organized, long, detailed explanations of the specific elements of the advertising plan will not be needed. It will be clear to those reading the plan what the market problems are and how this plan will solve them.

A. Target market.   The first step is the profile of the group of people to whom the advertising will be directed. This can be a brief summary of the consumer evaluation developed in Section II (Situation Analysis). The size of the market, geographics, demographics, psychographics, and past purchase history should be given, and finally, a rationale should be provided as to why the particular group of people was selected as the best prospects for sales messages. The clearer this statement is made, the better the chances for success in achieving the advertising objectives and also in getting approval for the plan.

An important part of this section is the quantification of the target market you have selected. Be as specific as possible in terms of number of people and where they are located geographically. This information is vital to support the creative and media recommendations that follow.

B. Advertising communication objectives.   This section spells out exactly, in quantifiable, measurable terms, what sales message will be communicated in what time period to the target market. Generally, advertising goals are stated in terms of the communication effects that are expected to occur—for example, creating awareness, imparting knowledge about the product benefits, developing preference, and the like. Unless your recommendation is for direct response advertising, your goals should not include sales or marketing objectives. This is where advertising plans often fall apart. The planner writes into the advertising program activities or actions that advertising alone simply can't accomplish. (See Chapter 1.)

No matter what goals are set for the advertising plan, they must be measurable and specific. For example, here's just one of the advertising goals taken from a recent plan:

> During the first four months of the campaign, to make 60 percent of the target market aware of the new coast-to-coast service being offered by Whiz-Bang Airlines.

Note that the objective is specific. It gives a goal against which actual results can be measured. It specifies the group that will be measured, and it sets a time limit for the accomplishing of the goal. Finally, the objective to be measured is specific: the awareness of "coast-to-coast" service being offered by the airline. That's the way to write effective advertising objectives.

C. Creative strategy. The advertising strategy defines the message to be communicated in the advertising campaign. It is the companion to the advertising communication objective because it states what is to be communicated. Often, the strategy is stated in the form of a "promise" to be made to the target market. The creative strategy simply sums up the solution to the advertising problem that has been identified as being one faced by the brand or the company. If the first sections of the plan have been properly developed, the creative strategy should be the logical solution to the problem or problems that have been developed in Sections II and III.

D. Executions. The executions (or tactics) are the form the actual advertising will take. They carry out the strategy that has been developed, and put it in a form that allows it to be transmitted to the target audience. Generally, this section contains the actual elements to be used in the campaign, such as storyboards, layouts, and radio scripts. If a central theme for the campaign has been developed, it should be featured here along with any other specific creative recommendations being made.

E. Plans. This section may or may not be required in your formal document. It generally includes a brief description of how the creative executions will be accomplished. For example, if new television commercials are to be produced based on results of what happens in a distribution drive in the field, you might want to sketch out a general timetable for the production of those commercials. Or, alternatively, it might include a commitment timetable for production cost elements and at what point they must be approved. In short, it is a section that can be used to explain or bring forward specific steps that are contingent on activities within the campaign or will occur as a result of portions of the program.

VI. Media Recommendations

In this section, the planner should outline the complete details of the media program that will be used to get the advertising message to the target market.

A. Key media problem. This section starts with the major media problem to be solved, usually in the form of a brief question facing the advertising planner for the campaign. For example, in the advertising objective set for Whiz-Bang Airlines, the goal was to make 60 percent of the target market aware of "coast-to-coast" service from the airline. The problem here might be how to identify and reach persons who are prospects for transcontinental airline service. Many people fly on airplanes, but not all of them fly on transcontinental routes. Thus, the question facing the campaign planner is how to locate and communicate with prospects most effectively and efficiently. On the other hand, other media questions, such as how to compete in a category in which the brand is being outspent by competition by a substantial amount, might be more important in other situations. This section can often be handled in one or two paragraphs; it should sum up the problem the media plan is designed to resolve.

B. Media objectives. These are the specific message delivery goals established by the campaign planner. They should be stated as quantifiable, measurable objectives within a certain time period. In many cases, these goals will be stated in terms of reach and frequency against the target market for the time period outlined.

C. Media strategy. A statement of media strategy outlines and explains the various media to be used to achieve the plan's media objectives. For example, if television is to be used, network or spot should be specified. Or, if print is the major vehicle, will it be newspaper or magazines? In short, the planner should use this section to tell how the media objectives will be accomplished and give some support and rationale for the choices being recommended.

D. Media plan. After outlining what is to be accomplished through the media and the media to be used, the next logical section is the media plan. This section should outline, in as much detail as is needed, the specific scheduling for each medium. Depending on the complexity of the overall plan, and the specific brand for which the plan has been developed, the outline may consist of a single flowchart with one or two magazines listed, or it may consist of a number of specific media plans for individual markets or areas of the country.

The easiest way to illustrate media plans is with a flowchart (see Chapter 12), which gives a graphic illustration of how the media is to be used across the length of the plan, and can illustrate how the various media have been scheduled to work together.

Also, this section should include a media budget recap sheet. This sheet should show spending for each medium and a total for the campaign. In some instances, you may want to show quarterly or other expenditure patterns, depending, of course, on the needs of the brand.

VII. Other Marketing Communications Programs or Recommendations

Traditionally, the advertising plan has not included the recommendations for the other marketing communications tools, such as sales promotion, public relations, or direct marketing, which might be used in the overall marketing program. Although these tools might have been referred to in the overall marketing and communication plan, in the past, they were prepared separately by a functional specialist. Today, however, with the increasing importance of integrated marketing communications (see Chapters 1 and 2), many advertising planners are now either responsible for these other communications programs and thus include them, or, to give a clear picture of the overall programs, include a brief synopsis of what has been planned by other managers. Thus, if the advertising planner is responsible for some of these other functions, these sections are a logical addition to the plan. If not, consideration should be given to including them to provide a total picture of the overall communications program to management.

If these other marketing communications approaches are not being used, these sections can be easily deleted from the plan or adjusted as needed. We include sections on sales promotion, public relations, and direct marketing for the sake of completeness.

VII. 1. Sales Promotion Recommendations

Because sales promotion is becoming such an important part of the total spending for many brands and companies, the proposed sales promotion program should probably be included in the advertising campaign plan. Including the proposed sales promotion program will illustrate how the advertising and promotional efforts have been coordinated to achieve maximum effectiveness. As in the case of the advertising section, you'll want to include specific recommendations.

A. Sales promotion objectives.   These objectives should be stated in measurable, quantifiable terms. They should indicate exactly what the sales promotion program is expected to accomplish. Actual results may be listed in terms of sales or trial or conversion or similar behavioral activities by the target market. As will be shown in Chapter 13 on sales promotion, this is an area in which direct action can be expected. An example of a measurable sales promotion objective might be:

> Using sales promotion, the objective is to increase shelf facings by 25 percent in the top fifteen national supermarket chains during the eight months of the program.

B. Sales promotion strategy.   This section simply spells out what specific sales promotion techniques will be used to accomplish the goals stated earlier. Specific tools to be used are usually stated, for example, sampling, couponing, in-store displays, contests, and sweepstakes. In most instances, specific recommendations will be supported with some information on the strategy being used and the reasoning behind it. If there has been a major change in the marketplace that makes certain sales promotion strategies more practical during this planning period than in the past, that information should be included.

C. Sales promotion executions.   This section illustrates the specific details for each of the sales promotion strategies listed earlier. For example, if cents-off coupons are being recommended, the value of the coupons and how they will be distributed should be discussed. In discussing a contest, the contest theme should be described, along with the way in which the winners will be selected, the prize structure, the timing, how the promotion fits in with the advertising, and so on. In short, each of the sales promotion programs should be outlined in sufficient detail so that management can quickly and easily see what is planned. Be sure to relate the sales promotion plan to the advertising. In some instances, you may want to refer to the advertising media plan and the other elements so that management will have a clear view of how all the pieces fit together.

D. Sales promotion plan.   Finally, a brief outline of the overall sales promotion program should be prepared. This outline can be in the form of a flowchart or other device that shows the timing and length of each promotional activity. Preparing an overlay showing the advertising media plan in relation to the sales promotion schedule is a good way to show how everything is dovetailed together during the campaign period. In addition, this section should present the various costs for each scheduled element, including estimates of various redemption costs or units, such as the dollar amount for coupons, number and cost of premiums, and expected acceptance and value of trade deals. This is the section where all the detailed information needed to make a plan action oriented is located.

VII. 2. Public Relations

Public relations is a very sophisticated marketing communications technique. Whether PR is being used to try to solve complex corporate communications problems, to provide additional communication with the potential customer for the product, or as a technique to improve trade relations, a sound planning approach is needed. Such an approach would include objectives, strategies, and tactics.

A. Public relations objectives. As with other techniques, PR objectives should be stated in measurable, quantifiable terms. Commonly, these objectives have been set as the amount of print space or air time obtained in support of the project. Increasingly, however, PR objectives are being set in terms of measurable changes in attitudes, beliefs, or feelings by the target market as a result of public relations activities. For example, a measurable public relations objective might be stated as:

> The objective is to increase awareness among security directors at the top 200 U.S. airports of the availability of the new model ZYX metal detector, using trade publication new product press releases, from the present 25 percent to 50 percent in the next two months.

B. Public relations strategy. The specific public relations approaches that will be used are listed in this section. These might run the gamut from appearances on network talk shows to placement of the product in major motion pictures to the distribution of press releases to the trade. This section is key for management because it describes what public relations tools have been selected and why they were chosen.

C. Public relations executions. Even though it is often not possible to illustrate PR tactics prior to the time they are implemented, this section, in most cases, does include such things as lists of the publications that will be targeted with news releases, the dates and locations of informational meetings, the specific dates when plant tours will be conducted, and so on. Often the specific news releases, publicity photos, and the like are included to illustrate the approach that will be taken.

D. Public relations plan. A calendar flowchart should be included here to illustrate the various PR activities and how they flow throughout the year. It is also helpful to relate this PR plan to the other advertising, sales promotion, and direct marketing activities that will occur. This way, management can see how all elements fit together.

A general public relations budget, broken down into the broad areas of activities, if not included elsewhere, should be presented to give management a feel for the total investment being made.

VII. 3. Direct Marketing

One of the fastest growing areas in marketing communications is that of direct marketing. In the past, direct marketing was almost synonymous with direct mail. Thanks to the development of electronic data gathering and storage systems, direct marketing is much more than just an alternative communications medium. (We'll discuss direct marketing in more detail in Chapter 14.) For our purposes here, *direct marketing* is defined as any communications technique directed to a specific, identifiable audience with the goal of achieving a measurable response.

A. Direct marketing objectives.   In direct marketing, specific, measurable responses to various communications efforts are the rule, not the exception. Therefore, direct marketing objectives must be totally quantified, for example, to sell X number of units, to generate Y number of inquiries or Z number of qualified leads. Although there is doubtless some residual communications benefit from direct marketing activities, in general, the objectives are only those which are directly measurable and directly traceable to the direct marketing activities. For direct marketing, an objective might be stated as:

> We will drop 50,000 direct mail packages in support of Product Lambda on January 20 of the coming year. We will be mailing to the merged list of former users and level A prospects. We expect a response rate of 2.3 percent. Orders should peak two weeks after the mail drop.

B. Direct marketing strategies.   As with the other marketing communications approaches described earlier, there are several direct marketing alternatives. In direct marketing, strategic choices would include the type of list to be used such as existing clients or new lists; the type of offer to be made, for example, with or without a premium, credit or cash only, use of an 800 number for order receipts, and so on. In addition, the strategies might also include the media to be used, such as direct mail, telemarketing catalogs, magazines, and so on. In short, the strategy should describe the approaches that will be used to achieve the selected level of direct response.

C. Direct marketing executions.   In this section, a brief description of the contents of the direct mail package or the script for the telemarketing effort or an outline of the products to be included in the catalog should be given. In other words, you should include enough of a description or illustration of what is proposed to give the management a clear idea of the approach.

D. Direct marketing plan. As was suggested for other communications approaches, a brief outline of the total direct marketing effort along with a flowchart makes it easier to see and understand how the implementation will take place. It is also helpful to relate the direct marketing efforts to the efforts being made with advertising, sales promotion, and public relations.

If it is not included elsewhere, a budget outline should be included to show how much of an expenditure is being proposed. If, for example, direct mail is considered a part of the advertising program, that too should be noted.

VIII. Evaluation

It is essential to describe and illustrate very clearly exactly how the advertising campaign will be evaluated. If various steps need to be taken prior to the start of the campaign, such as a pretest, that should be noted. A brief description of the recommended methods and whether or not the costs are to be considered an advertising or a marketing expense should be included. For the most part, evaluation plans are included as an advertising expense.

IX. Conclusions

Depending on the persons to whom the plan is being addressed, you may or may not need to include this section. If the plan is being developed as an internal document, it probably is not necessary because you will have covered most of this "selling material" in the "Executive Summary." If, however, the plan is being developed by an advertising agency for submission to a client, a one- or two-page review of why the plan meets the needs of the brand, how it is designed to achieve certain preagreed upon objectives, and so on, is in order. In other words, this is the place to put the selling copy to convince a client or management to approve the plan and to "ask for the order." It's really the only chance to do some old-fashioned selling of the plan as developed. A caution though: Don't make this section redundant. If reasons have already been given on why certain things have been recommended within the body of the plan, don't just repeat them. Use this section, if it is used at all, to summarize the value of this plan compared to any others that might be developed or considered.

YOUR ADVERTISING PLAN—A WORKING MODEL

No perfect outline exists to fit every advertising campaign planner's needs. The following outline was developed with three major objectives in mind: simplicity, substance, and clarity. Use this model as a directional guide for the plan. Include things not listed but that are important in making the plan clear and complete. Likewise, drop those sections that do not relate. If it makes a better plan, change the sequence. For example, you may prefer to have the budget section at the end as a summary. If you follow this plan or at least include all the items listed as follows, all the major elements for an advertising campaign plan will be covered.

I. Executive Summary

On a single side of a sheet of paper, outline the major issues covered in the plan. It is usual that one or perhaps two elements are vital to the success of the proposal. It may be that you will need basic agreement on the proper target market, the creative strategy, or even the media plan. There usually are one or two issues with which your readers must agree if they are to approve the plan. Make sure those points come through loud and clear in this summary. And be sure you adequately support your views and positions with facts and information. If you can get these major issues down on one page, you're usually well on your way to gaining approval for the advertising plan.

To be sure that management understands the integrated nature of the overall plan, it is usually wise to add a few sentences about the other marketing communications programs that will be used in combination with advertising. A brief section on the sales promotion, public relations, and direct marketing plans should be included in this summary.

II. Situation Analysis

Dig up all the facts and information listed later. Then cut away the unimportant information and get down to the real basics. This section shouldn't run more than ten to fifteen pages.

A simple way to reduce the verbiage in your plan is to use pie charts, graphs, and growth curves. Many times, a small chart can replace hundreds of words of prose.

In terms of content, the following points should be covered or at least considered:

A. Relevant history of the product or brand.

1. Background of the product or brand
2. Past advertising budgets
3. Past advertising themes
4. Patents or technological history
6. Significant political or legal influence
7. Current creative theme being used in advertising or promotion

8. Current problems and opportunities facing the brand
9. Major events or activities that might affect the brand in the coming plan period
10. Relevant marketing data from the marketing plan that might be helpful in understanding why the advertising plan is prepared the way it is

   Note that most of the questions asked about the brand's history could also be asked about the major competitive brands. A historical comparison with the competition can be made in this section or separately under "Competitive Analysis." Use whichever is most easily understood by your readers.

B. Product evaluation.

1. How does the product compare to the competition in terms of features, ingredients, uses, consumer acceptance, and so on?
2. What has been added or improved in the last few years, deleted or dropped, new uses, new markets, and so on?
3. Do consumers perceive the product to be new and modern or old-fashioned? Is it a fashion product and affected by changing consumer mores?
4. How does the product stack up in terms of value? The price–value relationship?
5. Are present users satisfied?
6. Is distribution widespread? Is the product available?
7. How do retailers feel about the product? Do they want to stock and sell it? Is distribution adequate? And so on.
8. What about packaging? Labeling?
9. Is the brand name well known? How well accepted is it?
10. What about service, if provided, with the product?
11. What problems do consumers have with product, if any? Are they correctable?
12. Is there anything in the product or its features unique or different from those of the competition?

   Although just a partial list, it gives you an idea of what should go in this section. Include any relevant data that will give readers an understanding of the product, how it fits in the marketplace, and, most especially, why the proposed advertising plan will be effective.

C. Consumer evaluation.

1. Demographic profile. Occupation; marital status; household head; race; education; age; household income; presence of children in household; social class; locality type; geographic region; other geographical or market breakdowns, such as high or low CDI areas, county size, and so on.

2. Psychographic profile. Any VALS data available? Any psychographic information from Simmons or other life-style data bases? Any user data from previous primary research? Any data on life-style or how your product fits into the lives of your present customers or prospects? And so on.

3. Analysis of present customer's behaviors. Information on consumption, such as social influences, where used, how used, frequency of use, average amount used; attitudes about product, such as quality, price, packaging, styling, reputation of the brand; percentage of consumer awareness of present advertising or promotional activities. What problems does the product solve for the consumer? Is the consumer aware of these benefits? How loyal are present customers? Does brand-switching occur? If so, among this brand or others? Who are the best prospects for the brand? Where are they located? Can they be influenced? In short, include any and all relevant information about the present customers and prospects whom you have identified for the product or service.

D. Competitive analysis.

1. Direct competition
2. Indirect competition
3. Advertising strengths and weaknesses of competition
4. Current and past competitive advertising themes
5. Strengths or weaknesses of competitive packaging, branding, and so on
6. Past competitive advertising and sales promotion expenditures
7. Any research on effectiveness of competitive expenditures
8. Trade acceptance of or influence of competitive advertising or sales promotion programs
9. Any apparent weaknesses in competitive programs
10. Any geographic concentration of competitive expenditures
11. Any comments or feelings from the sales force or trade as to unusual strengths of competitive programs

III. Marketing Goals

Marketing goals can be taken directly from the marketing plan. Be sure to include information on such areas as what marketing objectives have been set in terms of sales, margins, or profits for the period the advertising will cover. Also include information on expected market share or share improvement, current and proposed market penetration, and where changes should occur.

More specifically, refer to the marketing plan to describe the proposed marketing strategy for the coming period. This is important because it enables the reader to see how the advertising plan fits in with the overall marketing strategy. Be sure to include a brief description of how these marketing objectives are being supported by the advertising campaign. That is particularly true if the advertising plan is expected to make a direct and major contribution to accomplishing marketing goals.

A brief description of the basic strategic marketing approach being taken for the brand should also be included. This description would include an outline of the various marketing mix elements and how each is either supported, featured, or reinforced by the advertising plan which follows.

IV. Budget

(See Chapter 8.)

V. Advertising Recommendations

These recommendations are the heart of the advertising plan. What follows is an outline of the elements you'll want to include:

A. Target market.   The best approach is to immediately identify the target market to whom the advertising will be directed. This may simply be a summary of the "Consumer Evaluation" section or it may be more detailed, depending on the needs of the readers. Here's where you outline in general terms the demographics and psychographics of the target market, identify how many of those types of people there are, and give some indication of why they are prospects—that is, are they present users, users of competitive products, or not users in the category? Also, be sure to support the recommendations for selecting the particular target market segment of the population here.

B. Advertising communications objectives.   This section covers the basics of what the advertising is supposed to accomplish. One of the easiest ways to do this is through a formal, structured approach. The ("Problem Statement") form that follows will help you present this information to management in a clear, easy-to-understand manner. It has two major sections:

The Problem Statement

1. Key fact (usually one or two sentences): A single-minded statement that sorts out all the information about the product, market, competition, and so on. It is the single element that is most relevant to the advertising need or plan. It identifies the reason the advertising is needed for the brand.

2. Primary market problem advertising can solve (one half page or so): This statement should grow out of and be directly related to the key fact. It may be a product problem, a marketing problem, or an image problem, but it must be related to an area in which advertising can have some influence.

C. The creative strategy.   Next comes the "what" you'll be saying in the advertising campaign. The creative strategy is the most important element in the entire program; if you select the wrong approach or feature an unimportant benefit, no matter how much media you buy or how creative your other communication ideas may be, the advertising campaign will likely fail.

We start the development of the creative strategy with a clear, concise description of the product or service for which the plan has been developed.

1. What is the product or service?
    a. In reality: What is the product this advertising is designed to sell? What is it made of? How is it made? Are there specific ingredients or elements that are unusual or different? In other words, give real product information. Facts. Facts. Facts.
    b. As perceived: How do consumers think of the product or service? Although high quality may have been built into the product, do consumers perceive it in that way? How do people feel about the product? Do they like it? Do they consider it to be useful? Worth the cost? And so on. Remember, to consumers, perceptions are their truth whether they are technically correct or not.

    The goal here is to try to understand how customers and prospects feel about the product or service, as they choose to use it or ignore it in the marketplace.

2. Who are the prospects?
    In this section, the target market must be brought to life for both management and others who will be involved in the implementation of the plan. Obviously, the number of prospects in the target market must be given, along with the growth potential, geographics, demographics, psychographics, media patterns, and the like. However, using only numbers and broad, general descriptions and definitions does little to help those who are going to implement the plan visualize the prospects as people. One of the best ways to aid this visualization is to describe a representative person in the target market. You can describe how they currently use the product or service and start to explain why or how the advertising program will help to convert them to the brand. This humanizes the target market, converting faceless statistical units into real people.

3. Who are the principal competitors?

   In two or three sentences, list the primary competitors of the brand. Tell why they are major competitors. Explain what these competitors are doing in the marketplace; how this advertising program will compete with or overcome their efforts. This section should not include a listing of all competitors in the marketplace, only those important ones against whom the brand competes on a regular basis.

4. What is the competitive consumer benefit?

   This is a summary statement of the message the target market wants to hear about the brand, product, or service in order to either start, continue, or increase their purchases of it, or give them a major reason why they should switch from another brand. It should be a single benefit, written from the customer's, not the marketer's, point of view. And, it must be a real benefit to the consumer, not just another snappy advertising slogan.

5. What is the support for the benefit? the reason why?

   This statement summarizes the reasons why the "competitive consumer benefit" can be stated. It explains and expands the benefit to make it possible and believable. Ideally, this statement should consist of one or two primary facts about the product, not a listing of all the possible claims that might be made.

6. What is the target market incentive statement?

   This is simply a summary statement of the advertising strategy written in a short, simple sentence. It recaps the entire strategy in this way.

   To (User Group or Target Market), (Name of Brand) is the (Product Category) that (Benefit of Brand) because (Reason Why).

7. What is the tone of the advertising?

   The tone is often called the "personality" or "manner" in which the advertising will be presented. For example, for a health care product, the tone might be serious. For a new product, newsy. For a children's product, fun or happy. In other words, this section describes the feelings or emotions that the advertising should generate in the target market with exposure.

8. What is the communication objective?

   This can be summarized by asking a few basic questions.

   a. What is the main point? In other words, what single, clear-cut message should the target market take away from this advertising?

   b. What action should be taken? After seeing or hearing the advertising, what should the target market do? Should they go to the store and buy? Change their opinion about the brand? Put the brand on a shopping list? Exactly what? These are among the most important points in the entire advertising strategy.

9. What are the divisional or corporate requirements?
    Listed here are any legal, company policy, or other statements, either written, graphic, or audio, that must be included in the advertising.

D. Executions.   This section shows how the creative strategy has been fulfilled. Include as much or as little of the actual creative product as is necessary to get the ideas across. This material may include but not be limited to:

1. Print layouts and copy
2. Radio scripts
3. Television storyboards
4. Theme lines and art
5. Package designs, illustrations, and so on
6. Brochure or catalog layouts
7. Outdoor board designs
8. Advertising specialties

E. Advertising plan.   Outline any details of how the advertising will be done or other special information. For example, if the advertising calls for special travel to photograph locations, specify why that location or area is important. A timetable for approval of the creative material might be included simply to enable production to be done in time for the media schedule. This is the area in which to cover those important details that need to be discussed and explained if management is to have a complete picture of the entire advertising program.

VI. Media Recommendations

In this section the proposed media program should be explained clearly and concisely. Depending on the complexity of the media plan, descriptive material may be needed or a simple outline may be sufficient. If the proposed media plan is radically different from that which has traditionally been used for the product or service, additional justification may be required. In other cases, where plans are simply being updated, a quick review of the history of the media program may be sufficient. At a minimum the following information should be included.

A. Key media problem.   This is where the primary problem that the media plan must solve is listed. An example might be:

> This media plan is unique to the brand because the marketing activities are being revised from national to regional and local coverage. This plan is designed to maximize media coverage in the twenty markets that have been selected to give the appearance of a national plan to dealers and the sales force.

The key media problem may be more specific than this example if the situation warrants, but, in general, it should set up the basic premise that management will need to approve to get final acceptance of the entire program.

B. Media objectives.   This section relates media to the overall marketing and advertising plan—in other words, the specific goal of the media plan in quantifiable terms. At a minimum, the following areas should be covered:

1. The target audience to be reached, in terms of demographics and psychographics (if they are pertinent)
2. Budget available and restrictions on its use
3. Reach and frequency needed
4. Effective reach levels needed
5. Continuity needed
6. Pattern of monthly and yearly continuity
7. Special geographic weighting needed
8. Merchandisability of media if necessary
9. Flexibility needed
10. Degree to which media will have to support promotions
11. Creative strategy implications

In addition, a rationale for each of the decisions should be included here to support the proposal.[1]

C. Media strategy.   This section covers the specifics of the media plan. That means each of the media proposed should be listed and then support given for that recommendation. In addition, each of the strategies must be related to one or more of the media objectives. In some instances, explanations of why other perhaps more obvious strategies were not used or why a new plan that doesn't follow historical tradition is necessary may be needed. At a minimum, strategies should include:

1. Media classes selected (e.g., network television or magazines)
2. Strategy for allocating the budget to geographic areas (rollout vs. national introduction; spot only or national plus spot heavy-up)
3. Allocation of budget to media classes (dollars and percentages of total)
4. Allocation of budget by months and/or quarters of year; introductory versus sustaining period strategy
5. Reach and frequency levels desired by months and/or quarters of the year

---

[1]Jack Z. Sissors and Lincoln Bumba, *Advertising Media Planning,* 3rd ed. (Lincolnwood, Ill.: NTC Business Books, 1989): 230–36.

6. Effective reach and frequency levels per typical month
7. Size of the primary and secondary target markets
8. Weighting of strategic targets
9. Geographical weighting requirements that must be used
10. Cost-per-thousand standards, if required
11. Explanations of why a strategy is different from previous ones
12. Specifications of the size of media units to be used (15- or 30-second commercials; full or fractional pages)
13. Criteria to be used for the selecting or scheduling of media (need for flighting)
14. Relationship of strategy to that of competitors, with special emphasis on certain key brands that must be dealt with specifically
15. A rationale for each strategy statement[2]

D. Media plan.   This section documents and details the specifics of the media proposal. This information is usually supported by media flow-charts showing exactly when each insertion or broadcast is scheduled, along with costs and other supporting information. Again, at a minimum, the media plan should include the following information:

1. A statement of criteria for determining media values
2. Proof that vehicles selected are the best of all alternatives (using media value criteria) for the budget (data plus words)
3. Data showing net reach and frequency for targets reached by a combination of all vehicles, including frequency distributions
4. Data showing gross impressions for a combination of all vehicles, especially for target audiences
5. Cost per thousand shown for all vehicles selected or considered
6. Cost summary tables showing each vehicle, number of times used per month, cost per insertion, and total cost per month
7. Yearly cost summary
8. Yearly flowchart (or schedule) showing vehicles, weeks of insertions, reaches, frequencies, and costs per month for the year
9. Any other data that will help buyers implement the plan[3]

VII. Other Marketing Communications Programs or Recommendations

As previously discussed, most advertising plans traditionally have not included sections or segments on other marketing communications pro-

---

[2]Sissors and Bumba, *Advertising Media Planning,* 3rd ed.: 236–39.
[3]Sissors and Bumba, *Advertising Media Planning,* 3rd ed.: 43–47.

grams. However, because the integration of all marketing communications, including advertising, is becoming increasingly important, the advertising planner may want to at least include a brief summary of what these elements are and how they have or will be dovetailed with the proposed advertising plan.

Increasingly, sales promotion, because it is so directly related to the advertising program, is either under the control of the advertising planner or is very closely coordinated with another manager or planner. Therefore, we develop the sales promotion portion of the advertising program in some detail. The sections on public relations and direct marketing, because they are, for the most part, under the control of other managers, are only summarized in the plan. (See Chapters 13 and 14 for more details on public relations and direct marketing.)

A. Sales promotion recommendations. Because sales promotion now accounts for 60 percent or more of many products' total promotional budget, these recommendations may represent a substantial portion of the overall plan. In some instances, the sales promotion program is handled as a separate document, or it may be included in the general advertising plan for the product or service. Here, we make the assumption that it is a part of the advertising plan.

1. Sales promotion objectives. Start first with a clear, concise, and complete description of what the sales promotion program is designed to achieve. This description can vary widely, but the more specific the recommendations, the better. For example, don't use broad, general ideas, such as "support the advertising campaign"; that's understood. Be specific: "Generate trial of Brand Q among 40 percent of the TM during the first six months of the budgeted period." With clear, measurable sales promotion objectives, management can easily see how your entire plan fits together.

    Some of the common objectives often set for the sales promotion program are
    a. Generate trial
    b. Hold present customers
    c. Load present customers
    d. Encourage repeat usage of the product
    e. Build more frequent or multiple purchases
    f. Introduce a new or improved product
    g. Introduce new packaging or different size package
    h. Neutralize competitive advertising or sales promotion
    i. Capitalize on seasonal, geographic, or special events
    j. Encourage customers to trade up to a larger size, a more profitable line, or another product in the line

2. Sales promotion strategy. These are the specifics of the sales promotion plan. At a minimum, the specific sales promotion techniques proposed should be justified. One of the basic differentiations in sales promotion that should be made is that between the consumer and the trade. In other words, identify what activities are designed to get consumer action and what is recommended to get trade support. Some of the basic sales promotion strategies that might be included are

    a. Consumer sales promotion strategies
        i. Coupons
        ii. Contests and/or sweepstakes
        iii. Bonus packs
        iv. Stamp and continuity plans
        v. Price-offs
        vi. In-packs, on-packs, near-packs, and reusable containers
        vii. Free-in-the-mail premiums
        viii. Self-liquidating premiums
        ix. Refund offers
        x. Sampling
        xi. Point-of-purchase materials

    b. Trade sales promotion strategies
        i. Trade deals
        ii. Trade coupons

    c. Special events

3. Sales promotion executions. To illustrate what is being proposed include examples of the specific sales promotional activities. These examples can consist of sketches or simply descriptions of the specific nature of the event. In general, rough sketches of art or illustrations of specific promotion are needed. For example, if items such as samples are proposed, a sketch of the mailer or distribution package along with any sales material or information that might be included should be illustrated. Some of the more common items often included in this section are

    a. Coupon advertisements or mailers
    b. Trial or sample packages
    c. Layouts of sweepstakes ads
    d. In-store take-one pads or display material
    e. Illustrations or sketches of premiums proposed
    f. Sketches of bonus pack labels or stickers

    Including examples of the specific sales promotion activities proposed will allay questions in the mind of management as to exactly what will be used in the sales promotion program.

B. Sales promotion plan.   An outline in calendar form usually follows examples of the illustrations of the sales promotion executions. This is done to give management a view of how all the various parts fit together and will interact in the marketplace. If it has not been done previously, include a recap of the cost of the sales promotion program, including not only immediate expenditures proposed for sales promotion activities but also a description of the reserves that will be necessary for such things as coupon redemption, premium purchases, and fulfillment of promotional programs.

In this section, also list the response expected for each of the activities. For example, what percentage of the coupons will be redeemed? How many premiums will be needed? What is the cost of the contest or sweepstakes prizes and judging? What will it cost to return refund coupons to those who participate?

C. Public relations recommendations.   A brief description of the public relations activities that will be used in support of the product or service should be stated here. This description is often taken from the public relations proposal prepared by another manager. If the proposal is not available, include, at a minimum, some idea of the scope and plan of the public relations activities that will be used to support the product, service, or brand.

Ideally, summary statements of the objectives, strategies, executions, and general public relations plan for the product or service should be included. This section obviously depends to a great extent on how closely the advertising and public relations people work together for the mutual benefit of the product or service.

D. Direct marketing recommendations.   Again, if it is practical and possible, the advertising planner should include some overview of the direct marketing activities that will be used on behalf of the product, service, or brand during the period of the proposed advertising plan. If direct marketing is under the control of the advertising planner, this section can be done in some detail. If it is not, usually, summary statements alone are possible. (See Chapter 14 for more information on direct marketing planning.)

VIII. Evaluation

A brief statement of how the advertising campaign is to be evaluated should be included. This statement should cover the proposed methods—for example, a telephone tracking study, or the purchasing of Nielsen or SAMI data, or the measurement of shelf space in retail stores—so that the stated objectives of the campaign can be evaluated. Usually, some specific details are given as to who will be responsible for this evaluation and how it will be carried out. Because the advertising campaign planner often relies on the research department or even an outside research organization for this portion of the plan, it is vital that direction and control be identified in detail.

Finally, the estimated cost of this evaluation plan should be included. This is particularly true if the evaluation plan is to be included as a part of the total advertising campaign cost.

IX. Conclusions

As previously stated, this section may or may not be included in the advertising plan, depending on the audience and the position of the advertising campaign planner. If it is included, it should be short and to the point. Don't repeat material previously included. If a "Conclusions" section is to be used at all, it should summarize and bring out the major factors that make the plan especially appropriate to the problems and opportunities facing the product or service.

SOME TIPS ON WRITING AN ADVERTISING PLAN

Although everyone has his or her own writing style, there are some general guidelines for the preparation of an advertising plan. These should be helpful to both professionals and novices.

1. Be brief. An advertising plan is not a test of literary ability. It is written to enable the advertising planner to communicate ideas and recommendations in a clear and concise fashion. Therefore, summarize, outline, categorize, cut out all excess words. Edit and trim. Make the plan lean and easy to read and follow.
2. Avoid redundancy. One of the biggest hazards of an advertising plan is repetition of the same ideas over and over. If the idea or concept is covered in a previous section, refer to it. Don't repeat it.
3. No pronouns. Readers of advertising plans don't really care who had the idea or suggestion. They want only facts. Therefore, leave out the references to "I" or "me" or "we" or "us." If you wrote the plan, the reader knows it. You don't need to remind him or her of it.
4. Inductive; not deductive. Start with the most important points and then support them. Advertising plans are not novels. They shouldn't be written to build up suspense.
5. A summary at the beginning. One of the best ways to develop an advertising plan is to put a brief summary at the beginning of each section. That way, the reader can quickly and easily see if that is the section that contains the detailed information he or she is seeking.
6. Show sources of information. A must for any advertising plan is to show the sources of data that are used. It lends much more credence

to the proposal to do so. Further, it illustrates that the recommendations are based on solid information not just opinion or guesswork.

7. Fifty to sixty pages maximum. Although there are occasions when this rule may have to be bent or broken, generally, no advertising plan should run over fifty to sixty pages. If it is longer than that, there's a good chance it's overwritten. One way to handle the "number of pages" problem is to move charts, graphs, and supporting material to an appendix and identify it as such. Then, if readers need more information, they have it available. Creating an appendix also assures that the basics of the plan are not cluttered with details.

In summary, be brief, be complete, but most of all, pack the plan with usable, useful information.

ADVERTISING INFORMATION SOURCES

Although most of the material needed for the advertising plan will be developed in the research section, here are some suggested sources of information that may be helpful in locating information about a company, an organization, a product, service, category, or the like.

I. Financial information sources
  A. Finding out what books exist on a subject
    1. Library card catalog
    2. *Cumulative Book Index*
    3. *Books in Print*
  B. Finding journal and newspaper articles
    1. *Funk and Scott Index of Corporations and Industries*
    2. *Business Periodical Index*
    3. *The Wall Street Journal*
  C. Financial services
    1. Moody's manuals
      a. *Moody's Industrial Manual*
      b. *Moody's OTC Industrial Manual*
      c. *Moody's Bank and Finance Manual*
      d. *Moody's Municipal and Governmental Manual*
      e. *Moody's Public Utility Manual*
      f. *Moody's Transportation Manual*
    2. Standard and Poor Corporation
      a. *Standard Corporation Records*
      b. New York Stock Exchange listed stock reports
      c. American Stock Exchange stock reports
      d. Over-the-counter and regional exchange stock reports
  D. Company information
    1. Annual reports (often available from stock brokerage firms)

      2. House organs

      3. Prospectuses

II. How to find information about an industry
- A. Guides to sources
  1. *Wasserman's Statistics Sources*
  2. *Encyclopedia of Business Information Sources*
- B. Other sources
  1. Standard and Poor's Industry Surveys
  2. U.S. Census publications
     - a. *Annual Survey of Manufacturers*
     - b. *Census of Agriculture*
     - c. *Census of Business*
     - d. *Census of Construction Industries*
     - e. *Census of Housing*
     - f. *Census of Manufacturing*
     - g. *Census of Mineral Industries*
     - h. *Census of Population*
     - i. *Census of Transportation*
  3. Survey of Current Business
- C. Directories listing corporations
  1. *Thomas Register of American Manufacturers*— includes alphabetical listing of trademarks
  2. *Conover-Mast Purchasing Directory*

III. How to find information about a geographical area
- A. U.S. Census publications (in addition to those listed above)
  1. *Statistical Abstract of the United States*
  2. *County and City Data Book*
  3. *County Business Patterns*
- B. State statistical abstracts
- C. State industrial directories
- D. "Survey of Buying Power Issue," *Sales and Marketing Management* magazine (annual)

IV. Special advertising sources
- A. Standard Rate and Data Service
  1. Consumer magazines
  2. Business publications
  3. Canadian Advertising
  4. Network Rates and Data
  5. Newspaper Rates and Data
  6. Spot Radio Rates and Data
  7. Spot Television Rates and Data
  8. Transit Advertising Rates and Data
  9. ABC Weekly Newspaper Rates and Data
  10. Print Media

          11.   Directorio de Medias

          12.   Newspaper Circulation Analysis

   B. *Standard Directory of Advertisers*

   C. *Standard Directory of Advertising Agencies*

   D. National Advertising Investments

V. Syndicated marketing studies

(*Note* that companies listed here will often provide "year-old" data to universities and colleges for cost of postage and handling.)

   A. Simmons Market Research Bureau

Audience exposure estimates and product-usage studies correlated with both broadcast and printed media. A major source of consumer research data and marketing studies for all major consumer product categories.

   B. A. C. Nielsen Company

Several kinds of syndicated services are available:

      1. NTI (Nielsen Television Index) is a national television rating service which estimates audience size for all the network TV shows using audimeters installed in approximately 1,200 U.S. TV households.

      2. NSI (Nielsen Station Index) is the Nielsen's service for measuring local TV audiences.

      3. Nielsen Food & Drug Index is a service that measures movement of products in retail stores. From these store audits, companies are able to estimate their brand shares.

   C. LNA-BAR

Leading National Advertiser-Broadcast Advertiser Reports (LNA-BAR) provides a monthly estimate of TV commercial expenditures and gross time billing for all major national brands. Also available are estimates of production costs for programs and talent costs along with station lineups. Network radio station lineups by program and advertiser is another service syndicated by LNA-BAR.

   D. SAMI (Selling Areas Marketing, Inc.)

This syndicated research company estimates inventory withdrawals by major food and drug chains and stores.

SUMMARY

The advertising plan is a very important element in the campaign because it forces the planner to consider all elements that might influence the success of the campaign and explain to others (i.e., top management) how the campaign will work. Key components of the plan are executive summary, situation analysis, marketing goals, budget, advertising recommendations, media recommendations, other marketing communications programs or recommendations, evaluation, and conclusions.

Case Studies

Sidley's Soft Drinks

Mort Sidley, president of Sidley's Soft Drinks, decided to hire an outside advertising agency in May 1989. Sidley's manufactured and distributed six soft drinks regionally. Their market area included retail outlets in North and South Carolina, Georgia, Alabama, Kentucky, and Tennessee. In the past, all promotional efforts had been handled in house and had consisted mostly of consumer sales promotions and store displays. Sidley's average market share was 10 percent, giving it a good showing behind the national brands. Sidley had decided to allocate more of his budget to advertising and to develop a campaign to be used throughout the region. With the heavy advertising and sales promotion spending from the national brands, he was afraid Sidley's was in danger of being lost in the shuffle. Accordingly, he contacted three agencies who had experience in the region and asked them to study the situation and submit a written plan outlining their analysis and solution. Sidley set a June 15 deadline for submission of the plans.

PLAN A

The three plans Sidley received were very different from one another, both in content and in format. Plan A contained a detailed analysis of the entire soft drink industry, outlining competitive expenditures and campaigns for the past five years. It also contained an in-depth look at the national brands' product lines—formulations, positioning, pricing, trade deals, and consumer promotions. The plan briefly outlined Sidley's activities and product characteristics, noting that the product was comparable to the national brands in quality and that its distribution was quite good in the region it served. Plan A identified price as the primary benefit. (Sidley's was priced an average of 10 percent below the national brands.)

The target market was defined as that sought by the national marketers, with special emphasis on young professionals aged 22–34. A psychographic study of these people revealed them to be very quality conscious, but also concerned about price. Sidley's was a known brand, but they were unaware of its high quality. This segment currently purchased national brands, but were not brand loyal, switching to whichever brand happened to be sale-priced at the time.

Marketing objectives included a 5 percent increase in market share during the first eight months of the campaign. The plan also recommended expanding distribution into Mississippi within the next eight months.

151

These objectives would be accomplished through the increased ad budget, which would be used to develop a major regional campaign.

The advertising campaign was centered around the theme "Quench it with Sidley's quality." Advertising would be carried over regional television and in regional magazines and would feature members of the target market drinking Sidley's after a day's activity (tennis, swimming, biking, etc.). The plan explained that, by using television, Sidley's would actively compete with the national brands.

Sales promotion activities would include coupons ("Sidley's quality for less than ever") and premiums, such as coolers and beach towels carrying the Sidley name. These premiums would help increase recognition.

The evaluation plan called for a straightforward analysis of sales increases.

PLAN B

Plan B began by briefly reviewing Sidley's activities and the competitors' spending in the region. Sidley's "home-grown" appeal was identified as the product's unique feature; the bulk of the plan was devoted to a detailed explanation of the advertising campaign that would bring this feature to the general public's attention. The "Drink of Dixie" would be advertised on television, radio, and billboards. With an appeal to all "true Southerners" to support the South's own soft drink, the campaign included such elements as a commercial showing Robert E. Lee and Stonewall Jackson enjoying Sidley's after a victorious battle, billboards where Sidley's grew on magnolia trees, and a jingle to the tune of "Dixie":

> Oh, I'm so glad I have my Sidley's,
> It's the drink that's really Dixie,
> Drink it down, drink it down,
> Drink it down, it's for me.

Plan B defined a target market that was very Southern in its orientation and primarily rural. It recommended that Sidley's set up soft drink machines in small towns throughout the area. The Dixie appeal would help strengthen Sidley's image against the national brands and was expected to increase market share 5 percent in six months.

PLAN C

Plan C began with a look at Sidley's growth over the past five years, its primary areas of strength (medium-sized communities and suburbs of larger cities), seasonality (like most soft drinks, sales dropped slightly from November to February), and distributor attitudes (well liked). It contrasted these findings with those for the national brands, which were stronger in the big cities. The plan also noted that retailers had no strong attitude toward the national brands, suggesting that they would be willing to support any consumer promotions Sidley's might institute as long as the money was right.

Consumers were described as liking Sidley's, and a large proportion of Sidley's buyers were identified as being fiercely brand loyal. The target market for the campaign was described as households of three or more persons living in suburban and nonmetro counties and having yearly incomes of $10,000+. The best prospects among this group were brand-switching national brand buyers.

Marketing goals were for a 7 percent market share increase after the first year, and a 30 percent increase in brand recognition.

The advertising campaign identified Sidley's as "The South's Favorite Son." Ads were to be run in local newspapers and were in the form of turn-of-the-century advertisements. Each ad would feature a tintype-style photo of a local resident with a can of Sidley's. Copy would explain that Sidley's was that person's favorite soft drink. The newspaper ads would be augmented by a radio commercial featuring a "politician" introducing "the South's favorite son—Sidley's." The plan explained that using newspapers would set Sidley's apart from the national brands and give it strong local appeal, particularly in the smaller towns.

Sales promotions would include coupons in the form of ballots ("Pick your favorite son—any of Sidley's six flavors at a savings"). Store displays would also be used.

Evaluation would consist of an analysis of sales increases by community type and a pre-post measure of brand awareness among the target market.

Questions

1. Based on the information given in the case, evaluate each plan. Is the information relevant to the situation? Adequate?
2. Does the analysis seem to justify and lead logically to the solution?

Hytek Industries, Inc.

Tracy Read, account executive at Komplex Advertising, was reviewing her notes from a recent meeting with the new product committee at Hytek Industries, a major client. Hytek had just given the go-ahead for Komplex to begin work on a marketing communications campaign for a new product that they expected to be a major factor in the consumer marketplace. Tracy knew that if Hytek were right, the account could mean a great deal of business for Komplex. Agency management had promised her the use of several assistant account people to help in researching the elements that would become part of the initial plan. However, Tracy also knew that she would have to think through a number of elements in order to give the assistants proper direction. The product was not a simple one, and neither Hytek nor Komplex quite knew how to go about defining the market or developing concrete objectives. Tracy began reviewing her notes.

THE PRODUCT

The product was a telephone caller identification service. Consumers who subscribed to the service and purchased the appropriate hardware (manufactured and sold by Hytek) would be able to identify the caller before they answered the telephone. A display screen would show the name of the calling party. Consequently, the product could be used to screen calls, so the consumer would only have to answer calls coming from people they wished to talk with at any particular time.

The hardware was relatively expensive, retailing for around $80. In addition, there was a monthly charge for the service. The service was also something that many people might regard as a luxury rather than a necessity. Though there was no identical product available, there were other products, such as answering machines and answering services, that could perform roughly the same service. Those products tended to be slightly more expensive, but had been on the market for some time and consumers were familiar with them.

MARKET FORECAST

Hytek's engineers, who'd developed the product, were convinced it would be a hit with the consumer market. During the meeting, they had been tossing around 60–70 percent penetration figures by the end of Year One. Tracy believed that estimate to be totally unrealistic, given the product's expensive price tag, its complexity, and its novelty. Fortunately, she'd noticed the marketing people rolling their eyes while the engineers were talking, and figured that meant they realized that the marketing task probably wouldn't be quite that easy. Still, she would need some facts to back up whatever projection the agency developed. Hytek tended to be product oriented, and Tracy suspected it would take some convincing to get them to see this product as anything other than a runaway success story.

Hytek was especially interested in the proper introduction of this product because it would provide them with their first entry in the telecommunications industry. Hytek's management firmly believed that telecommunications provided the best opportunity for continued expansion of the company in terms of sales and profits.

ENVIRONMENTAL CONCERNS

There was some chance that introduction and acceptance of the product might be hampered by government regulation. The product was in test in one area, and the test was being closely watched by both state and federal groups. Some concerns had been raised over possible privacy-related implications of the service. (Clearly, if the service were restricted there would be no market for the hardware.) However, there was no current legislation that would prohibit use of the product, and strong consumer acceptance could probably diffuse any negative legislative activity.

DISTRIBUTION

The Hytek hardware would be sold through retailers who carried other telecommunications and electronics products. Again, the Hytek engineers claimed that retailers would be very interested in selling the product and would probably contact Hytek to ask for the product. Tracy wasn't sure that the engineers were right on this score either. She suspected that some level of trade support would be needed.

If the current test proved successful, a national rollout would probably follow fairly quickly, with A and B counties targeted first. It would be important to get widespread distribution support to make it easy for interested consumers to find the hardware.

BUDGET

Hytek had not established a budget for the product. Traditionally, Hytek viewed marketing communications budgets as investments and expected a strong return on that investment within a year or two, depending on the product. Tracy suspected Hytek might be willing to stretch the payback period for this product, given its importance to the company's future activities.

Tracy had a number of resources at her disposal in addition to the account people. Komplex specialized in technical products and had an outstanding reference library. There was also a major university located nearby; Komplex people used the library there quite often.

Past dealings with Hytek suggested they'd approve some preliminary consumer research spending. Although results of the ongoing test were available to Tracy, she also wanted to talk to some prospective users to see how they reacted to the product concept. However, Hytek would probably want to see a preliminary plan outline before Tracy would have the chance to see any research results. And, of course, it would be nice to have a better idea of who the prospects for this product were before starting any primary research.

Finally, Tracy viewed this task as more than an advertising problem. Hytek had referred to a "marketing communications" program, and Tracy agreed that advertising alone would not be sufficient to sell this product. She would need to consider possible applications of sales promotion, public relations, direct marketing, and personal selling to work in conjunction with any advertising.

Tracy needed to put together a preliminary outline of tasks for the assistant account people. She would have to review a first-draft plan with her own management in a few days before taking the draft to Hytek the next week. Hytek would accept changes in the plan as new information was uncovered, but because of their keen interest in this product, Tracy knew that Komplex's job in the future would be much easier if she could impress Hytek with this preliminary plan. She would have to be careful to develop some realistic expectations for the product without ruffling the engineers' egos too much.

Questions

1. Help! Where would you start if you were Tracy? Specifically:
   a. What sources (or types of sources) might you look at to identify the type of people who might be interested in this product?
   b. What factors would you look at for the situation analysis portion of the plan for the Hytek product? If you could only expand on one area, what would it be? Why?
   c. What, if anything, would you include in the media recommendations portion of the plan at this point?
   d. What information would you look at in developing a more realistic market forecast for this product?
   e. What sort of evaluation period would you recommend for the Hytek product?

Give support for each of your recommendations. (Hint: you might want to review Chapters 1–3 for some ideas.) Keep in mind that each part of the plan must flow from and support the other parts.

5

Research
The Foundation for the Advertising Campaign

Few successful campaigns can spring full blown from the mind of the advertising planner. The products, the consumers, and the marketplace are simply too complex for campaign planners to rely totally on intuition and inspiration when developing an advertising campaign. And, the risks are too great as well. In spite of the massive use, and often misuse, of research, it is still one of the most helpful though misunderstood tools available to the advertising campaign planner.

THE REASONS FOR RESEARCH

Research is needed and must be used to develop an effective advertising campaign. The first reason, the increasing complexity of products, consumers and the marketplace, has already been alluded to. A few years ago, when there was less competition, fewer markets, fewer media, fewer distribution systems, and less communication, it was possible for a marketer and an advertising agency to sit down and develop a simple advertising campaign just by writing some rather winning prose about the product, putting it in the form of an ad, and then placing it in the local newspaper. It was possible because the customers and prospects were usually the friends and neighbors of the marketer and agency people. The advertisers knew the market and the people they were trying to communicate with. In addition, the product was often simple and the demand was great. That's not the case today. Now the marketer and agency are often separated from the market not only in terms of space and time, but also in terms of culture and social class. And, in most categories, there are too many products, too many advertising messages, and much, too much sales promotion competing for the consumer's attention. In our complex society and increasingly complex marketplace, research is vital.

Second, the penalty for failure in today's marketplace is tremendous. Where once the advertiser risked only a few hundred dollars on a newspaper advertisement, now a single 30-second television commercial, broadcast nationally, can run well into six figures. With that sort of money involved, advertisers and agencies, as a matter of good business practice, must remove as much of the risk from advertising as possible.

Third, if one truly accepts the marketing concept, that is, to fill consumer needs and wants, it is necessary to conduct research simply to learn what those consumer needs and wants are. In order to move from a production-oriented to a marketing-oriented system, research, with its resulting consumer and market information, is not only helpful, it's a must.

Although the research background is vital to the planner in developing a successful advertising campaign, there is one caution. Research can provide information on where a product or service stands in the marketplace and what product and services consumers want and need. Research might even indicate the direction in which an advertising campaign should move. It can provide the information base on which to make various advertising campaign decisions. It cannot dictate the actual method of accomplishing these goals. The direction the campaign goes in depends on the skill and talent of the advertising campaign planner. Once the planner knows the situation, the direction, and the potential rewards, he or she must set the advertising objectives and then develop the advertising plan and implementation to achieve those goals. In other words, research is a guide, not a definitive answer, and should be used as such.

TYPES OF RESEARCH

The campaign planner is often faced with a multitude of advertising and marketing needs, ranging from identification of present users, to competitive themes being used in the marketplace, to methods of evaluating the advertising campaign after it is completed. In addition, researchers often use a bewildering number of methods and techniques to gather information. And, to complicate matters even more, the planner often faces research results computed or analyzed by rather sophisticated statistical techniques, which the researcher may consider to be more important than the actual information being gathered.

Because this is not a text on how to conduct research, we assume that you, the advertising planner, are more interested in gathering the needed information than in being able to conduct the research in person. The key element for the planner is to understand the various research techniques used, be aware of the availability of information, and have a sufficient understanding of research analysis, so that the needed information can be gathered in the least possible time, at the lowest possible cost.

Marketing Research versus Advertising Research

The campaign planner typically uses two types of research in developing and evaluating an advertising campaign.

1. *Marketing research*—information on the market, competition, prospects, distribution, and pricing.
2. *Advertising research*—information directly related to the advertising campaign, normally in connection with the development, pretesting, placement, and evaluation of the actual advertising campaign or materials.

The planner should keep these two differing kinds of research activities clearly in mind. Although both marketing and advertising research are needed to develop, implement, and evaluate an advertising campaign, there are several differences in what information is gathered, what sources are used, and the availability of the information needed. Market research is covered in this chapter. Advertising research is discussed in Chapter 6.

The Five-Step Advertising Campaign Research Plan

For most advertising campaigns including the development, testing, and evaluation of the plan, research in five specific areas is needed.

Prospect, market, product, and competitive research.   Research in these areas involves gathering information to identify the target prospects for the product or service to be advertised, the size of the market, market location, distribution patterns, pricing, any product tests and/or evaluation, and identification of competition and competitive products. This research deals with the development of information necessary to market the product or service whether advertising or another form of promotion is used. Generally, these are rather broad studies and often come from existing sources or data. These types of information and the various research tools used to obtain them are discussed later in this chapter.

Strategy development research.   Research in this area deals with the sales message or type of appeal to be made to the target market. It may or may not include gathering additional target market information. Whether it does or not usually depends on the scope of market identification available from basic research. In general, after the basic marketing research has been conducted, strategy development research is the first step in the development of the advertising campaign. The objective of all strategy development research is to identify the single strongest competitive consumer benefit that can be developed from all alternatives. This is advertising research. It will be discussed in some detail in Chapter 6.

Advertising performance research.   The specific goal of advertising performance research is to determine how well the advertising performed or is performing in the marketplace. Measurement is usually based on how well the advertising communicates with prospective consumers. Further, attempts to determine consumer reactions to the advertising may be made. Often, this type of research is called advertising pretesting. It is discussed in detail in Chapter 9.

Media, media usage, and media placement research.   Another type of advertising research is conducted to determine media distribution, media availability, usage of the media by the consumer population, and size of media audiences. The goal of this research is to optimize the advertising budget in terms of its effectiveness and efficiency in reaching the target market with the advertising campaign messages. This research will be covered in detail in Chapter 12.

Measurements of the effects of the advertising campaign.   This is pure advertising research. It consists of activities and methods designed to evaluate the results of the advertising campaign among the target market. Often this is the only research plan developed and specified by the advertising campaign planner and included in the outline of the campaign itself. Most other forms of marketing and advertising research discussed previously are used only to plan and implement the campaign. Measurement research, however, is used to evaluate what the campaign did or did not accomplish. Thus, it is quite different from the other types of advertising research. Measurement research will be covered in Chapter 14.

The planner must have a sound grasp of the entire research spectrum to be able to marshal all the information and material needed to successfully advertise a product even on the lowest level. Although the areas and techniques may seem complex, the information on the following pages should provide a sound understanding of the various types of research.

Existing Product versus New Product Research

Although it might seem that the research task is already very complex, one additional caution should be made: The information needed to develop a campaign for a new product is often more complex and often quite different from that required for an existing product or one that has already been marketed in some fashion. This problem will be discussed as it relates to the development of a research plan.

DEVELOPING A RESEARCH PLAN

No matter what the product or service, where the market is located, or the size of the campaign to be prepared, all research information gathering must start with a plan. Without a planned approach to research, costs in time and money mount quickly. In addition, the planner may find her- or himself with too little or too much information on which to base a decision. Although there are as many ways to develop a research plan as there are researchers, the outline that follows has worked quite well in providing a research base of information for the development of an advertising campaign. It is management oriented and can be used with any type of product or service and for any type of campaign which is anticipated.

1. Define the advertising problem.
2. Determine specifically how research can help solve the problem:
    a. The data or particular information, for example, target market, size of market, creative direction, and message design needed to solve the problem
    b. The cost or time impact on the product to obtain or use the research
3. Determine what additional information is needed above what is already on hand.
4. List the alternative methods available to obtain the needed information and select the most effective and efficient ones:
    a. Secondary research
    b. Primary research
5. Estimate the cost of each form of research and weight the cost against the potential value in the development of the advertising campaign.
6. Develop the final research plan or proposal.

This outline focuses directly on that material needed in the development of the advertising campaign. The campaign planner inevitably finds some information that, while of value in developing the plan or interesting to know, is just too costly to collect. The cost–benefit relationship between the need for information and the need for precise information must be weighted against the cost of obtaining the data or achieving that precision. For example, it is quite unusual for an advertising campaign researcher to use a strict probability sample in a research study. The costs simply outweigh the potential benefits. The advertising planner is constantly making trade-offs between the ideal and the practical.

As noted above, the first step in a research plan is to define the research problem. Usually, that's the key to a successful research study. If the information to be gathered is clearly stated, the alternatives usually become quite clear. The vague, loosely worded, imprecise problem statement causes most research problems. If the information cannot be defined clearly, consumers or marketers or retailers or any other research source cannot be expected to give clear, precise answers to questions. It's simple.

A clear understanding and statement of the information provide a basis for a problem statement.

Three basic elements go into the makeup of a good research problem statement:

1. The information to be gathered must be measurable.
2. It must be relevant to the problem being considered.
3. The various pieces of information or knowledge to be gained must somehow be related.

A good example of a research problem statement follows:

> Sales of the 20-ounce size of Reckless Ralph's Window Cleaner have declined 10 percent in the past six months. Is the decline in sales due to a decline in the total category, the package size, or are sales being lost to another brand? If sales are being lost to another brand, which brand is it, and why?

This problem statement clearly and concisely sums up what information is needed and offers some direction toward solution. The research problem is measurable. The questions are relevant to the problem. And the information requested is directly related to the overall problem. The researcher can clearly identify the various sources of information needed and develop a sound research plan with this approach.

Three basic sources of information are used in the development of an advertising campaign plan: (a) secondary research, (b) primary research, and (c) observation. Generally, secondary research and observation are the basic methods of gathering information for products or services that are presently being marketed and advertised. Primary research is often used in planning the advertising to help in the introduction of a new product or the marketing of an existing product or service in a new area.

IDENTIFYING PROSPECTS, MARKETS, AND COMPETITION FOR EXISTING PRODUCTS OR SERVICES

For the most part, advertising campaign planners work with products that are already on the market. New product development also tends to grow out of experience with existing lines. So, by understanding how and where various types of information for existing products are available, the planner can often develop information bases for almost any type of new product.

Types of Information Needed

Four types of information are needed about presently marketed products:

1. Information on consumers or present users
2. Basic market information

3.   Information about the product or service to be advertised
4.   Information on competition and competitors

Information on consumers or present users.   Obviously, the best advertising prospects for a product or service are those already using the product or service or persons who resemble users in some way. This is especially true because in many product categories 20 percent of the users account for eighty percent of the purchases. That is why research begins with present users. In general, the planner needs to know who the users are geographically, demographically, and psychographically; how they buy the product (one at a time or in multiple units); when they buy it (in a particular season); and so forth.

Many other characteristics also must be defined. Where do users normally purchase the product and what price do they pay? How do they use the product and are they using it in familiar or unfamiliar ways? To what degree are users satisfied with the brand? Are they loyal to the brand or do they switch to other brands? Further, are there groups of heavy users, people who use more than the normal amount of the product? If so, who are they, where are they, and why do they use such a disproportionate amount? Obviously, it is necessary to know how consumers feel about the brand, what information they have, how past advertising has affected them, and so on.

Of course, in developing a research plan, each brand will have different needs and may require different information. Generally, the planner wants as clear a profile of present users as possible in order to understand to whom advertising should be directed, where they are located, and what sales messages might best motivate them to continue using or perhaps to increase their usage of the brand.

For example, assume you are in the baby food business as Gerber Products is. From your research, you will want to learn as much as you can about how mothers feel about baby food, what they consider important, what they are concerned about, and so on. Knowing how mothers feel and how they use your products will be particularly helpful in developing advertising to keep present customers purchasing and almost as important in getting new mothers to start and stay with Gerber baby foods.

The planner uses the profile of present customers and users to select and segment other population groups who might be likely prospects for the brand. By knowing present users, the planner should be able to expand the user base by bringing new users to the brand and getting others to switch from competitive brands.

Market information.   In addition to knowing who present users are and who prospects might be, the planner needs to know something about the marketplace in which these consumers operate. The place to start is with the general economic conditions in the country or the area where the advertising campaign will be placed. Among other things, the planner should know if there is inflation or recession, the level of unemployment, and consumer attitudes toward the economy. This information will help define how the product fits in the overall scheme.

From this general view, the planner moves to the product category in which the brand competes and learns as much as possible about that area. Necessary information includes the total value of sales in the category, the category sales trends, and usage trends. These data tell how the category is faring. Further, the planner needs to know information on such things as pricing and pricing stability, distribution patterns, and type of retailers who carry the product, as well as the general profile of persons who use a product in the category—their demographics, geographics, purchasing patterns, and the like, if they differ from those of present customers.

In short, the planner needs as clear a picture as possible of the total market for the particular product category and brand and the marketplace in which the brand is competing. For the specific brand, the planner needs to know the areas of and levels of distribution, types of retailers who stock the brand, existing pricing patterns, forms and methods of discounts given retailers and consumers, the type of sales force, and the like. This information is used to match the brand against the total market. Often, the standing of the brand in the market among both retailers and consumers dictates the way in which the advertising campaign can be developed.

Information about the product or service to be advertised.   It is important to have information such as the product's construction, contents, length of service, background, and its advantages and disadvantages when compared to competition, and to look at the brand from the consumer's view. The manufacturer of a brand may believe certain product ingredients are very important—for example, it has twice the amount of ingredient R as does the competition. If, however, these ingredients can't be translated into consumer benefits, they aren't truly important in terms of advertising potential. For purposes of the advertising campaign, the planner needs to gather as much information about the brand as possible and then compare it with competitive brands. This information includes more than just ingredients or manufacturing differences. Warranties, guarantees, product tests, previous advertising campaigns, and any psychological benefits built up over time should also be included.

Information on competition and competitors.   Advertising does not exist in a vacuum. It is necessary to know competitive products, their claims, distribution, pricing, customers, strengths, and weaknesses in order to develop the most effective advertising campaign possible. Only by knowing competition can the planner know what advertising may or may not be able to say.

One special note is important here. A product's or a brand's competitors are often more than just specific competitive brands in the category. There may be competition for sales from other categories as well. Thus, it is necessary to identify all general competition. For example, direct competition of the Disney World resort might be other Florida resorts. But indirect and, perhaps, more important competition for the tourist dollar might be resorts in Mexico, the Caribbean, California (particularly Disneyland), and other sunny spots. Going a step further, even less direct but, perhaps, as important competition for a Florida vacation might be the use of that ''vacation'' money to purchase a new automobile, a new home, a swimming pool, or a college education for the children. Thus, advertisers must look at all forms of competition for the money that would be spent to purchase their product or service, and attempt to relate to the most important ones. In a sense, all products and services in the marketplace are competing with one another for the consumer's limited funds. How the product is viewed and how the consumer can be led to view the product often are the responsibility of the advertising campaign planner.

From this discussion, it should be clear that different products and different brands have different research needs. A specific list of information and materials is required in order to develop the most effective advertising plan. In some instances, the information may already be on hand. In others, it may be necessary to locate or generate the information prior to developing the advertising campaign. In the next section, we look at some of the most common sources of consumer, market, product, and competitive information for consumer products, and where that information might be found.

Sources of Information

The campaign planner needs two basic kinds of information or material: (a) that which has already been gathered or exists in a form the planner may use; and (b) that which must still be gathered or collected in some way. Existing information is called secondary information. Research based on this information is called secondary research. If the information is not available and requires a research program specifically designed to get it, that kind of research is called primary research. In most cases, secondary research is used in planning much of the advertising campaign for an existing product. Because information for new products is often not available, primary research is required. It will be discussed later.

Company records or company marketing intelligence. The prime source of information for a brand and, unfortunately, one of the most overlooked, normally consists of sales records, product shipments, customer reports, and the like. The amount of information that is gathered and stored by a company and can be useful to the advertising planner is amazing. The secret is to locate it, and the key to obtaining and using existing company information is a clear, concise description of what is needed and what form it is needed in. If the needed information can be adequately described to the accounting or financial people, it can usually be obtained. In addition to existing records, many organizations also have what they may call a marketing intelligence or marketing information system. Such a system may consist of records and data on the product and product sales, competitive situations, customers, prospects, and the like.

Previous company research. In many cases, a great deal of information can be taken from previous research studies conducted by the company for reasons other than advertising. This information may consist of consumer data, product tests, distribution information, and pricing tests. In some instances, the information is held in the marketing department; in others, it may be found in a research department or even in the sales organization.

Syndicated market and consumer information. When specific research or information is not available for the individual brand, often general information about market and brand standing may be purchased from organizations that gather and make this type of information available. Some of these suppliers provide information that may be very general and include only such basic market data as the size of the total market, distribution patterns, and geographic dispersion. In other cases, the data may be brand specific and designed to provide only the information the planner needs to analyze the total market. In all instances, however, these data are gathered by an outside source, who usually also gathers the same data for other organizations and competitors as well, and provides the information for a fee. Some of the major sources of syndicated market and consumer data are described in Exhibit 5–1.

Trade and association studies. Many trade journals and associations conduct surveys of their readers and collect data about their particular field or industry as part of an ongoing service. Many trade associations develop quite sophisticated data and information for their members; these data may be available if the advertiser company is a member of the group. In many specialized or limited fields or activities, the trade association may be the only source of market and/or marketing information.

Exhibit 5–1   Major Sources of Syndicated Market and Consumer Data

Selling Areas—Marketing, Inc. (SAMI)
This organization provides continuous measurement of the sale and distribution of food and related products based on a computerized warehouse withdrawal technique. Dollar volume and share of market data are measured and reports are issued every four weeks. The base is products in 425 categories in forty-two retail markets. In addition, SAMI offers an on-line interactive system to facilitate analysis by subscribers.

Nielsen Retail Index
Nielsen provides a continuous national and regional measurement of consumer sales and sales-influential factors in retail outlets for numerous consumer packaged goods. The sales data are obtained every thirty or sixty days by auditing inventories and sales of carefully selected sample stores throughout the U.S. The audit data provide purchasers of the service with reports of total sales of the product class; sales of their own brand and that of competitive brands; retailer inventory and stock turn; retail and wholesale prices; retail gross margins; percentage of stores stocking; special manufacturer's deals and local advertising. The data are gathered and provided for the entire U.S. market and for Nielsen-defined geographic regions by type of store ownership groups and sales volume groups. Nielsen subsidiaries and affiliated companies conduct store audits similar to those conducted in the U.S. in a number of foreign countries.

Scanner Services

National Scantrack (Nielsen), **BehaviorScan** (IRI), **Supermarket Product Movement Data** (National Scanning Services)
These services all provide retail sales data derived from supermarket scanners. Sales results from a national sample of grocery stores are aggregated to form weekly reports on product movement in a number of categories. The data are available to subscribers through an on-line system.

Market Research Corporation of America (MRCA)
MRCA conducts a menu census based on a national sample of 4,000 families. These census data contain information on each menu served at each meal during a two-week period, including snack items and carryout foods for each member of the panel. The census also indicates whether the item was used as a basic dish, an ingredient, or an additive; how the item was prepared; who was present at the meal; what was done with the leftovers; and so on.

National Purchase Diary, Inc. (NPD)
NPD is the largest supplier of diary panel data in the U.S. The basic panel consists of 13,000 households selected to be representative of the entire U.S. population. Regional breakouts are possible, as are local market reports in a number of areas. Panel members are also identified by both PRIZM and VALS classifications.

The data base is built on monthly diaries submitted by panel members. Participants list their purchases in fifty basic consumer product categories. NPD data are reported by selected demographics, regions, product ownership, and media habits. Panel data format permits analysis of sales and share trends by brand, package size, product type, and retail outlet. Special analyses can provide information about heavy versus light users, users of a product class, dealing strategy, price ranges, and brand loyalty. On-line data are available.

Information Resources, Inc. (IRI)
In addition to its BehaviorScan scanner data reports, IRI has consumer panels in a number of markets. The households in these panels agree to have their grocery purchases monitored as well as their television viewing and other media use. In this way, purchasing behavior can be compared to advertising exposure for individual households.

Simmons Market Research Bureau (SMRB)
Simmons is a research firm that specializes

(continued)

Exhibit 5–1 (Continued)

in communications media and product usage research. The information form is an annual data base called SMRB Syndicated Media/Marketing Survey. This report contains audience measures for magazines, newspapers, radio, television, and outdoor media usage and attendance. Marketing data are also collected for over 500 product categories, including brands purchased and volume used. Media and purchase data are then cross-tabulated by various demographic and psychographic variables to provide tables of product usage and media-related information.

Locating these data and determining their accuracy are the major obstacles to their use. This information (we are not considering information collected by the government here), has been gathered for a purpose and usually has been funded by some organization. Care should be taken in analyzing the data-gathering method, sample size, and age of the information when it is being used for a research base. Most marketing research texts have excellent lists of sources of this information. Additional sources are available at most libraries or through various trade organizations.

Census and/or registration data. One of the most overlooked sources of information about markets and consumers is that developed or gathered by various governmental organizations. Federal, state, and local governments are particularly good sources of data on almost any subject. The federal government publishes information through the Census Bureau on such topics as population, housing, retail trade, wholesale trade, service industries, manufacturers, agriculture, and transportation. In addition, states also publish census data on such factors as population, retail sales, income levels, and employment. Moreover, even cities and counties issue census data on population trends and projections, income, economic and planning studies, traffic counts, and demographic factors. Virtually any large library can provide most types of census data. Because new census material is constantly being published, a thorough study of existing information should be made before additional research is undertaken.

Libraries and universities. Public and private libraries provide an almost endless source of information on all possible topics. Perhaps of most interest to the advertising campaign planner is the fact that most librarians can and will provide sources to the researcher and in many cases will actually locate and provide the information at no cost.

Universities are also a good source of information for the advertising planner. Many advertising and marketing departments conduct ongoing research in various phases of marketing, advertising, and advertising campaign planning. They often provide leads on ways to locate various types of information; they may even have the information available.

Miscellaneous sources.   The supply of data sources for the advertising campaign planner seems almost endless. Individual companies, market research organizations, and others often gather and publish data on various industries and various consumer categories. The same is true of advertising and marketing consultants, advertising agencies, and the like. A quick check of the telephone book and a few calls can often turn up additional sources or leads. Scanning current marketing or research journals is one of the best sources of information. This will often turn up leads, particularly when a bibliography is included. In short, data are usually available. It takes only a bit of investigative interest and creativity to turn up the leads and the material.

Extrapolation of Data

Although it is sometimes true that data often exist for products or services currently being marketed, and that the real task is to determine what data are needed and how they might be gathered, it is not always the case. For example, even though the product may have been on the market for a long time, the campaign planner may decide to develop a new strategy or advertise to another consumer segment or suggest another use for the product. In such cases, if the use is new and the consumer purchasing group isn't fully established, specific market, usage, or consumer data may not be available. This is where the advertising campaign planner really gets to take a creative approach toward research, converting existing data into usable information for another area. This technique is called *data extrapolation;* it is a very common practice in advertising and marketing research and should not be overlooked by the planner. Perhaps an example will illustrate the point.

Assume the planner's brand is in the coffee category. A new technique that has just been developed removes coffee acids without removing the caffeine. The resulting new brand tastes much smoother than other brands on the market. Of course, smooth taste is important to many coffee users, but the planner doesn't have much of a description of users of other brands other than knowing that they exist. However, the planner can develop a profile of prospective new users from existing market information by extrapolating some existing data.

The planner starts with people who have demonstrated they dislike black coffee, which seems to indicate that there was something about the coffee taste they didn't like. What do people add to their coffee to change its taste? Some add cream or nondairy creamers, some add sugar. The assumption can be made that people who use nondairy creamers don't like the taste of black coffee. In other words, they may be looking for a smoother tasting coffee. Because people use sugar for many things in addition to changing the taste of coffee, cream or creamer users might provide a better answer as to who prospects might be. The nondairy-creamer market is large; the information on who purchases and uses nondairy creamers should be available. Obviously, not all the users of nondairy creamers are prospects, but the planner can estimate a logical number who might be—that is, he or she can extrapolate a market for a smoother tasting coffee.

This is just one way existing market data can be used in developing information that can be helpful in the planning of an effective advertising campaign. The extrapolation of data is limited only by the ability and creativity of the person seeking the information. Research, just like advertising strategy and advertising executions, can be a very creative field.

Using Marketing Data to Determine Market Position

After information about the market, the consumer, and the competition has been gathered, the next step is to develop some method of identifying the brand's position in the marketplace. Identifying the brand's position is particularly important when it has varying levels of sales or penetration in markets across the country. Advertising and marketing people use a system of indices to illustrate the standing of the product in various markets: a category-development index (CDI) and a brand-development index (BDI), both of which are computed against the all-commodity volume (ACV) in the particular type of market. The calculation of these indices provides convenient numbers that help identify the best markets or the proportion percentage of distribution for individual products or services. All-commodity volume gives the total amount of sales in a given category. For products sold in food stores, for example, all food store sales would comprise the all-commodity volume. Because a small number of food stores often generates a large share of total food store sales, it is possible to achieve a high percentage of distribution of the ACV in a disproportionately small number of stores.

For example, if total sales of canned tuna fish in Tulsa are 2,000 cans per month, that would be the ACV, or total number of cans of tuna sold. Further assume that the sales by each supermarket chain by month were as shown in Table 5–1.

The ACV is 2,000 cans of tuna fish sold each month. Yet, these sales are not equally divided among the chains in the market nor among the individual stores. For example, Chain A has only 12 stores, yet sells 850 cans of tuna per month, an average of 70.8 cans per store per month. On the other hand, Chain D has 23 stores and sells 154 cans per month, or an average of 6.7 cans per store per month. Closer examination probably would show that sales by individual stores within a chain are not equal either. Some stores may sell much tuna, others almost none.

Table 5-1   Sales by All-Commodity Volume Index

Chain	Number of stores	Number of cans of tuna sold	Percent of ACV
A	12	850	42.5
B	16	420	21.0
C	19	180	9.0
D	23	154	7.7
E	4	103	5.2
All others	116	293	14.6
Total	190	2,000	100.0

A company that markets tuna obviously wants to get as wide a distribution as possible to take advantage of its advertising within the Tulsa market. By obtaining distribution in Chains A and B, whose 28 stores account for only 14.8 percent of the 190 stores in the market, a marketer would have distribution in stores doing 63.5 percent of the ACV. This instance is not at all unusual. In some product categories, 60 percent or more ACV distribution can be achieved in less than 30 percent of the retail outlets across the country. This is particularly true in the many markets dominated by one or two supermarket chains.

Category- and brand-development indices are calculated in a similar manner. For the CDI, total sales of the category may be indexed against sales for a certain geographic region or type of store. In a product category, such as soft drink mixes, for example, the category-development index may be quite high in the Midwest, say 130 (index = 100), while somewhat lower in the Southwest, say 89. Here, the CDI calculation is based on the percentage of total sales that occur in each geographic region.

The brand-development index is the comparison of brand sales indexed against total product sales calculated on a geographic or other basis. In the earlier example, Brand A might have a brand-development index of 125 in the Southwest, indicating that sales are very good in that region. This, however, would be offset to a certain extent because the CDI for that area is rather low. The use of these shorthand indices helps to better identify the present sales or potential market for a brand or category. They are widely used by commercial research organizations.

A major factor in any market analysis is the sales trend for the category or brand. Trend lines that show patterns of sales over several years are developed. Five-year trends are usually best because, frequently, there are wide fluctuations in the marketplace in one- or two-year periods. Trend lines are especially important for products that have shown consistent growth or decline for a number of years. Being able to spot a trend can often be very helpful in planning the campaign. Scanner data have proven especially helpful in mapping the effects of sales promotion activity on product sales.

IDENTIFYING PROSPECTS, MARKETS, AND COMPETITION FOR NEW PRODUCTS OR SERVICES

As stated in the previous section, the largest number of advertising campaigns are created for existing products or services. However, the most exciting task for the advertising campaign planner is often developing the plan for a new product or brand about to enter a new market. Although new product advertising campaigns may be the most exciting, they are also the most difficult and often the riskiest for planner and product because of the lack of information on which to make campaign decisions. With new products, services, or brands, there usually isn't adequate information on which to make the necessary estimates or evaluations. Thus, the campaign planner may be forced to rely on intuition and management judgment. The alternative course is some form of marketing research study. The true problem with new product research isn't that it can't be done, but that the research is costly and time consuming, and that consumers often are unable to verbalize what they might do in new purchasing situations.

As with research for existing products, there are two basic ways to gather information on new products: secondary research and primary research.

Secondary Research

Secondary research is the easiest and quickest source of information, although in the case of a product that is totally new, there is usually little published information available. As is the case with existing products, the first step is to check company records and marketing intelligence information. If the manufacturer or marketer has been planning the new product for some time, a file usually has been built up so there is some previous research information. With any new product, all company sources should be checked before going on to the other information.

Research organizations in many major cities often will do library or data searches on a product category for a fee. In addition, major research organizations have data files of previous research studies done in categories that might be of value. For example, a company planning to enter the pet food drink category might find that some organizations have gathered data on that product area and might make their findings available for a price. For other major sources of secondary information see those listed for existing products earlier in this chapter.

The alternative to finding existing information is to do extrapolations from other data. As was illustrated in the example on the new type of smooth coffee, a planner may be able to extrapolate market information from data gathered for another purpose, or data from a category similar to the one the company plans to enter.

A caution here on both previously gathered and extrapolated data: Use this information only as a general guide for planning. The planner should be sure to check the date of the material and the purpose for which it was gathered. The marketplace changes rapidly. It is possible to take a giant leap to error by using out-of-date or inconclusive secondary data.

Primary Research

Primary research is original research carried out to gather specific information about the problem being studied. Usually, primary research is conducted when existing information is not available, the existing information is suspect, or additional specific information is needed. Primary research may be carried out for either an existing product or a new product. The comments and suggestions that follow apply equally to both.

Four general types of primary research are used in advertising campaign planning: *exploratory or qualitative,* primarily used to better define the problem, the market, or the consumer, *descriptive or quantitative,* the most widely used type of research in advertising campaign planning; *experimental,* widely used in new product research that consists of laboratory tests in which a cause-and-effect relationship is sought; and *tracking or performance evaluation,* often used to evaluate the effects of an advertising campaign (see Chapter 15).

No matter which type of research is used, data are usually gathered either by observation or by survey research. In observation data gathering, consumers or users are observed as they shop, evaluate products or services, make purchasing decisions, or are otherwise involved with the product or service under study. Survey data gathering entails either asking a number of customers or prospects questions about products or services or having them keep a diary of their purchases, product use, or other measurable activity.

Exploratory or qualitative research.   Exploratory research is undertaken when the information needed is to be directional or diagnostic. Such research is usually done with fairly small groups of people, and the sampling is conducted on a quota or availability basis.

Definitive conclusions usually cannot be drawn from exploratory or qualitative research. Instead, an attempt is made to get a general impression of the market, the consumer, or the product. Two types of qualitative research can be quite helpful in the exploratory stages of the campaign. These are intensive data gathering and the use of "projective" techniques.

1. Intensive data gathering. The informal research approach consists of gathering information or data through discussions with interested groups or individuals, such as consumers, prospects, and retailers, who have knowledge about the product or service. An excellent source of information is often the sales force in direct contact with consumers and retailers.

   Conducting focus groups or doing individual "depth interviews" are more systematic and formal methods of data gathering. The interaction of focus groups usually generates a great deal of insight into the research problem and can lead to more detailed methods of information gathering.

   An alternative intensive data-gathering approach is the "depth interview." Interviews are conducted in the same way as those in a focus group, except they are done on an individual basis. Respondents are asked to discuss the product, the problem, or the situation. By asking carefully structured questions, the interviewer tries to probe the deeper feelings of the respondent rather than simply exposing surface opinions, which may be readily offered.

   Both focus groups and depth interviews are best carried out by a trained researcher. Untrained persons may obtain general information through focus-group discussion, but errors may creep in or the group may be inadvertently led to a false conclusion unless the person directing the questioning or analyzing the data has had adequate previous experience with this form of data gathering.

2. Projective techniques. Many forms of projective techniques may be used. All have the same basic approach: The person being interviewed is asked to involve himself or herself in a situation or experience in which he or she "projects" feelings and experiences about the product, brand, or problem set up by the interviewer. The assumption made in these projective techniques is that the person being interviewed, by involving himself or herself in a situation, will disclose underlying feelings, thoughts, and desires about the problem or situation which might not otherwise be revealed in direct questioning.

   Projective research projects can take many forms, from word association to role playing to cartoon completion to Thematic Apperception Tests. Only skilled, experienced researchers are capable of developing successful projective research instruments. If this methodology is contemplated, a commercial research organization should be consulted.

Exploratory or qualitative research should be used by the advertising campaign planner in the first stages of the development of the plan. Qualitative research is generally inexpensive; it can be done with small numbers of consumers, with selection based on a quota or availability sample. This type of research is often conducted to determine general trends or to identify areas that need further exploration.

Qualitative research may be sufficient to answer the campaign planner's questions. The information gathered, however, because of the limited sampling methodology, is subject to wide variations in reliability and validity. If exploratory or qualitative primary research is to be used as the basis of the campaign, this fact should be referenced in the campaign plan.

Quantitative or descriptive research.   Quantitative or descriptive research is usually primary research. The results can be projected to various portions of the market universe, and the laws of statistical probability can be applied to lend support to, or cause rejection of, the findings.

Boyd, Westfall, and Stasch differentiate between exploratory (qualitative) and descriptive (quantitative) studies.

> Descriptive studies differ from exploratory studies in the rigor with which they are designed. Exploratory studies are characterized by flexibility, while descriptive studies attempt to obtain a complete and accurate description of a situation. Formal design is required to ensure that the description covers all phases desired. Precise statements of the problem indicate what information is required. The study must then be designed to provide for the collection of this information. Unless the study design provides specified methods for selecting the sources of information (sample design) and for collecting the data from these sources, the information obtained may be inaccurate or inappropriate.
>
> Descriptive data are commonly used as direct basis for marketing decisions. After analyzing the data, the investigators attempt to product the result of certain actions.[1]

Thus, qualitative or exploratory research is used primarily to give direction to the advertising campaign planner, while quantitative or descriptive research is used in choosing between alternatives or in decision making.

Quantitative or descriptive research is also distinguished by the methods used to gather data. The two types are observation and survey. Because the first is not widely used in advertising campaign planning, only a brief overview will be given. More emphasis will be placed on survey research methodology.

1.   Observation. In quantitative research, the activities or habits of persons in the marketplace are observed either personally or through

---

[1] Harper W. Boyd, Jr., Ralph Westfall, and Stanley F. Stasch, *Marketing Research: Text and Cases,* 4th ed. (Homewood, Ill.: Richard D. Irwin, 1977): 48.

some mechanical means, such as is done in scanner panels. Because historical data are gathered according to what the given person was observed doing or had done in the past, many researchers believe predictions of what that person might do in the future based on observation are difficult to make.

Another form of observation is the so-called pantry check made in consumers' homes. Pantries are checked to determine the various brands that have been purchased and the amount of product on hand. By correlating this observed information with the demographic characteristics of the respondents, the present users (or general target market) for the product can be identified.

Observation is also used by several commercial research organizations, such as Nielsen or Audits & Surveys. These groups visit retail outlets and make shelf audits of products. They might, for example, gather data on what products are being stocked, what brands are available, what sizes are available, prices, and brands that are out of stock. This information is used by the advertiser to determine his or her position in the marketplace.

Observation can be helpful to the advertising campaign planner, but it is usually quite expensive because a large number of observations is required to develop a conclusive answer.

2. Survey. Survey research is the most common method of primary research data gathering used for advertising campaigns. As the name implies, data are obtained through a survey of present or prospective consumers of the product or service. The usual goal is to obtain information necessary to develop a profile of the target audience or to determine the most effective advertising message to be used.

Survey research methodologies differ according to the method of data gathering employed. The most common forms are personal interviews, mail surveys, consumer panels, and telephone interviews.

a. Personal interviews. Personal interviewing may take many forms, ranging from traditional door-to-door canvassing to intercepts in shopping malls and laundromats or outside food and drugstores. The key to success in personal interviewing is to find situations in which respondents have the time available to answer questions, a very precious commodity in today's marketplace. The usual data-gathering form is a series of questions, scales, evaluations, or other devices which allow the respondent to express his or her ideas, concerns, or opinions. Interviews in the home may last an hour or more; interviews with persons interrupted while shopping, such as in a mall intercept, must be confined to five or ten minutes. There is literally no limit to the type of data that can be gathered. In each case, the result depends on the kind of information desired and the situation in which the interview occurs.

The primary advantages of the personal interview are the opportunities to probe, to ask follow-up questions, and to use examples or samples of the product or advertising material. The major disadvantages are the extremely high cost of personnel and diminishing cooperation, particularly in door-to-door calls.

b. Mail surveys. Much useful information can be gathered through a mail survey. Respondents tend to give more complete answers because the interview is relatively anonymous. Respondents can also answer questions that might not be readily available in a personal or telephone interview. Because no one is there to give directions, the questionnaire form must be made as easy as possible to follow with primarily closed-end questions. The questionnaire may be any length and may cover almost any subject.

Data gathering by means of the mail questionnaire is relatively inexpensive. The main costs are for the mailing list, the questionnaire form, and postage. A nominal reward is sometimes included in a direct mail questionnaire to encourage response.

Mail questionnaires ordinarily have a fairly low return rate. A 30 percent to 40 percent response to a mail questionnaire is considered normal. Obtaining a return of 60 percent to 70 percent is exceptional. All results, however, depend on the product interest, the quality of the questions, and the mailing list.

c. Consumer panels. Preformed or existing panels of consumers have long been used for research data gathering. A number of commercial panels offer services that may be purchased, for example, National Family Opinions, Inc. (NFO).

Data gathering from consumer panels has the same disadvantage as do mail surveys in terms of time required. Response rates, however, often reach near 100 percent because the panels are established groups and are rewarded for participation. The representativeness of panels may be questionable because they answer many research questions during the course of a year.

The major advantage of panel data gathering is that the information obtained is more complete and more detailed. The panel is accustomed to furnishing information through questionnaires and tends to be quite cooperative. Based on total research expenditure, cost per response by a panel is usually lower than in most other types of interviews.

d. Telephone interviews. An increasingly important method of data gathering is the telephone interview. With the advent of Wide Area Telephone Service (WATS) lines, interviewing throughout the country can now be done from a central location that provides complete control over the interview. Costs of WATS line interviews are relatively low compared to other forms of data collection, and when time for data gathering is considered, this is probably the lowest costing of all research methods.

Telephone data-gathering usage has increased as samples have been improved. Originally, telephone samples were limited to persons whose names were listed in telephone directories. Newer systems of random digit dialing now make all connected telephones part of the sample frame, and every telephone home is a potential respondent, including the approximately 20 percent or more with unlisted numbers.

Telephone interviews are excellent for obtaining a relatively small amount of information from a large number of people. Because contact is by voice, only certain types of questions may be asked. Questions that require visuals or thorough understanding of a complex question are not practical. A telephone interview may last from ten to fifteen minutes with many closed-end questions, that is, questions for which a list of answers is supplied or made available. Some questionnaire callers have kept people on the line for thirty minutes or more. Surprisingly, telephone respondents may provide information they would not ordinarily give in a personal interview. Apparently, the telephone offers a certain amount of anonymity.

The major advantages of telephone interviews are low cost, a complete sample frame, the ability to call any geographic area (with WATS lines), and very rapid data gathering and reporting. Moreover, the telephone is the only practical method of conducting a coincidental survey, a study which is conducted at the same time the advertising is appearing.

Telephone surveys do have disadvantages, however. Answers usually must be shorter and not as indepth as those obtained through other methods. There is no opportunity to use props or other materials that might help explain the questions or to display package designs, advertisements, or other items that the subject must see to be able to respond to. And, as more companies engage in telemarketing of products and services, consumers may become suspicious of use of the telephone for "research purposes only," reducing response rates. Despite these disadvantages, more emphasis will likely be placed on telephone data gathering, particularly as the costs of personal interviews increase.

Experimental research.   Experimentation is a type of laboratory or otherwise controlled research in which a cause-and-effect relationship is sought. Strict controls are employed so that the variable that causes the effect can be identified. Experimentation is used only on a selective basis, because it is very difficult to control all marketing variables.

Several research organizations offer forms of experiments to gather data. One of the best known is Yankelovich, which has developed a testing method for new product introductions.

The most common form of experimental research in advertising is the use of a test market for new products or in new advertising campaigns. Two or more individual markets are matched as closely as possible according to such marketing variables as population, category sales, and household income. Using these matched markets, an advertising campaign is run in one market or set of markets and not in the others. Then the results are observed. An alternative method is to use differing advertising campaigns in a given set or sets of markets and to observe the differences that result. A third method is to use media weight tests. Here, varying levels of media promotion are used in matched test markets. Again, because other variables are held as nearly constant as possible, the influence of the media can be evaluated in terms of such effects as changes in attitude and awareness.

Experimentation, particularly in advertising, is an expensive method of obtaining information, because the effects may not be immediately observable. It is widely used for new products, however, for example, to test the viability of the product on a small scale or to test various advertising or marketing alternatives prior to a major national introduction.

Sampling for data gathering.   The success of any research design depends on the sample selected for data gathering. The major objective is to make sure that respondents to be interviewed are representative of the entire target population. It is important to determine who is to be sampled, the procedure to be used for selection of the sample, and the size of the sample.

1. Who is in the sample? Persons to be interviewed must be representative of the target population. If the planner wants to learn about cat food, owners of cats should be interviewed. In advertising and marketing research, this is done through screening questions such as, "Do you or your family own a cat?" Those who do not have a cat would not be included in the study; they would automatically be screened out of the sample.

   The research sampling frame for an advertising campaign study can be easily defined. It may be as broad as "all women from 18 to 49 years of age with children under 12 years of age in the home," or it might be as restrictive as "those persons owning canaries in the state of Idaho." The sampling frame depends on the type of specific data to be gathered and a general idea of the information sought. A common definition used as a sample frame is "present users of a product category or brand."

The key point in a sampling plan is to state clearly and concisely in advance the sample universe. If this is done, no confusion will arise as to whether an individual selected for interviewing is qualified.

2. Sample selection. There are two types of sampling techniques. Probability samples are those in which every known unit in the universe has an equal probability of being selected for the research. For example, if the universe were defined as drugstores in the city of Dallas with sales in excess of $1,000,000 annually, a complete list of potential stores could be developed from various sources, such as tax receipts and licenses. Knowing the names and locations of all the drugstores in Dallas which fit the qualification makes possible the development of a probability sample such that each store has an equal chance of being selected.

    Probability samples are used when the number of units to be measured is fairly small; a complete list of the items in the universe exists (such as all drugstores in Dallas); the cost per interview depends on the location of the items; and the need exists for precisely measuring the risk of sample error. Because of these conditions, the use of probability sampling in advertising and marketing research is quite limited, unless the universe can be very precisely defined.

    A nonprobability sample does not provide every unit in the universe with an equal or known chance of being included in the sample frame. If, in the earlier example, the restriction might be relaxed from stores doing over $1,000,000 in Dallas to simply those drugstores in North Dallas that are high volume and located within easy access of the freeway system, this then would not be a probability sample. It would be a nonprobability sample because not all drugstores would be included in the sample frame. For example, large stores that might qualify in every other respect might not be located near the freeway system, or might not be considered high volume by the researcher, and so on.

    Nonprobability samples are widely used in marketing and advertising research because in many categories no listing of the complete universe is available. Such samples are also used when the costs for a true probability sample are prohibitive because (a) the population members are widely dispersed geographically, (b) only a general estimate of the data is needed, (c) there is a possibility of obtaining a larger sample with a decrease in the magnitude of error, and (d) the nature and size of the bias can be estimated fairly accurately.

    Most advertising and marketing research studies are of the nonprobability type—for example, the planner doesn't really know the true universe of users of the product or competitive products. The dispersion of product users is normally great, particularly for those sold on a national basis. Error can be estimated based on sample size, and the amount of bias can also be determined. The primary reason for nonprobability sampling in advertising and marketing research is simply the cost of obtaining data. Once again, the advertising campaign planner is faced with the cost–benefit trade-off. Planners are usually willing to trade some validity and reliability to avoid the large costs entailed in developing a true probability sample.

3. Sample size. One of the most difficult tasks in planning or evaluating primary research is determining the sample size required to achieve a given level of confidence. Statistical techniques are available for developing confidence levels of probability samples. The problem becomes more complex with nonprobability studies because the true universe is usually unknown.

    A number of rules of thumb exist for determining sample sizes that are helpful to the advertising campaign planner. Although they lack precision, such rules do give general approximations of sample sizes for various types of nonprobability studies. In data gathering, such as depth interviews or focus groups, most ideas or answers concerning a product or service will be verbalized after the first thirty or so persons have been interviewed. This happens because most consumers have the same basic, general ideas about various products and services. Therefore, after about thirty persons have answered, repetition of the major ideas begins to mount rapidly. Similarly, interviews with 100 to 200 users of products or services, given a standard questionnaire in a limited geographic area, will tend to indicate the general attitudes of the population. After 100 interviews, reliability tends to mount as more and more respondents give the same answers to the questions being asked. For a regional study covering several cities or a few states, a sample of 300 to 400 qualified respondents is normally considered to be sufficient. A sample of 1,000 to 1,200 qualified consumers, selected according to a probability sample, will generally reflect the opinions and feelings of the national population on most subjects. Although these sample sizes are only estimates, they have been proven to the extent that only in unusual circumstances will major errors occur.

4. Problems. Four major problems are usually encountered with sample respondents: not-at-home, refusals, respondent bias, and interviewer bias.

    Not-at-home and refusals create more problems in a probability sample than in a nonprobability one. For a group to constitute a true probability sample, the actual persons selected in advance must be interviewed. Obviously, this is not always possible. Steps must be taken, therefore, to select a large enough original sample so that substitutions for nonrespondents can be made without destroying the representative makeup of the original sample.

The biases of both respondent and interviewer are most difficult to control. Respondent bias usually appears when the person is truly anxious to assist the interviewer and the respondent often gives answers that do not reflect his or her true feelings. In some cases, respondents, in an attempt to appear knowledgeable, give answers to questions on which they have no information.

Interviewer bias usually comes about when the interviewer, through either the question itself or the manner in which it is asked, indicates the type of answer that would be most acceptable or is generally regarded as correct. The advertising campaign planner should be aware of the bias problem, particularly if the sample is small, if the interviewers are not professionally trained, or if the interviewers or respondents have strong feelings about the particular subject under study.

SUMMARY

Research isn't a cure-all. It won't make a bad campaign a good one. But it can provide important information about the size and makeup of the potential market for the product, and it is the key to advertising campaigns as *planned* efforts. This chapter reviewed the basic kinds of information needed and how to use them effectively.

Case Studies

Duotest

Pat Williams, marketing services manager for the laboratory products division of Chemhealth, Inc., had just returned to her office following a meeting to discuss the progress the research and development department was making on a new product, Duotest. Things appeared to be moving along, and it wouldn't be long before R&D would be able to pinpoint a likely introduction date for Duotest. Once that date was set, Pat would work with the person assigned to manage Duotest to develop the initial marketing communications campaign for the product.

Chemhealth was a major manufacturer of chemical-based, health-related products. The company was divided into two major divisions: laboratory products and consumer products. Laboratory products included those items sold to hospital and university medical laboratories, such as materials to test blood for bacteria, drug detection tests, and the like. Chemhealth was the market leader in this area, but their lead over the nearest competitor was shrinking. A number of new competitors had come into the market in the past five years, and price competition was growing. Chemhealth generally priced their products according to what the market would bear, that is, at the highest premium they could get. There had been several cases in the last year where Chemhealth had lost an established customer to a lower-priced competitor. Feedback from the Chemhealth direct sales force suggested that the decision makers in the laboratories felt that Chemhealth products were of very high quality, but not that much better than the competition to justify the price differential.

In the past, Chemhealth had relied on the proven quality of its products, the company's excellent reputation, its strong customer service department, and the skill of its direct sales force to move the products and justify their higher price. The strategy that had worked for years was losing its effectiveness. Most of the blame could be placed on the competition, rather than Chemhealth itself. Several competitors had also set up customer service departments, and had hired away some of Chemhealth's salespeople. So, they could match Chemhealth in two key areas; they were also undercutting Chemhealth's prices.

Another important contributor to Chemhealth's slipping share was the change occurring in the organizational structure of many of Chemhealth's customers. Traditionally, the Chemhealth salesperson had only needed to sell the lab technician on the product to close a sale. It seemed that more and more people in the customer organization were becoming involved in the purchase decision. For example, the squeeze on hospital profits and consumer pressures to keep health care costs down were making hospital administrators and purchasing agents far more cost conscious than they had been in the past. Consequently, the lab technicians were being pressured to do more comparison "shopping" when buying testing materials. This situation allowed competitors to move in on Chemhealth customers, and although Chemhealth was still winning in many buying decisions, a few of those wins had come at the expense of the company's target profit margin.

Duotest had been developed according to Chemhealth's traditional process, that is, it was the result of an R&D breakthrough rather than a customer-driven development process. It was actually a combination of two existing tests that were used together in 75 percent of applications. Rather than running each test separately, a lab using Duotest could do both procedures at once, resulting in a time savings of up to two hours. Duotest was particularly attractive for Chemhealth because a competitor had been making significant sales inroads at the expense of one of the two tests it would replace. The concensus feeling was that no competitor would be able to duplicate Duotest for at least four years.

Pat's job in the development process would be to work with the brand manager to set up the advertising program for Duotest. Chemhealth used media advertising to generate awareness for new products and bring in leads for the sales force. Advertising dollars typically went to trade journals, direct mail (including postcard packs), and product literature. Pat would be the liaison between the brand manager and one of Chemhealth's advertising agencies. The agency would develop the advertisements based on the strategy provided by the brand manager. Generally, Pat had some say in strategy development. And, as part of the development committee for Duotest, she would also have input on the pricing of the product.

Before coming to Chemhealth, Pat had worked for another business-to-business firm. That company had relied heavily on marketing research to provide direction for communications strategies, product positioning, and pricing. Pat's job there had included working with outside research firms to set up specific studies. The situation at Chemhealth was quite different. Research other than that done in R&D was a rarity, especially in the laboratory products division. Most brand managers had moved up from the field sales force, and the feeling seemed to be that the "gut feelings" of the brand managers and their supervisors was as good a form of research as any. Because the introduction date for Duotest had yet to be set, the sales force hadn't been told much about the product and so there had been no feedback at all from anyone other than the members of the development committee.

Pat felt that research could provide a great deal of needed direction. How much would the lab technicians be willing to pay for the time savings

Duotest would provide? Should Duotest be positioned as a convenience product or a technological advance? How believable was the claim of being able to do two tests at once? How might the competition react to the Duotest introduction?

Probably the biggest question facing Pat was how she could sell the other members of the development committee on the need to do research. She knew that both the brand manager and the division director thought Duotest was a guaranteed winner—she'd heard "the lab boys'll love this one" at every meeting. She also knew that the brand manager was leaning toward recommending a price 20 percent above the combined cost of the two existing tests, figuring that the added convenience was worth the premium. Although that was fairly typical Chemhealth reasoning, Pat wasn't sure it was the right approach given the market situation. But, without research support, it would just be her gut feeling against the brand manager's.

Questions

1. Assume that you're the brand manager for Duotest. Argue *against* doing research in this situation.
2. Given the nature of this industry, confidentiality is always a big concern in new product development. What type of research might Chemhealth do to minimize confidentiality problems? What types of research would you recommend avoiding?
3. What sources would you use to try to predict how the competition might react to the Chemhealth's introduction of Duotest?
4. Assume that the needed research would require drawing a sample. Who would you recommend including in the sample? (Assume that cost and confidentiality are not considerations here.)
5. If the research for Duotest is successful (i.e., if it's obvious to all that it really helped in decision making), Chemhealth might be persuaded to do more research. What type(s) of research might Chemhealth consider as a way to develop more of a customer orientation?

Family Food Station

Jim Johnson had recently joined the marketing department at Family Food Station, Inc. Jim's background was in consumer research, and he had been hired with the hope that his expertise could help Family Food Station compete successfully in a marketplace that was becoming increasingly complicated.

Family Food Station was a chain of dinner restaurants located through-out the continental United States. Family Food Station restaurants were usually found in medium and small cities and towns. There were some Family Food Stations in the suburbs of large metropolitan areas, but the company's emphasis had always been on smaller markets where there was less competition from other restaurants, and where going out to eat was more likely to be regarded as a special occasion.

Family Food Station believed their chief competition to be other dinner restaurants. In most markets, the Family Food Station was one of the top three restaurants in town based on total sales. Of course, there was some variation from market to market, depending on the particular competitors there.

The Family Food Station menu was the same throughout the country and offered a variety of entrées including beef, chicken, pasta, and fish dishes. There was also a children's menu for the under-12 group. Some of the restaurants offered bar service, depending on the laws in the particular locality. Family Food Station restaurants were known for their generous portions, good food quality, and reasonable (though not low) prices. (The average dinner check, including appetizer, entrée, and dessert, was about $15.00 per person.) The chain consistently ranked in the top five in national surveys of restaurant patrons.

Decor was also standardized throughout the chain. Family Food Station restaurants were usually stand-alone units, often located near shopping centers. Each had its own parking lot. Inside was a fairly large lobby with seating for patrons waiting for a table (30–45 minutes waiting times weren't unusual on Friday and Saturday nights). The dining area was large and contained both booths and tables. Although it could get noisy when all tables were filled, there was enough space between groups of diners to allow for some privacy.

Family Food Station was especially proud of its restaurant staff. These people, many of whom had been at the same location for several years, were consistently rated high on friendliness, quality of service, and knowl-edge about the menu in customer surveys. Many of the middle- and upper-management people at the regional and corporate levels had been promoted from the restaurant staff, so they knew the business intimately.

All in all, Family Food Station seemed to be in good shape as far as image was concerned. The restaurants offered good food at a good value in a comfortable atmosphere. The frequent lines on weekend nights were testi-mony to the chain's popularity. Despite these strengths, corporate manage-ment was concerned about the future and believed that a staff researcher might be able to help them identify problem areas and potential solutions to those problems.

The restaurant industry was experiencing flat sales; several chains had posted losses in the last few years. Family Food Station's sales had grown, but the growth was a bit deceptive. Most of the growth was due to an increase in the number of Family Food Station units—thirty-five new restaurants had been opened last year and a similar number were expected to open this year. So, although total sales were up, sales per restaurant were actually down about .5 percent. Family Food Station was still in a better position than many of its competitors, but management obviously wanted to reverse the decline in sales.

Most economic indicators suggested that consumer disposable income was increasing and would continue to increase as the number of two-income families grew. Couples continued to wait longer before having children, leaving them with more money to spend on themselves. Working couples had less time (and interest) in preparing dinner at home, as a result, they dined out more frequently.

On the negative side, couples with children were more likely to be interested in saving money than spending it—they expected the costs of education to continue to rise and wanted to be prepared. Also, taking children to a restaurant was a much more complicated proposition than dining out as a couple. And, fast food restaurants were a more convenient dining alternative than a sitdown restaurant.

As a preliminary step in developing some research ideas, Jim had visited a number of Family Food Station restaurants in a variety of locations. He'd observed diners and also talked with managers and servers to get their perceptions. Some of his findings were

- Family Food Stations seemed to attract a very diverse group of people. Jim saw families with young children, couples (married and dating), groups of senior citizens, businesspeople, and groups of young adults. No one restaurant seemed to attract more of one group than another.

- The diners appeared to enjoy the Family Food Station experience. On the few occasions when Jim witnessed a complaint being made, the manager took care of the problem immediately and the diner seemed to be satisfied.

- Many diners seemed to regard Family Food Station as a place for a celebration. Every restaurant Jim visited had diners celebrating birthdays, anniversaries, and job promotions. He even saw several couples get engaged over a Family Food Station dinner.

- The restaurant managers and serving staff all agreed that although about 15–20 percent of their patrons were "regulars" (particularly common among the senior citizens), there was generally a great deal of turnover among patrons. (This was supported by some conversations Jim overheard. In one case, a family came in to celebrate the mother's birthday. Jim heard a daughter say, "I wonder if they'll have the same things as last year. Remember how good the spaghetti was?")

Armed with this information, Jim returned to the chain's headquarters to put together an initial proposal on how research might help Family Food Stations and what type of initial research study ought to be done. Jim anticipated that the research findings would help guide the areas of product (restaurant) development and advertising creative strategy development. (The current advertising campaign highlighted menu items and occasional price specials on particular entrées.)

Questions

1. Devise a list of questions that you would want to have answered in the initial research study. Remember, the company's objective is to turn around the per-unit sales decline. Keep in mind that this will be the first time Family Food Station has done any formal research.
2. Given your list of questions, what type of research should be conducted—exploratory, descriptive, experimental, or tracking?
3. Who should be included in the sample?
4. How would you choose the markets to include in the research study?

6 Advertising Strategy Research

After the very basic information on the marketplace has been gathered—
the product category, the consumer, the product or service to be advertised, the competition, and so on—the next step, the actual development
of the advertising campaign, starts with the development of the advertising strategy.

The development of the advertising strategy is probably the most important decision the advertising campaign planner will make. If the advertising strategy is wrong or poorly developed, the campaign will likely fail no
matter what media are used or how much money is invested. All too often,
though, it seems the advertising planner is too anxious to start writing advertisements or developing commercials without first defining what the
advertising strategy could or should be. This chapter focuses on this very
important area of advertising strategy research and development.

Advertising strategy involves "what" is to be said and "to whom" it will
be directed. The execution is the "how to say it." The "how often" and
"where" questions are answered by the media plan. Charles Ramond has
suggested that there are three steps in each of the areas of campaign development. Those are illustrated in Table 6–1.

SOME DEFINITIONS

Before proceeding, some basic definitions are needed.

- *Advertising objectives*—a clearly stated, measurable end result of an
  advertising message or messages. Usually the objective is measured in
  terms of a change in awareness, preference, conviction, or other communications effects.

Table 6–1 Steps in Campaign Development

To make this decision	One must choose a	Using techniques variously known as
What to say	Theme, copy platform	Concepts tests, positioning studies
To whom	Target audience	Market segmentation studies
How to say it	Copy, commercial execution	Copy research, commercial tests
How often	Frequency of exposure	Studies of repetition
Where	Media plan	Media research models, audience studies
How much to spend	Budget level	Sales analysis, marketing models

SOURCE: Charles Ramond, *Advertising Research, the State of the Art* (New York: Association of National Advertisers, 1976): 3–4.

- *Advertising strategy*—the formulation of an advertising message that communicates the benefit or problem solution characteristics of the product or service to the target market. It is usually developed for use in the mass media.
- *Advertising execution*—the physical form—art, illustration, copy, music, and so on—that the advertising strategy takes when it is presented to the target market to achieve the advertising objective(s).

These are the major terms used in this text. They will be referred to often.

WHERE TO START

In general, the advertising strategy is dictated by the marketing objectives. For example, if the marketing objective is to increase sales in a new territory by 15 percent in the coming year, the advertising challenge is quite apparent. The product must be explained to persons who are probably not familiar with it. Likewise, if the marketing goal is to generate additional use among present customers, clearly, the advertising objective is to give the present users new or additional ways to use the product or service.

In the "Situation Analysis" (described in Chapter 4), we saw that there are two basic sources of information about the prospects or customers: internal material, which often consists of sales and purchase data, and external information, which commonly is provided by outside suppliers, such as Simmons, Nielsen, MediaMark, and National Family Opinion, in a syndicated form. Or, it may be developed by primary research conducted by the company. This basic research information generally provides the planner with a basic view of the market and the current purchasers. It doesn't help much, however, in determining what to say about the product or service in advertising. That requires another type of investigation.

BASIC CONSUMER IDENTIFICATION HELPS IDENTIFY
THE ADVERTISING STRATEGY

The first step in deciding "what to say" about the product or service in advertising is to make some generalizations about the target market. Exhibit 6–1 is a model of the potential purchasers for almost any product or service.

Exhibit 6–1   Potential Purchaser Model

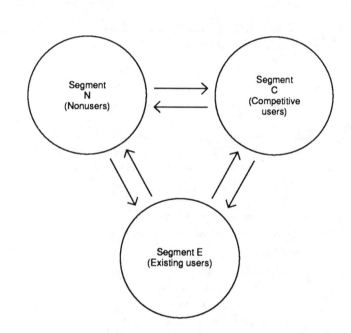

As can be seen, the total market is contained within the outer circle. Inside the broad category market circle are the three basic groups to which advertising can be directed. Circle N includes those persons not now presently using a product in the category. They are nonusers. Those in Circle C are predominantly users of competitive brands. The persons in Circle E are current or existing users predominantly of the advertiser's brand.

All the people in these groups are very mobile (as indicated by the arrows). For example, some people move between being a noncategory user to using competitive brands, and some to the advertiser's brand. Present customers also switch around between the advertiser's brand and that of a competitor. The market is quite fluid.

One of the first decisions the advertising planner needs to make is to decide against which of these basic groups—Circle N or nonusers, Circle C or competitive users, or Circle E or present users—the advertising will be directed. Obviously, users of the advertised brand know a great deal about it. They certainly know more about it than category nonusers. Obviously, a different advertising strategy is called for. Therefore, the decision to speak to present or prospective customers is the first decision the advertising planner must make.

Table 6–2 illustrates some of the alternatives that the advertising planner might consider in developing an effective advertising strategy.

Table 6–2 Objective–Market Group

Objective	Market group
Increase total number of customers	Entire market Segments N and C
Increase total demand for product category	Entire market
Rekindle interest in a mature product	Entire market Segments N and C
Rediscover former users	Entire market Segments N and C
Attract nonusers of the category	Segment N
Attract users of competitive brands	Segment C
Maintain current sources or use	Segment E
Increase usage rate	Segment E
Increase frequency of use	Segment E
Increase variety of uses	Segment E
Reduce time between purchases	Segment E

Often, to determine what will help achieve these types of marketing/advertising goals, research is needed. Some of the more common methods of advertising strategy research are described in the following sections. Although the advertising campaign planner need not be expert in these research techniques, he or she must know enough about them to intelligently select the proper approach proposed by market researchers.

CONDUCTING ADVERTISING STRATEGY RESEARCH

Research among Existing Users

As is true of market research, advertising research activities for strategy development can be divided between those for existing or new products and those for present and prospective users. Although some of the techniques are similar, the approaches often differ.

The objective of the research needed to develop an advertising strategy for an existing product is to learn why present users purchase and use the brand or why other persons purchase competitive products. The planner needs to determine, as accurately as possible, why various purchasing decisions are made and then match those purchasing-decision points against the various brands. This is not an easy task. What consumers purchase is fairly easy to determine. *Why* they do so is much more difficult to elucidate.

Often, even purchasers don't know the true reason why they prefer a certain brand over others. Even more difficult to learn is what would encourage them to switch to another brand. This is very true for commonly purchased, low-risk products such as beer, detergents, canned foods, and even bar candy. Consumers simply don't go through a deep mental process in determining which brand in a product category to buy. They have images in their minds of certain brands. They may remember a few catch phrases or even recognize the label among a host of others, but when asked why they purchased Detergent A over Detergent B, they often are hard put to come up with an answer.

In spite of these difficulties, the advertising planner must have some guidance in developing an advertising strategy. That guidance can only come from consumers. Obviously, Armstrong has done its research homework with consumers. (See Exhibit 6–2.) Apparently, they have learned that fear of making a mistake in cutting is one of the major concerns of persons installing their own sheet vinyl floors. Therefore, Armstrong has developed a "Trim and Fit" product and offered it along with a guarantee of replacement if there is a problem. It is likely that research told them this is a good way to reduce consumer concern and change the perception of the product.

Although there are many ways of gathering information and material for strategy development, seven basic approaches are widely used. These are (a) focus groups, (b) perceptual or brand mapping, (c) usage studies, (d) motivation research, (e) benefit segmentation, (f) projection techniques, and (g) problem detection studies. Each is briefly described in the following sections. Please note that although the techniques may seem simple, most require the skill and guidance of a trained research person to properly apply them in the marketplace. (More information on any of these methods can be found in most market or advertising research texts.)

Focus groups.   As discussed in Chapter 5, focus groups are comprised of "users" or "nonusers" who are asked to discuss a particular product or service category. The purpose is to determine what is important to these consumers, what is unimportant to them, and how they make a purchase in that product category. Often, the focus group mixes users of one brand

Exhibit 6–2   Armstrong Print Ad

Go on, cut. You'll be brilliant.
Armstrong guarantees it.

Install your new Armstrong sheet vinyl floor with a Trim and Fit™ kit, and if you goof while cutting or fitting, your Armstrong retailer will replace both the flooring and the kit. Free. That's the Fail-Safe™ Guarantee. Just see your local home center or building supply retailer for details.

For the name of your nearest Trim and Fit retailer and a free Floor Project Planning Pack, call

1 800 233-3823

toll-free between 9:00 a.m. and 8:00 p.m., Mon. thru Fri., E.S.T. Ask for Dept. 7AFHC.

If you'd like only the Planning Pack, write: Armstrong, Dept. 7AFHC, P.O. Box 3001, Lancaster, PA 17604.

Armstrong
so nice
to come
home to

with users of competitive products. The attempt here is to learn why purchasers of one product are different from those of competitive products, and to determine what they consider to be the key benefits they receive from the brand, how they think about the brand, talk about it, and so on. In general, focus groups provide only broad, general ideas or direction. Focus group hypotheses should be pursued through other forms of quantitative research.

Perceptual or brand mapping.   In an effort to understand how consumers have various brands positioned in their minds, and to learn more about how consumers feel about brands in a category, researchers often use an approach called brand mapping, which requires participants to evaluate existing brands in a product category. The term, *perceptual* or *brand mapping,* is used because the technique requires consumers to identify how they feel about or perceive various products in terms of certain benefits or attributes.

A five- or seven-point rating scale is constructed using bipolar adjectives that might apply to the product or the product category. (In some instances, the scale is used to determine which benefits or attributes are most important in the brand decision, and then the comparison is made.) For example, the scale might look like the grid in Exhibit 6–3. The respondent marks the position on the scale for the product being studied.

Exhibit 6–3   Rating Scale for Perceptual Mapping

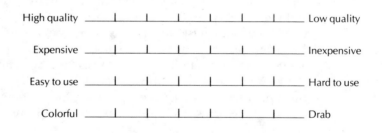

These adjectives may describe any attributes that are considered important to either the users or the marketer. Often these terms come from the results of focus group sessions in which various product benefits and attributes had been discussed.

Mapping is done to determine how the brand relates to competition in terms of these various benefits or features. These relationships are determined by constructing a two-dimensional matrix to compare the scores of

Exhibit 6–4   Two-Dimensional Matrix for Mapping

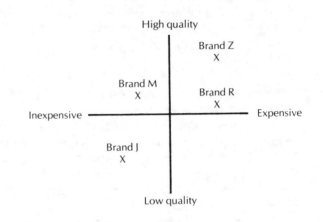

the brand being investigated with those of a competitor or group of competitors. (Exhibit 6–4 is an example.)

In Exhibit 6–4, Brands J, M, R, and Z are compared on the basis of the attribute's high or low quality and expensive or inexpensive price. The researcher averages respondents' scores and plots them on a grid. The result is a visual picture of how consumers view the various products or brands.

In this example, Brand R is viewed as being expensive but of not very high quality while Brand Z seems to be equated with relatively high price and high quality. This type of mapping approach is quite helpful in spotting weaknesses in the advertiser's brand or those of competitors. It is also useful in determining what perceptions consumers have or don't have about a brand. It should be noted that the consumers' assessment of a product may or may not be accurate. That isn't important. It's how they think or what they believe that is the key element in this research, because it is on these bases that consumers make their purchase decision.

Usage studies.   Often, research is conducted with existing users of the product or service to determine the reasons why they purchase the product. In these studies, which may be large or small, the intent is to determine the benefits the consumer seeks or finds in the brand, and to use this knowledge as part of a strategy to bring more users to the brand. The basic approach is to ask current users why they buy or what benefits they receive from the brand through some form of discussion or questionnaire.

For example, several years ago a manufacturer of baby shampoo was surprised to see sales of the product increasing while the birth rate was declining. Through usage studies, the marketer learned that because of changes in hairstyles, teenagers had started using the product. Because these teens washed their hair every day or at least several times per week, they were looking for a product that was mild. The baby shampoo gave them that benefit. The manufacturer picked up the new usage idea and turned it into an advertising campaign. The shampoo manufacturer now promotes the product to all age groups, but particularly to those people who wash their hair frequently.

Motivation studies.   Several years ago, motivation research (MR) was the rage. It has since declined in popularity, although it still has a rightful place among techniques used to learn more about products and brands. Motivational research uses a depth interviewing technique to determine why people act as they do, sometimes including why they use a product or brand or why they avoid it, how they feel about competitive brands, what they look for in a brand to purchase, and so on. The objective of MR is to discover some of the important aspects of purchase behavior that might not be uncovered in only casual, surface interviews. Often, MR is used to determine basic beliefs about the category or the brand. These beliefs can then be confirmed in more formal and quantitative research. In general, motivational research is conducted only by skilled researchers who have the ability to do the necessary probing interviews and then to interpret the results.

Benefit segmentation.   From the foregoing techniques, it should be obvious that one of the goals of all this research is to determine or identify important segments of the population. Few, if any, advertisers have products or services that interest the entire population. Even if the product were of interest, it would be practically impossible to finance a campaign directed toward the entire population. Although segmentation and segmentation research were discussed in Chapter 5, a brief review here will be helpful.

Segmentation studies attempt to group consumers in some fashion so that a specific advertising message might be directed at them. Some rather sophisticated computer programs that can group or assimilate consumers on a common basis have been developed as a result of various types of research. General segmentation studies attempt to group customers or prospects along various lines, such as demographics, geographics, psychographics, or life-style.

One of the major new methods of attempting to understand consumers is through scanner panel data. The basic technique developed by Information Resources, Inc., and called *BehaviorScan,* consists of recruited panels of consumers (usually entire households) in selected markets across the country. These panelists agree to carry a magnetic encoded card that, when their purchases are scanned in a supermarket or drugstore in one of the test cities, relates the purchases back to that household. Through this system, individual household purchases including price, size, brand, flavor, and so on, are captured. In addition, details of in-store activities, such as price adjustments, advertising features, and displays, are also recorded. Therefore, researchers can start to analyze and evaluate the impact of various promotional techniques and also look in more detail at the types of households that use particular products or brands. This approach is proving to be a fertile one in terms of better understanding of consumer purchase dynamics. Although this type of research is just now starting to be used in advertising development and evaluation, it holds great promise for the future.

Of perhaps more interest to the advertising campaign planner are benefit segmentation studies. Benefit segmentation attempts to determine the various benefits consumers seek from products, services, or brands and then to quantify consumers based on these benefits. For example, an early study of toothpaste determined there were four basic benefits consumers sought from the toothpaste they bought: (a) cavity prevention, (b) tooth whitening, (c) breath freshening, and (d) economy. Thus, in addition to basic geographics and demographics, advertising planners can separate or segment the population on the benefits they seek from toothpaste brands. By knowing the four basic benefits sought, advertising strategies could be developed for individual brands of toothpaste. Benefit segmentation is a complex research process, in many cases, but it can provide some valuable answers for the planner.

It's likely that the advertising planners for Aqua-fresh toothpaste have done some additional research on the various market segments in that category. In the ad in Exhibit 6–5, they are appealing to people who want protection from cavities, those who want fresh breath, and also those who want whiter teeth. All these benefits are rolled into the unique checkerboard advertisement.

Projection techniques.   Projection techniques ask the participant to project his or her feelings on to the product or service. For example, one of the questions asked might be, "What kind of a person do you think might use Brand X?" This question requires the participant to identify the kind or type of person that he or she sees using the product, providing the researcher with clues about the personality or perceptions of the brand. Another favorite technique is to ask the participants to humanize a brand, in other words, to give human characteristics to the brand. A typical question might be, "If the Ford Escort were a person, what kind of person would

Exhibit 6–5   Aqua-fresh Ad

SOURCE: Courtesy of Beecham Products USA.

the Escort be?'' Again, this is an attempt to understand how consumers feel about products or services or brands. Such understanding will give the advertising planner a better insight as to what kind of strategy can or should be used.

Problem detection.   The problem detection technique is an attempt to get customers to identify problems that they have and then to find solu-

tions that are to the benefit of the brand of the advertising planner. A typical approach would be to develop a long list of problems that might be
solved by the product to be advertised. This list is then shown to consumers who are asked a series of questions. The questioning might go
something like this:

1. Which of these problems is important to you?
2. Does the problem occur frequently?
3. Has the solution to the problem been offered by some other existing
    product?

From this line of questioning, using a scoring system for each of the
questions, the research can learn what problems are important and if competitive products have already established a position in the mind of the
consumer.

Other alternative research techniques are regularly developed, tested,
and evaluated by marketing and advertising researchers. Those listed earlier, however, seem to have emerged as the major approaches that can or
are used in gathering information on which to base an advertising strategy.

Research among New Users

Typically, focus groups, perceptual mapping, benefit segmentation, motivational research, and problem detection are all used in determining what
consumers might find most important about new products just as they are
used to test the appeal of existing products. One of the major approaches
that is used for new product strategy development is the need–want survey. In this approach, prospective consumers are surveyed about problems
that they have as they pertain to a particular product category. They are
asked in effect, "What are your needs and wants for fruit drinks for your
children?" Using this approach, researchers are able to determine what is
important to consumers. They can then match these needs with the benefits that the proposed product can provide. By making these comparisons,
the list of exploratory advertising strategy statements can be developed.

There is a basic difference, however, in new product research. Often, the
product isn't available or hasn't even been manufactured. In many cases,
only a description of what the product might be is used in the research.
When this is the case, the research methodology is often called a *concept
test*. Concept testing attempts to determine consumer interest in a product
or brand based simply on a description of what the product or brand
might be or might do. Then, the information gathered is used to determine
the best method of communicating that benefit.

In general, concept testing is a two-step procedure. First, the advertising
campaign planner must determine which of several potential product benefits is most important to the consumer. For example, if a company plans

to introduce a new, fortified, nonsugar-added fruit drink in a pouch container, the first step would be to determine which benefit would be of the most interest to the target market. Would it be the added vitamins and minerals? The absence of sugar? Or the unique pouch container? Even though the product is the same in each case, a separate concept statement would be written for each benefit. Then these concept statements would be tested with prospects. A good concept statement has three basic attributes:

1.   A statement of the problem that the product is meant to solve
2.   The type of solution that the product provides
3.   The necessary supporting attributes (physical and conceptual) that lend credibility to the product's ability to solve the problem[1]

Once the best concept statement has been selected, the next step is to determine the best way to communicate the corresponding benefit. This requires a concept statement of another sort. It's the alternative ways in which the benefit can best be communicated to be understood by consumers. For example, in the fruit drink case, assume consumers said that the most important benefit of the new product would be the absence of added sugar. The question then is, how best to use this as an advertising strategy. Here the planner constructs various ways the benefit can be communicated and puts this in the form of a strategy statement or advertising promise. When testing an advertising strategy, two points must always be included:

1.   The promise or the end benefit that the consumer will receive by purchasing or using the product
2.   Product attributes that provide a rational basis for the promise that's being made

In the no-sugar-added strategy mentioned earlier, the strategy statement might be phrased directly as "no sugar added"; it might be phrased obliquely, for example, "naturally sweet—nothing has been added"; it might be stated as "lower in calories because no sugar has been added." In any case, no matter how the benefit is stated, it must be clear, concise, and complete so that consumers can understand the idea in a very short period of time.

The use of concept testing is very widespread and, unfortunately, in many cases not very well done. A good concept statement is difficult to write, but it is a necessity with a new product. Additional information on concept testing can be found in most advertising or marketing research texts.

---

[1]Eugene F. Cafarelli, *Developing New Products and Repositioning Mature Brands* (New York: John Wiley & Sons, 1980): 110.

EVALUATING ADVERTISING STRATEGY RESEARCH

Throughout this chapter, a great deal of emphasis has been put on how research for advertising strategy development should be conducted and the various methods that might be used to gather the proper information. While research and research methods are important to the campaign planner, often, it is just as important or more so to be able to judge existing or just completed research. In many instances, the advertising campaign planner will not actually be doing the research. Instead, the research data may already exist or may be furnished either by the agency, the advertiser, or a research organization. In those cases, the ability to judge, evaluate, and extract information from the research studies is vital. If the campaign planner doesn't have an understanding of research, how it is done, the basis for sample selection, and so on, then that person is in a very precarious position. He or she must rely totally on whoever analyzed the research to be accurate in interpretation and conclusions. A better way would be for the planner to have a basic understanding of how to evaluate research studies so that he or she could be sure of the research base.

Criteria for Evaluation of Research

In any type of research, the key question is whether the results provide solid evidence on which to base advertising decisions. Knowing the answer to this question is especially important for the advertising campaign planner who may be proposing a new or unique approach. The crucial questions concern (a) the soundness of the research, (b) the issues of validity and reliability, and (c) whether the information is germane to the recommendations resulting from analysis of the data.

The Advertising Research Foundation has prepared a guide for evaluating advertising research. They recommend considering:

1. Under what conditions was the study made? Problems. Sources of finances. Names of organizations participating. Period of time covered. Date of report. Definition of terms. Questionnaire and instructions to interviewers. Collateral data. Complete statement of methodology.
2. Has the questionnaire been well designed? Dangers of bias. Unreasonable demands on memory. Poor choice of answers. Monotonous questions. Lack of space for answers. Was it pretested?
3. Has the interviewing been adequate and reliably done? Familiarity with prescribed interview procedure. Training. Maturity. Were spot checks made to ensure accuracy?
4. Has the best sampling plan been followed? Random samples are preferable. Quota sampling is more likely to be satisfactory for collecting qualitative rather than quantitative data.

5. Has the sampling plan been fully executed? Substitutions or other variations may destroy validity of data.
6. Is the sample large enough? If a probability sample is properly designed, reliability of results can be determined mathematically. In other samples, it is much more difficult to determine adequacy of sample size.
7. Was there systematic control of editing, coding, and tabulating?
8. Is the interpretation forthright and logical? If one factor is interpreted as cause, all others must be held constant. All basic data underlying interpretations should be shown. Validity of respondents' memory should not be overemphasized. Small differences should not be emphasized. Analysis should be clear and simple.[2]

Limitations of Research

In addition to the question of whether the actual research conducted is reliable and valid, a more basic question is, "What answers can research provide?" There are six basic limits to advertising and marketing research:

1. Research, even if expertly conducted under favorable circumstances, will not provide precise answers to marketing questions.
2. All research is based on past experience and conducted under certain conditions. If those conditions change—and the marketplace is constantly changing—research results may well also change. Thus, all research is time-and-situation specific.
3. Research is a business tool, not an answer to all business questions. Research may increase the probability of success; it may help to reduce losses. But doing research to find out why a brand's sales are falling may not produce the information necessary to stop the slide. (Research may give an indication, though, of how the slide may be reduced.)
4. Research is an out-of-pocket expense. Research costs usually are not recoverable. Most research is an investment in the brand or the business. The advertising campaign planner must recognize research costs as nonrecoverable and regard them as an expense against the brand.
5. Research is time consuming. There must be sufficient time in the advertising planning process to develop, conduct, and evaluate research.
6. Usually, there are limited personnel available for the research task. Persons who have the ability to conduct skilled research are in short

---

[2]*Criteria for Marketing and Advertising Research* (New York: Advertising Research Foundation, 1953).

supply. Therefore, there are limits to the amount of research that can be conducted, no matter how strong the desire for information.[3]

SUMMARY

In summary, research must be the basis for the development of the advertising strategy. Without sufficient research information to provide an understanding of the market, the consumer, and how the consumer thinks and talks about the product, the advertising campaign planner can drift into erroneous ideas and approaches. Research must provide the basis for determining what the advertising campaign is designed to achieve and what the advertising is to say. We look at these concerns when we start to set advertising objectives.

---

[3]Dorothy Cohen, *Advertising* (New York: John Wiley & Sons, 1972): 234.

Case Studies

Noile Shampoo

In February of 1989, the management team of the personal care division of Sullivan Industries met to discuss Noile shampoo. The product had been in national distribution for two years. Targeted at the consumer with oily hair, Noile's market share was .5 percent of the total shampoo market, and 4.9 percent of the oily hair category.

Noile was formulated with a strong cleaning agent to cut through dirt and oil and oil-free conditioners to protect after cleaning. The advertising campaign described the product as "the serious solution for a serious problem." Early research had identified a segment of consumers who were bothered by extremely oily hair.

Although the initial research had indicated that more women than men were in the "seriously oily" category, 68 percent of Noile's purchasers were men. Most of these men were young (20–35) bachelors. Many were very sports oriented, participating in tennis, skiing, or jogging regularly. Female purchasers also tended to be young and active.

Tom Dodge, the product manager, felt that sales might increase if a new advertising strategy was adopted. He believed that the "serious solution" theme had reached the limit of its effectiveness. Therefore, Dodge requested permission to have the research department conduct several usage studies to help identify potential new approaches. He was given the go-ahead.

Sullivan Industries had several established consumer panels. Panel A consisted of 200 female homemakers. One-third of these panelists did not work outside the home; two-thirds were employed in full- or part-time positions. The women were between the ages of 21 and 54 and were regular purchasers of one or more Sullivan products.

Panel B was made up of 200 men aged 21 to 54. Approximately 40 percent were professionals, 40 percent worked as skilled laborers, and 20 percent worked in semiskilled positions. They were also regular Sullivan customers.

Panel C consisted of 200 teenagers, half were male, half were female. These were students in grades 7 through 12.

Working with Dodge, the market research department developed a questionnaire to assess usage rates and perceived benefits for Noile. The questionnaire was sent to all members of Panels A and B. After six weeks, Dodge received the following report:

Noile Questionnaire Results

1. How often do you shampoo your hair?

Panel A		Panel B	
Daily	34%	Daily	28%
3–4 times/wk	52%	3–4 times/wk	49%
1–2 times/wk	14%	1–2 times/wk	23%

2. Is your hair:

Panel A		Panel B	
Dry	37%	Dry	29%
Oily	41%	Oily	44%
Normal	22%	Normal	27%

Panel A		Panel B	
Longer than shoulder length	26%	Longer than shoulder length	0%
Shoulder length	34%	Shoulder length	2%
Collar length	23%	Collar length	38%
Shorter than collar length	17%	Shorter than collar length	60%

3. Have you tried Sullivan's Noile shampoo?

Panel A		Panel B	
Yes	32%	Yes	57%
No	68%	No	43%

    (If yes, go to Question 4; if no, go to Question 8.)

4. How many times have you purchased Noile in the past year?

Panel A		Panel B	
Once	4%	Once	0%
2–4 times	48%	2–4 times	11%
5–8 times	37%	5–8 times	26%
9 times or more	11%	9 times or more	63%

5. Do you use Noile every time you shampoo?

Panel A		Panel B	
Yes	36%	Yes	83%
No	64%	No	17%

6. When using Noile, do you also use a cream rinse or conditioner?

	Panel A			*Panel B*	
Yes		87%	Yes		34%
No		13%	No		66%

7. What do you like most about Noile? (open ended, most frequent responses reported)

	Panel A			*Panel B*	
Helps control oil		61%	Cuts through oil & sweat		71%
Doesn't dry hair out		17%	Hair stays clean		53%
Hair stays clean longer		37%	Doesn't dry hair out		24%
Has conditioner		12%	Cleans and conditions		22%
(Skip to Question 9)					

8. Why haven't you tried Noile?

	Panel A			*Panel B*	
Don't have oily hair		54%	Don't have oily hair		55%
Too harsh		38%	Too harsh		21%
Like present shampoo		36%	Like present shampoo		38%
Haven't seen it		8%	Haven't seen it		10%
Too expensive		6%	Too expensive		3%

9. Your age:

	Panel A			*Panel B*	
21–25		12%	21–25		13%
26–30		18%	26–30		20%
31–35		21%	31–35		21%
36–40		20%	36–40		15%
41–45		10%	41–45		12%
46–50		11%	46–50		7%
50–54		8%	50–54		12%

10. You are:

	Panel A			*Panel B*	
Married		38%	Married		30%
Single		33%	Single		38%
Divorced		26%	Divorced		30%
Widowed		3%	Widowed		2%

NOTE: 72 percent (144) response from Panel A members and 77 percent (154) response from Panel B members. These figures are provided for your information and analysis. Cross-indexes are available upon request.

Dodge felt that the questionnaire results provided an excellent basis for developing a new strategy for Noile. After lunch, he decided, he would request some cross-indexes and set up a meeting with the ad agency account executive.

Questions

1. Would you have included Panel C in the questioning? Why or why not?
2. A cross-index (or cross-tab) compares two or more questions. For example, cross-indexing Questions 3 and 9 would reveal how many people aged 21–25 have tried Noile. Assume that because of time and computer cost restraints, Dodge can only request two cross-indexes. What do you think would be most helpful and why?
3. If Dodge were to assess Noile against competitors on a perceptual matrix, what attributes might he select for the axes?
4. Do you feel Noile might be a candidate for benefit segmentation?
5. Were there other usage or psychographic areas you would have included in the questionnaire?
6. What, if any, questions do the questionnaire results raise that you would like answered before developing a new strategy?

Replas Products, Inc.

Gene Sampson, president of Replas Products, Inc., was preparing an overview of his firm's current situation in the plastics marketplace. The overview would be given to a research firm to guide them in developing a study that would then be used by the Replas advertising staff in determining the approach to use in promoting Replas's newest product—a recyclable plastic for use in packaging applications.

Replas was a fairly new company, only ten months old. Sampson had previously been chief of production in the plastics division of a major manufacturing firm. That company had done some experimenting with recyclable plastics, but had been reluctant to invest heavily in the technology required for mass production. Because their current nonrecyclable products were profitable, and the division was required by corporate management to return a certain profit percentage quarterly, the decision had been made to put recyclable plastic testing on hold. Sampson had disagreed with that decision, believing that recyclable plastic would be the industry standard in the very near future. He obtained rights to the company's recyclable plastics process and left to form Replas. Several other top engineering and production people came with him.

In its first few months, Replas was concerned mainly with getting operations and production established. Sampson had found several environmentally concerned venture capitalists to invest in Replas, giving him the time and money to get the business on its feet. He had recently gotten orders from several large package goods food manufacturers to begin producing recyclable plastic packaging for some of their products on a test basis. So, things were looking up for Replas. But Sampson was also learning that there was a big difference between producing a product and marketing it.

Plastics and plastic packaging, in particular, are a growing environmental threat. Plastics production is growing at about 9 percent annually, faster than many other processed materials. The inherent benefits of plastic—strength, flexibility, light weight—make it appealing for many applications in packaging, automobile manufacturing, construction, and other industries. However, plastic is a major problem from a waste perspective. Many kinds of plastics are virtually indestructible; they do not deteriorate in landfills, cannot be incinerated because of toxic fumes, and pose health hazards to fish and wildlife. Plastics currently make up about 7 percent of the waste stream in the U.S. Paper products make up the greatest proportion of the waste stream, at 42 percent. But, 21 percent of the paper waste is recovered through some sort of recycling program. Less than 1 percent of the current plastic waste is being recovered.

Plastic bags and bottles make up the greatest part of plastic waste. The growing number of supermarket chains switching from paper bags to plastic testifies to the appeal of the plastic product. At the same time, environmental publications are full of photographs of plastic waste on beaches, sea gulls being choked by discarded plastic six-pack holders, and fish trapped in plastic bags. A number of states are considering legislation banning or severely restricting plastic packaging in response to these environmental concerns.

The type of plastic manufactured by Replas and several other plastics firms could solve many of the current problems. It was a recyclable plastic suitable for packaging applications. Packaging made from this plastic could be separated out from other refuse, recycled, and used in other applications. Because of the longer useful life of this plastic, it was actually cheaper in the long run than nonrecyclable plastic. When he started Replas, Sampson believed that the recyclable plastic would sell itself. His experience in the past few months showed that he'd been a bit optimistic.

Because of the inherent costs and risks in switching from one type of packaging to another, many manufacturers were reluctant to make the change to recyclable plastic unless they were forced to by legislation. (Replas was part of a plastics consortium that had hired a public relations firm to make sure that legislators in all states and at the federal level knew about the existence and benefits of recyclable plastic. They were hoping that the pending laws would differentiate between recyclable and nonrecyclable plastics, keeping recyclable plastics legal even if nonrecyclables were banned.) Sampson felt that consumer demand for recyclable plastic packaging might spur manufacturers to make the change more quickly. He was willing to spend some money on a campaign directed at consumers, but he had no idea what to say.

Sampson had studied the experiences of the aluminum industry in trying to get consumer support for recyclable aluminum. One thing was clear: active consumer participation was required to make a recycling program work. For maximum efficiency, consumers had to separate recyclable waste from nonrecyclable waste. Sampson knew that some areas had ordinances requiring such separation, but he didn't think that there was much active enforcement of those ordinances—he hadn't come across cases of people being heavily fined or jailed for not separating their trash! Even in areas where people were charged a deposit fee for aluminum packaging (such as Connecticut, where aluminum soft drink cans carry a 5-cent surcharge), a substantial portion of the packages weren't returned for refund.

So, Sampson wasn't sure where to begin—would consumers recognize the benefit of recyclable plastic through a simple informational campaign? Should advertising stress the broad societal/environmental benefit of the product? Or would an economic appeal have greater success (in the long run, recyclable plastic packaging would probably reduce retail prices by a few cents)? Who were the best prospects for a campaign—people who were used to recycling? people in areas with waste disposal problems? people who were heavy users of products packaged in plastic? Sampson knew that one campaign probably wouldn't change things immediately. But he hoped that a Replas campaign could start the ball rolling. There were a lot of potential benefits—more interest from his customers, the manufacturers; greater awareness of recyclable plastics among legislators; increased activity in the plastics industry. He hoped the experts at the research company would be able to help him.

Questions

1.   As a first step, develop some specific advertising objectives based on what Sampson hopes to get out of his advertising campaign.
2.   How might the concept of potential purchasers illustrated in Exhibit 6–1 apply to this situation?
3.   How would you use focus group research in this situation? Who would you want to include in the group? What would you hope to learn from them?
4.   Describe how you would use *either* perceptual mapping or motivation research in this situation. What would you hope to learn? Who would you question?
5.   Would a concept test be appropriate in this situation? Why or why not?

7

Identifying and Establishing Advertising Objectives

Once the preliminary work of analysis and identification of the market, competitive and consumer problems and opportunities facing the brand or company has been completed, the campaign planner is ready to determine exactly how the advertising campaign will be developed. The first step in that process is to identify and establish the advertising objectives or to set the goals the advertising will attempt to achieve. In other words, with an idea of what we want to achieve with advertising, we can start to put together the elements and plan that will achieve these objectives.

The setting of advertising objectives or goals is a very important step in the campaign process. These objectives determine the direction, methods, and even the tone the advertising will take. For example, all the physical elements of the campaign will be dictated by the objectives that have been set—what the advertising strategy will be, what media will be used, how sales promotion and direct marketing and public relations will be integrated into the program, how much money will be needed, and so on. All these actual parts of the advertising plan and advertising campaign will be influenced by the advertising objectives that are set at this point.

Although the setting of advertising objectives would appear to be a rather straightforward task, often it is not. Many times, the planner identifies several alternative strategic advertising approaches that might be used; for example, directing the advertising to present users to retain their business or to light or nonusers to bring them into the brand franchise; attempting to influence competitive users to switch brands; or, in some cases, trying to build demand for the category, which will then ultimately lead to more brand sales. In most cases, the outcome of the use of various strategies is a hotly debated issue among advertising people. Therefore, advertising objectives are often one of the most difficult parts of the advertising campaign development process.

211

There is sometimes confusion or misunderstanding on the part of clients and advertising agencies about exactly what advertising can or cannot do for the brand or company. This confusion can be a problem. Often, advertisers would like to be able to relate advertising directly to sales. With direct marketing and direct response, that's possible; but for most mass media campaigns, such direct correlation is an extremely difficult task because of the many intervening marketplace variables that exist.

A final problem is that, in some instances, the planner can clearly identify several alternative approaches for the campaign. Given finite financial resources, the question then becomes, "Which strategic approach should I propose?" That decision will determine exactly how and for what purpose advertising will be used in the overall communications program for the company or brand.

THE PURPOSE OF ADVERTISING OBJECTIVES

Why Set Advertising Objectives?

In general, there are five basic reasons for setting specific advertising objectives: agreement among all parties, financial control, development of the advertising elements, measurement and evaluation, and relationship of advertising to other marketing elements. A discussion of these reasons follows.

Agreement among all parties.   It is vital that all parties involved in the development, approval, and evaluation of an advertising campaign agree on what is to be done and what the advertising can accomplish. Without this formal agreement, the approval process for the various specific campaign elements becomes a most difficult one. If each person in the approval process brings his or her own ideas of what the objectives of the campaign are and remains tied to them, then the approval process will be more difficult, and often the end result of the campaign will be a disaster. If clear concise advertising objectives are set, they greatly simplify the task of those who must develop the specific elements of the campaign. In short, the advertising objectives are the baseline of the campaign. It is almost mandatory that all involved agree to what is to be achieved before any single element is considered.

Financial control.   Advertising objectives help management maintain financial control over the advertising investment. They also provide a method for determining the value of the advertising program in terms of the overall success of the company or brand. For example, it is much easier for management to approve an advertising budget when the specific objectives and potential outcomes are known rather than when the request is simply stated as, "We need $5,000,000 for advertising for this brand in the coming year."

Development of the advertising elements. Clearly, advertising objectives are needed as guidelines for those who develop the various elements in the advertising campaign. Without some idea of what the advertising is to achieve, the creative and media people are simply shooting in the dark. In addition, those who approve the various parts of the advertising program need some idea of what is to be accomplished in order to make a sound, objective judgment as to whether or not to approve a piece of creative work or a media plan or even an in-store merchandising program.

Measurement and evaluation. Increasingly, management is asking advertising people and advertising agencies, "What did we get for the advertising investment we made?" Without some predetermined advertising objectives or goals to refer to, it is most difficult for advertising people to provide management with a clear picture of the true value of the advertising investment. If the advertising objectives are set in advance, it then becomes a much easier task to evaluate the results of the campaign at the end.

Relationship of advertising to other marketing elements. Because integrated marketing communications will be the rule in the future, it is vital that advertising objectives be set so they can be coordinated with other communication elements. By clearly identifying what advertising can or is expected to do throughout the campaign, it is much easier to establish its relationship to the other elements in the communications program.

HOW TO ESTABLISH ADVERTISING OBJECTIVES

As has been stressed throughout this text, advertising must flow from or "cascade" out of the more basic goals and plans set for the entire business unit. Although it might seem that the objectives for a specific brand's advertising are only distantly related to the overall objectives of the corporation, in truth, they are a direct result of plans and decisions that have been made at higher levels. A brief review of those decisions should be helpful in putting the advertising objectives in perspective.

The Corporate Business Plan

The objective of most organizations is to achieve a profit; several factors influence the way the organization goes about reaching that goal. It is important for the advertising planner to have some idea of how advertising is viewed by corporate management, if he or she is to develop a sound advertising proposal that will further the organization's goals.

Five factors, in general, have much to do with how advertising is viewed within any specific business organization. A discussion of the factors—the corporate strategic plan, product or market orientation, the prime industry, competition, and management—follows.

The corporate strategic plan. Most major organizations follow some form of strategic business plan (as described in Chapter 1). Although advertising people may find it hard to believe, not all organizations' strategic plans emphasize growth or expansion. Some companies find themselves better served by harvesting existing businesses and maintaining a low but stable return on their investment. The strategic plan being followed by these organizations has a direct impact on their view of advertising, its importance, their willingness to invest in advertising, and even the content of various advertising approaches. In these cases, advertising is of minor importance to the overall plan of the company.[1]

Product or marketing orientation. The strategic plan for the organization is generally determined by the business orientation of the company. As you will recall from Chapter 1, there are five basic concepts under which organizations conduct their marketing, and, therefore, their advertising activity. They are (a) the production concept, (b) the product concept, (c) the selling concept, (d) the marketing concept, and (e) the societal marketing concept. Depending on the approach that the company takes to the marketplace, advertising can be very important or not important at all. It is vital that the advertising planner understand the approach the organization is taking to be able to set realistic advertising objectives.

In general, for purposes of understanding their approach to advertising, we might group most companies into one of two camps. Those who view advertising as a necessary or perhaps unnecessary business expense and those who view advertising as a business-building investment. In other words, there are production-oriented companies and marketing-oriented companies. The difference between the two is quite dramatic: The marketing-oriented organization views the market from the consumer's standpoint and determines how to best meet the consumer's wants. The production-oriented organization, however, takes the approach that manufacturing and distribution of products are most important.

Production-oriented organizations concentrate their efforts on developing more efficient means of producing or distributing a given product. The

---

[1]Philip Kotler, *Marketing Management: Analysis, Planning, Implementation, and Control* (Englewood Cliffs, N.J.: Prentice-Hall, 1988): 13–30.

production-oriented company takes the view that "if you build a better mousetrap, the world will beat a path to your door." The marketing-oriented company provides the opportunities and even the path to their product for the consumer to take. The goals of each company are strongly influenced by the type of market orientation taken, and that orientation, obviously, influences the value of advertising to the organization.

Prime industry.   The prime industry in which the organization is involved has much to do with its corporate goals. If the industry is research oriented, then the orientation of the company may well be more toward research than marketing. The pharmaceutical drug business is a good example of a research-oriented industry. Companies in this field believe research is most important and marketing is a minor ingredient in their success.

In addition, the industry in which the company operates often has an impact on the value it places on advertising. In some industries, such as food, cigarettes, and beverages, advertising is a very important part of the marketing mix. In others, such as industrial products, and, up until a few years ago, health care and financial services, advertising was not considered to be very important at all. Historically, the industry in which the organization operates has much to do with how it has viewed advertising.

Competition.   The strength and activity of competition also influences corporate goals and, ultimately, marketing and advertising goals. If the business arena is highly competitive, the corporate goal may be market share first and profits second. If competition is limited, the goal may be optimization of profits or the obtaining of a sufficient share of available profits with minimum investment. Many companies also believe that if their competition advertises, so should they. So, competition also impacts advertising goals.

Management.   The approach of management in directing the organization has a major impact on the goals that may be set for the corporation. If management is aggressive and growth minded, corporate goals will be different than if management is conservative and is content to simply "tend the store" until someone else takes over. The effect of management on company direction and, ultimately, on advertising is quite clear.

The objectives that management set for the company have much to do with what advertising and marketing goals are established. For example, if the company were following a "harvesting" strategy with its various divisions or brands, the use and importance of advertising would be minimal. Similarly, if research were the basic goal of the corporation, then that goal would affect the amount and type of advertising used. Obviously, the advertising goals of a marketing-oriented, consumer package-goods operation seeking to maximize sales and generate market share would be totally different from those of a research-oriented firm. Again, one of the first things a campaign planner has to evaluate is the corporate goals of the organization and their impact on the specific advertising campaign being planned.

Marketing goals for the company and the brand flow directly out of the organization's corporate goals. These goals are specified in the marketing plan.

MARKETING OBJECTIVES

Once the corporate goals are established, the marketing plan for the company or brand is written. The marketing plan outlines and details all the marketing activities that the company will undertake for a given period. In general, there is a long-term marketing plan developed for a period of five years or more. This plan is supplemented by an annual marketing plan. The annual plan details the specific marketing activities that will be used during the coming year.

The five-year plan looks in broad strokes at what has happened the previous year, the budget for the coming year, the actual results for the current year on a monthly basis, and then presents a forecast for the next three years.

Of more direct interest to the campaign planner is the annual marketing plan. The annual marketing plan consists of all data, both physical and financial, that relate to the production, distribution, pricing, and promotion of the brand. Most marketing plans can be summarized as follows:

A *marketing plan* is a written document that (a) examines the major acts in a marketing situation of a product or service; (b) identifies the problems and opportunities in the situation; (c) proposes long-range strategy to meet these problems and opportunities; and (d) recommends tactics of selling and advertising for the coming year to carry out this strategy.[2]

Although the advertising planner may or may not be involved in the development of a marketing plan, knowing its contents is very helpful. An outline for a marketing plan, developed by the Association of National Advertisers, can be found at the end of this chapter (see Exhibit 7–8).

The marketing plan incorporates the various aspects of the advertising plan, including very broad promotional objectives to be achieved. Thus, until the marketing plan is developed, it is often quite difficult to develop any specific advertising plan or campaign and, therefore, to establish any definitive advertising objectives. The advertising objectives must be di-

---

[2]Herbert West, "Why You Need a Master Strategy Blueprint," *Advertising Age,* 18 (January 1959): 59.

rectly related to the marketing plan, for that is the basic guiding document for the brand or company.

UNDERSTANDING ADVERTISING OBJECTIVES

The advertising campaign, although it is important, is usually only one of the tools needed to execute the marketing plan. Because there is sometimes confusion between advertising and marketing objectives, a brief review of the differences will help in planning.

Differences in Marketing and Advertising Objectives

Sales versus sales messages.   In general, marketing goals are defined in terms of sales and profits. Advertising goals are usually set in terms of delivering sales messages to the target audience, or some other communication effect. Marketing goals are measured in concrete terms of dollars and cents. Advertising goals are measured by change in awareness, attitude, and information shifts among consumers.

Current versus lagged effects.   Marketing objectives are evaluated for a single specific time period, such as one year. The program either achieves or fails to achieve the sales or profit objectives that have been established for that time. Future sales are not taken into account. Advertising, however, in many cases has a lagged effect; that is, advertising dollars may be invested in this calendar year, but results may not occur until a later period. Often, specific marketing activities don't have this sort of lagged effect, but the effects of advertising may take some time to develop.

Tangible versus intangible results.   Part of the difference between marketing and advertising goals is the final result. Marketing goals are usually stated in concrete terms, such as units moved, sales or profits, distribution achieved, shelf facings in stores, and the like. Advertising goals, on the other hand, can often be quite intangible. They may include such things as shifts in attitudes, changes in opinion, entry into and establishment in the evoked set, and the like. Therefore, it can be quite difficult to measure the rather soft objectives of advertising in terms of the hard, discrete data, available from marketing goals.

Factors Influencing the Establishment of Advertising Objectives

Today, for most consumer and many industrial products, advertising is considered as simply another method of delivering sales messages. Advertising is a surrogate for trying to see and talk to each prospect individually. Advertisers recognize that personal, face-to-face sales presentations are, for the most part, the most effective selling method. However, for products with broad distribution and usage and high household penetration, this face-to-face selling simply isn't possible or practical. So, advertising is used.

If we view advertising as a method of delivering sales messages on behalf of the product, service, company, or brand, we start to get a better understanding of how advertising objectives can be set. We know, for example, that every salesperson doesn't make a sale every time he or she talks to a prospect or even every time a formal sales presentation is made. We need to view advertising in the same way. Advertising is the delivery of a sales message and, as such, there are some factors that will have an impact whether or not the sales message is received, how it is acted upon, and ultimately how successful it will be.

Pertinence of the sales message.   People pay the most attention to things that are most important to them. For example, a cure for cancer will get more attention than will the introduction of a new household detergent. So, the results of advertising and, therefore, the setting of advertising objectives are greatly influenced by the type of product and the importance of that product or service to the target market.

Length of purchasing decision.   Some products have a long purchasing decision process. For example, the purchase of a new computer system for a company may sometimes take several years. Other purchasing decisions are made rather quickly, such as the purchase of a soft drink or candy bar. Delivery of a sales message for a soft drink, therefore, will likely have a much quicker impact on the prospect than will the sales message for a product that requires careful consideration, such as a computer system. Because advertising objectives are influenced by the length of decision time for the purchase of the product, the number of people involved in the decision, the value of the purchase, and so on, these factors must be taken into account when setting advertising objectives.

Competition and clutter.   The more competitive products there are available, the greater the likelihood of conflicting sales messages being addressed to members of the target audience. Therefore, the prospect will likely have greater difficulty in sorting out those messages that are important or useful to him or her. Likewise, the greater the competitive activity, the more competitive messages there are in the media. So, simply getting the attention of the consumer is a major factor in setting the overall advertising objectives for the campaign in many product categories.

Product life cycle.   The phase the product is in in its life cycle greatly affects the impact advertising can have. If the product is in a mature category, has little competitive advantage, and has been available for some time (in the latter stages of its life cycle), it is much more difficult to deliver sales messages through advertising. Most consumers simply assume they know the category, have had experience with the brand or brands, and, therefore, have little need for more information or material to make a purchase decision. This situation often greatly influences the setting of advertising objectives.

Intervening marketing variables.   The advertising planner has little or no control over any of the marketing mix elements except the advertising for most consumer products sold through self-service outlets. Therefore, although the advertising may promise availability of the product at a certain price in certain locations, there is no guarantee that those stores will stock, price, or promote the product as the advertising planner envisioned. Stock outs, pricing discrepancies, competitive activities, and a host of other marketing variables have a major impact on what advertising objectives can be set or achieved.

In spite of all these problems, advertising objectives are still vital to a successful campaign. The key is for the advertising planner to recognize these factors and the other influences and take them into account when setting the advertising objectives.

Types of Advertising Objectives

Most advertising planners use one or more of three types of advertising objectives—sales, behavioral effects, and communication effects.

Sales.   Some types of marketers, primarily those involved in direct response, can easily set and measure their advertising objectives in terms of unit or dollar sales or specific sales leads. They can do that because advertising is the only form of marketing and selling used in moving their brand to the final consumer. Their marketing system goes directly from the manufacturer through the media to the consumer. The consumer either reacts with an order or doesn't. Commonly, direct or direct response marketers set this type of sales goal for their advertising.

In addition, it is often possible for retail advertisers to set specific sales goals for their advertising. Because they work in much the same way as a direct marketer—there is no lag or distribution channel between them and their customer—they can set specific sales goals for their advertising and measure the effects in that way.

When it is possible or practical, setting sales as the advertising objective is the most acceptable way of measuring advertising impact.

Behavioral effects.   When advertising goals can't be set directly in terms of final sales, some type of behavioral activity by consumers can be used as a measure of the effect of the advertising messages. For example, some advertisers attempt to get advertising respondents to take a specific action short of making a purchase, such as sending for more information, returning a reply card, calling a dealer, or visiting a retail location. This approach is common to many forms of industrial advertising because the advertiser knows most industrial products are sold only through face-to-face negotiation between a salesperson and a buyer. Many industrial marketers use advertising to generate leads for the sales force. Thus, customers or prospects who ask for more information or send in coupons can be correlated with advertising exposure.

The advertiser may measure many types of activities or actions suggested through the advertising. This will enable the advertiser to identify who is responding to the advertising and what results are being obtained. In cases where direct sales cannot be measured, a surrogate measure of behavior or interest in the product generated by advertising is often used as a measure of success.

Communication effects.   In the case of most consumer package goods or products purchased on a regular basis and through various forms of trade channels, the advertising objectives must be even softer than a measure of behavior. In other words, a measure of the effects the advertising has in terms of either awareness, knowledge, preference, or some other mental effect on the consumer is used. Because this type of measurement makes up the greatest portion of the advertising objectives of consumer product advertisers, it will be discussed in detail on the following pages. Before doing so, however, we must look at some of the factors that influence the type of objectives the advertising campaign planner can set.

Choosing Sales, Behavior, or Communication Effects

Several factors determine whether the advertising planner should set sales or behavior or communication effects as the objective for the campaign. A discussion of some of the factors that influence this decision follows.

Marketing channel.   The channel through which the product or service is marketed has much to do with the type of advertising objectives that can be set. For example, direct marketers can set sales goals. Consumer product marketers, distributing brands primarily through self-service retail operations, usually attempt to measure only communication effects.

Type of message.   Not all advertising is designed to generate an immediate response. For example, an oil company attempting to explain the energy situation to the consumer public really isn't trying to sell additional product. It is advocating a position or explaining its operation. The same is true of many corporate advertising campaigns whose goal is only to change attitudes or opinions about situations, events, or activities. In these cases, no actual sales may result. Thus, the type of information in the message to be communicated through the advertising campaign usually will be quite different from the information given by a company trying to generate, for example, a point-of-purchase sale.

Long- or short-term effects.   The intended effect of the message also has much to do with establishing the advertising objectives. For example, an attempt to build an image of the organization in the minds of the consumers may require quite a long time to achieve. Convincing consumers the XYZ Corporation makes high-quality automobiles may take several years. A product sales message, however (the 70 model of XYZ is a high-performance auto), may require only a few months exposure to change attitudes or opinions. The campaign planner must consider the length of time required for response when setting advertising objectives.

Intended audience.   The audience for the advertising campaign also has an effect on the advertising objectives. For example, it is usually much easier to get existing users of a product to use more of the product or to use it in additional ways than it is to get new users to try the brand. It may be much easier to get established retailers to perform some type of sales promotion function in their stores than to try and get new stores to stock the product.

These are just a few of the factors the advertising planner must take into consideration when deciding what advertising objective to set, for example, sales, behavior, or communication effects. Most mass media advertising goals are essentially based on communication effects; therefore, we look at this area in much greater detail because these are the more typical advertising objectives with which most planners work.

SETTING ADVERTISING OBJECTIVES

While there are three basic types of advertising objectives—sales, behavioral effects, and communication effects—at the same time, there are several views of how advertising objectives and results should be established and measured.

Colley's DAGMAR Approach

Russell Colley wrote *Defining Advertising Goals for Measured Advertising Results* (DAGMAR) for the Association of National Advertisers in 1961.

He did much to convince advertisers that communication effects should be the basis for most advertising evaluations. Another result of Colley's efforts was the general idea of establishing advertising objectives and then measuring results of the advertising campaign against those objectives.[3]

Because Colley's recommendation established most of the concepts still used today for advertising objectives and advertising measurement, it is worthwhile to examine his ideas in some detail.

Specifically, Colley states that advertising's job, purely and simply, is to communicate to a defined audience information and a frame of mind that stimulates action. Advertising succeeds or fails depending on how well it communicates the desired information and attitudes to the right people at the right time at the right cost.[4]

Colley's approach to measuring advertising results is based on the following six principles:

1. An advertising goal is a succinct statement of the communication aspects of the marketing job. (It expresses the particular work advertising is uniquely qualified to perform and does not encompass results that require a combination of several different marketing forces.)
2. The goal is expressed in writing—in finite, measurable terms. (If there is agreement among all of those concerned on what advertising is expected to accomplish, then it is no great chore to reduce it to writing. If there is a lack of agreement as to purpose, the time to find this out is before the advertising is prepared, not afterward.)
3. Goals are agreed upon by all concerned, at both the creative and approval levels. (Planning is separated from doing. Agreement is reached on what needs to be said to whom before time and money are spent on how best to say it.)
4. Goals are based on an intimate knowledge of markets and buying motives. (They express realistic expectancy in light of carefully evaluated market opportunities. They do not express mere hopes and desires arrived at without factual foundation.)
5. Benchmarks are set up against which accomplishments can be measured. (State of mind—knowledge, attitude, and buying propensity—are appraised before and after the advertising, or among those reached versus those not reached by the advertising.)
6. Methods to be used at a later date in evaluating accomplishments are set up at the time goals are established.[5]

[3]Russell H. Colley, *Defining Advertising Goals for Measured Advertising Results* (New York: Association of National Advertisers, 1961).

[4]Colley, *Defining Advertising Goals:* 21.

[5]Colley, *Defining Advertising Goals:* 14.

Colley's primary theme throughout the DAGMAR approach is that good advertising objectives are both specific and measurable. In his view, the key to measuring advertising results involves, first, being able to define the advertising goals to be accomplished. This decision is one of the most difficult parts of the task. Colley suggests a "6 M" approach, which he outlines as follows:

Merchandise	What are all the important benefits of the products and services to be sold?
Markets	Who are the people to be reached?
Motives	Why would these people buy or fail to buy?
Messages	What are the key ideas, information, and attitudes to be conveyed (to move the prospect closer to the ultimate aim of a sale)?
Media	How can the prospects be reached?
Measurements	What method is proposed to measure accomplishment in getting the intended message across to the intended audience?[6]

To be able to measure the effect of the advertising message, the campaign planner must be able to detect a change in the consumer's perceptions, attitudes, or actions. Colley proposes the following hierarchy of stages in the communication process designed to achieve the ultimate goal of advertising—persuading the consumer to act. The four stages of "commercial communication" suggested by Colley are

1. Awareness. The prospect must be made aware of the brand or product.
2. Comprehension. The prospect must comprehend what the product is and what it will do for him.
3. Conviction. The prospect must arrive at a mental disposition or conviction to buy the product.
4. Action. Finally, the prospect must take action.[7]

The primary thrust of Colley's approach is that the response to communication can be measured in many instances with existing research tools and methodologies. Colley offers the example (see Table 7–1) of the effects advertising might have on consumers. He uses two different products and compares the effects before and after advertising communication.

Colley does not specifically deal with how the benchmarks are established or the methodology of measurement. His key point is the impor-

---

[6]Colley, *Defining Advertising Goals:* 23.
[7]Colley, *Defining Advertising Goals:* 38.

Table 7–1 Effect of Advertising on Consumer Response

Product: Filter cigarette	Before advertising (percent)	After advertising (percent)
Aware of brand name:		
Unaided recall	20	40
Aided recall	40	80
Comprehended messages:		
Message A	6	12
Message B	10	20
Message C	8	16
Favorably disposed to buy	4	8
Demonstrated action	2	4
Image: Industrial chemical division		
Aware of corporate name	85	88
Aware that corporation is a leading supplier of industrial chemicals	15	30
Comprehended key messages:		
Message A	6	12
Message B	4	8
Message C	5	10
Favorably disposed to buy	5	10
Action leading to purchase	3	6

SOURCE: Colley, *Defining Advertising Goals:* 39.

tance of the identification of specific communication goals from the start of advertising to the close of the campaign.

In summary, Colley's DAGMAR approach is best described as a written measurable communications task involving a starting point, a definite audience, and a fixed period of time.

A RECOMMENDED APPROACH TO SETTING ADVERTISING OBJECTIVES FOR MEASURABLE RESULTS

The DAGMAR approach is, for the most part, conceptually sound and practicable in the marketplace. There is, however, one problem. The hierarchy of steps from awareness to action is somewhat ill-defined. The DAGMAR approach has much to recommend it, and when combined with a different hierarchy of effects model can provide an effective method of setting measurable advertising objectives. The Lavidge and Steiner model, illustrated in Exhibit 7–1, is more specific than Colley's "four stages of commercial communication." We believe it provides a better method of establishing and measuring advertising results.

Exhibit 7–1 Effect of Advertising on Consumers: Movement from Awareness to Action

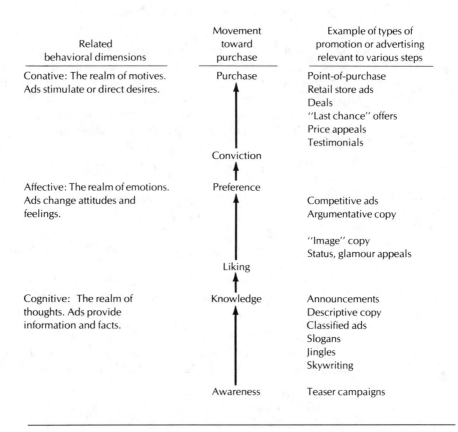

Related behavioral dimensions	Movement toward purchase	Example of types of promotion or advertising relevant to various steps
Conative: The realm of motives. Ads stimulate or direct desires.	Purchase	Point-of-purchase Retail store ads Deals "Last chance" offers Price appeals Testimonials
	Conviction	
Affective: The realm of emotions. Ads change attitudes and feelings.	Preference	Competitive ads Argumentative copy "Image" copy Status, glamour appeals
	Liking	
Cognitive: The realm of thoughts. Ads provide information and facts.	Knowledge	Announcements Descriptive copy Classified ads Slogans Jingles Skywriting
	Awareness	Teaser campaigns

SOURCE: Robert J. Lavidge and Gary A. Steiner, *Journal of Marketing* (October 1961): 61.

Lavidge and Steiner describe their model as follows:

> Advertising may be thought of as a force, which must move people up a series of steps:
> 1. Near the bottom of the steps stand the potential purchasers who are completely unaware of the existence of the product or service in question.
> 2. Closer to purchasing, but still a long way from the cash register, are those who are merely aware of the product's existence.
> 3. Up a step are prospects who know what the product has to offer.
> 4. Still closer to purchasing are those who have favorable attitudes toward the product—those who like the product.

5. Those whose favorable attitudes have developed to the point of preference over all other possibilities are up still another step.
6. Even closer to purchasing are consumers who couple preference with a desire to buy and the conviction that the purchase would be wise.
7. Finally, of course, is the step which translates this attitude into an actual purchase.[8]

The Lavidge and Steiner model, although not proven in actual practice for all types of products or situations, has great intuitive and common-sense appeal—it talks in terms of how many consumers are likely to make purchases in various product categories. We recommend the use of the L&S model as the hierarchical measure for the basic Colley approach.

Since the introduction of the Lavidge and Steiner model, several researchers have raised questions about its use with some products in some situations. The advertising campaign planner should be aware of some of these questions.

1. For some products, consumers might not go through the sequence as it is set out, that is, they may start and stop, or they may make mistakes and start over, and so on.
2. Feedback at various stages might allow later events to have an influence on earlier activities.
3. Some consumers might collapse the entire process into a split second, particularly for low-risk, low-cost products.
4. Some consumers might not follow the process at all. They might make purchasing decisions under some other system.

An alternative to the L&S model was presented by Robertson and is illustrated in Exhibit 7–2. Vaughn described it as follows:

This modified "hierarchy" model proposes that some consumers, under some conditions, for some products, might follow a sequential path. The dotted lines [in Exhibit 7–2] are feedbacks which can alter outcomes. Other decision patterns on the right, track consumers as they violate the formal sequence of the hierarchy. Thus, consumers can learn from previous experience and swerve from the awareness-to-purchase pattern.[9]

In spite of these irregularities, the L&S model still provides a very sound method of establishing measurable advertising objectives for the campaign planner.

---

[8]Robert J. Lavidge and Gary Steiner, "A Model for Predictive Measurements of Advertising Effectiveness," *Journal of Marketing,* 24 (October 1961): 59–62.

[9]Richard Vaughn, "How Advertising Works: A Planning Model," *Journal of Advertising Research*, 20, 5 (October 1980): 28–29.

Exhibit 7-2   Altered Hierarchy Model

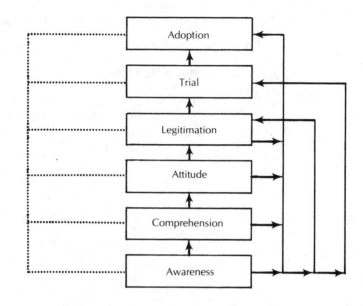

SOURCE: Vaughn, "How Advertising Works": 29. Copyright Foote, Cone & Belding Communications, Inc., 1979. Reprinted by permission.

The Expanded Three-Order-Hierarchy Models

As mentioned, the major concerns about the L&S hierarchical approach to understanding advertising effects (and therefore how to set advertising objectives) revolve around the facts that (a) there are a series of possible reactions, and (b) these reactions occur in some predetermined order. Most experts agree that three reactions called cognitive, affective, and connotative exist. The question is the order in which they occur. In other words, the model assumes that learning occurs before attitude change which leads to behavior. In fact, many studies in psychology, marketing communications, and advertising research provide evidence that this order is not always the same in every case.

One approach that has been suggested is that of Ray[10] who argues that there are three possible hierarchies. Each is briefly reviewed in the following sections.

---

[10]This section is adapted from Michael L. Ray, *Advertising and Communication Management* (Englewood Cliffs, N.J.: Prentice-Hall, 1982): 182–88.

The Learning Hierarchy: Learn–Feel–Do. The "learning hierarchy" is similar to that proposed by Lavidge and Steiner, that is, it is a step-by-step process that assumes that learning must occur before attitude and behavior can change. The model is illustrated below as Exhibit 7–3.

Exhibit 7–3   Learning Hierarchy

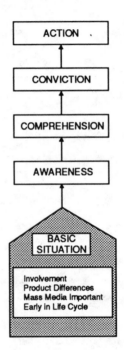

It appears that the learning hierarchy is most likely to occur for products and their attendant advertising where there is consumer involvement, product differentiation, and an emphasis on the use of mass media communication. Further, it seems to occur most often when the product is in the early stages of the product life cycle and the traditional adoption process is occurring.

The Dissonance-Attribution Hierarchy: Do–Learn–Feel. This hierarchy is the reverse of the learning hierarchy. In other words, behavior occurs first, then attitudes change and, finally, learning occurs. This situation seems to be most prevalent when the consumer is faced with choices and the products are perceived to be very similar or their differences are hard to immediately determine or the chances of a wrong choice have major implications. A prime example is the purchase of a new automobile. Following the purchase of an automobile, many buyers often seek out advertising or other material that will help support their choice or reinforce their belief that they made the right decision. In other words, they are trying to reduce the dissonance from communication or advertising which makes them feel that they had not made the right purchase decision. The basic model of this hierarchy is illustrated in Exhibit 7–4.

Exhibit 7–4   Dissonance-Attribution Hierarchy

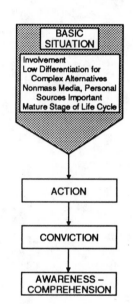

Typically, situations which seem most appropriate for the dissonance-attribution hierarchy are those in which the consumer is involved in a purchase decision whose alternatives have no real distinguishing factors. In addition, nonmass media or more personal communication sources are important, and products are in the mature stage of the product life cycle. In other words, the consumer is familiar with the product category and perhaps even the brands but has difficulty distinguishing between them and, therefore, justifying the purchase made.

The Low-Involvement Hierarchy: Learn–Do–Feel. The low-involvement concept was developed by Herbert Krugman. He suggested there were categories in which the consumer had little involvement with either the product or the advertising. Therefore, because of this low involvement, there was little perceptual defense against the advertising messages. Over time, and after much message repetition, a shift in the cognitive structure might occur. Therefore, when faced with a product-purchasing situation, the name of the product might come quickly to mind, the purchase decision would be made, and the attitude about the product would subsequently change as a result of the product experience. (Exhibit 7–5 illustrates the model.)

Exhibit 7–5   Low-Involvement Hierarchy

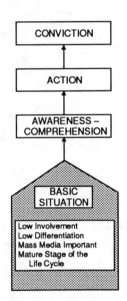

In the case of products that seem to best fit this low-involvement hierarchy, there are few apparent differences among competitive brands; mass-media advertising, particularly broadcast, is important; and the product is in the mature stage of the product life cycle.

Given the much more time-pressured, sophisticated consumer, the more complex marketplace, and the vastly expanded communications systems of the 1990s, the three-order: hierarchy models do appear to give a better explanation of why advertising effects are often very different from product to product and even brand to brand.

Although the L&S hierarchy is much easier to understand and much easier to apply in advertising planning and measurement, it does seem somewhat simplistic in its approach. Nonetheless, we recommend that the planner start first with the L&S or learning hierarchy model. Test either model against known consumer behavior and purchasing patterns. If it fits, use it as the basis for setting the advertising objectives. If it does not, try one of the other hierarchical models and then select the one which most closely fits what is known about how consumers go about making purchase decisions.

The key point is that no matter which model is chosen, the planner and management must agree on how consumers purchase or consider the purchase of the advertised product. Most advertising people subscribe, even if unknowingly, to one of the three hierarchies when developing an advertising campaign. Assumptions about which model is being used must be stated up front; they clearly identify and suggest how the advertising objectives have been set and how evaluation of the campaign should be conducted.

In summary, whatever measurement approach is used and however the measurement is conducted, the advertising campaign planner must establish clear, concise, measurable advertising objectives at the beginning of the advertising campaign. The following example of an objective offered by Colley provides a guideline for almost any type of advertising objective:

> To increase among thirty million homemakers who own automatic washers the number who identify Brand X as a low-sudsing detergent and who are persuaded that it gets clothes cleaner—from 10 percent to 40 percent in one year.[11]

If advertising objectives are stated in this way, they can be measured and the results can be evaluated. It's as simple as that.

Some Practical Examples

Several alternative ways in which advertising objectives may be stated have been shown. The best illustrations, however, are practical examples. The statement of advertising objectives in Exhibit 7–6 is taken from a student advertising plans book for a "real-world" client. Note how specifically the advertising objectives are stated, for example, to achieve 70 percent awareness of the product in a very specific target market. Notice also how the advertising campaign objectives are separate from the marketing objectives in Numbers 4 and 5. These final objectives deal specifically with behavior, and because there are intervening variables, such as marketing and promotional programs, they are separated from the advertising objectives that deal only with communication effects.

Advertising objectives can also be much more complex than those illustrated in Exhibit 7–6. For example, the statement of advertising objectives in Exhibit 7–7 illustrates a different set of objectives for an advertising campaign. This plan involved a national overlay program plus a heavy-up campaign in fifty-five additional high-potential markets. As is shown, separate advertising objectives were developed for each portion of the campaign based on the differing levels of media weight and market conditions.

---

[11]Colley, *Defining Advertising Goals:* 7.

Exhibit 7–6   Advertising Objectives—A Student Plan

1. To create awareness of Brand X among 70 percent of our target market (primarily women in the top 100 markets, ages 18 to 49, with one or more children under age 18, and having annual household incomes of approximately $15,000 plus) by the end of Year 1, the introductory year of our national campaign.

2. To have 70 percent aided recall among our target market of our advertising promise as stated in the creative strategy.

3. To have 65 percent of our target market report a preference for Brand X over other competitive brands.

Through a combination of advertising and marketing efforts:

4. To generate a 39 percent trial rate in our target market within the designated distribution areas by the end of the introductory year.

5. To achieve a 65 percent repurchase rate (an average of five purchases per year/six packages per purchase) in our target market by the end of the introductory year.

The awareness goal nationally, for example, was set at 30 percent while, in the heavy-up markets, the objective was 75 percent.

Again, the advertising objectives and marketing objectives have been separated. In these examples, advertising is evaluated in terms of communication effects. Marketing is evaluated according to trial, repurchase rate, and franchise obtained.

Advertising objectives, as illustrated by these examples, can be made measurable. For proper evaluation of the campaign results, they must be measurable. The use of very specific advertising objectives in the advertising plan greatly simplifies the advertising campaign planner's task. If the objectives are clear, complete, and measurable, the advertising campaign development program is made much easier.

SUMMARY

One of the keys to success is knowing what you want the advertising campaign to do. This goal can vary greatly for different organizations, but it must be stated clearly before the campaign itself is developed. The planner must first understand the corporation's overall objectives, and then its marketing objectives. Next comes a standard for measuring the outcomes. Is the advertising supposed to create greater awareness or greater liking, or is it supposed to increase trial of the product or market share? These are very different objectives and will influence the way in which the campaign is developed. But it is important to establish advertising objectives to lend in the development of the campaign elements, to provide a basis for approval, and to enable the campaign results to be measured.

For those not familiar with traditional package goods marketing plans, the following examples illustrates the various elements and how a plan is organized. This example may be helpful to the planner reviewing a marketing plan prior to developing the advertising campaign. (See Exhibit 7–8.)

Exhibit 7–7   Advertising Objectives—A National Program

	National overlay (percent)	Heavy-up markets (55) (percent)
Awareness	30	75
Correct image perception	20	60
Liking	15	50

(In addition to these three objectives, which can be linked directly to advertising, three behavior-related objectives of the total advertising, marketing, and promotion program were stated:)

Ultimate objectives of advertising, marketing, and promotion

	National overlay (percent)	Heavy-up markets (55) (percent)
Trial	10	40
Repurchase rate	50	50
Franchise	5	20

The national objectives are explained as follows:

1. Awareness. When asked to name all brands that come to mind, 30 percent of the target market will name Brand X.

2. Correct image perception. 20 percent of the target market will acquire the correct perception of the product image from Brand X's advertising messages. Image perception is measurable by checklists, semantic differentials, and projective techniques.

3. Liking. 15 percent of the target market will prefer Brand X to other brands in the product category. Liking can be measured by rank order of preference or by rating scales.

4. Trial. 10 percent of the target market will purchase one package of Brand X once during the first year. Trial can be measured by store audits or surveys as well as by coupon redemption.

5. Repurchase rate. 50 percent of those who try the product during the first year will purchase it again. This can be measured by diaries or tracking studies.

6. Franchise. The end results of trial and repurchase rates will constitute our market share or franchise.

Exhibit 7–8   Format for the Annual Marketing Plan

Brand Name 19__ Marketing Plan

Outline	Description
I. Current Year Performance	1–2 short paragraphs summarizing how the brand performed this year relative to sales, share and budget objectives; the reasons for significant variations from plan; the major events that occurred affecting the market, if any; etc.
II. Recommendation	2–3 sentences stating the brand's objectives in total shipping units and in sales value, the total expenditures to support the brand, and the share objective.
III. P & L Effect of the Recommendation	Summarize in a brief table the basic P & L differences between recent performance and the new fiscal year, showing the ratio of each figure to sales, as follows:

	Last year	Current year	New year
Volume			
(value)	$—	$—	$—
(units)	—	—	—
(% increase/decrease)		— %	— %
Share	— %	— %	— %
Cost of goods	$—(%)	$—(%)	$—(%)
Adv./prom.	$—(%)	$—(%)	$—(%)
Other costs	$—(%)	$—(%)	$—(%)
Pre-tax profit	$—(%)	$—(%)	$—(%)

IV. Background
1. Market
   - Size — 2–3 short paragraphs on the size of the market in units and/or volume, plus its growth rate. Competitive brands and share position versus the company brand should be shown. If the list of competitive brands is extensive, mention only the major brands.
   - Consumer — 1–2 short paragraphs describing the consumer profile (age, income, etc.) and indicating what the total consumption of this product category is by major geographic areas.
   - Pricing — A brief table, preferably without comment, showing competitive and company retail price structures, by unit size. If appropriate, cost per ounce/unit may also be shown.
   - Competitive spending — A table breaking out the previous year's competitive media and promotional expenditures by six-month periods, e.g., Jan.–June vs. July–Dec., plus competitive volume consumed during these two periods if available. Estimates of promotion costs should include only regional and national promotions, and not tests. This table should be arranged as follows:

	1st 6 months				2nd 6 months			
	Vol.	Med.	Prom.	Total	Vol.	Med.	Prom.	Total
Brand A	—	$—	$—	$—	—	$—	$—	$—
Brand B	—	$—	$—	$—	—	$—	$—	$—

SOURCE: F. Beaven Ennis, *Effective Marketing Management* (New York: Association of National Advertisers, 1973): 13–16.

Exhibit 7–8 Format for the Annual Marketing Plan

Outline	Description
	Following this table, brief comments may be made on any significant changes from the above pattern which may be taking place currently.
• Other	State any other facts or statistics about the market that would be helpful to management in reaching a decision on this proposal.
2. Brand	
• Product	1–2 sentences on the general makeup of the product's formula, points of uniqueness, a table on the sizes/variety it is sold in, and the profit margin by size.
• Manufacturing	A short paragraph on existing plant capacity, next year's capital investment requirements if known, and any production or purchasing problems encountered to date. This is an optional section and is primarily concerned with new products.
• Product research	A brief summary of the major pieces of research relating to the brand and its performance. Emphasis should be placed on actual research scores obtained rather than on editorial comments.
• Market research	This encompasses all other significant research studies performed on the brand, to include items such as the major scores obtained from the latest advertising research, test market shares, name and packaging research, etc., if appropriate.
• Other	State any other facts or statistics about the brand that would be helpful to management in reaching a decision on this proposal.
V. Opportunities and Problems	
1. Opportunities	In support of this recommendation, list the key areas of opportunity from which the brand expects to obtain its growth or sales objectives in the coming year.
2. Problems	Similarly, outline the major factors that might jeopardize the brand's ability to meet its objectives, explaining what steps have been taken to minimize these risks.
VI. Strategies	
1. Marketing	A concise, well-defined paragraph or two on the brand's basic objective and marketing strategy. The length of this section will vary according to individual brand needs, but should be limited to approximately a half page.
2. Spending	This section is optional and is primarily intended for brands with heavy advertising expenditures which may vary significantly according to sales areas or marketing opportunities.
3. Copy	This should consist of three brief statements: the first devoted to the primary copy objective, the second to the strategy to achieve this objective, and the third to the brand's TV/print pool or rotation policy. As a guide, this entire section should be about a half page in length.

(continued)

Exhibit 7–8 (Continued)

Outline	Description
4. Media	As with Copy, this section should consist of three elements. The first is a statement of objective and the second the strategy to achieve the objective. Every effort should be made to make these two statements as specific as possible, particularly in terms of coverage, frequency of commercial exposure, wave advertising, etc.

The third element of this section should be a table showing sales volume versus media expenditures by major sales areas, the current year compared to the new year, arranged as follows:

Area	Current year			New year		
	Vol.	Med.	Exp'd/unit	Vol.	Med.	Exp'd/unit
1	—	$—	$—/cs	—	$—	$—/cs
2	—	$—	$—/cs	—	$—	$—/cs
etc.						

Significant changes in expenditures per unit in any sales area, from one year to the next, should be explained briefly beneath this table. Depending upon the number of sales areas used, the entire Media Section should probably not exceed three-fourths of a page. Brands with little or short-term media should eliminate the above table entirely.

5. Promotion

Similarly, the three elements of this section should consist of a promotion objective, a well-defined strategy statement, and a table showing the differences in expenditure and deal-pack volume, by major sales areas, from one year to the next, as follows:

	Area 1	Area 2	Area 3	Etc.
Expend./unit				
Current year	$—	$—	$—	
New year	$—	$—	$—	
% Vol. in trade deals				
Current year	—%	—%	—%	
New year	—%	—%	—%	

As a guide, the Promotion Section should probably be no longer than one page.

VII. Tests/Research

This is a brief statement on what major tests and/or research the brand will conduct in the coming year, e.g., media or promotion tests, product tests, package research, etc. Simply give the nature, purpose, and cost of each activity. The entire section should not exceed a half page.

This concludes the written portion of the Annual Marketing Plan, to which the four recommended financial marketing exhibits should be attached.

Case Studies

America Helps

America Helps is a national fund-raising organization founded in 1971. Designed to provide funds to public service groups in the nation's small towns and rural areas (communities with populations under 10,000), America Helps allocated funds of between $1,000 and $10,000 to over 4,000 groups in nearly 450 communities last year. Donations to America Helps totaled $28 million in the same time period, a 6 percent increase over the previous year's level.

Areas that receive funds from America Helps are referred to as "America Helps Communities." Contributors can specify that their money go to a particular community or a particular organization; this was the case for roughly 35 percent of all donations each year. The organization's chief purpose is to ensure that service groups can spend the majority of their time in serving, not raising money. Among those receiving funding from America Helps are 4-H clubs; counseling groups, such as Alcoholics Anonymous; and a variety of other organizations. The community groups are required to undergo a rigorous financial and organizational audit to qualify for America Helps funds and are reassessed every nine months.

Juliana Coffman had recently joined the staff of America Helps as Director of National Advertising. This was a new position; America Helps had traditionally left any advertising to the local groups. Coffman had been brought in with the hope that a national advertising campaign could help redirect the organization in several areas.

Long-range corporate plans called for America Helps to be active in 600 communities, spread throughout the fifty states, within three years. To meet this goal, a regular increase in yearly donations was essential. Since its inception, donations to America Helps had increased from year to year at a rate of between 4 and 7 percent. Donations came from several sources, and last year had been a typical year in terms of breakdown by source.

Seventy-seven percent of the donations received last year had come from individuals. Ninety percent of these were from people who lived in or near an America Helps community. Corporations had donated 11 percent of the total. This percentage represented several large contributions from firms with plants in or near America Helps communities. The remaining 12 percent of donations came from miscellaneous sources, such as foundations, estates, and community fund raisers.

In response to difficult economic conditions, the board of directors of America Helps wanted to attract a broader donation base, including contributions from persons and businesses that have no direct ties to America Helps communities. The board reasoned that the types of organizations that received America Helps funds would earn the interest and support of many potential individual and corporate donors. Despite the considerable competition for charitable dollars from larger fund-raising organizations, America Helps felt their grassroots image could make an impact in larger areas. Coffman's job was to begin to tap that potential through advertising.

Because national advertising was a new concept at America Helps, Coffman felt it was vital to establish some clear-cut objectives that would be discussed with the board of directors before any advertising dollars were spent. She reasoned that having preestablished objectives would not only facilitate the development of the advertising campaign, but also provide positive proof of the campaign's success, proof that would be very important when she presented her budget for succeeding years.

After reviewing the history of America Helps (particularly last year's results) and the board's stated objectives, Coffman developed the following advertising objectives for her first-year campaign:

1. To create awareness of America Helps among 75 percent of the national population
2. To lay the groundwork for the expansion of America Helps to fifty new communities next year
3. To have 60 percent knowledge among the *Fortune* 500 companies of America Helps' methods and services
4. To increase overall giving by 11 percent
5. To increase corporate giving from 11 percent of total donations to 22 percent
6. To increase donations from persons outside of America Helps communities from 8.5 percent of the total to 14 percent

Questions

1. Is each objective measurable? What additional information, if any, might Coffman need to prove the success of her campaign based on these objectives?
2. Is each objective an *advertising* objective, a goal that can be achieved through advertising?
3. Based on the objectives, what type of plan might Coffman develop? Who would be the target audience? What media might she use?
4. Are Coffman's objectives in keeping with corporate strategy?
5. Are Coffman's objectives appropriate for the time frame of a first-year advertising campaign?
6. Refer to the section on "Factors Influencing the Establishment of Advertising Objectives" (pp. 217–219) of this chapter. Have all the factors been considered in Coffman's objectives?
7. Evaluate Coffman's objectives using the Lavidge and Steiner model.

Purr-fect Punch

Debbie Wilder and Audrey Curtis, product manager and advertising manager respectively at Allen Pet products, were meeting to develop advertising objectives for the second year of an Allen product, Purr-fect Punch. Purr-fect Punch was a nondairy, milk-flavored, vitamin-enriched beverage for cats. The product was sold in shelf-stable (no refrigeration needed), 18-ounce boxes with a built-in pour spout. The product required refrigeration after it was opened.

Allen had introduced Purr-fect Punch to the Cincinnati market six months earlier. Initially, they had had problems getting distribution for the product, but after four months, the major grocery chain in the market had agreed to give them shelf space. Purr-fect Punch was now in 80 percent of Cincinnati's grocery stores.

The cat food and cat treat categories were interesting areas. Cat ownership in the U.S. was up, having passed dog ownership a few years ago. Demographic trends were believed to be largely responsible—as more and more people moved to urban areas and lived in smaller households and smaller dwellings (particularly apartments), the benefits of cat ownership became more obvious. Unlike dogs, cats could live comfortably in a fairly small space. They did not require as much attention as dogs, and could be left alone overnight more easily. People who wanted the companionship of a pet but felt their schedule was too busy to accommodate the demands of a dog were likely to adopt a cat instead.

Cat foods came in a variety of forms. Canned cat foods were available in a range of flavors, prices, and sizes, from expensive "gourmet" products to store brands. Semimoist cat foods, which were chewy-textured flavored shapes, were also available, as were dry cat foods. In consumer research studies, cat owners often reported that their pets were very finicky. A cat might eat one flavor of food exclusively for several weeks and then suddenly refuse to touch it. Or, a cat might refuse to eat the same flavor two days in a row. Some cats would only eat canned food, while others would only eat dry. Most cat owners said they usually kept a small inventory of cat food on hand in hopes of always having something handy that the cat would eat at any particular time. They also admitted to buying "human" canned fish or other delicacies for their cats from time to time. Growth in the cat food category had kept pace with increases in cat ownership.

The cat treat category grew more quickly. These products included highly flavored semimoist products, catnip-flavored products, and the newcomer, Purr-fect Punch. Cat owners used treats to reward their pets for good behavior, and to ease their own consciences after leaving their pet alone for a day or two. Many cat owners who purchased cat treats were convinced that their pet really enjoyed the products, looked forward to receiving them, and could recognize the package.

Cat food and cat treats were shelved together in supermarkets, along with cat litter products. They were usually located either next to or across the aisle from dog foods and dog treats (the dog treat category had many more products than did the cat treat category).

Allen had invested heavily in the shelf-stable packaging for Purr-fect Punch so that the product could be shelved next to other cat treats rather than in the refrigerated "human" beverage section. The front of the Purr-fect Punch package had a picture of a cat with Purr-fect Punch droplets on its whiskers. The cat was licking its face, apparently trying to get at the droplets. The Purr-fect Punch name was in large red type and a subheading reading "Milk-flavored drink cats love" appeared beneath the picture of the cat. The package back explained Purr-fect Punch's vitamin content and health benefits for cats.

As mentioned, Purr-fect Punch had been in widespread distribution in Cincinnati for two months. One of the stores that had accepted the product early on had recently sold Allen its scanner records for the product. In the four-month period covered by the data, Purr-fect Punch had gained a 30 percent share of the cat treat market in that store. All purchasers had bought one package at a time; 15 percent had used a 20-cent discount coupon Allen had distributed through the Cincinnati newspapers. The store manager reported that no one had complained about or returned the product, and he believed that some of the buyers were repeat purchasers.

In response to the apparent success of Purr-fect Punch, the leading manufacturer of catnip-flavored treats had launched an aggressive sales promotion to encourage consumer stockpiling (a buy-two-get-one-free offer). That promotion had only been running for two weeks, but did not appear to have affected Purr-fect Punch sales yet.

Several other cat treat manufacturers had also stepped up their advertising efforts in Cincinnati by running newspaper advertisements and offering co-op advertising dollars to the supermarkets. In fact, Allen believed that the increased competitive activity had been a key factor in the initial difficulty in gaining distribution for Purr-fect Punch. But, now that the product was selling well (and bringing in above-category-average margins for the retailer), the company doubted they would lose any distribution.

Allen's advertising effort in the Cincinnati market included television spots shown during early and late newscasts. The spots showed people treating their cats to Purr-fect Punch, with each person serving the product in a cup chosen to match the cat's personality. For example, a Persian cat was shown drinking Purr-fect Punch from a crystal goblet, while a scruffy tomcat was shown drinking from a beat-up plastic bowl. Although the cat and container changed, the cat's obvious enjoyment of Purr-fect Punch remained constant.

As mentioned earlier, Allen had also distributed a coupon through a newspaper advertisement. In addition, some local-edition magazine advertising was scheduled to break in a month. The magazine ads would not carry a coupon. Each ad would feature three of the cats from the television spots, each with their different cup, drinking Purr-fect Punch. All advertisements featured a clear product shot and instructed consumers to look for the product "beside your regular cat food."

Because of the product's success in Cincinnati, Allen was planning to go into national distribution during the following year. Wilder and Curtis had to develop advertising objectives for the national campaign. They had studied Purr-fect Punch's performance in Cincinnati, as well as the results of various consumer research studies with cat owners. (No specific research had been conducted for Purr-fect Punch, other than taste tests with cats. However, Allen had a library of research studies conducted for its other cat food products as well as general studies of pet owners.)

Questions

1. Which of the three hierarchies discussed in this chapter (learning, dissonance-attribution, and low involvement) do you feel is most applicable to the Purr-fect Punch purchasing decision? Why?
2. What are the implications of your answer to the first question in terms of setting objectives for Purr-fect Punch?
3. Would you set advertising objectives for Purr-fect Punch in terms of sales, behavior, or communications goals? Why?
4. Discuss the role any two of the influences described on pages 217–219 would likely play in setting objectives for this product.
5. Which step or steps in the Lavidge and Steiner hierarchy would you suggest focusing on for Purr-fect Punch? Write an objective that deals with one of the levels you've chosen.

Determining the Advertising and Promotion Budget

Our initial focus in this chapter will be on the total communications budget. That focus is important because the advertising planner must understand what role advertising will play in the overall marketing, communication, and promotional plan that is being designed for the brand or company. From there, we move into advertising budgeting because that is our primary concern.

Setting advertising objectives and establishing an advertising budget are directly related. The objectives establish what the planner *wants* to do, and the budget limits what the planner *can* do. In actuality the two must be dealt with together rather than separately. We separate them here only for the organization of the text. The final step, of course, is *how* to meet objectives, which is where most advertising efforts are concentrated.

Although objectives and budgeting are inseparable—that is, each one influences the other—this chapter deals primarily with the *hows* and *whys* of budgeting.

WHAT MARKETING COMMUNICATIONS IS SUPPOSED TO DO

The amount of money an organization allocates to promotion and/or marketing communications is, in general, directly related to the expectations management has for these activities; in other words, how much management thinks promotion or marketing communications can impact the sales and profits of the business. Therefore, some companies in a given industry will have substantial promotional budgets, while others allocate almost nothing. The reason for the difference is simple. It is the belief in, or evidence for, what promotion, marketing communications, and, eventually, advertising, can do to achieve the overall goals of the organization that its managers have.

By spending money on promotional activities, including marketing communications, managers believe that they can better achieve, or be more likely to achieve, one or a combination of three basic goals: (a) maximize profits, (b) maximize sales, or (c) maximize market share. Sometimes, the company objective may be to achieve some combination of these three goals but, most often, one of the goals is uppermost in the minds of management. This is a key element for the advertising planner to understand. If the goal is profits, marketing communications is often considered to be a minor element in the plan. If the goal, however, is sales or market share, communications may play a much more important role in the overall brand or company plan.

THE CONCEPT OF MARGINAL ECONOMIC RETURNS

The evaluation of marketing communications as an activity that can help achieve profits, sales, or market share goals is often based on the concept of a marginal return on investment. The idea of marginal investment is simple. The organization will continue to invest in any business activity as long as the return on the investment is greater than the cost. As this relates to advertising, the company will continue to invest in advertising as long as the return on the advertising investment is greater or the same as the cost of the advertising. For example, the company would spend an additional dollar on advertising as long as it got back at least a dollar in return.

Although the concept is simple, the allocation and evaluation process is quite difficult. First, in the case of a marketing communications budget, the allocations are made to several activities, such as advertising, sales promotion, and public relations. Therefore, just allocating additional funds to marketing communications is not the answer. The question is, To what marketing communications activity should the funds be allocated? Assuming that the various available promotional activities do not provide the same return, either a decision has to be made as to which activity should be funded and which should not, or some method of allocation must be found. This, in itself, is a difficult task.

A second question is, What is the return and how do we measure it? Sales promotion and direct marketing, in general, are considered to be much easier to measure in terms of their relatable return than is advertising and/or public relations. Often, in sales promotion and direct marketing, it is easier to tie the activity more directly to the sales or profit impact. With advertising and public relations, we are often dealing with the delivery of sales messages; it becomes more difficult to judge impact. It is often very hard to say which message actually resulted in a sale or a behavioural change. When we consider the lagged effects (see Chapter 2), such as are commonly found in advertising and public relations, the evaluation and, therefore, the budgeting process becomes even more difficult. As a result, advertising and public relations planners often have advocated that their own communications activities should be measured on the basis of the number of message units distributed, not on the results the messages achieve. Although a case can be made for this approach, if the advertising planner hopes to compete with other marketing communications managers for finite funds, some sort of measurable result must be established to support the proposed advertising expenditures.

BUDGETING BASED ON ADVERTISING EFFECTS

In spite of the complexity of the problem, a marketing communications and, ultimately, an advertising budget must be set. One approach, based on the marginal return concept, was developed by Longman. His concept of relating advertising to sales is illustrated in Exhibit 8–1.[1]

Exhibit 8–1   Sales Related to the Advertising Expenditure

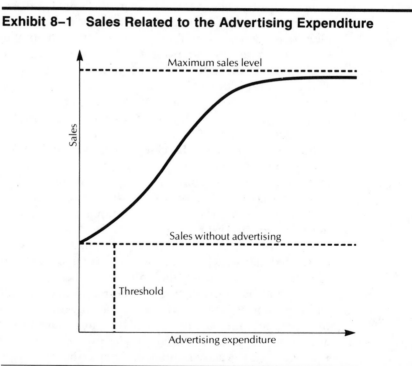

SOURCE: From Kenneth A. Longman, *Advertising,* 1971.

---

[1]Kenneth A. Longman, *Advertising* (New York: Harcourt Brace Jovanovich, 1971).

Longman contends that advertising for a brand or company can only be effective between two basic sales points, the threshold point and the maximum sales point. He suggests that a certain level of sales will be generated without any advertising at all. He calls that the "threshold" level. Further, there is a maximum point above which sales cannot rise. This limit may be due to plant capacity, market saturation, raw ingredient availability, or other factors. It is between these two points, the threshold and maximum sales level, that advertising can actually have some effect on sales response. In Longman's model, the key to successful advertising is to generate the greatest amount of sales dollars between these two points with the minimum advertising investment. This maximum sales point can be measured through marginal analysis, in other words, the point at which sales reach the maximum and advertising is most efficient. Although the actual calculation of marginal utility is somewhat out of the scope of the average advertising planner, this idea of a maximum and minimum attainable sales level and the understanding of where advertising investments operate is a key concept in developing and determining an advertising budget. The general idea is to spend the least amount of money and achieve the greatest amount of additional sales dollars. Sometimes, in the advertising planning process, when planners start to think about various advertising alternatives and options, that basic idea gets lost.

WHAT ADVERTISING CAN DO

In spite of all these budgeting, analysis, and relationship problems, there are some specific things that good advertising can accomplish. Assuming that the other parts of the marketing mix are correct (sometimes a big assumption by advertising planners), that is, that the product is correct and acceptable, the distribution is adequate, the pricing is competitive, and so on, advertising can effectively accomplish some very important tasks for a brand or company. Ray has identified eight functions that advertising can perform:

1. For new products, advertising may help consumers consider a trial.
2. For established products, advertising can assist consumers in considering new or increased usage of the brand.
3. When a brand has been on the market for some time, advertising can help remind people of their reason for preferring the brand; it helps maintain brand purchasing or loyalty.
4. Advertising can help confirm the reputation of the brand already established by showing high quality, high price, examples of people who use the brand, and so on.
5. Advertising can also be effective in helping consumers change their thinking about a brand or product. For example, advertising can be used to add attributes to the brand that may have been overlooked,

or can encourage people to reevaluate the importance of the product's attributes in terms of a particular need, and so on.

6. For marketers with a family branding approach, advertising can help build acceptance for the brand family; this acceptance may lower the requirements for advertising support for each individual product in the group.

7. Where personal selling is necessary to close the sale, as in the case of many business-to-business or consumer durable products, advertising can pave the way for a personal sales call or presentation by a salesperson.

8. For some service establishments, such as restaurants, banks, or the like, advertising can give the consumer a "feeling" for what it is like to be in such a facility.[2]

These are some of the functions advertising might serve as steps to an actual measurable sales effect. If the planner clearly identifies what he or she is trying to achieve, advertising can be just as measurable as any other marketing communications technique. The keys are to set the objectives in advance; implement the plan; and measure the results. With supportable evidence of past advertising success, the advertising budgeting process is greatly simplified.

WHERE MARKETING AND ADVERTISING DOLLARS COME FROM

One of the major complaints of some advertisers is that advertising planners and advertising agencies sometimes recommend advertising programs that the brand or the company simply can't afford or whose cost, based on anticipated results, simply can't be justified.

This problem sometimes comes about because the advertising planner or the agency people simply don't understand the economics of the brand or the company. They just don't know where a brand or company's marketing and advertising dollars come from nor do they understand how contribution margins and, therefore, profits are generated.

A brief review of the economics of a typical package-goods brand might help in the understanding of how to develop an advertising budget. Table 8–1 is a hypothetical "combined operating statement" for a typical consumer product. (Note that the letters at the left of each of the entries are used for descriptive purposes only.)

Assume you are the brand manager for Ferd's Food Company. Your primary brand responsibility is canned marinated eggrolls. The eggrolls are

[2]Michael L. Ray, *Advertising and Communication Management* (Englewood Cliffs, N.J.: Prentice-Hall, 1982): 151–52.

Table 8-1 Hypothetical Operating Statement for a Nondurable Consumer Product

A.	Retail price 69¢ per can/12 per case		$8.28	
B.	Anticipated retailer's margin @ 20%		1.66	
C.	Gross price to retailer		6.62	
D.	Less trade promotions/deals @ 2%		.13	
E.	Net price to retailer		6.49	
F.	Wholesale/broker commission @ 7%		.45	
G.	Net sales price		6.04	(100%)
H.	Cost of goods		3.32	(55%)
J.	Fixed costs, 20%	$ .66		
K.	Variable costs, 80%	2.66		
L.	Gross margin		2.72	(45%)
M.	Distribution expense		.12	(2%)
N.	Contribution margin		2.60	(43%)
P.	Direct expenses			
Q.	Advertising	.16		(6%)
R.	Consumer sales promotion	.24		(4%)
S.	Management and sales expense	.92		(15%)
T.	Research and development	.06		(1%)
U.	Total direct expenses		1.58	(26%)
V.	Product margin		1.02	(17%)

packaged in 14-ounce cans containing approximately seventeen eggrolls and are shipped twelve cans to the case. The normal retail price (out-of-store) is 69¢ per can.

Line A illustrates the retail price of a case of twelve cans of eggrolls at 69¢ each. From the retail price of 69¢, the retailer usually obtains a gross margin of 20 percent. Thus, on a per-case basis, the retailer's gross profit is $1.66 (Line B). Ferd's Food's gross price to the retailer on the case of eggrolls is $6.62 (Line C).

From the gross trade price, a deduction for trade promotions or deals often must be made (Line D). In this case, Ferd's Food plans to offer trade promotions amounting to 2 percent of gross sales to the retailer. The discount will be offered on all purchases made during the year if the retailer will run a reduced-price feature on eggrolls during the Chinese New Year promotion. The cost of the trade promotion is deducted from the gross price to retailer to give a net price to retailer (Line E). Thus, the net price (per case) to the retailer is $6.49.

Ferd's eggrolls are not sold directly to the retailer but through a broker or wholesaler system. The broker's commission, therefore, must be deducted. The average commission to the broker (or the margin required by a wholesaler) is 7 percent of the gross price (Line F), in this case, 45¢. This amount is deducted from the net price to retailer, leaving a net sales price for the eggrolls of $6.04 per case (Line G). This is the amount that Ferd's Food Company will receive for the sale of each case of marinated eggrolls.

The cost of manufacturing and packaging the eggrolls must be deducted from the net sales price. The total cost-of-goods, as determined by the production and accounting departments, amounts to $3.32 per case, or 55 percent of the net sales price. The fixed costs (Line J), the eggrolls' share of the company's general overhead, is calculated at 20 percent of the cost-of-goods, or 66¢ per case. The variable costs (Line K) are calculated at 80 percent of the cost-of-goods of the product, or $2.66 per case. The variable costs include such items as raw materials, manufacturing cost, filling and packaging the eggrolls, and storage and handling until the products are put into the distribution system. Thus, deducting cost-of-goods (Line H) from the net sales price yields the gross margin on the product (Line L). The gross margin is the amount available for transportation and marketing expense plus any profit to Ferd's Food Company on the sale of each case of eggrolls.

From the gross margin available (Line L) of $2.72 per case, distribution expense must be deducted (Line M). This is the actual cost of physically moving the product from the manufacturing plant to the wholesale warehouse or retail store. Here the distribution expense is estimated to be 2 percent of net sales, or 12¢ per case. Subtracting the distribution expense from the gross margin leaves a contribution margin of $2.60 per case (Line N). If there were no selling or other expenses, this contribution margin would be the amount each case of eggrolls could contribute to the profit of the company. Realistically, however, there are promotional expenses, which are referred to as direct expenses (Lines P and U).

Direct expenses include all promotional costs, such as advertising (Line Q), consumer sales promotion (Line R), management and sales expense (Line S), and an allocation for research and development of new or improved eggrolls (Line T). These costs are combined as total direct expenses (Line U).

Although the final profit on each case of eggrolls is shown as product margin (Line V) and appears to be what is left after all costs and expenses have been deducted, the format is somewhat misleading. Usually, management of Ferd's Food Company, after reviewing sales and expense forecasts for all company products and brands for the coming year, assigns a profit margin percentage (or a total dollar figure) to the eggroll brand manager as a goal for the coming year. This goal is determined on the basis of projecting an adequate return on the company's investment in the eggroll brand and as a proper contribution to the overall financial income and profit of the company. Thus, in actuality, using the profit goals established by the management for the brand, the funds available for marketing—including advertising, promotion, sales, and research and development—is the difference between the contribution margin (Line N) and the product margin (Line V) or, in this case, $1.02 per case of eggrolls sold. It is from this total direct expense amount (Line U) that the brand manager must make the allocation for an advertising campaign.

There are, of course, circumstances that might help to increase or decrease the funds available for total direct expense (Line U). For example, a price increase with no cost increase would provide a greater margin. Or, as manufacturing economies of scale are realized, a factor such as increased sales might reduce the variable cost of the product (Line K). The possibility exists of reducing or completely deleting all trade promotions/ deals (Line D). If sales could be concentrated closer to the manufacturing plant, distribution expenses (Line M) might be lowered. A change in any of these costs will directly affect the number of dollars available to the product manager for total direct expenses (Line U). For purposes of this illustration, however, the assumption is made that the sales forecast is fairly firm, the trade promotions and deals are already established, and distribution expenses will not vary. It is within this framework that the brand manager and the advertising agency must determine how best to allocate the available marketing funds, which include the funds for the advertising campaign.

In most instances, management and sales expense (Line S) and research and development costs (Line T) are most difficult to manipulate. For example, management and sales expenses (Line S) commonly consist of the salaries and expenses of the sales force who call on the trade. In a multi-product company, these expenses are usually allocated to individual brands on the basis of total sales volume, or brand managers determine how much of the sales force's time they would like devoted to the brand. The cost to the brand is then determined as a percentage of overall sales costs. In addition, the salaries of the product manager, any assistants, and the clerical staff are included in this figure. Therefore, reduction of management and sales expenses is a difficult task, although some options are available.

The same is true of research and development costs (Line T). In this instance, because Ferd's Food Company manufactures many products, a general research and development program for the entire company is operated under an R&D unit. Because this group works on behalf of all brands, costs of their efforts are allocated on an equalized basis. The eggroll brand pays a prorated share of all costs of research and development with the understanding that the group is working on behalf of the eggroll brand a proportionate share of the time. R&D expenses charged to the eggroll brand often are allocated by top management and are difficult to reduce.

From a study of this example, it quickly becomes evident that the actual funds available for an advertising campaign are greatly constrained. The funds available are the result of sales and expense forecasts made by brand or top management. Any increase in funds available for advertising must be a direct result of increased sales or reduced costs. That's a key point to remember when budgeting for any brand.

WHAT GOES IN THE ADVERTISING BUDGET

Having looked at the conceptual structure of how advertising budgets are established and where and how advertising funds are generated, we now look at the actual advertising budgeting process. One of the first questions most planners ask is, What exactly goes into the advertising budget? In many cases, this is a knotty question, indeed.

Although planners like to keep the advertising budget clean and involved strictly with the campaign, often it isn't possible. If by company policy or tradition, for example, the annual distributor's picnic and outing is considered an advertising expenditure and is included in the advertising budget, then the expense reduces the amount available for the actual campaign.

In general, the campaign planner has little control over what is charged against the advertising budget. This decision is usually made by management and/or the brand manager, often based on history or tradition. But, no matter who decides what goes in, the planner must keep any noncampaign charges in mind when establishing the overall brand advertising campaign budget. Although uncampaign charges may not be as great a problem as they once were, the planner may sometimes find some rather unusual items and expenses charged against advertising simply because the company has always done it that way or has no other place to put the charges. When this is the case, these costs must simply be included in the budget and acknowledged as one of the campaign planning problems. These costs or charges, however, should not be included when an evaluation of the campaign results is made (see Chapter 15).

Over the years, several attempts have been made to try and identify the costs that legitimately should be charged against an advertising program. Although company policy and tradition may contradict some of these rules of thumb, they do provide the advertising planner with an outline of the common wisdom in the industry.

Patti and Frazer have compared three studies in which major advertisers were requested to classify items as a *white* charge (definitely should be in the advertising budget), a *gray* charge (uncertain as to whether or not it should be in the advertising budget), or a *black* charge (definitely should not be in the advertising budget). The studies compared are a 1960 study by *Printer's Ink* magazine, an update of that study done by Patti and Blasko in 1981, and a study among business-to-business advertisers done by Patti and Blasko in 1984. The results are illustrated in Exhibit 8–2.[3]

---

[3]Charles H. Patti and Charles F. Frazer, *Advertising: A Decision-Making Approach* (New York: Dryden Press, 1988): 260–61.

Exhibit 8–2 Charges to the Advertising Budget: Three Studies*

Expense	Printer's Ink (1960)	100 LCA (1981)	100 LIA (1984)
Media costs (time, space)	White	White	White
Local cooperative advertising	White	White	White
Consumer research	White	Black	White
Institutional advertising	White	White	White
Advertising in Yellow Pages	Black	White	White
Advertising department travel and entertainment	White	Black	White
Advertising department salaries	White	Black	Black
Catalogs for sales staff	Black	Black	White
Advertising aids for sales staff	Black	Black	White
Test-marketing programs	Black	Grey	Black
Point-of-purchase materials	Black	Grey	Black
Sample requests by advertisers	Black	Grey	Black
Dealer-help literature	Black	Grey	Black
Direct mail to dealers	Black	Grey	Black
Contributions to industry advertising funds	Black	Grey	Black
Cost of merchandise for tie-in promotions	Grey	Grey	Black
Employee fringe benefits	Black	Grey	Grey
Coupon redemption costs	Grey	Grey	Grey
Package design and artwork	Grey	Grey	Grey
House-to-house sample distribution	Grey	Grey	Grey
Testing new labels and packages	Grey	Grey	Grey
Public relations consultants	Grey	Grey	Grey

SOURCE: Charles H. Patti and Charles F. Frazer, *Advertising: A Decision-Making Approach:* 261.

White charge refers to those items properly charged to the advertising budget; *Black charge* refers to items that are properly charged to an account other than the advertising budget; *Grey charge* refers to items that do not have a clearcut line in any one budget.

From this list, the advertising planner can get a general idea of what should and shouldn't be included in an advertising budget.

OTHER FACTORS THAT INFLUENCE THE ADVERTISING BUDGET

Up to this point, we have assumed for purposes of advertising budgeting that all products are alike, all companies alike, and all brands alike, which, of course, is not the case. Although the same basic, general principles might be used to consider and tentatively set an advertising budget, each budget is actually a very individual and personal project for that brand and company and that category alone. We will now consider some of the factors that influence the budget for an individual brand or company.

New or Existing Product

Whether the product is just being introduced or has been on the market for several years usually has a great effect on the budget required. (Recall the discussion of the product life cycle from Chapter 3.) Often, established products require only maintenance advertising schedules. These schedules can be much less expensive than a campaign designed to introduce the brand and initiate first-time trial. The difference between planning and budgeting for an existing and new product is described in detail elsewhere in this chapter.

Push or Pull Strategy

Most basic marketing strategies can be broadly classified as either a "push" or a "pull." A *push* strategy means that the major emphasis is on moving the product onto the retailer's shelves or into the distributor's warehouse. It is then the responsibility of the retailer or distributor to generate consumer interest and demand. With a *pull* strategy the marketing emphasis is placed on the ultimate consumer. The assumption here is that if sufficient consumer demand can be generated, the product can be "pulled" through the distribution system. Although, in truth, most companies use marketing and promotional strategies that are a combination of "push" and "pull," the need for and use of advertising is dramatically different in each. In general, a push strategy requires more sales promotion and personal selling than advertising. A pull strategy relies heavily on building consumer demand through the use of advertising and public relations. As a result, the decision as to whether to use a push or a pull strategy has a great deal to do with the level of advertising needed for the company or brand.

Exhibit 8–3   Distribution Channels and Their Implications for Advertising Expenditures

Used by direct-response marketers for a wide variety of goods. Most common channel for business-to-business goods (raw materials, component parts, and capital equipment, for example). Advertising has one audience — the ultimate buyer or user.

Used by manufacturers of autos, clothing, furniture. Advertising has two audiences — the ultimate buyer (to stimulate demand) and the retailer (to encourage stocking of merchandise).

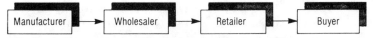

Used by manufacturers of consumer convenience goods (groceries, drugs and cosmetics, toys, etc.) and some business-to-business manufacturers (office equipment and supplies). Advertising has three audiences — wholesalers and retailers (to encourage inventory stocking) and the ultimate buyer (to stimulate demand).

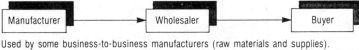

Used by some business-to-business manufacturers (raw materials and supplies). Advertising has two audiences — wholesalers (to maintain and/or expand distribution) and buyers (to encourage product usage and brand preference).

SOURCE: Patti and Frazer, *Advertising: A Decision-Making Approach*: 267.

Exhibit 8–3 illustrates the differences in various types of advertising strategies and their impact on the various audiences.

Complexity of the Product/Product Benefit

The complexity of the product or the product benefit has much to do with the amount of advertising needed and, therefore, the required advertising budget. If the product is simply an alternative brand in a known category, the required advertising investment might be nominal. If, however, the product and the category require a great deal of explanation or require consumers to make a major change in their usage habits, the advertising requirement may be substantial. For example, banks and financial institutions, prior to deregulation, traditionally invested very little in advertising. The financial instruments that they sold and the services that they provided were all about the same and had been available for years. With deregulation, major changes occurred in how banks and financial institutions did business and the products they offered. The marketplace, products, and usage became much more complex and competitive. Today, banks and financial institutions are one of the major advertising categories and their investment in advertising has grown tremendously.

Advertising Response Functions

Closely allied to the question of product and benefit complexity is the way in which the advertising planner believes consumers respond to advertising, in other words, the shape of the advertising response function. For most products, the assumption is that advertising works or consumers respond to advertising as a result of several exposures to the message. The typical response curve or function is thought to be an S-curve, as shown in Exhibit 8–4A. This concept is based on the so-called learning curve, the basis of which is that consumers must see the advertising a number of times before it becomes effective. Advertising response builds over time in much the same way that we ''learn'' to swim or drive a car or ice skate, that is, with practice. For some products, however, the advertising may well get a response on the first exposure. The curve would be similar to that shown in Exhibit 8–4B.

This convex curve suggests that the first exposure to the advertising is the most important. Additional exposures have some impact, but at a constantly decreasing rate. In other words, the first exposure is the most important and all others do very little to move the consumer to action.

The advertising planner's belief about the shape of the advertising response function for the particular product or service has much to do with how the advertising is planned and implemented. It is of critical importance in the development of the media schedule. (More will be said about this in Chapter 12.)

Competition, Clutter, and Media Inflation

The strength and number of competitors have much to do with the amount of advertising money needed to achieve some advertising objectives. For example, if there are a large number of competitors and they are all advertising extensively, then simply having a brand message heard may require a heavier than normal advertising investment. A very competitive marketplace is usually a costly advertising arena.

Exhibit 8–4   Advertising Response Curves

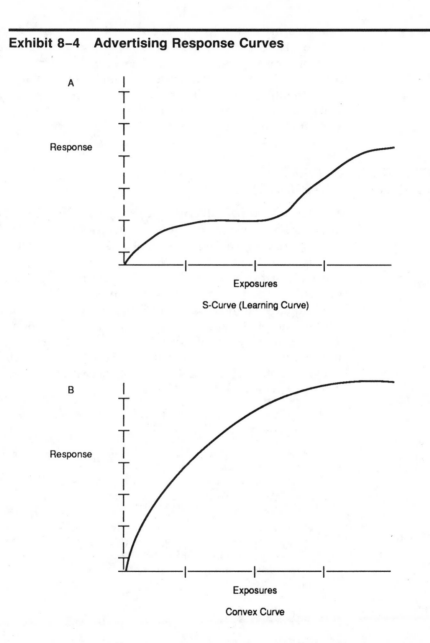

S-Curve (Learning Curve)

Convex Curve

Because there are limited media advertising opportunities for all advertisers, there is much "clutter" in the media. *Clutter* simply means there are many advertising messages directed to an audience. Although all of these messages may not be directly competitive to the brand, they are certainly competitive in terms of attention by the prospective audience.

Another factor is media inflation. For the past thirty or so years, the cost of media has continually increased. So, each year, the advertiser buys fewer and fewer exposures and impressions for the same amount of money. This trend is expected to continue at least in the foreseeable future.

Competition, clutter, and media inflation are not likely to subside. They will probably only become more of a problem for the advertising planner. Therefore, understanding the marketplace in terms of these three important factors is a must in terms of advertising budgeting.

STEPS IN PLANNING AND IMPLEMENTING AN ADVERTISING BUDGET

As with most other advertising campaign development areas, the establishment and implementation of an advertising budget is best done with a carefully developed, step-by-step plan. Simon Broadbent suggests the following approach[4]:

Conceptually, we might think of advertising budgeting as depending on three factors that the marketer can manipulate—the price of the product, the amount spent on advertising (adspend in the illustration), and promotion spend (or the amount invested in sales promotion). We might also add the expenditures for direct marketing, public relations, and so on, but to simplify, we deal with only these three. The end result of these factors is the contribution margin that the product provides. (See Exhibit 8–5.) Broadbent continues:

> Thus decisions on adspend are made, while at the same time considering these questions.
>
> - How do I expect advertising to affect volume short term?
> - How does adspend affect price?
> - How does adspend affect (sales) promotions:
>   –As a support?
>   –As an alternative?
> - What are the priorities in agreeing on both volume and contribution?
> - What are company long-term objectives in:
>   –The saleability of the brand?
>   –Volume and contribution?[5]

This approach is illustrated in Exhibit 8–6.

[4]Simon Broadbent, *The Advertiser's Handbook for Budget Determination* (Lexington, Mass.: Lexington Books, 1988: 51.
[5]Simon Broadbent, *The Advertiser's Handbook:* 52.

Exhibit 8–5   Advertising Budgeting Factors

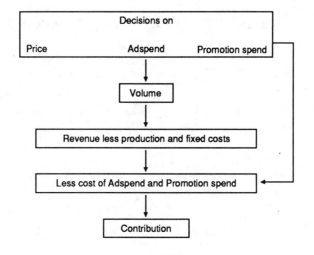

Exhibit 8–6   Adspend Decision Sequence

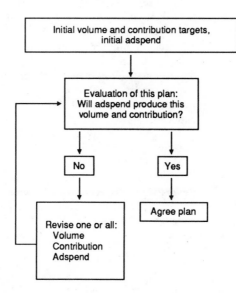

Broadbent summarizes his approach with the process chart shown in Exhibit 8–7.[6]

Exhibit 8–7   The Advertising Budgeting Process

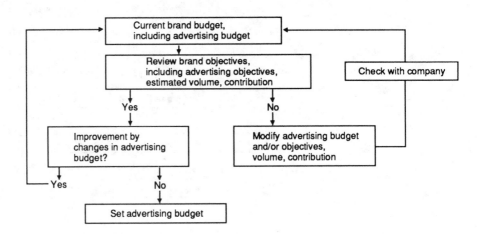

Broadbent's steps include:

1. Review
   - Long-term and immediate brand objectives, especially advertising objectives
   - Current, draft, and recent actual brand budgets
   - Category, major competitors, and brand marketing history and forecast
   - Evidence of advertising effects in the long and short terms and on consumers and trade
2. Review and use several methods to estimate the working media spend, especially
   - Objective and task
   - Brand history
   - Modeling (if available)

   Estimate and add nonworking media spend to obtain the first range of advertising budgets. Estimate what the media spend will buy.
3. Check whether brand objectives and budget constraints are met.[7]

[6]Simon Broadbent, *The Advertiser's Handbook:* 76.
[7]Simon Broadbent, *The Advertiser's Handbook:* 76

With these concepts in mind, we now turn to the actual step-by-step development of an advertising budget.

Because there are as many ways to plan an advertising budget as there are planners, a well-conceived, step-by-step process is usually the best. Often the budgeting procedure for each brand is time and situation specific. However, the planning sequence developed by David L. Hurwood and James K. Brown works for most products or services in most situations. It should work as well for you whether you're an experienced planner or a novice. (See Exhibit 8–8.)[8]

Finally, with any proposed advertising budget recommendation, the advertising planner should end the planning process by reviewing the following five questions suggested by Rossiter and Percy:

1. What is the current level of advertising expenditure (established brand)? Or the most likely level of advertising expenditure (new brand)?
2. What would sales be if advertising expenditures were zero?
3. What would maximum sales be if you could spend as much as you wished on advertising and what would this expenditure have to be?
4. What would sales be if the current (or most likely) level of advertising were halved?
5. What would sales be if the current (or most likely) level of advertising were increased by half as much again?[9]

If the planner will test his or her proposed advertising budget against these five questions, it will quickly put the entire process, particularly those questions about relatively small amounts of money, in much better perspective. Also, it will cause the planner to think more carefully about advertising and its likely impact on the overall goals of the brand or company.

METHODS OF ADVERTISING BUDGETING

With background on the nature of advertising budgets, and the considerations that influence the budget and the planning sequence, the next step is to review the major methods by which advertising budgets are established. In all, Broadbent has identified twelve typical budgeting methods. Each of them is reviewed briefly as follows[10]:

Advertising to Sales (A/S or Percentage of Sales)

The sales revenue for the coming budget period is estimated. Either the past or current sales year may be used. From this, a fixed proportion is al-

---

[8]David L. Hurwood and James K. Brown, *Some Guidelines for Advertising Budgeting* (New York: Conference Board, 1972): 22–23.

[9]John R. Rossiter and Larry Percy, *Advertising and Promotion Management*: 73.

[10]Simon Broadbent, *The Advertiser's Handbook*: 78–118.

Exhibit 8–8   A Process for Planning and Evaluating the Advertising Budget

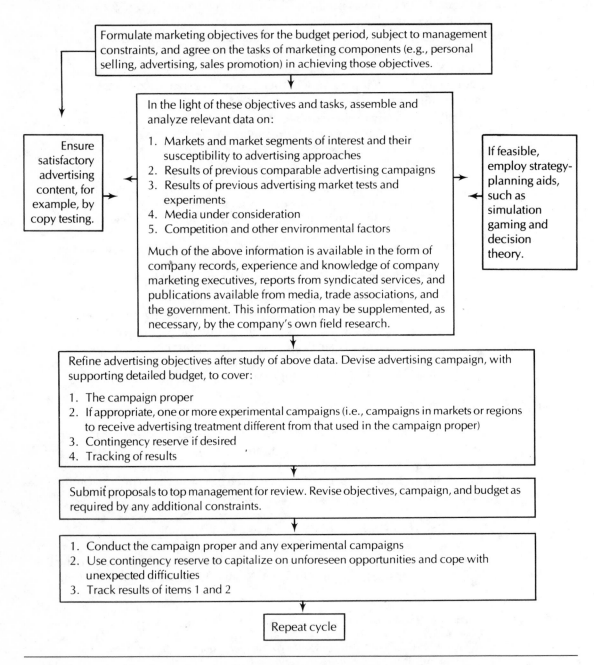

Formulate marketing objectives for the budget period, subject to management constraints, and agree on the tasks of marketing components (e.g., personal selling, advertising, sales promotion) in achieving those objectives.

In the light of these objectives and tasks, assemble and analyze relevant data on:

1. Markets and market segments of interest and their susceptibility to advertising approaches
2. Results of previous comparable advertising campaigns
3. Results of previous advertising market tests and experiments
4. Media under consideration
5. Competition and other environmental factors

Much of the above information is available in the form of company records, experience and knowledge of company marketing executives, reports from syndicated services, and publications available from media, trade associations, and the government. This information may be supplemented, as necessary, by the company's own field research.

Ensure satisfactory advertising content, for example, by copy testing.

If feasible, employ strategy-planning aids, such as simulation gaming and decision theory.

Refine advertising objectives after study of above data. Devise advertising campaign, with supporting detailed budget, to cover:

1. The campaign proper
2. If appropriate, one or more experimental campaigns (i.e., campaigns in markets or regions to receive advertising treatment different from that used in the campaign proper)
3. Contingency reserve if desired
4. Tracking of results

Submit proposals to top management for review. Revise objectives, campaign, and budget as required by any additional constraints.

1. Conduct the campaign proper and any experimental campaigns
2. Use contingency reserve to capitalize on unforeseen opportunities and cope with unexpected difficulties
3. Track results of items 1 and 2

Repeat cycle

SOURCE: Hurwood and Brown, *Some Guidelines for Advertising Budgeting:* 22–23.

located for advertising. For example: The average factory price of a case of goods is estimated to be $9.00. The sales forecast is that 900,000 cases will be sold. The advertising allocation ratio to sales is set at seven percent (or A/S = 7 percent). The advertising budget is, therefore, $9.000 × 0.07 × 900,000 or $567,000.

Although the percentage of sales method is quick, easy, and accepted by many firms, it has an inherent weakness. When sales are good, the advertising budget increases. When sales are bad, advertising is reduced. The basic principle at work is that advertising becomes a result of sales, which is contrary to the basic belief that advertising should generate sales.

Exhibit 8–9 illustrates examples of the top 100 U.S. advertisers using advertising as a percentage of sales for 1986 and 1987. As can be seen, the percentages used by various companies in various industry categories are subject to wide variations.

Advertising to Margin (A/M)

The gross margin for the brand or company is estimated for the next budget period. A fixed proportion of this margin is allocated for advertising. Sometimes, profit is used in place of margin, and, sometimes, the previous year is used as the base. For example, gross margin in the Ferd's Foods example in Table 8–1 is expected to be $2.72 per case. If we estimate that we will sell 5,000,000 cases of Ferd's eggrolls and that we are willing to spend 18 percent of our gross margin on advertising, the budget would be established at $2.72 × 0.18 × 5,000,000 or $2,448,000. Examples of the advertising investment as a percentage of gross margin for various industries is shown in Exhibit 8–10.

Per Case Allowance (Case Rate)

Unit volume is estimated for the coming year. This volume can be in any form of units; it need not be only in cases. (It is also possible to use either a past year or the current year.) A fixed sum per unit is allocated for advertising. For example, we are willing to invest one half of the entire contribution margin for each case of Ferd's eggrolls (Table 8–1) we plan to sell in the coming year. That amount is $1.30 (Line N = $2.60 divided by 2 or $1.30). We estimate 3,500,000 cases will be sold. Therefore, the advertising budget is $1.30 × 3,500,000 or $4,550,000.

Other Allowances

A fixed sum per unit may be allocated for advertising. The units can be almost anything—the number of households in an ADI, the number of retail

Exhibit 8-9   Advertisers by Primary Business

Top 100 advertisers by primary business

Primary business	Rank	Advertiser	U.S. ad spending 1987	U.S. ad spending 1986	U.S. sales 1987	U.S. sales 1986	Sales/$1 adv. 1987	Sales/$1 adv. 1986	1987 worldwide Sales	Earnings	Return on sales
AIRLINES	55	AMR Corp.	$152,609	$131,098	NA	NA	NA	NA	$7,197,974	$198,407	2.8
	80	Delta Air Lines	108,636	105,056	NA	NA	NA	NA	6,915,000	306,800	4.4
	68	Texas Air Corp.	124,343	132,576	NA	NA	NA	NA	8,474,967	(466,146)	(5.5)
	64	UAL Corp.	137,790	137,047	6,932,790	6,145,141	50.31	44.84	8,292,790	335,117	4.0
AUTOMOTIVE	88	BMW AG	99,456	61,740	NA	NA	NA	NA	10,502,400	202,388	1.9
	14	Chrysler Corp.	568,722	503,571	23,685,400	20,489,000	41.65	40.69	26,276,500	1,289,700	4.9
	84	Daimler-Benz AG	105,018	79,697	NA	NA	NA	NA	37,540,300	99,100	0.3
	9	Ford Motor Co.	639,510	650,875	55,302,000	50,034,000	86.48	76.87	71,643,000	4,625,000	6.5
	3	General Motors Corp.	1,024,852	838,912	86,421,900	91,343,100	84.33	108.88	101,781,900	3,550,900	3.5
	37	Honda Motor Co.	245,365	205,307	NA	NA	NA	NA	12,677,000	453,000	3.6
	52	Hyundai Group	164,336	93,673	NA	NA	NA	NA	3,500,000	75,000	2.1
	56	Mazda Motor Corp.	151,884	156,524	NA	NA	NA	NA	11,527,000	32,000	0.3
	47	Nissan Motor Co.	181,438	180,042	NA	NA	NA	NA	33,950,000	516,000	1.5
	76	Subaru of America	113,233	58,534	NA	NA	NA	NA	1,785,038	NA	NA
	33	Toyota Motor Corp.	257,738	259,761	3,213,000	4,943,000	19.21	28.03	50,000,000	1,779,000	3.6
	49	Volkswagen AG	167,257	176,353	NA	NA	NA	NA	23,867,000	273,000	1.1
CHEMICALS & PETROLEUM	34	American Cyanamid	250,376	229,181	2,618,000	2,536,000	10.46	11.07	4,166,000	276,000	6.6
	65	Dow Chemical Co.	135,689	138,931	5,946,000	5,165,000	43.82	37.18	13,377,000	1,240,000	9.3
	59	E.I. du Pont de Nemours & Co.	149,749	110,681	20,796,000	18,758,000	138.87	169.48	30,468,000	1,786,000	5.9
	50	Mobil Corp.	166,285	167,874	22,350,000	19,250,000	134.41	114.67	56,716,000	1,258,000	2.2
	99	Monsanto Co.	84,689	88,563	4,883,000	4,638,000	57.66	52.37	7,639,000	436,000	5.7
ELECTRONIC EQUIPMENT	7	Eastman Kodak Co.	658,221	610,192	8,040,000	7,398,000	12.21	12.12	13,305,000	1,178,000	8.9
	32	General Electric Co.	272,607	287,744	37,517,000	33,543,000	137.62	116.57	40,515,000	2,915,000	7.2
	39	International Business Machines	240,846	295,518	24,937,000	25,362,000	103.54	85.82	54,217,000	5,258,000	9.7
	82	Philips NV	107,226	83,842	5,690,600	6,439,000	53.07	76.08	25,229,400	390,000	1.5
	42	Tandy Corp.	225,052	219,673	NA	NA	NA	NA	3,793,800	316,400	8.3
ENTERTAINMENT & MEDIA	36	Walt Disney Co.	249,823	163,925	NA	NA	NA	NA	2,876,800	444,700	15.5
	93	MCA Inc.	91,366	104,521	2,072,809	1,925,830	22.69	18.43	2,589,623	137,254	5.3
	45	Time Inc.	196,579	190,026	NA	NA	NA	NA	4,193,000	250,000	6.0
	79	Warner Communications	110,428	79,579	2,696,494	2,353,115	24.42	29.57	3,403,563	328,142	9.6
FINANCIAL	44	American Express Co.	212,479	202,213	14,685,000	13,946,000	69.11	68.97	17,768,000	533,000	3.0
	58	ITT Corp.	151,321	124,331	14,634,000	13,555,000	96.71	109.02	19,524,854	1,018,875	5.2
	74	Loews Corp.	115,200	146,467	NA	NA	NA	NA	9,323,705	696,165	7.5
	78	Prudential Insurance Co.	111,319	70,320	NA	NA	NA	NA	29,019,000	867,000	3.0
FOOD	43	BCI Holdings Corp.	223,208	293,375	NA	NA	NA	NA	NA	NA	NA
	98	Borden Inc.	84,743	80,464	5,355,000	4,044,000	63.19	50.26	6,514,000	267,000	4.1
	41	Campbell Soup Co.	230,708	208,610	3,664,500	3,575,900	15.80	17.14	4,490,400	247,300	5.5
	72	CPC International	115,329	121,747	1,600,000	1,680,000	13.87	13.80	4,903,000	355,000	7.2
	13	General Mills	572,233	550,436	NA	NA	NA	NA	5,178,800	265,400	5.1
	38	H.J. Heinz Co.	245,264	218,574	3,053,000	2,781,000	12.45	12.72	5,244,000	386,000	7.4
	48	IC Industries	169,309	161,653	3,422,400	3,064,600	20.21	18.96	4,027,000	251,700	6.3
	17	Kellogg Co.	524,865	371,382	2,491,500	2,268,700	4.75	6.11	3,793,000	395,900	10.4
	22	Kraft Inc.	400,699	468,334	7,540,900	5,771,900	18.82	12.32	9,876,000	489,000	5.0
	28	Nestle SA	340,825	311,015	NA	NA	NA	NA	25,500,000	NA	NA
	1	Philip Morris Cos.	1,557,846	1,451,170	18,228,000	17,568,000	11.70	12.11	27,695,000	1,842,000	6.7
	19	Pillsbury Co.	473,895	495,150	5,350,000	5,510,000	11.29	11.13	6,191,000	69,000	1.1
	27	Quaker Oats Co.	344,414	306,219	NA	NA	NA	NA	5,329,800	255,700	4.8

Rank	Company	(1)	(2)	(3)	(4)	(5)	(6)	(7)	(8)	(9)
GUM & CANDY										
21	Ralston Purina Co.	436,606	478,031	NA	NA	NA	NA	5,868,000	523,000	8.9
5	RJR Nabisco	839,589	894,237	11,721,000	11,338,000	13.96	12.68	15,766,000	1,209,000	7.7
31	Sara Lee Corp.	278,141	256,599	NA	NA	NA	NA	10,424,000	325,000	3.1
97	United Biscuits (Holdings) PLC	84,758	64,213	1,244,000	1,176,600	14.68	18.32	3,081,230	231,700	7.5
53	U.S. Dairy Associations	161,372	177,897	NA	NA	NA	NA	NA	NA	NA
69	Hershey Foods Corp.	122,809	111,010	NA	NA	NA	NA	2,433,793	148,171	6.1
24	Mars Inc.	378,559	317,435	NA	NA	NA	NA	NA	NA	NA
77	Wm. Wrigley Jr. Co.	112,462	96,183	528,034	493,026	4.70	5.13	781,059	70,145	9.0
95	Franklin Mint	86,620	50,651	NA	NA	NA	NA	NA	NA	NA
MISCELLANEOUS										
90	Goodyear Tire & Rubber Co.	95,027	124,972	5,908,000	5,590,000	62.17	44.73	9,905,000	771,000	7.8
91	Hallmark Cards	93,913	61,032	NA	NA	NA	NA	NA	NA	NA
67	Hasbro Inc.	134,308	135,511	933,293	977,850	6.95	7.22	1,345,089	48,223	3.6
94	Marriott Corp.	88,523	69,507	NA	NA	NA	NA	6,522,200	223,000	3.4
29	U.S. Government	311,299	307,059	NA	NA	NA	NA	NA	NA	NA
PHARMACEUTICALS										
23	American Home Products Corp.	390,391	392,503	3,536,200	3,681,500	9.06	9.38	5,028,272	845,081	16.8
60	Bayer AG	145,392	126,149	4,189,900	3,789,200	28.82	30.04	20,700,000	860,500	4.2
26	Bristol-Myers Co.	358,934	333,488	3,949,800	3,594,800	11.00	10.78	5,401,000	709,600	13.1
20	Johnson & Johnson	459,271	410,959	4,167,000	3,972,000	9.07	9.67	8,012,000	833,000	10.4
46	Pfizer Inc.	182,059	171,686	2,651,000	2,483,000	14.56	14.46	4,920,000	690,000	14.0
35	Schering-Plough Corp.	250,184	212,376	1,595,000	1,416,000	6.38	6.67	2,699,000	316,000	11.7
15	Warner-Lambert Co.	558,115	553,314	1,864,000	1,747,000	3.34	3.16	3,484,700	295,800	8.5
RESTAURANTS										
8	McDonald's Corp.	649,493	591,808	10,576,000	9,554,000	16.28	16.11	14,330,000	549,000	3.8
81	Wendy's International	107,599	108,412	NA	NA	NA	NA	1,058,557	4,505	0.4
RETAIL										
11	K mart Corp.	631,845	573,719	NA	NA	NA	NA	25,627,000	692,000	2.7
73	Kroger Co.	115,263	108,207	NA	NA	NA	NA	17,659,730	246,644	1.4
18	J.C. Penney Co.	513,497	495,924	14,771,000	14,117,000	28.77	28.47	15,332,000	608,000	4.0
4	Sears, Roebuck & Co.	886,529	1,105,398	NA	NA	NA	NA	48,440,000	1,649,000	3.4
96	Southland Corp.	86,134	60,015	NA	NA	NA	NA	8,125,008	(66,422)	(0.8)
SOAPS & CLEANERS										
87	Clorox Co.	102,132	90,367	NA	NA	NA	NA	1,126,044	104,899	9.3
30	Colgate-Palmolive Co.	279,813	259,284	2,486,930	2,286,007	8.89	8.82	5,647,460	54,022	1.0
89	S.C. Johnson & Son	96,397	151,022	NA	NA	NA	NA	2,000,000	NA	NA
2	Procter & Gamble Co.	1,386,710	1,500,268	12,423,000	11,805,000	8.96	7.87	19,336,000	1,020,000	5.3
12	Unilever NV	580,656	543,242	4,457,000	5,757,000	9.91	8.20	30,948,000	946,000	3.1
SOFT DRINKS										
25	Coca-Cola Co.	364,737	370,117	3,277,900	3,459,100	9.48	8.86	7,658,300	916,100	12.0
6	PepsiCo Inc.	703,973	641,538	7,884,200	9,515,400	13.52	12.29	11,485,000	595,000	5.2
75	Dr Pepper/Seven-Up	114,117	85,330	NA	NA	NA	NA	NA	NA	NA
TELEPHONE										
100	Ameritech	83,445	68,763	NA	NA	NA	NA	9,536,000	1,188,000	12.5
16	American Telephone & Telegraph	531,018	522,551	NA	NA	NA	NA	33,598,000	2,044,000	6.1
63	Bell Atlantic Corp.	138,618	114,141	NA	NA	NA	NA	10,298,400	1,240,400	12.0
62	Nynex Corp.	142,798	112,369	NA	NA	NA	NA	12,084,000	1,277,000	10.6
TOBACCO										
57	American Brands	151,371	143,919	2,815,800	2,390,600	18.60	16.61	9,152,906	522,679	5.7
83	B.A.T. Industries PLC	105,294	98,241	5,835,000	5,499,000	55.42	55.97	27,126,691	751,943	2.8
TOILETRIES & COSMETICS										
54	Beecham Group PLC	153,307	113,918	1,023,900	903,000	6.68	7.93	3,796,286	647,743	17.1
71	Cosmair Inc.	117,224	120,701	NA	NA	NA	NA	750,000	NA	NA
85	Gillette Co.	103,831	131,437	1,166,300	1,100,900	11.23	8.38	3,166,800	229,900	7.3
66	Noxell Corp.	134,876	111,871	377,152	414,287	3.07	3.37	489,463	43,579	8.9
51	Revlon Group	165,239	171,402	NA	NA	NA	NA	2,400,000	NA	NA
WINE, BEER & LIQUOR										
10	Anheuser-Busch Cos.	635,067	643,893	NA	NA	NA	NA	9,019,100	614,700	6.8
61	Adolph Coors Co.	144,664	131,101	NA	NA	NA	NA	1,350,739	48,148	3.6
92	E&J Gallo Winery	93,602	116,561	NA	NA	NA	NA	NA	NA	NA
40	Grand Metropolitan PLC	231,574	232,055	2,711,880	2,468,958	11.71	10.64	8,994,150	815,944	9.1
70	Seagram Co.	122,325	112,443	1,686,000	1,778,000	13.78	15.81	3,815,000	521,000	13.7
86	Stroh Brewery Co.	102,878	128,294	NA	NA	NA	NA	1,430,000	NA	NA

Source: Sales and earnings are from public documents and reflect the latest fiscal year. Advertising expenditures are for calendar year only and are Advertising Age estimates. Notes: Dollars are in thousands.

SOURCE: "Top 100 Advertisers by Primary Business: 100 Leading National Advertisers, Part 1," *Advertising Age* (Special Issue), September 28, 1988: 152.

Exhibit 8–10 Ad Investment as a Percentage of Gross Margin

Industry	SIC no.	Ad dollars as % of sales	Ad dollars as % of margin	Annual growth rate (%)	Industry	SIC no.	Ad dollars as % of sales	Ad dollars as % of margin	Annual growth rate (%)
Abrasive, Asbestos, Misc Minrl	3290	1.7	4.9	7.4	Deep Sea Foreign Transport	4411	4.9	11.1	9.0
Adhesives And Sealants	2891	4.2	9.0	12.5	Dental Equipment & Supplies	3843	0.3	0.9	5.5
Advertising	7310	1.2	3.6	26.4	Detective & Protective Svcs	7393	0.2	1.0	5.3
Advertising Agencies	7311	0.1	0.5	25.8	Direct Mail Advertising Svcs	7331	0.2	0.9	12.6
Agricultural Services	700	1.7	4.8	13.3	Drawng, Insulatng Nonfer Wire	3357	3.2	19.8	(4.8)
Agriculture Chemicals	2870	0.7	3.5	29.4	Drugs	2830	4.4	7.1	0.1
Agriculture Prodtn-Livestock	200	0.6	2.3	(9.5)	Drugs And Proprietary-Whsl	5122	0.4	3.4	3.9
Agriculture Production-Crops	100	2.9	8.4	4.2	Durable Goods-Wholesale, Nec	5099	0.7	2.8	7.4
Air Cond, Heating, Refrig Eq	3585	1.5	5.7	13.7	Educational Services	8200	5.0	9.5	17.0
Air Courier Services	4513	2.1	12.2	9.3	Elec Apparatus & Equip-Whsl	5063	0.1	0.3	14.0
Air Transportation, Certified	4511	1.8	14.6	10.6	Elec Appliance, TV, Radio-Whsl	5064	0.8	3.9	8.2
Aircraft	3721	0.7	2.6	(29.5)	Elec, Electr Mach, Eq, Supply	3600	1.8	5.8	13.7
Aircraft And Parts	3720	0.5	2.4	(36.6)	Elec Meas & Test Instruments	3825	2.5	4.5	6.7
Aircraft Engine, Engine Parts	3724	0.8	2.2	15.3	Elec Transmission & Distr Eq	3610	1.1	3.2	8.0
Aircraft Parts, Aux Eq, Nec	3728	0.9	3.4	7.8	Electr Coil, Transfrm, Inductr	3677	1.9	4.9	5.0
Alarm & Signaling Products	3666	2.2	5.7	5.5	Electric Lighting, Wiring Eq	3640	1.1	2.8	7.5
Auto Dealers, Gas Stations	5500	0.5	1.8	5.5	Electrical Industrial Appar	3620	2.5	9.2	2.3
Auto Mdse Mach Operators	5962	1.7	2.9	8.5	Electronic Comp, Accessories	3670	1.1	3.1	(5.5)
Auto Rent & Lease, No Drivers	7510	2.9	4.3	12.6	Electronic Components, Nec	3679	2.3	6.5	11.5
Auto Repair, Services, Garages	7500	4.0	16.6	11.9	Electronic Computing Equip	3680	1.2	2.5	7.7
Automatic Regulatng Controls	3822	1.5	6.0	(30.5)	Electronic Parts & Eq-Whsl	5065	1.3	4.2	7.6
Autos & Other Vehicles-Whsl	5012	2.6	20.2	19.8	Engines And Turbines	3510	1.8	6.3	12.3
Bakery Products	2050	1.9	4.2	7.2	Engr, Architect, Survey Svcs	8911	0.8	3.0	8.1
Ball And Roller Bearings	3562	1.1	4.7	(1.0)	Engr, Lab And Research Equip	3811	1.7	4.0	18.9
Beet Sugar	2063	0.3	1.2	7.5	Equip Rental & Leasing Svcs	7394	3.5	5.2	5.7
Biological Products	2831	1.7	3.8	11.2	Fabricated Plate Work	3443	0.4	1.9	(2.3)
Books: Pubg, Pubg & Printing	2731	3.8	6.4	11.1	Fabricated Rubber Pds, Nec	3069	1.1	3.7	10.5
Business Credit Institutions	6150	0.1	0.1	10.2	Fabricated Structural Metal	3440	1.6	7.0	(3.4)
Business Services, Nec	7399	5.3	12.9	13.8	Farm Machinery And Equipment	3523	1.6	9.3	2.6
Catalog Showrooms	5334	3.7	15.5	2.8	Farm & Garden Machinery & Eq	3520	3.4	10.9	5.9
Chemicals & Allied Pds-Whsl	5161	3.5	6.1	15.0	Finance Lessors	6172	0.8	1.1	8.6
Chemicals & Allied Prods	2800	2.6	6.4	14.3	Finance-Services	6199	0.7	6.0	(6.7)
Cmp Program & Software Svcs	7372	3.5	9.0	17.8	Fixed Facility, Svc-Air Trans	4580	0.4	4.1	10.0
Coating, Engraving, Allied Svc	3470	2.6	4.7	(1.0)	Flat Glass	3211	0.2	0.5	16.0
Comm & Signaling Devices, Nec	3669	1.2	3.7	(0.3)	Floor Covering Mills	2270	1.1	3.0	17.6
Commercial Printing	2750	1.2	4.1	8.1	Food And Kindred Products	2000	7.3	35.0	13.6
Commercial Testing Labs	7397	0.6	2.0	12.9	Footwear, Except Rubber	3140	3.2	8.2	(4.4)
Comml Machines & Equip-Whsl	5081	1.9	7.5	15.3	Freight Forwarding	4712	3.6	20.4	24.6
Communication Services, Nec	4890	4.1	16.9	(6.6)	Gen Bldg Contractors-Nonres	1540	0.2	2.4	4.4
Computer Disk & Tape Drives	3684	1.2	4.0	19.1	Gen Med & Surgical Hospitals	8062	0.3	2.3	22.7
Computer Equipment, Nec	3689	1.9	4.8	16.5	General Industrial Mach & Eq	3560	0.3	1.0	4.7
Computer Graphics Systems	3686	0.8	1.5	13.6	Glass Containers	3221	6.1	12.3	47.2
Computer Peripherals	3688	2.3	6.4	6.0	Glass, Glasswr-Pressed, Blown	3220	2.0	5.7	7.5
Computer Related Svcs, Nec	7379	1.6	2.7	4.2	Grain Mill Products	2040	9.3	19.3	10.0
Computer Stores	5995	1.0	4.0	18.3	Guided Missiles & Space Vehc	3760	0.6	2.4	7.3
Computer Terminals	3683	1.6	3.6	3.3	Hardwr, Plumb, Heat Eq-Whsl	5070	6.4	50.1	17.7
Computer & Data Process Svcs	7370	0.1	0.1	16.3	Health Services	8000	3.3	26.0	24.2
Computers-Mainframe	3682	1.3	2.1	14.5	Health & Allied Services, Nec	8091	0.9	2.5	15.5
Computers-Mini & Micro	3681	5.1	10.1	9.6	Heating Eq, Plumbing Fixture	3430	3.3	8.6	17.7
Concrete, Gypsum And Plaster	3270	0.7	2.2	2.3	Hospitals	8060	5.8	35.4	17.8
Concrete Pds, Ex Block, Brick	3272	1.0	3.1	20.1	Hotels, Other Lodging Places	7000	0.4	0.5	(27.0)
Connectors, Electr Applicatns	3678	1.2	2.8	14.9	Indl Process Furnaces, Ovens	3567	0.2	0.8	(7.2)
Constr, Mining, Matl Handle Eq	3530	1.0	3.1	(5.9)	Indl Trucks, Tractors, Trailrs	3537	0.9	4.8	4.8
Construction Machinery & Eq	3531	1.3	5.2	9.6	Industrial Controls	3622	1.7	8.3	16.8
Construction-Special Trade	1700	9.8	20.1	25.1	Industrial Mach & Eq-Whsl	5084	2.0	5.8	20.4
Convrt, Paprbrd Pd, Ex Contain	2640	1.9	4.2	7.1	Industrial Measurement Instr	3823	1.7	4.1	7.0
Credit Reporting Agencies	7321	0.9	3.6	8.5	Ins Agents, Brokers & Service	6411	0.6	2.3	4.9
Crude Petroleum & Natural Gs	1311	0.2	0.3	3.6	Insurance Carriers, Nec	6399	0.0	0.0	(100.0)
Dairy Products	2020	4.9	17.8	4.6	Investors, Nec	6799	0.0	0.0	(100.0)
Data Processing Services	7374	1.2	3.5	6.9	Iron And Steel Foundries	3320	1.0	3.8	12.2

SOURCE: Schoenfeld & Associates, *Business Marketing*, October, 1988: 104–6.

Legend: SIC – Standard industrial classification. N/A – No data available for this value. NEC – Not elsewhere clas-

Exhibit 8–10 Ad Investment as a Percentage of Gross Margin

Industry	SIC no.	Ad dollars as % of sales	Ad dollars as % of margin	Annual growth rate (%)	Industry	SIC no.	Ad dollars as % of sales	Ad dollars as % of margin	Annual growth rate (%)
Lessors Of Real Property, Nec	6519	0.4	0.8	(17.7)	Photographic Equip & Suppl	3861	3.2	6.5	9.5
Lumber And Constr Matl-Whsl	5030	2.2	12.3	4.6	Plastic Matl, Synthetic Resin	2820	1.4	7.2	22.2
Lumber And Wood Pds, Ex Furn	2400	0.5	2.0	16.6	Plastics, Resins, Elastomers	2821	1.6	4.9	(13.7)
Machine Tools, Metal Cutting	3541	2.0	7.7	(1.2)	Pollution Control Machinery	3558	0.8	2.8	7.4
Machinery And Equipment-Whsl	5080	1.3	4.3	7.3	Prefab Metal Bldgs & Comp	3448	0.7	3.8	9.6
Mailing, Repro, Comml Art Svcs	7330	0.4	0.7	32.2	Prefab Wood Bldgs & Componts	2452	1.2	5.2	11.2
Meas & Controlling Dev, Nec	3829	1.1	2.3	0.2	Prim Smelt, Refin Nonfer Metl	3330	0.1	0.6	15.8
Measuring, Controlling Instr	3820	4.8	23.2	13.5	Printing Trades Machy, Equip	3555	1.3	3.4	13.4
Meat Packing Plants	2011	1.3	9.8	14.5	Pumps And Pumping Equipment	3561	1.2	3.3	2.8
Medical Laboratories	8071	0.9	2.1	2.9	Pwr Distr & Speclty Transfrm	3612	0.0	0.1	21.1
Medicinal Chems, Botanicl Pds	2833	4.9	5.9	25.8	Radio, TV Comm Eq, Apparatus	3663	0.8	3.2	(19.0)
Metal Cans	3411	1.7	8.8	4.0	Radio Broadcasting	4832	8.8	22.3	21.0
Metal Doors, Frames, Mold, Trim	3442	0.3	1.0	2.8	Railroad Equipment	3743	0.0	0.0	(100.0)
Metal Forgings And Stampings	3460	1.8	6.3	1.9	Real Estate	6500	1.5	4.2	16.2
Metal Office Furniture	2522	1.5	4.4	23.1	Real Estate Agents & Mgrs	6531	2.8	10.4	13.4
Metals Service Centers-Whsl	5051	0.1	0.9	15.9	Real Estate Dealers	6532	0.0	0.2	2.1
Metalworking Machinery & Eq	3540	5.4	13.6	6.5	Real Estate Investment Trust	6798	1.4	2.1	7.6
Mgmt, Consulting & P R Svcs	7392	1.8	8.5	(3.0)	Refrig & Service Ind Machine	3580	2.1	5.9	5.0
Misc Chemical Products	2890	2.8	7.6	8.6	Refuse Systems	4953	0.8	1.9	24.5
Misc Elec Machy, Eq, Supplies	3690	2.8	10.6	10.3	Research & Development Labs	7391	2.0	10.1	18.8
Misc Fabricated Metal Prods	3490	0.8	2.7	7.2	Robotics	3695	1.5	3.5	(15.5)
Misc Fabricated Textile Pds	2390	1.0	4.4	13.8	Rubber And Plastics Footwear	3021	4.1	9.8	10.8
Misc Machinery, Ex Electrical	3590	1.7	4.9	3.9	Rubber & Plastic Hose,Beltng	3041	1.4	5.2	3.0
Misc Manufacturng Industries	3990	2.2	5.8	7.9	Sanitary Services	4950	1.0	6.0	22.0
Misc Plastics Products	3079	2.3	6.8	10.5	Savings & Loan Associations	6120	0.7	1.6	4.3
Miscellaneous Publishing	2741	1.1	2.0	16.9	Sawmills, Planing Mills, Gen	2421	0.2	0.7	6.2
Miscellaneous Services	8900	1.1	2.1	8.6	Search, Navigate, Guide Sys, Eq	3664	1.5	6.2	5.6
Mng, Quarry Nonmtl Minerals	1400	1.7	4.2	17.6	Security Brokers & Dealers	6211	3.2	7.9	13.0
Motor Vehicle Part, Accessory	3714	1.6	6.1	12.6	Security & Commodity Brokers	6200	3.8	43.4	0.0
Motor Vehicles & Car Bodies	3711	1.6	9.0	9.1	Semiconductor, Related Device	3674	1.2	2.7	11.6
Motors And Generators	3621	1.0	2.9	5.9	Sheet Metal Work	3444	1.3	5.7	15.9
Musical Instruments	3931	3.3	10.8	9.4	Ship & Boat Bldg & Repairing	3730	2.3	18.7	(39.8)
News Syndicates	7351	0.1	0.2	(13.2)	Soap, Detergent, Toilet Preps	2840	7.6	16.4	9.0
Newspaper: Pubg, Pubg & Print	2711	3.9	9.2	25.7	Social Services	8300	1.6	4.5	14.9
Office Automation Systems	3687	2.3	4.1	13.5	Solar Energy Equip & Comp	3437	3.1	17.8	(27.0)
Office, Computing, Acctng Mach	3570	1.2	2.0	10.0	Special Cleaning, Santn Preps	2842	14.5	25.3	7.9
Office Furniture	2520	1.4	3.8	6.3	Special Industry Machinery	3550	1.7	5.8	9.3
Oil And Gas Field Expl Svcs	1382	0.8	2.1	(13.7)	Steam Supply	4961	2.6	6.0	3.0
Oil Field Machinery & Equip	3533	0.5	2.9	(7.7)	Structural Clay Products	3250	2.4	7.1	(1.6)
Operative Builders	1531	1.9	11.6	34.9	Surgical, Med Instr, Apparatus	3841	2.6	5.0	13.6
Operators-Nonres Bldgs	6512	3.8	7.7	7.3	Svcs Allied With Exchanges	6281	8.2	15.1	15.1
Ophthalmic Goods	3851	2.0	8.0	14.6	Svcs To Dwellings, Oth Bldgs	7340	1.9	10.0	(2.8)
Optical Character, Laser Scan	3685	1.1	3.0	10.5	Tele & Telegraph Apparatus	3661	1.6	3.5	10.1
Optical Instruments & Lenses	3832	1.5	3.3	11.5	Telegraph Comm (Wire, Radio)	4821	2.7	10.6	13.8
Ordnance & Accessories	3480	2.3	9.8	17.7	Telephone Comm (Wire, Radio)	4811	1.9	4.3	2.3
Ortho, Prosth, Surg Appl, Suply	3842	1.8	4.2	10.0	Telephone Interconnect Sys	4892	0.6	1.9	12.7
Outpatient Care Facilities	8081	1.1	11.5	23.4	Television Broadcasting	4833	2.7	7.5	14.2
Paints, Varnishes, Lacquers	2851	3.1	8.4	5.6	Textile Mill Products	2200	1.1	2.4	3.4
Paper And Allied Products	2600	3.8	14.4	10.7	Tires And Inner Tubes	3011	3.1	9.7	(1.8)
Paper Mills, Ex Bldg Paper	2621	2.9	9.0	5.5	Tobacco Manufacturers	2100	0.6	1.4	(14.5)
Patent Owners And Lessors	6794	1.9	6.0	11.1	Totalizing Fluid Meters	3824	2.4	5.6	39.3
Paving And Roofing Materials	2950	2.2	3.8	(7.7)	Training Equip & Simulators	3665	1.6	7.5	12.4
Pens, Pencils, Oth Office Matl	3950	5.2	11.0	7.2	Transportation Services	4700	0.0	0.1	14.2
Periodical: Pubg, Pubg & Print	2721	3.4	6.2	3.5	Truck And Bus Bodies	3713	1.1	7.2	15.0
Personal Services	7200	3.7	13.0	4.8	Trucking, Except Local	4213	0.1	1.2	24.9
Personnel Supply Services	7360	4.6	30.2	53.4	Trucking, Local, Long Distance	4210	0.4	4.8	10.7
Petroleum, Ex Bulk Statn-Whsl	5172	2.2	50.2	(35.9)	Valve, Pipe Fittings, Ex Brass	3494	1.0	2.1	19.7
Petroleum Refining	2911	0.2	0.8	0.3	Water, Sewer, Pipe Line Constr	1623	0.3	(0.3)	(21.3)
Pharmaceutical Preparations	2834	7.0	10.5	9.3	Water Transportation	4400	1.9	4.9	7.2
Photofinishing Laboratories	7395	1.8	4.4	7.4	X-Ray, Electromedical Apparat	3693	1.3	2.4	11.7

sified. Ad dollars as % of sales – Ad expenditures/net sales. Ad dollars as % of margin – Ad expenditures/(net sales—cost of goods sold). Annual growth rate of advertising dollars.

outlets stocking the brand, the number of automobiles estimated to be sold, and so on. For example, based on average sales per store, we can profitably allocate up to $150 per store per year for advertising. If we were to allocate that amount for all 30,500 supermarkets doing in excess of $2,000,000 per year in sales, our advertising budget would be $150 × 30,500 or $4,575.000. An example of this approach for the automobile business is shown in Exhibit 8–11.

Inertia

The budget from last year is simply extended for the coming year. In other words, "If it ain't broke, don't fix it." For example, if $4,500,000 was allocated for advertising last year and the company or brand had a successful year, the coming year's budget would be set at $4,500,000. The assumption here is that something is working for the brand or company. It might well be the advertising. So, don't change it.

Media Inflation Multiplier

The media budget for the past year is used as the base. An estimate is made of what increases are likely in the media to be used as compared with last year. This percentage increase is used to increase the budget for the coming year. For example, the working media budget for the past year was $5,000,000. Media costs are estimated to increase by 15 percent for the coming year. Therefore, the budget would be set at $5,000,000 × 1.15 or $5,750,000.

Competitive Comparisons

Using this method, advertising expenditures for the total category in which the brand or company competes are determined first. Then, competitive advertising expenditures are estimated. Relating share of market, share of units, or other factors to the share of advertising, a ratio is established. From this, the advertising planner then seeks to achieve a "share of voice" or share of advertising which is, in general, equal to the share of market which the brand holds. For example, if it is determined that total advertising expenditures in the eggroll market are estimated to be $50,000,000 and Ferd's has a 15 percent share of market, then Ferd's advertising budget would be set at $50,000,000 × 0.15 or $7,500,000. In some instances, the share of voice is set higher than the share of market in the belief that it is necessary to overspend in the category to achieve growth. One of the most well-accepted approaches is that developed by

Exhibit 8–11   Advertising per Vehicle Sold

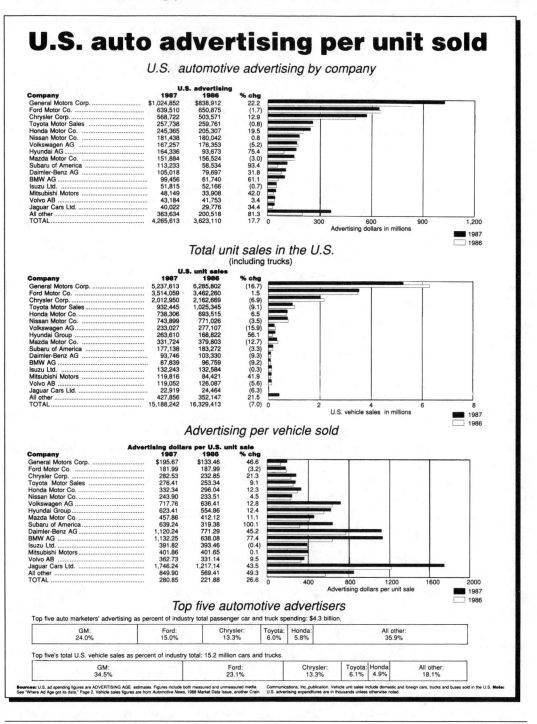

U.S. auto advertising per unit sold

U.S. automotive advertising by company

Company	U.S. advertising 1987	1986	% chg
General Motors Corp.	$1,024,852	$838,912	22.2
Ford Motor Co.	639,510	650,875	(1.7)
Chrysler Corp.	568,722	503,571	12.9
Toyota Motor Sales	257,738	259,761	(0.8)
Honda Motor Co.	245,365	205,307	19.5
Nissan Motor Co.	181,438	180,042	0.8
Volkswagen AG	167,257	176,353	(5.2)
Hyundai AG	164,336	93,673	75.4
Mazda Motor Co.	151,884	156,524	(3.0)
Subaru of America	113,233	58,534	93.4
Daimler-Benz AG	105,018	79,697	31.8
BMW AG	99,456	61,740	61.1
Isuzu Ltd.	51,815	52,166	(0.7)
Mitsubishi Motors	48,149	33,908	42.0
Volvo AB	43,184	41,753	3.4
Jaguar Cars Ltd.	40,022	29,776	34.4
All other	363,634	200,518	81.3
TOTAL	4,265,613	3,623,110	17.7

Advertising dollars in millions

■ 1987 □ 1986

Total unit sales in the U.S.
(including trucks)

Company	U.S. unit sales 1987	1986	% chg
General Motors Corp.	5,237,613	6,285,802	(16.7)
Ford Motor Co.	3,514,059	3,462,260	1.5
Chrysler Corp.	2,012,950	2,162,669	(6.9)
Toyota Motor Sales	932,445	1,025,345	(9.1)
Honda Motor Co.	738,306	693,515	6.5
Nissan Motor Co.	743,899	771,026	(3.5)
Volkswagen AG	233,027	277,107	(15.9)
Hyundai Group	263,610	168,822	56.1
Mazda Motor Co.	331,724	379,803	(12.7)
Subaru of America	177,138	183,272	(3.3)
Daimler-Benz AG	93,746	103,330	(9.3)
BMW AG	87,839	96,759	(9.2)
Isuzu Ltd.	132,243	132,584	(0.3)
Mitsubishi Motors	119,816	84,421	41.9
Volvo AB	119,052	126,087	(5.6)
Jaguar Cars Ltd.	22,919	24,464	(6.3)
All other	427,856	352,147	21.5
TOTAL	15,188,242	16,329,413	(7.0)

U.S. vehicle sales in millions

■ 1987 □ 1986

Advertising per vehicle sold

Company	Advertising dollars per U.S. unit sale 1987	1986	% chg
General Motors Corp.	$195.67	$133.46	46.6
Ford Motor Co.	181.99	187.99	(3.2)
Chrysler Corp.	282.53	232.85	21.3
Toyota Motor Sales	276.41	253.34	9.1
Honda Motor Co.	332.34	296.04	12.3
Nissan Motor Co.	243.90	233.51	4.5
Volkswagen AG	717.76	636.41	12.8
Hyundai Group	623.41	554.86	12.4
Mazda Motor Co.	457.86	412.12	11.1
Subaru of America	639.24	319.38	100.1
Daimler-Benz AG	1,120.24	771.29	45.2
BMW AG	1,132.25	638.08	77.4
Isuzu Ltd.	391.82	393.46	(0.4)
Mitsubishi Motors	401.86	401.65	0.1
Volvo AB	362.73	331.14	9.5
Jaguar Cars Ltd.	1,746.24	1,217.14	43.5
All other	849.90	569.41	49.3
TOTAL	280.85	221.88	26.6

Advertising dollars per unit sale

■ 1987 □ 1986

Top five automotive advertisers

Top five auto marketers' advertising as percent of industry total passenger car and truck spending: $4.3 billion.

GM: 24.0%	Ford: 15.0%	Chrysler: 13.3%	Toyota: 6.0%	Honda: 5.8%	All other: 35.9%

Top five's total U.S. vehicle sales as percent of industry total: 15.2 million cars and trucks.

GM: 34.5%	Ford: 23.1%	Chrysler: 13.3%	Toyota: 6.1%	Honda: 4.9%	All other: 18.1%

Sources: U.S. ad spending figures are ADVERTISING AGE estimates. Figures include both measured and unmeasured media. See "Where Ad Age got its data," Page 2. Vehicle sales figures are from *Automotive News*, 1988 Market Data Issue, another Crain Communications, Inc.,publication. Vehicle unit sales include domestic and foreign cars, trucks and buses sold in the U.S. **Note:** U.S. advertising expenditures are in thousands unless otherwise noted.

SOURCE: "U.S. Auto Advertising per Unit Sold: 100 Leading National Advertisers, Part 1," *Advertising Age* (Special Issue), September 28, 1988: 150.

J.O. Peckham using Nielsen data. From his studies, Peckham found that to hold market share, the advertiser should spend at the same level as share of market. To gain sales, it was necessary to spend at 1.5 to 2.0 times market share. Therefore, the industry rule-of-thumbs have been established at that rate. More on this method in the section on the "Competitive Expenditure Approach" in this chapter.[11] To return to the Ferd's example, to gain market share, Ferd should allocate $50,000,000 × 0.15 × 1.5 or $11,250,000.

Task or Objective and Task

This method is essentially the one that we have followed in first setting specific advertising objectives and then determining how to reach those objectives. The budget is the result of identifying the advertising activities that will be needed to reach the objectives and then estimating a cost for those activities. The sum of those costs then becomes the advertising budget. Obviously, adjustments must be made because it is unlikely that most brands or companies can afford the cost of reaching all their objectives. Therefore, the objective and task method is essentially one of adjustment and negotiation to reach a point where the set objectives can be met with a budget that the company or brand can afford.

An example of the objective and task method: The company wants to increase trial of its brand of cat food. Previous television schedules had used a 65 reach and a 3 frequency against the target market. As a result of some market tests, it was found that increasing the reach to 70 and the frequency to 4 against cat owners generated the desired trial. Because the previous television schedule had cost approximately $3,000,000, the new budget was set at $4,000,000 to make possible the new 70 reach and 4 frequency media goal. An estimate by the media department indicated that it would cost an additional $200,000 to achieve these 70 reach and 4 frequency goals in the selected markets. Therefore, using the objective and task method, the advertising planner would either (a) have to allocate additional $200,000, (b) reduce the number of television markets, (c) lower the reach and frequency requirements, or (d) see if the sales goals for the brand could be adjusted.

Some variations on the objective and task method include:

Effective frequency.   In this approach, media planners estimate the number of persons who will be exposed to the advertising one, two, three, and so on, times during the schedule. This estimate is made in the belief that the advertising must be exposed a certain number of times for it to be

[11]J.O. Peckham, *The Wheel of Marketing* (Scarsdale, N.Y.: privately published, 1975): 73–76.

effective. Therefore, the advertising plan is to have the selected number of persons exposed to the advertising the chosen number of times. The cost of this "effective frequency" then becomes the advertising budget, subject to the adjustments in the task method discussed earlier.

Zero-based budgets.   This approach assumes that nothing is taken for granted. Just because certain media, approaches, or techniques were used in the past does not assure they will be used in the future. In other words, a bottom-up approach is used; each and every advertising decision must be justified. In general, the justification of these decisions is the task to be achieved by the advertising.

Affordable (Residual)

The advertising budget in this method is essentially set as a result of what is left after the other costs of doing business have been covered or after company or brand profits have been obtained. Returning again to Ferd's eggrolls, the budget in this instance (Table 8–1) would be set from the "contribution margin" (Line N). In this example, the advertising budget would be set as part of the overall direct expenses of the brand and would be considered in terms of its value in achieving the goal of the "bottom line," just as sales promotion, research and development, management, and sales expense, and the like, are. If management requested a larger product margin than was planned (in this case $1.02 on Line V), then advertising or one of the other direct expense items would have to be reduced.

Brand History Review

This approach requires a complete review of the brand, marketplace, competition, and the like. From this review, the advertising planner should be able to identify trends, associations, and averages that will give a clue as to the dynamics of the brand in the marketplace. In other words, one might expect to find some indications of what is effective in advertising and what is not, which brands are succeeding, their advertising expenditures, and so on. Using this information, an initial estimate of the budget is made and from this estimation the task method may be employed.

If the planner has conducted a thorough review of all the market factors that might have an impact on the brand or company (as suggested in the first seven chapters of this text), this method should be relatively easy to implement and can be most effective. This approach, which is a type of profit-planning approach described later in this chapter, is highly recommended.

Modeling

Some marketing organizations and their advertising agencies, using past advertising spending experience and brand or company sales data, have attempted to relate the two in some sort of a model. The model itself relies on mathematical equations that attempt to relate the advertising expenditures to product pricing, distribution, market share, and eventually sales. The goal is to develop a "model" that explains the relationship among the various elements and that would enable the modelers to forecast future results. As a result of the availability of scanner panel data, many advertising experts and academicians are busily trying to develop models that will be helpful to advertising planners. At this point, those models that have been developed are proprietary or have not proven to be generalizable to the broad range of products or services that would make them usable in the marketplace.

Experiments

The experimental approach is the next step beyond modeling. In this instance, rather than using past history to validate a model, the advertising expert uses tests and experiments in one or more market areas to determine the results of variations that might be tried. The most common example of this is the advertising weight test. Using such techniques as split cable homes in a specific area (Household A gets Commercial X and Household B, which may be next door, gets Commercial Y; or Household A is exposed to twice as many commercials as Household B; and so on), adjustments in the amount of advertising to which the household is exposed, the commercial content, scheduling, and so on, can be made. Because, in many cases, household purchases of products are captured through scanners in retail stores, relationships between the advertising and actual purchases can be determined. By varying the experiments and reading the purchases, advertising researchers can start to develop models that identify the proper mix of advertising and other elements to achieve the brand or company goals. (Note: For a more detailed description of all these budgeting methods, particularly "modeling" and "experiments," the reader is again referred to Simon Broadbent, *The Advertiser's Handbook for Budget Determination:* Chapter 5.)

Fixed Amount

Often this is called "management decision" for, in fact, it is just that. Management sets the amount to be spent on advertising. The advertising planner's only task is to allocate the available funds. The management decision may be the result of past experience, estimated effects of advertising, financial requirements, or simply a management control tool. In any event, the allocation may have all or nothing to do with the needs of the brand in the marketplace. But, it is management's prerogative to set budgets of this sort.

An advertising planner who finds him- or herself working under the fixed amount type of budgeting should (a) prepare the budget using the approaches recommended in this text, or (b) present the budget recommendations to management with proper supporting documents to see if the budget can be adjusted. (c) If no adjustment is possible, use the objective and task method to adjust to the available funds. In many cases, advertising agencies find themselves in this "fixed amount" budgeting situation. The budget has been set by marketing management at high levels and the agency's only job is to develop a creative and media plan within that allocation. Here again, the agency should make recommendations based on a thorough analysis of the market, the brand, the advertising objectives, and so on, but should recognize that, generally, once the advertising budget is set and included in the financial plans of the brand and the company, it is not easily adjusted.

BUT, WHAT IS THE RIGHT WAY TO BUDGET?

Given all these alternatives, the advertising planner may be shaking his or her head saying, "But what method should I use?" In the following section, a recommended approach is given. But, as an overview of how other major companies develop their advertising budgets, Table 8–2 presents conclusions to several studies, dating back to 1975, summarized by Broadbent.[12]

A RECOMMENDED APPROACH TO BUDGETING FOR EXISTING PRODUCTS OR SERVICES

One of the major problems advertising planners often face is developing an advertising budget for an existing or established brand or company. The planner may find that previous budgets had been inadequate and/or that sufficient advertising funds had not been invested in the brand. In those instances, the planner generally develops a new plan requiring a larger budget to achieve established goals. This problem often occurs when a new advertising agency or a new planner starts to work on a brand. The new agency's first recommendation always seems to be to increase the advertising budget and advertising expenditure. Although these increases may be justified, often the feeling of advertisers is that the planner or agency believe all the brand's sales, marketing, and advertising problems

---

[12]Simon Broadbent, *The Advertiser's Handbook:* 119–20.

Table 8–2 Methods of Setting an Advertising Budget

- Advertising budget-setting is "largely an art. That is, most firms are 'budgeting by ear.' For many of them, however, this is not arbitrary decision making, but reflects considered judgment based on experience and the reported impracticality of more sophisticated budgeting methods."
- It is common to use more than one method.
- The advertising to sales ratio is the most common method used, more often of anticipated sales but quite often of last year's sales.
- Per case allowance, or a budget based on unit sales, is common; again more often of anticipated than last year's unit sales.
- Affordable is the second most frequent method quoted, although it is hard to believe that it is not a criterion always applied.
- The task method (or objective and task) is used by a minority, with a variety of ways of determining the task.
- Arbitrary methods are quite common, presumably meaning the person answering the survey did know how the budgets are set.
- Modeling is rare, used only by a sophisticated few.

SOURCE: Simon Broadbent, *The Advertiser's Handbook:* 119.

can be solved with increased spending. Sometimes this is the case, but often it isn't. Only through a careful analysis of one brand's past history can the proper budget be established. A recommended approach follows.

The Profit Planning Approach to Advertising Budgeting

For existing consumer products, under the brand management system, it should be clear that advertising budgeting is often less a case of budgeting and more a case of allocating available funds. In practice, there is a basic approach to budgeting and allocation that takes into account the situation described earlier and gives the advertising planner a sound, proven method of budgeting. It's called the profit planning approach. Its four basic steps follow:

1. Develop an accurate forecast of predicted sales for the coming budget period. This assumes the planner has a reasonably firm estimate of fixed and variable product manufacturing costs.
2. Convert the sales forecast into a contribution margin for the product or brand (Table 8–1).
3. The planner must have an understanding of the desired profit margin for the product, company, or brand, either in total dollars or as a percentage of net sales price or gross margin.

4. The planner then allocates the available direct expense funds for marketing to advertising, promotion, selling expense, and research and development budgets and, if appropriate, public relations, direct marketing, and so on.

This method permits the planner to approach advertising budgeting from a managerial standpoint. The emphasis is on achieving the desired profit margin for the brand by adjusting sales forecasts or direct expenses as necessary to achieve those goals. Each step of the profit planning approach is outlined in the following sections.

Step 1: Forecast accurately.   Profit planning budgeting places primary emphasis on the ability of the planner to understand three basic things: the fixed and variable manufacturing costs for the product at all levels of sales; the specific percentage or dollar amount desired as a profit margin for the company, product, or brand; and the competitive market situation and consumers so that an accurate sales forecast can be made.

Table 8–1 shows that, with a top line established by the sales forecast and a bottom line dictated by the desired profit margin, the product manager and/or advertising planner can manipulate only a few variables in developing an advertising budget. Once the desired profit margin has been established, assuming a competitive pricing situation, the only true variables are the number of units forecast to be sold, the variable product cost, and the direct expenses to be allocated. Thus, primary emphasis in the profit planning approach to budgeting is on developing the sales forecast.

Initially, the sales forecast should be made in units rather than dollars. The unit forecast can then be converted into dollars based on the selling price less the necessary discounts. This leads to the second step.

Step 2: Estimate the contribution margin.   Once the net sales price of the product has been determined, the cost-of-goods on the forecasted sales is deducted. This calculation gives the gross margin. Distribution expense is then deducted, leaving the contribution margin (see Table 8–1). This contribution margin truly defines the funds available for all marketing expenditures, including advertising.

Step 3: Deduct the desired product margin.   Once the product margin has been established, either as a lump sum or as a percentage of net sales price, it is deducted from the contribution margin of the product. The result is the total amount available for marketing (direct expenses).

Step 4: Allocate the marketing funds.   The total available marketing funds ("direct expenses" in Table 8–1) are now known. Based on that amount, the planner can then allocate the available funds among sales expense, advertising and promotion investments, public relations, direct marketing, research and development, and so on, to achieve the best return. At this point, the planner knows the true alternatives available. It is also the point at which the effects of various expenditures for personal sales versus advertising or advertising versus sales promotion or public relations versus advertising or direct marketing versus sales promotion, for example, can be estimated with some accuracy.

The major differences between the profit planning method and more traditional budgeting approaches involve viewing the advertising budget within the framework of the entire product operating sheet rather than as a separate entity. Advertising is a function directly related to the profit margin and is a part of the total mix of product income and expense. Advertising is not theoretical. It's a practical device that can be used by the campaign planner to increase sales and profits.

In the profit planning approach—because advertising is directly related to the sales forecast—effective advertising results in increased advertising dollars. Advertising and sales are inextricably intertwined. Also, the advertising budget is in the hands of the person responsible for the sale and profit of the product. By developing the sales forecast, estimating sales and costs, and knowing the other expenses that are to be charged against the product, the planner can justify the advertising investment to management.

The profit planning approach may not be feasible for some advertising budgeters because of lack of information on such factors as costs and profit margins desired. However, it is a sound, real-world approach to establishing an advertising budget.

ADVERTISING BUDGETING FOR NEW PRODUCTS

Budgeting advertising for a new product or brand requires a different approach from those already discussed. The most common technique is based on a payout plan. Its rationale developed from the belief that a new brand or product requires a heavier investment in advertising, packaging, sales promotion, public relations, direct marketing, and so on, to get started than may be needed by established brands. Because the new brand has no sales income to pay for the advertising, the company must forego profits on the brand until it can pay its own way. Therefore, the parent company should invest funds in promotional activities for the new brand until it is established. As the new brand achieves sales and profits in the market, the investment money and previously lost profits can be repaid to the parent company. Because this payback procedure usually cannot be accomplished in one budgeting period (ordinarily one year), a payout plan is developed in which the advertising planner for the new brand budgets the payoff of the parent investment over a period of several budgeting periods (usually one to three years) for a consumer product.

The procedure for developing a payout plan consists of four steps discussed later and illustrated in Table 8–3.

Table 8–3   Three-Year Payout Plan: Hypothetical Consumer Product

		Theoretical marketing years		
		Year 1	Year 2	Year 3
A.	Total marketing in units	20,000	22,000	23,000
B.	Average percent of market share goals . .	8	10	11
C.	Market sales in units	1,600	2,200	2,530
D.	Pipeline in units	288	50	28
E.	Factory shipments in units	1,888	2,250	2,558
F.	Net trade sales @ $6.00 per unit	$11,328	$13,500	$15,348
G.	Less fixed and variable cost of goods			
H.	@ $3.50 per unit	$ 6,608	$ 7,875	$ 8,953
J.	Gross margin	$ 4,720	$ 5,625	$ 6,395
K.	Less distribution expense @ 10¢ per unit	$ 189	$ 225	$ 256
L.	Contribution margin	$ 4,531	$ 5,400	$ 6,139
M.	Advertising	$ 3,000	$ 2,500	$ 2,000
N.	Promotion	$ 5,000	$ 1,000	$ 1,000
O.	Product margin (or loss)	$(3,469)	$ 1,900	$ 3,139*
P.	Product margin as a percent of sales . . .	—	14.1	20.4
Q.	Cumulative product margin (or loss)	$(3,469)	$(1,569)	$ 1,570

*Product pays out at Month 30.

Estimate the Share Goal

The total market must be determined for the product category the new brand is entering. This estimate is usually based on research. Using the total estimated market, a growth projection based on the budget period is then prepared. This projection usually covers three to five years.

As illustrated in Table 8–3, the total market for the hypothetical product illustrated is estimated at 20,000 units in Year 1. The market is expected to grow by 10 percent to 22,000 units in Year 2 and by 4.5 percent or to 23,000 units in Year 3 (Line A).

The new brand's estimated share of the total market must then be determined. Because a new brand's sales typically start slowly and increase until reaching a certain level, an average share for the year is often used. For example, the average market share goal for Year 1 is 8 percent (Line B). For the company to achieve that goal, the brand share would have to be above 8 percent at the end of Year 1 to average out to that level. Most new brands, depending on use-up and repurchase rates, reach their peak sales share between six and nine months after introduction. After that time, they may slowly decline to a stable position, as new triers either become loyal users or switch again to another brand.

Determine the Trade Inventories (Pipeline)

In addition to consumer sales, an estimate of the sales that will be made to the trade to stock the warehouses and shelves at retail must be made. This is called the *pipeline.* Typically, pipeline sales occur only at introduction. However, as a brand's distribution increases or more product is stocked on retail shelves, additional sales may be made into the pipeline. All pipeline sales are one time only and usually decline dramatically after Year 1 (see Line D).

When introducing a new product, several methods of estimating the amount of product going into the pipeline may be used. One is a straight-line projection based on the percentage of estimated sales of the product for the year. This figure varies widely depending on the speed with which the product sells and how large a display is normally found in the store.

A more widely used method is to estimate the number of units of the product that would be on display plus the amount stocked as backup (that found in the storeroom of the retail outlet). This sum is then multiplied by the number of stores in which distribution is expected to be achieved. For example, assume a planner is working on the planned introduction of a new line of packaged dry soup mixes. The soup is packed twenty-four packages to the case per flavor for three flavors. Normal retail display is one case of twenty-four packages per flavor per store. Because the sales volume of dry soup mix is fairly high, the retail store usually maintains one additional case per flavor per store in the back room for restocking the shelves. In other words, the planner estimates that, for all the stores in which distribution is obtained, there will be two cases per flavor in the pipeline. If the estimated distribution volume of 10,000 stores is achieved nationwide, there would be 60,000 cases of the product in the pipeline (2 cases per flavor × 3 flavors = cases per store × 10,000 stores = 60,000 cases of the product). There are alternative methods of determining what is in the pipeline, but this is a common approach.

Determine the Advertising/Promotion Expense

No hard-and-fast rules exist for budgeting advertising and sales promotional expenditures for a new product because there are so many variations in product, market, consumer acceptance, and the like. There are, however, some rules of thumb that have proven successful for a number of marketers.

As shown in the hypothetical example (Table 8–3), advertising and promotion expenditures are normally heavier in the introductory year than in the following years (see Lines M and N). This is logical because the product is unknown to the consumer and the trade. It simply costs more to get consumer interest and trial in a new product than to maintain an existing known product.

Three basic methods for budget allocation are used.

The buy-your-way-in approach.   This allocation entails budgeting enough money in dealer incentives and activities, such as promotional discounts or price allowances, to achieve the needed retail distribution. At the same time, heavy advertising and consumer sales promotion are used so that, once the product is on the dealers' shelves, consumers are encouraged to try it. The budget is set by estimating the cost of the required trade and consumer advertising and sales promotion and then allocating that amount. For example, some food retailers require substantial allowances from manufacturers simply to stock the item. (More on this in Chapter 13 on "Sales Promotion.") Although the method is expensive and not always successful, in some instances, it is the only approach that will generate distribution and consumer sales.

Competitive expenditure approach.   The competitive expenditure approach to budgeting is widely used. The rule of thumb says the advertiser must spend at a rate of one and one-half to two times the annual advertising rate per share point of competitors to reach a share objective. For example, assume Brand V has an 8 percent market share goal for the first year (see Table 8–3). Studies are made of competitive market shares to learn which brand has approximately that same share. Assume Brand Z has an 8 percent market share. Based on that fact, an estimate is then made of the annual advertising expenditure for Brand Z. If it is $1,500,000, the company should invest between $2,250,000 and $3,000,000 for Brand V, approximately one and one-half to two times the annual rate for competitive Brand Z and its 8 percent share.

Over a period of several years, J.O. Peckham gathered evidence of a strong correlation between what is invested in advertising as a share of the category total and the share of market achieved. Examples of several brands in the food and household-products categories are illustrated in Exhibit 8–12. The first set of bars illustrates the share of sales attained by each brand over a two-year introductory period. The second set of bars illustrates the share of advertising for each brand over the same two-year period. The ratio is obtained by dividing share of advertising by share of sales. For the food product category, the average ratio of share of advertising to share of sales was 1.7 and the median 1.5. In the toiletry product category, the average ratio of share of advertising to share of sales was 1.5 and the median 1.5.

The cases illustrated here are only examples, and doubtless there is some variation. In general, however, the rule of thumb of a ratio of approximately 1.5 to 2.0 share of advertising to share of sales is needed for the successful launching of a new brand in the marketplace.[13]

The profit planning approach. Although buy-your-way-in and competitive-expenditure approaches have often been successful, they ignore the basic reason for the payout planning program, namely, the payout. In most consumer, nondurable product companies, there is an acceptable payback period for new products, usually between twelve and thirty months. With this as a guideline, the same budgeting approach that was recommended for existing products profit planning can be used to determine the introductory budget.

Using the profit planning approach, the length of the payout period is determined. Based on that, the advertising budget for the new product introduction can be calculated. For example, in Table 8–2, the hypothetical product illustrated has a payout or break-even point at approximately Month 30. (Sufficient profit will accrue in the sixth month of Year 3 to erase the carry-over deficit from Year 1 and 2, as illustrated by Lines P and R.) Had there been a management decision that the new product had to pay out in twenty-four months, the only options would have been to raise the product price (Line C), raise the market share goal (Line B), or reduce the advertising or promotion expenditures during the introductory periods (Lines M and N). Either of these steps would have allowed an earlier payout as required by management.

Although the profit planning approach is a more complex new product budgeting procedure than the alternatives previously discussed, it adopts a management viewpoint that is guided by the needs of the brand and the entire company. Other allocation methods lack this profit-oriented view, particularly the buy-your-way-in approach, which conceivably could end up as a major expense, rather than a payout, to the company.

Determine the payout period. The final step in the development of a payout plan in the profit planning approach is the determination of the length of the payout. The actual calculation is a straightforward one. The cumulative product margin (Line R) is carried from period to period until the product margin (Line P) exceeds the amount previously invested. At

---

[13]J.O. Peckham, *The Wheel of Marketing:* 73–76.

Exhibit 8–12   Two-Year Summary: Share of Advertising–Share of Sales Relationships for New Brands of Food and Household Products

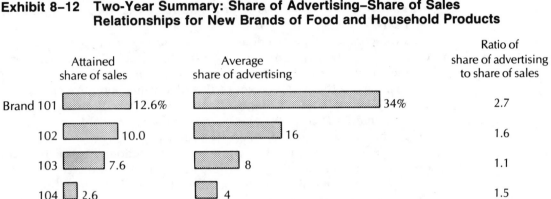

	Attained share of sales	Average share of advertising	Ratio of share of advertising to share of sales
Brand 101	12.6%	34%	2.7
102	10.0	16	1.6
103	7.6	8	1.1
104	2.6	4	1.5
105	2.1	3	1.4

Two-Year Summary: Share of Advertising–Share of Sales Relationships for New Brands of Toiletry Products

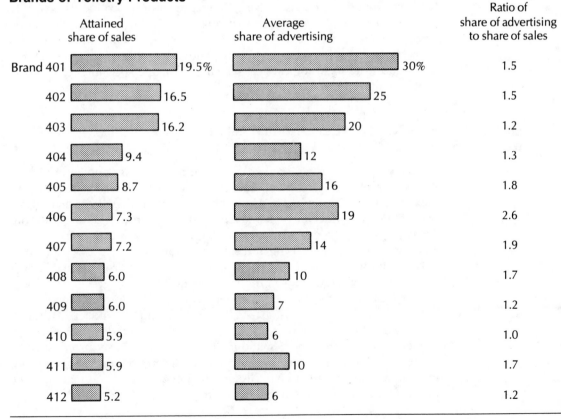

	Attained share of sales	Average share of advertising	Ratio of share of advertising to share of sales
Brand 401	19.5%	30%	1.5
402	16.5	25	1.5
403	16.2	20	1.2
404	9.4	12	1.3
405	8.7	16	1.8
406	7.3	19	2.6
407	7.2	14	1.9
408	6.0	10	1.7
409	6.0	7	1.2
410	5.9	6	1.0
411	5.9	10	1.7
412	5.2	6	1.2

SOURCE: Peckham, *The Wheel of Marketing,* 1975.

the point where the product margin gains exceed the cumulative product margin losses, the brand has returned all the initial seed money to the company and is now on a profit-making basis.

In the competitive expenditure and buy-your-way-in approaches, the calculation of the payout period is a result of the calculations, not a pre-planned length of time. In the profit planning approach, however, it is an integral part of the development of the advertising and sales promotion budget, because the payout time is the basis on which the available funds are determined. This use of payout time is another reason the profit planning approach is suggested for a new product.

Management decisions on new product introductions are usually based on (a) the amount of money risked the first year should the goals not be achieved and an absolute disaster occur, and (b) the sales and brand share the first year after the payout is achieved. Sales and brand share after payout are usually indicative of the return that can be expected from the new brand on an ongoing basis. Using these two figures, management can then determine the ratio of the risk to the return when the plan is compared to alternative uses of the funds.

Determination of an advertising budget for a new product is probably the least precise of any budget that might be developed for a company. There is no past experience on which to base one's plans, and there is no successful way of knowing the future. The only option is to approach the problem in the most logical and systematic manner possible, that is, the profit planning payout plan.

ALLOCATING FUNDS BETWEEN ADVERTISING AND SALES PROMOTION

As has been previously discussed, the need today is for an integrated marketing communications plan, one in which all elements fit together to maximize the effects of each. Although public relations, direct marketing, packaging, and other elements are important, perhaps the greatest concern for package goods marketers today is the relationship between the amount spent on advertising and sales promotion.

Up until the last few years, the major portion of the promotional budget was spent on advertising—in the neighborhood of 70 percent or so. Today, that ratio is almost the reverse, with sales promotion now accounting for 65–70 percent of most package goods product's budget. Although there are a number of reasons for this change, including the growing power of the retailer, the demand for more immediate, short-term results by management, and the lack of meaningful differentiation between products, advertising is still a vital force in the development and maintenance of a brand and a brand's consumer franchise.

There is more and more evidence that advertising and sales promotion work best when used in combination, rather than singly. Therefore, it is increasingly important that advertising and sales promotion be considered together, particularly in the budgeting process. Although it is not within the scope of this text to look deeply at sales promotion budgeting, there is little question that there must be a relationship between the advertising budget and the sales promotion budget. One should not dominate the other. They must work in harmony.

In Chapter 13, we will look at sales promotion in more detail. There we will illustrate the need for proper allocation between sales promotion and advertising to achieve the goals of the brand, the company, and the planner.

SUMMARY

After the advertising objectives have been set, the next step is to determine how much money is needed to accomplish those goals. That figure determines the advertising budget. The basic approach to advertising budgeting is from marginal economic analysis. This concept suggests that advertising spending should continue as long as it is profitable. Using a basic profit-and-loss sheet for a typical package goods brand, the planner is able to see how advertising dollars are generated and the potential constraints that exist. Major questions in advertising budgeting revolve around exactly what goes in the advertising budget and what the legitimate charges against this budget are. A conceptual plan for developing an advertising budget leads to a discussion of several alternative ways of establishing an advertising budget. The profit planning approach to advertising budgeting has been shown to be a sound one for both existing and new products.

Case Studies

Cristel Products

Charles Dobbs was faced with his biggest challenge since joining Cristel Products two years earlier. During his time with Cristel, a major food marketer, Dobbs had worked as an assistant brand manager on several products. He had recently been appointed brand manager for a new product, frozen french fries. Dobbs had worked with a top-level committee to develop objectives for the product, which would be Cristel's first new product introduction in several years and its first national frozen food entry.

Frozen potato products, primarily french fries, were purchased by 45 percent of all U.S. homemakers (35,680,000). The market was dominated by one brand, which had accounted for 55 percent of all sales last year. The rest of the market was divided among six small brands and various regional distributors and store brands.

Cristel had decided to enter the category for several reasons:

1. They had a ready source of potatoes.
2. French fries could be packaged and processed using present equipment, although additional workers would have to be hired.
3. The company was eager to expand into the frozen food area.
4. Despite the market's dominance by one brand, Cristel felt their established name and reputation of quality would give them an excellent entry into the market.

A Year 1 share goal of 6 percent had been established for the french fries, increasing to 12 percent in Year 3. Cristel anticipated no problems in gaining distribution equivalent to 83 percent of "all commodity volume," because they had long-standing relationships with many retailers.

In line with the market share goal, the following objectives had been established for the advertising campaign:

1. Achieve 80-percent awareness among french fry purchasers
2. Among those aware, achieve 70-percent knowledge of Cristel's product as a quality french fry
3. Among those with knowledge, achieve 60-percent preference
4. Among those with preference, achieve 45-percent conviction to purchase Cristel french fries
5. Among those with conviction, achieve 40-percent actual purchase of Cristel

Dobbs was working to prepare the three-year budget/payout plan for the product. He had before him figures on various cost elements, but had yet to determine the advertising and promotion budget.

	Year 1	Year 2	Year 3
Market sales in units (case of 30 2-lb. bags) .	46,108,000	47,952,320	49,390,889
Market share goal	6%	10%	12%
Market sales in units . . .	2,766,480	4,795,232	5,926,907
Pipeline	15,000	8,000	4,000
Factory shipments	2,781,480	4,803,232	5,930,907
Sales @ $45.36/unit ($1.19 retail price) . . .	$126,167,933	$217,874,604	$269,025,942
Fixed & variable costs @ $32.50/year 1	90,390,100		
$29.50/year 2+		141,685,344	174,961,757
Gross margin	35,769,833	76,189,260	94,064,185
Distribution @ $11.75/unit	32,682,390	56,437,976	69,688,157
Contribution margin . . .	$ 3,087,443	$ 19,751,284	$ 24,376,028

In addition to the established objectives, there were several other points Dobbs needed to take into account in setting a recommended advertising and promotion budget:

1. The market leader had spent an estimated $20 million on advertising during the past year and was expected to continue spending at that level.
2. Cristel sales reps had suggested an additional $3.00/case allowance in Year 1 to ensure that retailers would give the new product freezer space. Similar on-going allowances would probably be needed to hold that space.
3. The category was characterized by heavy couponing.
4. Cristel traditionally maintained an advertising to sales ratio of 2.5 percent.
5. Management, although eager for the product to succeed, was not eager to spend a tremendous amount on advertising.

Questions

1. Using the share of voice = share of market technique, what would the Cristel advertising budget be for Years 1–3?
2. What would the Year 1 advertising budget be under Cristel's traditional 2.5 advertising to sales ratio?
3. In addition to the suggested $3/case allowance to retailers, what other types of costs might be included in the sales promotion budget?
4. How might Dobbs take advantage of Cristel's strong reputation in determining his advertising budget?

5. Can you see any problems with using the share-of-voice approach in this situation?
6. What information would Dobbs need to use the DAGMAR approach in his budgeting?

Easy As Pie Mixes

Brian Ford, brand manager at Pixie Baking Products, Inc. (PBP), was putting together a preliminary budget and profit projection for PBP's newest product, Easy As Pie Mixes. Although PBP had a long history of new product successes, it had been several years since their last introduction, and Brian knew that changes in the marketplace made the situation for this product quite different from that of past PBP introductions. His budgetary recommendations would require a great deal of thought and support to get approval from his superiors.

PBP marketed a variety of baked goods including dry cake mixes, frozen prepared pie shells, a variety of flours, and a complete line of bread products. PBP enjoyed a fairly good relationship with most supermarket retailers, but had had to decrease its margins in the cake mix and pie shell lines recently because of increased competitive pressure and an accompanying need to increase trade dealing activities.

The new product, Easy As Pie Mixes, was a departure from PBP's other products and also something of a novelty in the pie mix category. Each Easy As Pie mix contained a pouch of prepared filling (in several fruit flavors, plus banana and coconut creams) and a tube of pie crust dough (in a form similar to packaged bread and roll doughs). All the consumer would need to do was roll out the dough, place it in a pie pan, add the prepared filling (and a top crust, depending on the variety), and bake it in an oven.

The product had performed well in consumer testing. It appealed primarily to working women who enjoyed baking but didn't feel they had the time to make a pie from scratch. Focus groups had suggested that Easy As Pie would be viewed as a nice compromise between baking from scratch and heating a frozen pie. Frozen pies were clearly seen as more convenient than Easy As Pie mixes, but much less personal because so little effort was needed. Easy As Pie was viewed as being closer to homemade but still relatively convenient. It was also viewed as more convenient than buying a frozen pie shell and a can (or cans) of pie filling. (PBP realized that Easy As

Pie might cannibalize their frozen pie shell sales, but because of the growing difficulty in maintaining shelf space in the crowded freezer section of the supermarket, they were willing to risk hurting sales of the frozen shell.)

Easy As Pie would be stocked in the refrigerated section of the supermarket, another crowded, highly competitive area. PBP knew that a substantial trade support program would likely be needed to get into that section, but expected that Easy As Pie's unique characteristics and apparent consumer appeal would make it a quick success and help them hold on to distribution. The hope was that Easy As Pie would be located near other refrigerated baking foods, such as bread and roll dough.

Ford felt that frozen pies would be Easy As Pie's primary competition. The leading brand in that category had recently launched an aggressive advertising campaign positioning its brand as a way for the cook to do something nice for her family and/or friends, who would think the pie was made from scratch. Several trade journals had estimated media spending in that campaign at about $6 million.

Ford was also using the frozen pie category as the basis for his market projections. Unit sales of frozen pies last year were 12,300,000. Growth was projected at 1 percent annually, and Brian didn't expect Easy As Pie to expand the category substantially. He felt that the product could capture an average 9 percent share the first year (the leader had a strong 38% share), 15 percent in Year 2, and 20 percent in Year 3. Pipeline sales would probably be about 15 percent of his Year-1 sales projection, falling to 3 percent in Year 2 and 1.5 percent in Year 3.

PBP was planning to price Easy As Pie at $2.75 to the trade, which would likely result in a retail price of $3.50, competitive with the average frozen pie price of $3.99. PBP's cost of goods on the product was $1.10 per unit. Because of the need for refrigerated transport, distribution expense would run about 15 cents per unit.

Brian anticipated that nearly equal advertising and sales promotion weight would be required in the first year, the advertising to position Easy As Pie in face of the frozen brand leader's heavy spending, and the sales promotion to get the necessary refrigerated distribution. He also felt that PBP would be willing to investment spend for a few years to get Easy As Pie established, as long as the brand was meeting its share goals.

Questions

1. Using the information given, construct a three-year payout plan for Easy As Pie. (With the given data, you can get through the contribution margin, following the example, in Table 8–3.)

2. Budget for advertising and sales promotion in Year 1 using the share-of-voice technique. How much will you spend? What will PBA's profit/loss be that year?

3. Advertising to sales ratios for food products average 7.3 percent. What would Easy As Pie's advertising budget be using that method? Do you think the advertising to sales method is an appropriate budgeting technique in this situation? Why or why not?

4. Industry experts predict that the leading frozen brand will cut its media spending in half for Year 2 of your payout period. Using share of voice, what would your Year-2 advertising budget be?

9

The Advertising Strategy
Key to Advertising Success

Think back to the Introduction and Chapter 1. You'll recall that we said the most important thing about advertising was the opportunity it gave to deliver sales messages for the product or service. We now come to the actual development of that sales message, the creative portion of the advertising campaign. It is, without doubt, the most important step in the campaign process. With a good, solid, benefit-oriented message, all the other elements of the campaign are magnified. Without this kind of message, it makes little difference how much is spent, where the advertising is placed, what other communications techniques are used, and so on—the advertising program will likely fail.

To this point, much time and effort has been spent learning who the prospective customers are or might be, where they are, how or why they might want or need the product or service, and even a bit about why they might respond to the product. By this time, the planner should have filled his or her head with all the information, knowledge, and attributes of the product or service, the marketplace, and the competition. Now, it's time to put all that material to work in the development of the best possible sales message. That's where the advertising campaign really starts to take life. This development of the selling message is generally the toughest, yet the most important step in advertising campaign planning.

ADVERTISING THAT'S STRATEGIC AND INTEGRATED

As we have stressed throughout this text, advertising is only one element of the overall promotional campaign for the product or service. Yet, the development of the advertising campaign sets the direction, tone, and, in some instances, the execution of the other marketing communication techniques. For example, advertising is generally used to signal to consumers the type, quality, style, value, cost, location, and even the image of the product or service. From this advertising strategy, other elements of the marketing communications mix are generated. Public relations tries to build on the advertising. Sales promotion is used to reinforce what is being said in the advertising. Packaging is designed to reflect the image being created in the advertising. This means the advertising really must have a strategic focus. It must be advertising that motivates consumers to act and react; has long-term potential for extension, development, and improvement; and can be supported and extended in other forms of marketing communication.

Strategic advertising always starts with the consumer. What benefit does the consumer desire? What need or want is to be filled by the product or service? What reward will the consumer get from purchase or use of the product? In other words, the emphasis is on what the consumer wants to buy, not what the manufacturer or marketer wants to sell.

People buy things—products or services or even ideas—for only two basic reasons. The product or service or idea will (a) solve a problem they have or perceive they might have, or (b) it will allow them to hold onto or improve on some of the good things they enjoy or want to enjoy. In other words, people buy the benefits of a product or service, not necessarily the product or service itself. For example, few people want a can of motor oil. There's really not much you can do with it. But, people do want the benefits of a can of motor oil if it helps keep their automobile running smoothly, gives them better gas mileage, helps reduce auto repair costs, and the like. By the same token, people want a specific automobile not just for the metal and plastic and rubber from which it is made. Instead they want the transportation it will provide or the convenience compared to public transportation or the prestige it will give them in their peer group. People don't buy products or services, they buy the benefits those products or services provide. Recall the Aunt Jemima Pancake Mix salesperson from the Introduction. No one wants buttermilk in the mix, they want the light, tasty pancakes that the inclusion of buttermilk will provide. No one really wants a half-inch drill. They want the holes that half-inch drill will make. Benefits, not attributes, are the key to a successful sales message and to a successful advertising campaign. That's the strategic part of the advertising campaign development process.

At the same time, the advertising campaign must be capable of being integrated into the other marketing communication techniques. To make that possible, the advertising campaign must have one clear, concise message which can then be translated by the other planners into their particular form of marketing communication.

The reason for this needed integration is simple. Consumers get information and ideas and concepts and perceptions of products and services from a multitude of sources, not just from advertising. Information about a new model automobile may come from a neighbor who has seen or driven one (word of mouth), from personal observation, or from simply seeing the new car parked in lots or on the street. Information and impressions can come from news stories in the media, from visits to dealer's show rooms, talks with salespersons, plus product literature and brochures. It can also come from sales promotional material in the media, from auto shows, from reading such publications as *Consumer Reports* and other sources. As important as the sources of information, however, is the fact that consumers don't appear to differentiate between what is advertising, what is news, what is information, and so on. They seem to simply gather all the available information, material, concepts, ideas, suggestions, and so on; sort them out; and draw some conclusion or form some images of the product or service. This multiple input system is why the advertising campaign planner must have a very clear idea of the benefit to be offered and the message to be delivered for, in general, it is from the advertising campaign that most of the other marketing communications programs are formed. As our media systems expand, there is an increasingly critical need for one clear, concise, complete message about the product or service. And, commonly, formulating that message is the task of the advertising planner.

SOME DEFINITIONS FOR CLARIFICATION

One of the things that often creates confusion in advertising campaign development is the widely varying way in which advertising people use certain terms. To make sure we're all talking the same language, here's how we define the following:

- *Advertising objective*—the clearly stated, measurable end result or effect of an advertising message, messages, campaign, or program. Usually, the advertising objective is measured in terms of growth or changes in awareness, preference, conviction, or other communication effect. The objective is "what the advertising is supposed to do."
- *Advertising strategy*—the benefit, problem solution, or other advantage, either physical or psychological, that is the value of the product or service that the advertising attempts to communicate to the target market. The strategy is "what the advertising is attempting to communicate."
- *Advertising execution*—the physical form in which the advertising message appears. This would include such areas as art, copy, music, and so on, and how these elements are aggregated or constructed in an effort to communicate the strategy to the customer or prospect to achieve the advertising objectives. The execution is the "how" the advertising appears or is distributed.

With these definitions in mind, we now start the development of an advertising strategy.

A STRATEGY IS THE ADVERTISING ROAD MAP

Today, many advertising planners use some form of advertising strategy development process to help them organize the information and their own thoughts about the product, their understanding of the prospective customer, their view of competition and competitive products, and so on, into some form of logical development process. The terminology for this system and approach goes under many names from "copy platform" to "creative strategy." No matter what it is called, the system tends to be a logical, step-by-step process which leads to the development of the most effective advertising message or messages.

The strategy process and the resulting advertising strategy form are important for a number of reasons.

1. The advertising strategy document serves as a method of obtaining total agreement from all levels of management on the target market, advertising objectives and strategy, and the general direction of the campaign. This is most important, for all persons involved must agree as to basic, general direction before any attempt is made at developing any of the advertising executions, media alternatives, promotional activities, and so on.

2. The document serves as general direction for the other persons who will be involved in the advertising process. For example, the creative and media people, because they may not have been involved in the information gathering and assembling process on prospects, competitors, or product features, use the advertising strategy as the basis for their development work. It's their guide to what is to be accomplished in the campaign and how to go about it.

3. The advertising strategy form can serve as direction for others who are developing other forms of marketing communications. For example, those involved in public relations, sales promotion, or direct marketing, and so on, would use the advertising strategy document to get an idea of the general thrust of the advertising campaign.

4. Finally, the advertising strategy document serves as a checkpoint for advertising executions, media plans, merchandising options, and the like. The planner and even management can use the developed strategy as the basis for evaluating the various forms of advertising tactics that might be proposed. This, in itself, may be one of the most important uses of the advertising strategy form.

BUT, JUST WHAT IS AN ADVERTISING STRATEGY?

So far, we've spoken about advertising strategies and the advertising strategy form in abstraction. Although we've made a good case for their use, little has been said specifically about what an advertising strategy is. An example will help put the advertising strategy into perspective.

In a visit to any supermarket or grocery store you will find a wide variety of detergent products. Some if not all of the brands listed would likely be on display. Each brand attempts to appeal to a segment of the detergent-buying population. This segmentation process is clearly demonstrated in the advertising strategy being used. For example, the following detergents have the following sales messages:

Oxydol—Bleaches as it washes

Dreft—The detergent for baby's laundry

Ivory Snow—Softens as it cleans

Gain—A clean you see, a fresh you smell

Cheer—All-temperature Cheer

Bold 3—Detergent plus fabric softener

Tide—America's favorite

Dash—Low-suds concentrate

Some might ask, "Why do consumers need all these different detergents?" After all, they're all designed to do pretty much the same thing, that is, to remove the dirt and odor from clothing and other washables, when used in an automatic washing machine. So, why are there so many brands? Why so many claims?

The answer is simple. Over the years detergent manufacturers have successfully segmented the laundry washing market by offering products with different features, ingredients, or benefits. Each brand has been developed to fill a consumer need or want. As we can see, some consumers want the advantage of a bleach in their detergent. Others want low suds. Still others want a product that can be used in all water temperatures.

To communicate the various benefits of each brand, the manufacturer first developed the product to fill the need. The advertising planner then translated that benefit into an advertising strategy that summed up in a phrase or a few words what the product would do or the benefit it offered the purchaser. Because all the detergents will accomplish, more or less, the same task of cleaning items in the laundry, the thing that really sets them apart from each other in the consumer's mind is the benefit they provide—the problem the product will solve. The advertising strategy sums up the competitive product benefit that differentiates it from other products. That's the main purpose of an advertising strategy.

Oh, by the way, these detergents are all manufactured by the same company, Procter & Gamble. Over the years, P&G has almost perfected market positioning, segmentation, and advertising strategy development. All these laundry products compete in the same detergent category and, to a certain extent, among themselves. Their primary job, however, is to compete against non-P&G brands. To do so, the advertising strategies must be very clear, very complete, and very concise, as they are here. Because advertising is the primary way in which consumers learn about detergent products, if the strategy were not as on target as are those listed earlier, consumers could not or would not be able to differentiate the various brands. Each would lose its clear, concise market positioning and, ultimately, sales in the marketplace.[1]

THE IMPORTANCE OF A BENEFIT-ORIENTED ADVERTISING STRATEGY

Several years ago, to determine the differences in the effect of advertising headlines, Dr. Alfred Politz, famed marketing and advertising researcher, conducted a series of split-run print studies. Using a home study course in the operation of television equipment as the advertised product, Dr. Politz developed two identical advertisements in terms of size, offer, copy, details, and look. The only difference in the two was the headline—the "what" being said about the home study course. In one advertisement the headline was:

New Jobs Offered in TV Station

In the second advertisement, the headline was:

Television Course for $11.97 per Week

Although Dr. Politz was testing the individual effects of the headlines, he was also testing the strategy. (The first advertisement was based on a strategy of offering job opportunities, while the second was built around a strategy of economy or low price for the course.)

Dr. Politz placed these two advertisements in a split-run edition (that is, one half the issues carried advertisement A, the other half advertisement B) of a magazine that would reach persons who might logically be interested in such a home study course. Again, the advertisements were identical with the exception of the headline and the response key that identified the advertisement to which consumers were responding.

Can you guess which ad pulled the best response? It was the first. It got over five times more inquiries than the "economy" strategy and headline. The "what you say" about your product or service does make a major dif-

---

[1]Adapted in part from Don E. Schultz, *Essentials of Advertising Strategy* (Chicago: Crain Books, 1981): 32.

ference in the results of an advertising campaign as Dr. Politz showed. The same can happen for any planner if a sound strategy is developed.[2]

As you can see from this example, the key ingredient for any advertising strategy is that the planner understand and think about the customer or prospect first, last, and always in the development process. As you move to the development of an actual advertising strategy, you might want to consider these questions:

1. Whom are we talking to now? In other words, what has our previous advertising been saying? Does it fit the target market?
2. Where are we now in the mind of the consumer? Is our product an important part of the prospect's life or simply something that is purchased and repurchased with little thought given to the use or brand?
3. Where is the competition in the mind of the consumer? What feelings or attitudes or experience do consumers have about competitive products? What will our advertising have to overcome to make the prospect give our brand consideration?
4. Where would we like to be in the mind of prospect consumer? Can we become the favorite brand or at least one of a considered set? What's our real objective with this advertising campaign?
5. What is the consumer promise? What can we say that will really bring home the benefit of what we have to offer? This is the key ingredient for any strategy.
6. What supporting evidence can we provide that will give the prospect a reason to believe our sales message?[3]

With these six questions in mind, we're ready to move to the actual development of the advertising strategy.

FORMALIZING THE ADVERTISING STRATEGY: A RECOMMENDED FORM

Over the years most major advertisers and agencies have developed some formal method of developing an advertising strategy. Some use a form, others a step-by-step development process, others simply list the basics of the product and the promise to be made to the consumer. Why do they formalize the advertising strategy? Why go to the trouble of developing a strategy when it seems that everyone knows what needs to be done? In the

---

[2]Adapted in part from Alfred Politz, "The Decline of Creative Advertising," *Journal of Marketing,* 25 (October 1960): 1–6.

[3]Adapted in part from A. Jerome Jewler, *Creative Strategy in Advertising,* 3rd ed. (Belmont, Cal.: Wadsworth Publishing, 1989): 38–39.

answers to those two questions lie the reasons why most advertisers and agencies formalize the advertising strategy.

1. A standard form or approach assures that everyone involved in the development of the creative product is in agreement as to who the target market is, what the message is to achieve, what benefit of the product is to be featured, and so on.
2. The development of an advertising strategy focuses the emphasis of the creative work on the message and not on the advertising tactic or the media delivery.
3. The development of an advertising strategy helps assure that the advertising message is developed from the point of view of the consumer and not the advertiser.

The advertising strategy form that follows has been developed, improved, and refined over the years. It works and has worked for all types of companies, products, clients, agencies, and students. The complete form is illustrated in Table 9–1. Here's a step-by-step outline of how to go about developing a successful advertising strategy.[4]

Step One—The Problem Advertising Can Solve

1. The Key Fact. The client has a problem concerning his brand, product, or company. That's the reason for the advertising campaign. To develop the proper strategy, you must first define the key fact or the key problem that you, as the advertising planner, are trying to solve. The problem must be related to and identified from the consumer's point of view. The fact that the brand's sales are declining is of no concern to the consumer. The real question is, Why have consumers stopped buying the brand?

This key question or key fact is crucial to the development of an effective advertising program. What is the key problem? Is it lack of brand awareness? Misconceptions about what the brand is, does, or the benefit it provides? Is the problem a more powerful advertising message from competitors? In other words, what is the key problem or key fact that summarizes why consumers aren't buying now?

The advertising strategy can only deal with one key fact or problem. It is your job to isolate that problem and get everyone's agreement that this is indeed the problem you will try to solve with the advertising strategy.

2. The Marketing Problem Advertising Can Solve. Several issues must be specified here. First, the marketing problem must flow from the

---

[4]This section is adapted from Don E. Schultz and Stanley I. Tannenbaum, *Essentials of Advertising Strategy,* 2nd ed. (Lincolnwood, Ill.: NTC Publishing, 1988): 56–65.

key fact. If the key fact is a declining sales curve because of more effective advertising by a competitor, then a statement of the marketing problem must respond to that. For instance, would you define the marketing problem as: the advertising campaign must be designed to (a) get new customers away from competitors by offering a stronger competitive benefit; (b) get our present customers to use our product more often thus preventing them from using the competitors'; (c) attract customers who have never purchased in the product category before; or (d) hold onto the customers we presently have by providing them reasons not to switch? It's the identification of the marketing problem that advertising can solve that really determines what your campaign will be all about.

By distilling all the information you have about the client's problem, you are in a position to define the essence of the marketing problem.

Let's say that the marketing problem is to get present customers to use the product more often. Now, the question to be asked is, Can advertising solve that problem?

Maybe, yes. Maybe, no. Take the case of Shredded Wheat cereal. Millions of people buy it, but few eat it very often. Most eat it about once every two weeks. Can advertising motivate them to use it more often?

If the key fact is that sales are down because distribution is poor, is this a marketing problem advertising can solve? Sometimes, yes. But generally, no.

If the key fact is that sales are down because competitors have undercut the price by 20 percent, can advertising solve this marketing problem? Sometimes, yes. But generally, no.

To objectively answer the question of "the marketing problem advertising can solve," a great deal of original information and thinking about the vitality of the product in relation to the state of the market is mandatory.

These two points—the key fact and the marketing problem advertising can solve—must be agreed upon and written down to generate insight into the total problem. It must be written, without prejudice, before the actual writing of the strategy statement. Now, let's move on to the strategy itself.

Step Two—The Creative Strategy

1. The Product.

A. Reality.   In reality, what is the product you are trying to sell? What are its ingredients? How is it made? Where is it grown? Who grows it? Who makes it? State real product information—facts—that will help those who will develop the creative and media portions of the campaign have a real feel for the product.

If you're selling canned peas, try for interesting facts about the product that may help distinguish it from other canned peas. Are the farmers who

Table 9-1   Advertising Strategy Form

Step One

The Problem

1. The Key Fact
2. The Marketing Problem Advertising Can Solve

Step Two

The Creative Strategy
1. What Is the Product? Or Service?
   a. In reality?
   b. As perceived?
2. Who Are the Prospects?
   a. Geographics
   b. Demographics
   c. Psychographics
   d. Media patterns
   e. Buying/use patterns
3. Who Is the Principal Competition?
4. What Is the Competitive Consumer Benefit?
5. What Is the Support for the Benefit? The Reason Why?
6. The Target Market Incentive Statement
7. What Is the Tone of the Advertising?
8. What Is the Communication Objective?
   a. What is the main point?
   b. What action should be taken?
9. Mandatory or Legal Requirements

grow the peas conscientious? What time do they start picking the crop? When do they stop? Is there a special kind of dirt the product is grown in? A special kind of rainfall? An angle of the sun that is most conducive to growing? Do the pickers wear gloves? Are they clean? Are they proud? When is the picking season? What is the price of the product? The package—what's it like? Where is the product bought? Does it taste good? Why?

These are but a few of the questions that should be asked to build the product reality section of the strategy. Leo Burnett once said, "There is inherent news in any product—and this can always be found if you dig hard enough into the product—and dig for facts."

The purpose of the product reality section is to obtain all the facts about the product: (a) to lead to a dramatic selling claim, and (b) to get common agreement on what the product is, what it does, and how it acts and feels. Even an objective statement of the product's shortcomings should be noted.

B. Perception.   Perceptions of the product are as important as the reality—often, they are more important. How do people feel about Shredded Wheat? Is it cold, impersonal? Strawy? Healthy? Tasty? Medicinal? Good for kids? A pain to eat? A laxative? Does it provide memories of childhood? Of Mom and Dad? Of Sunday breakfast?

Everyone concerned with the brand—at the agency and the advertiser—must be aware of how the brand is perceived by the customer or potential customers. Decisions then must be made: Shall advertising build on the positive perceptions? If so, how? Or are the negative perceptions so strong that advertising should attempt, overtly, to turn them around? Or, perhaps, these negative perceptions are so strong that they simply can't be changed with advertising.

Consumers' perceptions can be hypothesized on the basis of personal experiences. Generally though, the information should be gathered from quantitative and qualitative research. This research should be conducted among the user group defined in the marketing position section of the strategy.

In this section of the strategy the need to briefly describe the perceptions of the product category you are dealing with is also important. For instance, if you are placing Shredded Wheat in the cereal category, you need to find out how people feel about that category. Are cereals considered junk foods? Healthy? A necessity? Calorie-ridden? A tradition? You'll need all this to give a complete picture of how the product and category are perceived.

2. The Customer.   Who is the person most likely to buy your product? Age? Income? Education? All the vital statistics are helpful. But, remember, two families living next door to one another can have the exact same demographics, but one family eats no cereal, the other eats Shredded Wheat. Why?

Are their needs and wants at breakfast different? Again, why? What do they do for exercise? Hobbies? How do they relate to cereals? What is their favorite breakfast? How do they shop? When? Do they eat breakfast alone? Do they eat differently on weekends? On vacation? To develop a successful advertising campaign you have to know the customer as if he or she were your sister, brother, or mother.

Don't stop at just the demographics of a customer. Age and income figures alone never lead to a good campaign. If you don't have the luxury of other data, make your own hypothesis about the customer's life-style and habits. Talk to people you know. Ask people in stores how they feel about the product. Use your imagination to determine who would be most likely to use the product. You'll be surprised how close your hunch will be to the real thing.

To summarize, we are writing this strategy to decide what competitive benefit we can offer a target customer to take business away from a competitor, expand our own business by getting people to use our product more often, or open up a whole new category for our product.

So far, we've analyzed the product and the customer. Now, let's look at the competition.

3. The Competition.   Who are we competing against? What are their strengths? Their weaknesses? What are they offering the consumer—in reality? Perceptually? Are they vulnerable? Are consumers loyal to them? How loyal? What shares of market do each have? How much do they spend on advertising?

You must know the competition in order to compete. In the case of Shredded Wheat, are you competing against tiny Wheat Chex? Or are you competing in the hot cereal category against Cream of Wheat or Quaker Oats oatmeal? Or, perhaps, against vitamin pills? Or are you competing against general cereals like Corn Flakes, Rice Krispies, or Wheaties? Or against bacon and eggs?

Where do you hope to get your business from? Where does your brand have the most leverage by offering the most persuasive competitive benefits?

You now know what your product is, what the consumer wants, and who the competition is and what they are offering the consumer. Now, how can you take business away from the competition—business that will contribute significant dollar volume to your brand? This leads you to the most important point of the strategy statement—the competitive consumer benefit.

4. The Competitive Consumer Benefit.   If your strategic thinking is correct, the competitive consumer benefit is simply the key to what the consumer wants to hear about your product. It is nothing more than a factual statement based on your product, the consumer, and the competition of what your brand can uniquely offer that will make the consumer's life a bit better or solve one of the consumer's problems.

 The competitive benefit must be a single benefit that can be dramatically executed in advertising. Very often, seasoned professionals, as well as beginners, try to crowd two or more promises into the benefit statement. This usually results in chaos. Creative people end up going off in several confusing directions and the advertising shows it. Strategies based on two or more benefits usually communicate little and almost always lack persuasiveness.

If you can offer one simple benefit in a believable, persuasive strategy, you're well on your way to a sale.

It is vital to remember that the benefit must be competitive. You must make the consumer believe that your product does something better for him or her than other products in the competitive category. In other words, the benefit is not competitive if it simply says, "My product gives you good taste."

The benefit must be competitive. "My product tastes better than all other products in the competitive frame."

The competitive benefit must be something that solves a consumer problem or makes the consumer's life easier. The consumer, when hearing the benefit, has every right to ask, "What's in it for me?" If the answer is wishy-washy, then it is clearly not a benefit. If the answer is the same as that of other products, then the benefit is not competitive.

Many people have difficulty in distinguishing product features or product attributes from competitive benefits.

A product feature is something a product does—for example, a washing machine with fewer moving parts. But the benefit of "fewer moving parts" is that you will have fewer repair bills—or less worry.

A product attribute is something the product has—for example, a cereal made from whole grain wheat. The competitive benefit is that it gives you energy, or makes you feel good about what you put in your body.

Again, people buy quarter-inch holes, not quarter-inch drills. Tell consumers how to solve a problem or how to improve their life, and they'll buy your product. Tell them what makes your product tick or they'll click to another channel.

5. The Support? The Reason Why?   In order for the competitive consumer benefit to be effective, it must be believable to the consumer. First, it must jibe with the consumer's realm of experience. If you tell the consumer that you have a hair cream that will make him look younger, he won't believe you. If you tell a consumer you have a hammer that will make him or her an expert carpenter, that consumer will have a hard time accepting the idea.

The benefit must be relevant to the consumer's needs, wants, and experience. If the benefit of the product is "more energy," is that important to a twelve year old who has trouble expending his natural energies?

The benefit must be supported by a set of reasons to cause belief. In other words, as the Leo Burnett agency puts it, the consumer must be given "permission to believe."

The reason to believe, or benefit support, should come out of the product reality. It should be one fact, something the product does that makes the benefit supportable and believable. It should give the consumer permission to believe the benefit.

The support should be specific and brief. For instance, the claim that a washing machine has 28 percent fewer moving parts than any other washer would clearly support the benefit "less repair bills."

The reason "72 percent more prime wheat" clearly supports a competitive benefit of better health or nutrition.

Commonly, we can summarize the "Reason Why" as the "because" phrase which makes the competitive benefit possible.

6. Target Market Incentive Statement.   At this point, the strategy can be summed up—and checked out—with a piece of shorthand called the "target market incentive statement."

In one sentence, it recaps the whole strategy statement up to this juncture: "To (User Group, Name of Brand) is the (Product Category) that (Benefit of Brand)."

For instance, if you were developing a strategy for Shredded Wheat, had targeted it against adult breakfast eaters, decided to compete in the cereal category, and wanted to offer a competitive benefit of more nutrition, here is how the target market incentive statement would be written: "To adult breakfast eaters, Shredded Wheat is the brand of cereal that gives you more nutrition than any other cereal."

If you are developing a strategy to convince children who use vitamins to switch to Shredded Wheat, had decided to compete against bottled vitamins, and wanted to offer a benefit that this vitamin is more fun to take than any other vitamin, here is the way the target marketing incentive statement would read: "To children who take vitamin pills, Shredded Wheat is the brand of vitamin that is more fun to eat than other vitamins."

7. Tone.   One of the most important ingredients of the strategy statement is the section called "tone" or "personality" or "manner." This section should flow logically from the rationale behind the strategy. It should express the personality that the advertising will give the product, based on the benefit the product is offering, the consumer, and the competition. For example, if the benefit is offering fun to youngsters, obviously the tone of the advertising will not be "scientific." If all competitors are offering fun through animated characters, perhaps the tonality section should state that the advertising must offer fun but must do it differently, for example, with puppets or movie stars.

8. Action Statement.   As a result of the strategy and the creative execution that comes from it, what is supposed to happen? At this point, two action statements should be written. First, what is the main point—the one point—you want the consumer to take away from the advertising? That it's cute? Or funny? Or that it tells him what the product can do for him or her? The main point "take away" should really be the benefit that is contained in the strategy. It should literally fill out the statement. "I should buy this product because...." That, after all, is the intention of the advertising: to offer one persuasive reason why the prospect should purchase the product.

This main point of communication is a basic criterion on which the advertising should be judged. If the advertising does not communicate the benefit, then the communication is wasted.

The second action statement is what the consumer should do as a result of seeing the advertising. Do you want the viewer to think more favorably of your product? Fill out a coupon for more information? Buy your product? Tell a friend about it? Here again, measurable criteria can be applied and areas of accountability can be designated.

As stated earlier in this chapter, an advertising strategy as outlined here is not to be mechanically filled out. It is a thinking process that logically takes you through a consideration of the product, the consumer, and the competition, and should lead you to a meaningful competitive benefit that, in turn, will lead to a compelling, persuasive sales message.

9. Mandatory or Legal Requirements.   In many product categories, financial and automobile, in particular, there are certain legal explanations or addenda that must appear in the advertising. Likewise, many advertisers have specific requirements regarding the use of the logotype, brand names, brand characters, and the like. Legalities should be noted and, if necessary, explained in this section. If there is some requirement that must appear in the advertising executions, it should be listed here so that it will not be overlooked.

A Final Test of the Strategy Form

The advertising strategy form also serves another use. If the advertising planner can't complete the suggested form in detail, some material, information, or support is probably lacking. The planner should review the process and gather the necessary information and material before proceeding any further.

As a final review, look, at the advertising strategy form and evaluate it in these four ways:

1. Simplicity. Is the strategy easy for all the persons who will be involved in the approval to understand? Can you make it clearer or shorter or better?
2. Specificity. Is it clear? Complete? Concise? Does it state the advertising problem faced and provide a clear solution?
3. Durability. Will the strategy last a long time? Can it be overcome or offset by competitors quickly or easily? Is it something the advertiser can live with for several years?

4. Advertisability. Does this strategy offer the creative and media people latitude to develop really outstanding advertising? Is it too restrictive? In short, can great advertising come out of this strategy?

With this review of the advertising strategy basics, an example of how to develop and complete an advertising strategy form follows.

EXAMPLE OF AN ADVERTISING STRATEGY FORM

Here's an example of how an advertising strategy form should be completed. Of course, it's fictional but it will give you the idea. (See Table 9–2.)

Assume a new client has come to you with a new product. You've never seen this product before. In fact, the client, named Groves Unlimited, has just discovered it. The company calls it an ORANGE.[5]

The Client's Description of the Product

Here is the client's description of the product. It is typical of the briefing an advertising planner might get on a new product.

Groves Unlimited is a newly formed company based in Orlando, Florida. They have just developed and patented a new food product. This product, called an ORANGE, is a round citrus fruit that is approximately four inches in diameter. The ORANGE has a semihard skin or peel that is considered inedible. However, the meat of the fruit, under the skin, is delicious.

Groves Unlimited has tested the product and can claim that one ORANGE supplies the full recommended daily supply of vitamin C and niacin, as determined by the Food and Drug Administration. The meat of the ORANGE can be eaten directly. It is best eaten in its raw state. It is good at room temperature or refrigerated. It is also possible to squeeze the juice from the ORANGE to make a beverage that requires no sweetening.

- Pricing. Groves Unlimited plans to distribute the ORANGE with a recommended list price of forty-nine cents per pound. This is approximately eight to ten cents per orange.
- Packaging. The ORANGE will be sold in single units (loose) or prepackaged in plastic or net sacks with approximately three pounds or five pounds per sack.
- Distribution. Groves Unlimited will initially introduce the ORANGE to retail food stores throughout the United States. They recommend it be sold in the produce sections.

---

[5]The following section is adapted in part from Don E. Schultz and Stanley I. Tannenbaum, *Essentials of Advertising Strategy:* 67–74.

- Promotion. Groves Unlimited has asked you as the advertising planner to develop an advertising strategy to promote the use of this product.

Step One—The Problem Advertising Can Solve

The client has given you his thoughts. As the advertising planner, the assignment is to initially develop a strategy for the ORANGE. From that, an advertising campaign can be developed.

1. Key Fact.   The strategy begins with the statement of the key fact. What do you think is the key fact from all that you now know about this product? (Remember, you've never heard of the ORANGE before.) Is it that Grove wants to make millions? Or will the orange establish a new taste trend for America? Or is it a discovery that will shake the earth?

The key fact is simply this: There is a new product called the ORANGE and the world has never heard of it.

2. The Marketing Problem Advertising Can Solve.   Now, the question is, Is this a marketing problem that advertising can solve? The answer, obviously, is yes. The product seems right, the price is right, distribution will be achieved, and advertising should help sell it. But ask yourself—should you go after present users of citrus fruit? Try to expand the category? Or get into a new category? Obviously, there are no current users of ORANGES to pursue. So, for the purposes of this illustration, you could write the marketing problem statement like this: To get new users to try this product by offering a competitive consumer benefit.

Step Two—The Creative Strategy

1. The Product.   Now, look at the product. In reality, what is it?

The Product—Reality.   List the product's most important features:

1. Round fruit with thick skin and juicy meat
2. Tastes slightly sour—slightly sweet
3. Satisfies your thirst
4. Has vitamin C (healthy)
5. Has the same color as the sun
6. Good at breakfast or as a snack
7. Mixes well with alcohol
8. Tasty ingredient for other recipes

Some of the important attributes of the product are listed. Perhaps you can list more. There are some negative features of the product, and they, too should be listed:

1. Skin tastes awful
2. Too many seeds
3. Sloppy—squirts when cutting
4. More expensive than other fruits, like grapefruit

The Product—Perception.   In this section, you deal with the perceptions of the product. Usually, you conduct some research to find out what potential consumers think and feel about the product before and after they use it. Let's hypothesize some perceptions—both positive and negative. Add as many as you see fit:

Positive:

1. Better tasting than lemons
2. Pretty—has color of the sun
3. Healthy, natural food with vitamins

Negative:

1. Hard to get open
2. Seedy
3. Hard to get juice out
4. Not as good tasting as milk

2. The Customer.   Now, take a look at the customer. Here are some easy, though arbitrary, demographics:

Age: 25–45 years old
Sex: Female
Household Income: $70,000
Education Level: H.S. +

How do you build a strategy on these statistics? You have to know more about the customer. What does she do for a living? Does she love her kids? Her job? Does she work long hours? Does she feel guilty about working and being away from her children? Her husband? Does she wish she had more time to prepare meals? How can the orange solve her problems or make her life easier?

Put down in a simple paragraph some information about this woman's life-style and what she may want from the product:

> We are targeting the woman who chooses to work but still feels devoted to her family. She is always looking for new ideas in meals, snacks, entertainment, and decorating that will please her family and still be convenient to her schedule.

3. The Competition.   Now, who is our competition for the orange? From where will business come? A snap judgment will say we'll get it from other citrus fruits, like grapefruit and lemon. But why those old standbys? People have been using and drinking them for years. And they're loyal. Can we take business away from these established products? What benefit will people believe makes our product better? Does the world need another citrus fruit? Is there another category we can compete in successfully? Why not against cereals? Or vitamins? List the main forms of competition for the orange, as if it were a new product today:

1. Product Class: Breakfast Juice
   Brand Names: Grapefruit Juice
                  Prune Juice
                  Tomato Juice
2. Product Class: Cereals
   Brand Names: Rice Krispies
                  Total
                  Cap'n Crunch
3. Product Class: Vitamins
   Brand Names: One-A-Day
                  Therm-a-Gard
                  Flintstones
4. Product Class: Snack Foods
   Brand Names: Twinkies
                  Milky Way
                  Fritos
5. Product Class: Decorative Accessories
   Brand Names: Candelabra
                  Vases
                  Horn of Plenty
6. Product Class: Alcoholic Beverages
   Brand Names: Bloody Mary
                  Gimlet
                  Martinis

In which competitive frame should we compete? In which product category can we make the most money? Which is most vulnerable to this new product entry? Consider what our new product is and the strengths and weaknesses of all the competitors. Then, consider the needs and wants of our target consumer and determine whether our product—the ORANGE—can uniquely and competitively solve her problem or make her life easier.

4. The Competitive Consumer Benefit.   As was outlined earlier, this woman would welcome a product that provides new ideas in meals, snacks, entertainment, and decorating—a product that will please her family and still be convenient to her schedule.

Knowing this woman and what she wants, ask yourself, Why let the orange compete in a tight, competitive category against other juices or cereals or vitamins? Why not open a whole new category for your product alone and provide this competitive consumer benefit:

> The orange makes you feel like a more caring mother and wife than if you used any other combination of products.

5. The Support? The Reason Why?   The reason why—or support—could be stated this way:

> Works different ways to make your family's life better, easier, and happier. Dozens of innovative ways to use the product: quick snack, breakfast food, table decoration, furniture polish, meal ingredient, cold drink, beverage mixer, vitamin source, and more.

6. Target Market Incentive Statement.   The incentive for the target market could be stated: To mothers of young families, the ORANGE is a citrus fruit that makes them seem more caring than if they used a combination of other products.

7. Tone.   The tone or personality, of the advertising will, of course, flow from the benefit statement and dramatize it in the context of the target customer.

The tone statement in the strategy could read as follows:

> Highly emotional—allows the wife and mother to feel like a heroine to her husband and kids. She's the smart one who discovered this new product.

8. Action Statement.   What do you want the consumer to do as a result of our advertising?

1.   Think that she is a more caring mother if she uses ORANGES instead of other products in meals.
2.   Buy our product and use it in different ways each day.

9. Mandatory or Legal Requirements.   Because the FDA has approved our claims about vitamin C, there are no other requirements.

When given this hypothetical problem, most people would probably set up the orange as a citrus drink competitive with grapefruit and tomato juice. Although this positioning may be sound, the idea behind this example is to illustrate how the development of a strategy opens your mind to other ways of selling. It gives you the opportunity to objectively analyze the product, the needs of the customer, and the entry positions into the market. It further gives you the opportunity to be creative in your strategic thinking. By not accepting the obvious course, you may open a market that gives you much more leverage to compete in and is much more lucrative.

Table 9–2   A Completed Advertising Strategy Form

Creative Strategy Development for the ORANGE

Step One

A. The Problem
   1. The Key Fact: There is a new product called the ORANGE and the world has never heard of it.
   2. The Marketing Problem Advertising Can Solve: To get new users to try this product by offering a competitive consumer benefit.

Step Two

B. The Creative Strategy
   1. What Is the Product?
      a. In reality?
         1. Round fruit with thick skin and juicy meat
         2. Tastes slightly sour/slightly sweet
         3. Satisfies your thirst
         4. Has vitamin C (healthy)
         5. Has the same color as the sun
         6. Good at breakfast or as a snack
         7. Mixes well with alcohol
         8. Tasty ingredient for other recipes
         9. Skin tastes awful
         10. Too many seeds
         11. Sloppy—squirts when cutting
         12. More expensive than other fruits, like grapefruit

      b. As perceived?
         1. Better tasting than lemons
         2. Pretty—has color of the sun
         3. Healthy, natural food with vitamins
         4. Hard to get open
         5. Seedy
         6. Hard to get juice out
         7. Not as good tasting as milk

   2. Who are the Prospects?
      Females 25–45 years old with household incomes above $70,000 and with more than a high school education. We are targeting the woman who chooses to work but still feels devoted to her family. She is always looking for new ideas in meals, snacks, entertainment, and decorating that will please her family and still be convenient to their schedule.
   3. Who Is the Principal Competition?
      No direct competition for our benefit. A number of products would be needed to provide all the benefits of the orange.
   4. What Is the Competitive Consumer Benefit?
      The orange makes you feel like a more caring mother and wife than if you used any other combination of products.

(continued)

Table 9–2   (Continued)

5. What Is the Support for the Benefit? The Reason Why?
   Works different ways to make the family's life better, easier, and happier. Dozens of innovative ways to use the product: quick snack, breakfast food, table decoration, furniture polish, meal ingredient, cold drink, beverage mixer, vitamin source, and more.
6. The Target Market Incentive Statement: To mothers of young families, the *orange* is a citrus fruit that makes them seem more caring than if they used a combination of other products.
7. What Is the Tone of the Advertising?
   Highly emotional—allow the wife and mother to feel like a heroine to her husband and kids. She's the smart one who discovered this new product.
8. What Is the Communication Objective?
   a. What is the main point?
      Think that she is a more caring mother if she uses ORANGES instead of other products in meals.
   b. What action should be taken?
      Buy our product and use it in different ways each day.
9. Mandatory or Legal Requirements
   None required. FDA has approved vitamin C claims.

The final strategy is clear and concise. In addition, as you can see, the strategy statement gives the creative and media people a clear, sharp course to pursue. In no way does it inhibit creativity. In fact, it encourages it. The strategy gives the knowledge that can only help lead to more effective approaches. It also narrows the avenues of pursuit. It lets the creative and media people spend time searching for uniqueness in their areas. The strategy also provides an excellent way to measure the selling power of the creative executions and gives you criteria for evaluating the advertising.

WHAT TYPE OF STRATEGY APPROACH TO USE

To this point, it would appear that advertising strategies are all about the same. That is, all products or services can be approached in about the same way using a generalized strategy format. Such is not the case. Ever since advertising progressed from simple written signs to formal media systems, advertising experts have been trying to find the best way to develop an advertising strategy and from that, an advertising campaign. Although there is still no one right way, several very sound approaches have been developed over time.

These different methods of developing an advertising strategy (and therefore an advertising campaign) have been identified by Patti and Frazer. They are compared in Table 9–3. As you will see, each of the seven listed approaches has some situations and conditions under which it works best. In addition, there are some generalized reactions that competitors might take. Although there is no one perfect method of strategy development, this approach will help put the most well known and recognized into some frame of reference.

With this look at advertising strategy development, we're ready to move on to the advertising execution.

SUMMARY

With a soundly developed advertising strategy and a clear-cut advertising promise supported by a sound reason why, many advertising campaign planners believe they have devised an advertising campaign that is sure to succeed. Although we, too, believe that "what you say" is of much greater importance than "how you say it," the advertising strategy is a critical element of success. A sound strategy will usually succeed at some level; a truly outstanding advertising execution can increase the response to the campaign by a thousandfold. The difference between a "good" and a "great" campaign is often the result of the advertising execution—the next step in advertising campaign development.

Table 9–3   Creative Strategy Alternatives: A Summary

Strategy	Description	Most suitable conditions	Competitive implications
Generic	Straight product or benefit claim with no assertion of superiority	Monopoly or extreme dominance of product category	Serves to make advertiser's brand synonymous with product category; may be combated through higher order strategies
Preemptive	Generic claim with assertion of superiority	Most useful in growing or awakening market where competitive advertising is generic or nonexistent	May be successful in convincing consumer of superiority of advertiser's product; limited response options for competitors
Unique selling proposition	Superiority claim based on unique physical feature or benefit	Most useful when point of difference cannot be readily matched by competitors	Advertiser obtains strong persuasive advantage; may force competitors to imitate or choose more aggressive strategy (e.g., "positioning")

(continued)

Table 9–3 (Continued)

Strategy	Description	Most suitable conditions	Competitive implications
Brand image	Claim based on psychological differentiation; usually symbolic association	Best suited to homogeneous goods where physical differences are difficult to develop or may be quickly matched; requires sufficient understanding of consumers to develop meaningful symbols/associations	Most often involves prestige claims that rarely challenge competitors directly
Positioning	Attempt to build or occupy mental niche in relation to identified competitor	Best strategy for attacking a market leader; requires relatively long-term commitment to aggressive advertising efforts and understanding consumers	Direct comparison severely limits options for named competitor; counterattacks seem to offer little chance of success
Resonance	Attempt to evoke stored experiences of prospects to endow product with relevant meaning or significance	Best suited to socially visible goods; requires considerable consumer understanding to design message patterns	Few direct limitations on competitor's options; most likely competitive response is imitation
Affective	Attempt to provoke involvement or emotion through ambiguity, humor, or the like, without strong selling emphasis	Best suited to discretionary items; effective use depends upon conventional approach by competitors to maximize difference; greatest commitment is to aesthetics or intuition rather than research	Competitors may imitate to undermine strategy or difference or pursue other alternatives

SOURCE: Charles H. Patti and Charles F. Frazer, *Advertising: A Decision Making Approach* (New York: Dryden Press, 1988): 304.

Case Studies

T. White and Associates

T. White and Associates, a Stamford, Connecticut-based rehabilitation consulting firm, recently opened a branch office in Richmond, Virginia. Other branches are located in Baltimore, Maryland, and Youngstown, Ohio. Each office is staffed by a branch manager, four to fifteen counselors, and supporting clerical staff.

T. White was formed in 1968 under the auspices of the Phoenix Mutual Casualty Insurance Company. T. White and similar companies were organized in response to the desire on the part of both insurance carriers and attorneys specializing in workers' compensation claims for an outside agent to supervise rehabilitation efforts. Through the counselor approach, claimants are provided with a trained, concerned intermediary who is presumably less likely to be biased in favor of economic concerns over the time and quality elements of the rehabilitative effort. Carriers benefit because an outside consultant relieves some of the workload formerly carried by claims representatives. Also, the counselor's specialized training often leads to quicker rehabilitative results. Although not all major insurance carriers utilize counseling firms, acceptance is currently estimated at 55 percent.

Persons filing job-related injury claims are assigned a counselor who oversees any medical care needed and supervises physical and vocational rehabilitative efforts. The counselor's efforts may include working with an employer to modify the physical requirements of a job if the claimant is to return to his preinjury employment. If the nature of the injury is such that the claimant can no longer perform the same type of work, the counselor works with the claimant and attorney to identify areas of vocational interest suitable to the claimant's physical capabilities. The counselor then ensures that necessary training is provided and aids the claimant in obtaining a job in the field. Supervision is maintained for up to one year to ensure a proper "fit" between the claimant and the job.

Some counseling supervision is strictly medical, while other cases call for psychological counseling and a high degree of vocational support. A relationship of mutual trust between claimant and counselor is vital for successful rehabilitation. Counselors usually have either medical (RN) or psychological training. T. White requires that all counselors undergo a six-week on-the-job training period that includes specialized classes in vocational and medical guidance. Counselors are also expected to attend seminars on work-related topics, and tuition fees for applicable courses are paid by the company. A typical counselor caseload involves working with ten to fifteen persons in varying stages of rehabilitation.

Although originally established by the Phoenix Company, T. White now works with a number of carriers. Case references are also obtained through physicians and corporations familiar with past cases, as well as attorneys specializing in workers' compensation cases. All fees are handled through the involved insurance company, and bills are submitted monthly. Carrier approval must be obtained for any rehabilitative efforts, such as physical therapy and vocational training. The claimant's attorney is also consulted on all major decisions.

The Richmond office was opened to service the claims resulting from the involvement of a regular T. White client, Timber Mutual, with a large paper-processing plant located in Richmond. After six months of operation, Scott Miller, the branch manager, filed a report with the home office. He noted that the number of cases from Timber Mutual was currently thirty-seven, a workload that the four Richmond counselors were easily able to handle. Miller predicted that this figure would remain fairly constant, taking into account the flow of completed cases and new claims. Although income from this business source was more than sufficient to justify the office's existence, Miller was eager to solicit other clients. He felt that the Richmond market was very attractive for several reasons:

• Several large manufacturing plants were located in or near the city.
• Many of the major insurance carriers had established regional offices in the area.
• The number of personal injury claims had increased slightly from the past year, in comparison with a decline in the national trend.

On the negative side, Miller noted that there were four other rehabilitation consulting firms of varying size operating in the city. Each counted one or more of the large insurance carriers among its major clients. The environment for new referrals was somewhat competitive.

After reviewing Miller's report, the home office informed him that they had decided to make Richmond a test ground. The field of rehabilitation consulting had been reluctant to use advertising as a marketing tool in the past, being content to rely upon counselors' personal contacts with insurance carriers. T. White management felt that, if properly done, advertising could prove effective for tapping new sources of business, as well as reinforcing old contacts. Therefore, Miller was to develop an advertising campaign for the Richmond office. Management placed the following stipulations on the campaign:

1.   Its fundamental strategy was to be readily transferrable to other offices.

2. It must result in a 75 percent increase in case referrals within nine months of inception. (Approval was given for the hiring of additional counselors as needed.)
3. It was to be accomplished within a budget of $500,000.

Although the main office's enthusiasm was greater than he had anticipated, Miller realized that he now had an opportunity to put some of his marketing ideas to work. All he needed to do was review the media vehicles available to him and start spending money.

Richmond is served by two daily newspapers and several community weeklies. Four broadcast television stations are based in town, and viewers can also pick up several Washington, D.C. stations. Cable television penetration is close to 45 percent. There are twenty-six radio stations, encompassing a variety of formats.

Feeling that rehabilitation consulting was still relatively unknown and that broad public awareness was the key, Miller bought a full page in each of the daily papers and ran an advertisement that outlined T. White's services. He also taped a 30-second radio spot to be broadcast on an all-news station exhorting listeners to "check today's paper for important news regarding your health and future." Two weeks later, only one referral had come in attributable to the "campaign." Realizing that perhaps there was more to successful advertising than he had thought, Miller asked a friend in marketing for advice. After listening to a description of the company's services (he hadn't seen the newspaper ads) and reading Miller's original report, the friend suggested that Miller answer the following questions before spending any more money:

- Who was the primary audience? insurance companies? corporations? unions? doctors? lawyers? potential claimants?
- Having identified the audience, what type of message would best attract them? Would they need basic information as to what the company is and offers, or would they be more interested in how it differs from similar companies?
- What media vehicles would be most likely to get the message to the right audience?

Questions

1. Develop advertising strategies for at least two of the potential audiences. Include a justification for addressing that particular audience.
2. Which potential strategy do you feel would be most effective? Why?
3. If T. White were to stress new business solicitation through carrier contacts as a primary aspect of counselors' responsibilities, would the advertising strategy change? Why or why not?

Health Heels

Mike Young, a copywriter at Smith & Smythe Advertising, was working to develop a creative strategy for a new line of women's shoes. His agency handled several lines for a major manufacturer of athletic and street shoes. This new line was made up of women's high-heeled shoes that were built to provide the sort of foot cushioning usually found only in athletic shoes.

Mike had been through a series of meetings with the agency exec assigned to the account and the client's product manager for the line. At the last meeting, Mike had agreed to take a stab at drafting a creative strategy for the national launch of the line. Now he was reviewing his notes from the meetings as well as the results of some consumer concept and product testing. Mike firmly believed that this was an innovative product that would win consumer favor. Now, if he could just come up with what to say about the product.

Health Heels (the client's working name for the line) had been developed after some extensive research and testing by the client's design group. The idea for the product had come from the company's financial vice president, a fitness- *and* fashion-conscious woman. One day in a product development brainstorming session, she mentioned that she was getting tired of the working woman's common shoe struggle—wearing athletic shoes to get to and from work and changing into "fashion/business" shoes once she got there. "It's not a major headache," she said, "just one of those irritating little things where you find yourself thinking, 'There's got to be a better way!' I have to admit that I really like the way a pair of nice looking high heels can set off an outfit, but they'll rip your feet up if you wear them for too long. At least, that's what they do to my feet. And these aren't cheap high heels! Is there anything we can do about that problem?"

A comfortable, athletically sound high heel proved hard to develop. The company's designers went through a number of prototypes before coming up with Health Heels. Both the heel and sole of the shoe had several layers of special cushioning to help absorb the impact of walking, particularly the extra impact associated with the design of any high-heeled shoe. Health Heels were both comfortable and fashionable—but that unique combination of attributes came at a price. In order to recover the invested research costs and provide adequate margins for both the company and its distributors, Health Heels would likely sell for about $100 a pair at retail.

Secondary research into women's shoe purchasing habits showed that about 20 percent of shoes sold were priced in the $75–$125 range. About 65 percent of women over the age of 18 owned at least one pair of athletic shoes. However, Mike wasn't sure how many of those women were also buyers of shoes in the Health Heels price range.

Concept testing had shown that many women reacted positively to the Health Heels concept, seeing it as a solution to a very real problem. Of the women surveyed, 75 percent owned athletic shoes and 25 percent did not. Of the 75 percent owning athletic shoes, 25 percent reported they were involved in a walking program as part of their regular exercise routine. These "walkers" were especially excited about the Health Heels concept, but the other groups were also positive.

Reported likelihood of purchase fell significantly when women were told how much Health Heels would cost. The decline was lowest among the walking group and highest among the 25 percent of the sample who did not currently own athletic shoes. Results of a probing question asked of those who changed their purchase intention suggested that believability became a problem at the high price; that is, women felt that $100 was a lot to pay for a pair of high heels that might not really be all that comfortable.

After the concept test, some prototype pairs of Health Heels were made and given to a group of twenty-five women to wear. Twenty of these women currently owned athletic shoes and ten were "walkers." All twenty-five of the women gave the shoes excellent ratings after a month of wear. Some of their comments included: "These are the most comfortable shoes I've ever worn. And I don't just mean the most comfortable heels—I mean the most comfortable shoes of any kind!" "I love these shoes—I've worn them almost every day. After the first week, I stopped wearing my sneakers to and from work and just wore these. They're great! Do they come in navy blue?" "I've never really thought of my high heels as uncomfortable. But these shoes feel so much better, I actually hated having to put on a pair of $250 slingbacks to wear to a dinner the other night. Those used to be my favorite shoes!"

Twenty of the women said they would be willing to pay the $100 price. Of the other five, two said the price was appropriate for the shoes, but out of their budget. Three felt $100 was too high, but said they'd be sure to buy Health Heels if ever they were marked down by a retailer.

Based on the positive results of the product use test, the company decided to stay with the $100 price. Mike's job was to come up with a creative strategy that would convince women who had never tried Health Heels to pay $100 for a pair. In his first draft, he came up with the following:

CREATIVE STRATEGY FOR HEALTH HEELS

Step One: The Problem

1. The Key Fact: Women need to be made aware of Health Heels and have to believe in the product's benefits enough to be willing to pay $100 a pair at retail.
2. The Marketing Problem Advertising Can Solve: We need to convince women to buy Health Heels to replace their regular high-heeled shoes.

Health Heels probably won't replace dressy high heels worn for special occasions or with special outfits, but should replace those high heels worn on an everyday basis—work shoes.

Step Two: The Creative Strategy

1. What is the Product?
    A. In reality. A women's high-heeled shoe specifically designed to wear like an athletic shoe. The shoe has special cushioning to protect the foot and absorb the normal impact of walking, and the particularly harsh impact caused by high heels. The shoes look like a standard pair of women's pumps, and come in all the basic colors—black, taupe, gray, white, and navy. The retail price will be about $100 a pair.
    B. Perception: Women will like the idea of a comfortable high heel. But, because comfort isn't usually associated with high heels, they'll likely be somewhat skeptical that Health Heels are as comfortable as we claim. And, with the $100 price tag, that sketicism/concern will probably be increased. "Are these shoes that much more comfortable than other high-heeled pumps that I should pay $100 for them? They look like other high heels."
2. The Prospects:
    A. Geographics: No particular geographic area—total U.S., particularly urban areas, where there are more women working in jobs that demand the type of clothing high heels usually accompany—suits, dresses, and so on.
    B. Demographics: Women employed full or part time in professional and clerical jobs; most aged 18–54; personal income of $20,000 and over; most will be at least high school graduates; married, single, divorced.
    C. Psychographics: Concerned about looking good at work, primarily for her own personal satisfaction. Also concerned about comfort—either takes public transportation to and from work and has to walk from a transportation stop to the office and her home or does a lot of walking on the job. May be involved in regular exercise program. Willing to try new product, though not necessarily a risk-taker. Considers herself a "smart shopper."
    D. Media Patterns: Watches television in the evening for 1–3 hours. Heavy reader of magazines, primarily women's publications. Listens to the radio while getting ready for work in the morning. Sees transit advertising and outdoor on the way to and from work. Gets a lot of direct mail, has bought by mail in the past.

E. Buying/Use Patterns: Buys 2–5 pairs of high heels for work yearly. Buys these for fashion (color, style) and for comfort, although has found that what's comfortable in the store isn't always comfortable on the job. Owns a pair of athletic shoes that she wears to and from work, changing once she gets to the office. Usually spends about $60–$75 for work pumps. Spends more for dress shoes. Athletic shoes cost her about $30–$40. Likes the comfort of her athletic shoes, but won't leave them on at the office because they don't go with the outfit she carefully selected to wear. When she's wearing something for the first time, she often leaves the athletic shoes at home.

3. Principal Competition: Traditional high-heeled pumps, particularly those positioned as "career" shoes. Athletic shoes are not direct competition, because they have other uses besides office wear. Health Heels would not completely replace athletic shoes, but might replace standard pumps.

Questions

At this point in the strategy, Mike got called to a meeting for another client. Your task is to complete the strategy: Competitive Consumer Benefit, Support for the Benefit, Target Market Incentive Statement, Tone, and Communications Objective. Develop two separate approaches, using any two of the methods discussed in Table 9–3: generic, preemptive, unique selling proposition, brand image, positioning, resonance, or affective. (Note: you may refine the target market description if you wish; Mike's first draft describes a fairly general target.)

From Strategy to Execution

GETTING PEOPLE TO ACT AND REACT TO ADVERTISING

Because we have invented new and more sophisticated media techniques to get messages to consumers, one of the biggest problems most advertising planners face today is getting the consumer's attention in an extremely cluttered media marketplace. The consumer's capacity to receive and process all this new information hasn't expanded. In truth, the sheer amount of advertising in today's marketplace is almost overwhelming. So, the big question the planner must ask is: What can I say and how can I say it so that my message is important enough for the consumer to give me enough of his or her attention and his or her very valuable time to understand and to react to my sales message?

The answer the planner provides to this question separates the excellent one from the one who is only average. The reason: to achieve excellence the planner must truly understand the person he or she wishes to reach with the advertising. The planner must be able to empathize with the problem the consumer has that can be solved by the product or service. The problem and the solution must be clearly and concisely stated—so that the consumer receives the message and is able to act on it easily.

We've said before that people buy things—products or services or even ideas—for only two basic reasons: the product or service or idea must (a) solve a problem the consumer has or perceives she or he might have, or (b) allow consumers to hold onto or improve on some of the good things they enjoy or want to enjoy. If your strategy is correct, the next step is the execution or presentation of the sales message.

Starting at the Wrong End

A common problem in the development of an advertising campaign is that the inexperienced planner (and, unfortunately, some of the more experienced ones too) start at the wrong end of the advertising campaign. They start with the advertising execution, not the product benefit. They start with an idea for a commercial or an advertisement or a media buy or an event or a sales promotion premium. They start with the execution or translation of the advertising campaign, not with the strategy or the primary selling message or benefit that is to be offered to the consumer through the advertising.

Today, unfortunately, much mass media advertising appears to have been developed based on the availability of a neat, new creative or technological gimmick—for example, ultra slow motion photography. Or computer animation. Or strobe lights. Or the use of outrageous rock musicians. In other words, the emphasis in the campaign has been put on the technique used to get attention, not on the ultimate benefit the consumer will receive from the advertising as a result of using the product. You might think about it this way:

> Let's assume you are a door-to-door salesperson. Your job is to go to homes in your city (just like the Aunt Jemima Pancake Mix salesperson in the introduction) and attempt to persuade homeowners to install another layer of insulation in their ceiling. You have a good story. Your product can actually reduce the annual heating cost for the homeowner by about 35 percent. And, based on the average home, the product will pay for itself in about two winters.

What would you do when you got to the door of the homeowner? Would you:

1. Start to sing a finger-snapping jingle?
2. Show a picture of a well-known celebrity?
3. Do a tap dance on the front step?
4. Tell a joke?
5. Start talking about how to save 35 percent on heating bills?

Although the example may seem a bit farfetched, it's not when you consider the type of advertising to which most of us are exposed every day. Advertisers try to entertain us. Amuse us. Make us laugh. They use celebrity spokespersons. They use music and songs and dancing and even tell jokes. All in an attempt to call attention to their product or service. The problem is, consumers aren't interested in the jokes or songs or celebrities or even the product or the advertising. They're interested in what problem the product will solve or the way it might help them improve their life. Remember, good advertising is simply good selling. Get to the benefit and get to it quickly.

Enhancing the Strategy with a Strong Execution

There's little question the "what you say" is the most important decision in an advertising campaign. All other decisions simply reinforce or help magnify that decision. But the advertising execution or the "how the advertising strategy is communicated to the prospect" does have a very major impact. In general, a sound strategy will succeed regardless of the execution. If "what you say" is of benefit to the prospect or solves a prospect's problems, some response will usually occur. However, if the strategy is presented in an interesting, exciting, and memorable way, it is more likely that larger numbers of prospects will respond quickly. Thus, to qualify this position a bit, although the "what you say" is vital, the "how you say it" can really prove to be the difference between a successful campaign and an outstanding one.

Here's an example. Quaker Oats Company's Life cereal was first introduced in 1961. After several moderately successful attempts to sell this new nutritional, ready-to-eat cereal to different target markets, Quaker Oats and the advertising agency at that time, LaRoche, McCaffrey & McCall, developed the basic strategy of promoting Life as "the nutritional cereal which tastes good." After several years and several different advertising executions, this new "what to say" strategy about the product had started to generate interest among consumers. Sales were growing, but the product was not an overwhelming success.

In early 1968, sales of the cereal took off. That growth is directly due to a new advertising execution. Specifically, it was a television commercial developed by the Doyle Dane Bernback Agency that has come to be known simply as "Mikey." (See Exhibit 10–1.) The strategy did not change. The execution did. The "Mikey" commercial immediately got the attention of ready-to-eat cereal buyers and users, and Life began its sales climb. The decision to feature "taste" in the advertising as the "what to say" started the cereal on the road to success. The translation of that strategy through the "Mikey" commercial really provided the impetus to make it a major winner. Some twenty years after the "Mikey" commercial first appeared, it was still winning new customers for Life cereal.

Similarly, John Hancock, a well-known and respected insurance company, found a very unique way to present its messages about financial services in an extremely crowded and cluttered media environment. John Hancock's basic strategy focused on the consumer. What the consumer wanted and needed in financial services, that is, answers to problems or anticipated problems or questions was basic to the strategy. But the execution really brought the message to life. Where most of the competitive advertising consisted of corporate symbols presented in various ways, John Hancock, with its real world, real life approach, really stood out and got noticed. (See Exhibit 10–2.)

Exhibit 10–1   Life Cereal's "Mikey": Execution Improves Success

1ST BOY: What's this stuff?
2ND BOY: Some cereal. Supposed to be good for you.

1ST BOY: D'you try it?
2ND BOY: I'm not gonna' try it, you try it.

1ST BOY: I'm not gonna' try it.

2ND BOY: Let's get Mikey!
1ST BOY: Yeah!

2ND BOY: He won't eat it. He hates everything.

2ND BOY: He likes it!

Hey Mikey!
ANNCR: (VO) When you bring Life home, don't tell the kids it's one of those

nutritional cereals you've been trying to get them to eat. You're the only one who has to know.

SOURCE: Reprinted courtesy of Quaker Oats Company.

Exhibit 10–2   John Hancock Storyboard

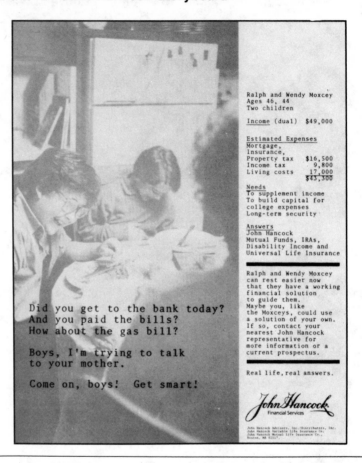

SOURCE: Reprint permission granted by John Hancock Mutual Life Insurance Company, Boston, Massachusetts.

The "Big Idea"

Great advertising campaigns, particularly those which are brought about by great advertising executions, are usually the result of what is termed a "big idea." As with the "Mikey" and John Hancock examples, the "big idea" is usually very simple, but it brings a realism, an understanding of the marketplace, and an empathy with the target market that literally makes the advertisement jump off the page or off the television screen and into the life of the reader or viewer.

Selling an intangible is tough even in person-to-person situations. It's even tougher through the media. But, American Express has done the job beautifully over the years. Their "Do You Know Me?" campaign, in which people with famous names, but not famous faces, told of the advantages of the American Express card, ran for over ten years. It got the point across that even if you aren't known, the American Express card certainly is. This "big idea" broke through the clutter and got the American Express sales message across cleverly, convincingly, and most important, interestingly. The strength of that idea carries over into a more recent print campaign (see Exhibit 10–3): "The American Express Card. It's part of a lot of interesting lives." The emphasis has moved from celebrities and "near celebrities" to everday, interesting, people.

The light beer category has been a unique American phenomenon. Miller introduced the category in 1974 and grew to be the dominant brand. In 1982, Anheuser-Busch introduced Budweiser Light, a competitive product. The original Budweiser Light theme was "Bring Out Your Best." Because Miller was so dominant, the name "lite" was almost synonymous with the category. Therefore, in a bar, when a person ordered a "light beer" or a "light," they were most often served Miller.

As a result of this bartender bias, the basic problem Budweiser Light faced was to get consumer trial. That could only come about by getting them to ask for the brand by name. The first step was to shorten the name to Bud Light. That was done in 1984, at the same time the new advertising campaign developed by DDB Needham Worldwide, called "Gimme a Light," was introduced. In the advertising campaign, the situation was always the same: a customer came into a bar, asked for a "light beer," saying "Gimme a light." He or she was presented with some unique form of light ranging from lasers to a dog jumping through a burning hoop. The customer then realizes the mistake and says, "I meant a Bud Light." Thus, the brand name was firmly established in what has been one of the most successful advertising campaigns in the category. (See Exhibit 10–4).

Another example of the "big idea" is that of *Rolling Stone* magazine. *Rolling Stone* was born in the late 1960s. It quickly became the voice of the "antiestablishment" with a unique editorial view. As times changed, so did *Rolling Stone,* but the original image of the publication readers as "hippies," protesters, and off-beats remained. To change the view of advertisers and agency people, particularly media planners and buyers, *Rolling Stone* launched a dramatic advertising campaign in the trade press. Called "Perception–Reality," the series compares what advertisers likely perceive the reader of *Rolling Stone* to be with what he/she really is. The same is done to illustrate the type of products *Rolling Stone* readers use and buy to show the value the publication has as an advertising vehicle. *Rolling Stone,* with a strong strategy and an unique execution, is successfully changing the way advertisers and advertising agencies think of the publication's audience. A big idea makes a sound strategy even stronger. (See Exhibit 10–5 for an example of *Rolling Stone's* "big idea.")

Exhibit 10–3   AMEX Print Ad

The American Express Card.
It's part of a lot of interesting lives.

SOURCE: Reprinted courtesy of American Express.

Cheer detergent has been on the market for a number of years. The basic consumer benefit the product provides is that it works equally well in all water temperatures. That strategy really hasn't changed in more than fifteen years. But, a unique presentation of that idea, a man washing clothing in ice water, provided a "big idea" that sent Cheer sales soaring. The exe-

Exhibit 10–4   Bud Light Commercials

SOURCE: Reprinted courtesy of Anheuser-Busch.

cution really gets the all-temperature water message across in a memorable way. The basic consumer benefit and the brand are burned into the memory of the consumer. Most important, though, the advertising stands out in the sea of detergent commercials that surround the consumer every day. Another "big idea" strengthens, expands, and enhances the advertising strategy. (See Exhibit 10–6.)

Exhibit 10–5   *Rolling Stone*'s "Big Idea"

Exhibit 10–6   Cheer Storyboard

SOURCE: Reprinted courtesy of Procter & Gamble.

How to Develop a Big Idea

A "big idea" is generally quite simple. For example, showing various forms of lights as Bud Light did or demonstrating how the product works under unusual circumstances as in the Cheer commercial is not really conceptually very difficult. Yet, these commercials are considered to be quite "creative," and the persons who came up with the ideas to be some of the best in the advertising business. And, they are. But they're successful not just because they are creative, but because they have used what is called "controlled creativity"; that is, these advertising executions not only get attention, they get the sales message across. Most of all, they convince the consumer that the product really does provide a competitive benefit.

The big question, though, is how does one go about coming up with a really great idea that will turn a sound strategy into a winning advertising campaign—a "Mikey" or a "Perception–Reality"? That is usually the result of what is called ideation or the generation of ideas. Can you as an advertising planner do it? Can anyone learn to generate ideas, to come up with new and exciting concepts and approaches that will grab the attention of the audience and literally drive the sales message home in an interesting and effective way?

The answer is yes. Although there are some people who seem to have an innate gift for generating ideas, most anyone can be taught to develop sound advertising executions. A big idea is usually more the result of perspiration than inspiration. If you use a sound, logical, proven approach as preparation for having ideas, they will come. Not all will be a "Do You Know Me?" but they will be sound, exciting advertising ideas that get consumers to sit up and take notice.

Basic psychological literature on creativity comes from several theories. All attempt to explain creativity and how it occurs. These range from the psychoanalytic theories of Freud, Kris, and Kubie; to the Gestalt theories of Wertheimer; to the association theories of Mednick; to the composite theories of Koestler, Gruber, and Hadamand. All have contributed something to our understanding of how the mind works and how people generate new approaches, new concepts, and new solutions to old problems.[1] Although a thorough review and an explanation of theories of creativity are beyond the scope of this book, four particular concepts and techniques should prove helpful in understanding how ideas come about or in actually helping generate effective ideas for advertising.

---

[1]Thomas V. Busse and Richard S. Mansfield, "Theories of the Creative Process," *Journal of Creative Behavior,* 14, 2 (1980): 91–103.

The James Webb Young "Technique for Producing Ideas"

The best known and, perhaps, the most widely accepted method of developing advertising ideas is that proposed by James Webb Young, a creative executive with J. Walter Thompson advertising agency. Young developed his concept of idea generation in 1940. It has been widely quoted and discussed since that time. In summary, Young suggests that a "new idea is nothing more or less than a *new combination* of old elements." Young, in his book, *A Technique for Producing Ideas,* suggests five specific steps in how to create new combinations of old elements and generate ideas.

> First, the gathering of raw materials—both the materials of the immediate problem and the materials which come from a constant enrichment of your store of general knowledge.
> Second, the working over of these materials in the mind.
> Third, the incubation state, where something besides the conscious mind does the work of synthesis.
> Fourth, the actual birth of the idea—the "Eureka! I have it!" stage.
> And fifth, the final shaping and development of the idea to practical usefulness.[2]

Young's formula sounds very simple. Perhaps a few words of explanation will illustrate the process better.

Gathering raw materials.   Young suggests there are two types of materials to be gathered, the specific and the general. Specific refers to those elements and information directly related to the product or service to be advertised. The general materials are all those things about life and events that a person gathers in living and being interested in the things around him or her. Because all ideas are simply new combinations of old elements, obviously the more elements available for this combining procedure, the greater the possibility of developing a combination that can be truly exciting and effective.

Working over the materials in the mind.   Young likens the ideation process to eating food, that is, masticating the materials for digestion. We start by turning all the materials over in the mind. Young says, "[You] take the different bits of material which you have gathered and feel them all over, as it were, with the tentacles of the mind. . . . [F]acts sometimes yield up their meaning quicker when you do not scan them too directly, too lit-

---

[2]James Webb Young, *A Technique for Producing Ideas* (Chicago: Crain Books, 1975): 53–54.

erally." In other words, look for the meaning, not the absolute facts in the combinations.

The incubation stage. "In this third stage you make absolutely no effort of a direct nature. You drop the whole subject and put the problem out of your mind as completely as you can." In other words, turn the problem over to the unconscious mind. Let it do the work. It is here that new combinations, new processes, and new meanings generally occur.

The birth of the idea. According to Young, "Now, if you have really done your part in these three stages of the process, you will almost surely experience the fourth. . . . Out of nowhere the idea will appear. . . . It will come to you when you are least expecting it."

In other words, there is no explanation of how the new combination of old elements comes about; it simply occurs as a result of the first three steps. That's the mysterious but always exciting part of the process. But, there is one final stage.

The final shaping and development of the idea. Once more, quoting Young, "[This is] the stage which might be called the cold, grey dawn of the morning after." Not every idea is totally complete. Often it requires work and/or adaptation to make it exactly fit the situation. At this stage, Young suggests many good ideas are lost simply because the idea generator wasn't patient enough to go through this final adaptation process, this final shaping of the raw idea into a really big idea.[3]

Young's method has worked for many successful advertising people. But, it is not the only way to develop a big idea. Here are some others.

Arthur Koestler's "The Act of Creation"

Although Arthur Koestler's concepts of how ideas are developed and created are not directly related to advertising, they have had much influence on how people believe the mind works. Koestler's basic notion is the idea of *bisociation*. That simply means a new idea often occurs when two thoughts collide and combine. He describes it more fully as occurring when two frames of reference ("matrices") coincide. The coincidence or collision of these matrices results in a combination that previously had not been considered or had not been thought of. In other words, two rather common concepts or thoughts or situations or even events, when brought together through bisociation, result in a new and original idea. In fact, he describes it as being "an act of liberation—the defeat of habit by originality."[4]

---

[3]Young, *Technique for Producing Ideas:* 30–54.
[4]Arthur Koestler, *The Act of Creation* (New York: Macmillan Co., 1964): 96.

One need only look at various advertising executions to see how Koestler's bisociation concept works. It's in the "Mikey" commercial, "a nutritional cereal that tastes good." It's in Bud Light's "Gimme a Light," showing why a specific light, Bud Light, should be ordered, and so on.

David Bernstein, author of *Creative Advertising*, provides an excellent example of Koestler's concept of bisociation. The following example illustrates how ideas come into conflict and create a new idea.

PROPOSITION

Lowenbrau is very expensive but it is the best quality beer you can buy. The Lowenbrau proposition gives you little to work on. If there were a "product plus"—an ingredient, strength or price advantage—an idea would be easier to arrive at. . . . If you were launching the first ever German beer on the domestic U.S. market, you could simply state that fact. . . . But if you accept that premise in this case you end up with a headline such as:

"Lowenbrau—supreme quality"
or
"Lowenbrau—when only the best will do"
or
"The mark of excellence"

And so on. Ad nauseam (which is a good name for this sort of advertisement). Brian Palmer has a favorite all-purpose headline for this proposition. "Preferred by those who like it best." It has the merit of sounding impressive and being totally acceptable to Weights and Measures Inspectors . . . . To return to the Lowenbrau proposition. . . and the idea.

IDEA

"When they run out of Lowenbrau, order champagne."

OBSERVATIONS

1. The idea re-presents the proposition. It says that Lowenbrau is a top quality beer without saying, "Lowenbrau is a top quality beer."
2. The idea is a relationship. The product has been associated with another, more accepted, symbol of quality. The association, moreover, justifies the price.
3. The idea is a reversal of normal thought processes. Instead of the beer being an acceptable alternative to champagne, it suggests the reverse.[5]

(Note: The above campaign was used successfully in Europe.)

As Bernstein demonstrates, two ideas that were normally thought not to be even related and even in conflict have collided and produced another, even more compelling idea. That's how bisociation works. And, that's how ideas are born.

---

[5]David Bernstein, *Creative Advertising: For This You Went to Oxford?* (London: Longman Group, 1974): 86–88.

Edward deBono's "Lateral Thinking"

Edward deBono, in his book, *Lateral Thinking for Management,* defines *lateral thinking* as:

> Vertical thinking is traditional logical thinking. It is called vertical thinking because you proceed directly from one state of information to another state. It is like building a tower by placing one stone firmly on top of the preceding stone; or like digging a hole by making deeper the hole you already have.[6]

He contrasts vertical thinking with what he calls lateral thinking. Lateral thinking generally can be considered to be "discontinuity" or "change for the sake of change" thinking. Perhaps the best way to explain lateral thinking is to contrast it with the more traditional or vertical thinking which most of us practice. DeBono gives several examples.

1. Vertical thinking is selective; lateral thinking is generative.
2. Vertical thinking moves only if there is a direction in which to move; lateral thinking moves in order to generate a direction.
3. Vertical thinking is analytical; lateral thinking is provocative.
4. Vertical thinking is sequential; lateral thinking can make jumps.
5. With vertical thinking one has to be correct at every step; with lateral thinking one does not have to be.
6. With vertical thinking one uses the negative in order to block off certain pathways; with lateral thinking there is no negative.
7. With vertical thinking one concentrates and excludes what is irrelevant; with lateral thinking one welcomes chance intrusions.
8. With vertical thinking categories, classifications, and labels are fixed; with lateral thinking they are not.
9. Vertical thinking follows the most likely paths; lateral thinking explores the least likely.
10. Vertical thinking is a finite process; lateral thinking is a probabilistic one.[7]

In short, lateral thinking seeks to explore new relationships among elements or situations or events or even activities to generate new and unique ideas. These new relationships are necessarily simple because we tend to think in patterns or in some sort of self-organizing system. Although these

---

[6]Edward deBono, *Lateral Thinking for Management* (New York: American Management Association, 1971): 4. Copyright 1971 by the American Management Association. All rights reserved. Reprinted by permission of the publisher.

[7]Edward deBono, *Lateral Thinking: Creativity Step by Step* (New York: Harper & Row, 1970): 39–46. Copyright 1970 by Edward deBono. Reprinted by permission of Harper & Row publishers.

thought patterns are highly advantageous in dealing with the myriad of rather mundane but necessary activities required to survive in our environment, they tend to inhibit any new approaches or new concepts from being developed. Lateral thinking attempts to break out of these patterns and to look at new and previously unexplored relationships or areas of possibility. In summary, deBono describes lateral thinking as follows:

> The purpose of lateral thinking is the generation of new ideas and escape from the old ones. The need for lateral thinking arises from the patterning behavior of the mind which is not good at restructuring ideas to bring them up to date and allow full use of available information. The traditional habits of thinking are very effective at developing ideas but not very good at restructuring them. Lateral thinking is designed to supplement traditional thinking and especially to introduce discontinuity that is necessary for restructuring ideas. The basic process of lateral thinking is the escape from old ideas and the provocation of new ones. The ideas generated by lateral thinking are selected and developed by traditional thinking methods.
>
> The principles of lateral thinking could be summarized as follows:
>
> 1. Recognition of dominant or polarizing ideas.
> 2. The search for different ways of looking at things.
> 3. The relaxation of the rigid control of vertical thinking.
> 4. The use of chance and provocative methods in order to introduce discontinuity.[8]

DeBono lists several methods that can be used to stimulate lateral thinking and to break the vertical thinking pattern. Among those are such things as (a) generate alternatives to present situations; (b) challenge present assumptions; (c) innovate; (d) suspend judgment for a period of time; (e) reverse a common approach; (f) develop analogies for the situation; (g) brainstorm.[9] The primary idea is to look at things differently, in nontraditional, lateral thinking patterns. In other words, turn the idea upside down and look at it a different way.

Gordon's Synectics

William J.J. Gordon has developed a program to train creative thinking which is essentially associative in nature. It is based on metaphor (lifting an idea out of context and using it in another context to suggest resemblance to some other concept) and analogy (an indication of form, process, or relationship which explains steps and procedures). The system is called *Synectics* and is based on forcing metaphors and analogies.

---

[8]DeBono, *Lateral Thinking for Management:* 50–51.
[9]DeBono, *Lateral Thinking for Management:* 50–51.

Gordon bases his approach on three types of analogical approaches. The first, *direct analogy,* is a metaphorical comparison between a key element of the problem and a rough similar concept in a new context. In the second, *personal analogy* is developed by trying to empathize with the problem, for example, trying to imagine how an umbrella would feel opening in a storm. The third approach is called *compressed conflict,*—new ideas are created by combining two word descriptions of words that contradict each other such as "delicate aggressor."

The Synectics exercises are built around a simple logic formula: "A is to B as C is to what?" As the foundation of analogical thinking, it becomes creative by using free association to stimulate the wildest possible connections.[10]

If you are responsible for the development of the basic advertising strategy and the execution of that strategy, you may find one of these four approaches helpful in getting the creative juices flowing to help develop the "big idea."

Executing the "Big Idea"

Having the "big idea" and translating that idea into effective, motivating, selling-based advertising are often many steps apart. One of the best ways to make sure the "big idea" becomes "big advertising" is through a set of guidelines. The following checklist will assure that the idea tracks and turns into a sound, effective execution. Part of the "Sixteen Guidelines System" was developed by Don Kanter, for many years the creative director of Stone & Adler, Chicago.

In addition to Kanter's twelve guidelines, four others have been added. Again, as Kanter says, these are merely guidelines. They are not straight-jackets. They are suggestions that will help keep the idea development on track and make sure that the big idea comes through clearly, quickly, and completely.

Guideline One: Know the Product.
The first guideline is that you do not write a word until you have studied your product or service and dug out every possible benefit you can . . . along with the selling points. Talk to people. Talk to the buyer, the product manager, the account executive . . . whoever. Look at ads and mailing for competitive products or services. If it's possible, try the product or service yourself.

Then build your copy skeleton. List the benefits and selling points. Rank them. Outline them. This is the tough part of copywriting. And it is partic-

---

[10]Adapted from Sandra E. Moriarty, *Creative Advertising: Theory and Practice* (Englewood Cliffs, N.J.: Prentice-Hall, 1986): 4–5.

ularly hard for writers who think they are quote-writers-unquote and want to get to the typewriter and start writing. Yet it is the most vital and important part of copywriting because it undergirds every word you write. I repeat: If you realize that your job is to sell, you will realize that you cannot sell until you know as much as possible about what you are selling.

Guideline Two: Know Your Market.

Now that you know your product, learn your market. To whom is this product or service going to be sold? What is he or she (or they) like? What are their demographics, their life-styles? Where do they live?

Again, don't try to reason this out for yourself. Talk to people to find out.

Then visualize your prospect and talk directly to him or her, as if you were selling in person. Keep in mind that you are selling, and that you are substituting the written word for the spoken word.

One obvious caution here: I am not telling you to write precisely as you would speak—far from it. As anybody who's read transcripts of tapes know, literal spoken dialogue does not make very good written copy. I am telling you to write directly to your prime prospect.

This market knowledge is another part of the writing process that lies underneath that part of the iceberg which is visible: your copy. But like product knowledge, market knowledge undergirds what you write.

With the product and market knowledge, and with the outline done, we are now ready—honest—to start writing copy.

Remember, I said guidelines, not rules. And remember that there are exceptions to everything. I've found these guidelines to be valid and helpful, but I'll occasionally go against them—*if* there is a good and valid reason to do so.

Guideline Three: Talk to Your Prospect.

Talk to your prospect—not to everybody. You know, this is where the copywriter has an advantage over the face-to-face salesperson. A salesperson will generally sell one product or line of products—to one audience. As writers, we get the chance to sell many different kinds of products and services to many different audiences. It's almost like being an actor: talking with kings and princes . . . and with peasants and paupers . . . and talking to each group so that they understand you—and more important, believe you.

Guideline Four: Make a Promise.

Make a promise to your prospect—and then prove that you can deliver what you promise.

That's really putting the benefit/selling point theory into practice: the benefit is the promise you make, and the selling points are the way you prove that you will deliver on the promise. It's an obvious point, but worth repeating: unless there is something of value in it for the prospect, he or she is not interested.

Guideline Five: Get to the Point.

Make that promise right away. In other words, get to the point.

It's amazing how much copy wanders around, tries to tease or tell stories . . . and takes forever to get to the point—by which time you've probably lost the prospect.

How many times have you heard a writer say, "Well, I've got this tremendous teaser line, and everybody who sees it will be beside himself or herself with curiosity."

You know, all of us are human beings. We have problems: the kids are sick, we've got to pay the bills somehow, the Cubs (or the Cards or Mets) blew last week's game—you know, important things to think about.

But somehow, we assume that everybody in America is vitally interested in our copy—that they dash home, throw off their coats, and grab the magazine or the newspaper or that day's mail so that they can ponder every word of what we wrote. Baloney; they have lots of things to worry about more important than our copy. We're lucky if we can get their attention, much less sell them anything—and we will get their attention only if we tell them quickly what's in it for them . . . if we make that promise and make it fast.

Get to the point.

Guideline Six: Be Germane.

Be germane and specific to your selling proposition.

There's a fairly simple test for this. Look at your major headline, or headline and subhead combination. If you could use that for anything other than the specific product or service you are selling, something's wrong. Fix it.

Guideline Seven: Be Concise.

There's a relatively simple test for this one, too: Take what you write—then cut it by 20 percent. Almost without exception, you will find that not only hasn't it hurt your copy, it has really improved it by making it sharper and more to the point.

Guideline Eight: Be Logical.

Once you've hooked your reader with your promise, lead him or her through your selling proposition logically, smoothly. Don't jump to one subject, then to another, then back to the first one again.

Guideline Nine: Be Enthusiastic.

If you don't believe in what you're selling, how do you expect your prospect to believe in it?

Caution: Enthusiasm doesn't mean adding an exclamation point to every other sentence. That doesn't make your copy enthusiastic. Enthusiasm is when you believe that what you are selling is good, and a good value . . . and this comes through in your copy.

Guideline Ten: Be Complete.
You are the only salesperson there is, and if you leave something out, there's nobody the prospect can ask. You may well do a brilliant job of organizing, researching, outlining and writing...only to lose the sale because you forgot to include the size...or some other obvious point.

Guideline Eleven: Don't Try to Dazzle.
Don't try to dazzle your audience with the brilliance of your craft. If anybody says, "Gee, that's a great ad (or a great mailing piece or a great commercial)," you've gotten the wrong reaction. The reaction you want is, "Gee, that's a great product (or service)—I've got to have that." Save your brilliant word-smithing for the Great American Novel I'm sure you've already started.

Guideline Twelve: Respect the English Language.
This is the tool with which you earn your living, and every good craftsman treats his tools with respect and care. The English language is a beautiful thing. It has its rules, and I believe they should be observed. I still cringe when I hear phrases like "will everybody take their seats"...or when somebody doesn't know whether or not to include an apostrophe in the word "i-t-s"...Respect the language.[11]

Guideline Thirteen: Empathize.
Be able to empathize with customers and prospects. Most great advertising comes about because the writer is able to put himself or herself in the place of the person to whom they are writing or speaking. To use the old phrase, they are "able to walk in the other person's shoes." That simply means being able to understand what it is like to have the problem the product or service will solve; what it is like to be the person to whom the advertising is being directed.

For example, can you imagine what it would be like to be a mother with a sick child? What would it be like to be sixty-five years old and on the last day at your job? What would it be like to be a farmer who is trying to decide whether to buy a new tractor for the farm or to send one of his children to college? Or what would it be like to live in a small town in South Dakota? If you can imagine what it would be like to be in those situations, you're well on your way to being able to translate sound advertising strategies into outstanding advertisements.

Guideline Fourteen: Have a Specific Response in Mind.
One of the biggest problems many advertising writers have is that "they are simply writing advertising." They really don't have a purpose in mind, other than to get the ad done and into the newspaper, or on the radio, or

---

[11]From a presentation by Don Kanter to students at Medill School of Journalism, Northwestern University, Evanston, Ill., 1982. Used with permission of Mr. Kanter.

on TV. And the advertising shows it. The copywriter really doesn't have a clear idea of how the prospect is to respond or what the prospect should do as a result of seeing the advertisement. In short, what is supposed to happen? Is the reader/listener/viewer supposed to change his or her opinion or image of the product? Should they put the brand on a shopping list? Should they mentally jot the product down as a "possibility" on the next shopping trip? Or should they leap from their chair, rush to their nearest dealer, and make a purchase as quickly as possible? Be clear on what the reader or listener or viewer is to do as a result of seeing the advertising.

Guideline Fifteen: Offer Benefits, Not Gimmicks.
Too often today, advertisements tend to rely on new technology such as computer animation, new lighting, overprinting, or visual effects to take the place of sound, logical, usable consumer benefits that will occur as a result of using the product. The benefit of the product or service is often lost in the final presentation or execution simply because customers and prospects wouldn't, couldn't, or didn't dig through all the gimmicks to find the offer or the promise or the benefit that was available to them. Or, because the gimmick totally overwhelmed the sales message. The elements of the advertising execution should be meaningful, and the benefits should be relevant and clear. That's what makes advertising memorable. Not gimmicks. Not tricks. Not the latest fad. Good, solid, honest benefits for the consumer dressed up in an interesting and informative way.

Guideline Sixteen: Ask for the Order.
Too often in advertising translations, the writer or art director or others involved in the ad forget they are in the selling business. They forgot that the idea of advertising is to make a sale, at least a mental, if not a physical, one. Yet, too many times advertisements simply present the product benefits or the solution to the consumer's problem and then stop. The message simply sits there. No one asks the customer to buy, or to make a mental pledge to try, or to consider the product or service being advertised. In short, the advertising writer almost seems embarrassed that the advertising is supposed to sell things or to help people buy things. That's a big mistake.

The ad must ask the reader or listener or viewer to buy. It must try to "close the sale." If not, nothing will happen.

"Closing the sale" doesn't mean that every advertisement must end with a "Buy now!" tag line. It can be any form of action, either physical or mental, but the ad should ask the prospect to do something or think about something or make a mental commitment to the product. Every ad or commercial must ask for the order.

Effective Media Translations

The various media available to the advertising planner offer different creative strengths and opportunities to enhance the "big idea" through sound executions. Just as all products and ideas are not equal, neither are all media. Each medium offers unique possibilities. The key is to take advantage of those inherent strengths to help maximize the impact of the advertising execution.

Although the planner may not be charged with the actual translation of the strategy into the media and may have only final approval or control over how the advertising is to appear, some general rules exist for the use of each of the media. These rules can help assure success in the marketplace. The following guidelines will assure that you make the best possible use of each medium.

Guidelines for Print.

1. **Is the message clear at a glance? Can you quickly tell what the advertisement is all about?** Today, most readers are simply scanners of the print media. To be successful, the print ad must tell the scanner quickly and clearly the message and benefit of the advertisement. It must generate additional attention to get the copy read. Is this advertisement a clear message?

2. **Is the benefit in the headline?** With scanners, those who only see the headline and the illustration, it's vital for the headline to quickly and clearly tell the prospect the value or benefit or problem solution being offered. Involved, complicated, difficult-to-understand headlines don't work in today's fast-paced information situations. Is the headline a benefit-oriented message?

3. **Does the illustration support the headline?** The headline and the illustration must work in concert. Does the illustration lend support to or explain the headline? It should. It should demonstrate why the advertiser can make the claim made in the headline. Support the promise. Does the illustration support and tie into the headline?

4. **Does the first line of the copy support or explain the headline and the illustration?** Print ads must present a united idea. Immediately supporting the benefit in the headline with a statement of why that benefit is available or why the claim can be made assures that casual scanners get the total message in just a few seconds. If there is interest, they will read on. First, however, make sure the support for the claim is stated immediately. Does the first line of copy support the headline and the illustration?

5. **Is the ad easy to read and easy to follow?** With the average reader spending only fractions of a second deciding whether or not to stop or to move on, the print advertisement must be or appear to be easy to read and easy to follow. That includes both the layout and the composition. Does the ad invite readership?

6. **Is the type large and legible?** In the last few years a mass of "creative" or "artistic" type faces have been developed. Although they have their place, usually advertising isn't one of them. Clear, sharp, easy-to-read, and most of all, legible type is a must in print advertising. People simply won't work to learn what you have to say. Is the type in your ad easy to read?

7. **Is the sponsor clearly identified?** Again, is it clear who is making the offer in the ad? Too many advertisers seem almost embarrassed to present themselves as the seller or the purveyor of the ideas or products or services offered. People want to know who they are dealing with and how to contact them. They want to buy from people they know. Is the advertiser clearly identified in the ad?

8. **Are there any excess words, phrases, or even ideas that could be deleted?** People are busy. They don't want and won't take time to read extra words and extra phrases that have little or nothing to do with the benefits they seek or the problem they want to solve. If the information is important and helpful, they'll read literally volumes, but if it's simply "fluff," they'll drop it in a second. Are there any words here that could come out? Cut the copy to the bone, but make it complete.

9. **If there is a coupon or a clip-out, is it easy to remove or easy to get?** In some art director's zeal to make the advertisement a work of beauty, key elements, such as coupons, maps, directions, and so on, get lost in a wash of creative genius. If the object of the advertisement is to get a person to clip a coupon, make it easy to do. Put it in the corner. Make it big enough to read. If the name is to be added, make sure there is enough room. In short, do everything possible to help the reader, even if it means giving up an art direction award. Are the elements of the ad easy to understand?

Guidelines for Radio. Radio is one of the most misunderstood and misused media today. Radio is more than just music and jingles and shouting announcers. It's the arena of the mind and the imagination. Below are just a few suggestions on how to evaluate radio commercials.

1. **Does the commercial intrude?** Today, radio is primarily a background medium. People are doing something else while they are listening. Therefore, you must intrude to get attention. That doesn't mean irritating, but it does mean that it is necessary to break out of the drone and either offer a benefit or gain attention so that prospects will hear the message. Does the commercial intrude enough to get attention?

2. **Is the commercial written for the ear and the mind?** As the first video generation, many advertising people assume there is a picture available to support their words, whether there is or not. Radio must play on the mind through the ears. That means it must involve the imagination. That's done with sound effects, words, pauses, and so on. Effective radio allows the listener to add content and contrast to the commercial to further support the idea being heard. Take advantage of this unique aspect of radio. Does this commercial involve the imagination?

3. **Does the commercial involve the listener?** Closely allied with point two is involvement. One of the major problems with much radio today is that, not knowing how to use it, some advertisers simply have announcers read print advertisements over the air. That is a massive waste of the medium. Radio has the unique ability to involve listeners, to get them to add to and supplement what is actually being said or heard. Does the radio commercial involve the listener or simply present a mass of facts and data? It makes a big difference.

4. **Is there only one sales message?** Because radio is so easy to produce and so easy to change, many advertisers make the mistake of thinking that they can use radio as one would a laundry bag—simply stuff ideas into the time frame until it is full. Nothing could be further from the truth. Good radio commercials have only one major selling point. And that selling point is repeated and embellished during the commercial. Good radio is *not* what can be crammed into sixty seconds. It's how well the time can be used to build a story for the listener and discuss the benefits of the product or service. Does the commercial have only one main idea?

5. **Is the brand clearly identified?** Because radio is fleeting and a background medium, too often the brand name or the sponsor is lost. Radio, unlike print, can't be referred to or reviewed. Once the commercial is broadcast, it's gone forever. Therefore, it is impossible to repeat the brand name or the product benefit too often in radio. Remember when you've tried to recall an address or a telephone number from a radio commercial? It's very difficult to do. The radio commercial should have enough brand and benefit identification so the message gets across.

6. **Does the commercial sound the way the target market speaks?** The spoken word and the written word are totally different. Radio commercials, written as literary gems, usually fail because thoughts, ideas, and concepts are compressed when spoken. People don't speak in complete sentences or even complete phrases. Radio should be written to communicate—to get ideas and information and benefits across to the audience. That means writing for the ear rather than for the eye in the way most people talk. The best thing:

read the commercial aloud. Is that how you would tell your benefit in person? If not, loosen up and write as you speak.

A caution here: Writing as you speak doesn't mean using poor grammar or incorrect sentence construction. It simply means using the written word the way you use it in conversation, not as you use it in print. Is your commercial in written or spoken language?

Guidelines for Television.   Because of its great range, television is a medium unto itself. To execute successful television commercials, keep the following points in mind when evaluating or developing commercials for the campaign.

1. **Does the commercial interrupt?** Although politeness is generally considered a virtue, it really has no place in a television commercial. People go to television to be entertained, not to see commercials. Therefore, the commercial must break through their relaxation and get their attention. If radio must intrude, television commercials must interrupt. They must break through the wall of interest in the program content and literally call attention to the product and message. This does not mean that a television commercial should be rude or vulgar or irritating, but it does mean that it must interrupt the programming and get attention for the message being presented. So, first check to see if the commercial interrupts and gets attention.

2. **Is the commercial a visual idea?** Many television commercials are simply stand-up announcers pitching the product to the audience. This is probably the worst possible way to use television. Television is visual. It is movement. It is action. Without those three things, you might as well use print or radio. You can test that by asking yourself, "Is my sales message a visual idea?" If it isn't, you're not taking full advantage of the medium.

3. **Does the commercial demonstrate the benefits of the product or service?** This follows very closely with the previous point of television being visual. The major feature television offers is the opportunity to actually demonstrate the benefit being offered or the problem being solved by the product or service. Almost every product or service can be demonstrated, if not the actual thing that the product does then the benefit the user receives or the psychological satisfaction of using the product or service. Does your television commercial demonstrate the benefit you offer?

4. **Is there very clear brand identification?** One of the major problems in television is misidentification; that is, viewers see commercials for one brand and attribute them to another. Some studies have shown that this misidentification runs as high as 50 percent for brands in some categories. You must visually and vocally tie the benefit of your product to your brand.

A key point in developing sound television executions is to avoid what are called generic claims, in other words, benefits and problem solutions that are common to the category and cannot be tied directly to the brand. For over 100 years, Ivory soap has used the line "99 and 44/100% pure, it floats." That's a clear brand identification and a clear product benefit. The benefit being offered must be inexorably connected to the brand. Is it?

5. **Is there only one clear sales message?** Perhaps because of the wide and varied opportunity to insert additional claims either in the audio or video portion of the commercial, too many advertisers try to insert "just one more idea to reach another group of people who may be watching." This is a mistake. Commercials that try to reach everyone with something usually end up reaching no one with anything. Have one clear sales message and one clear idea directed to one clear target market. If the product has other benefits and strategies for them, write additional commercials. Don't confuse your audience. Is your commercial single minded?

6. **Does the commercial properly represent the product?** Finally, does the general tone of the commercial properly represent the product? For example, if the product is high-priced, prestigious, does the commercial portray that image? Take a close look at the product and the people who might buy it. Would the commercial appeal to them? If not, change it now before it gets on the air.

In line with this, beware of "Vampire Video," in which the execution totally overwhelms the sales message. This is probably a bigger problem in television than in any other medium. The opportunity to have dramatic pictures, exciting music, thrilling movement, and dulcet announcer tones all at the same time often results in a commercial that is well remembered as a commercial but whose sales message is forgotten. Make sure your message doesn't get lost in the translation.

HOW TO JUDGE ADVERTISING EXECUTIONS

Sometimes, as it has been assumed up to now, the campaign planner and the advertising copywriter are the same person. In many instances, that's the case. In others, however, it isn't. For example, a brand manager or advertising manager for a manufacturer or marketer may be directly involved in the development of the advertising strategy, but dependent on the advertising agency creative personnel or, perhaps, creative people in her own organization to provide the actual physical translations. Similarly, an agency account executive or other manager may have a large part in developing the strategy but rely on the creative department to translate that strategy into the actual advertisements or commercials. If either of these is the case, the question then becomes how does the planner evaluate the executions—determine whether advertising translations will be effective? How can the planner recognize a "big idea"? Is there a way to assure that what is presented will work in the marketplace?

What follows is a list of guidelines or checkpoints that have proven effective over the years. Remember, these are simply guidelines or checkpoints, not rules. Sometimes there is a good reason for breaking the "rules." It's knowing when and why to break them that separates the good advertising campaign planner from the average one. Use these checkpoints to make sure that the advertising really is and does what it is supposed to do in the campaign.

Is the Advertisement on Strategy?

This sounds simple but often it's the biggest problem with a campaign. The strategy is planned to say one thing and the advertising ends up saying another. So, look at the strategy statement first. Then look at the advertising execution. If the execution doesn't translate the strategy, toss the execution out and start over. Start over no matter how cute, how clever, how exciting the actual advertisement or commercial or poster or whatever seems to be. The first and guiding rule: The advertising must say what it set out to say in the strategy. That means the execution must follow the strategy. No exceptions. (This is the only guideline that should never be broken.)

Will the Execution Appeal to the Right Audience?

A great deal of time has been spent defining and locating the target market for the advertising message. The question now, assuming the ad is on strategy, is, "Will this execution appeal to that group of people?" If the answer is no, toss it out and start over.

If you really know your target market, you should have a strong idea of whether or not a specific execution or interpretation of the strategy will appeal to them, and that means in terms of layout, style, grammar, music, tone, and so on. The execution should fit the audience.

Would You Say This to Your Prospect in Person?

If you were calling on your prospect in person, would this be what you would say to convince him or her to buy? Strangely enough, advertisers often hide behind their advertisements when it comes to trying to sell someone something. The anonymity of the printed page or the radio commercial or even the sales brochure seems to open up the doors to all sorts of inane ideas. We put "bells and whistles" on advertisements and commercials that do nothing more than make the message more difficult to read, see, hear, or understand. Is that advertisement how you would sell the product in person?

From the Marketer's or Consumer's View?

Is the advertisement written from the marketer's or the prospect's viewpoint? One good check of an advertising execution is simply to ask, "Does this ad help my prospect buy or simply try to help me make a sale?" And there's a big difference in that view.

Is the Execution Clear, Concise, Complete, and Convincing?

A big problem with many advertisements is that the writer often assumes the prospect knows as much about the product as he or she does and is as interested in it as the writer is. When this happens, the reader or listener or person on the other end of the advertisement is often left far behind. So, first, the advertisement must be clear. Is it easy to follow? Are all the benefits listed and supported? Is the advertisement complete? Is there anything important left out—anything the target market might need to know or to have to make a decision in favor of the product or service advertised?

Also, the advertisement must be complete. A good check of this is to ask, "If the prospect never saw another advertisement or commercial for this product or service, would he or she know enough about how to buy and where to buy so that a sale could occur?" If the answer is no, this is the time to make necessary changes.

Does the Execution Overwhelm the Message?

A common failing of many advertisements, but in particular television advertisements, is that they succeed in getting themselves, but not the product or the product benefit, remembered. When this happens, it usually is the result of the advertising execution simply overwhelming the advertising message. The layout or color or animation or whatever is so outstanding that it totally overshadows the message the advertiser is trying to get across. Remember, the advertising is there to sell or influence the purchase of a product or service. If it can entertain or amuse or thrill or even bring a tear, wonderful. But the primary job is to sell a product, a service, or an idea. Don't let the execution get in the way.

Is There a Call to Action?

Surprisingly, a great deal of advertising does not ask for any commitment from the viewer, reader, or listener. No effort is made to make the sale. No attempt to get some action or commitment from the prospect. The purpose of advertising is to get someone to do something he or she isn't doing now. That something can be a change of opinion, the trial of the product, a mental pledge to consider the product at the next buying opportunity. Or whatever. But advertising should be designed to get some sort of response. And, if the advertisement doesn't ask directly for the desired response, that response probably won't come.

Are You Proud Enough of the Advertisement to Show It to Someone Close to You?

In other words, is this piece of advertising something you are proud of, something you would want your name on if ads were signed? If not, start over. Advertisements you aren't proud of rarely gain response from others, particularly those you're trying to sell. People hardly ever buy from rude or crude or pushy salespeople. The same thing is true of advertisements. If you want your advertising to succeed, it must make friends with your prospects and customers. Does the execution you're judging accurately reflect you and your product? If not, change it now.

Those are basic questions a planner can and should ask about the translation of every advertising strategy. These questions won't make someone an expert on creative executions, but if the answer to each of the eight questions above is yes, the advertising execution has a big lead on advertising that doesn't qualify on all these points. No one can predict the success of an advertising execution, not even the testing services, but these simple questions can assure that almost everything possible has been done to insure success.[12]

SUMMARY

The translation of the advertising strategy is a key element in the success of the advertising campaign. The strategy is the "what you say about the product or service," while the execution or translation is "how you say it." The job of the execution is to deliver the sales message to the target market.

---

[12]Adapted in part from John M. Keil, "Can You Become a Creative Judge?" *Journal of Advertising,* 4, 1 (1975): 29–31.

Most executions are the result of what is called the "big idea." This chapter discussed four basic methods of developing ideas: Young's "Technique for Producing Ideas," Koestler's "Act of Creation," deBono's "Lateral Thinking," and Gordon's "Synectics."

Guidelines for creating the "big idea" are helpful. They include such factors as know the product, know the market, talk to the prospect, make a promise, get to the point, be germane, be concise, be logical, be enthusiastic, be complete, don't try to dazzle, respect the English language, empathize, have a specific response in mind, offer benefits not gimmicks, and ask for the order.

Finally, there are specific guidelines to evaluate executions in print, radio, and television which build and expand on the strength of the medium itself.

Case Studies

Potato Flips

Perfectly Potato Products had been marketing a line of potato chips called "Potato Flips" for ten months. The product had not been a major success story, having gained only 2 percent national market share, far short of the 20 percent share that had been forecast.

Flips differed from other potato chips in that they were made with one-third less oil. They had been taste tested extensively and had out-scored all the existing national brands. Test participants described them as "light," "fluffy but crunchy," and "very potatoey-tasting."

Although preliminary market and consumer research had suggested that PPP might be able to segment the potato chip market successfully by positioning Flips as a lower-calorie chip to appeal to diet-conscious consumers, top management had vetoed the idea. Corporate pride insisted that a big splash be made in a big, mass market. Consequently, an advertising campaign was developed that focused on the "fun" aspects of the product. Television commercials showed a variety of celebrity look-alikes "flipping" over Flips. The print ads were similar, showing a person "flipping" over Flips. Copy points included the product's great potato taste and briefly mentioned the one-third less oil feature.

Nine months after the national introduction of Flips, PPP was acquired by a large national food conglomerate. Soon after the acquisition was completed, Greg Jeffries, the brand manager for Flips, was summoned to give an accounting for his product. Jeffries correctly assumed that Flips' future was in jeopardy and decided to go on the offensive with his presentation.

"Ladies and gentlemen," he began, "right now, Flips is a perfect example of a good product being hurt by poor strategy. There's no doubt that the product *is* good—taste-test results and extremely high repurchase rates prove that it's a good product. People who try Flips love them. The problem is, not many people are trying them. Why? Because they like the chip they're used to buying, and we haven't given them a really good reason to buy ours instead. The 'Flipping over Flips' campaign has been great for getting recognition—just about everybody's heard of Flips. But when they go to the store, they aren't buying them."

Jeffries then distributed copies of the research study that had suggested segmenting the market. "I believe that the positioning described in this study is the right answer for Flips. Right now, there are basically two types of potato chips—regular, and chips for dips. So why not a brand of chips for slim hips? Seriously, consumer studies show that there are a lot of nutrition-conscious and calorie-conscious people for whom potato chips are almost taboo. With a lower-calorie positioning based on the one-third less oil feature, we'd not only attract buyers of other chips, but also people who haven't bought a bag of potato chips in months. I think there's a lot of potential here."

After several minutes of conferring with his colleagues, the marketing vice president spoke. "OK, Jeffries, you may be right. Get together with the agency. We want to see ideas for an ad campaign based on the lower-calorie positioning two weeks from today. We'll decide then on the future of Flips."

Jeffries called the Flips account executive immediately. He outlined the situation, emphasizing that this was do or die. "Can you put your creative people to work on this? I'd like four separate approaches within the week. You and I can pick which is best and get a big presentation together on it in time for the meeting."

The AE promised to do his best. He called in four of the agency's resident creative geniuses and presented the problem to them. "I know this is a rush job, but this Flips account could be the intro to big billings with the new parent company. So, I've got copies of the segmentation study, taste-test results, and product samples for each of you. Give it your best shot."

Five days later, Jeffries was looking at storyboards illustrating these four alternatives:

1. **UFO:** Scene is a military air traffic control room. A large group of people is gathered around a radar screen. *Audio:* "F-17, this is Control. Do you have visual?" "Negative, Control. Repeat coordinates." "We have you on screen, F-17. Object should be at two o'clock." "Wait, Control. We have visual. It's . . . it's . . . it's a bag of potato chips." Close-up on amazed faces. Then cut to bag of Flips floating alongside jet fighter. *Audio:* "Correction, Control. Not potato chips, Potato Flips." "They must have gotten out of a grocery bag. Come back in, F-17. Oh, and bring the Flips with you. We're hungry." *Voiceover* (while the bag continues to float onscreen): "Potato Flips. One-third less oil than regular potato chips makes them *very* light."

2. **The Exploding Potato:** Close-up on a potato. As rumbling noises start underneath, the potato begins to rock back and forth. The noise builds and the potato rocks faster. Potato explodes with a boom and Potato Flips flutter down into a Flips bag. *Voiceover:* "Potato Flips— one-third less oil and terrific potato taste."

3. **Falling Flips:** No sound. Snow, as seen from a distance, fills screen. As camera closes in, crunching sounds begin. Sounds get louder, and snow is seen to be Potato Flips. *Voiceover:* "Potato Flips are extra light and crunchy, because they're made with one-third less oil than other potato chips." Cut to bag of Flips. *Voiceover:* "And less oil here may mean . . ." Split screen; Flips and bathroom scale. *Voiceover:* "Less here."

4. **Potato Diet:** Woman sitting on a park bench, drinking a diet beverage and eating Flips. She's joined by another woman, who has another diet drink and a container of yogurt. Woman #2: "What happened to your diet?" Woman #1: "Nothing! I'm still eating light." #2: "Come on! Potato chips are hardly diet food." #1: "These are *not* potato chips. They're Potato *Flips.*" (Close-up on Flips bag.) #2: "C'mon. Chips or Flips, I still . . ." #1 (interrupting): "Flips are made with a third less oil than potato chips. So, they're still crunchy and potatoey, but not nearly as fattening." #2: "Can I try a Flip?" #1: "OK, but just one. This *is* my lunch." Close-up on Flips bag. *Voiceover* (#2): "Just one more, please?"

Questions

1. Which execution(s) do you feel is most "on strategy"? Why?
2. Which execution would be most effective in attracting the target market?
3. Which execution is most convincing?
4. Imagine each execution on television. Would they cut through the clutter?
5. Are the executions visual ideas?
6. Do the executions demonstrate the product's benefit?
7. Assume each execution must be translated into an accompanying print ad. What are some potential headlines?
8. If you were Jeffries, which execution would you select to present to the board as the "salvation" for Flips?

Silver Screen Videos

Tim Conners, creative director at Conners Doyle Advertising, a small Detroit agency, was trying to come up with some executional ideas for a new client, Silver Screen Videos. SSV operated video stores in several large metropolitan areas and was getting ready to break into the Detroit market. Conners Doyle had the job of creating an exciting introductory campaign.

Detroit already had a number of video stores competing for VCR owners' time and dollars. In addition to three other video chains and a host of independent video stores, the two leading supermarket chains and the leading drug chain all had video rental departments. And, two convenience store chains also rented a limited number of titles. People in Detroit did not have to go far from home to rent a video tape.

SSV had done a thorough study of the Detroit market before deciding to expand there. SSV management felt that their product was better than that of any of the competitors. SSV had been successful in other markets with a similar amount of competition; they had driven small operators and even a chain out of business in other areas.

SSV defined their target market as the VCR owner, including both VHS and Beta owners. (The president of SSV had been one of the first people to buy a videocassette player, and didn't feel that Beta owners should be penalized for being innovators. Consequently, all SSV stores carried both VHS and Beta tapes.) SSV believed that most of their customers were heavy users of video tapes—people who rented movies 2–3 times a week. SSV's experience in other markets suggested that new members would be people already belonging to one or more video clubs. SSV's goal was to become those people's first choice club—the one they would rent from most frequently.

SSV had provided the agency with a long list of attributes that they felt differentiated them from all of the competition:

- More videos (SSV would carry more titles in *each* store than any of the competitors)
- Longer hours (SSV stores would be open from 8 A.M.–2 A.M.)
- Both VHS and Beta videos (only one Detroit chain carried Beta videos, and only in some of its stores)
- Low rental rates (equal to those of any other chain)
- A reservation system (people could call in during the day to reserve a tape for that night)
- Good locations (SSV had obtained prime space throughout the city and suburbs)
- Used tapes available for purchase at a discount
- Video cassette recorder repair (again, both VHS and Beta)

The real question facing Conners was how to communicate the SSV message. The other chains had been in the Detroit market for several years and were currently running occasional "reminder" newspaper advertisements tied to the video tape release of especially popular movies. SSV wanted to use both newspaper and television ads for its introductory campaign. Tim's thinking was that the print ads could be used to highlight a number of the SSV attributes from the list above. The TV spots would need to create an image for SSV, an image that would set it apart from the competition and that could carry over to the newspaper ads.

In tossing ideas around with a couple of other creatives at the agency, the phrase "complete video store" kept coming up. SSV's point of differentiation was that it had *everything* a consumer could want in a video store. At the same time, Tim knew that the small independent stores were fairly popular in Detroit, and he was afraid that there might be a fine line between presenting SSV as a complete, supervideo store and making it seem too big and impersonal.

Tim came up with a few ideas: a spot playing off images associated with movie premiers—limos pulling up, stars getting out, searchlights on the marquee. The marquee would be for an SSV store, and the "stars" would be videotapes "dressed" in formal wear talking about how much they were looking forward to appearing in SSV stores. The TV spots would be tied to the print by keeping the searchlight graphic and the line, "Now appearing at SSV . . . ."

Another idea was to play off Detroit imagery—shots focusing on the Pistons, the Silverdome, and other Detroit icons. SSV would be presented as taking its place among Detroit's emblems, another "best" of its kind comes to Detroit. The print ads would also carry the "best" label.

A third idea was to use an "average consumer" spokesperson who would talk about this great new video store coming to Detroit. The spokesperson would explain that he knew about SSV because he used to live in Cincinnati (an SSV market), and SSV was the only thing he really missed when he moved to Detroit. This would be a continuing campaign—the spokesperson would talk about a different SSV attribute in every spot. The same spokesperson would be featured in the print ads.

Tim felt that each of the three ideas had merit. The "stars" idea would play off the excitement and involvement people felt when a big movie was being released. The "best" idea would tie in to civic pride, which might help SSV compete with the small independent stores. The "coming to Detroit" spot might encourage consumer word of mouth. And, each of the ideas could be used in both TV and print executions.

Questions

1. Review the criteria for judging executions given in this chapter. Then, judge each of the three ideas on the following:
   (a) Is the idea on strategy?
   (b) Does the idea have audience appeal?
   (c) Is each idea something you would tell people in person?
   (d) Does the idea present SSV from the marketer's view or the consumer's view?
   (e) Does the execution overwhelm the message?
2. Which idea would you recommend Tim go with? Why?

11

Pretesting the Advertising Campaign

Once the advertising strategy has been developed and executed, the next logical question to ask is whether or not the advertising will achieve the objectives set for the campaign. To determine how well the advertising communicates the sales message and if it will be effective in the marketplace, many major advertising elements and most proposed advertising campaigns are pretested in some way. There is an inherent belief in the value of pretesting. The point of debate is over how this testing should be done. Many practitioners argue that unless you have a testing system that is acceptable, pretesting is not worth the time or effort and experienced judgment is better. For example, major industry organizations, such as the Advertising Research Foundation, have wrestled with the copy testing problem for years without a totally satisfactory solution.

The discussion of pretesting can be put in proper perspective by reviewing what Russell Colley wrote in *Defining Advertising Goals for Measured Advertising Results* in 1961.

> The purpose of an advertisement is not just to get itself seen. It is not just to get itself heard or read. The purpose of an advertisement is to convey information, an attitude about a product (service, company, cause) in such a way that the consumer will be more favorably disposed toward its purchase. The purpose of an advertisement is to bring about changes in knowledge, attitudes and behavior of people with respect to the purchase of the product.[1]

Keeping this basic purpose of advertising in mind, perhaps we can better understand the reason for and methods of pretesting.

---

[1]Russell H. Colley, *Defining Advertising Goals for Measured Advertising Results* (New York: Association of National Advertisers, 1961): 35.

TO TEST OR NOT TO TEST

The discussion of whether or not to pretest any advertising continues to be heated. Most creative people are opposed to pretesting. They argue that a creative idea can't be subjected to ranking or numbering. For example, they question whether or not anyone is capable of evaluating and ranking the Mona Lisa against the Michelangelo's David as works of art; or if it's possible to measure and put a number on the way in which any creative form affects an individual. Furthermore, because advertising is considered a form of creativity, they believe advertising pretesting stifles that creativity. On the other hand, clients and advertising executives are hesitant to invest millions of dollars in an advertising campaign with only their own intuitive guidance as to how effective the campaign might be. The controversy may never be resolved; nonetheless there are five very good reasons to pretest or evaluate advertising prior to its use in the media or as a part of the final campaign.

To Prevent Disaster

In general, advertising pretesting gives only a limited amount of information, but that information can be very important. The primary objective is to determine whether or not the advertising campaign is an absolute disaster; that is, will the proposed advertising actually drive people away from the brand? Advertising pretesting is usually quite reliable in meeting this objective.

To Test New Approaches to Old Problems

Most advertising campaigns submitted for pretesting are those for existing or established products. In those cases, the advertiser usually knows how the previous advertising has performed or at least has some idea of what effect it had on consumers. Thus, there is a standard against which new advertising can be measured to determine if it is more effective, delivers the sales message more clearly or more efficiently, is better understood, or is more relevant, than that which had been done previously. If, for example, it was found the new advertising was actually less effective, the advertiser would make changes prior to any major investment in the campaign or, perhaps, simply revitalize the present campaign.

To Evaluate Alternative Methods of Communicating the Brand's Sales Message

As is the case in any sales situation, several things can be said in several ways to communicate the benefits of the brand or to present the brand's solution to the consumer's problem. Some ways will be better or more effective than others. Usually, however, it is impossible to tell which way is best without actually trying the alternatives out using consumers. Therefore, the success of a new campaign isn't simply a judgment that can be made by the advertising's creators. The advertiser really needs to try the proposed alternative creative approaches with consumers to get their reactions and see which alternative works best. Pretesting, no matter how effective, can't identify what the single best approach may be, but it can identify the best of the alternatives being tested.

To Determine How Well the Advertising Achieves Its Objectives

The pretest gives the planner an opportunity to see how well the proposed new advertising campaign performs in terms of the objectives that have been set. If for example, the major objective of the campaign is to generate brand name awareness, then that can be measured in the pretest. If the advertising doesn't perform well, changes can then be made. In a pretest, many objectives, such as information communicated, knowledge gained by consumers, and changes in conviction, can be measured. Thus pretesting advertising provides a preliminary measure of how the advertising might perform in the marketplace in achieving the objectives that have been set for the campaign.

To Improve the Proposed Advertising before It Is Used

Obviously, the planner wants to use the strongest, most effective advertising possible in the campaign. The pretest provides an opportunity to identify any unforeseen weaknesses and correct them before the actual campaign. Not only can the advertising be improved, but major savings in production costs may result as well.

In summary, perhaps the best view of why advertising pretesting should be used and what it is all about is provided by Alan Hedges, a market researcher in England:

> We too often speak of testing advertising (a term which should be struck from all our vocabularies) as if we were submitting the piece of film or print to a testing machine (which happens to be made up of consumers) which will accept or reject it; just like the quality control process at the end of a production line which rejects items which are over or under weight, or whatever it may be.
>
> This is a very misleading way of looking at creative research, and one which I believe is responsible for a good deal of the misdirected activity which we find in this field. We are not *testing* the advertising since we do

not have, and cannot have, any such machine. We are *studying consumers* in order to gain some better understanding of the way they are likely to react to stimuli of different kinds, the stimuli being advertisements or advertising ideas. Since both the stimuli and the repertoire of possible responses are highly complex (and since the research situation is a very unusual one), we know that we cannot make any precise and simple formulation of what a given advertisement will achieve—but we *can* improve our understanding to the point where we are better able both to produce relevant and effective ideas and to judge when we have a campaign which is adequate for our purposes.

Therefore advertising research should seek to enrich our *understanding* of the way a particular advertisement is likely to affect people.[2]

WHEN TO PRETEST

It is best to test any advertising at the earliest stage possible—usually at the advertising strategy or development stage, or at the time when the central benefit to be communicated to the consumer is being identified. Unfortunately, however, much advertising pretesting occurs much farther down the line, after copy has been approved, television commercials bid and sometimes even produced, and the battle lines drawn between those who believe the advertising sound and good and those who think it can be improved. In general, advertising can be pretested at four basic stages: the concept stage, the creative strategy or competitive consumer benefit stage, the rough stage, and the stage at which the advertising is finished.

The Concept Stage

The most basic measurement of the value of a product or brand is often taken at the concept stage. Although concept testing is not an actual advertising testing technique, it is widely used for new product ideas or suggestions and new approaches for existing products. Thus, it is often the first step in the development of an advertising campaign.

The concept statement is a few sentences that outline the attributes, uses, and advantages of a product or a brand to the consumer. Eugene Cafarelli suggests a concept statement should consist of three main points:

1. A statement of the problem that the product is meant to solve
2. A definition of the type of solution that your product provides
3. The necessary supporting attributes (both physical and communications) that lend credibility to the product's ability to solve the problem[3]

---

[2]Alan Hedges, *Testing to Destruction* (London: Institute of Practitioners in Advertising, 1974): 36–37.

[3]Eugene J. Cafarelli, *Developing New Products and Repositioning Mature Brands* (New York: John Wiley & Sons, 1980): 110–11.

Frequently, the concept statement is accompanied by an illustration or picture of the product as it looks or will look when produced, or of the solution it might provide. The combination of this illustration and the accompanying statement is called the concept board. It is used to help the consumer visualize what the product might be or might do. Cafarelli offers these rules of thumb about preparing concept boards and statements:

1. Use normal language. Often the concept board will be used when no one is around to explain what a word or term means. Also, make sure the sentences are short. You're not writing a traditional English composition. You are writing more in the style of advertising, without attempting to interject creative twists (there are no slogans, etc.)
2. The verbal section of the concept board should have a number of paragraphs. Avoid long, involved paragraphs, particularly when you are referring to several kinds of supporting attributes. It is better to break them into paragraphs that contain one, or at most, a few supporting attributes.
3. It is best to avoid catchy names in concept statements, unless the name is an integral part of the product concept or aids in the communication of the concept. It is best if the name indicates the function of the product. For example: "A SAFE TRICYCLE" will be better than "HEAVY WHEELS" if you are talking to mothers who are prospective purchasers of a tricycle type toy that will not tip over. Ultimately, you might want to call it something like "HEAVY WHEELS." But that would be a result of what you learned in your positioning research. It almost never is a good idea to use names in concept statements. I must say, though, that like most statements, this must be tempered. In the area of cosmetics, the name often becomes a part of the total package. Therefore, in areas like cosmetics and toiletries, sometimes a name has to be part of the concept statement. It is an area in which you need to use good judgment.
4. Finally, the concept should have a one- or two-sentence summary that puts the concept in perspective.[4]

More than one concept statement can be developed for the same product, and the alternative concepts can be tested against one another. For example, two concept summaries for the same product might read as follows:

Concept A: A home computer that can run a wide variety of software. Hundreds of programs are already available and more are being written daily to provide you with a wide range of options.

Concept B: A home computer that thinks like you do. Keys are labeled in clear language and basic programs operate in a sensible fashion. You won't have to spend months trying to decipher every command.

---

[4]Cafarelli, *Developing New Products:* 110–11.

As you can see, each concept focuses on a different set of product attributes. The concepts would be tested against one another to see which is most attractive to prospective consumers.

The Creative Strategy or Competitive Consumer Benefit Stage

The creative strategy (or advertising strategy) or benefit statement is the basic sales message or the idea of the advertising. This statement really is a summation of what problem solution the advertising is supposed to communicate to the consumer. It is the real "heart" of the advertising campaign. Therefore, it is vital that this statement is sound, believable, relevant, and persuasive to the consumer; otherwise, the advertising is certain to fail no matter what else is done.

As was discussed previously, the strategy or benefit statement must offer a consumer a benefit or provide the solution to a consumer problem. Often the strategy is pretested in the form of a promise statement. An example follows:

> The Grumman American airplane gives you superior fuel and speed efficiency compared with similar models from Piper, Cessna, and Beechcraft.

For pretesting purposes, the statement may be written in a form that provides a summary of the offer, "If you buy this brand, you will get this benefit or it will solve this problem." The statement is often accompanied by an illustration of the product or the benefit offered to help the consumer visualize the offer.

The goal of most creative strategy pretesting is to determine which of several alternative sales messages that might be used with the brand is the strongest. Therefore, the strategy testing should take place at a very early stage in the development of the campaign. This is the basic reason for pretesting. If the promise made the consumer isn't effective, believable, or persuasive, no advertising, no matter how creative, can make the campaign successful.

The Rough Stage

The most common form in which advertising is pretested is in a rough form—one stage prior to final production. The newspaper or magazine advertisement is done with rough art and the copy may or may not be set in type. The visuals need only illustrate, in a general way, the action, event, or situation taking place.

For broadcast, a radio "scratch track" is often used. This scratch track simply is a recorded rough approximation of what the finished commercial would be. For example, a piano might be used to carry the basic tune although a full orchestra is planned for in the finished version. Television is usually tested in the form of a storyboard that may be shown to the respondents in its rough art form or photographed in some way as to illustrate what is going to take place in the commercial. Many commercials are put into rough storyboard form and are then transferred to sound on a film called an *animatic*. The sound and the storyboard illustrations can be synchronized so that they represent a very rough version of the final commercial. These animatics may be either very rough or close to finished commercial form depending on the method of testing to be done. Another form of rough commercial gaining popularity is the "steal-o-matic," a rough representation using frames edited from existing commercials. The frames are put together to give a sense of the new commercial.

Generally, roughs are used when testing alternative ideas, such as benefit statements or strategies. They may also be used to test various executions of the same strategy to see which one best communicates the sales message.

Finished Advertising Form

The pretesting of finished advertising is done primarily by large advertisers for major campaigns, and it is a fairly common practice for them. The form used is the finished print ad or commercial in almost exactly the same form that the consumer would actually see should the campaign be approved for release. The most common reason for pretesting finished advertising is that many sales messages and advertising executions, particularly those that make use of image or mood, cannot be totally or accurately rendered except in final form. Thus, the argument is made that only a finished ad or a finished commercial can truly elicit what the consumer's actual response to the advertising might be.

Most of the syndicated services that pretest advertising use a finished commercial or a finished print ad for testing. Although testing finished advertising is much more expensive than testing at the earlier stages outlined, it is often required with certain types of campaigns.

Although the preceding discussion might have made it seem that advertising pretesting in various forms is an either–or situation, it is not. In fact, some advertisers pretest their advertising at all of the stages mentioned. This is particularly true for advertising being developed for new products, or when major changes are planned for existing products. The pretesting scheme should be developed and implemented by the campaign planner just as the other parts of the campaign are. Budgets for this pretesting must also be set and included in the overall plan.

WHAT TO MEASURE

Obviously, what is to be measured in the pretest is often determined by the form or the stage at which the advertising will be tested. For example, with product concepts, it is difficult to test much more than varying levels of appeal. With finished television commercials, however, it is possible to test several things, including understanding, recall, and information communicated. Thus the planner should determine in advance what is to be pretested, when, and in what form.

Measure against Objectives

The first rule of any advertising pretesting is to set objectives for the measurement. In other words, it must clearly be stated what is being measured and what the objectives of the test are. If the importance of varying new product concepts is to be measured, the real objective is to determine if the product as described will actually solve consumer problems or offer strong enough benefits to generate trial. On the other hand, if the objective is to measure the effects of a rough commercial, totally different objectives may be set for the advertising, such as implanting the brand name, getting the sales message across, and building knowledge of the product. Therefore, the advertising pretest should reflect the objectives of the advertising campaign. If the objective is to build awareness of the brand name in the marketplace, then the advertising should be evaluated on the basis of how well it communicates the brand name, not on how well the spokesperson is remembered. A simple rule: The results of the pretest should be measured on the same basis as the objectives that have been set for the campaign.

Results Must Be Measurable

As stated earlier, the results of the pretest must be measurable. Objectives that can't be quantified should not be used. For example, it is most difficult to measure whether or not respondents "liked" an ad or a commercial. Liking has components that are often hard to measure. It is much better to measure quantifiable objectives, such as recall of the sales message, believability of the message, persuasiveness, or a change in attitude.

One must always keep in mind that in any pretest situation the goal of the pretest is not to measure the mere popularity or entertainment value of the advertising. The goal of advertising is to communicate a sales message. That, not how much people liked the advertising, should be the basis of the test.

Effects Measured

In general, three basic effects can be measured in pretesting—perception, comprehension, and reaction.

Perception.   Perception is the lowest form of communication or understanding of the advertisement. It simply means the person understands that this is an advertisement and that it contains a sales message. Perception is primarily used to determine what the advertising means to the respondent. In other words, the pretest will show how the person perceives what is being said or how he or she interprets the message of the advertisement. It does nothing more.

The measure of perception is important because advertisers often use attention-getting devices or other means of attracting attention or methods of demonstrating the value of the brand outside a straight sales message. It is important that consumers perceive the same message the advertiser is sending.

Comprehension.   Do consumers understand what the advertiser is trying to communicate? In other words, do the words and pictures being used properly communicate the sales message? If the goal of the advertising is to demonstrate that the brand is more effective than the competition, it is important to know if consumers take away from the advertising the message that the advertiser intended.

Comprehension is normally measured by asking the consumer to play back or describe the intended message of the advertisement. The consumer's answer can then be checked against the stated objectives of the advertisement.

Reaction.   The consumer's reaction is normally the final and most important factor measured in a pretest. In other words, if the consumer perceived the ad and also comprehended it, what is his or her reaction to the message? Most often, the pretest attempts to determine if the message persuaded respondents to change their attitudes or behavior toward the brand after seeing it. If the goal of the advertising is to stimulate a change in attitude, the pretest can be used to determine whether or not that particular advertisement changed the attitude or simply reinforced an attitude that was already there.

By setting measurable objectives for the advertising pretest and then measuring the various levels of perception, comprehension, and reaction, the campaign planner should have a fair idea of whether or not the advertising will be effective when used in the actual advertising campaign.

HOW TO PRETEST ADVERTISING

There are two basic methods of pretesting: (a) through a custom-developed pretest plan, and (b) through the services of a syndicated or formal pretesting organization. In each case, the methods used are determined by the need or level of measurement required, and these needs dictate the form of the advertising to be pretested. Despite a number of variables (e.g., Is it a concept test, creative strategy, or benefit statement, or is the advertising in the rough or finished stage?), there are some basic factors that apply to all pretests.

Test with the Target Market

There is one cardinal rule in any pretesting situation: The persons with whom the advertising is being pretested should be members of the proposed target market. Although this seems to be a very simple concept, it is often overlooked. Because a convenience sample of some sort is usually used to provide the respondents for the pretest, the persons actually evaluating the advertising may or may not be logical prospects for the product, service, or brand. In most cases, it is worthless to pretest the advertising on those who are not in the target market for the brand. For example, testing advertising for a teenage product with women in their 40s or testing an advertisement for work clothes designed for low-income, blue-collar workers with white-collar workers makes little sense. But although this point sounds obvious, the pretest audience is so often not the target market that much advertising pretesting is of little value to the advertiser. Pretest your advertising with your target market to get accurate results.

Testing Concept Statements, Creative Strategies, and Benefits

There are two basic methods of pretesting concepts, strategies, and benefit statements—through personal interviews or in focus group situations.

Personal interviews. The traditional way to pretest concept statements, strategies, and benefits is the personal interview. The most common sites for interviews are in the home, at shopping malls, in or near retail outlets, or even at major airports. The primary objective is to find persons fitting the target market description and then conduct the interviews. A prescreening of respondents is often used to make sure the respondent is in the target market. For example, interviews for a new food product concept might be conducted in the food store with persons waiting in the checkout line. The prospects usually have time to answer questions; they are in a shopping situation and have their minds on food and food products.

The procedure may take many forms. A typical concept test method is to have the various ideas written on cards that are handed to the respondents. After reading the cards, respondents are asked to summarize the concept in their own words. The summary confirms that the statement is interpreted as intended.

After reading the concepts, the respondent is then asked to rank/order the concepts based on their appeal. Frequently, questions are asked, such as why the particular selection was made. Demographic data also are gathered to ensure that the respondent is a member of the selected target market (if this has not already been determined in a prescreening). A sample of 50 to 100 respondents is usually sufficient to identify the most salient concept or strategy among those offered. With this number of respondents, responses tend to stabilize; little beyond verification is gained with larger numbers.

Focus groups.   An alternative to the personal interview is the *focus group,* so called because the attention of the entire group is focused on the product category, concept, or strategy being evaluated.

A group of eight to ten respondents from the prospective target market is asked to meet to discuss a particular topic. Led by a trained interviewer, the respondents are shown the material to be tested. The interviewer then guides the group in a discussion. The purpose is to obtain information on the subject, not necessarily direct answers. Discussions are usually tape-recorded and often videotaped. After the session, the interviewer or an interpreter analyzes the conversations and develops a summary or consensus of the group. This interpretation gives valuable insight into the deeper feelings of the group members. It also determines how they talk about the product and discloses the language they use.

As in the personal interview technique, small samples, such as two or three focus groups, of the target market are usually sufficient to give an indication of the value of various concepts or strategies being tested.

The results of both personal interview and focus group methods usually are directional only. Because the sample is small and subject to error, the result of either type of testing should be regarded as a "prevention of disaster" test, or directional guidance for further research, rather than absolute truth.

Testing Rough or Finished Advertisements

There are two basic methods of pretesting rough or finished advertisements, one internal and one external.

Internal checklists, rating scales, and readability formulas.   One of the easiest and most common methods of advertising pretesting is an internal evaluation by the advertiser or agency. This evaluation, commonly done for many industrial product print advertisements, may be accomplished by means of a checklist or rating scale system. Checklists are used to (a) ensure that all the various components of the advertisement are included, such as coupons, ordering information, sizes, colors, and delivery time; and (b) ensure that the major selling points of the product, service, or brand are included in the advertisement.

Very elaborate checklists, which include such topics as checking for "a benefit-oriented headline," "the use of the word *you* in the copy," and the inclusion of the brand name a certain number of times in the copy, have been developed by advertisers. Although checklists seem somewhat mechanical, they can play an important part in ensuring that advertisements are complete and that no obvious errors are present.

Some advertisers have developed rating scales that can be used to evaluate and compare alternative advertisements. They might include such subjective evaluations as, "Does the first paragraph follow the headline and lead to the body copy?" or "Is the brand name of the product visible at a glance in the layout?" The usual method is to develop a rating scale based on a five-point measure, such as a "Very Good" to "Very Poor" scale. By rating different advertisements on these scales and then totaling the results for each advertisement tested, one can select a winner. These rating scales are often completed by the management of the company, the sales force, or others in a position to judge the merits of the advertisement.

The final method of internal evaluation is a readership test for print ads. Such tests are designed primarily to determine how easy the advertisement is to read and comprehend. Several formulas are available, including the Flesch Formula developed by Rudolph Flesch. Flesch's formula is computed based on

1. the average sentence length;
2. the average number of syllables;
3. the percentage of personal words used; and
4. the percentage of personal sentences in a 100-word sample of the writing.

The formula determines whether the writing can be read and understood by the average person. Phillip Ward Burton has said that the Flesch formula shows that the most readable copy contains 14 words per sentence, 140 syllables per 100 words, 10 personal words, and 43 percent personal sentences in total.[5]

---

[5]Phillip Ward Burton, *Advertising Copywriting,* 3rd ed. (Columbus, Ohio: Grid, 1974): 366–75.

Checklists, rating scales, and readability levels of advertising are low in cost, easy to apply, and usually reveal glaring errors. These types of pretests, however, do little to evaluate how the advertisement affects the consumer.

Consumer panels.   A consumer panel is simply a group of prospective consumers for the product or service who are exposed to and evaluate the proposed advertising in either rough or finished form. Consumer panels may take many forms, from prerecruited ongoing groups to persons contacted for a simple interview in the local supermarket or bus station. Regardless of the type of panel used, the primary objective is to get prospective customers' considered opinions of the product and combine the responses to form a single opinion. A few of the more common evaluation methods using consumer panels include:

1. Order-of-merit test. The order of merit is a simple ranking test of a group of advertisements by respondents. For example, respondents are asked to look at several alternative advertisements and then to rank them in some way. Ranking may be made on almost any basis, but one of the more common ones is the persuasive ability of the advertisement. Questions such as "Which of these advertisements would you most likely read if you saw it in a magazine?" "Which of these headlines would interest you the most in reading further?" "Which advertisement convinces you most of the quality of the product?" and "Which layout do you think would be most effective in causing you to buy?" are commonly used in an order-of-merit test.[6]

    In addition to ranking, respondents may be asked to describe why they selected certain advertisements or why they consider one to be better than others. This helps give the researcher or planner a better understanding of the decisions and why they were made.

2. Portfolio. In the portfolio test, unidentified test advertisements are placed in a folder or portfolio with a number of other advertisements that are not being tested. Sometimes the portfolio is made up to simulate a normal magazine or newspaper and may even include editorial content. Respondents are then shown the portfolio and allowed to look at it for as long as they like. After viewing the portfolio, they are asked to recall which ads they saw, what they remembered about each ad, which ad they liked best and why, and so forth. This questioning helps determine how the advertisement should score when placed in a normal environment. In the portfolio test, advertisements must be in a finished form, or else the balance of the materials must be at the same stage of development as the test ad

[6]James F. Engel, Martin R. Warshaw, and Thomas C. Kinnear, *Promotional Strategy,* 6th ed. (Homewood, Ill.: Richard D. Irwin, 1987): 408.

to permit a fair evaluation to be made. From five to ten ads can be evaluated by the portfolio method at one time. Portfolio tests are probably a stronger method of pretesting than order-of-merit tests or rankings.

3. Rating scales. Rating scales are often used for evaluation of appeals or parts of individual advertisements. They provide an opportunity to isolate dimensions of opinion and can be repeated with other groups for comparisons.

    A method called the semantic differential is often used for this type of pretest. Adjectives that are opposite in meaning are used to either describe the advertisement or to identify claims made in the advertisement. For example, in the illustration in Exhibit 11–1, a series of bipolar adjectives describing the content of an advertisement has been developed. They describe how the brand works based on the advertisement that has been prepared. Respondents, after reading the advertisement, check the various scales to indicate what information they received from the advertisement or how the brand was described. By evaluating these responses, the planner can determine whether or not the advertisement is achieving the objectives that have been set.

Exhibit 11–1   Semantic Differential

After reading this advertisement, would you say that Brand X is

	Very -3	Quite -2	Slight -1	0 0	Slight +1	Quite +2	Very +3	
Hard to use	___	___	___	___	___	___	___	Easy to use
Low quality	___	___	___	___	___	___	___	High quality
Unpleasant	___	___	___	___	___	___	___	Pleasant

The terms used can be applied to the product, the brand, or the advertisement. Rating individual advertisements and their communicative powers makes possible an identification of the best of the group of advertisements being tested.[7]

Other rating scales, such as a scale of the important values the advertisement should contain, or of how the brand and its claims compare to competition, can also be used. The inherent problem in scales of this sort is the subjective development of the factors to be evaluated.

---

[7]Engel, Warshaw, and Kinnear, *Promotional Strategy:* 409.

4. Paired comparisons. In this methodology, several advertisements are given to panel members. Respondents are then asked to rate each ad individually against the others. For example, if there are three ads to be tested, A would be rated against B, A against C, and B against C. Each ad is thus rated in comparison with each of the others. With this technique, the best ad may be selected through comparison, not simply by ranking. This technique is usually limited to approximately eight ads which require a total of twenty-eight comparisons. Respondent fatigue often develops beyond that number.

5. Mock magazines. In this method special magazines are printed or regular editions of known magazines are obtained prior to distribution. Sample advertisements are printed and inserted in place of or in addition to those which appear regularly. These specially constructed magazines are then distributed to subscribers or readers. After a suitable time, the respondents who received the magazines are contacted and asked questions about the magazine and the advertising.

    This pretesting technique uses recall as the measure of success. The main advantage is that the advertisement is tested in an actual reading situation rather than in a "forced viewing." Other finished advertisements, however, can be tested, and the investment in production must be made before testing and may be wasted on those ads that are rejected.

6. Projective techniques. Although not widely used, various forms of projective techniques—such as the puzzle game, word association, sentence completion, and role playing—are valid for pretesting. The puzzle game is a good example. Respondents are given a partially completed advertisement, for example, the ad might be complete except for the headline or the illustration. Several alternative headlines and/or illustrations are given to respondents, and they are asked to complete the advertisement using the parts furnished. The respondent selects the headline and illustration that he or she thinks would be most suitable. The assumption is that the headline and illustration most often selected would be the most effective. In other forms of projective techniques, respondents are asked to fill in blanks or draw pictures that indicate what would most appeal to them.

7. Storyboard tests. Television storyboards are often tested with consumer juries using roughly the same techniques previously discussed. Respondents, however, are usually shown more than just layouts. The television commercial may be shown in slide form with a prerecorded audiotape. Respondents are usually able to make the transition from rather rough art and single-voice recordings to a finished commercial. Also, if needed, particular scenes can be isolated for discussion and evaluation. The major advantage, of course, is the low cost, because expensive television production is not required.

Artists' drawings of the various frames to be used appear to be quite satisfactory for testing purposes. As with other forms of testing, a rather small number of respondents is needed because basic reaction comes rather quickly and additional respondents only quantify the results. Normally, thirty to fifty responses are sufficient for general direction.

8. Mail tests. Although not widely used, the mail test is still effective. Alternative copy appeals are printed on postcards which are then sent to prospective customers. Offers are made on the cards using various copy approaches. The appeal that draws the most returns is judged to be best. Because this technique requires an offer and a rather long period of time for reply, it is normally used only to test direct mail or direct response advertising prior to major mailings.

9. Focus groups. Although not technically a consumer panel, a focus group is often used to pretest advertising, particularly television advertising. The focus group seems to work quite well with children or younger people who often have trouble expressing themselves individually to adults but do quite well in a group setting.

This is certainly not a complete list of consumer jury techniques that may be used to pretest advertising. Other techniques include measures of predisposition to buy, forced switching test, first- and second-brand choices, and even projective buying games. All are designed to achieve the same goal—to obtain a preliminary evaluation of various alternatives by the prospective target market.

The major advantage of these types of pretests is that consumers generally can separate the good advertisements from the bad. Because the advertisements are tested against consumers rather than advertising experts or other groups, a rather basic understanding of how they would work in the marketplace can be gained. They are fast and easy to use and are usually low in cost because samples are limited in size.

Doing one's own pretesting does have some limitations, such as obtaining a representative sample for the test, and the artificial nature of the testing situation. In addition, all of these situations are "forced viewing"; that is people are required to read the advertising, whereas in a real world situation they might not even notice it. Thus, although the pretesting of advertising with forms the planner can do her- or himself is better than no pretesting at all, the campaign planner must keep in mind that most results are only directional in nature; they are guides to better advertising, not an assurance that the best advertising available or possible has been done.

Pretesting Hazards

Although the preceding pages have given a rather descriptive view of the various techniques and approaches used in advertising pretesting, some basic rules of thumb on the hazards of *any* form of pretesting should be pointed out.

Pretesting judges only the best of the lot tested.   Any pretesting procedure gives one the opportunity to find the best of those advertisements being tested, not the best of all possible approaches. If all the advertisements being tested are, in truth quite poor, only the best of the worst will be selected, not the best possible approach.

Pretests should be realistic and practical.   Although it is always tempting to ask consumers to make many evaluations in a pretest, keep in mind what consumers can and can't judge from the advertising being shown them. They can't, for example, tell whether or not an advertisement will turn the brand's sales around or whether or not it will generate the level of awareness or comprehension the planner is seeking. Respondents can tell you only what the advertising does to them and how they react.

Try to prevent respondent prejudice.   One of the most difficult tasks in advertising pretesting is preventing respondents from becoming "advertising experts." This simply means that respondents have a tendency to judge advertising by offering improvements, rather than responding as consumers. When this happens, the opinions given are often worthless. Although "advertising expertise" is a difficult problem to overcome, efforts should be made to limit respondents' opinions and comments to their proper role as consumers of, not as creative directors. Some suggestions are given in the next section on how to avoid this respondent prejudice.

Campaigns can't be tested.   All advertising pretesting is for individual advertisements in a given situation. Consumers can't tell you what the effect would be of multiple exposures over time or how differing executions for the same strategy might affect them when coupled with other marketplace activities. Remember, individual advertisements are being tested, not a campaign.

Recognize the inherent problems in pretesting.   Some common situations often occur in advertising pretests. These involve the problems arising from the difference in viewing advertising in a controlled setting as compared with normal viewing. For example, advertisements with negative appeals usually score poorly in pretests, but are sometimes successful in the marketplace. Similarly, advertising that is entertaining, humorous, or light usually scores very well in advertising pretests, although it may not perform as well in the normal media channels. Finally, "hard sell" facts about the product or service usually score the lowest of all on pretests. Yet, there is ample evidence that "hard sell" advertisements and commercials may be most effective in communicating with the intended audience. Certain types of advertisements may also score well depending on the specific pretest measure used (i.e., commercials with music, commercials with a great deal of action, etc.). It is important to keep these problems in mind when evaluating the results of a pretest.

Ways to Avoid Respondent Prejudice

As mentioned earlier, one of the biggest problems in advertising pretesting is simply that consumers or respondents usually consider themselves to be experts in advertising. Thus, they often try to go far beyond what they are capable of doing in terms of judging or evaluating advertisements. In addition, if they know the advertising is being pretested, they seem to assume there is something wrong with it. Thus, they are anxious to help spot errors or make changes. Advertising is a very personal thing to most people, and as a result, they are tempted to give opinions or make suggestions on how advertising should be improved. For these reasons, there are always respondent prejudices involved in any pretesting situation. However, there are some things that can be done to help overcome these prejudices. They are as follows:

1. The respondent should not be preconditioned or influenced toward a desired direction to support a preconceived notion. Because most consumers quickly learn that the test is for advertising, the researcher must try not to influence the test in one way or another. Don't lead or guide the respondent in any of the answers he or she may give.

2. Direct questions should be asked, not those that will solicit opinions. As an example, the question, "How do you like this ad?" usually leads to opinion answers. The more direct question, "Would this type of advertisement make you want to purchase the product?" is more specific and helps avoid opinions. Short, direct, to-the-point questions should be asked in an advertising pretest.

3. Questions that can be answered logically by the respondent should be asked. Sometimes the respondent is assumed to have knowledge he or she may not have. Thus, if a person is asked, "What do you think are the advantages of alternating current in an electric razor?" it is likely the answers would vary widely. Most people don't know the answer. When faced with this type of problem, they often make up an answer or guess rather than appear ignorant.

4. Respondents should not be asked to project their answers to others. Even the most informed parents really can't answer how their children would feel or react to a product or an advertisement. Therefore,

putting respondents in the position of guessing how others might feel or react only asks for trouble. Respondents know only about their own feelings. When they are asked to project to others, they are being asked to guess. When that situation occurs, respondents often believe it is acceptable to guess in other areas, too.

5. Questions should probe. The first answer may represent the true feelings of the respondent, but often, it is just that—an answer. Follow up by asking such questions as, "Why do you say that?" and "What do you mean by that?" Try to get the truth, not merely a superficial answer. When respondents know a probe will follow, they will often dig a bit deeper to give true facts and not just "top-of-mind" replies.

Certainly, these are not all the available methods of preventing respondents from becoming "advertising experts," or having respondent prejudices. These methods may, however, help overcome these very common problems in pretesting.

HOW TO PRETEST ADVERTISING—SERVICES AVAILABLE

Over the years, a number of advertising pretesting organizations and testing systems have been developed. Several have been in operation for quite some time and are widely used. On the other hand, new methods and new companies are constantly springing up with new techniques that may seem to offer exciting new opportunities. Because many facilities and techniques are similar, with only minor methodological differences, only the major services and those that have proven themselves over time are discussed here. More specific information can be obtained on each type of pretesting system or approach from any market research text or from the organizations themselves.

Generally, separate research organizations have developed for pretesting print and broadcast. Certainly, broadcasting pretest services are more widespread than print services, simply because the demand for these services from large advertisers is greater. In addition, most advertising practitioners feel themselves capable of evaluating print advertising better than advertising for radio or television. Over the years, four basic types of formal advertising pretesting methodologies have developed. Each is discussed briefly in the following sections.

Objective Mechanical Methods

These techniques are called "objective" because they rely on mechanical means for physiological measurement rather than opinions or replies from respondents. Tests are usually conducted with individuals in a laboratory setting. These pretesting approaches have not gained widespread use; many are still regarded as experimental rather than conclusive.

1. The Eye Camera. Eye camera testing tracks the respondent's eye movement through the layout of an advertisement, showing which elements of the ad are noticed first, and which are given the most attention.
2. The Tachistoscope. The tachistoscope records the speed of response to various portions of an advertisement. Tests have shown that quick recognition of elements in an ad leads to high advertising readership.
3. GSR/PDR. These are measures of advertising attention attraction. Galvanic skin response (GSR) measures changes in skin temperature; elevated skin response is taken to indicate interest in a stimulus. Pupil dilation response (PDR) measures changes in pupil size while viewing advertising, measuring the amount of advertising information processed by the respondent.[8]

Although the above tests have the advantage of being objective, some concern has been expressed about their interpretation and the understanding of exactly what the results mean.

Print Services

Two organizations, Daniel Starch and Gallup & Robinson, offer widely used print pretesting services in which preprinted advertisements are tipped into test magazines. These magazines are then circulated to respondent groups. Following an opportunity to read the magazine, respondents are contacted and interviews are conducted concerning the magazine and the advertisements being pretested. The tests are primarily of recognition and recall and provide an effective evaluation technique prior to full-scale schedules in media.

Broadcast Services

The largest number of pretesting services has been developed for broadcast advertising, particularly television. The major difference between the techniques is the situation in which the test commercials are viewed by respondents. Four basic broadcast pretest methodologies are available, three of which rely on artificial settings while the fourth attempts to measure response in a natural viewing environment.

In-home. A small-screen, self-contained projector is taken into the homes of potential target market viewers. Respondents are asked a series of questions, shown the test commercials, and then asked another series of

---

[8]Engel, Warshaw, and Kinnear, *Promotional Strategy:* 411–12.

questions. The in-home technique has the advantage of gaining the complete attention of the respondent. It is extremely expensive and thus not widely used.

Trailer tests.   For the purpose of getting closer to the actual point of decision by the respondents, pretesting is sometimes conducted in a natural-setting/forced-viewing situation. One method is to set up a trailer in a shopping center parking lot. Shoppers are invited to enter and are offered prizes for cooperation. First, respondents are asked a series of questions about the products to be tested and are given an opportunity to select a number of brands in a simulated shopping situation using cents-off coupons or similar incentives. The respondents then view the test commercials along with other material. After seeing the commercials, respondents are given another set of coupons to be used in the stores in the shopping center. Later, coupons given the respondents are retrieved from the stores where they were used. By correlating the choices made prior to viewing the commercials with the coupons used in the actual shopping situation, inferences are drawn about the strength of the commercials in affecting purchasing behavior.

Theater tests.   A widely used technique for pretesting is forced viewing in a theater setting. ASI Market Research and ARS, Inc., ask respondents to come to a theater supposedly to view a potential new television series. At the beginning of the show, respondents select brands of products from among the categories to be tested. (They are told that the selections are door prizes.)

The actual test consists of showing a nontelevised pilot or another entertainment piece followed by a series of commercials and more entertainment. After the showing, respondents are again asked to make brand selections from various categories. Differences between the brand choices prior to viewing the commercials and those after the viewing are assumed to indicate the persuasive power of the commercials. Other evaluations are made in this type of setting through questionnaires and mechanical devices to measure such factors as attention value, effect of "clutter," and recalled sales points.

Theater testing is fast, fairly inexpensive, and can be replicated if necessary. Another advantage is that research organizations have tested many commercials in most consumer categories. Test commercials may be compared with previously tested commercials or the "norms" that have been established. These comparisons give an indication of the relative strength of the test commercial compared with others that have been tested. A disadvantage is the forced-viewing situation and the fact that the audience is often in the theater to be entertained. These conditions sometimes lead to false assumptions of how the commercial will do in a real-world situation.

On-air/recruited natural environment.   On-air commercial tests have been developed to try to overcome the problems of forced viewing. It is hoped that placing the respondent in as natural a setting as possible will improve predictability.

These tests, typified by Burke Marketing Services and Gallup & Robinson, use an unassigned channel on a cable television system or programming on a regular UHF station as the pretest vehicle. Prospective respondents are either recruited to watch the programming on the channel during the time the test commercials will be shown or selected afterward based on proven recall of the programming. Because respondents are not told which commercials are being tested, real-world viewing is simulated as closely as possible. After the commercial has appeared, the recruited respondents are telephoned and asked a series of questions concerning what they saw and remember about the test commercials that were shown. Response to the questions and recall of the test commercials are the normal measures used to rate success.

The major advantage of this technique is the real-world atmosphere in which the commercial appears with all the normal distractions and competition from the programming and other commercials. The major disadvantage is the fairly high cost of the technique and the lack of projective ability with respect to what will happen in repeated viewings.

A variation of these techniques has been developed by Burke's AdTel. Test sites are located in several communities in which matched samples of homes have been connected to cable television. Respondents keep diaries of such factors as purchases and television viewing. By controlling the source of the programming through the cable system, the research organization is able to show one commercial in one set of homes while a different commercial is seen by the other sample. Respondents are not aware of what is being tested. Through a comparison of the purchasing behavior of each group of viewers and their exposure to the alternatives, the commercials can be evaluated. Although this technique completely simulates the actual conditions under which commercials are seen, it is quite expensive and only a limited number of advertisers can use the system at any one time.

Sales Tests

The sales test attempts to replicate the actual response the advertisement would receive in the real world. Three techniques deserve mention, although they are not as widely used as might be expected.

Inquiries.   Inquiry tests are conducted by means of running advertisements in regular media and judging the effectiveness according to the number of inquiries generated. The standard approach is to run different advertisements at different times in the same publication or at the same time in different publications. Based on the number of inquiries received, the advertisement to be used on a broad scale or continuing basis is selected.

Split runs.   Split-run testing simply means that different advertisements are run in the same edition of a publication. This can be done by having the publication use different ads in alternating issues or by running one ad in half the press run and a different ad in the other half. Advertisement elements, such as headlines, appeals, and offers, can be evaluated according to the response achieved.

The major advantage of these two sales test forms is that the advertising is being evaluated under real-world conditions. The disadvantage is that these approaches can be used only for print advertising and are limited to those publications that have split-run capabilities. Also, split-run testing may not work for all types of products. An appeal for an automobile, for example, would be difficult to test in an inquiry or split-run technique, because such a purchase is made infrequently.

Scanner tests.   Variations of the AdTel split cable with recruited panels are now being used by a number of organizations, particularly Information Resources, Inc. (IRI). These involve recruiting panels of people, usually in somewhat isolate markets with cable service, and giving them user identification cards. Through the use of scanners in food and drug stores, each person's purchases can be monitored over time through the coded card and scanner. The research company can control the television advertising that goes into the home through the cable. Thus, because the advertising that was sent into the home is known, and sales are measured through the use of the personalized purchasing card through the scanners in stores, individual purchases can be monitored. With this system, a true advertising-related-to-sales measurement can be made of varying advertising messages and campaigns (and other promotional elements) over time. These new types of sales measurements of advertising effects have great promise for advertising pretesting in the future.

WHAT MAKES A GOOD ADVERTISING PRETEST?

A number of major factors must be considered in any type of pretest. Some of the more important ones have been identified.

Determine first *how* the advertising should be judged. Should recall, persuasion, or communication of a specific product benefit be used and at what level? Usually, determining this need clarifies what techniques should be used.

When deciding to pretest, describe the problem to be solved not the methodology to be used to the research people involved. This is especially important if outside research organizations are to be used.

Whenever and wherever possible, disguise the true purpose of the pretesting, the name of the advertiser, and other campaign themes. Try to have the respondent react to the advertising as a consumer and not as an advertising expert.

Be sure the right sample is selected, that is, that the respondents logically are in the target market and are prime prospects for the product or service.

If possible, use several markets to avoid geographic bias in the pretest.

Understand the results of the study. The scores on pretests are only approximations. What is the range of the scores? What is the confidence level of the study? Understand the statistical and methodological terminology used in the results.

Test only one thing, not several things, at one time. If several of the test items are varied, there is no way to know what stimulated the response. Hold everything constant in the pretest except the item to be evaluated.

Use good judgment. Don't rely totally on the results of pretests. If something sounds unusual or the results seem out of the ordinary, go back to the study. Check the verbatim comments (most pretesting organizations will report these along with summary tables). Understand what the respondents were trying to say. Use common sense.[9]

Other rules-of-thumb in advertising pretesting can be cited, but those described here seem to cover the major points. Advertising pretesting should be used primarily to guard against disasters. Guaranteed techniques and completely foolproof tests simply do not exist.

REVISING—OR WILL YOU ACCEPT THE TRUTH?

One of the most difficult things to accept in advertising pretesting is the result. Much work has gone into the development and formulation of the campaign, much research has been done, long hours have gone into developing appeals and, yet a group of fifty consumers in a period of only a few minutes can totally reject the entire premise of a campaign. One's natural reaction is to seek another jury, find another group who truly understands the campaign. Test and retest.

Unfortunately, although results of pretesting are only directional, they may uncover major flaws in the thinking and planning of a campaign. If that is the case, accept the truth. Determine, if possible, exactly what went wrong. Learn why the theme or appeal is weak or has little potential.

---

[9]Kenneth Roman and Jane Maas, *How to Advertise* (New York: St. Martin's Press, 1976): 104–5.

Most of all, learn to accept the fact that not every campaign will test well, not every campaign idea is a winner. If the pretest should prove that the campaign is a poor one, certainly an attempt should be made to determine why. But, a vendetta against the "dummies in the market" who don't understand the campaign approach is the fault of the planner, not the respondents. Accept the results as a guide for improvement. That is often one of the most difficult parts of advertising campaign development.

SUMMARY

The major source of controversy about pretesting relates to the problem of establishing objectives. Just as a planner must ask what a campaign is supposed to accomplish when setting objectives for a campaign, the planner must ask what the pretest is going to measure. The concept stage, the strategy stage, the benefit stage—these are some key times to test an advertising execution. Whether it is done internally by the organization or is conducted by an outside service, at its best, testing can help creative people and can be used to develop better advertising.

Case Studies

Demeter Teas

Demeter Teas, an Aberdeen, North Carolina-based company, marketed a nationally distributed line of decaffeinated teas. Their twenty-item line consisted of a variety of fruit-, spice-, and herb-based teas packaged in boxes of forty teabags. Demeter had been operating for five years.

The market for bagged teas last year was as follows:

- Households drinking tea = 52,268,000 (65.9%)*
- Average number of cups per day = 1.8

Demeter, the only national decaffeinated brand, had an 11 share of the market last year.

Although Pat Lynn, vice president for marketing, felt these results were good, given the company's relative newness, she also believed there was a great deal of room for growth. Decaffeinated drinkers made up roughly 22 percent of all coffee drinkers,[†] and she believed that the tea market held similar potential. The key to tapping that potential was in product presentation through advertising.

Demeter's present advertising campaign, which had been in use for three years, consisted of monthly half-page, four-color advertisements in six national women's magazines. Also, an advertisement with a coupon was run quarterly as a free-standing insert in Sunday newspapers in the top 100 markets. The coupon was usually for 25 cents off on the purchase of one box of tea bags. (Average retail price was $1.79 per box.) The coupon was usually good for any flavor, even if the accompanying advertisement introduced a new flavor.

Although actual copy varied, Demeter's advertisements always focused on the teas' natural goodness, citing the fruit, spice, and herb flavors and tying the product to the mythical Demeter, the Greek goddess of agriculture. Although the product was described as caffeine-free tea, the no-caffeine feature was not emphasized.

Lynn called a meeting with the three managers in charge of fruit, spice, and herb teas, respectively. After reviewing the current advertising campaign and some recent sales figures (market share holding steady through the past two quarters; category growth at 2 percent), she explained why a

---

*Mediamark Research, Inc., 1986.
†Mediamark Research, Inc., 1986.

new emphasis on no caffeine was desirable. She went on to say, "I'd like some suggestions from you on how we should present the no-caffeine benefit to the consumers. You are all very familiar with the tea market and the tea consumer. We'll meet again next week to discuss your ideas."

When the group reconvened the following week, Lynn called on Susan Allison, the fruit tea manager.

"It seems to me," Allison began, "that we should define Demeter as the *only* caffeine-free tea available to consumers. I think that most people are aware of caffeine's effects. Pointing out that we're the only tea without caffeine should attract health-conscious drinkers."

Alan Henry, the spice tea manager, spoke next. "I disagree, Susan. I don't think people associate caffeine with tea the way they do with coffee. A lot of people who drink tea assume it doesn't have caffeine to begin with. Yes, we need to say that we're caffeine-free, but first we've got to point out that tea does have caffeine."

"I think you're both a bit off track," said herb tea manager Constance Lee. "I agree that people know about caffeine's effects, and I think they associate caffeine with tea. But, I think most tea drinkers, especially the cup-a-day group, think that tea's weaker than coffee, so it's got less caffeine. They figure it'll take longer for the caffeine in tea to affect them. You know, two cups of coffee equals four cups of tea, that kind of reasoning. I think we should show that a cup of tea and a cup of coffee both have about the same amount of caffeine and then say that we take care of the problem because we don't have any caffeine."

"Let me see if I understand each of you," said Lynn. "Susan, you say people know about caffeine, so all we need to say is that 'we're caffeine free' and they'll know why that's good. Alan says most people don't think tea has any caffeine, so we should ask them, 'Did you know all tea has caffeine—except Demeter?' Constance says people know tea's got caffeine, but they think it's negligible and we need to tell them, 'Your cup of tea has as much caffeine as a cup of coffee—unless it's Demeter.' "

"It seems to me that you're all saying the same thing, just in a different way. Frankly, I don't know which is best. No matter what we go with, we'll be reinforcing our current 'natural' image, so I don't think we're likely to lose any customers. But, I'm not sure which appeal is likely to bring in the most new Demeter drinkers. I'd like to think on what you've said for a few days."

Questions

1. Would an advertising pretest be helpful in this situation? Why or why not?
2. How would you test this case: as a concept, a benefit statement, a rough, or in finished form?

3. Assume you are each of the three managers. What would you expect your alternative to accomplish in terms of comprehension?
4. Can you establish one comprehension-related objective against which all three alternatives could be measured?
5. Who would the target market be for this advertising pretest?
6. Would you recommend that the alternatives be tested through personal interviews or focus groups? Why?
7. Can you see any obvious hazards in this pretest situation?

Metropolis Aquarium

Paul Thomson, marketing director at Metropolis Aquarium, had just met with representatives from an advertising agency that had donated its services to creating some alternative campaign ideas for a new program the Aquarium was planning to start in six months. The agency had come up with three separate creative approaches that might be used to promote the new "Make Friends with a Fish" fund-raising program.

Metropolis Aquarium was located in a large southeastern city. Founded in 1941, the Aquarium housed fish and other marine life from all over the world. Its most popular exhibits were a penguin colony and a sea otter group. Metropolis Aquarium charged admission and also sold family and individual memberships that were good for a year's admission.

Attendance figures at Metropolis Aquarium had remained steady over the past three years. Tourism in Metropolis had actually increased substantially during that same period, but the Aquarium competed for visitors with seven museums, two zoos, and a nearby amusement park. Paul was happy with the attendance figures; several of the museums had seen a drop in attendance in the last two years. At the same time, no major new exhibits were scheduled to open at the Aquarium in the next two years, so it was unlikely that attendance would increase dramatically in the foreseeable future.

Maintenance and operating costs continued to increase. The behind-the-scenes job of caring for and feeding the fish and animals and keeping the exhibit areas clean was very complex and very expensive. The Aquarium received financial support from a number of government and private funding sources, and had an ongoing development program. However, more money was always needed. The "Make Friends with a Fish" program was designed to get financial support for the Aquarium from the general public.

"Make Friends with a Fish" was modeled after programs in place in a number of zoos nationwide. A yearly maintenance cost was assigned to each type of animal (or fish). Then, sponsors would select a fish based on how much they were willing to contribute to the program. The sponsor received a photograph of "their" fish and an "adoption" certificate. The sponsor(s) name would be posted next to the exhibit housing "their" fish. For example, a piranha fish could be sponsored for $55 a year, while sponsorship of a blowfish cost $40. Charges ranged from $5 for a striped garfish to $500 for a hammerhead shark.

Similar programs at zoos had been very successful. The actual cost of running the adoption programs was relatively low, with the supporting promotional campaign accounting for the bulk of the cost. The photographs, certificates, and name plaques cost very little. Program costs decreased after the first year, because many sponsors regularly renewed their "adoption," so promotional costs dropped after the initial campaign.

In talking to program directors at zoos with adoption programs, Paul had learned that the initial promotional effort was critical for a successful program. Unfortunately, it seemed that every zoo had taken a different approach to promoting the program, and everyone had their own ideas on the "best" way to advertise the adoption program. Paul had gotten sample ads from a number of zoos and given these to the agency, but he had pointed out that none of the samples really fit the Aquarium's situation.

Paul had also made sure the agency knew that both of the zoos in Metropolis had on-going animal adoption programs. He thought that each was moderately successful. Another consideration was that the creatures in the two most popular Aquarium exhibits, the penguins and sea otters, would not be included in the program. Both of those exhibits had been funded by area businesses, and one of the conditions of the funding was that those companies would receive sole credit for the exhibits.

With that background in mind, Paul reviewed the agency's suggestions. All three campaigns were designed to be executed primarily through direct mail to the Aquarium's standing list of attendees and members, plus the circulation list of *Metropolis* magazine.

"WE NEED YOUR HELP"

This version emphasized the high costs associated with running the Aquarium and included photos of behind-the-scenes activities to show the scope of the Aquarium's operations. The "Make Friends with a Fish" program was featured as a new way to help support the Aquarium. Different dollar levels of support were listed and the sponsor was told that the Aquarium would select the particular fish based on the dollar pledged.

"GET PERSONAL"

This version focused on the fun involved in sponsoring a fish, emphasizing that having your name posted in the Aquarium and knowing that you were responsible for a particular fish would make your next visit to the Aquarium even more fun than usual. There was little discussion of the financial needs that had prompted the program. The mailing piece featured pictures of a number of kinds of fish. The sponsor was able to select the particular type of fish they wanted to support.

"GIVE A FISH"

This approach suggested giving a fish as a gift to that hard-to-buy-for person or your child. The fish adoption program was described as an unusual present, one that would amuse the recipient and help the Aquarium at the same time. Again, the gift-giver was able to select the particular fish to be "given." The mailing piece was illustrated with drawings of different kinds of fish, each imaginatively "gift wrapped." Although the mailer didn't go into the Aquarium's financial needs in detail, it did make it clear that the adoption would help keep the Aquarium operating.

Paul felt that all three campaigns might be effective, but he wasn't sure which would work the best. The current membership campaign was similar to the "We Need Your Help" campaign in that it focused on the scope of the Aquarium's activities and the kind of money that was needed to keep the Aquarium afloat financially. But, he didn't know if that was the right approach for the adoption program or whether one of the "fun" approaches might not be better.

The agency had suggested that it might be best to pretest the three alternatives to see which one would be most effective in getting the "Make Friends with a Fish" program off to a good start. They were willing to have their research department do the testing at cost. Paul would have to decide whether to spend the money for the testing, or, if not, which approach to use.

Questions

1. Would you pretest the three alternatives? Why or why not?
2. What criteria would you use to test the three alternatives?
3. Keeping in mind Paul's desire to keep the testing inexpensive, (a) who would you select as your testing sample? (b) What type of test would you use?
4. If cost were not a major concern, how would your answers to Question 3 change? Why?

12 Media Planning
Optimizing Message Delivery

The "big idea" of the advertising campaign rarely originates with the media planner, but the financial consequences of media strategy are widespread. For some products media may be the largest item in the advertising budget and in some instances, particularly for consumer products, it may be the largest portion of the entire marketing effort. For many products and services, millions are invested in advertising annually. The pressures to optimize budgets are enormous. Even with so much riding on the development of effective media strategy, it is important to keep in mind that the best media plan cannot rescue a poor creative execution. Sound execution, on the other hand, is wasted if inefficiently delivered or improperly directed to the wrong prospects. Effective advertising requires both first-rate copy and proper message delivery.

Prior to the emergence of television in the 1950s, media selection was relatively simple. Newspapers, several large magazines, and radio were the choices. Television did more than add another vehicle. It altered people's lives by becoming the primary entertainment force and the major news source for most people and started a technological evaluation that is still exerting substantial influence on the advertising industry.

THE CHANGING MEDIA WORLD

Today's media world is vast and complex. The TV industry is composed of over 1,100 commercial and 300 public TV stations. Dozens of cable TV networks provide programming to 9,000 cable systems. Nearly 8,800 ra-

This chapter was contributed by William P. Brown, Vice President for Media Services, the Quaker Oats Company, Chicago, Illinois.

dio stations, over 1,700 daily newspapers, and hundreds of consumer magazines exist. Countless additional media vehicles are available to reach general audiences and specialized groups.

Obviously, the enormity of this array of media makes the planning process complicated and perhaps awesome. Yet the sheer magnitude of choice creates opportunities for advertisers and allows many who cannot afford expensive Super Bowl commercials to effectively promote their products and services in less expensive but effective ways. The complexity of the media world can be viewed as a blessing also.

Advertisers are always seeking better ways to sell ideas, services, and products. Advertising media likewise are extremely dynamic. Television, the advertising darling of package goods manufacturers, produced stable, growing audiences from the late Fifties to the late Seventies. Agencies, advertisers, and TV executives could count on these viewers—always present in larger numbers habitually watching more TV. Then came cable, video cassette recorders, and subscription TV. The audience research showed strange aberrations. At first, there were merely minor shifts in audience patterns, but recently pronounced declines in traditional viewing are appearing.

The transitory nature of the advertising media world requires innovation and demands originality in approaching the media planning process. Such changes enable opportunity, but creative exploration of media alternatives is increasingly vital.

MEDIA BUILDING BLOCKS: BASIC MEDIA CONCEPTS

Several important terms and concepts have been developed to explain the dynamics of media planning. These are discussed in this section.

Rating

Sometimes referred to as coverage, a *rating* is the percentage of a specified population exposed to a single issue of a print or broadcast vehicle. The group measured must be defined but can be any target audience (women, men, children, households, etc.). Table 12–1 shows a simple rating group.

TV programs, radio shows, newspaper audiences, outdoor billboard traffic, virtually any medium's audience can be expressed as a rating. Some typical ratings for women are shown in Table 12–2.

Up to this point, national ratings have been discussed. Ratings generally relate to standard geographical areas, metropolitan statistical areas, or more commonly an area of dominant influence, the latter an Arbitron research service term for 212 separate TV areas in the U.S.

Table 12–1 Sample Rating Group

	Total women	Women 18–49
U.S. population	94.0 million	60.0 million
Reader's Digest readers	27.3 million	15.6 million
Reader's Digest ratings	29%	26%

Table 12–2 Typical Ratings for Women

	Women	Men	Teens	Children
Prime network TV program	10	8	6	6
Daytime network TV program	4	1	1	1
Early news network TV program	7	7	3	2
Late night network TV program	4	4	2	—
Saturday morning network TV program	1	—	4	7
Early morning local radio show	2	3	3	—
Network radio news program	1	1	1	—
Women's service magazine	20	2	4	—
Men's magazine	2	10	2	—
Daily newspaper	25	30	3	1

Gross Rating Points

The arithmetic sum of all the individual ratings in a media schedule is called *gross rating points.* GRPs are a measure of the total intensity or pressure of a media plan. The period of time represented by the GRPs should be specified (week, four weeks, length of the campaign, etc.).

In Table 12–3, television and magazine women's ratings are added to sum 200 total gross rating points for the schedule.

Cumulative Audience

GRPs tell how much weight or total pressure is expected by the number of advertising messages but they do not tell how many different people are exposed to the messages. That is the function of *reach,* the number or percentage of a given population exposed to at least one of the advertising messages over the course of a schedule. Synonyms are cumulative (cume) audience, net audience, or unduplicated audience.

Reach or the dispersion of an advertising schedule is determined by the number of dayparts, programs, stations, media, magazines, etc., employed.

Table 12–3 Sample Media Schedule

TV	Ratings (women)	Number of announcements or insertions	GRPs
Who's the Boss?	15	2	30
All My Children	7	3	21
Good Morning America	3	4	12
General Hospital	6	1	6
As the World Turns	4	2	8
Sunday Night Movie	9	1	9
Evening News	6	2	12
Magazines			
Better Homes & Gardens	25	2	50
Family Circle	23	1	23
Reader's Digest	29	1	29
Total GRPs			200

For instance, the largest TV audiences and, thus, the largest reach levels are generated at night when most people are home from work, school, or other activities. TV reach is increased by running announcements in the late evening, morning, and afternoon so they will be seen by people who work during the evening and may be available during the afternoon. Because magazines appeal to specific groups of people, the greater the number of titles used in a campaign, the greater the reach of the schedule. Size of magazine is important also. Large circulation magazines like *TV Guide* and *National Geographic* reach more people than do those that are more specialized (*Golf Digest, Soap Opera Digest*).

Reach divided into gross rating points produces average frequency, a measure of a campaign's depth. *Frequency* is the number of times a person sees the advertising message. In the example of 200 gross rating points, assume 50 percent of all women are exposed to at least one message. The average frequency is four.

$$\frac{\text{Gross rating points}}{\text{Reach}} = \text{Average frequency}$$

$$200/50 = 4$$

The formula is usually expressed in this fashion: $R \times F = GRPs$. To facilitate the use of these concepts, the advertising profession has developed tables of reach and frequency. Computers are often used to generate these numbers.

The earlier example is typical of a daytime TV schedule composed of serials and game shows. During the prime evening hours, 200 GRPs would generate broader reach—approximately 80 percent of women, resulting in an average frequency of 2.5 times. Thus, varying the mix of dayparts influences reach and frequency of an advertising schedule. The total number of spots aired and the number of different programs employed also affects reach/frequency patterns. In radio, the number of spots, dispersion of spots across the day, and number of stations used influences reach/frequency relationships. As the number of magazines and their editorial differences increases, the greater the reach.

Reach and frequency help in evaluating alternative schedules in planning. If reach is the most important criteria, the schedule that produces the greatest reach would be chosen. If frequency of exposure is more important, then the schedule concentrating the most exposures has the advantage. At a given budget level and similar GRPs, reach and frequency analysis is invaluable in deciding the best alternative to achieve the objectives of the advertising program.

Cost per Thousand

The universal calculation of media efficiency is cost per thousand (CPM), the cost of delivering one thousand impressions of a specified population.

$$\text{CPM} = \frac{\text{Cost (dollars)}}{\text{Impressions or People (in thousands)}}$$

Table 12–4 shows some typical women 18–49 CPMs.

Table 12–4   Typical CPMs

	Cost	W 18–49 impressions	Calculation	CPM
Prime network TV (:30)	$100,000	4,800,000	$\frac{\$100,000}{4,800}$	$20.83
Day network TV (:30)	15,000	2,000,000	$\frac{15,000}{2,000}$	7.50
Reader's Digest (page 4-color)	115,000	15,600,000	$\frac{115,000}{15,600}$	7.37

CPM cuts through different audience sizes and costs to create one simple expression of efficiency: the cost to reach 1,000 people as specified.

Effective Reach

A refinement of the reach concept used more frequently in media circles is the idea of effective reach, sometimes confusingly referred to as effective frequency. Take your pick, the term *effective reach* seeks to answer the old question: How much advertising is enough? Effective reach is simply how many people receive sufficient frequency of the advertising to become aware of the message and comprehend its content.

The optimum level of frequency for any product depends upon a host of factors, including the product purchase cycle, complexity of the message, competitive position and communications, brand awareness, and communication properties of media vehicles (which will be discussed more completely later). Numerous studies have been undertaken to determine the optimum level of advertising frequency. The conclusions are the same: it depends. However, for most branded package goods, these observations are generally recognized:

1. One exposure is of little value.
2. A second adds some value.
3. Three exposures a month (or during a purchase cycle) are needed to produce sufficient communication.
4. After a certain level of frequency, succeeding exposures produce increasingly *less* value.
5. At certain frequency levels, the commercial execution becomes ineffective. Negative reactions may result.

In the theoretical model in Exhibit 12–1, people exposed less than three times are of little value. The optimum level of exposure is six messages. But after eight exposures people grow weary of the message, succeeding impressions are less effective, and negative attitudes may be generated.

Frequency Distribution

Users of reach and frequency sometimes forget that frequency is an average. Some people see more impressions, and an equal number see fewer impressions than the average. To visualize more clearly the flow of impressions, a frequency distribution chart or table similar to the one in Exhibit 12–1 should be consulted.

Another means of looking at frequency distribution is to divide the population into groups based on exposure behavior. For instance, Table 12–5 shows a typical TV quintile analysis. The total TV audience is divided into five equal parts based upon overall viewing patterns—heaviest to lightest TV viewing.

Exhibit 12–1   Effective Reach and Frequency

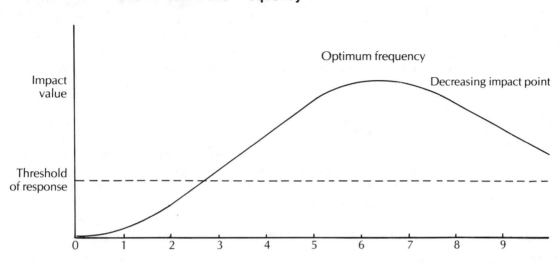

Note that the two heaviest viewing quintiles (40 percent) account for 76 percent of the total GRPs, a typical TV relationship.

Quintile and frequency distribution charts aid in determining how to schedule advertising in a medium and give some insight into when to add a second or third medium to a campaign. For instance, in the above quintile distribution, 40 percent of the TV viewers account for 76 percent of total exposures of the TV schedule. If a magazine schedule were added to that campaign, more impressions would be delivered to the lighter viewing quintiles. People who are heavy readers of magazines are lighter TV viewers. Subsequently, when print is added to a TV schedule, impressions build against lighter viewing quintiles, evening out or flattening frequency of exposures. Thus, instead of adding more frequency on top of the origi-

Table 12–5   Sample TV Quintile Analysis

	Reach	*Frequency*	*GRPs*
Heaviest viewing 20%	12.4	9.2	114
Next heaviest viewing 20%	12.4	6.5	80
Third heaviest viewing 20%	12.4	2.9	36
Fourth heaviest viewing 20%	12.4	1.6	20
Lightest viewing 20%	12.4	0.4	5
Average	62.0	4.1	255

nal frequency, the planner, through the use of quintile analysis, can see when to stop using TV and when to add magazines or radio or some alternative medium. As in the case of reach/frequency analyses, computer programs are now available to assist in constructing quintile distribution charts.

Armed with the basic media concepts, the planner is ready to build the media strategy and plan.

BUILDING MEDIA STRATEGY

Media planning is dependent upon marketing objectives and strategy, and the media plan becomes an integral part of the overall marketing plan. Media interacts with all elements of marketing strategy. The first step in media planning is a thorough review of all marketing information. The planner must understand the advertising and marketing goals so that the media plan supports those objectives.

Relating Media Planning to Marketing

Marketing objectives.   Critical to proper media planning are the marketing objectives that set the overall goals of all promotional, advertising, and merchandising activities. Marketing objectives address sales goals and marketing budget, prime prospects for the product or service, geographical sales and sales potential, sales seasonality, promotions, creative direction, and competitive issues.

Product characteristics and consumption patterns.   The nature of the product itself can determine media employed. Certain personal items are inappropriate for early evening TV, for example, while other products may require complex copy. Consumption patterns are critically important in determining where to promote products. Regional peculiarities must be considered as well as what types of people might consume or need the item.

Distribution patterns.   The geographical distribution channels and availability of products and services must be evaluated in structuring strategy. Even though products may be consumed nationally, individual brands may not be sold across the country or attain sufficient strength to justify universal advertising support.

Promotion and merchandising strategies.   During the 1970s inflation altered America's economic structure and the nature of marketing changed as well. Promotion and merchandising activity increased as consumers became more cost conscious. The relationship between advertising and promotion narrowed and is highly interrelated today. Advertising works hand in hand with couponing, point-of-sales promotion, sampling, and merchandising tools.

Competitive activity.   Media planning requires thorough knowledge of competitive marketing and advertising efforts. Plans often address threats of new or existing competitors and category spending. Standard industry sources provide the base for competitive expenditure analysis.

Financial constraints.   Media budgets sometimes are established by marketing people unfamiliar with the realities of the media world. The planner must have adequate financial footing to achieve advertising's role in the marketing plan. Budget parameters must be established before planning commences.

Creative execution.   Creative strategy and particularly the kinds of executions to be utilized are vital to media planning. Unless copy conforms to the media recommended, time is wasted.

Establishing Media Objectives

Media objectives are positive statements of what the media budget will achieve in the promotional plan. Media objectives answer five universal questions plus other considerations unique to the particular marketing situation. Objectives tell *what* will be done, not how it wil be accomplished.

Who is to be reached?   The target audience for advertising communications is identified as precisely as possible. Prospects are commonly defined in terms of socioeconomic characteristics (age, sex, income, education, race, family size, employment status, etc.). Two other means of defining the target audience are source of business (users/buyers) or psychographical/life-style characteristics. If more than one target audience is employed, the relative importance (weighting) of each needs to be established. Indirect secondary groups (sales force, agents, employees, etc.) important to the plan should be noted.

What is to be accomplished?   What is the media plan to accomplish against the target audience? Increase awareness of the brand or service? Alter an attitude about the product? Introduce a product? Reinforce promotional activities? Remind customers of the product? Block or meet a new competitive product? Encourage sales force response? Precise identification of the primary tasks of the media process should be outlined.

When does the advertising appear? This goal establishes the proper timetable for spending. Is the purpose of the advertising to

- lead the peak sales season?
- conform to monthly sales?
- support promotions?
- counter competitive threats?
- remind shoppers prior to purchase (time of day)?
- relate to weather, holidays, or quarters?

Where does the advertising occur? Establishing geographical priorities for spending emphasis ties directly back to consumption, distribution, and sales patterns. Some issues to consider include:

- National versus regional versus local support
- Actual brand sales development versus category sales characteristics
- Problem areas due to competitive introductions or testing
- Population density (city, suburban, rural promotion)

How much advertising should be scheduled? This objective determines the required advertising pressure necessary to accomplish results. Often, advertising weight goals are defined in terms of reach and frequency during flights or on a monthly basis. If season or geographical emphasis changes, the resulting reach and frequencies are also detailed.

Other considerations: special needs of the situation. Exceptional marketing or advertising goals should be specifically addressed beyond the above five areas. Special trial or inducement marketing activities may need communication support. Flexibility in commiting budgets or the need to cancel plans should be detailed. Matching peculiar creative ideas might be required. The need for testing alternative strategies, copy, or marketing approaches for future efforts is critical and is established in the media objectives. Any special company standards (i.e., avoiding certain media vehicles, etc.) as well as significant competitive issues should be addressed.

The media objectives establish goals of the plan. The remainder of the plan goes about the business of accomplishing the tasks and outlining specific media elements to be used during the course of the plan, usually a year.

Strategic Issues

Media strategies are solutions to the media objectives and tell how those goals will be achieved. Addressing these issues is challenging and requires a generous amount of judgment.

Geographical strategic allocations.   Products nationally distributed have three basic spending options:

- One hundred percent directly into national media
- A mix of national and local media
- Local media only across the country or a significant portion of the country

To aid in solving this issue, managers often analyze brand and category sales. An easy method is to index brand sales and category sales to construct a BDI or brand development index. In Table 12–6, brand geographical sales are related to overall category sales to show where the brand is

Table 12–6   Brand Development Profile

	Brand		Category		
	Sales (units)	%	Sales (units)	%	Brand development index
Eastern region	50	24	150	25	96
Baltimore	10	4	50	8	50
Boston	20	10	60	10	100
New York	20	10	40	7	143
Southern region	70	33	100	17	194
Jackson	20	10	20	3	333
Atlanta	15	7	30	6	117
Dallas	35	16	50	8	200
Central region	30	14	100	17	82
Chicago	5	2	20	3	67
Detroit	10	5	40	7	71
Minneapolis	15	7	40	7	100
Western region	60	29	250	41	71
Los Angeles	20	10	50	8	125
Denver	15	7	100	17	41
Kansas City	15	7	50	8	88
San Francisco	10	5	50	8	63
Total U.S.	210	100	600	100	—

strong or weak compared to the entire market. Eastern region sales represent 24 percent of the brand's total sales and 25 percent of the category's total sales. Thus, the BDI is 96 (24/25). Brand sales nearly match category sales in the Eastern region. Not so in Baltimore, however, where brand sales are below category sales (50 index). In New York brand sales are quite strong (143 BDI). An index is merely a percentage relationship between two other percentages. Indices are an easy method to uncover differences among many statistics.

If brand sales closely match category sales, spending may conform to the market. However, if sales deviate substantially from the overall category, strategic decisions have significant impact on possible results. A very successful strategy is to follow the brand's sales pattern. This conservative approach is to identify markets or areas having growth potential and invest (overspend) in these (Western region in the example). Still another approach is to identify weak markets and promote in these (Baltimore for instance).

Another helpful way to focus on product and category strategic issues is to group markets in a matrix (see Exhibit 12–2).

Exhibit 12–2   Media Strategies: BDI/CDI System

	Category development	
Brand development	**High**	**Low**
High	• Saturation brand and category sales • Incremental spending unproductive • Defensive spending • Sustained advertising	• Brand strong but consumer spending low • Added spending ineffective • Seek to build category frequency of purchase
Low	• Competition strong; brand relatively weak • Investment spending potentially effective • Build frequency at key periods (peak sales) • Seek intensive or flighted activity	• Limit advertising to peak sales periods • Is advertising necessary? No sales potential; brand weak • Support promotions to avoid distribution losses

Target audience analysis.   Because several groups may be important to the product or service, weighting of the relative significance of each group should be established. How much advertising weight or emphasis should be given each target is often a marketing decision. Sometimes research must be conducted to decide where to place emphasis.

In this example of a woman's product, the planner determines whether to target media strategy against category or brand users. Category users are younger, but the individual brand's franchise is middle aged. In selecting media and individual vehicles, it makes significant difference which profile to target advertising to. (See Table 12–7.)

Table 12–7   Sample Target Audience Analysis for a Woman's Product

Women	% population	% category users	% brand users
18–34	36	45	25
35–54	31	30	50
55 +	33	25	25

In the next example of an all-family product, advertising might be directed to both women and children. Although all ages consume the product, children on a per capita basis consume twice as much as any other group. Women exceed children in total consumption and are the major family food shoppers. These groups probably exert much more influence over other family members in the purchase decision. (See Table 12–8.)

Table 12–8   Sample Target Analysis for an All-Family Product

	% population	% consumption
Women	39	32
Men	35	25
Teens	10	12
Children	16	31

Should one target advertising to women (buyers) or children (major consumers), or perhaps both? Media reaching women (daytime TV, women's service magazines) and children (Saturday morning TV) or perhaps vehicles that attract both groups, such as early evening situation comedy TV shows, could be employed.

Strategic weighting, based upon the relative significance of several important consuming groups, is another possible approach. For instance, in the all-family product example, a combination of TV dayparts selected in such a way to deliver advertising impressions in the same proportion (weight) as consumption might be attempted in developing a media strategy. (See Table 12–9.)

Table 12–9   Sample Strategic Weighting

	% consumption	Day TV	Weekend TV	Sports TV	Combined
Women	32	75	3	18	32
Men	25	10	2	63	25
Teens	12	5	20	11	12
Children	31	10	75	8	31

% of total impressions delivered

Note that the combination of day, weekend children's, and sports programming distributes weight exactly in proportion to consumption. Similar advertising weighting can be accomplished using various media to reach a certain mix of women of different ages—daytime soap operas for younger women and evening news programs to reach older women who might not be busy preparing family meals at that time of day.

Reach and frequency issues.   Another major question for which no definitive research is available is how much reach and frequency is enough. Many factors—marketing and media objectives, competitive positioning and pressure, brand's marketing position, and a host of others—can affect this judgment. As a broad gauge, reach or frequency are emphasized in these instances unless other factors preclude the strategies:

Reach situations	Frequency situations
New products	Strong competitors
Expanding category	Complex story
Flanker brand	Frequently purchased category
Strong brand franchise	Weak loyalty to brand
Undefined target market	Narrow target market
Infrequent purchase cycle	Consumer resistance to brand or category

Scheduling options.   The ideal advertising situation is strong, year-around support at high effective reach levels, but of course, that's impractical for virtually all advertisers. Like other strategic issues, scheduling involves the planner's judgment. There are several major methods of scheduling advertising, each with its benefits and trade-offs.

Continuous advertising is weight scheduled throughout the advertising period. Variations in sales plus high media costs generally preclude continuous pressure. Continuous scheduling might be used in these instances:

- Expanding market situations
- Frequently purchased items
- Tightly defined buyer category

Continuous scheduling

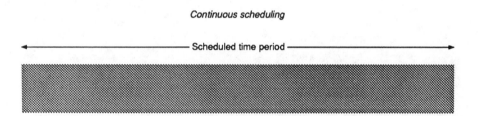

Flighted advertising comes in periodic waves separated by periods of no activity (hiatuses). Most brands employ some form of flighting due to media costs.

Situations lending themselves to flighting include:

- Limited funding
- Relatively infrequent purchase cycle
- Seasonal items
- Market share building programs

Flighting

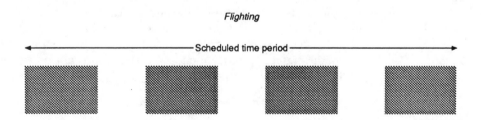

Communication models indicate that forgetting occurs during periods of inactive advertising. Usually the loss is gradual, although numerous factors spread memory delay (competitive clutter, product importance, campaign maturity, seasonality, budget size, copy execution, etc.). Scheduling can dramatically influence campaign results.

In this example, two sixteen-week campaigns are scheduled differently, yet at the end of the sixteen-week period average reach and frequency are equal:

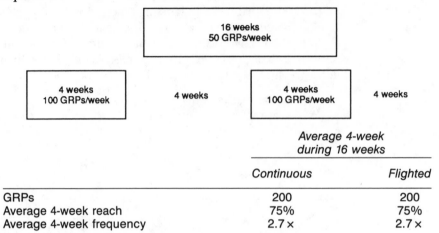

| | Average 4-week during 16 weeks | |
	Continuous	Flighted
GRPs	200	200
Average 4-week reach	75%	75%
Average 4-week frequency	2.7×	2.7×

However, during advertising periods, pressure and reach are surprisingly dissimilar:

| | Average 4-week flight | |
	Continuous	Flighted
Total GRPs	200	400
4-week reach	75%	89%
4-week frequency	2.7×	4.5×

Compromise scheduling strategies have been developed to draw upon the strengths of continuous (no voids) advertising and flights (increased intensity of exposure). The first, pulsing, is continuous advertising at low weight levels reinforced periodically by waves of heavier activity. If some media vehicles can be identified that efficiently concentrate on a portion of the target audience, continuous support at low weights may be feasible. Then, at strategic points, such as consumer promotion or peak seasonal periods, more intense pressure is activated.

Pulsing

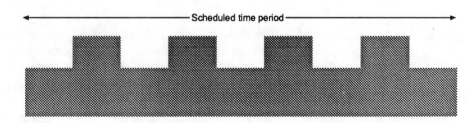

Blinkering, another compromise, is total-in and total-out advertising periods of short duration. Blinkering generates strong pressure while advertising and keeps hiatuses short. The brand may appear as a continuously advertised product without doing so.

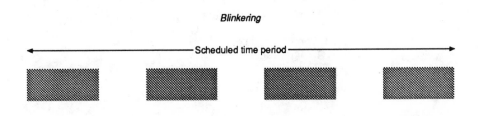

Blinkering

Blinkering and pulsing represent economical ways of blending the two original scheduling strategies, but both require extremely careful implementation and can lead to inefficiencies in strong marketplaces.

Media mix.   Advertising campaigns in a single medium tend to build impressions against a portion of the population because each medium has a hard core of listeners, viewers, or readers. Using a number of media tends to disperse advertising impressions more effectively than a single medium. Mixing several media tends to balance frequency.

If people are divided into groups based upon patterns of media consumption, we can see how advertising impressions accumulate against these groups. (See Table 12–10.)

Varying message delivery by media generally produces better advertising results than concentration in a single medium or area within a medium (e.g., early morning in the case of TV or a selected group of magazines):

1. As indicated earlier, using several media can level out impressions against target audiences and avoid intense concentration against a single portion of the audience. Caution: sometimes this characteristic is desirable, especially if the medium concentrates impressions against a good cross section of the desired audience for the advertising campaign.
2. Sometimes a synergistic effect on advertising recall or awareness is generated through a combination of media. TV messages are reinforced and recreated in the mind's eye when a related jingle is heard. This "imagery transfer" greatly improves effectiveness.
3. A second medium usually increases frequency against lighter users of the first medium. Thus effective reach can be enhanced.
4. Media mix is only valuable when sufficient resources are available to add a second or third medium. Achieve effective reach levels in the primary medium before dispersing advertising impressions via other media.

Table 12–10   Cumulative Effects of Advertising Impressions

	Adults	Adults 18–49 $40,000+ income, and some college	Index
Heavy TV viewers/light magazine readers	32%	17%	53
Light TV/heavy magazine	32	54	169
Heavy TV/light radio	33	24	73
Light TV/heavy radio	33	43	130

Creative values and audience adjustments.   Most advertising practitioners believe that media communicate in unique ways. An impression in one medium is not the same as an exposure in another. Media have individual "impact" values. TV commercials produce different results compared with radio commercials or newspaper ads. TV commercials within the TV medium may also produce differing effects. (A commercial for breakfast products may be more meaningful in the morning when people eat breakfast.)

Judgment is needed to determine creative values. Usually a combined agency/client judgmental decision is established based upon campaign objectives. Print may be best for a long, complicated story. Newspapers serve to announce new information forcefully. TV provides visual demonstrations. Radio reinforces many campaigns adding extra intensity near the time of purchase. Each medium has unique communication characteristics.

Closely related to creative values is the concept of audience adjustment. Fortunately, more research is available here, but considerable judgment is needed to properly employ the concept in planning. Most media research measures vehicle audience, not commercial or ad delivery. Audiences should be adjusted downward to reflect the fact that not everyone who watches a program or reads a magazine sees the commercial or the ad. Through various print and broadcast studies, factors have been established to reflect the lower commercial audiences. These adjustments are based upon broad-scale averages, however, and should not be taken as gospel. These "eyes on" and "pages turned" kind of research can be used to refine inter- and intra-media comparisons.

Often agencies will combine creative values and audience adjustments into comparisons. Table 12–11 is an example.

Once creative values and audience adjustments factors are taken into account, effective reach takes on additional meaning, especially when the media planner is attempting to decide upon the relative advertising impact of several potential media strategies.

Table 12–11   CPM Comparison—Women 25–54

Vehicle	Gross vehicle CPMs	Index	"Eyes-on" factor	Creative impact weight	Adjusted W 25–54 CPMs	Index
Prime net TV	$20.00	(100)	68%	1.00	$29.12	(100)
Day net TV	7.50	(38)	60	1.00	12.50	(43)
Magazines	10.00	(50)	85	.50	23.53	(80)

(Magazines = $10.00 ÷ 85% = $11.76 ÷ 50 = $23.53)

Product life cycle strategies.   Most products, certainly most branded consumer goods, have a life cycle. New products are introduced to the market, grow to maturity, and eventually are forced into decline by competitive or innovative new items. In broad terms, these stages call for significantly varying media strategies, as noted in Table 12–12.

From this point the media planner has established media goals and addressed overall strategic issues. These strategies should relate back to the media goals. The next job is to marry media vehicles with the strategies to produce the optimum message delivery.

Table 12–12   Product Life Cycle Media Strategies

	New product	Growing product	Mature product	Declining product
Target audience	Widespread (possibly unknown or unclear)	Defined	Users	Users
Advertising reach/ frequency	Reach with effective frequency	Frequency on prospects	Frequency on narrow group of users	Reach among users
Geographical emphasis	National	Natural/basic, additional emphasis on opportunity areas	Best markets	Best areas
Advertising pattern	Strong introduction, continuous following anticipated sales	Heavy during season	Leading into and during seasonal peaks	Support promotions only

Market–Media Research Services

The client marketing research group may provide considerable information to the media planning function concerning target audiences, sales, distribution patterns, and other marketing elements. Sometimes this information is not available internally and must be obtained from other sources. A number of media research firms supply syndicated market and media research data. Mediamark Research, Inc., and Simmons Market Research Bureau, Inc., are two of the most widely used services for product usage and media audience data.

The two services are highly competitive, employ different methodologies, and produce a wealth of market information. As an example of the extensiveness of the data provided, MRI breakouts for ready-to-eat cereals are shown in Exhibit 12–3. Demographic consumption data can be cross-tabulated with a host of media vehicles. On-line time-sharing enables numerous cross-tabs and manipulation of these extensive data banks across hundreds of product/service categories, thousands of brands, and numerous media audiences.

MRI reports can be intimidating but are not difficult to understand. Breakfast cereals are purchased primarily by female homemakers who are categorized in the left column and cross-referenced to all demographic and other categories reported by MRI. Column "A" tells how many female homemakers are users/purchasers of the brand. MRI categories are those who use/purchase any cereal; degree of use is noted in the groups to the right (heavy, medium, light). The "B" column under each usage describes users in terms of demographics. Note that the four education breaks add to 100 percent. The same is true for each demographic subgroup.

The last two columns are quite helpful in marketing and media planning. Column "C" indicates the relative consumption by all the categories listed on the left. This column is also indexed ("D"). A high index (over 100) means that the group (education, for instance) purchases more than would be expected based upon its proportion of all people. A low index (below 100) means below average consumption for this group. Similiar data are available in MRI for individual brands and categories of brands (presweets, regular, natural cereals, etc.).

Close inspection of the indices can provide considerable insights into category and brand target consumers and the media that reach them. Note that MRI data cover most major media types, specific vehicles, and various quintile categories.

Another interesting market media research organization is Claritas Corp's PRIZM. PRIZM is based upon groupings of neighborhood areas into forty homogeneous clusters based upon census blocks and zip codes. Claritas profiles a business against the forty socioeconomic zip clusters using company-generated and syndicated data. The profile provides a means

Exhibit 12–3 Sample Mediamark Research, Inc., Breakouts

BREAKFAST CEREALS (COLD)

INDIVIDUAL PORTIONS/LAST 7 DAYS

BASE: FEMALE HOMEMAKERS	TOTAL U.S. '000	ALL A '000	B % DOWN	C % ACROSS	D INDEX	HEAVY MORE THAN 8 A '000	B % DOWN	C % ACROSS	D INDEX	MEDIUM 4-8 A '000	B % DOWN	C % ACROSS	D INDEX	LIGHT LESS THAN 4 A '000	B % DOWN	C % ACROSS	D INDEX
ALL FEMALE HOMEMAKERS	79236	70921	100.0	89.5	100	17933	100.0	22.6	100	25578	100.0	32.3	100	27410	100.0	34.6	100
WOMEN	79236	70921	100.0	89.5	100	17933	100.0	22.6	100	25578	100.0	32.3	100	27410	100.0	34.6	100
HOUSEHOLD HEADS	27114	23388	33.0	86.3	96	4211	23.5	15.5	69	8686	34.0	32.0	99	10491	38.3	38.7	112
HOMEMAKERS	79236	70921	100.0	89.5	100	17933	100.0	22.6	100	25578	100.0	32.3	100	27410	100.0	34.6	100
GRADUATED COLLEGE	12005	10991	15.5	91.6	102	2902	16.2	24.2	107	4054	15.8	33.8	105	4034	14.7	33.6	97
ATTENDED COLLEGE	13697	12249	17.3	89.4	100	3281	18.3	24.0	106	4095	16.0	29.9	93	4874	17.8	35.6	103
GRADUATED HIGH SCHOOL	33217	29887	42.1	90.0	101	7917	44.1	23.8	105	10869	42.5	32.7	101	11102	40.5	33.4	97
DID NOT GRADUATE HIGH SCHOOL	20318	17794	25.1	87.6	98	3833	21.4	18.9	83	6560	25.6	32.3	100	7401	27.0	36.4	105
18-24	7140	6302	8.9	88.3	99	1099	6.1	15.4	68	2280	8.9	31.9	99	2924	10.7	41.0	118
25-34	19497	17952	25.3	92.1	103	5191	28.9	26.6	118	6295	24.6	32.3	100	6466	23.6	33.2	96
35-44	15715	13838	19.5	88.1	98	4629	25.8	29.5	130	4494	17.6	28.6	89	4715	17.2	30.0	87
45-54	11324	10255	14.5	90.6	101	2399	13.4	21.2	94	3599	14.1	31.8	98	4257	15.5	37.6	109
55-64	11154	9959	14.0	89.3	100	2366	13.2	21.2	94	3826	15.0	34.3	106	3787	13.7	33.8	98
65 OR OVER	14406	12616	17.8	87.6	98	2249	12.5	15.6	69	5085	19.9	35.3	109	5282	19.3	36.7	106
18-34	26637	24255	34.2	91.1	102	6290	35.1	23.6	104	8575	33.5	32.2	100	9390	34.3	35.3	102
18-49	48167	43385	61.1	90.0	101	12295	68.6	25.5	113	14936	58.4	31.0	96	16134	58.9	33.5	97
25-54	46536	42045	59.3	90.3	101	12220	68.1	26.3	116	14387	56.2	30.9	96	15438	56.3	33.2	96
EMPLOYED FULL TIME	34842	30845	43.5	88.5	99	7211	40.2	20.7	91	11002	43.0	31.6	98	12633	46.1	36.3	105
PART-TIME	7143	6383	9.0	89.4	100	2202	12.3	30.8	136	2051	8.0	28.7	89	2129	7.8	29.8	86
NOT EMPLOYED	37251	33694	47.5	90.5	101	8520	47.5	22.9	101	12525	49.0	33.6	104	12648	46.1	34.0	98
PROFESSIONAL	6473	5937	8.4	91.7	102	1722	9.6	26.6	118	1946	7.6	30.1	93	2270	8.3	35.1	101
EXECUTIVE/ADMIN./MANAGERIAL	4555	4075	5.7	89.5	100	898	5.0	19.7	87	1633	6.4	35.9	111	1544	5.6	33.9	98
CLERICAL/SALES/TECHNICAL	18435	16303	23.0	88.4	99	3851	21.5	20.9	92	5796	22.7	31.4	97	6656	24.3	36.1	104
PRECISION/CRAFTS/REPAIR	1000	953	1.3	95.3	106	*239	1.3	23.9	106	*290	1.1	29.0	90	423	1.5	42.3	122
OTHER EMPLOYED	11522	9961	14.0	86.5	97	2703	15.1	23.5	104	3389	13.2	29.4	91	3869	14.1	33.6	97
H/D INCOME $50,000 OR MORE	14304	12808	18.1	89.5	100	4015	22.4	28.1	124	4447	17.4	31.1	96	4346	15.9	30.4	88
$40,000 - 49,999	9821	8835	12.5	90.0	101	2475	13.8	25.2	111	3217	12.6	32.8	101	3142	11.5	32.0	92
$35,000 - 39,999	6500	6083	8.6	93.6	105	1422	7.9	21.9	97	2155	8.4	33.2	103	2506	9.1	38.6	111
$25,000 - 34,999	13806	12602	17.8	91.3	102	3394	18.9	24.6	109	4368	17.1	31.6	98	4840	17.7	35.1	101
$15,000 - 24,999	15616	13958	19.7	89.4	100	3478	19.4	22.3	98	5216	20.4	33.4	103	5264	19.2	33.7	97
LESS THAN $15,000	19190	16635	23.5	86.7	97	3149	17.6	16.4	73	6174	24.1	32.2	100	7313	26.7	38.1	110
CENSUS REGION: NORTH EAST	16966	15354	21.6	90.5	101	4060	22.6	23.9	106	5738	22.4	33.8	105	5555	20.3	32.7	95
NORTH CENTRAL	19582	17694	24.9	90.4	101	4921	27.4	25.1	111	6183	24.2	31.6	98	6590	24.0	33.7	97
SOUTH	27346	24521	34.6	89.7	100	6041	33.7	22.1	98	8519	33.3	31.2	97	9960	36.3	36.4	105
WEST	15342	13353	18.8	87.0	97	2910	16.2	19.0	84	5138	20.1	33.5	104	5305	19.4	34.6	100
MARKETING REG.: NEW ENGLAND	4656	4176	5.9	89.7	100	1117	6.2	24.0	106	1500	5.9	32.2	100	1559	5.7	33.5	97
MIDDLE ATLANTIC	13652	12399	17.5	90.8	101	3275	18.3	24.0	106	4693	18.3	34.4	106	4431	16.2	32.5	94
EAST CENTRAL	11204	10082	14.2	90.0	101	2853	15.9	25.5	113	3493	13.7	31.2	97	3737	13.6	33.4	96
WEST CENTRAL	12679	11561	16.3	91.2	102	3212	17.9	25.3	112	4137	16.2	32.6	101	4212	15.4	33.2	96
SOUTH EAST	14499	13246	18.7	91.4	102	3405	19.0	23.5	104	4706	18.4	32.5	101	5135	18.7	35.4	102
SOUTH WEST	9288	8051	11.4	86.7	97	1695	9.5	18.2	81	2764	10.8	29.8	92	3593	13.1	38.7	112
PACIFIC	13258	11406	16.1	86.0	96	2377	13.3	17.9	79	4286	16.8	32.3	100	4743	17.3	35.8	103
COUNTY SIZE A	32384	28350	40.0	87.5	98	6605	36.8	20.4	90	10614	41.5	32.8	102	11131	40.6	34.4	99
COUNTY SIZE B	23508	21425	30.2	91.1	102	5631	31.4	24.0	106	7420	29.0	31.6	98	8374	30.6	35.6	103
COUNTY SIZE C	12456	11210	15.8	90.0	101	3070	17.1	24.6	109	3898	15.2	31.3	97	4242	15.5	34.1	98
COUNTY SIZE D	10888	9937	14.0	91.3	102	2628	14.7	24.1	107	3646	14.3	33.5	104	3663	13.4	33.6	97
MSA CENTRAL CITY	28381	25036	35.3	88.2	99	5699	31.8	20.1	89	9119	35.7	32.1	100	10219	37.3	36.0	104
MSA SUBURBAN	32254	28942	40.8	89.7	100	7736	43.1	24.0	106	10397	40.6	32.2	100	10808	39.4	33.5	97
NON-MSA	18601	16944	23.9	91.1	102	4498	25.1	24.2	107	6062	23.7	32.6	101	6383	23.3	34.3	99
SINGLE	8850	7522	10.6	85.0	95	1112	6.2	12.6	56	2746	10.7	31.0	96	3664	13.4	41.4	120
MARRIED	50063	45917	64.7	91.7	102	13613	75.9	27.2	120	16265	63.6	32.5	101	16038	58.5	32.0	93
OTHER	20323	17483	24.7	86.0	96	3209	17.9	15.8	70	6567	25.7	32.3	100	7707	28.1	37.9	110
PARENTS	31882	29804	42.0	93.5	104	10689	59.6	33.5	148	9950	38.9	31.2	97	9165	33.4	28.7	83
WORKING PARENTS	19985	18561	26.2	92.9	104	6479	36.1	32.4	143	6163	24.1	30.8	96	5919	21.6	29.6	86
HOUSEHOLD SIZE: 1 PERSON	13148	10817	15.3	82.3	92	1149	6.4	8.7	39	4062	15.9	30.9	96	5606	20.5	42.6	123
2 PERSONS	23406	20545	29.0	87.8	98	3603	20.1	15.4	68	8078	31.6	34.5	107	8864	32.3	37.9	109
3 OR MORE	42682	39559	55.8	92.7	104	13181	73.5	30.9	136	13439	52.5	31.5	98	12940	47.2	30.3	88
ANY CHILD IN HOUSEHOLD	34747	32364	45.6	93.1	104	11111	62.0	32.0	141	11052	43.2	31.8	99	10201	37.2	29.4	85
UNDER 2 YEARS	5971	5586	7.9	93.6	105	1639	9.1	27.4	121	2127	8.3	35.6	110	1820	6.6	30.5	88
2-5 YEARS	13551	12754	18.0	94.1	105	4545	25.3	33.5	148	4237	16.6	31.3	97	3972	14.5	29.3	85
6-11 YEARS	16228	15245	21.5	93.9	105	5814	32.4	35.8	158	4877	19.1	30.1	93	4554	16.6	28.1	81
12-17 YEARS	15479	14312	20.2	92.5	103	5164	28.8	33.4	147	4897	19.1	31.6	98	4251	15.5	27.5	79
WHITE	68615	61924	87.3	90.2	101	15927	88.8	23.2	103	22194	86.8	32.3	100	23803	86.8	34.7	100
BLACK	8816	7420	10.5	84.2	94	1741	9.7	19.7	87	2819	11.0	32.0	99	2860	10.4	32.4	94
HOME OWNED	54889	49584	69.9	90.3	101	13737	76.6	25.0	111	17729	69.3	32.3	100	18119	66.1	33.0	95
DAILY NEWSPAPERS: READ ANY	46387	41920	59.1	90.4	101	10943	61.0	23.6	104	15045	58.8	32.4	100	15932	58.1	34.3	99
READ ONE DAILY	37130	33434	47.1	90.0	101	8706	48.5	23.4	104	11967	46.8	32.2	100	12761	46.6	34.4	99
READ TWO OR MORE DAILIES	9258	8486	12.0	91.7	102	2236	12.5	24.2	107	3078	12.0	33.2	103	3172	11.6	34.3	99
SUNDAY NEWSPAPERS: READ ANY	49444	44400	62.6	89.8	100	11851	66.1	24.0	106	15705	61.4	31.8	98	16843	61.4	34.1	98
READ ONE SUNDAY	43413	38895	54.8	89.6	100	10136	56.5	23.3	103	13807	54.0	31.8	99	14952	54.5	34.4	100
READ TWO OR MORE SUNDAYS	6031	5505	7.8	91.3	102	1715	9.6	28.4	126	1898	7.4	31.5	97	1892	6.9	31.4	91
HEAVY MAGAZINES - HEAVY TV	20671	18671	26.3	90.3	101	4901	27.3	23.7	105	7197	28.1	34.8	108	6573	24.0	31.8	92
HEAVY MAGAZINES - LIGHT TV	18757	16973	23.9	90.5	101	4737	26.4	25.3	112	5770	22.6	30.8	95	6466	23.6	34.5	100
LIGHT MAGAZINES - HEAVY TV	20250	17831	25.1	88.1	98	3787	21.1	18.7	83	6627	25.9	32.7	101	7418	27.1	36.6	106
LIGHT MAGAZINES - LIGHT TV	19558	17446	24.6	89.2	100	4508	25.1	23.0	102	5984	23.4	30.6	95	6954	25.4	35.6	103
QUINTILE I - OUTDOOR	15906	14343	20.2	90.2	101	3803	21.2	23.9	106	4750	18.6	29.9	93	5790	21.1	36.4	105
QUINTILE II	16049	14063	19.8	87.6	98	3456	19.3	21.5	95	5209	20.4	32.5	101	5398	19.7	33.6	97
QUINTILE III	15880	14290	20.1	90.0	101	3849	21.5	24.2	107	4918	19.2	31.0	96	5523	20.1	34.8	101
QUINTILE IV	15886	14445	20.4	90.9	102	3793	21.2	23.9	105	5549	21.7	34.9	108	5104	18.6	32.1	93
QUINTILE V	15515	13781	19.4	88.8	99	3033	16.9	19.5	86	5153	20.1	33.2	103	5595	20.4	36.1	104
QUINTILE I - MAGAZINES	15649	14315	20.2	91.5	102	3781	21.1	24.2	107	5238	20.5	33.5	104	5296	19.3	33.8	98
QUINTILE II	15680	14043	19.8	89.6	100	3809	21.2	24.3	107	5290	20.7	33.7	105	4944	18.0	31.5	91
QUINTILE III	16383	14868	21.0	90.8	101	3987	22.2	24.3	108	4980	19.5	30.4	94	5901	21.5	36.0	104
QUINTILE IV	15915	14274	20.1	89.7	100	3660	20.4	23.0	102	5072	19.8	31.9	99	5542	20.2	34.8	101
QUINTILE V	15608	13422	18.9	86.0	96	2697	15.0	17.3	76	4998	19.5	32.0	99	5727	20.9	36.7	106

(continued)

Exhibit 12–3 (Continued)

BREAKFAST CEREALS (COLD)

		ALL				INDIVIDUAL PORTIONS/LAST 7 DAYS: HEAVY MORE THAN 8				MEDIUM 4 - 8				LIGHT LESS THAN 4			
BASE: FEMALE HOMEMAKERS	TOTAL U.S. '000	A '000	B % DOWN	C % ACROSS	D INDEX	A '000	B % DOWN	C % ACROSS	D INDEX	A '000	B % DOWN	C % ACROSS	D INDEX	A '000	B % DOWN	C % ACROSS	D INDEX
ALL FEMALE HOMEMAKERS	79236	70921	100.0	89.5	100	17933	100.0	22.6	100	25578	100.0	32.3	100	27410	100.0	34.6	100
QUINTILE I - NEWSPAPERS	15995	14417	20.3	90.1	101	3760	21.0	23.5	104	5258	20.6	32.9	102	5399	19.7	33.8	98
QUINTILE II	16180	14633	20.6	90.4	101	3783	21.1	23.4	103	5184	20.3	32.0	99	5665	20.7	35.0	101
QUINTILE III	15913	14459	20.4	90.9	102	3977	22.2	25.0	110	4945	19.3	31.1	96	5537	20.2	34.8	101
QUINTILE IV	15578	13725	19.4	88.1	98	3364	18.8	21.6	95	4900	19.2	31.5	97	5461	19.9	35.1	101
QUINTILE V	15571	13688	19.3	87.9	98	3049	17.0	19.6	87	5291	20.7	34.0	105	5349	19.5	34.4	99
QUINTILE I - RADIO	14915	12958	18.3	86.9	97	3072	17.1	20.6	91	4992	19.5	33.5	104	4893	17.9	32.8	95
QUINTILE II	15953	14140	19.9	88.6	99	3256	18.2	20.4	90	5000	19.5	31.3	97	5884	21.5	36.9	107
QUINTILE III	15994	14566	20.5	91.1	102	4046	22.6	25.3	112	5010	19.6	31.3	97	5511	20.1	34.5	100
QUINTILE IV	16206	14652	20.7	90.4	101	4098	22.9	25.3	112	5057	19.8	31.2	97	5496	20.1	33.9	98
QUINTILE V	16169	14607	20.6	90.3	101	3462	19.3	21.4	95	5520	21.6	34.1	106	5625	20.5	34.8	101
QUINTILE I - TV (TOTAL)	16081	14542	20.5	90.4	101	3099	17.3	19.3	85	5705	22.3	35.5	110	5739	20.9	35.7	103
QUINTILE II	16635	14716	20.7	88.5	99	3648	20.3	21.9	97	5507	21.5	33.1	103	5561	20.3	33.4	97
QUINTILE III	15833	14290	20.1	90.3	101	3824	21.3	24.2	107	5272	20.6	33.3	103	5195	19.0	32.8	95
QUINTILE IV	15262	13540	19.1	88.7	99	3518	19.6	23.1	102	4670	18.3	30.6	95	5352	19.5	35.1	101
QUINTILE V	15425	13833	19.5	89.7	100	3844	21.4	24.9	110	4424	17.3	28.7	89	5564	20.3	36.1	104
RADIO WKDAY: 6-10:00 AM CUME	45107	40243	56.7	89.2	100	10084	56.2	22.4	99	14499	56.7	32.1	100	15661	57.1	34.7	100
10:00 AM - 3:00 PM	28138	24953	35.2	88.7	99	6424	35.8	22.8	101	8971	35.1	31.9	99	9558	34.9	34.0	98
3:00 PM - 7:00 PM	28380	25163	35.5	88.7	99	6506	36.3	22.9	101	8655	33.8	30.5	94	10002	36.5	35.2	102
7:00 PM - MIDNIGHT	11776	10550	14.9	89.6	100	2515	14.0	21.4	94	3654	14.3	31.0	96	4380	16.0	37.2	108
RADIO AVERAGE WEEKDAY CUME	61019	54460	76.8	89.3	100	14147	78.9	23.2	102	19363	75.7	31.7	98	20949	76.4	34.3	99
RADIO AVG. WEEKEND DAY CUME	51317	45664	64.4	89.0	99	11293	63.0	22.0	97	16421	64.2	32.0	99	17950	65.5	35.0	101
RADIO FORMATS: ADULT CONTEMP	20565	18721	26.4	91.0	102	4852	27.1	23.6	104	6375	24.9	31.0	96	7494	27.3	36.4	105
ALBUM ORIENTED ROCK (AOR)	7130	6313	8.9	88.5	99	1390	7.8	19.5	86	2479	9.7	34.8	108	2444	8.9	34.3	99
ALL NEWS	2636	2278	3.2	86.4	97	560	3.1	21.2	94	1013	4.0	38.4	119	705	2.6	26.7	77
BLACK	2071	1839	2.6	88.8	99	*493	2.7	23.8	105	627	2.5	30.3	94	719	2.6	34.7	100
CLASSICAL	1948	1699	2.4	87.2	97	426	2.4	21.9	97	737	2.9	37.8	117	536	2.0	27.5	80
CHR/ROCK	13663	12253	17.3	89.7	100	2853	15.9	20.9	92	4511	17.6	33.0	102	4888	17.8	35.8	103
COUNTRY	14237	12935	18.2	90.9	102	3444	19.2	24.2	107	4742	18.5	33.3	103	4749	17.3	33.4	96
EASY LISTENING	7216	6466	9.1	89.6	100	1648	9.2	22.8	101	2269	8.9	31.4	97	2549	9.3	35.3	102
GOLDEN OLDIES	2876	2441	3.4	84.9	95	725	4.0	25.2	111	829	3.2	28.8	89	887	3.2	30.8	89
MOR/NOSTALGIA	4109	3707	5.2	90.2	101	910	5.1	22.1	98	1288	5.0	31.3	97	1509	5.5	36.7	106
NEWS/TALK	5386	4689	6.6	87.1	97	1250	7.0	23.2	103	1805	7.1	33.5	104	1634	6.0	30.3	88
URBAN CONTEMPORARY	3270	2779	3.9	85.0	95	674	3.8	20.6	91	881	3.4	26.9	83	1225	4.5	37.5	108
RADIO NETWORKS: ABC CONTEMP	4434	4038	5.7	91.1	102	1100	6.1	24.8	110	1381	5.4	31.1	96	1557	5.7	35.1	102
ABC DIRECTION	3493	3096	4.4	88.6	99	890	5.0	25.5	113	1212	4.7	34.7	107	994	3.6	28.5	82
ABC ENTERTAINMENT	5261	4813	6.8	91.5	102	1111	6.2	21.1	93	1965	7.7	37.4	116	1737	6.3	33.0	95
ABC FM	2808	2585	3.6	92.1	103	763	4.3	27.2	120	868	3.4	30.9	96	954	3.5	34.0	98
ABC INFORMATION	7527	6760	9.5	89.8	100	1663	9.3	22.1	98	2840	11.1	37.7	117	2257	8.2	30.0	87
ABC ROCK	3370	3107	4.4	92.2	103	707	3.9	21.0	93	1199	4.7	35.6	110	1200	4.4	35.6	103
CBS	5188	4605	6.5	88.8	99	1263	7.0	24.3	108	1788	7.0	34.5	107	1554	5.7	30.0	87
CONCERT MUSIC NETWORK	900	784	1.1	87.1	97	*276	1.5	30.7	135	*235	.9	26.1	81	273	1.0	30.3	88
INTERNET	23077	20448	28.8	88.6	99	4950	27.6	21.4	95	7411	29.0	32.1	99	8088	29.5	35.0	101
KATZ RADIO GROUP	25173	22508	31.7	89.4	100	5482	30.6	21.8	96	8326	32.6	33.1	102	8700	31.7	34.6	100
MUTUAL	6769	6204	8.7	91.7	102	1619	9.0	23.9	106	2187	8.6	32.3	100	2398	8.7	35.4	102
NBC	4808	4346	6.1	90.4	101	1205	6.7	25.1	111	1503	5.9	31.3	97	1639	6.0	34.1	99
NBN	1407	1202	1.7	85.4	95	*188	1.0	13.4	59	*473	1.8	33.6	104	541	2.0	38.5	111
RADIORADIO	3198	2865	4.0	89.6	100	794	4.4	24.8	110	1005	3.9	31.4	97	1067	3.9	33.4	96
SATELLITE MUSIC NETWORK	3680	3215	4.5	87.4	98	648	3.6	17.6	78	1166	4.6	31.7	98	1402	5.1	38.1	110
SHERIDAN	1787	1435	2.0	80.3	90	*263	1.5	14.7	65	*426	1.7	23.8	74	746	2.7	41.7	121
THE SOURCE	3294	2956	4.2	89.7	100	563	3.1	17.1	76	1059	4.1	32.1	100	1334	4.9	40.5	117
SUPERNET	16028	14141	19.9	88.2	99	3446	19.2	21.5	95	5083	19.9	31.7	98	5613	20.5	35.0	101
TRANSTAR	4324	3821	5.4	88.4	99	1008	5.6	23.3	103	1235	4.8	28.6	88	1579	5.8	36.5	106
US1	4060	3598	5.1	88.6	99	926	5.2	22.8	101	1154	4.5	28.4	88	1517	5.5	37.4	108
US2	4128	3673	5.2	89.0	99	1040	5.8	25.2	111	1338	5.2	32.4	100	1295	4.7	31.4	91
WALL STREET JOURNAL NETWORK	3222	2831	4.0	87.9	98	759	4.2	23.6	104	1091	4.3	33.9	105	982	3.6	30.5	88
TV WKDAY AV 1/2 HR:7-10:00AM	7432	6852	9.7	92.2	103	1586	8.8	21.3	94	2596	10.1	34.9	108	2671	9.7	35.9	104
10:00 AM - 4:30 PM	12732	11341	16.0	89.1	100	2935	16.4	23.1	102	4060	15.9	31.9	99	4346	15.9	34.1	99
4:30 PM - 7:30 PM	20201	18140	25.6	89.8	100	4259	23.7	21.1	93	7132	27.9	35.3	109	6749	24.6	33.4	97
7:30 PM - 8:00 PM	31577	28104	39.6	89.0	99	6150	34.3	19.5	86	10919	42.7	34.6	107	11035	40.3	34.9	101
8:00 PM - 11:00 PM	37214	33530	47.3	90.1	101	7831	43.7	21.0	93	12587	49.2	33.8	105	13112	47.8	35.2	102
11:00 PM - 11:30 PM	23262	20907	29.5	89.9	100	4606	25.7	19.8	87	7875	30.8	33.9	105	8426	30.7	36.2	105
11:30 PM - 1:00 AM	6802	6049	8.5	88.9	99	1340	7.5	19.7	87	2140	8.4	31.5	97	2569	9.4	37.8	109
TV PRIME TIME CUME	63663	57082	80.5	89.7	100	14297	79.7	22.5	99	20617	80.6	32.4	100	22168	80.9	34.8	101
PROGRAM-TYPES:DAYTIME DRAMAS	7150	6530	9.2	91.3	102	1979	11.0	27.7	122	2303	9.0	32.2	100	2248	8.2	31.4	91
DAYTIME GAME SHOWS	3743	3425	4.8	91.5	102	1020	5.7	27.3	120	1155	4.5	30.9	96	1251	4.6	33.4	97
EARLY MORNING TALK/INFO/NEWS	5875	5440	7.7	92.6	103	1562	8.7	26.6	117	1861	7.3	31.7	98	2017	7.4	34.3	99
EARLY EVE. NETWK NEWS - M-F	11664	10429	14.7	89.4	100	2868	16.0	24.6	109	4021	15.7	34.5	107	3540	12.9	30.3	88
FEATURE FILMS - PRIME	11260	10100	14.2	89.7	100	2890	16.1	25.7	113	3366	13.2	29.9	93	3844	14.0	34.1	99
GENERAL DRAMA - PRIME	11800	10739	15.1	91.0	102	2482	13.8	21.0	93	4190	16.4	35.5	110	4067	14.8	34.5	100
PVT DET/SUSP/MYST/POL.-PRIME	11952	10917	15.4	91.3	102	2887	16.1	24.2	107	3977	15.5	33.3	103	4053	14.8	33.9	98
SITUATION COMEDIES - PRIME	9559	8463	11.9	88.5	99	2435	13.6	25.5	113	2923	11.4	30.6	95	3106	11.3	32.5	94
CABLE TV	36901	33623	47.4	91.1	102	9284	51.8	25.2	111	11521	45.0	31.2	97	12818	46.8	34.7	100
PAY TV	20291	18587	26.2	91.6	102	5224	29.1	25.7	114	6238	24.4	30.7	95	7124	26.0	35.1	101
HEAVY CABLE VIEWING (15+ HR)	12402	11305	15.9	91.2	102	3049	17.0	24.6	109	4057	15.9	32.7	101	4199	15.3	33.9	98
CABLE NETWORKS: A&E	4381	3996	5.6	91.2	102	974	5.4	22.2	98	1319	5.2	30.1	93	1702	6.2	38.8	112
BET (BLACK ENTERTAINMENT TV)	973	833	1.2	85.6	96	*217	1.2	22.3	99	*317	1.2	32.6	101	*299	1.1	30.7	89
CNN (CABLE NEWS NETWORK)	14023	12817	18.1	91.4	102	3402	19.0	24.3	107	4429	17.3	31.6	98	4986	18.2	35.6	103
CNN HEADLINE NEWS	9263	8429	11.9	91.0	102	2222	12.4	24.0	106	3059	12.0	33.0	102	3148	11.5	34.0	98
CBN CABLE NETWORK	6935	6328	8.9	91.2	102	1622	9.0	23.4	103	2512	9.8	36.2	112	2194	8.0	31.6	91
THE DISCOVERY CHANNEL	4376	3992	5.6	91.2	102	963	5.4	22.0	97	1462	5.7	33.4	103	1568	5.7	35.8	104
ESPN	11260	10167	14.3	90.3	101	2668	14.9	23.7	105	3455	13.5	30.7	95	4044	14.8	35.9	104
FNN (FINANCIAL NEWS NETW'K)	642	617	.9	96.1	107	*138	.8	21.5	95	*242	.9	37.7	117	*237	.9	36.9	107
THE LEARNING CHANNEL	993	907	1.3	91.3	102	*160	.9	16.1	71	*310	1.2	31.2	97	*437	1.6	44.0	127
LIFETIME	6205	5803	8.2	93.5	104	1491	8.3	24.0	106	1991	7.8	32.1	99	2322	8.5	37.4	108
MTV	7162	6545	9.2	91.4	102	1598	8.9	22.3	99	2358	9.2	32.9	102	2589	9.4	36.1	104
THE NASHVILLE NETWORK	7147	6405	9.0	89.6	100	1612	9.0	22.6	100	2432	9.5	34.0	105	2361	8.6	33.0	95
NICK AT NITE	3628	3477	4.9	95.8	107	1071	6.0	29.5	130	1186	4.6	32.7	101	1220	4.5	33.6	97
NICKELODEON	5936	5564	7.8	93.7	105	1593	8.9	26.8	119	1880	7.4	31.7	98	2090	7.6	35.2	102
USA NETWORK	8059	7380	10.4	91.6	102	1967	11.0	24.4	108	2646	10.3	32.8	102	2767	10.1	34.3	99
VH-1 (VIDEO HITS ONE)	2138	1996	2.8	93.4	104	*512	2.9	23.9	106	700	2.7	32.7	101	784	2.9	36.7	106
THE WEATHER CHANNEL	9846	8886	12.5	90.2	101	2572	14.3	26.1	115	3012	11.8	30.6	95	3302	12.0	33.5	97
WTBS	13102	12034	17.0	91.8	103	3352	18.7	25.6	113	4252	16.6	32.5	101	4429	16.2	33.8	98

Exhibit 12–3

BREAKFAST CEREALS (COLD)

BASE: FEMALE HOMEMAKERS	TOTAL U.S. '000	ALL				HEAVY MORE THAN 8				MEDIUM 4-8				LIGHT LESS THAN 4			
		A '000	B % DOWN	C % ACROSS	D INDEX	A '000	B % DOWN	C % ACROSS	D INDEX	A '000	B % DOWN	C % ACROSS	D INDEX	A '000	B % DOWN	C % ACROSS	D INDEX
ALL FEMALE HOMEMAKERS	79236	70921	100.0	89.5	100	17933	100.0	22.6	100	25578	100.0	32.3	100	27410	100.0	34.6	100
AMERICAN BABY	2410	2320	3.3	96.3	108	747	4.2	31.0	137	715	2.8	29.7	92	858	3.1	35.6	103
AMERICAN HEALTH	2494	2273	3.2	91.1	102	529	2.9	21.2	94	953	3.7	38.2	118	790	2.9	31.7	92
AMERICAN WAY	425	405	.6	95.3	106	*65	.4	15.3	68	*190	.7	44.7	138	*151	.6	35.5	103
ARCHITECTURAL DIGEST	1519	1418	2.0	93.4	104	*237	1.3	15.6	69	568	2.2	37.4	116	613	2.2	40.4	117
AUDUBON	607	530	.7	87.3	98	*168	.9	27.7	122	*154	.6	25.4	79	*209	.8	34.4	100
BABY TALK	1563	1373	1.9	87.8	98	*384	2.1	24.6	109	506	2.0	32.4	100	483	1.8	30.9	89
BARRON'S	*280	*241	.3	-	-	*45	.3	-	-	*94	.4	-	-	*102	.4	-	-
BASSMASTER	*456	*431	.6	-	-	*92	.5	-	-	*145	.6	-	-	*195	.7	-	-
BETTER HOMES & GARDENS	20796	19129	27.0	92.0	103	5024	28.0	24.2	107	7142	27.9	34.3	106	6964	25.4	33.5	97
BHG/LHJ COMBO (GR)	34816	32270	45.5	92.7	104	8619	48.1	24.8	109	12000	46.9	34.5	107	11652	42.5	33.5	97
BLACK ENTERPRISE	795	647	.9	81.4	91	*104	.6	13.1	58	*189	.7	21.3	66	*374	1.4	47.0	136
BON APPETIT	2955	2651	3.7	89.7	100	703	3.9	23.8	105	956	3.7	32.4	100	992	3.6	33.6	97
BRIDE'S MAGAZINE	2046	1891	2.7	92.4	103	*389	2.2	19.0	84	739	2.9	36.1	112	763	2.8	37.3	108
BUSINESS WEEK	1379	1205	1.7	87.4	98	*265	1.5	19.2	85	419	1.6	30.4	94	522	1.9	37.9	109
BYTE	*239	*220	.3	-	-	*65	.4	-	-	*86	.3	-	-	*70	.3	-	-
THE CABLE GUIDE	6681	6093	8.6	91.2	102	1515	8.4	22.7	100	2052	8.0	30.7	95	2527	9.2	37.8	109
CABLETIME	2677	2380	3.4	88.9	99	630	3.5	23.5	104	903	3.5	33.7	104	848	3.1	31.7	92
CAR & DRIVER	*351	*303	.4	-	-	*66	.4	-	-	*121	.5	-	-	*116	.4	-	-
CAR CRAFT	*202	*196	.3	-	-	*19	.1	-	-	*74	.3	-	-	*103	.4	-	-
CHANGING TIMES	1296	1170	1.6	90.3	101	*260	1.4	20.1	89	409	1.6	31.6	98	500	1.8	38.6	112
CHICAGO TRIBUNE MAGAZINE	1190	1085	1.5	91.2	102	299	1.7	25.1	111	319	1.2	26.8	83	467	1.7	39.2	113
COLONIAL HOMES	1650	1505	2.1	91.2	102	489	2.7	29.6	131	516	2.0	31.3	97	501	1.8	30.4	88
CONDE NAST LIMITED (GR)	14096	12859	18.1	91.2	102	3345	18.7	23.7	105	4530	17.7	32.1	100	4983	18.2	35.4	102
CONDE NAST WOMEN (GR)	17272	15611	22.0	90.4	101	3806	21.2	22.0	97	5431	21.2	31.4	97	8375	23.3	36.9	107
CONSUMERS DIGEST	1495	1390	2.0	93.0	104	*472	2.6	31.6	139	427	1.7	28.6	88	491	1.8	32.8	95
COSMOPOLITAN	8257	7405	10.4	89.7	100	1618	9.0	19.6	87	2769	10.8	33.5	104	3018	11.0	36.6	106
COUNTRY HOME	3325	3126	4.4	94.0	105	878	4.9	26.4	117	1225	4.8	36.8	114	1023	3.7	30.8	89
COUNTRY JOURNAL	1085	1023	1.4	94.3	105	*353	2.0	32.5	144	*384	1.5	35.4	110	*286	1.0	26.4	76
COUNTRY LIVING	4948	4566	6.4	92.3	103	1488	8.3	30.1	133	1429	5.6	28.9	89	1649	6.0	33.3	96
CREATIVE IDEAS FOR LIVING	1377	1212	1.7	88.0	98	*388	2.2	28.2	124	*367	1.4	26.7	83	457	1.7	33.2	96
DELTA SKY (AIR GROUP ONE)	592	564	.8	95.3	106	*106	.6	17.9	79	*142	.6	24.0	74	*317	1.2	53.5	155
DIAMANDIS MAGAZINE NTWK (GR)	2979	2726	3.8	91.5	102	702	3.9	23.6	104	1120	4.4	37.6	116	906	3.3	30.4	88
DISCOVER	1119	1003	1.4	89.6	100	*158	.9	14.1	62	441	1.7	39.4	122	404	1.5	36.1	104
DISNEY CHANNEL MAGAZINE	2938	2784	3.9	94.8	106	903	5.0	30.7	136	1182	4.6	40.2	125	699	2.6	23.8	69
EAST/WEST NETWORK (GR)	2172	1949	2.7	89.7	100	407	2.3	18.7	83	642	2.5	29.6	92	900	3.3	41.4	120
EBONY	4282	3602	5.1	84.1	94	950	5.3	22.2	98	993	3.9	23.2	72	1660	6.1	38.8	112
ELLE	1021	903	1.3	88.4	99	*184	1.0	18.0	80	421	1.6	41.2	128	*299	1.1	29.3	85
ESQUIRE	938	791	1.1	84.3	94	*158	.9	16.8	74	*320	1.3	34.1	106	*313	1.1	33.4	97
ESSENCE	1969	1678	2.4	85.2	95	*288	1.6	14.6	65	748	2.9	38.0	118	642	2.3	32.6	94
FAMILY CIRCLE	19404	17713	25.0	91.3	102	4539	25.3	23.4	103	6839	26.7	35.2	109	8335	23.1	42.9	94
FAMILY COMPUTING	438	406	.6	92.7	104	*179	1.0	40.9	181	*82	.3	18.7	58	*146	.5	33.3	96
FAMILY HANDYMAN	1163	1078	1.5	92.7	104	*341	1.9	29.3	130	*425	1.7	36.5	113	*312	1.1	26.8	78
FIELD & STREAM	2281	2012	2.8	88.2	99	599	3.3	26.3	116	763	3.0	33.5	104	650	2.4	28.5	82
FLOWER & GARDEN	1599	1418	2.0	88.7	99	*438	2.4	27.3	120	581	2.3	36.3	113	*401	1.5	25.1	72
FOOD & WINE	1182	1007	1.4	85.2	95	*261	1.5	22.1	98	410	1.6	34.7	107	336	1.2	28.4	82
FORBES	659	608	.9	92.3	103	*156	.9	23.7	105	*190	.7	28.8	89	*262	1.0	39.8	115
FORTUNE	1009	921	1.3	91.3	102	*235	1.3	23.3	103	*248	1.0	24.6	76	438	1.6	43.4	125
4 WHEEL & OFF ROAD	*254	*242	.3	-	-	*82	.5	-	-	*134	.5	-	-	*25	.1	-	-
GLAMOUR	6161	5501	7.8	89.3	100	1326	7.4	21.5	95	2090	8.2	33.9	105	2085	7.6	33.8	98
GOLF DIGEST	926	853	1.2	92.1	103	*196	1.1	21.2	94	*288	1.1	31.1	96	*369	1.3	39.8	115
GOLF DIGEST/TENNIS (GR)	1339	1185	1.6	87.0	97	*286	1.6	21.4	94	395	1.5	29.5	91	483	1.8	36.1	104
GOLF MAGAZINE	402	398	.6	99.0	111	*98	.5	24.4	108	*101	.4	25.1	78	*199	.7	49.5	143
GOLF MAGAZINE/SKI (GR)	935	876	1.2	93.7	105	*177	1.0	18.9	84	*259	1.0	27.7	86	439	1.6	47.0	136
GOOD HOUSEKEEPING	18146	16706	23.6	92.1	103	4743	26.4	26.1	115	6181	24.2	34.1	106	5782	21.1	31.9	92
GOURMET	1755	1633	2.3	93.0	104	440	2.5	25.1	111	575	2.2	32.8	101	618	2.3	35.2	102
GQ (GENTLEMEN'S QUARTERLY)	1054	946	1.3	89.8	100	*207	1.2	19.6	87	*382	1.5	36.2	112	*357	1.3	33.9	98
GUNS N' AMMO	*394	*341	.5	-	-	*104	.6	-	-	*160	.6	-	-	*77	.3	-	-
HARPER'S BAZAAR	1597	1416	2.0	88.7	99	*262	1.5	16.4	72	503	2.0	31.5	98	651	2.4	40.8	118
HEALTH	1797	1650	2.3	91.8	103	*422	2.4	23.5	104	506	2.0	28.2	87	721	2.6	40.1	116
HEARST MAN POWER (GR)	2517	2227	3.1	88.5	99	637	3.6	25.3	112	844	3.3	33.5	104	745	2.7	29.6	86
HEARST WOMAN POWER (GR)	42337	38673	54.5	91.3	102	10271	57.3	24.3	107	14097	55.1	33.3	103	14305	52.2	33.8	98
HG (HOUSE & GARDEN)	6132	5600	7.9	91.3	102	1518	8.5	24.8	109	2094	8.2	34.1	106	1987	7.2	32.4	94
HOME	1334	1237	1.7	92.7	103	*285	1.6	21.4	94	*367	1.4	27.5	85	585	2.1	43.9	127
HOME MECHANIX	736	685	1.0	93.1	104	*211	1.2	28.7	127	*238	.9	32.3	100	*236	.9	32.1	93
HOMEOWNER	838	750	1.1	89.5	100	*203	1.2	24.2	107	*241	.9	28.8	89	*305	1.1	36.4	105
HOT ROD	732	702	1.0	95.9	107	*176	1.0	24.0	106	*296	1.2	40.4	125	*230	.8	31.4	91
HOUSE BEAUTIFUL	4242	3905	5.5	92.1	103	1136	6.3	26.8	118	1155	4.5	27.2	84	1613	5.9	38.0	110
HUNTING	*368	*355	.5	-	-	*72	.4	-	-	*138	.5	-	-	*145	.5	-	-
INC.	655	491	.7	75.0	84	*116	.6	17.7	78	*166	.6	25.3	79	*209	.8	31.9	92
INSIDE SPORTS	*416	*343	.5	-	-	*44	.2	-	-	*90	.4	-	-	*209	.8	-	-
JET	2963	2678	3.8	90.4	101	631	3.5	21.3	94	988	3.9	33.3	103	1059	3.9	35.7	103
LADIES' HOME JOURNAL	14020	13141	18.5	93.7	105	3595	20.0	25.6	113	4858	19.0	34.7	107	4688	17.1	33.4	97
LIFE	6552	5938	8.4	90.6	101	1616	9.0	24.7	109	2055	8.0	31.4	97	2267	8.3	34.6	100
MADEMOISELLE	2734	2471	3.5	90.4	101	645	3.6	23.6	104	790	3.1	28.9	90	1038	3.8	37.9	110
MCCALLS	14158	12850	18.1	90.8	101	3433	19.1	24.2	107	4846	18.9	34.2	106	4570	16.7	32.3	93
MCCALLS NEEDLEWORK & CRAFTS	3957	3503	4.9	88.5	99	1097	6.1	27.7	122	1101	4.3	27.8	86	1305	4.8	33.0	95
MCGRAW-HILL NETWORK (GR)	1719	1580	2.2	90.8	101	*380	2.1	22.1	98	550	2.2	32.0	99	627	2.3	36.5	105
METRO SUNDAY COMICS	12795	11501	16.2	89.9	100	3088	17.2	24.1	107	4105	16.0	32.1	99	4308	15.7	33.7	97
MODERN BRIDE	1188	1046	1.5	88.0	98	*173	1.0	14.6	64	*445	1.7	37.5	116	*428	1.6	36.0	104
MODERN MATURITY	14403	12949	18.3	89.9	100	3177	17.7	22.1	98	5037	19.7	35.0	108	4735	17.3	32.9	95
MODERN PHOTOGRAPHY	731	670	.9	91.7	102	*70	.4	9.6	42	*309	1.2	42.3	131	*291	1.1	39.8	115
MONEY	2083	1844	2.6	88.5	99	421	2.3	20.2	89	705	2.8	33.8	105	718	2.6	34.5	100

(continued)

Exhibit 12-3 (Continued)

BREAKFAST CEREALS (COLD)

BASE: FEMALE HOMEMAKERS	TOTAL U.S. '000	ALL A '000	B % DOWN	C % ACROSS	D INDEX	HEAVY MORE THAN 8 A '000	B % DOWN	C % ACROSS	D INDEX	MEDIUM 4-8 A '000	B % DOWN	C % ACROSS	D INDEX	LIGHT LESS THAN 4 A '000	B % DOWN	C % ACROSS	D INDEX
ALL FEMALE HOMEMAKERS	79236	70921	100.0	89.5	100	17933	100.0	22.6	100	25578	100.0	32.3	100	27410	100.0	34.6	100
MOTHER EARTH NEWS	811	691	1.0	85.2	95	*175	1.0	21.6	95	*211	.8	26.0	81	*305	1.1	37.6	109
MOTOR HOME/TRAILER LIFE (GR)	465	428	.6	92.0	103	*51	.3	11.0	48	*225	.9	48.4	150	*152	.6	32.7	94
MOTOR TREND	*246	*216	.3	-	-	*51	.3	-	-	*72	.3	-	-	*94	.3	-	-
MS.	1010	901	1.3	89.2	100	*206	1.1	20.4	90	*327	1.3	32.4	100	*368	1.3	36.4	105
MUSCLE & FITNESS	693	678	1.0	97.8	109	*181	1.0	26.1	115	*238	.9	34.3	106	*259	.9	37.4	108
NATIONAL ENQUIRER	9906	8904	12.6	89.9	100	2038	11.4	20.6	91	3210	12.5	32.4	100	3656	13.3	36.9	107
NATIONAL GEOGRAPHIC	11668	10641	15.0	91.2	102	3042	17.0	26.1	115	3960	15.5	33.9	105	3638	13.3	31.2	90
NATIONAL GEOGRAPHIC TRAVELER	1286	1217	1.7	94.6	106	*344	1.9	26.7	118	475	1.9	36.9	114	*398	1.5	30.9	89
NATIONAL LAMPOON	*338	*289	.4	-	-	*93	.5	-	-	*89	.3	-	-	*108	.4	-	-
NATURAL HISTORY	521	442	.6	84.8	95	*166	.9	31.9	141	*118	.5	22.6	70	*159	.6	30.5	88
NEWSWEEK	7025	6445	9.1	91.7	103	1880	10.5	26.8	118	2192	8.6	31.2	97	2373	8.7	33.8	98
NEW WOMAN	2146	1937	2.7	90.3	101	442	2.5	20.6	91	662	2.6	30.8	96	833	3.0	38.8	112
NEW YORK MAGAZINE	496	471	.7	95.0	106	*117	.7	23.6	104	*194	.8	39.1	121	*160	.6	32.3	93
NEW YORK TIMES (DAILY)	895	831	1.2	92.8	104	*134	.7	15.0	66	335	1.3	37.4	116	362	1.3	40.4	117
NEW YORK TIMES MAGAZINE	1337	1219	1.7	91.2	102	*242	1.3	18.1	80	468	1.8	35.0	108	508	1.9	38.0	110
THE NEW YORKER	792	726	1.0	91.7	102	*179	1.0	22.6	100	*273	1.1	34.5	107	*274	1.0	34.6	100
OMNI	1152	1060	1.5	92.0	103	*255	1.4	22.1	98	*309	1.2	26.8	83	496	1.8	43.1	124
1,001 HOME IDEAS	2807	2508	3.5	89.3	100	600	3.3	21.4	94	861	3.4	30.7	95	1048	3.8	37.3	108
ORGANIC GARDENING	1173	1043	1.5	88.9	99	*249	1.4	21.2	94	*430	1.7	36.7	114	*364	1.3	31.0	90
OUTDOOR LIFE	1850	1671	2.4	90.3	101	*484	2.7	26.2	116	743	2.9	40.2	124	*444	1.6	24.0	69
PARADE	28451	25560	36.0	89.8	100	6611	36.9	23.2	103	8953	35.0	31.5	97	9996	36.5	35.1	102
PARENTS' MAGAZINE	6527	6108	8.6	93.6	105	1860	10.4	28.5	126	2193	8.6	33.6	104	2055	7.5	31.5	91
PC MAGAZINE	*257	*205	.3	-	-	*38	.2	-	-	*79	.3	-	-	*88	.3	-	-
PC WORLD	*320	*285	.4	-	-	*70	.4	-	-	*123	.5	-	-	*92	.3	-	-
PENTHOUSE	780	689	1.0	88.3	99	*188	1.0	24.1	106	*165	.6	21.2	66	*337	1.2	43.2	125
PENTON EXECUTIVE NETWK (GR)	1317	1215	1.7	92.3	103	*269	1.5	20.4	90	*363	1.4	27.6	85	584	2.1	44.3	128
PEOPLE	15106	13455	19.0	89.1	100	3602	20.1	23.8	105	4739	18.5	31.4	97	5115	18.7	33.9	98
PERSONAL COMPUTING	561	519	.7	92.5	103	*72	.4	12.8	57	*282	1.1	50.3	156	*166	.6	29.6	86
PETERSEN MAGAZINE GROUP (GR)	3112	2893	4.1	93.0	104	588	3.3	18.9	83	1294	5.1	41.6	129	1011	3.7	32.5	94
PLAYBOY	2528	2290	3.2	90.6	101	630	3.5	24.9	110	738	2.9	29.1	90	924	3.4	36.6	106
POPULAR HOT RODDING	*292	*246	.3	-	-	*64	.4	-	-	*126	.5	-	-	*57	.2	-	-
POPULAR MECHANICS	1125	1010	1.4	89.8	100	*334	1.9	29.7	131	*397	1.6	35.3	109	*278	1.0	24.7	71
POPULAR SCIENCE	1017	895	1.3	88.0	98	*282	1.6	27.7	123	*306	1.2	30.1	93	*307	1.1	30.2	87
PREVENTION	4694	4271	6.0	91.0	102	1174	6.5	25.0	111	1560	6.1	33.2	103	1537	5.6	32.7	95
PSYCHOLOGY TODAY	2262	1989	2.8	87.9	98	442	2.5	19.5	86	683	2.7	30.2	94	864	3.2	38.2	110
PUCK	8696	7857	11.1	90.4	101	2035	11.3	23.4	103	2618	10.2	30.1	93	3203	11.7	36.8	106
READER'S DIGEST	24753	22864	32.0	91.6	102	5927	33.1	23.9	106	8431	33.0	34.1	106	8306	30.3	33.6	97
REDBOOK	9389	8580	12.1	91.4	102	2160	12.0	23.0	102	3215	12.6	34.2	106	3205	11.7	34.1	99
ROAD & TRACK	*339	*305	.4	-	-	*119	.7	-	-	*103	.4	-	-	*83	.3	-	-
RODALE ACTIVE SPORTS (GR)	868	793	1.1	91.4	102	*140	.8	16.1	71	*319	1.2	36.8	114	*333	1.2	38.4	111
ROLLING STONE	1516	1326	1.9	87.5	98	*241	1.3	15.9	70	578	2.3	38.1	118	507	1.8	33.4	97
RUNNER'S WORLD	*359	*328	.5	-	-	*52	.3	-	-	*147	.6	-	-	*129	.5	-	-
SATURDAY EVENING POST	2023	1875	2.6	92.7	104	*367	2.0	18.1	80	788	3.1	39.0	121	720	2.6	35.6	103
SCIENTIFIC AMERICAN	427	382	.5	89.5	100	*99	.6	23.2	102	*171	.7	40.0	124	*112	.4	26.2	76
SELF	2116	1950	2.7	92.2	103	525	2.9	24.8	110	626	2.4	29.6	92	800	2.9	37.8	109
SEVENTEEN	2961	2697	3.8	91.1	102	693	3.9	23.4	103	1009	3.9	34.1	106	995	3.6	33.6	97
SHAPE	1332	1241	1.7	93.2	104	*307	1.7	23.0	102	*524	2.0	39.3	122	*410	1.5	30.8	89
SKI	533	478	.7	89.7	100	*79	.4	14.8	65	*158	.6	29.6	92	*240	.9	45.0	130
SKIING	514	489	.7	95.1	106	*95	.5	18.5	82	*184	.7	35.8	111	*210	.8	40.9	118
SMITHSONIAN	3306	2861	4.0	86.5	97	682	3.8	20.6	91	886	3.5	26.8	83	1293	4.7	39.1	113
SOAP OPERA DIGEST	3353	3113	4.4	92.8	104	855	4.8	25.5	113	1127	4.4	33.7	104	1131	4.1	33.7	98
SOUTHERN LIVING	6662	5977	8.4	89.7	100	1680	9.3	24.9	110	2070	8.1	31.1	96	2248	8.2	33.7	98
SPORT	690	587	.8	85.1	95	*117	.7	17.0	75	*145	.6	21.0	65	*325	1.2	47.1	136
THE SPORTING NEWS	*490	*489	.7	-	-	*151	.8	-	-	*205	.8	-	-	*134	.5	-	-
SPORTS AFIELD	454	*426	.6	93.8	105	*145	.8	31.9	141	*127	.5	28.0	87	*154	.6	33.9	98
SPORTS ILLUSTRATED	3191	2833	4.0	88.8	99	879	4.9	27.5	122	970	3.8	30.4	94	984	3.6	30.8	89
STAR	5756	5305	7.5	92.2	103	1242	6.9	21.6	95	1905	7.4	33.1	103	2159	7.9	37.5	108
SUNDAY MAG/NET	17695	15850	22.3	89.6	100	4520	25.2	25.5	113	5525	21.6	31.2	97	5804	21.2	32.8	95
SUNSET	2399	2138	3.0	89.1	100	387	2.2	16.1	71	677	2.6	28.2	87	1074	3.9	44.8	129
TENNIS	413	*312	.4	75.5	84	*90	.5	21.8	96	*107	.4	25.9	80	*114	.4	27.6	80
TIME	9394	8534	12.0	90.8	101	2613	14.6	27.8	123	2953	11.5	31.4	97	2987	10.8	31.6	91
TOWN & COUNTRY	1161	997	1.4	85.9	96	*210	1.2	18.1	80	372	1.5	32.0	99	415	1.5	35.7	103
TRAVEL & LEISURE	1303	1163	1.6	89.3	100	*301	1.7	23.1	102	398	1.6	30.5	95	464	1.7	35.6	103
TRAVEL/HOLIDAY	654	553	.8	84.6	94	*121	.7	18.5	82	*175	.7	26.8	83	*257	.9	39.3	114
TRUE STORY	3660	3326	4.7	90.9	102	850	4.7	23.2	103	1285	4.9	34.6	107	1212	4.4	33.1	96
TV GUIDE	20917	18669	26.3	89.3	100	5089	28.4	24.3	107	6454	25.2	30.9	96	7125	26.0	34.1	98
U.S. AIR MAGAZINE	518	453	.6	87.5	98	*171	1.0	33.0	146	*180	.7	34.7	108	*102	.4	19.7	57
U.S. NEWS & WORLD REPORT	3651	3334	4.7	91.3	102	823	4.6	22.5	100	1374	5.4	37.6	117	1137	4.1	31.1	90
US	2509	2242	3.2	89.4	100	*480	2.7	19.5	86	794	3.1	31.6	98	958	3.5	38.2	110
USA TODAY	1267	1225	1.7	96.7	108	*371	2.1	29.3	129	482	1.9	38.0	118	372	1.4	29.4	85
USA WEEKEND	11657	10533	14.9	90.4	101	2845	15.9	24.4	108	4115	16.1	35.3	109	3573	13.0	30.7	89
VANITY FAIR	940	882	1.2	93.8	105	*259	1.4	27.6	122	*293	1.1	31.2	97	*330	1.2	35.1	101
VOGUE	4215	3798	5.4	90.1	101	921	5.1	21.9	97	1186	4.6	28.1	87	1691	6.2	40.1	116
WALL STREET JOURNAL	1180	1078	1.5	91.4	102	*219	1.2	18.6	82	*375	1.5	31.8	98	485	1.8	41.1	119
WEIGHT WATCHERS	2955	2749	3.9	93.0	104	796	4.4	26.9	119	957	3.7	32.4	100	996	3.6	33.7	97
WOMAN	1459	1279	1.8	87.7	98	*341	1.9	23.4	103	*386	1.4	25.1	78	572	2.1	39.2	113
WOMAN'S DAY	18340	16887	23.8	92.1	103	4604	25.7	25.1	111	6186	24.1	33.6	104	6117	22.3	33.4	96
WOMAN'S WORLD	4214	3924	5.5	93.1	104	1100	6.1	26.1	115	1248	4.9	29.6	92	1576	5.7	37.4	108
THE WORKBASKET	2743	2514	3.5	91.7	102	754	4.2	27.5	121	863	3.4	31.5	97	897	3.3	32.7	95
WORKBENCH	704	679	1.0	96.4	108	*235	1.3	33.4	147	*333	1.3	47.3	147	*111	.4	15.8	46
WORKING MOTHER	1791	1651	2.3	92.2	103	*376	2.1	21.0	93	614	2.4	34.3	106	661	2.4	36.9	107
WORKING WOMAN	2410	2097	3.0	87.0	97	545	3.0	22.6	100	796	3.1	33.0	102	758	2.8	31.4	91
YANKEE	1468	1351	1.9	92.0	103	*398	2.2	27.1	120	420	1.6	28.6	89	534	1.9	36.4	105

Exhibit 12-3

BREAKFAST CEREALS (COLD)

BASE: FEMALE HOMEMAKERS	TOTAL U.S. '000	BOO BERRY A '000	B % DOWN	C % ACROSS	D INDEX	CAP'N CRUNCH A '000	B % DOWN	C % ACROSS	D INDEX	CAP'N CRUNCH CRUNCHBERRIES A '000	B % DOWN	C % ACROSS	D INDEX	CAP'N CRUNCH PEANUT BUTTER CRUNCH A '000	B % DOWN	C % ACROSS	D INDEX
ALL FEMALE HOMEMAKERS	79236	1088	100.0	1.4	100	8885	100.0	11.2	100	3083	100.0	3.9	100	2558	100.0	3.2	100
WOMEN	79236	1088	100.0	1.4	100	8885	100.0	11.2	100	3083	100.0	3.9	100	2558	100.0	3.2	100
HOUSEHOLD HEADS	27114	*339	31.2	1.3	91	2093	23.6	7.7	69	799	25.9	2.9	76	681	26.6	2.5	78
HOMEMAKERS	79236	1088	100.0	1.4	100	8885	100.0	11.2	100	3083	100.0	3.9	100	2558	100.0	3.2	100
GRADUATED COLLEGE	12005	*210	19.3	1.7	127	1311	14.8	10.9	97	282	9.1	2.3	60	*256	10.0	2.1	66
ATTENDED COLLEGE	13697	*122	11.2	.9	65	1439	16.2	10.5	94	630	20.4	4.6	118	*444	17.4	3.2	100
GRADUATED HIGH SCHOOL	33217	497	45.7	1.5	109	4351	49.0	13.1	117	1615	52.4	4.9	125	1209	47.3	3.6	113
DID NOT GRADUATE HIGH SCHOOL	20318	*258	23.7	1.3	92	1784	20.1	8.8	78	556	18.0	2.7	70	650	25.4	3.2	99
18-24	7140	*162	14.9	2.3	165	1269	14.3	17.8	159	717	23.3	10.0	258	*539	21.1	7.5	234
25-34	19497	*350	32.2	1.8	131	3722	41.9	19.1	170	968	31.4	5.0	128	707	27.6	3.6	112
35-44	15715	377	34.7	2.4	175	2003	22.5	12.7	114	783	25.4	5.0	128	*663	25.9	4.2	131
45-54	11324	*113	10.4	1.0	73	1226	13.8	10.8	97	*435	14.1	3.8	99	*350	13.7	3.1	96
55-64	11154	*37	3.4	.3	24	*505	5.7	4.5	40	*100	3.2	.9	23	*110	4.3	1.0	31
65 OR OVER	14406	*48	4.4	.3	24	*160	1.8	1.1	10	*81	2.6	.6	14	*188	7.3	1.3	40
18-34	26637	512	47.1	1.9	140	4991	56.2	18.7	167	1685	54.7	6.3	163	1247	48.7	4.7	145
18-49	48167	953	87.6	2.0	144	7766	87.4	16.1	144	2781	90.2	5.8	148	2123	83.0	4.4	137
25-54	46536	840	77.2	1.8	131	6951	78.2	14.9	133	2185	70.9	4.7	121	1721	67.3	3.7	115
EMPLOYED FULL TIME	34842	515	47.3	1.5	108	4158	46.8	11.9	106	1404	45.5	4.0	104	1020	39.9	2.9	91
PART-TIME	7143	*111	10.2	1.6	113	1355	15.3	19.0	169	*524	17.0	7.3	189	*257	10.0	3.6	111
NOT EMPLOYED	37251	462	42.5	1.2	90	3371	37.9	9.0	81	1156	37.5	3.1	80	1281	50.1	3.4	107
PROFESSIONAL	6473	*82	7.5	1.3	92	974	11.0	15.0	134	*200	6.5	3.1	79	*179	7.0	2.8	86
EXECUTIVE/ADMIN./MANAGERIAL	4555	*13	1.2	.3	21	386	4.3	8.5	76	*152	4.9	3.3	86	*57	2.2	1.3	39
CLERICAL/SALES/TECHNICAL	18435	*299	27.5	1.6	118	2277	25.6	12.4	110	878	28.5	4.8	122	559	21.9	3.0	94
PRECISION/CRAFTS/REPAIR	1000	*41	3.8	4.1	299	*144	1.6	14.4	128	*20	.6	2.0	51	*62	2.4	6.2	192
OTHER EMPLOYED	11522	*190	17.5	1.6	120	1732	19.5	15.0	134	678	22.0	5.9	151	*420	16.4	3.6	113
H/D INCOME $50,000 OR MORE	14304	*238	21.9	1.7	121	1790	20.1	12.5	112	396	12.8	2.8	71	*355	13.9	2.5	77
$40,000 - 49,999	9821	*122	11.2	1.2	90	1209	13.6	12.3	110	*341	11.1	3.5	89	*324	12.7	3.3	102
$35,000 - 39,999	6500	*82	7.5	1.3	92	854	9.6	13.1	117	*185	6.0	2.8	73	*241	9.4	3.7	115
$25,000 - 34,999	13806	*145	13.3	1.1	76	1744	19.6	12.6	113	763	24.7	5.5	142	*394	15.4	2.9	88
$15,000 - 24,999	15616	*298	27.4	1.9	139	1939	21.8	12.4	111	812	26.3	5.2	134	651	25.4	4.2	129
LESS THAN $15,000	19190	*203	18.7	1.1	77	1348	15.2	7.0	63	586	19.0	3.1	78	593	23.2	3.1	96
CENSUS REGION: NORTH EAST	16966	*287	24.5	1.6	115	2035	22.9	12.0	107	479	15.5	2.8	73	590	23.1	3.5	108
NORTH CENTRAL	19582	*349	32.1	1.8	130	2542	28.6	13.0	116	1055	34.2	5.4	138	752	29.4	3.8	119
SOUTH	27346	*360	33.1	1.3	96	2978	33.5	10.9	97	835	27.1	3.1	78	822	32.1	3.0	93
WEST	15342	*112	10.3	.7	53	1330	15.0	8.7	77	714	23.2	4.7	120	*394	15.4	2.6	80
MARKETING REG.: NEW ENGLAND	4656	*71	6.5	1.5	111	551	6.2	11.8	106	*123	4.0	2.6	68	*95	3.7	2.0	63
MIDDLE ATLANTIC	13652	*214	19.7	1.6	114	1607	18.1	11.8	105	427	13.9	3.1	80	546	21.3	4.0	124
EAST CENTRAL	11204	*188	17.3	1.7	122	1302	14.7	11.6	104	497	16.1	4.4	114	429	16.8	3.8	119
WEST CENTRAL	12679	*266	24.4	2.1	153	1718	19.3	13.5	121	698	22.6	5.5	141	479	18.7	3.8	117
SOUTH EAST	14499	*223	20.5	1.5	112	1574	17.7	10.9	97	507	16.4	3.5	90	468	18.3	3.2	100
SOUTH WEST	9288	*69	6.3	.7	54	1022	11.5	11.0	98	*232	7.5	2.5	64	*191	7.5	2.1	64
PACIFIC	13258	*57	5.2	.4	31	1111	12.5	8.4	75	600	19.5	4.5	116	*351	13.7	2.6	82
COUNTY SIZE A	32384	318	29.2	1.0	72	3260	36.7	10.1	90	915	29.7	2.8	73	883	34.5	2.7	84
COUNTY SIZE B	23508	*431	39.6	1.8	134	2997	33.7	12.7	114	1149	37.3	4.9	126	851	33.3	3.6	112
COUNTY SIZE C	12456	*234	21.5	1.9	137	1535	17.3	12.3	110	535	17.4	4.3	110	*395	15.4	3.2	98
COUNTY SIZE D	10888	*104	9.6	1.0	70	1094	12.3	10.0	90	*485	15.7	4.5	114	*430	16.8	3.9	122
MSA CENTRAL CITY	28381	*452	41.5	1.6	116	2989	33.6	10.5	94	1007	32.7	3.5	91	835	32.6	2.9	91
MSA SUBURBAN	32254	388	35.7	1.2	88	3763	42.4	11.7	104	1164	37.8	3.6	93	996	38.9	3.1	96
NON-MSA	18601	*248	22.8	1.3	97	2133	24.0	11.5	102	912	29.6	4.9	126	727	28.4	3.9	121
SINGLE	8850	*128	11.8	1.4	105	889	10.0	10.0	90	*317	10.3	3.6	92	*260	10.2	2.9	91
MARRIED	50063	751	69.0	1.5	109	6448	72.6	12.9	115	2138	69.3	4.3	110	1832	71.6	3.7	113
OTHER	20323	*209	19.2	1.0	75	1548	17.4	7.6	68	628	20.4	3.1	79	467	18.3	2.3	71
PARENTS	31882	790	72.6	2.5	180	6231	70.1	19.5	174	2150	69.7	6.7	173	1783	69.7	5.6	173
WORKING PARENTS	19985	513	47.2	2.6	187	3837	43.2	19.2	171	1230	39.9	6.2	158	937	36.6	4.7	145
HOUSEHOLD SIZE: 1 PERSON	13148	*53	4.9	.4	29	365	4.1	2.8	25	*128	4.1	1.0	25	*112	4.4	.9	26
2 PERSONS	23406	*120	11.0	.5	37	1298	14.6	5.5	49	378	12.3	1.6	42	*426	16.7	1.8	56
3 OR MORE	42682	914	84.0	2.1	156	7222	81.3	16.9	151	2579	83.7	6.0	155	2019	78.9	4.7	147
ANY CHILD IN HOUSEHOLD	34747	843	77.5	2.4	177	6853	74.9	19.1	171	2402	77.9	6.9	178	1810	70.8	5.2	161
UNDER 2 YEARS	5971	*43	4.0	.7	52	1153	13.0	19.3	172	*502	16.3	8.4	216	*415	16.2	7.0	215
2-5 YEARS	13551	*384	35.3	2.8	206	2637	29.7	19.5	174	989	32.1	7.3	188	616	24.1	4.5	141
6-11 YEARS	16228	476	43.8	2.9	214	3316	37.3	20.4	182	1134	36.8	7.0	180	962	37.6	5.9	184
12-17 YEARS	15479	474	43.6	3.1	223	2993	33.7	19.3	172	949	30.8	6.1	158	864	33.8	5.6	173
WHITE	68615	985	90.5	1.4	105	7874	88.6	11.5	102	2679	86.9	3.9	100	2092	81.8	3.0	94
BLACK	8816	*79	7.3	.9	65	826	9.3	9.4	84	*342	11.1	3.9	100	*409	16.0	4.6	144
HOME OWNED	54889	719	66.1	1.3	95	5577	62.8	10.2	91	1795	58.2	3.3	84	1502	58.7	2.7	85

for targeting advertising and media investments. Clarita's zip-clusters are labeled with clever names, such as "Money and Brains"—swank town-houses, and mid-rise apartments on tree-lined urban streets. "Furs and Stationwagons" are young, well-educated professionals living in new suburban neighborhoods. "Bunker's Neighbors" is a take-off from the TV show.

Other marketing media research firms provide surveys on several areas, such as upper income groups, business professionals, and product categories. Some media audience research companies exist to supply tailor-made audience profiles for TV, radio, magazine, newspaper, and outdoor media and their respective trade organizations.

SELECTING AND BUYING MEDIA

Finding and selecting the optimum combination of media vehicles is dependent upon the objectives of the plan, the resulting strategic decisions, plus a background knowledge of the various media and how people relate to these media. The media planner systematically searches through available media types evaluating each against the criteria established by the objectives and strategies. Factors that are considered include:

- Target audience
- Geographical pattern
- Seasonality
- Competitive activity
- Budget flexibility

- Budget size
- Promotions
- Timing of audience response
- Creative

Of course, before selecting the media, the planner must understand the media and what each can do in the advertising program.

Broadcast Television

Television is available in nearly all American homes. Color penetration exceeds 95 percent, more than 65 percent of American homes have two or more TV sets, and over 55 percent are able to receive cable programming.

Advertising is purchased nationally through the three networks (each with approximately 200 affiliates), in the 212 local markets (called TV areas of dominant influence or ADIs) or nationally through syndicators who build à la carte networks market by market. Table 12–13 illustrates the composition of audiences by the typical TV time periods, source of origination, and types of programs offered.

Total audiences vary during the day and by programming type. (See Tables 12–14 and 12–15.) Audiences are highly seasonal, peaking in the winter months and turning lowest in the summer. (See Table 12–16.) Men, teens, and children follow seasonal viewing patterns. Television reaches

Table 12-13   Percent Composition of Viewing Audiences

	Women	Men	Teens	Children
Total U.S.	38	35	11	16
Daytime	67	19	7	7
Early evening	43	32	7	18
Prime	46	35	8	11
Late evening	51	43	4	2
Sports	31	52	8	9

Table 12-14   Percent Composition of Audiences by Type of Program

Daytime	Women	Men	Teens	Children
Serials	69	16	8	7
Games	57	24	7	12
Prime				
Drama	48	32	9	11
Movies	44	38	10	8
Sit coms	43	31	11	15

Table 12-15   Elements of the Typical TV Day

	Time period (E.S.T.)	Source of program	Program types
Early morning	Mon.–Fri./7 A.M.–9 A.M.	Network	News, talk
Morning	Mon.–Fri./9 A.M.–10 A.M.	Local	Talk, reruns, movies
Daytime	Mon.–Fri./10 A.M.–4:30 P.M.	Network	Quiz shows, specials, sit coms
Early evening	Mon.–Fri./4:30–7 P.M.	Local	Talk, reruns, movies, local news
Early news	Mon.–Fri./7–7:30 P.M.	Network	News
Access	Mon.–Fri./7:30–8 P.M.	Local	Game shows, reality shows, sit com re-runs
Prime	Mon.–Sun./8–11 P.M.	Network	Various
Late news	Mon.–Sun./11–11:30 P.M.	Local	News
Late evening	Mon.–Sun./11:30 P.M.–1 A.M.	Network	Talk, news, movies, drama reruns

Table 12–16   Hours: Minutes of Women Viewing Weekly

	November	February	March	July
Daytime	6:16	6:55	5:59	5:54
Early evening	5:01	5:27	4:08	3:45
Prime	10:51	11:37	9:54	8:17
Late evening	3:01	3:10	3:05	3:01
Other times	8:22	9:09	7:02	6:23
Total	33:31	36:18	30:08	27:20

Table 12–17   Cumulative Weekly Reach

	Women	Women 18–54	Working women
Daytime	63%	63%	45%
Early evening	79	76	75
Prime	89	88	88
Late evening	47	49	46

Table 12–18   Typical Television Costs

		Cost (:30)	Household	
			Rating	CPM
Daytime	Network	$ 15,000	5.0	$3.26
Prime	Network	100,000	12.0	9.09
Evening news	Network	55,000	9.0	6.62
Tonight Show	Network	40,000	6.0	7.27
Early and late fringe	Spot	Varies	6.0	6.50

large numbers of people as typified by the medium's penetration among women, younger women, and working women. (See Table 12–17.) Note that nearly half of all working women watch some daytime TV (10 A.M.–4:30 P.M.) during the week.

Although television cost efficiencies vary seasonally and by programming type, in general, relative costs are lowest during the daytime hours and highest in the evening when more people view TV. (See Table 12–18.)

Network television is employed to efficiently reach broad national audiences. The medium is highly intrusive, for commercials are wedged into programs in fairly short commercial "pods." The level of commercialization is relatively low, ranging from ten minutes per hour on network affiliates in prime time to sixteen minutes during nonprime hours. Various programming options provide some degree of selectivity (daytime for women, men in sports, children on Saturday morning). The vast majority of Americans can be reached in prime time.

To properly employ network, however, large budgets are required and the medium is not considered flexible in terms of budgeting options. Commitments are made months prior to air dates, especially in long-term, upfront negotiations. But the primary drawback is uneven delivery by market. This lack of geographical precision can be overcome by "filling in" with local spot.

Spot, like network, is a highly impactful medium which permits excellent flexibility geographically for both advertising weight and copy. Shorter lead times are needed than with network buys. However, spot is less efficient than network with significant variations in costs by market. Some markets are expensive while others are priced attractively. While network commercials are embedded in programs, many spot availabilities are between shows and viewed less intently.

Because television programming is subject to quick changes and TV audiences shift with alterations in shows, weather conditions, and other factors, buyers must provide a stewardship or postanalysis reports. These reports recap budget and audience goals and then provide actual final schedule costs and audience deliveries. The postanalysis tells if the TV schedule performed as anticipated and planned.

Radio

Radio is the most ubiquitous medium because radios are mobile and are found everywhere—in the home, in the car, and recently on the street via headphone sets. The typical household has six radios. As a commercial medium, radio is extremely local because most station signals are limited and people listen to hometown stations. However, numerous wired and nonwired radio networks exist. (See Table 12–19.)

Network programming is confined to short-form news and informational shows throughout the day and occasional hour-long special concerts and entertainment programs. Local programming consists of talk, news, or music. The variety of choice is almost unlimited ranging from album rock, progressive rock, standard rock, to beautiful music or symphonic music, or country music, and so on.

Table 12–19 Network Radio

Network	Formats	Number of affiliates	Key audience appeal
ABC			
Contemporary	Contemporary Hits	238	12–49
Directions	Country	420	25–54
Entertainment	Country, Adult Contemporary	515	35–54
FM	Urban Contemporary	143	12–34
Information	News/Talk/Sports	507	25–54
Rock	Rock	108	12–34
Talk	Talk/Call-in/Interviews	109	35–54
CBS	News/Talk/Sports	426	25–54
Radio Radio	Adult Contemporary/Oldies	135	18–34
CMM	Classical	33	25–54
Mutual	Country/MOR/Sports	800	25–54
NBC	News/MOR	375	25–64
The Source	Rock	118	18–34
Talknet	Talk, Adult Music	264	25–64
Premiere Network	Five formats (CHR, AOR, Urban Contemporary, Comedy)	1080	Varies
Satellite Music Network	Eight different music feeds	1000	25–54
Sheridan	Black Contemporary Gospel, R&B	120	18–49/ 25–54
Transtar I	Various	750	18–54
Transtar II	Life, Soft Rock	575	18–54
United States I	Adult Contemporary	173	18–49
United States II	Various	233	25–54
Wall Street Journal Network	News, Classical	95	25–54
Westwood One	News, Talk, CHR, Country, AOR	4300	Various

The radio day is divided into segments based upon available audiences:

Mon.–Fri.	6 A.M.–10 A.M.	Morning
Mon.–Fri.	10 A.M.–3 P.M.	Housewife time
Mon.–Fri.	3 P.M.–7 P.M.	Afternoon drive
Mon.–Sun.	7 P.M.–12 M.	Evening
Sat.–Sun.	6 A.M.–7 P.M.	Weekend

Radio prime time is morning drive. (See Table 12–20). Radio is bought much differently than TV. Many stations compete for available audiences, and people tend to be "loyal" to a limited number of stations. For these reasons, radio is purchased on a "cume" basis. Packages of announcements (12, 18, 24, etc.) are spread throughout the day and week on numerous stations in order to build reach. Because of stable, loyal audiences, frequency is generated easily. Reach is more difficult to achieve.

Table 12–20   Percent Listening to Radio during Average Quarter Hour

Monday–Friday	Men	Women	Teens (12–17)
6 A.M.–10 A.M.	22	27	14
10 A.M.–3 P.M.	18	21	8
3 P.M.–7 P.M.	17	17	16
7 P.M.–12 M.	8	8	13

Spot radio is usually employed along with network radio. Network radio has exceptionally wide variations in market-to-market deliveries, and local stations are normally added to compensate in poorly covered areas. Radio is most efficient on a CPM basis, especially network, but on a national basis, the medium can absorb large out-of-pocket budgets if significant reach is desired. Many spots are needed and the cumulative cost builds quickly. For this reason, radio has become primarily a local advertising medium.

Although network radio is efficient compared to TV and builds frequency, the medium is less intrusive than TV. Radio is a background medium and requires large budgets to achieve high reach. Local radio enables the advertiser to quickly move into a market, change copy easily, tie-in to local events with hometown personalities and to selectively support areas of importance. Radio complements TV in a media mix.

Consumer Magazines

Magazines are employed to reach large general audiences (*TV Guide, Time, Reader's Digest*) or a multiplicity of special interests. In recent years, the trend is toward specialized publications carefully edited to appeal to designated audiences. This editorial direction has meant increasing ability to target advertising toward very narrow groups:

- Geographically by regions, markets, zip codes
- Demographically by income, occupation, behavior
- Space unit by size (pages, partial pages, etc.) and coloration

Standard Rate & Data lists over fifty types of magazines that cover just about every interest.

Magazine advertising costs vary widely, but generally there is a relationship based on size of circulation and narrowness of the editorial appeal. (See Table 12–21.)

Table 12–21   Representative Magazine Costs

	Cost page 4/C ad	Circulation (000)	CPM
TV Guide	$104,600	16,900	$ 6.19
Woman's Day	73,000	5,160	14.31
People	75,500	3,275	23.05
House & Garden	23,750	615	38.62
Golf Digest	54,000	1,330	40.60

Another important factor in magazine selections and cost relationships is the proportion of a magazine's audience that reads the issue in the household that pays for it (primary audience) and the percentage that receives the book from someone else (pass-along readers). Primary readership is considered advantageous; those who pay are more intent readers. (See Table 12–22.)

Table 12–22   Magazines: Primary and Pass-Along Readership

	% primary	% pass-along
Sunday supplements (Parade, Family Weekly)	95	5
Reader's Digest	80	20
Newsweeklies (Time, Newsweek)	45	55
Women's service (McCall's, Redbook)	40	60
Fashion/glamour (Vogue)	20	80

Magazines offer numerous advertising advantages:

1. Demographic, geographic selectivity
2. Long life of message
3. Excellent color reproduction
4. Numerous size and coloration options
5. Long message potential
6. Couponing availability
7. Reasonable efficiencies
8. Compatible editorial positioning possibilities

But magazines require fairly long lead times (about three months for monthlies), slow accumulation of readership, premium prices for geographical editions, and uneven market-to-market circulation like most national media.

Newspapers

Because almost all newspapers are published and printed locally, the medium is evaluated as a local medium. A few papers are national in scope (*Wall Street Journal, USA Today, National Enquirer*) but have limited penetration in any specific local area. Newspapers are available daily or weekly and on Sundays.

Newspapers are accepted and read by a broad cross section of people but tend to skew somewhat toward people 35 and older, higher incomes ($35,000) with some degree of advanced education. Generally speaking, however, newspapers penetrate deeply among all adults in a market.

General newspapers tend to be relatively expensive compared to other consumer media because fairly large space sizes are employed, and papers have such deep penetration reaching 50 percent or more of households. Newspapers immediately penetrate a local market (one day), enable excellent geographical flexibility (county, metropolitan area, suburban, city editions), are highly promotable to the trade distributors, permit numerous ad size possibilities, and can be used in a matter of days.

Running a schedule of several ads requires a large budget because of the depth of newspaper exposure. Additionally, newspapers, with the exception of high-cost preprinted sections and weekend magazines, do not enable good color reproduction. Although much progress has been achieved recently in standardizing newspaper ad sizes and costs, local publishing requirements and varying cost efficiencies have hampered newspapers as a national medium.

Space does not allow a complete discussion of all the various advertising media available today. The basic four—TV, radio, magazines, and newspapers—are the primary vehicles employed to promote and advertise consumer products. Many other media can be brought into a campaign to reach specialized audiences or enable unique creative approaches. The planner has to evaluate other media as occasions arise.

Media Models

The advertising profession has invested considerable amounts attempting to duplicate the advertising process, especially media dynamics, in computer-based models. Today these simulations are employed as tools to aid in sifting through the many media vehicles and to simplify the planning process. Thanks to syndicated media planning systems, both large and small advertising agencies have access to computer models that rapidly and inexpensively perform some analysis functions:

1. Help in assessing alternative media plans by tabulating reach, frequency, CPMs, and descriptive summaries of plans for evaluation.
2. Analyze media and marketing data bases to organize information in establishing media objectives and strategies. Computers may analyze market segments to determine best prospects, cross-tabulate two groups (say, age and sex) to determine the interaction of demographic characteristics on consumption.

   Independent media computer firms like Telemar and IMS (Interactive Market Systems) provide these general data analyses.
3. Other more specialized functions are found among a few marketing research firms or large advertising agencies. Simulations of test market strategies, sales prediction systems, market share forecasting, and consumer behavior prediction models are not universally available or recognized.

At one time, perhaps fifteen to twenty years ago, computers and models were expected to totally perform the media planning process. Time and experience have shown that the planning function is too complex to be handled solely by linear programming or heuristic methods. Models and computer simulators have been a tremendous asset to the advertising profession in simplifying media analysis and assuming complex computational chores. However, human judgments and creative evaluations are vital to advertising media planning.

NEW MEDIA DEVELOPMENTS

During the 1980s two new television media expanded dramatically and greatly influenced the way Americans watch television. Cable, originally employed to improve picture quality in areas with poor reception, developed into a meaningful programming alternative to the networks. Both basic cable (with commercials) and pay cable (no advertising) now attract significant audiences in prime time. With cable approaching 60 percent penetration, the medium now gathers sufficient funding to secure better programming and may rival the networks in the 90s for audiences.

VCR penetration exploded in the 80s and more than 60 percent of households have a tape machine (see Table 12–23). VCRs have affected TV viewing in two ways. They permit playback of recorded TV programs at the convenience of the viewer, thereby adding to program audiences. But at the same time, VCRs have drawn some people from regular TV by allow-

Table 12–23 Percent U.S. Penetration

	1982	1985	1990
Basic cable	34	43	55
Pay cable	19	26	30
VCR	3	14	65

ing them to watch prerecorded films and other material when they might have been viewing regular TV. Daytime soap operas and evening feature films are the most frequently recorded TV programming; their audiences are slightly larger due to the tape machine. Saturday night viewing is slightly depressed today because of VCR replay of rented or purchased films. The value of taped viewership is somewhat questionable in the case of advertising for many viewers bypass or zip through commercial pods when watching shows.

The overall influence of cable and VCRs on traditional over-the-air TV has been to lower or erode audiences and drive up the cost to advertisers. Cable programming, by and large, has been priced efficiently, and many advertisers allocate a portion of national TV budgets to various cable networks. Table 12–24 shows that although cable homes spend more hours with TV, they view less network programming. As cable networks become stronger financially and invest in better original programming, erosion of network audiences will continue.

Table 12–25 lists many of the advertising-supported cable networks. Most concentrate on a specific type of programming, called narrow-

Table 12–24 Average Hours Viewed per Week

	Noncable homes		Cable homes		Pay cable homes	
	Prime	Day	Prime	Day	Prime	Day
Network affiliates	10.2	6.8	8.8	5.8	9.0	6.3
Other over-the-air stations	3.1	2.3	3.1	2.3	2.7	2.5
Cable-originated TV	—	—	2.5	1.9	2.4	2.1
Pay cable	—	—	—	—	2.5	1.2
Total	13.3	9.1	14.4	10.0	16.6	12.1

Table 12–25   Satellite-Fed Advertiser-Supported Cable Networks

Network	Programming	U.S. 1989 penetration (%)
ACTS	Christian programming	77
Arts & Entertainment	Comedy, drama, performing arts	40
Black Entertainment (BET)	Black programming, sports	25
CBN Family Channel	Family programming, twenty-four hours	48
CNN	National and international news, twenty-four hours	53
CNBC	Business news, consumer issues	(new)
Discovery Channel	Science, nature, human adventure	41
ESPN	Sports	55
FNN	Financial news, stocks, options	22
Galavision	Spanish language programming	4
Headline News	News headlines every thirty minutes	38
Learning Channel	Educational and career programming	16
Lifetime	Women's entertainment and information	46
Movietime	News and interviews about films	12
MTV	Rock & roll video music in stereo	48
TNN	Country & western concerts, sports	47
Nickelodeon	Children's programming, family shows	44
Nostalgia Channel	Entertainment for 45 + year-old audience	5
Prevue Guide	Cable programming listings	10
TBS	Superstation, general entertainment	52
TNT	Movies, specials, children's programming	30
USA Network	Broad-based entertainment network	52
VH-1	Music network for 25–49 year olds	33
The Weather Channel	National and local weather	42
WGN	Superstation from Chicago	30
WOR	Superstation from New York	25

SOURCE: Cabletelevision Advertising Bureau, Inc.

casting—news, weather, sports, children's shows, teen music, and so on. Pay channels (not listed) and some basic cable networks seek broad-based appeal by programming general entertainment and movies.

Cable rates to advertisers remain relatively low compared with the networks reflecting small audiences. Even so, cable offers several values:

1. Low unit prices for advertisers with small budgets
2. Inexpensive testing facility
3. Ability to build frequency of exposure at affordable rates
4. Highly selective audiences in the case of narrowcast networks
5. Flexibility in copy length (2-minute commercials are affordable)
6. Inexpensive sponsorship opportunities
7. Compatible programming adjacencies
8. Commercial tag possibilities (i.e., adding time to commercials locally via insert equipment at local cable companies)
9. Franchise positioning in compatible programming (beer in sports, etc.)

On a local basis, cable advertising is just now beginning to become a factor, primarily with local advertisers. In many metro areas, cable companies have joined together to form "interconnects" which permit advertisers to broadcast their messages to a long list of communities at the same time. An advertiser, for instance, can insert the commercial into programming for suburban communities only or advertise only in towns with a certain income. In addition, numerous regional sports channels offer advertisers the opportunity to schedule ads in certain geographical areas if distribution is limited.

Cable offers the low cost and frequency of radio, the video of TV, the selectivity of magazines, and the local interest of newspapers. Cable today is a relative child when compared with other established media; nonetheless, the new video medium promises to alter viewing life-styles and advertising approaches. The process is gradual, but it is happening.

THE MEDIA PLAN

Media Plan Document

1. Executive summary. One- or two-page review of basic strategy and plan elements for senior client executives not intimately involved in product marketing operations.
2. Background commentary and situational analysis. Briefly describes the market situation for the product or service, recaps marketing and advertising goals, and indicates creative direction.

3. Media objectives. Specific, actionable statements of what the media plan will accomplish.
4. Media strategies. Planned options to achieve media objectives; strategies outline how media objectives will be achieved.
5. Plan description. Executional elements of the media plan, alternative strategies considered, justification for recommendations. All tactical components are included in this section.

A sample media plan follows later in the chapter.

Evaluating the Media Plan

Evaluations of media plans involve reviewing alternatives presented and considering the effectiveness of the options. The first step is to ask if objectives support overall marketing goals. Assuming basic direction is on target, the next step is to determine which recommended strategies are the most efficient, effective combinations of media to fulfill the objectives. The properly written media plan will expedite evaluation by outlining alternative possibilities and rationalizing the recommended course of action.

Several other elements make for good planning. Are the planning group's assumptions and judgments clearly outlined? Were innovative ideas considered even if not recommended? Were any tests proposed as a learning tool for future planning? Are cost elements specifically and accurately outlined? Does the plan leave room for adjustments should marketing conditions change? Is substantiation thorough and clear? In the end, judgments will play a major role in evaluating media plans, but the plan must and should relate directly to marketing goals and other advertising plans.

Sample Media Plan—Goody Cereal

The following ready-to-eat cereal product media plan illustrates organization and style of media plans. Some of the tactical detail, primarily supporting exhibits, has been removed; but the essence of the strategic issues remains. Goody Cereal is a competitively priced, all-family, ready-to-eat (RTE) product. Its main attributes are good taste and appeal to adults and children alike. Introduced seven years previously, Goody Cereal enjoyed continuous growth until the last year when shipments plateaued. In the year ahead, additional budget is authorized in an effort to reestablish the brand's historical growth pattern.

Goody Cereal Media Plan

EXECUTIVE SUMMARY

- Planned spending will be up 18 percent over last year:

This year's plan $13,000M
Last year's plan $11,000M

Real dollars, which take into consideration media inflation, reflect a 10 percent increase in expenditures.
- An all-television media plan will be continued in light of

— its effectiveness in relaying the copy message.
— the competitive influence on TV.

Heavier national levels will be implemented this year to support a revitalized creative campaign.
- A print–TV option will be tested at 20 percent incremental spending.

Objectives/Strategies

1. Direct advertising support toward the Goody Cereal target audience defined as follows:
   - Women 25–54 primarily
   - Teens and children secondarily
   - $35,000 household income
2. Geographically, direct support in line with the product's sales.
3. Advertising will be flat throughout the year reflecting the lack of seasonal sales skews.
4. Plan Summary:

Vehicle	W 25–54 weekly GRPs	Number of weeks	$(000)	%
Prime network	29	26	7,200.0	57
Day network	39	26	3,800.0	26
Total network	68		11,000.0	83
Spot TV (45% U.S.)	32	26	2,000.0	14
Total media			13,000.0	97
Production			500.0	3
Total advertising			13,500.0	100

Background

Goody Cereal has enjoyed excellent growth since its introduction seven years ago. Last year, sales followed the industry pattern and were flat for the first time. The corporation wishes to renew Goody's growth trend. To return Goody to upward sales momentum, advertising budgets will be increased and creative will be freshened.

Independent promotions will run in the first quarter to build volume. By this time, the cumulative effects of new creative will be felt and brand awareness will begin building. Goody is expected to grow 10 percent next year and achieve a 3 percent year-end share.

The challenge facing Goody's franchise is to renew growth despite stagnation in the ready-to-eat category. Growth must derive from increased penetration that is below industry norms. Achieving this penetration through sales promotion initially and improved awareness from advertising later is the focus of next year's marketing plan.

Marketing budgets have been established at levels higher than inflation in order to achieve the company's growth target.

Media Objectives

1. Within the $13 million media budget, increase Goody Cereal awareness and reestablish growth, especially in areas where the brand has shown above-average sales development.
2. Direct advertising to the primary purchasing agent in households with $35,000+ income, women 25–54. Secondarily, target advertising to children 6–11 and teens 12–17 who consume 40 percent of the product.
3. Achieve minimum four-week reach of 75 percent and 3.5× average frequency against the primary target. Expand reach/average frequency to 85 percent/4.5 × in high potential areas.
4. Provide strong national support complemented by additional emphasis in high volume/BDI markets where growth has exceeded national rates.
5. Maintain year-around advertising because of flat seasonal sales.
6. Recognize that the brand has been successfully built with an established TV campaign that is revitalized for the upcoming year.
7. Test a 20 percent increase in budget to determine if adding women's service magazines can significantly improve awareness. Funding will be incremental. Test area to be determined and schedule prepared during first quarter of the year.

Media Strategy

A medium that can effectively reach both adult women family food shoppers and children/teens is vital to the Goody advertising strategy:

Age of user	% Goody volume	Index to RTE volume
–6	5	87
6–8	13	122
9–12	12	130
13–18	15	132
19–34	19	101
35–54	23	136
55+	8	36

Television remains Goody Cereal's advertising medium because of the

- proven effectiveness in providing broad reach efficiently against the primary and secondary targets.
- audio/video capabilities.
- strong competitive presence in this medium; ready-to-eat cereals concentrate their efforts in TV.

Prime network.   Prime network will be utilized to generate broad reach and rapid awareness. A base of prime is recommended to reach approximately 65 percent of women 25–54 an average of once every two weeks while advertising. The program environment and higher viewer attentiveness of the daypart will provide an impactful presentation of the Goody message.

Element	Attentiveness levels as a % of prime
Prime	100
Day	92
Late night	97
Early news	95

The chart that follows details the weekly reach potential among the primary and secondary audiences:

	Weekly reach potential by day-part (%)		
Element	Women 25–54	Teens 12–17	Children 6–11
Prime (M–Su/8–11 P.M.)	92	86	94
Day (M–F/10–4:30 P.M.)	63	60	66
Late night (M–F/11:30 P.M.–1 A.M.)	50	35	19
Early fringe (M–F/4:30–7:30 P.M.)	80	76	91

In addition, prime network will generate visibility for Goody Cereal because it has the least commercial clutter of all TV dayparts:

Element	Commercial minutes allowed per hour
Prime	10.0
Day	16.0
Late night	16.0
Early news	16.0

Day network.   Day network represents the most efficient media vehicle to reach women 25–54, even when adjusted by relative media values:

Element	Unadjusted W25–54 CPM	Index	Impact values	Adjusted CPM	Index
Day	$ 9.60	100	70	$13.71	100
Prime	22.56	235	100	22.56	165
Late night	16.73	174	85	19.68	144
Early news	21.30	222	75	28.40	207
Early morning	10.38	108	60	17.30	126
Early fringe spot	14.44	150	75	19.25	140
Magazines	9.90	103	70	14.14	103

Day network is utilized to provide additional reach as well as frequency of exposures against the prime prospect:

W25–54, average 4-week R/F	Prime only	Prime and day	Index
Reach	65	76	117
Frequency	1.8	3.6	200

Spot TV. The addition of spot television to the network base plan insures adequate spending behind the high BDI/high volume markets. Goody cereal will cover 45 percent of the U.S. in spot. These areas account for 55.2 percent of total volume (average BDI 123). Without spot television, the high BDI/high volume areas would be underdelivered based on sales contribution:

Spending versus Ideal

	% U.S. pop.	% volume	BDI	Ideal dollars*	Dollars allocated
Spot areas	45	55.2	123	7,176,000	6,950,000
Remainder U.S.	55	44.8	81	5,824,000	6,050,000
Total	100	100.0	100	13,000,000	13,000,000

*Ideal dollars = % volume × $13,000,000 budget

Scheduling. Due to the continuous purchasing pattern of ready-to-eat cereals, TV activity will be scheduled year-around. Network will run for 26 weeks in 4- to 5-week flights. Local TV is broken out into three priority groups:

	% U.S.	Number of weeks of spot TV
Group I	36	26
Group II	6	25
Group III	3	22

RTE and Goody Cereal sales are relatively flat throughout the year:

Quarter	Total RTE Index*
JFM	98
AMJ	102
JAS	104
OND	96

PLAN DESCRIPTION

Flowchart	Alternative Plans
Impression Analysis	Spot TV Allocation
Comparison with Previous Year	

*5 years of SAMI data

Goody Cereal Flowchart (W25–54 TRPs)

STANDARD BROADCAST MONTH	JANUARY	FEBRUARY	MARCH	APRIL	MAY	JUNE	JULY	AUGUST	SEPTEMBER	OCTOBER	NOVEMBER	DECEMBER
WEEK BEGINNING MONDAY	1 8 15 22 29	5 12 19 26	5 12 19 26	2 9 16 23 30	7 14 21 28	4 11 18 25	3 10 17 24 31	7 14 21 28	4 11 18 25	2 9 16 23	30 6 13 20 27	4 11 18 25

	JAN	MAR	APR/MAY	JUL	SEP	NOV
Coupon markers (X)	X		X	X	X	
Coupon type	ON-PACK COUPON		DIRECT MAIL COUPON	F.S.I. COUPON	ON-PACK COUPON	
PRIME NETWORK $7,200.0	29	29	29	29	29	29
DAY NETWORK $3,800.0	39	39	39	39	39	39

TOTAL NETWORK
W25-54 4-WK.
R&F 76%/3.6X
ER 68%

SPOT TV $2,000.0
GROUP I
GROUP II
GROUP III

TOTAL SPOT
W25-54 4-WK.
R&F 45%/2.8X
ER 44%

COMBINED
W25-54 4-WK.
R&F 87%/4.6X
ER 76%

| SPENDING BY QTR. | 23% | | 25% | | 25% | 27% | | | 25% |

Impression Analysis (Thousands)

Element	Women 25–54	Teens 12–17	Children 6–11
Prime network	315,398	130,187	124,051
Day network	424,156	59,176	46,519
Total network	739,554	189,363	170,570
Spot TV (45% U.S.)	155,671	77,171	89,854
Total	895,225	266,534	260,424
% by target	63%	19%	18%

Goody Cereal Recommended Plan versus Previous Year

	Previous actual	Recommended	Index
Number of weeks	24	26	108
Total budget	$11,000.0	$13,000.0	118
W25–54 avg. 4-wk. R/F			
Spot universe:			
R	85	87	102
F	4.3	4.6	107
Remainder U.S.:			
R	72	76	106
F	3.0	3.6	120
Impressions (MM)	706.5	895.2	127
CPM	$15.58	$14.52	93
Adj. impressions (MM)	575.2	729.1	127
Adj. CPM	$19.12	$17.83	93

ALTERNATIVE PLANS

The following alternatives have been examined:

- Alternative I   Prime and day network
- Alternative II   Prime/day network and magazines
- Alternative III Prime/day network, spot TV, and magazines

Alternative I

Description:

- All network plan
- Utilize the same network elements—prime and day
- Weekly network GRPs higher

Reasons for rejection:

- Provides comparable reach/frequency levels against national schedule
- Underdelivers against the spot areas, which accounts for 55.2 percent of volume in 45 percent of U.S.

W25–54 spot universe	Recommended	Alternative I	Index
R	87	80	92
F	4.6	4.0	87
3+	58	47	81
Total unadj. imp. (MM)	488.5	395.3	81
Total adj. imp. (MM)	392.3	327.5	83
Remainder U.S.			
R	76	80	105
F	3.6	4.0	111
3+	42	47	112
Total unadj. imp. (MM)	406.7	483.1	119
Total adj. imp. (MM)	336.8	400.3	119

Alternative II

Description:

- Total national plan/no spot
- Utilize prime/day network and magazines
- Weekly network GRPs are identical to recommended plan
- Magazines substituted for spot TV

Reasons for rejection:

- Underdelivers against the spot areas, which accounts for 55.2 percent of volume in 45 percent of U.S.

W25–54 spot universe	Recommended	Alternative II	Index
R	87	89	102
F	4.6	4.3	93
3+	58	60	103
Total unadj. imp. (MM)	488.5	425.3	87
Total adj. imp. (MM)	392.3	340.3	87

Remainder U.S.

R	76	76	100
F	3.6	3.6	100
3+	42	42	100
Total unadj. imp. (MM)	406.7	519.8	128
Total adj. imp. (MM)	336.8	415.9	124

Alternative III

Description:

- National and spot plan
- Utilize prime/day network, spot TV and magazines
- Eight weeks of prime eliminated in the most expensive quarters to afford a magazine schedule

Reasons for rejection:

- Deletion of eight weeks of a historically proven and impactful prime daypart; as a base media type, eighteen weeks of prime time are unacceptable

W25–54 spot universe	Recommended	Alternative III	Index
R	87	89	102
F	4.6	4.8	104
3+	58	60	103
Total unadj. imp. (MM)	406.7	469.9	111
Total adj. imp. (MM)	392.3	416.1	106
Remainder U.S.			
R	76	80	105
F	3.6	3.8	106
3+	42	47	112
Total unadj. imp. (MM)	469.9	541.2	116
Total adj. imp. (MM)	336.8	365.0	108

SPOT TV ALLOCATION

1. **Selected markets with significant BDIs/volume contribution.** A market list was compiled by the brand group indicating markets with

- BDIs over 100, and
- Goody Cereal volume contribution above .65 percent

Within the list, markets were prioritized into three groups.

2. **Equal weight methodology.** Based on marketing input, each of the selected markets was to receive equal weekly weight. A goal of 95 W25–54 GRPs (network and spot) was set for each market.

Network delivery in the individual markets was first taken into consideration. Spot GRPs were then derived by subtracting the network GRPs from the total weekly goal of 95.

3. **Market prioritization.** Markets were prioritized into three groups based on volume contribution, BDI and volume/share trends. The number of weeks scheduled for each priority group follows:

Group	% U.S.	Number of weeks	Total cost
I	36	26	$1,600,000
II	6	25	250,000
III	2	22	150,000
Total	45		$2,000,000

Goody Cereal Spot TV Allocation (95 GRP goal/ 35 markets)

	Markets	Percent U.S.	Average weekly W25–54 GRPs Network	Average weekly W25–54 GRPs Spot	Number of weeks in spot
Group I:	Albany	.55	63	32	26
	Baltimore	1.14	60	35	
	Boston	2.42	54	41	
	Buffalo	.79	61	34	
	Chicago	2.95	54	41	
	Cleveland	1.87	65	30	
	Denver	1.03	63	32	
	Des Moines	.42	69	26	
	Detroit	2.30	71	24	
	Flint	.57	80	15	
	Indianapolis	1.01	67	28	
	Los Angeles	5.17	61	34	
	Milwaukee	.89	63	32	
	Philadelphia	3.32	67	28	
	Pittsburgh	1.54	82	13	
	Providence	.67	73	22	
	Sacramento	.91	67	28	

	Markets	Percent U.S.	Average weekly W25–54 GRPs		Number of weeks in spot
			Network	Spot	
	San Diego	.79	60	35	
	San Francisco	2.42	58	37	
	Seattle-Tacoma	1.16	58	37	
	Syracuse	.43	63	32	
	Tampa	.84	65	30	
	Washington	2.01	51	44	
	Subtotal	36.20			
Group II	Columbus	.71	73	22	25
	Grand Rapids	.69	71	24	
	Harrisburg	.60	71	24	
	Minneapolis	1.32	54	41	
	Omaha	.43	77	18	
	Phoenix	.74	71	24	
	Rochester	.42	63	32	
	Salt Lake City	.59	62	33	
	Wilkes-Barre	.55	84	11	
	Subtotal	6.05			
Group III	Cincinnati	.87	63	32	22
	Hartford	1.04	55	40	
	Portland	.84	65	30	
	Subtotal	2.77			
	Grand total	45.02	63	32	

Case Studies

G & T Associates

Brian Harper, an account executive with G & T Associates, a Washington, D.C. advertising agency, was faced with a difficult situation. His chief client, a major savings and loan institution, was reducing its advertising budget by 55 percent in response to corporate losses and the economic situation. In the past, the company had handled its own media buying, relying on the agency only for creative. However, as part of the streamlining, the corporate media buyer position had been eliminated and placement responsibility had also been turned over to the agency.

Harper met with Linda Britten of the agency's media department to discuss strategy. His review of the situation included these facts:

> The area's three leading savings and loans had combined net income of −$49,575,000 last year. Our client had the lowest loss, and currently has a market share of 23.6 percent, the number one position. The market is highly competitive and has become more so with recent changes in banking regulations. Area savings and loans have introduced an average of five new accounts this year, each with heavy advertising support. In response to consumer confusion, most of this advertising has been very informational in nature (i.e., long copy print ads).
>
> In terms of year-round corporate advertising, savings and loan services in the Washington area are advertised through daily and weekly newspapers (46.6 percent), consumer magazines (3.3 percent), outdoor, spot radio (16 percent), local television (6.7 percent), exhibits, the Yellow Pages, and point-of-purchase items, such as brochures.
>
> Our client has been the leading spender ($1,867,000 last year). Here's how we compare to the competition:

	Advertising $	Share of voice	Share of market
Our client	$1,867,000	41.3%	23.6%
S&L B	934,000	20.6	23.1
S&L C	594,000	13.1	22.6

Harper went on to observe:

> Based on the share of voice = share of market theory, spending hasn't been very efficient, because market share should be much higher. I believe there are two primary reasons for the problem. First, in the past, the advertising strategy was very general. Basically, we just said, "We're the biggest," suggesting that being the biggest was the same as being the best. We've refined that; now we're stressing that we're a "strong, well-managed" savings and loan so that people will feel confident about letting

us handle their money. We think this is a key concern, especially because two area S&Ls closed down last year and three others were forced to merge to survive. Second, our media strategy (and the competition's) has been to spend continuously and spread the message broadly. There has not been any attempt to target consumers through strategic media placement. It seems to me that careful targeting and scheduling can help overcome the negative effects of the budget cutback. With the 55 percent reduction, the 1990 budget will be $840,150. That's still more than the number three S&L spent last year. Both our chief competitors lost money too, so I doubt their spending will increase much, if at all.

Britten asked, "How locked in are these people? What I mean is, would they be responsive to some major changes in their media strategy? If so, I think there are several things we can do that might prove very effective."

"I don't think they'd be averse to something different," Harper said. "I'm not going to tell them their past strategy was lousy, but I think they know the results weren't what they might have been. As long as you've got good support for your recommendations, I think there's an excellent chance they'll support a change. Some things to keep in mind, though: there'll probably be at least two more new account introductions next year. Plus, a new securities investment service will be opening in several of the branches. Those will have to be planned for. Can you come up with the basics by next week?"

Britten agreed to present her recommendations to the S&L's marketing vice president the next week.

Questions

Recommend media vehicles (and scheduling guidelines, i.e., flighting, continuous, etc.) that might prove effective for the S&L. Justify each. Be creative! The following information on the Washington metro area is provided to help you in your recommendations.

	Population (000)				
	18–24	25–34	35–44	45–64	65+
Women	254	429	308	463	174
Men	251	398	302	391	140

Households: 1,310,600

Consumer spendable income: $57,269,600

Spendable income per household: $43,697

Retail sales per household: $17,230

Media: 30+ radio stations; variety of formats. Costs for 60-second spot range from $15 to $600; 30 seconds, from $12 to $480.

Three network affiliated TV stations
Three independent stations
Two public stations
Cable penetration approximately 26 percent
Pay TV penetration approximately 18 percent

Two areawide daily newspapers:
Washington Post: circ. 894,557 (68% of HHs)
   $244/column inch daily edition
   $44/column inch extra in weekly business magazine
   $298.50/column inch Sunday edition

Washington Times: circ. 85,135 (6% of HHs)
   $25/column inch

15+ daily or weekly community papers, average $55/col. inch

Washington circulation of selected consumer magazines

Magazine	Circulation*
National Geographic	227,898
Family Circle	331,000
Reader's Digest	424,488
TV Guide	520,315
Better Homes & Gardens	214,000
Time	195,000
Woman's Day	199,000
Business Week	29,171

National savings data

Percentage of population having

Checking account at an S&L	16.4
Savings account at an S&L	18.7
IRA at an S&L	3.2
CDs at an S&L	6.8
S&L loan	4.4
S&L mortgage	9.3

SOURCES: Population, cable penetration: *The Washington DC Media Market,* Mediamark Research, Inc., 1986. Newspaper costs and circulation: SRDS, *Newspapers,* 69, 3 (March 12, 1987). Radio costs: SRDS, *Spot Radio,* 69,9 (September 1, 1987). Financial data: Simmons Market Research Bureau, Inc. (1986): Volume P-5. Magazine circulation: SRDS, *Consumer Magazines,* 69, 6, (June 27, 1987).

*All circulation figures are for Washington/Baltimore area.

CompStar, Ltd.

CompStar, Ltd., a major manufacturer of personal, midsize, and mainframe computer hardware, was in the final stages of preparation for the launch of its first major new product entry in five years. CompStar was the industry leader in terms of installed units in the business segment of the market. Its products were regarded as the industry standard for computer hardware. However, five years without introducing a new product had tarnished that image. The lag had given competitors a chance to bring out equipment that met the CompStar standard at a lower price. CompStar viewed the new product as their means to solidifying their number one position for the foreseeable future.

CompStar's existing line offered a variety of computer software for a variety of applications, from the home computer user to the small businessman to the large *Fortune* 500 company. While CompStar's mainframe products were the undisputed category leader, it had faced its stiffest competition in the personal computer area. The new product line was made up of a group of five units offering unsurpassed processing speed, state-of-the-art software, and top-quality graphics.

CompStar itself was a *Fortune* 50 firm, with a long history in the data processing industry. They had held off on entering the personal computer category, but once in quickly took the dominant position. CompStar had a history of doing things in a big way and was fiercely protective of its corporate image and superior product positioning. This attitude pervaded the company, from the CEO to workers on the production line. The unwritten company motto was, "When CompStar does something, it does it *right.*"

The new line of personal computers was not really designed for home use, but was more of a total business system, with the different models engineered to meet the computing needs of any size company. The new units were also designed to be compatible with CompStar's midsized and mainframe computers, further supporting the "total system" concept. CompStar's engineers were convinced that the new models were far superior to anything any competitor could offer, and would be unmatched for at least three years. Excitement over the new line of PCs was high throughout the company.

CompStar's market research department had conducted a wealth of studies of business computer buyers and could identify decision makers within companies of any size by job title. The advertising department, working with one of the top U.S. advertising agencies, sometimes used these titles to make trade journal buys or send out direct mail pieces.

The advertising department and the agency were also very excited about the new product introduction, seeing it as a chance to make a real impact with an exciting new campaign. Although the details were being kept secret, it was rumored that the television ads for the new campaign featured some terrific talent, and the print ads highlighted the new line's incredible graphic capabilities. Several competitors had introduced new products in the last few years with multipage inserts in leading business publications; the talk around CompStar suggested that the advertising department was determined to outdo those.

The media plan for the introductory blitz of the campaign called for six 30-second spots on the leading network station during the most heavily viewed weeknight primetime programming. National reach for the six-spot schedule would come close to seventy percent for the one night. Although the night's advertising would be expensive on an out-of-pocket basis, the agency felt that the CPMs were quite reasonable, especially given the national impact of the schedule. By the end of the evening, millions of people would know about CompStar's new line. Additionally, the multi-page insert would have broken three days earlier in the leading weekly business publication. The insert highlighted the new line's many exciting features and was very colorful. The agency intended to use excerpts from the insert as two-page spreads for the remainder of the campaign.

The introductory plan had been approved by the CEO and board of directors, all of whom were very excited about the impact CompStar would be making. Though many of them did not regularly watch the particular television programs on which the commercials would be running, they had all heard of the shows and knew they were highly rated. The vice president for marketing and advertising took pride in pointing out that the numbers two and three competitors were rarely seen on primetime network television and likely wouldn't "know what hit them."

The executives were also impressed by the actual commercials. These featured some very well-known television actors whom audiences would recognize immediately. The campaign was likely to generate a lot of viewer interest, hopefully translating to word-of-mouth support for CompStar's product. And, several shots focused on the new computer's graphics capability and processing speed. All in all, it was a very exciting campaign.

After the meeting, the VP for marketing and advertising rode down in the elevator with the head of the market research department, who had been uncharacteristically quiet during the discussion. The following conversation took place:

MKTNG VP: What's wrong? Didn't you like the ads?

RES DIR: It's not that I didn't like them. I agree that they're very exciting and that they'll probably really catch people's attention and get them talking.

MKTNG VP: So, what's wrong?

RES DIR: Well, I'm just not sure that the people who'll be talking are the right people.

MKTNG VP: What do you mean, not the right people? We're going to get 70 percent reach!

RES DIR: I know, but I've seen the demographic profiles on those programs, and I also know from our own research what our decision makers tend to watch on television. Those people watching those shows *aren't* in any of our target groups. Those shows are all situation comedies—our target watches news programs and some hour-long dramas. They just aren't the same people.

MKTNG VP: But these are the highest rated shows on television. Our commercials will make a really big splash. Everyone knows our spokespeople. Think how jealous our competition's going to be!

RES DIR: I agree that the spots will make a big splash with the people watching those programs. I'm just not sure we'll get much carryover to the target. And, to be honest, although the people watching the shows are going to recognize our spokespeople, I'm really not sure that our target knows who those actors are or will recognize them so quickly.

MKTNG VP: Well, the agency seems sure this is the way to go. And we really want to show our support for the new line. So, although I appreciate your comments, I'm going to respectfully disagree with you. Anyway, we'll soon find out who's right—aren't you planning to do some day-after recall testing on these spots? We'll see how they did then.

Questions

1. Give arguments supporting the views of both the marketing VP and the research director. Why does broadcast network television make sense for this situation? Why doesn't it?
2. What do you think is driving the decision to introduce the new product line in this way?
3. Briefly outline an alternative way of introducing the product. What media would you use? (Assume the creative can be adapted to any media.) Explain why your plan is more efficient, more effective, or both.

Sales Promotion

Over the past few years, investments in sales promotion have grown very rapidly. Manufacturers, retailers, and service organizations have invested a larger and larger percentage of their marketing funds in sales promotion as compared with more traditional media advertising. Exhibit 13–1 shows this growth of sales promotion spending by major manufacturers between 1975 and 1985. This upward trend is expected to continue.

Because of this dramatic growth and the emphasis placed on sales promotion by many advertisers, it is important to the advertising planner to have at least a working knowledge of the area to properly integrate it into the overall campaign. In addition, advertising and sales promotion are increasingly being planned at the same time by the same person so that all campaign elements work together. This chapter will provide the basics of sales promotion for package goods as it is planned and used by major marketing organizations today.

WHAT IS SALES PROMOTION?

Everyone seems to have a different definition of sales promotion. The American Marketing Association has defined *sales promotion* as:

> Media and non-media marketing pressure applied for a pre-determined, limited period of time at the level of consumer, retailer or wholesaler in order to stimulate trial, increase consumer demand or improve product availability.[1]

---

[1]Peter D. Bennett, *Dictionary of Marketing Terms* (Chicago: American Marketing Association, 1988): 179.

Exhibit 13–1   Sales Promotion Growth Chart

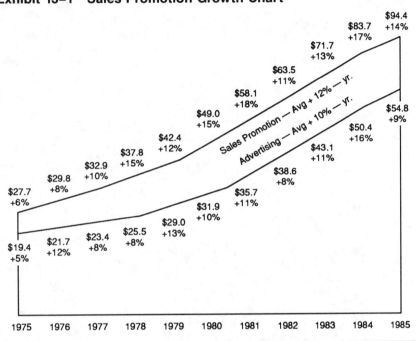

SOURCE: Russel Bowman, "Sales Promotion: The 1985 Annual Report," *Marketing & Media Decisions* (July 1986): 172.

We'll use this as a working definition initially but will expand the concept of sales promotion in the latter portions of this chapter.

Basically, sales promotion is an attempt by the seller to change the customer or prospect's view of the price–value relationship for the product or service for a limited period of time. These sales promotion efforts can be used to generate either consumer or channel demand or both. For example, the use of a sweepstakes (see Exhibit 13–2) is an attempt to change the price–value relationship of Oscar Mayer products by offering the ultimate consumer an opportunity to win free groceries. The same is true of the rebate offer by Jimmy Dean Biscuits and Muffins in Exhibit 13–3. All these examples are attempts by marketers to change or enhance the value that consumers traditionally perceive to be found in the products or service in hopes of generating a brand switch or additional demand. Similarly, sales promotion programs, such as off-invoice discounts or display and advertising allowances, are used to influence retailers in the same way.

Almost all sales promotion is based on the seller's belief that a demand curve exists for his or her product or service. Thus, as the price is lowered or value is increased in some way, demand for the brand or product or ser-

Exhibit 13–2   Sweepstakes Offer

SOURCE: Photographs courtesy of the Oscar Mayer Foods Corporation. Oscar Mayer is a registered trademark of

the Oscar Mayer Foods Corporation.

Exhibit 13–3   Rebate Offer

SOURCE: Reprinted courtesy of the Jimmy Dean Meat Company and Static Graphics, Dallas, Texas.

Exhibit 13–4   Traditional Demand Curve

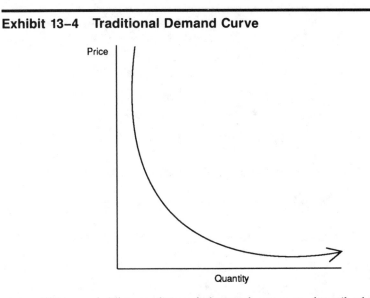

vice will expand. This traditional demand curve as described by economists and as accepted by marketers is illustrated in Exhibit 13–4.

As the American Marketing Association definition implies, sales promotion is used to influence consumers, retailers, and wholesalers. The most visible examples of sales promotion are those directed toward consumers, which appear in the media, on packages, or in retail stores. Although consumer promotion is the most visible, it is not the area in which the most marketing funds are invested. That distinction goes to sales promotion designed to influence the trade, that is, the wholesaler or retailer. For example, in the *Donnelley Marketing Eleventh Annual Survey of Sales Promotion Practices,* it was reported that among the manufacturers responding, trade promotion accounted for 44.3 percent of all sales promotion investment in 1988 while consumer sales promotion accounted for 24.7 percent. Media advertising was third in amount of investment with 31.0 percent of the funds. (See Table 13–1.)

Sales promotion activities, not usually of great importance to the advertising planner, can be used to motivate the sales force, for example, through the use of sales or display contests or volume goals. Prizes of cash, travel, or merchandise may be offered for meeting or exceeding sales goals. These types of sales promotion events may be conducted for either the internal (company-employed salespeople) or external sales forces, such as brokers, warehouse, or distributor salespeople. Although this form of sales promotion is generally developed and executed by the marketing organization, we include it here because the advertising planner is sometimes asked to provide suggestions or ideas for these sales promotional programs too.

Table 13–1   Shares of Promotional Dollars for Principal Categories in 1986, 1987, and 1988

	Percentage of respondents			Percentage point difference
	1986	*1987*	*1988*	*1988 versus 1986*
Consumer promotion	24.5	24.6	24.7	0.2
Trade promotion	43.1	44.7	44.3	1.2
Media advertising	32.4	30.7	31.0	(1.4)
Total	100.0	100.0	100.0	
Bases	(65)	(65)	(65)	

SOURCE: *Donnelley Marketing Eleventh Annual Survey of Promotional Practices* (Stamford, Conn.: Donnelley Marketing): 3.

WHY SALES PROMOTION HAS GROWN

Although there is little doubt that marketers' investments in sales promotion have grown dramatically, in some cases at the expense of traditional media advertising, many times advertising planners don't understand why the spending emphasis has changed or why marketers are more willing to invest in sales promotion than in media advertising.

To understand the growth of sales promotion, particularly against the trade, it is important to first review why and how this form of activity has traditionally been used. To simplify the discussion, we'll look at sales promotion as would the brand or the product manager of a package-goods company.

Sales promotion has traditionally been used by marketers with retailers to achieve four goals:

1. To generate additional product movement from the factory into retail channels. To reach economies-of-scale in manufacturing, trade promotions have been used to build volume so that the factory could operate at efficient levels. They have also been used to move excess inventory or simply to generate additional volume for a period of time.

2. To effect short-term price adjustment. Rather than reduce the price of the product permanently, many marketers have used sales promotion to adjust prices to reflect efficiencies in manufacturing and seasonal adjustments in availability of raw materials, and, certainly, as a competitive tool to meet marketplace demands. Thus, the manufacturer

can adjust the price up or down to the trade as needed with sales promotion, but continue to maintain some form of established price level.

3. To reward some type of performance by the retailer. Most manufacturers have found that displays, price reductions, and advertising or merchandising by the retailer create a great deal of product movement. Therefore, the manufacturer is willing to reward the retailer for some kind of extra activity at the store level to build sales. Often this is done with a short-term sales promotion event.

4. To differentiate parity products. When there is little new to be said about the product or service, marketers have often used sales promotion activities at the trade level to call attention to the product. Thus, they have used sales promotion techniques rather than improved or increased product benefits to attempt to generate both trade and consumer demand.

When viewed in a traditional marketing strategy sense, media advertising and consumer trade promotions have been used as the primary elements in a marketer's "pull" strategy. Trade promotion has generally been viewed as reflecting a "push" marketing strategy. As the U.S. marketplace has changed so have marketer's approaches. Therefore, the traditional view of "push" and "pull" has changed as well.

A Changed and Changing Marketplace

Beginning in the late 1970s, the U.S. marketplace underwent a dramatic change in structure and organization. Retail chains began to consolidate through purchase, acquisition, and simple market growth and expansion. This concentration of retail outlets began first with food and drugstores but quickly occurred in fast foods, hardware, mass merchandisers, and then in department stores and electronics outlets. As retailers became larger and more powerful, they gained greater and greater control of the distribution channels. With the sales of large quantities of consumer merchandise in the hands of a relatively small number of retailers, it became increasingly important for the manufacturer to secure the distribution of the product first, and then be concerned with the promotion of the product to the ultimate consumer. As a result, we have seen a major shift of manufacturer's marketing dollars from an attempt to influence the ultimate consumer's purchasing decision to assuring that the product is stocked on the retailer's shelves.

Obviously, there have been other marketplace changes that have encouraged the growth of sale promotion. Some include:

1. The drive for short-term, measurable results. As competition has increased, marketing managers have come under increased pressure

from management to show what has been achieved with the dollars invested. Because sales promotion often generates more immediate and measurable sales responses than does advertising, the shift of funds has become an obvious choice for brand managers.

2. The "changing" consumer. Today's consumer is better educated, more sophisticated, and more market experienced. The result has been that he or she has become less brand loyal, more willing to shop at the store shelf for special offers, and more responsive to in-store promotional efforts by the manufacturer and retailer. If products are perceived to be at parity, then price becomes the major decision-making variable.

3. The surplus marketplace. With the rise of global competition, more and more brands have flooded the market. There are simply too many products, too many stores, and too much promotion for today's slow to no-growth economy. When there is a surplus in the marketplace, price competition generally emerges. As a method of making short-term price adjustments, sales promotion has been the favored strategy over general media advertising.

Because sales promotion directed toward the trade has a much faster and a greater impact than that directed to the consumer, there has been a major shift in emphasis from consumer-oriented activities, such as media advertising or consumer-oriented sales promotion, to trade promotion. It is not likely this shift will reverse itself in favor of media advertising in the near future. Therefore, it is very important that the advertising planner understand the pressures on the manufacturer, and the need to maintain a substantial budget in trade promotion to assure product distribution and availability. Indeed, this shift in manufacturer emphasis makes it imperative that the advertising planner integrate the advertising plan with the sales promotion and merchandising plan to assure final market success.

With this brief overview of the importance of sales promotion and the reasons why marketers have shifted their former emphasis on media advertising to that of integrated marketing communications, and particularly sales promotion, we are ready to look at how sales promotion fits in an advertising campaign.

THE BASICS OF CONSUMER SALES PROMOTION

Because the advertising planner is most interested in the development of activities aimed at the ultimate consumer, we deal first with basics of consumer sales promotion. To understand how sales promotion works, however, we must first look at how consumers buy and use products.

Exhibit 13–5 illustrates the normal pattern of consumer purchase and consumption of a product. The consumer purchases a supply of the product (on our scale, 100) at point 100. Over time that supply is used up. An-

Exhibit 13–5   Normal Purchase Pattern without Deals

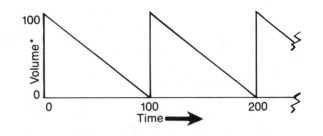

SOURCE: John C. Totten and Martin P. Block, *Analyzing Sales Promotion: Text and Cases* (Chicago: Commerce Communication, 1987): 46.
*Average Purchase Volume Index = 100; Average Interpurchase Time Index = 200.

other purchase is made at point 200 where the supply is again replenished up to point 100. That too, is used up over time, and so on. The objective of all sales promotion, merchandising, and the like is to attempt to change this normal, traditional, consumer purchasing pattern.

There are three ways in which a consumer can alter this patterned purchase and usage model. Exhibit 13–6 illustrates what happens when the consumer accelerates the purchase time. In other words, rather than purchasing at point 100 and 200, and so on, the time of purchase is moved forward. Thus, although there is no change in purchase volume, there is a 25 percent acceleration in repurchase time.

Exhibit 13–6   Accelerate Purchase Time

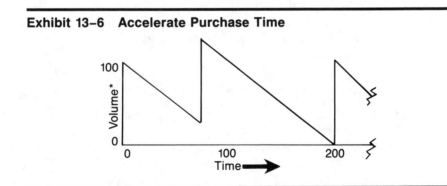

SOURCE: John C. Totten and Martin P. Block, *Analyzing Sales Promotion: Text and Cases*: 46.
*This example indicates no change in purchase volume, but a 25 percent acceleration in repurchase time.

Exhibit 13–7   Stockpiling

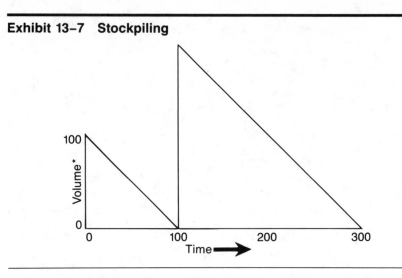

SOURCE: John C. Totten and Martin P. Block, *Analyzing Sales Promotion: Text and Cases*: 46.
*Purchase twice as much product, time to next purchase is twice as long.

Another change that consumers can make in purchasing is to stockpile. (See Exhibit 13–7.) In this instance, the consumer purchases twice as much product at time 200 (up to volume level 200) and takes twice as much time to use up and to repurchase.

The final alternative is for the consumer to increase consumption of the product. Increased consumption is illustrated in Exhibit 13–8. In this case, the consumer purchases at the normal volume during a period, but uses the product up more rapidly and is back in the market to purchase earlier than normal, before time 200.

Exhibit 13–8   Consumption Increase

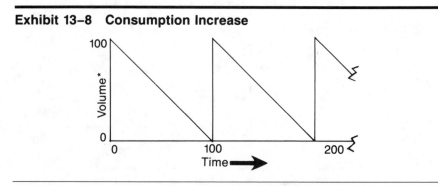
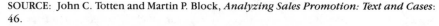

SOURCE: John C. Totten and Martin P. Block, *Analyzing Sales Promotion: Text and Cases*: 46.
*Purchase normal volume, but back into the market faster than normal.

The importance of these models of consumer purchasing behavior to the sales promotion person is quite clear. An attempt to influence the normal purchasing patterns of consumers in some way is made with sales promotion techniques.

In general, we can say sales promotion has three basic goals:

1. To obtain trial
2. To load the consumer with the product
3. To build continuity of purchase

The first objective, to obtain trial, is fairly clearcut. Using either a reduced price or another incentive, the marketer hopes to get the consumer to try the product. The assumption is that once the consumer tries the product, even at a reduced price, if they are pleased with its performance, they will then return to make another purchase at full price. This is the initiation of the normal purchase pattern as shown in Exhibit 13–5. Some common sales promotion techniques used to build trial are couponing, sampling, and free offers.

The second basic objective is to "load" the consumer. The idea is to get the consumer to accelerate the purchase time (Exhibit 13–6), stockpile (Exhibit 13–7), or increase consumption (Exhibit 13–8). The belief is that if the product is offered on promotion, the consumer will purchase sooner than planned, and if the product is on hand, it will be used up. Alternatively, if the sales promotion event encourages the consumer to stockpile, that is to keep a larger than normal supply of the product on hand, that will insulate the consumer from sales promotion activities by the competition. Therefore, the marketer is willing to adjust the price–value relationship of the product for a limited period simply to achieve this second objective. Commonly used sales promotion tactics to load the consumer include buy one/get one free offers, bonus packs, multiple purchase coupons, and rebates.

The third general goal of sales promotion is to build continuity of purchase. Given the low risk inherent in the purchase and use of most consumer products today, brand switching has become a major activity for most consumers and a major problem for most marketers. Thus, the marketer uses sales promotion to convince consumers to continue purchasing the same product brand time after time. Some of the most common sales promotion techniques used to provide continuity of purchase are rebate offers that require multiple purchases, timed release coupons (coupons that become valid over a period of time), and stamp or coupon saving plans.

This explanation of consumer purchasing patterns and the general goals of sales promotion should make it clear that certain sales promotion techniques are designed to achieve certain marketing goals. We'll discuss these techniques in more detail later in the chapter. For the moment, the planner should understand there are two basic tasks in planning any sales promotion event: (a) developing a knowledge of the consumer's purchasing and usage patterns, and (b) having clear-cut objectives in terms of changing basic purchasing patterns with sales promotion techniques.

THE BASICS OF TRADE AND RETAILER SALES PROMOTION

In general, the goal of most sales promotion directed to the retailer or trade is to stimulate activity at the retail level in order to generate greater than normal product and sales movement. Trade promotion is important because the retailer's efforts to generate sales volume are many times more productive than those of the manufacturer. (An example of the sales volume retail promotion can achieve in a one-week period is illustrated in Exhibit 13–9.

Exhibit 13–9   Sales Response to Promotion

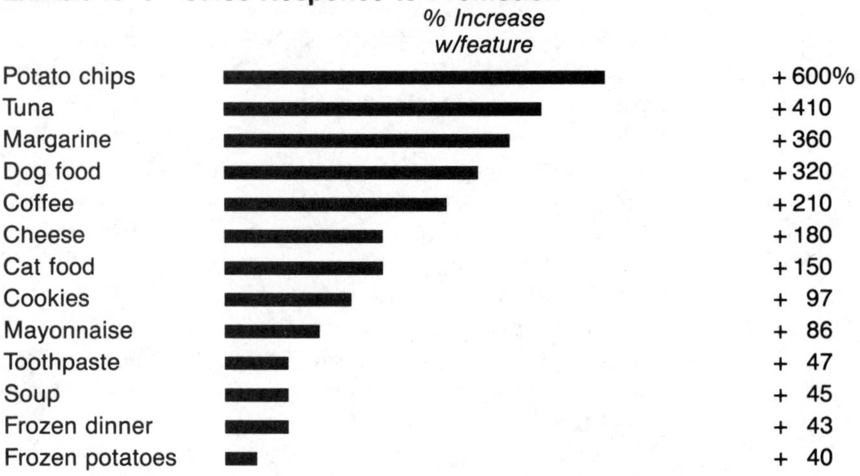

% Increase w/feature

Product	% Increase w/feature
Potato chips	+ 600%
Tuna	+ 410
Margarine	+ 360
Dog food	+ 320
Coffee	+ 210
Cheese	+ 180
Cat food	+ 150
Cookies	+ 97
Mayonnaise	+ 86
Toothpaste	+ 47
Soup	+ 45
Frozen dinner	+ 43
Frozen potatoes	+ 40

SOURCE: *The IRI Marketing Factbook,* 1984.

To be effective, however, these types of promotions must have a reduction in shelf price plus an in-store display or a newspaper advertising feature or some other effort.

With the retailer able to generate a high level of sales increase, most manufacturers are anxious to get in-store trade support for their products. In addition, retailer support commonly can enhance manufacturer-originated sales promotion programs many fold.

It is important here to understand what motivates the trade or retailer. If we think of the retail store as simply a big box in which the retailer puts items and the consumer takes those items out, several factors become clear. First, as with any type of container, there is a finite amount of space. Only a certain number of products can be stocked. So, the retailer's choices are limited. If something is to be added to the store, something must come out. Second, the retailer wants to put items in the store that customers will want. No wanted items, no traffic and no sales. Because the retailer's largest single cost is commonly inventory, he or she tries to find items that will sell quickly. This is turnover—how fast the item moves through the store: the faster the inventory turnover, the more profit for the retailer (assuming, of course, a profit is made on the item). Third, the retailer wants to stock products that bring people to the store. Because most retailers rely heavily on impulse purchases in the store, the greater the store traffic generated, the greater the sales. Therefore, the retailer wants products that will help him or her generate impulse purchases as the customers move through the store. Fourth, the retailer wants to stock items that give him the greatest margin (or difference) between what he pays for the product and what he sells it for. So, the real goal of all retailers is to stock products with fast turnover and high margins.

To give the retailer an incentive to stock and promote a product, a manufacturer may (a) offer sales promotion activities that change the margin the retailer makes on the product, such as a price reduction, free goods offer, or the like; (b) promote events that bring traffic to the store, such as multi-product promotions, demonstrations, and the like; and (c) sponsor activities that help improve the movement of the product (turnover). Typical trade or retail promotions that speed turnover include distributing consumer coupons, and sharing the cost of advertising (co-op) or displays with advertisers.

One thing that some manufacturers have difficulty understanding is that the goals of their promotion are quite different from those of the retailer. In most cases, the retailer really doesn't care which brand of a product he or she sells, assuming that the margins and turnover are about the same. The retailer is interested only in selling something to every person who enters the store. In most instances, the retailer makes about the same profit on competing brands; there is little reward for his or her efforts to get consumers to switch. Alternatively, the manufacturer is primarily interested in the sale of his or her particular brand. Therefore, most manufacturer advertising and promotional activities are designed to sell the brand, while most retailer activities are designed to generate store traffic and to sell something. These are the reasons for much of the conflict between manufacturer and retailer in the promotional area.

Manufacturers have three basic objectives or goals for most sales promotion that is directed against the retail trade:

1. To hold onto or to obtain additional shelf space in the store.
2. To convince the retailer to build or maintain in-store displays on behalf of the promoted product.
3. To encourage the retailer to support the brand and/or promotion in the retailer's own advertising. Commonly, this sort of support consists of newspaper features, television advertising, and the like.

The most common method used by manufacturers to generate retailer support is some sort of short-term price adjustment. Some of the more common approaches include reducing the price of the product for a limited period of time or on a limited amount of volume, or offering various types of allowances based on the purchase of a certain volume of the product. These allowances are usually related in some way to the price of the product, or give the retailer some incentive to do something out of the ordinary in the store. They often involve offering advertising allowances to cover the cost of brand advertising in the retailer's local advertising; or shelf or stocking allowances designed to partially pay the retailer's cost of allocating shelf space to the brand (often this is called a "slotting allowance" when applied to new products or to get new space in the store). Another alternative is to offer a display allowance to help offset the retailer's cost of building special displays in the store on behalf of the brand being promoted.

As the trade has increased in importance to the manufacturer, the number of trade or retail promotional activities has increased as well. For example, most supermarket chains today can provide major promotions for about twenty to twenty-five brands each week (that is, to provide a newspaper feature, an off-shelf display, or end-of-aisle display). Most major supermarket chains are presented with 200 or more offers each week on the more than 10,000 items they commonly stock from manufacturers seeking in-store promotion. Thus, most retailers can use only about ten percent of the "deals" being offered to them. Because of the limited capability of the retailer, the acceptance of a promotional offer from a manufacturer is a major consideration for the retailer and a major goal of the manufacturer. We'll deal more with this subject in developing sales promotion strategies for the trade in a later section. Now, we look at what sales promotion can and can't do for brand marketers.

WHAT SALES PROMOTION CAN AND CAN'T DO

From the earlier discussion, it might sound as if sales promotion in the hands of an expert can achieve most of a marketer's goals. This is simply not the case. Although sales promotion, if properly planned and executed, can create fairly substantial shifts in consumer purchasing, there are limitations on what sales promotion can and can't do.

Sales promotion can accomplish six specific things:

1. Sales promotion can help make a sale. By adjusting the price–value relationship, sales promotion can be used to generate immediate sales.
2. Sales promotion can help maintain present customers. One of the key things that marketers are learning is that their present customers are likely their best customers. Therefore, there is increasing emphasis on activities that attempt to hold onto or build brand loyalty.
3. Sales promotion can increase purchase frequency. As we've already discussed, sales promotion is quite successful in getting consumers to purchase and use the product more frequently.
4. Sales promotion can increase the size and number of purchases made by consumers. (See Exhibits 13–6, 7, and 8.)
5. Sales promotion can be used to support the image that the brand currently has. It can also be used to reinforce the advertising messages that are being delivered. Advertising and sales promotion must work together to present the same message and same feel for the product in all tactical activities. This is perhaps one of the most important factors that the advertising planner should consider.
6. Sales promotion can help generate sale channel support. We will deal more with this in the section on trade and retailer promotion but, in general, sales promotion is a most effective approach to get retailers and others in the channels to promote and merchandise the product at the store level.[2]

There are some things that sales promotion alone simply can't do:

1. Sales promotion can't change negative attitudes. If the product is not well received or well thought of, sales promotion cannot change consumers' opinions.
2. Sales promotion can't reverse a declining sales trend. Although sales promotion may, on occasion, give a sale bump or may help flatten or slow down the decline curve, alone, it cannot reverse the sales trend. For example, no amount of sales promotion on behalf of slide rules would have prevented consumers from converting from them to electronic calculators.
3. Sales promotion can't create a brand image, with the exception of that of a promotional brand. Although sales promotion for Marlboro can help support and reinforce the "cowboy" image which has been

---

[2]Adopted in part from Don E. Schultz and William A. Robinson, *Sales Promotion Management* (Chicago: Crain Books, 1982): 51–67.

established, sales promotion alone could not have created that image. It requires advertising, public relations, and other communication techniques.

4. Sales promotion cannot compensate for inadequate levels of advertising. One of the most dangerous strategies a marketer can take is to convert a substantial amount of the available marketing funds to sales promotion and ignore advertising, public relations, direct marketing, and the like. It takes a combination of market communications, including substantial amounts of advertising, to build and maintain a brand. Advertising and sales promotion work hand in glove. Therefore, they must be planned and implemented together.

5. Sales promotion cannot overcome basic product problems. If there is a product problem, sales promotion, because of its ability to build purchase and trial, will do more to highlight product problems than almost any other promotional approach. If the product is no good, no one will want to buy it, no matter how much promotional activity is used.

6. Sales promotion alone cannot generate channel loyalty. Some marketers believe if they consistently promote, they will gain the support and loyalty of the trade and retailers. Trade partners are just that, partners. They will always be driven by what is best for them. So although they will promote the marketer's products, they will do so only as long as it improves their own business. When it doesn't, they will stop.[3]

With an understanding of these basics of sales promotion, we can start to consider the organization and planning of specific sales promotion activities.

HOW THE UPC CODE AND SCANNERS CHANGED SALES PROMOTION

Before moving into the specifics of strategy and planning of sales promotion, it's important to understand how the electronic gathering of information on product sales and movement has changed the ways in which sales promotion is planned and executed.

Up until the early 1970s most records of product shipment and movement were kept in very gross measures. For example, the manufacturer counted the cases of products shipped to the retailer but spent little time analyzing such things as package size, flavors, and the like. The retailer did much the same. The retailer knew what volume he or she had sold but did little analysis of why or how, relying primarily on experience and instinct

[3]Adopted in part from Don E. Schultz and William A. Robinson, *Sales Promotion Management* (Chicago: Crain Books, 1982): 68–74.

for repurchase. Most manufacturer's information on what was moving, where it was moving to, pricing, competitive activity, and the like was based on estimations of activity in a sample of stores across the country. This was then projected to the whole. Retailers usually used some form of estimating procedure as well.

In the mid-1970s, the Universal Product Code (UPC) was introduced. These bar codes have been placed on each specific item (sku) stocked in the store. This UPC bar code allows each product to be identified when passed over a scanner in a retail outlet. The UPC code identifies the product, brand, size, flavor, retail price, and so on. Almost overnight, retailers began to know exactly what products were selling through their stores. Likewise, research organizations formed to gather this UPC code/scanner data from retailers and offered it, along with analysis, to the manufacturers. For the first time, manufacturers and retailers alike knew exactly what products were being sold, at what stores, at what time of the year, in what volume, at what price, and so on. In addition, with some analysis, it became possible to measure the various combinations of sales promotion techniques, for example, price adjustment, displays, features, and amount of shelf space, and determine the optimal mix in terms of sales, volume, return on investment, and so on.

With the development of a more sophisticated computer program, retailers turned from looking simply at sales to examining the specific profit on each of the more than 10,000 items in the store. Called Direct Product Profit (DPP), this new analysis provided the retailer with not just sales volume, movement, and turns, but with a record of the actual profit each product in the store provided. For example, although sugar has great overall sales volume, it is bulky, takes up a great deal of shelf space, has a low margin, and is easily damaged. So, today, when a retailer looks at the sugar category, he or she knows the product must be stocked, but because the DPP is low, the amount of shelf space, the number of brands carried, and so on are reduced. Alternatively, a product like a cold remedy takes up little space, has a high margin, and although it doesn't turn over as often as some other products, it does provide a substantial DPP. So, the retailer expands the space for cold remedies and perhaps even the number of brands, while the space and number of brands for sugar is reduced.

Today, this is the sort of sophisticated analysis the retailer undertakes to determine which products and which brands will be stocked and promoted in the store. And, DPP is the type of very complex, computer-based analysis that most brand managers must use in an attempt to influence the retailer to either increase the shelf space, display, or promotion of their individual brands. Advertising planners must understand that planning sales promotion today is a very complex and sophisticated process, one which goes far beyond just preparing a coupon drop or inserting a premium in the carton.

BASIC SALES PROMOTION STRATEGY FOR THE MANUFACTURER

We now look at the basic approaches that manufacturers of package goods can use to plan strategic sales promotion programs. Although each product, each category, and each brand is different, these are some generalized strategies that can be applied to most consumer products.

Two basic promotional strategies are available to most consumer product marketers, "push" or "pull" or a combination of the two. A "push" strategy puts the emphasis on getting the product into the distribution channels, assuming that once there, the retailer will do the necessary promotion to move the product to the ultimate consumer. The alternative, "pull," puts most of the promotional emphasis on the consumer, assuming that if consumer demand can be built, the consumer will go to the store, ask for the product and, the retailer, sensing consumer demand, will stock and promote it. We treat each of these approaches as if they were black or white; in truth, most marketers use a combination of the two by promoting to both the retailer and the consumer. For purposes of discussion, however, we'll look at push and pull separately, as a basis of comparison.

SALES PROMOTION WITH A PUSH STRATEGY

With a push strategy, the emphasis is on the trade or retailer. Therefore, the objectives of the manufacturer are (a) to get the product into the store and stocked on the shelf in the largest display possible; (b) to get the retailer to display the product in some way out of the ordinary, generally off the shelf; or (c) to get the retailer to feature the brand in some way either with a price reduction, a sign, or an advertisement, alone, or with some other attention-attracting device.

The Growing Power of the Retailer

One of the key concepts the planner should consider in any kind of promotional activity is the great power of the retailer to move large volumes of merchandise in short periods of time. And, the retailer's ability to increase sales grows each day as more and more consumers place their loyalty with the retailer and his or her store, rather than with the manufacturer's brand.

Exhibit 13–10 shows the results which can be obtained on average through promotion for a broad number of product categories in a wide number of retail food stores.

As can be seen, a 10 percent price discount generally results in about a 20 percent sales increase during the week of the promotion. When a feature is added, that is, the addition of the reduced price offer in a newspaper advertisement, the increase is approximately 78 percent. When an

Exhibit 13–10   Trade Promotions Average Category Response

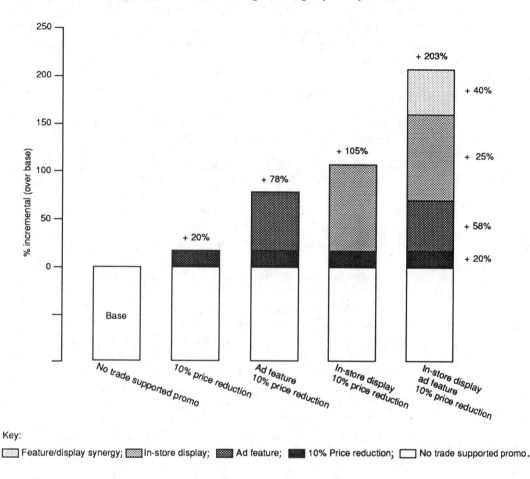

Key:

▦ Feature/display synergy; ▦ In-store display; ▦ Ad feature; ■ 10% Price reduction; ☐ No trade supported promo.

SOURCE: John C. Totten, "Health and Beauty Aids: A Sharp Pencil Is Needed" (unpublished paper, 1985): Figure 9.

in-store display is used with the price reduction, sales increase 105 percent and when all three are used in combination, sales generally increase by over 200 percent. Although these figures apply only to food stores, similar results are often obtained in drug chains and mass merchandising outlets. There are two lessons of value here for the advertising planner. First, the retailer can move large volumes of merchandise with promotion. There is practically nothing an individual manufacturer can do alone that will generate a 200 percent sales increase in a single week. Therefore, the manufacturer really needs the retailer's help to make promotion work. Second, it is apparent that synergy exists between the various promotional elements. Although price reductions and features and displays alone work well, the use of these techniques in combination is even more powerful. The advertising planner should keep these concepts in mind when developing promotional plans.

General Objectives of Trade Promotion

Having discussed the power of the retailer to move merchandise, we can now outline the general objectives of trade promotion.

1. Gain retailer support. Most trade promotion seeks to get the retailer to either support the manufacturer's promotion or to develop a promotional program on the local level.
2. Build or manage inventories. Often the manufacturer, to achieve economies of scale in manufacturing, will offer promotions to move inventory from the plant or warehouse into the retail channels. As an alternative, the manufacturer might plan to introduce a new package or a new product. In such cases, the manufacturer might offer some sort of promotion to move the new product into the retail store or to get the old product off the retail shelf.
3. Launch a new product. Given that most stores are fully stocked now, often the manufacturer will offer some type of sales promotion either to gain shelf space or to get movement for a new product.
4. Widen distribution. Promotion to the trade is widely used in an attempt to either widen or improve distribution of the product in the retail outlets. Sometimes, the goal is to get more shelf space. Other times it is to get the product stocked in more stores or new types of stores. In any case, sales promotion is used as some form of incentive to get retailer support for the product.

Sales Promotion Decisions

When the planner is starting to think about trade promotion, the first step is to determine what objective the promotion is designed to achieve. Basic trade promotional planning consists of decisions about the following:

1. What product is to be promoted? This would include consideration of questions about package size, flavors, color, and the like.
2. What is the goal of the promotion? Is the objective to achieve a shelf price reduction? An off-shelf display? A combination of the two?
3. What shelf price is desired during the promotion period? If the goal is a reduction of the shelf price for a period of time, how much of a

reduction? Or, what level of promotional pricing compared to the competition?

4. What length of time for in-store activity? Most promotional programs by retailers run for one week. Is that long enough for the brand? How long should the promotion last?

5. What level of allowance? The final question is, What level of trade allowance, discount, or promotional activity is needed to achieve the objectives which have already been determined?

To achieve these goals, the manufacturer has only a few strategic alternatives available. First among them is that of price reduction or adjustment. By reducing the price the hope is the retailer will receive a greater margin and will thus be interested in promoting the sale of the brand to the store's customers to generate this additional profit. Second is the offering of funds, materials, or assistance to help the retailer either generate store traffic or develop some sort of in-store activity that will encourage the consumer to purchase more of the brand, use it more often or at a greater level for a period of time. Third, increasingly as manufacturers understand the goals of the retailer, programs are being developed in which the manufacturer helps the retailer to sell not just more of the marketer's brand, but of other products in the store as well. For example, a soup company might develop a combination product in-store program that also helps sell crackers, or bread for sandwiches, or the like.

For the most part, push strategies involve the use of tactics that help the retailer generate additional sales of the brand within the store with some emphasis on generating store traffic and the sale of complementary products as well. We look now at the tactics that are commonly used in a push strategy.

Push Strategy Tactics

Because most of the emphasis is on gaining distribution and assisting the retailer in getting brand movement, the tactics used are generally variations on the same theme, money off or money to help the retailer build his or her own local promotional program.

The most common tactics include:

1. Price deals. These are usually special price concessions, over and above normal discounts, granted by the manufacturer for a limited period of time. These concessions may take the form of a price-off or off-invoice allowance. These are simply additional reductions of the list price of the product. A second approach is that of free goods or extra cases of the product when a minimum amount is purchased. For example, one free with twelve, or buy four, get one free. The

hope is that the retailer will pass this reduced price along to the consumer thus creating additional in-store demand for the brand.

2.   Performance deals. An alternative to the price deal is to add some sort of requirement for the retailer to "earn" the price reduction or bonus offer. For example, to receive the $3.00-per-case-off-invoice allowance, the retailer must insert a mention of the product in his or her regular newspaper advertisement, or must build a display in the store or give extra shelf space to the brand for a period of time. Generally, the retailer must provide some form of proof that the activity required was performed, such as a tear sheet of the advertisement or a picture of a display.

3.   Allowances. In an attempt to get the retailer to support the brand in his or her advertising and promotion, the manufacturer may provide an allowance to help pay a part of the cost of local advertising or to help pay for the cost of building a display. In general, these allowances are for advertising, display, or other in-store merchandising. Again, the retailer must provide some sort of evidence that the performance took place through an affidavit, picture, tear sheet, or the like.

4.   Cooperative advertising. Realizing that retailer promotion, particularly promotion that is location and price specific, works very well, many manufacturers have set up systems to share the cost of local advertising with the retailer. In these agreements, the manufacturer offers to share the cost, commonly up to 50 percent, of advertising that the retailer runs to support the brand at the local level. Most of these agreements cover newspaper advertising, but an increasing number are also now available for radio, television, and even circulars and flyers developed by the retailer. Although there are some problems with cooperative agreements, such as the advertising rate to be paid, the media to be used, and sometimes the aesthetics of the advertising itself, more and more manufacturers are finding that localized advertising, particularly that which offers some type of retailer promotion, is a very effective way of moving merchandise.

5.   Point-of-purchase materials. The increasing emphasis on shelf shopping by consumers, which results in in-store brand purchasing decisions, has contributed to the renewed interest in the whole area of point of purchase. The most common type of material is developed and paid for by the manufacturer and shipped to the individual retailer for local display. These include such items as shelf-talkers, wire hangers, posters, and dump bins. Although there is much waste in this approach, with in-store support, its effectiveness in terms of moving large amounts of the brand often makes it worthwhile.

Increasingly, point-of-purchase materials are becoming permanent store fixtures. For example, cigarette stands, case dividers, aisle and direction signage, and clocks promote individual brands while serving a useful purpose in the store. In some cases, in-store displays—shopping cart signs, checkout videos, electronic price markings—have actually become and are sold as regular media. As more and more consumer decisions are made in the store, it becomes more and more important for the planner to find or devise ways to get customers' attention at the point of purchase to reinforce the advertising message.

6. Dealer loaders. A dealer loader is designed to do exactly what the name implies—load the dealer with a product. One type of dealer loader packs the product in a display, such as a wheelbarrow, wagon, or other valuable premium. The premium and product are used as a display unit. When the product has been sold, the retailer keeps the premium.

    Dealer loaders may take almost any form, from a small, impersonal gift to sporting goods, clothing, or even expensive foreign trips for the retailer and his family. Dealer loaders are often tied to a specific-size purchase, with the value of the loader being proportionate to the value of the offer. This type of promotion is frequently used to support a new advertising program with the loader tied to the theme of the campaign.

7. Contests. Dealer contests have grown in size and importance over the years. It is not unusual for retailers to have opportunities to win very expensive prizes in contests sponsored by advertisers. Contests are usually tied to specific achievements by the retailer, such as purchases, total sales, sales based on quotas, sales increases over previous periods, or sales of a new or existing product line.

    Contests often work better with independent retailers than with chain stores. Many chain store operations have very strict rules about contests, premiums, and gifts that may be given or awarded to their store managers. In these instances, clearance is required from the chain's headquarters before any type of contest can be conducted with employees.

8. Push money. Often called "spiffs" or "PM," push money is money paid by the advertiser directly to salespeople, in general those on the retail floor, to promote specific items in the product line. A refrigerator manufacturer, for example, might offer "PM" or "spiff" on a certain model. During the time the promotion is in effect, the retail salespeople are encouraged to personally promote that particular model because they will be rewarded with an additional cash prize. Usually spiffs or PM works only for those products in which the retail salesperson is a key selling factor. The device is not effective for products sold in self-service situations or those with a low selling price.

In nearly every case, the use of PMs requires the cooperation and approval of the store manager or the headquarters office of the retail store. Because offering money to employees is regarded as an inducement, retail management must be consulted prior to the offering of such a program to their employees.

Although push money is still used, the legality of the practice has been questioned, and many advertisers are reviewing their use of this promotional tool.

9. Sales meetings. A final, widely used trade promotional tactic is the sales meeting conducted for retailers by the advertiser's sales representative or the broker sales force.

    Sales meetings take many forms, from a simple meeting in a hotel room with a small group to a formal, traveling, professional show. The determining factor is the importance of the announcement to the advertiser and the wholesaler. The advertising campaign is usually a key feature of a sales meeting program. Special emphasis is often given to the geographic areas represented by the retailers present. Thus, part of the development of many consumer-product advertising campaigns is a brief outline of how the material will be presented to the retailers and the sales force.

Legal Restrictions on Trade Promotion

Federal controls on all forms of trade promotion are spelled out in the Robinson-Patman Act, and administered by the Federal Trade Commission. The act requires that all trade promotion offers by a manufacturer or through a distributor for the manufacturer must be made equally available and in proportionate value to all retailers in the market area. In other words, manufacturers must treat all retailers alike or on an equal basis. Thus, if a volume discount is offered to a very large retail chain, a proportionate discount must be made to smaller retailers as well. The Robinson-Patman Act has been defined as being applicable in individual market areas, commonly in the form of ADIs or DMAs or SMSAs. Therefore, a manufacturer can offer one promotion in the Denver market and another in the Salt Lake City market. For the advertising and promotion planner, the key words in Robinson-Patman are "proportionately equal." Therefore, almost any promotion can be developed as long as it meets the "proportionately equal" test and is not in restraint of trade.

Hazards of Trade Promotion

From the earlier discussion, it might appear that trade promotion is the answer to all the manufacturer's advertising and promotion problems. Simply offer enough deals and the retailer will "push" the product out the door. Unfortunately, it isn't quite that simple. There are some major hazards to trade promotion as well:

1. No pass through. Probably the biggest problem with trade promotion is that when the manufacturer offers a reduced price to the retailer, he or she assumes the retailer will pass it along to the consumer. That's not always the case. Sometimes, the retailer simply takes the price reduction and improves his margin on the product. So, although the manufacturer had hoped for a change in the retail price and perhaps some additional effort on the part of the retailer, the retailer simply absorbed the extra discount and improved his margin for a period of time.

    The most obvious solution is, of course, the requirement that the retailer perform some sort of price reduction or activity on behalf of the brand to earn the discount or deal. Coupon requirements, for example, are that the retail price be lowered, signage placed in the store, and the product be featured in local advertising. This is generally a good solution, but it is very hard for the manufacturer to enforce. If the retailer doesn't perform as agreed, and the retailer is a major account, how far can the manufacturer go in enforcing the terms of the agreement. So, although trade promotion can generate substantially increased sales, in some cases, it results in only substantially increased margins for the retailer and little or no reward for the manufacturer.

2. Expectation for the future. Once the manufacturer starts to promote continuously—offer price discounts or other incentives on a regular basis—the expectation of the retailer is that such events will continue. The retailer, like the consumer, becomes deal prone. He starts to buy and promote the product only when a deal is offered. In short, the special price soon becomes the normal price. The saying in the business is, "Trade promotion is easy to start but hard to stop." Advertising planners should be wary of continuous or regularly scheduled promotional discounts even though they do move product volume. These kinds of promotions can all too often take the place of good, solid advertising and selling of the product.

3. Part of the retailer profit. Today, there is so much trade promotion that, in many cases, these manufacturer-originated activities have become a part of the retailer's profit margin. In other words, the retailer depends so much on the manufacturer discounting the product or offering other forms of price deals, that they have factored that into the profit margin of the store. When this becomes the case, the retailer pressure for discounts or deals simply to help maintain margins becomes intense. So, if the manufacturer doesn't continue to promote, the retailer often replaces the nonpromoted brand with a pro-

moted brand to maintain or improve the margin of the store. In such cases, sales promotion has ceased to be a strategy and becomes only a tactic to keep the product on the shelf.

4. Forward buying. The retailer who takes advantage of a manufacturer's short-term promotional offer or deal and buys a great deal more of a product that can be sold during the promotional period is "forward buying." In other words, the retailer buys enough to last well into the future. The retailer does this because the promotional offer is for a limited period of time. If the retailer buys now and warehouses the excess stock, he or she can take the full margin on the reduced-price merchandise by selling it out at normal price over time. As long as the cost of warehousing and the value of invested capital are lower than the reduced price offered by the retailer, it is profitable for the retailer to forward buy. Until there are some restrictions imposed by the manufacturer, forward buying will continue. And, manufacturers will find that less and less of their volume is sold at anything close to the regularly established price.

5. Diversion. Diversion is just an extension of forward buying. In this case, however, the retailers stock up not for future use, but with the intent of offering the reduced-price merchandise to another retailer, usually in another part of the country. Thus, the buyer for a supermarket chain in Tampa, may well buy twice the anticipated needs of a promoted product. He or she may then call another retailer in Buffalo and offer the merchandise at something over the reduced price that the manufacturer is offering. Because there is no lower price in the Buffalo area at that time, the Buffalo retailer can buy at a discount, which makes him or her more competitive in that market. The retailer in Tampa takes the shipment from the manufacturer, holds part of the inventory, and ships the balance to the retailer in Buffalo. The Tampa retailer then bills the Buffalo retailer at the slightly higher rate. Both retailers are happy but the manufacturer isn't. The manufacturer offered the promotional price, assuming he would get activity in the Tampa stores. However, a large portion of the volume went to Buffalo, where the manufacturer may or may not get any sort of merchandising for the discount he offered.

Both forward buying and diversion are major problems for manufacturers today. Although the advertising planner has little control over these types of activities, he or she should know they exist and factor them into any type of merchandising or promotion plan that might be developed.

SALES PROMOTION WITH A PULL STRATEGY

With a pull strategy, the emphasis is on the consumer—getting the consumer to create sufficient demand for the product so that the manufacturer will have to stock it in the store and the consumer can then purchase there. Traditionally, marketers have relied on sales promotion to build brand usage, that is, the manufacturer has offered the product at a reduced price or with a changed price–value relationship, assuming that trial and satisfaction is tantamount to generating long-term sales. For example, Exhibit 13–11 illustrates how sales promotion at the consumer level is supposed to work. Having a certain market share level, the marketer develops and implements a sales promotion program. As a result of the promotion, sales go up. As a result of that additional trial and usage, the share for the brand should grow (in our example, from 10 to 11 percent share of market).

Exhibit 13–11   Consumer Promotions Are Supposed to Work Like This

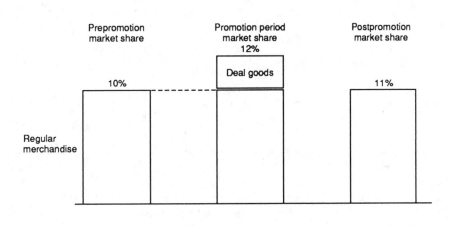

SOURCE: Adapted from Don E. Schultz and William A. Robinson, *Sales Promotion Management* (Chicago: Crain Books, 1982): 97.

In truth, most sales promotion programs perform like the one illustrated in Exhibit 13–12. The promotion does drive volume and share up during the time of the promotion. However, once the promotion is over, the share generally falls back to the base level or may even fall below it.

Thus, the basic concept of sales promotion—to offer a reduced price to get trial, assuming that repurchase at full price will occur later—is not borne out by current scanner data analysis. Today, there seems to be three basic reasons why sales promotion doesn't perform as we always thought it did:

1. **Brand switchers.** There are a large number of persons who switch brands on a regular basis, that is, they have an acceptable set of

**Exhibit 13–12 But Only Too Frequently They Work Like This...
or Even Like This!**

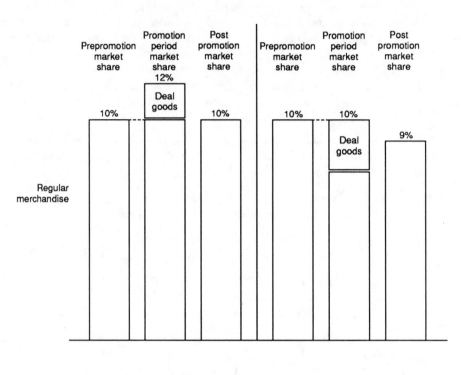

SOURCE: Adapted from Don E. Schultz and William A. Robinson, *Sales Promotion Management:* 98.

brands from which they shop. They simply buy the one currently being featured. Therefore, when there is a promotion, they will buy the promoted brand. When there isn't, they will purchase another acceptable brand on promotion. Their loyalty seems to be only to price.

2. Parity products. Many of the package goods offered have few differentiating features. In addition, the large amount of comparison advertising also seems to have convinced consumers that there is little difference between brands. Therefore, brand loyalty declines and consumers seem more and more to base their purchasing decisions on what is on sale rather than what brand benefits are available.

3. Shelf-shopping and consistent promotion. Because many consumers are pressed for time, they now do their shopping at the shelf, rather than from a predetermined shopping list. Because there is usually some brand in a category on promotion in the retail store at all times, it is easier to shop among those brands than to carefully analyze the differences. Thus, although the consumer may have entered the store with the intention of buying Brand A, the promotional program of Brand B, in the store and at the shelf, sways the purchasing decision.

Why Manufacturers Want to Promote Direct to Consumers

In spite of the problems of gaining long-term benefits from sales promotion, most marketers continue to attempt to influence consumers with sales promotion for three basic reasons:

1. Brand franchise. One of the major concerns of the manufacturer is to maintain the image or franchise for the brand that exists among consumers. Because the brand image has been built up over time and often at great expense, the manufacturer wants to maintain that image through the sales promotion program. Retailers, however, are primarily concerned with product movement; often their promotional activities have a detrimental effect on the brand and its image. Therefore, the manufacturer generally prefers to develop and implement the sales promotion program direct to consumers. That way he or she has control over the type of promotion used, which can enhance or maintain the brand image and franchise.
2. Control. Marketers prefer spending their promotional funds directly against the consumer because it gives them greater control over the type of promotion program that is used, and more control over its timing and activity level. When using a push strategy, the promotional programs are usually planned to fit the retailer's needs, not those of the manufacturer. Thus, consumer promotion gives the manufacturer greater control over the planning and implementation of the sales promotion program.
3. Creativity/lower cost/nonprice promotions. Most retailers, because they know price promotion works, use that approach on a regular basis. Often, the manufacturer, because he or she has a better understanding of the consumer and the product category, is able to plan and implement sales promotion programs that can build the brand and still generate sales, often at a lower cost than that of price promotion. In addition, most manufacturers feel that nonprice sales promotion can be more effective than traditional retailer price promotion if done in a creative manner.

The Consumer Franchise Building Concept of Sales Promotion

Most marketing experts agree that continuous price promotion probably has some long-term effect on the brand image and the brand franchise. Over the past twenty years, Robert M. Prentice has been developing the concept of "consumer franchise building" or CFB. Prentice's position, which he has backed up with a fairly large number of in-market tests, is that some sales promotion techniques contribute to the value of the brand image and franchise while others tend to detract or erode that image. Prentice's rationale for his CFB approach follows:

1. To generate profit over an extended period, a brand must build a strong consumer franchise. It must establish a significant, lasting value in the minds of an important segment of consumers.
2. But value isn't enough. Consumers must believe that the brand's value is worth the price. If they don't, the marketer will have to reduce the price or increase the value to the point where they are willing to buy it—to the point where consumers believe that value and price are in balance.
3. A brand's share of market at any given time reflects how consumers perceive the brand's price–value relationship in comparison with other brands.
4. How does the consumer arrive at his or her perception of brand value? Obviously, a lot depends on experience with the product and on its unique performance and the satisfaction it provides. But, a lot also depends on the ideas the consumer gets about the brand which make it uniquely different—in important respects—from competitive brands. These ideas arise from the brand's name, its positioning, the package, and the various marketing activities that implant unique and important ideas about the brand in the mind.
5. What kinds of marketing activities do this? I call them consumer franchise building (or CFB) activities. They include:

   Advertising. Perhaps the most common way to register such ideas (although some advertising, we have to admit, does a fairly poor job in this respect).

   Certain types of promotion. If they register unique and important selling ideas about the brand, including:

   Sampling—because the package highlights the product's advantages, because the proof of the pudding is in the eating, and because a descriptive folder with a strong selling message usually accompanies the sample—an ad, if you will.
   Cents-off coupons—distributed by the manufacturer by mail, or in print ads, or in or on a package. These coupons can also regis-

ter unique and important ideas about the brand—provided that
an effective selling message accompanies the coupon or appears
on it.

Demonstrations—either in-store or before economic or other
groups of consumers, are CFB activities. Service, material, recipes, and so on, which enhance the image of a brand and register
ideas of its unique superiority and value, are also CFB activities.

All these CFB activities perform two functions: (a) they build long-
term brand preference, and (b) they generate immediate sales (often more effectively than many people realize).

6. All other activities I classify as non-CFB activities. Their job is to accelerate the buying decision to generate immediate sales, but they
generally do not implant unique and important ideas about the brand
in the consumer's mind. Instead, they simply reduce the price or add
temporary, extraneous value (as in the case of most premiums and
contests) or help obtain retail distribution or cooperation. These are
important and necessary functions—but they do not register important and unique ideas about a brand in the mind.[4]

Although all sales promotion executives do not agree with Prentice's approach, he found that among the brands he studied, those that invested
less than 50 to 55 percent of their combined advertising/sales promotion
budget in CFB activities did not do as well in sales and profits as those who
did—a strong argument for the Prentice approach.

Sales Promotion Strategy versus Sales Promotion Tactics

Traditionally, most sales promotion activities have been very tactical in nature. It has only been within the past few years that sales promotion has
taken on a strategic approach with planners and managers setting objectives and using techniques to achieve both short- and long-term goals. Examples of sales promotion techniques that are usually tactical include basic
cents-off coupons, price-offs, and many rebate programs. The idea of such
promotions is apparently to give the consumer a price reduction in hopes
of getting an immediate sale. The problem is that there is very little value
to such promotion events beyond the immediate sales of the product.
They generally do little or nothing to enhance the brand, nor do they have
much, if any, long-term value for the brand or the company.

Exhibit 13-13 illustrates a more strategic approach as used by Philip Morris for its Marlboro brand of cigarettes. The Marlboro Country Store is a

[4]Robert M. Prentice, "How to Split Your Marketing Funds between Advertising and Promotion," *Advertising Age* (January 10, 1977): 49.

collection of self-liquidating premiums that will not only generate immediate sales, but also has some long-term value for the brand. The premiums in the Country Store associate Marlboro with high quality and enhance Marlboro's western image. In addition, each time the consumer uses the premium, he or she will be reminded of Marlboro. That's the difference between strategic and tactical sales promotion.

Exhibit 13–13   A Strategic Sales Approach

OBJECTIVES OF CONSUMER PROMOTION

With this general understanding of consumer or "pull" strategies, we can now start to consider the basic objectives of most consumer sales promotion. First, though, we must look at how much consumers take advantage of sales promotions to get some idea of the importance of planning this type of activity.

Exhibit 13–14 shows the value and importance of price promotion of food products in the U.S. households over the past few years. This chart was constructed from scanner data, therefore, the consumer may or may not have recognized that the products purchased were on promotion at the time of purchase. As you can see, a relatively small number of households make few purchases that don't have some form of promotional offer attached. Quite honestly, it would be almost impossible to buy all products at full price in a given year because sales promotion is so widely used today. From the chart it would appear that about 17 percent of U.S. households buy about 15–20 percent of their food store purchase on some sort of promotion.

Exhibit 13–14   How Households Use Price Promotions

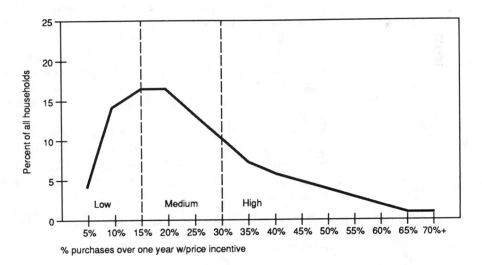

SOURCE: Gian M. Fulgoni, "Evaluating Price Sensitivity and Promotion Effectiveness Using UPC Scanner Data," presentation at Marketing Institute Trade Promotion Management Seminar, March 1983.

This chart shows how important promotion has become in the purchases of food products by American consumers. It is more than likely that sales promotion will become even more important in terms of influence and usage among consumer purchasers in the future.

The basic objectives of most sales promotion programs planned by manufacturers follow. These are the strategic goals that are usually set for sales promotion:

1. Trial. Loading. Continuity. By far, the most common objectives of sales promotion are to encourage consumers to either try, purchase multiple units, or continue to purchase certain brands of products. (Refer to basic objectives of sales promotion as outlined earlier in this chapter.)

2. Reach new users. Sales promotion is often used to get trial purchases from new users or new customers. Often, the promotion is run when the product is expanded into a new retail channel.

3. Trade up. Sales promotion can be used to encourage consumers to move up to a brand that offers better quality or carries a higher price.

4. Introduce a new product. Because consumers don't know of the benefits of a new product, sales promotion tactics are often used to reduce the cost of trial (couponing) or to encourage immediate trial (sampling).

5. Hold current users. In most product categories, the old 80–20 rule seems to hold true, that is, 80 percent of the volume is purchased by 20 percent of the customers. Because current users are so important, sales promotion is often used to maintain that usage or to try and build purchase continuity.

6. Increase usage. The "recipe" is the most common sales promotion technique employed to attempt to get consumers to use more of the product. Sales promotion tactics that show how to use the product or how to use the product more often or in greater quantity are important here.

7. Reinforce advertising. Often, sales promotion is used simply to reinforce the brand's advertising. Over the years, Virginia Slims cigarettes has offered a number of premiums, all of which have related to and extended and enhanced the feminine image that Slims has created through the advertising.

Understanding Consumer Segments for Sales Promotion

When advertising planners start to develop sales promotion programs one of the assumptions they often make is that all consumers are about the same. Nothing could be further from the truth. There are specific consumer segments in the market for almost all products. An understanding of these segments is vital to the planning of a successful promotion. One of the best ways to understand the consumer market when planning a sales promotion program is through the use of a segmentation scheme developed by Leigh McAlister, a marketing professor at the University of Texas. Her segmentation scheme is shown in Exhibit 13–15.

Exhibit 13–15   Segmentation Scheme

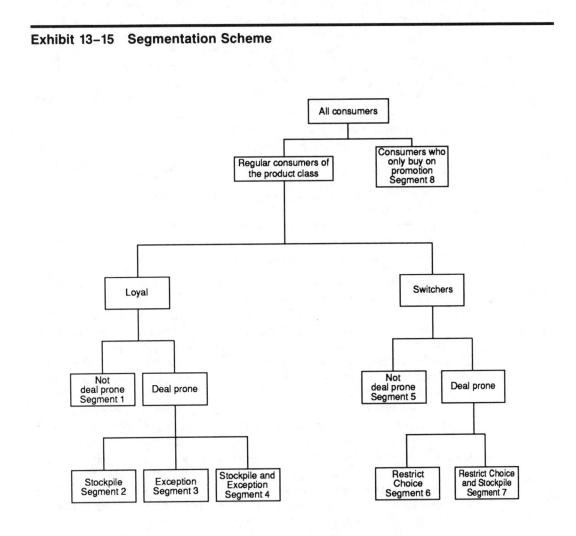

SOURCE: Leigh McAlister, "The Impact of Price Promotions on a Brand's Market Share, Sales Patterns and Profitability," *Marketing Science Institute Working Paper* (December 1986): Report 86–110.

As you can see, there are two basic groups of consumers. Those who are regular consumers of the product class (Segments 1 through 7) and those who buy only on promotion (Segment 8). Increasingly, scanner data show that there is a fairly large group of consumers in Segment 8. (Obviously there is some variation by product category but the general concept holds true). There are consumers who buy only when the product, brand, or category is on promotion. In other words, if Oscar Mayer Wieners are on sale, these people will make a purchase. When Oscar Mayer Wieners aren't on sale, they will either not buy wieners or buy another brand. The point is, the only time Oscar Meyer can make a sale to this group of consumers is through some form of promotional activity, usually a price reduction. These consumers will practically never buy Oscar Mayer Wieners at regular price. Unfortunately, for most package-goods product categories this group of consumers is growing thus making sales promotion more and more important in the overall marketplace.

The regular purchasers in the category can then be divided between those who are brand loyal and those who are brand switchers. Loyalty is generally defined as consumers who buy the same brand 75 percent of the time or more. Switchers are those who buy a specific brand less than 75 percent of the time.

Using this basic approach, we can start to identify groups of consumers who respond or don't respond in certain ways to promotional activities. McAlister has identified five basic groups:

- Group One: Not promotion sensitive (Segments 1 and 5). These consumers are not promotion or deal sensitive. They buy the same amount of the brand at the same rate regardless of any promotional activity. These groups will not increase purchases or consumption as a result of promotion. Marketers who promote to them actually lose money because the promotional price adjustment or promotion cost reduces the bottom-line profit and does not result in any additional volume or profit.
- Group Two: Loyal customers who stockpile in response to promotion (Segment 2). These consumers increase their purchases as a result of promotional activities, but these sales really only borrow from the future. In other words, consumers will buy now at a lower price and use up the excess when the product has returned to its regular price. Marketers who promote to this group lose money. They are simply selling volume now at a lower price that probably would have been sold later at a normal margin.
- Group Three: Exception and restrict choice (Segments 3 and 6). These consumers respond to promotion but only among a limited number of brands and only for a particular promotion. In other words, these consumers are swayed by promotion at a certain point but then return to

their regular purchase habits after the promotion has ended. Commonly, only one or a few units are purchased by these consumers as a result of the promotion. Therefore, the marketer makes incremental income on the promotion. The reason: The promotion holds the consumers of Segment 3 who might respond to competitive promotions and gains volume from the Segment 6 consumers who are switchers. This, of course, assumes that the promotional price is profitable to the marketer.

- Group Four: Stockpile and exception/restrict choice and stockpile (Segments 4 and 7). These consumer segments respond to promotion but rather than buying just one unit, they stockpile or purchase multiple units. The marketer makes money on both these groups through sales promotion (again, assuming the promotional price is profitable). Segment 4 consumers are retained by the brand as a result of the promotion because they would respond to promotion by other brands. Future sales are taken at a lower price now, but they would likely have been lost to competitive promotions at a future time. Segment 7 switches to the brand and stockpiles. As a result, the marketer gets present sales (and future usage) that probably would not have been obtained except with the promotional activity. Without the promotion, Segment 7 consumers would have responded to competitive promotions and stockpiled, thus taking them out of the market and, therefore, making them unavailable to the nonpromoted brand at any price.
- Group Five: Category expansion (Segment 8). This group was described in detail earlier.

Using this segmentation scheme, the planner can understand the various potential consumer groups that might respond to the promotion and start to plan promotional activity to appeal to those who are most attractive in terms of both sales and profits.[5]

Three Critical Consumer Characteristics

No matter what target group is selected by the advertising planner, scanner data analysis tends to show there are three characteristics among consumers that are critical in predicting future product purchases: past product use, brand or store loyalty, and deal-proneness.

1. Past product use. If someone has used a product in the category in the past, he or she is the best prospect for continued use of the brand. This supports the concept of the importance of the present

[5]Adapted from Leigh McAlister, "The Impact of Price Promotions on a Brand's Market Share, Sales Patterns and Profitability."

customer. If a person bought the brand in the past, he or she is the one most likely to purchase it again in the future.

2. Brand or store loyalty. The second significant characteristic is the loyalty that the consumer has demonstrated to the brand or to the store. Increasingly, it appears that consumers are relying on the retailer to make the brand decisions for them. In other words, the consumer may have some brands that he or she favors but if that brand is not stocked, then he or she will switch to the brand that is available in the store. Therefore, it is vital for the advertising planner to know the distribution pattern of the brand before starting to plan consumer promotions.

3. Deal-proneness. The final characteristic is the deal-proneness that the consumer exhibits when purchasing products in the category. If there is high deal-proneness, then it is likely that the promotion will get one-time purchasers who will not purchase again until the brand is promoted again (see discussion of McAlister model). Therefore, if there is high deal-proneness in the category or for the brand, the planner must assume that sales promotion will have little long-term effect on purchase habits.

Once we understand these basic strategic concepts of consumer sales promotion, we are ready to consider the tactics that can be used to implement these strategies.

Tactics for a Pull Strategy

In general, we might classify consumer sales promotion tactics as being either based on price or price-value adjustments, or on interest, that is, tactics that build consumer interest, involvement, or activity of some sort. We have separated the eight tactics or techniques into price promotion and interest promotion groups. In addition, there is another area of sales promotion, special events, that deserve separate treatment but is beyond the scope of this text.

Price promotion techniques.   The four price or price–value adjustment techniques that are available to the planner are couponing, refunds/rebates, value packs, and continuity programs.

Coupons.   Coupons are one of the oldest and one of the most effective sales promotion tools available to the campaign planner.

There are two types: *Manufacturer-distributed coupons* make an offer on a particular brand by the manufacturer of the product. These coupons may be redeemed at any retail store that carries the product. *Store coupons* are redeemable only at the store that offers the coupon. Stores develop their own coupons to generate promotional activity or, in some cases, to tie-in with manufacturer promotions. In some cases, manufacturers work with the retailer and agree to redeem the store's coupons for promotional considerations.

Manufacturer coupons allow the advertiser to reduce the price of his or her product at retail by a specific amount without relying on cooperation from the retailer. Coupons are used to induce trial of a new product or to gain trial of a new or improved product. They may also be used as distribution-forcing devices, as competitive weapons against promotional activities by competitors, and as control techniques to limit the number of redemptions of certain types of promotions.

Couponing can take many forms. The most traditional is a cents-off coupon distributed through media channels. Coupons may also be distributed by attaching them to or including them in the package. Another approach is the "cross-ruff"—a coupon for one product is either packaged with or printed on the package of another, often complementary product (not necessarily from the same manufacturer). Another popular method of coupon distribution is through cooperative mailings to selected homes. In these co-op mailings, an independent organization gathers the coupons of several marketers and mails or delivers them in a single envelope to consumer homes. The distribution cost is thus split among the participants.

The value of coupons varies as widely as the products on which they are used. The range for package goods coupons is usually from 25¢ to $1.00, although there are no prescribed norms. The average coupon face value is now 38¢, although this tends to increase according to the retail price of the product.

One of the major difficulties in a couponing program is determining the estimated level of redemption the coupon may achieve. Few, if any, coupons are ever redeemed at 100 percent rate. In addition, the method of distribution of the coupon has a direct effect on the redemption. Exhibit 13–16 shows the average redemption rate for the various types of grocery product coupons.

Coupon promotion costs are not limited to the value of the coupon. Several other factors must be included as well. Traditionally, coupons redeemed through retail stores allow an amount for retail handling. Currently, retailers receive 8¢ per retail coupon for handling regardless of coupon value. This amount is subject to change by agreement with the retailers or their trade organizations. In addition, a charge is made by the clearinghouse or other organization that gathers the coupons, reimburses the retailer, and bills the manufacturer. Although costs vary tremendously according to type of coupon, distribution, and other factors, the rule of thumb is to include about 4¢ per coupon for this service. Thus, a 25¢ coupon actually will cost the manufacturer about 37¢ for each redemption made (25¢ coupon value + 8¢ retailer handling + 4¢ clearinghouse = 37¢ total).

Exhibit 13–16   Grocery Products Coupon Redemption Rates by Media, 1988

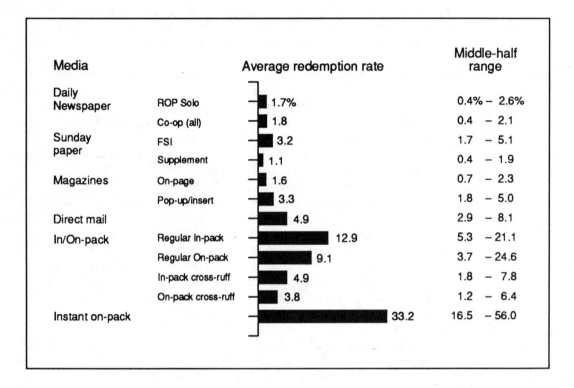

Redemption time is also a question. In most instances, an expiration date is included on the coupon. A cents-off coupon is usually valid from six months to one year after distribution. Although the majority of redemptions will occur in the first three months, redemptions may continue for the length of the coupon offer and sometimes after if retailers fail to honor the expiration date and continue to redeem the coupons at retail. Sufficient funds must be set aside by the campaign planner for estimated coupon redemption when this type of promotion is being planned.

Misredemption, that is, incorrectly or fraudulently redeemed coupons, is a major factor to be considered in any coupon redemption cost. Misredemption can occur anywhere along the distribution channel from the consumer to the retailer to the wholesaler.

A factor that affects the number of redemptions is the value of the coupon itself. Obviously, a coupon good for $1.00 off has much more appeal than one for 10¢. Other factors that affect redemptions include the product category, whether the product is purchased regularly or occasionally, the amount of discount off the regular retail price, and the percentage discount off the purchase price that the coupon allows. Most clearinghouses have developed estimates of redemption based on their experience with various types of coupons. These estimates may be used to help determine the amount that should be set aside to help cover the cost of a couponing program.

Refunds/rebates.   Refunds or rebates are offers to return all or part of the product's purchase price when a certain requirement is met, such as supplying proofs of purchase or purchasing a certain number of units. Many advertisers believe that this type of promotion builds brand loyalty. When consumers take advantage of refund offers, the advertiser obtains their names and addresses. Thus, using refunds/rebates helps pinpoint the user market and also offers follow-up sales opportunities.

Although refund offers can be designed to have many purposes, the basic objectives usually are to (a) obtain product trial, (b) reward customers, and (c) provide some form of continuity purchase program for the brand. Refund offers designed to generate trial typically appear in media advertising. Offers that seek to reward present users appear in or on the package.

Refunds are particularly attractive to many advertisers because of their relatively low cost. With many refund offers, consumers will start to save for the refund and never get around to collecting enough proofs of purchase or simply forget to send them in. This is called "slippage" and occurs with almost all refund offers. Typically, the refund offer will not redeem more than 1 to 2 percent of the media circulation in which the offer is made. Thus, the advertiser gets the benefit of the promotion, but its actual cost may be relatively low.

The primary disadvantage of the refund offer is that it actually amounts to a discount on the product. Although the offer must be large enough to gain attention, making it too great may result in the majority of refunds going to present users so that no additional sales result. In addition, many refund offers hold low interest for consumers. For example, brand-loyal customers don't respond to refund offers for competing products, so there is little trial among this important group. Finally, most refund offers don't generate immediate sales increases. Because it takes time for consumers to purchase and use the product, sales results often aren't noticeable for several weeks.

Several cost factors must be considered in a refund offer. First is the value of the refund. Second, most offers are handled through clearinghouse organizations which charge for handling the redemption plus the return postage. With a charge of approximately 15¢ for each redemption handled plus the return postage, 37¢ must be added to the value of the refund offer to determine redemption costs to the advertiser.

Many advertisers like to use refunds because response can be varied simply by manipulating three factors: (a) by varying the value of the refund, (b) by raising or lowering the number of proofs-of-purchase required for the refund, and (c) by varying the ways in which the offer is advertised.

Price-offs and value packs.   The two most common forms of price pack are a cents-off label or a two-for-the-price-of-one offer.

Since the FTC investigations into the misuse of these promotions in the early 1960s, stringent rules have been developed on the use of cents-off labels and price packs. The FTC has developed a series of "Guides against Deceptive Pricing." These cover such areas as former price comparisons, retail price comparisons, comparable value comparisons, advertising retail prices that have been established or suggested by manufacturers or other nonretail distributors, and bargain offers based on the purchase of other merchandise.

The price-off technique offers the advertising campaign planner broad promotional opportunities. For example, with the cents-off label, a significant price reduction can be promoted to the consumer with the assurance the savings will actually be passed along and not absorbed in the retail channels. The price pack offers the same advantages as the retail coupon but has none of the accompanying redemption costs for retailers or clearinghouses. Additionally, accurate estimates of the promotion costs can be determined in advance. Finally, the use of special product labels can actually turn the package into a sales promotion tool at the retail level.

Value packs.   Another form of price promotion is the value pack or bonus pack. This is usually a larger size of the standard package or a standard pack with additional merchandise offered at the current price. It is widely used in the food and health and beauty aids categories.

Value packs, like price-offs, appeal primarily to present users. They are used to encourage more or additional use of the brand by those who already buy because the offer acts as a reward for purchase. They can also be used to "load" customers with the product, that is, give them additional product they might not have had. The bonus pack is also used to try and hold present users in the face of some competitive sales promotion or advertising activity.

Generally, bonus packs do little to induce trial or help to build the brand image of the product. They also can be quite expensive because they often require special packaging and additional handling in the plant and in the retail store. The bonus pack offers the campaign planner an effective tool when the objective of the campaign is to either build total volume for the brand or to reward present users.

Continuity plans.   Continuity plans are simply promotional programs in which the consumer either collects stamps, coupons, or receipts and redeems them for free or reduced prices on gifts or prizes. By collecting the required proofs of purchase, the consumer is encouraged to either purchase a brand on a regular basis or to shop at a particular retail store to fulfill the particular game plan. Continuity programs are particularly widespread among supermarket chains, some of which seem to have an endless parade of continuity plans, such as a set of dishes, pots and pans, jewelry, lawn furniture, and the like.

Continuity plans seem to rise and fall in popularity with the public and with marketers. A few years ago, nearly every supermarket and gasoline service station had some type of trading stamp. Today, hardly any feature this type of continuity sales promotion program.

A prime example of a continuity plan among consumer brands is the General Mills program featuring Betty Crocker coupons. On General Mills consumer food products ranging from ready-to-eat cereals to cake mixes, the consumers can find Betty Crocker coupons either in or on the packages. By saving these coupons, the consumer may order flatware, kitchen utensils, and the like, from a catalog at greatly reduced prices. The plan has been in existence since 1930. (Today, one of the most common forms of continuity plans is that of the frequent purchaser or frequent flyer. Because these are very complex, long-term promotional programs, we only note them here.)

Interest promotion techniques.   There are four promotional techniques that rely primarily on building interest in either the category, the product, or the brand. These are sampling, premium packs, mail-in premiums, and contests/sweepstakes. A discussion of each follows.

Sampling.   Often, one of the primary marketing objectives is to obtain trial usage. Because most prospective customers already use an established brand, simply getting a presently satisfied user of a competitive product to switch to a new brand may be a Herculean task. Sampling has proven to be an effective approach to generate trial.

Sampling can take many shapes and forms. For low-priced products, the least expensive sampling unit is often the regular product. For more expensive products or those in which several uses or servings are purchased at one time, a sample package may be developed. The purpose of a sample is to provide a sufficient supply of the product so the consumer can judge its merits.

Although samples are commonly distributed to prospects at no charge, the sale of a trial package at retail is growing in importance. This package is usually a special size of the product for which the advertiser charges a price to offset some of his or her costs. The trial-size offer has appeal to the retailer, who receives a profit on the sale of the product rather than seeing it given away.

The chief problem inherent in any sampling program is finding an effective yet cost-efficient method of distribution. Four basic approaches are used: through the mail, hand delivery to the prospect's door, on-packs with an existing product, and in-store sampling by demonstrators.

The through-the-mail method offers the advertiser the obvious advantage of being able to control where and when the product is distributed fairly closely. This control permits demographic or geographic targeting. Cost and postal limitations on some products are usually the primary problems with through-the-mail promotions.

The problem of cost is the major disadvantage of delivery to the prospect's door. The opportunity to control where and when the samples are distributed, and the fact that almost any product can be distributed are almost overwhelmed by the sheer cost of personal delivery. Cooperative ventures—several products are distributed at once—often help reduce the cost problem of door-to-door delivery.

The on-pack sample is very low in cost but its distribution is limited to those persons who purchase the product with which it is packaged. Thus, packing a sample of a new soy sauce with a brand of chow mein limits the product trial to purchasers of the specific brand of chow mein selected.

In-store sampling is becoming increasingly important in many areas. A person, called a "demonstrator," sets up a table or booth, prepares the product, and offers samples to shoppers. This approach is particularly effective for food products because the consumer has an opportunity to taste the product prior to purchase. In addition, the "demonstrator" can often deliver a sales message during the sampling. The major disadvantages are the extremely high cost and limited number of stores in which the promotion can be conducted. It requires space, product, personnel, and a great deal of planning. It can, however, be one of the most effective of all sampling methods.

New and unique methods of sampling through the media are being developed. Often samples of the product can be bound into a magazine or included in the local newspaper.

The campaign planner has several cost factors to consider in a sampling program. First is the cost of the sample itself. Second is the cost of distribution. Often special packages or promotional literature to accompany the sample must be printed. When a coupon is included to encourage trial, its cost must also be included. Sampling is expensive but can be worth it.

Premium packs.   These techniques usually consist of in-packs, on-packs and near-packs. The major difference between the in-pack and on-pack premiums is the manner in which it is included in the package. The major advantage of these offers is that the product must be purchased for the consumer to obtain the premium. If a very desirable premium is available and promoted, substantial sales may be achieved that would not otherwise occur. Because all in-pack and on-pack premiums will eventually be distributed, premiums are usually low cost or are built into the retail price of the product.

For campaign planners, the advantages of the in-pack or on-pack premium are the known cost of the promotion and the opportunity to promote the premium. Each package is known to contain the premium and ensures that promotional expenditures will not be wasted by the lack of premium availability at the retail level.

Near-pack premiums offered by the manufacturer are not attached in any way to the package. The near-pack premium offer is usually made by offering the premium with the purchase of the product. The near-pack premium generally cannot be attached, so it is stocked nearby (near-pack). The offer is made on the package or through promotional signs. The near-pack is simply a method of offering a large or bulky premium with the purchase of the product.

Mail-in premiums.   There are two basic types of these premiums: those offered free in the mail and self-liquidating type. An offer of a free premium or gift, which is sent through the mail, is made to the consumer. Typically, this offer is made on the basis of sending in proof-of-purchase symbols or other signs that the product has been purchased. Normally, more than one proof-of-purchase symbol is required in order to obtain the premium.

Free-in-the-mail premiums, unlike other premiums, do not immediately reward the purchaser, because there is usually a delay in receiving the premium and an even greater delay when multiple proofs of purchase are required. In spite of this, this technique seems to work very well in competitive situations in which there is little or no product difference. In many cases, the premium offered, because it must be ordered and then shipped, can be personalized or made more attractive in some way. To be effective, most free-in-the-mail premiums must be promoted through media advertising that calls attention to the offer. Thus, the advertising is additional expense involved with this type of promotion.

The primary goal of most free-in-the-mail promotions is to reward present customers and to keep them buying. It also works in creating a trial or brand switch if the premium is attractive enough. In most instances, free premiums tend to have utilitarian value and are closely allied to the product being promoted. It is assumed that the premium will continue to remain with the consumer and serve as a reminder of the brand. Thus, many free-in-the-mail premiums are imprinted with the name of the manufacturer, a brand, or logotype.

Self-liquidating premiums.   Self-liquidating premiums are items offered, usually with proof of purchase of the product, at a price that covers the out-of-pocket cost of the item. The price paid by the consumer covers the actual premium cost plus postage and handling. Because self-liquidating premiums are purchased in large quantities by the advertiser, the price is usually much lower than if the same item were purchased at retail. Thus, there is a savings to the consumer.

Self-liquidators offer the advertiser several advantages. First, the cost of the premium is borne by the consumer. Second, the premium is often tied directly to the advertising campaign or theme, and thus the advertising message is extended at no cost.

The major disadvantage of the self-liquidating approach is the usual requirement by the premium supplier that the sales of a certain number of the premiums be guaranteed. If the premium is a success, there is no problem. However, if the premium redemption does not achieve the guaranteed number, the advertiser may find him- or herself holding a large supply of premiums that have little appeal to the consumer or that are tied to last year's advertising.

Contests and sweepstakes.   Contests and sweepstakes generate a great deal of interest among consumers, especially if the prize structure is appealing. The major question, however, is whether running the contest or sweepstakes will contribute to product sales. Most of the promotion supporting a sweepstakes or contest is directed only to the contest, not the brand. Unless the campaign is carefully planned, the brand's sales message may easily get lost in the excitement of the promotion. The contest or sweepstakes may be a success, but the advertiser may fail to achieve the desired promotional goals.

Although contests and sweepstakes are often lumped together in the same promotional category, a major difference exists between them. Contests are promotions in which participants compete for a prize or prizes based on some sort of skill or ability. Usually this competition consists of answering questions, completing sentences, or writing phrases or paragraphs about the product or its advantages, all of which require some form of talent. Sweepstakes, on the other hand, require only that the entrant submit his or her name to be included in a drawing or other form of awarding prizes. Because of the additional effort required of contest entrants, sweepstakes promotions usually draw about ten times more entries than contests.

Contests and sweepstakes appear to work best in generating interest in parity products, or in a product that has no particular promotional advantage. They may also be used to help renew enthusiasm for the product at the retail level, or to help in revitalizing an existing advertising campaign theme.

In addition, sweepstakes and contests do increase the readership of the advertising in which they are promoted. Consumers who have an interest in the promotion usually read the advertising more thoroughly than they do normal product advertising. Another advantage of a contest or sweepstakes is the opportunity to tie the promotion directly to the creative approach being used in regular advertising.

Finally, advertisers can often develop a large sweepstakes or contest prize list for a relatively small amount of money. Many manufacturers are willing to sell their products at less than retail cost to sweepstakes or contest promoters simply to obtain the additional advertising exposure their products will receive.

A major consideration in a contest or sweepstakes is preventing the event from becoming a lottery, which is illegal under federal laws. Lotteries have three basic elements: luck or chance prizes or awards, and consideration on the part of the contestant. The consideration portion of a lottery is where problems usually occur. Any campaign planner contemplating a contest or sweepstakes should consult qualified promotion and legal experts to ensure compliance with all federal, state, and local regulations.

Hazards of Pull Strategy Promotion

As with a "push" strategy, there are inherent hazards to the use of sales promotion directed to consumers through a "pull" strategy. The greatest concern, and certainly one that deserves serious consideration from manufacturers and retailers alike, is that there is increasing evidence that continuous price promotion for a brand or even for a category tends to build deal-proneness among consumers. In other words, because the brand or category is continuously or almost continuously price promoted, the deal or feature price tends to become the consumer-perceived "real" price. A prime example is in the cola soft drink category. The cola brands promote so much and so often that the promoted price has become to many consumers the regular price. Thus, when cola brands try to return to the "regular shelf price," sales generally fall off dramatically.

Along with the development of deal-proneness among consumers is the declining consumer response to brand promotional activities. Because there is so much sales promotion today, consumers simply can't keep up with all the offers or are simply flooded with alternatives. Thus, the response rate to an individual brand's promotion declines, creating fairly large waste in consumer promotion budgets. Indeed, it appears that much of the present consumer promotion simply rewards present users rather than generates brand trial or brand switching. Although customer reward is a good practice, in many cases, the promotion ends up being a discount to those who would have purchased the brand without promotion and at full margin.

Finally, there is the problem of coupon misredemption. Some studies have shown that misredemption can range up to 20 to 25 percent of all coupons redeemed. Some of this misredemption is the result of honest mistakes by consumers and store personnel. In other cases, organized crime groups obtain, falsify, and redeem coupons from manufacturers and retailers alike. So, although there is known misredemption of many sales promotion offers, there is little that can be done about the problem except to recognize it exists and to try and take as many measures as possible to prevent it from occurring.

PLANNING SALES PROMOTION

To this point, most of our discussion has been on the specifics of sales promotion, such as objectives and tactics. Although the planner will likely include sales promotion as part of an overall promotional program along with advertising, public relations, direct marketing, and the like, sales promotion is planned somewhat differently than the other communication approaches. Below is a fourteen-step outline commonly used to plan a successful sales promotion program.

- Step One: Analyze the market situation. The planner should look at category trends, economic trends, consumer behavior, and so on to determine the situation of the category and the brand. Most likely, this analysis will have already been done when planning the advertising, but it should be reviewed in terms of any changes or impact that might be specific to the sales promotion needs.
- Step Two: Evaluate the promotional environment. Look at what is happening in the areas of advertising, sales promotion, public relations, direct marketing, packaging, and so on particularly in the product category.
- Step Three: Assess competitive activity. How active are competitors in the area? What are they doing? What are they likely to do? How high are the promotional barriers that have already been erected in the brand category?
- Step Four: Identify the problem to be solved. Often the problem is more complex than it first appears. You need to pinpoint the specific objectives that need to be achieved, and make sure they can be accomplished through sales promotion.
- Step Five: Develop sales promotion objectives. As previously discussed, these must be clear-cut, specific and, in most cases, measurable. Be sure you are dealing with objectives and not tactics.
- Step Six: Identify the target audiences for the promotion. Who is to be reached and motivated by the promotional event? Is it the ultimate consumer? The sales force? Distributors? The trade? Be specific.

- Step Seven: Define the strategies that will be used. Refer to the section where the differences between sales promotion objectives and sales promotion strategies was discussed. The major question to be asked is, Will these strategies meet the objectives which have been set?
- Step Eight: Outline the tactics. These should flow naturally from the objectives and strategies. Refer to the techniques in both the "push" and "pull" strategies listed earlier in this chapter. Do they support the strategies?
- Step Nine: Develop a budget. Pull all the costs together and be sure to include redemption, handling, and other costs for on-going programs. What will it cost to conduct the program outline? How does that compare to available funds?
- Step Ten: Create the "Big Idea." Here's where you consider all the executional alternatives. What is to be communicated? What is the tone? What involvement devices would help extend and expand the message? All these go into making sure that the sales promotion program really stands out in a very crowded marketplace.
- Step Eleven: Choose the promotional media. What media will be used for the sales promotion program? FSI? TV? Magazines? P.O.S.? Telemarketing? Direct Mail? In other words, what is the most effective and efficient way to get the promotional program to the target market?
- Step Twelve: Pin down the promotional timetable. Include all the important dates—sell-in, in-field date, length of promotion, evaluation deadline, and so on.
- Step Thirteen: Pretest evaluation. All major sales promotion programs should be pretested. How will it be done? Through market tests? Consumer groups? Trade/dealer screens?
- Step Fourteen: Posttest evaluation. How will the results of the sales promotion event be measured? Will you use volume or share data? Consumer response? Attitude and awareness studies? Executive judgment? What? It's important to determine in advance just how the program will be measured and evaluated.

With this checklist, any planner should be able to develop sound, effective sales promotion events. There are a few final planning questions which should be asked, however.

1. Are your objectives realistic?
2. Do strategies support the objectives?
3. Is the idea clear?
4. Can the sales promotion event be executed as planned?
5. Is the program cost efficient?
6. Will the event appeal to the target audience?
7. Is the creative approach unique enough to break through the clutter?

When the questions have been answered affirmatively, more than likely the sales promotion program will not only support the advertising campaign, it will enhance it as well.[6]

EVALUATING THE SALES PROMOTION PROGRAM

Because this text is designed primarily for advertising planners, the evaluation of sales promotion programs will not be dealt with in great depth. The planner, however, should at least be aware of the common approaches to sales promotion evaluation currently being used.

In the past, and in some instances today, the impact of sales promotion programs has been measured in terms of product movement, volume increases, share gains, and so on. Most of this measurement has been done on a very broad scale, for example, through store audits and warehouse withdrawals. This approach gives marketing managers a very crude view of the impact their promotional programs had or were having. As a result, managers discovered approximately how much volume specific promotional events generated, but they didn't know if that was additional or new volume or simply the replacement of future volume. And, most important, they had little information on whether or not specific events generated profits or the promotional cost exceeded the additional income.

Over the past few years, two basic approaches to sales promotion have developed: (a) lost revenue or break-even analysis, and (b) incremental case analysis.

Lost revenue analysis simply looks at what the cost of the promotion is in dollar or case terms. Then a calculation is made to determine how many new dollars must be generated or how many additional cases must be sold to cover the cost of the actual promotion—the price reduction, allowance, premium offered, and so on. In other words, it determines how much additional volume or how many dollars have to be generated by the promotion to break even, that is, to pay for the cost of the promotion. This is the most basic promotional evaluation technique.

The second evaluation technique is cost-per-incremental case analysis. This technique takes (a) a prepromotion measure, (b) a measure during the period of the promotion, and then (c) a postpromotion measure. The prepromotion period is used as the base. Then, an analysis is made of the sales increases that occur during the promotion period to see what volume or sales or profit increases are achieved. Then, another measure is made of the same length of time as the prepromotion period after the promotion is over. Here, an attempt is made to see what kind of residual effect may have

---

[6]Adopted from Don E. Schultz and William A. Robinson, *Sales Promotion Management* (Chicago: Crain Books, 1982): 139–44.

occurred as a result of the promotion. It is hoped that the promotion will provide more impact than just the sales during the promotional period. Both pre- and postpromotion calculations are relatively simple to do; more detailed explanations can be found in most sales promotion text books.

Given the growth and availability of scanner and scanner panel data, new and more sophisticated forms of sales promotion analysis are being developed. In many instances, manufacturers are now able to calculate the actual profit per case as a result of the sales promotional event. No doubt, more sophisticated approaches will follow.

INTEGRATING SALES PROMOTION WITH THE ADVERTISING CAMPAIGN

Traditionally, we have thought of sales promotion as simply a short-term incentive to build immediate sales. There is a changing view of sales promotion among the more sophisticated marketers, however. Increasingly, forward-thinking marketers are looking beyond the immediate effects of the sales promotion event and trying to develop programs that not only generate immediate sales and profits but have some lasting value as well.

There is a new definition of *sales promotion*, one that is particularly appealing:

> Sales promotion focuses on the building of brand loyalty and share growth through the strategic use of long-term and/or a series of short-term programmed events.

In other words, sales promotion must do more than just generate immediate sales without regard for the future. Strategically, two new aspects of sales promotion must be considered:

1. *The residual market value of the promotion*—the image-enhancing communication about the product or service that remains after the promotion is over.
2. *The relationship value of the promotion*—the bonds, both actual and perceptual, that are created between the customer, the marketer, and the brand by the specific promotional event.

If the advertising planner will judge the sales promotion events proposed or created on the basis of these two new concepts, he or she will be well on the way to developing a truly integrated marketing communications program.

Case Studies

RealCream

Bossy Products' powdered dairy creamer, RealCream, had been in national distribution for two months when Bob Cubbin, the brand manager, met with top management to review the situation.

RealCream was currently stocked in stores representing 40 percent of national all-commodity volume. The goal for the end of Year 1 had been set at achieving distribution representing 65 percent of ACV. Cubbin felt this objective was still feasible, noting that Bossy's overall distribution represented 75 percent ACV. RealCream was being sold in every major market, but only by small chains and independents. In the large chains, the sales force had not yet been able to gain shelf space. The reason was twofold: First, the creamer section traditionally generated only an average margin for the supermarkets. Consequently, grocers were unwilling to expand the shelf space allotted to the category, and established brands were firmly entrenched. Second, because RealCream was a new product and still an unknown, buyers for major chains had adopted a "wait and see" attitude.

RealCream had been introduced to the trade under Bossy's traditional terms: one case free with the purchase of twelve. However, the nondairy creamer manufacturers offered a one free with ten allowance. RealCream was also higher priced than nondairy creamers.

Consumer acceptance of RealCream, while good, had not been as strong as expected. In its two months on the market, the product had accounted for 3 percent of the creamer category sales. Year 1 goal had been set at 15 percent. (Bossy's other products, powdered milk and canned condensed milk, had respective market shares of 30 percent and 25 percent.)

According to preliminary scanner data analysis, RealCream's sales had not come at the expense of any one nondairy creamer. The major competitors had experienced slight losses, but overall creamer sales had increased, suggesting that RealCream was bringing new users to the category. Cubbin pointed out that although some category growth had been expected, new users were only a secondary target and the main thrust of the promotional campaign had been to attract competitive users. He reviewed the campaign:

> Full-page, four-color advertisements had been placed in seven major women's magazines, *Reader's Digest,* and *TV Guide.* The ad pictured the RealCream jar sitting beside a coffee cup and a woman's hand stirring the coffee. The headline read: "RealCream: It's the Cream in My Coffee." Copy read as follows: "It seems we use so many substitutes these days. Some, like

salt substitutes, were developed for health reasons. Those are good substitutes. But others, like nondairy creamers, are used because they're more convenient, not better. I don't use a nondairy creamer anymore, because now there's RealCream. Same convenient powder form, but it's a real dairy food, made with real cream. Mmm, RealCream, I'd be lost without you."

Cubbin had asked Bossy's consumer researchers to conduct two focus groups, one with people who had tried RealCream and one with those who had not. The people who had tried the product had very positive comments. They liked the taste and the idea that it was a real dairy product. Most reported that they had seen the ad. Several had bought RealCream because of the Bossy name (featured prominently on the package). All intended to buy the product again. They agreed it was expensive in comparison to nondairy creamers, but they felt the expense was justified because of the "natural" aspect.

Nonusers were somewhat skeptical of RealCream's real dairy claim. "Who ever heard of powdered cream?" asked one panel member. Most participants felt that the product was too expensive in comparison with other creamers. The Bossy name suggested quality, but it was not strong enough to overcome questions about the price–benefit relationship.

In summary, Cubbin stated that he believed RealCream could still achieve the established goals. He reported that 30 percent of the promotional budget had been spent on introductory phase advertising. He wanted permission to allocate at least half of the remaining funds to a sales promotion effort in an attempt to attract competitive users to RealCream.

Bossy had always been reluctant to use major sales promotion plans for their products. Past efforts had been limited to cross-ruff coupons on company products. For example, powdered milk might carry a coupon for Bossy condensed milk. However, the management committee gave Cubbin their approval of his request.

Questions

1. Obviously, one way to increase distribution would be to offer a more competitive case allowance. However, Bossy would prefer not to do this because of corporate margin requirements. What other trade measures might you recommend?
2. Do you agree that sales promotion (consumer and/or trade) would be effective for RealCream?
3. Which of the basic consumer sales promotion techniques might be effective for RealCream?
4. Outline a sales promotion campaign for RealCream that ties into the advertising campaign. Remember that users of competitive products are the primary target.

Power Oats Cereal

Doug Gibson, account executive at Gentry Promotions, was reviewing a sales promotion plan he intended to present the next day. Doug's client was a major cereal manufacturer, and the sales promotion plan was for a new brand the manufacturer was planning to launch, Power Oats Cereal.

Power Oats would be positioned in the Adult Bran/Fiber segment of the cold cereal category, where it would be competing for shelf space and consumer dollars with about fifteen other brands. Power Oats was a vitamin-enriched, high-oat-bran product that would provide 100 percent of the consumer's minimal daily requirement of vitamins and minerals and at the same time aid in reducing cholesterol. The cereal manufacturer believed that this positioning would adequately differentiate them from other brands in the category. Although they hoped to bring some new users into the Adult Bran/Fiber segment, their primary goal was to take share from the two leading brands in the segment, both of which were manufactured by one of their leading competitors.

Doug knew that the ready-to-eat cereal category was highly competitive. RTE cereals took up a greal deal of supermarket shelf space, but also generated fairly high profit for the retailer. Consumer prices ranged from 9 to 20 cents per ounce, and the products in the Adult Bran/Fiber segment were among the highest priced in the store. Power Oats would retail for around 17 cents per ounce, slightly higher than the leading brands in the segment.

The Adult Bran/Fiber segment was the second largest in the category, just behind the All Family cereal brands. Dollar growth for the total cereal category was around 9 percent annually, although the increase was primarily due to increases in price, not in consumption. The Adult Bran/Fiber segment was growing the most quickly, while presweetened children's cereal sales were falling.

Getting adequate grocery store distribution was critical for a cereal brand, because 98 percent of cereal purchases were made in grocery stores. To maintain their precious shelf space, cereal manufacturers regularly offered retailers case allowances of 6–8 percent off the standard price.

A great deal of consumer sales promotion went on in the category. New products often offered trial sizes, although retailer acceptance of these was usually low. The two most frequently used consumer techniques were couponing and premiums. Premiums tended to be used more by cereals positioned at children; these brands would differentiate themselves through the "prize" carried inside the cereal package. Cereals positioned at adults relied more heavily on coupons, which were distributed through free standing inserts (FSIs) in Sunday newspapers or on the boxes themselves. Coupon face values averaged around 50 cents.

Adult Bran/Fiber cereals spent the bulk of their advertising dollars in print, primarily in women's magazines and health-oriented publications. However, new product introduction sometimes received spot TV support in major markets, and that was the plan for Power Oats.

Analysis of scanner data suggested that most cereal consumers fell into Segment 6 of the McAlister Model, that is, they were deal-prone switchers who tended to restrict their brand choice. (There was also a smaller group of nondeal-prone switchers.) Consumers did not like to always eat the same brand of cereal, and would settle on two or three brands within a segment. Then, their actual purchase would be determined by the brand that was offering the best deal at the time of purchase.

Based on this information, Doug had set some specific objectives for the Power Oats sales promotion program.

1. Get fifty percent ACV distribution by the end of the first full month of product availability.
2. Obtain at least two shelf facings per store.
3. Within three months of introduction, gain trial from 60 percent of consumers now buying Adult Bran/Fiber brands.
4. Within three months of introduction, gain trial from 20 percent of consumers not currently buying Adult Bran/Fiber brands.
5. In months four through six, encourage consumer stockpiling of Power Oats to combat expected competitive reaction.
6. For the remainder of the year, and for succeeding years, make Power Oats a member of the restricted choice brand set for 25 percent of segment consumers.
7. Support the advertising campaign that would position Power Oats as a premium entry in the Adult Bran/Fiber segment.

Doug felt confident that the Power Oats brand manager would agree with his objectives. He knew that his goals were fairly aggressive, but the manufacturer had indicated that they wanted to make sure this brand was successful and were willing to spend money to support it. Doug's next task would be to come up with tactics to support each of his objectives.

Questions

1. Briefly discuss how each of the critical consumer characteristics discussed in this chapter (usage patterns, brand/store loyalty, deal proneness) relate to this situation.

2. What specific techniques would you recommend to meet Objectives 3, 4, 5, and 6 above? Why? How would you expect consumers to react to those techniques?

3. What specific techniques would you recommend to meet Objectives 1 and 2? Why? How would you expect retailers to react to the techniques you have suggested?

4. How would you expect competitors to react to your recommendations for Questions 2 and 3?

5. Do the tactics you've recommended meet Objective 7? Why or why not?

14

Direct Marketing

One of the fastest growing areas in the overall promotion mix is direct marketing. Investments in direct marketing have grown phenomenally in the past four decades. The major reasons for this growth were

1. The growth of computer capability. Because direct marketing relies heavily on the capture, storage, and manipulation of large masses of information, such as names, addresses, and purchasing histories of customers and prospects, the increased capacity and capability of computers have been responsible for much of the growth. And, as computer technology and capability have grown, costs have declined. Therefore, it is now economically practical for marketers to make use of direct marketing capabilities, such as personalization, segmentation, and customer targeting.
2. Advanced statistical techniques. Partially as a by-product of increased computer technology, more advanced statistical techniques and procedures have been developed. These techniques allow direct marketers to accurately project the results of small-scale tests to larger population segments or data bases. For this reason, direct marketing has become one of the more reliable methods of marketing communications.
3. Measurability. With reliable projections and known response rates, marketers have become able to accurately measure the financial results of their efforts. In the era of "accountability" this measurability has great appeal.
4. Segmentation and personalization. As former mass markets have been fragmented and segmented by marketers with niche products,

there has been more and more emphasis on identification of target markets. With that identification has come the potential for personalization. New technology in computers, printing, and mailing now permit direct marketers to identify, personalize, and individualize messages, markets, responses, and even products to serve individual segments of the population.

5. Credit cards. Widespread acceptance and use of credit cards as a medium of exchange has made distance purchasing possible and practical. When using an 800 telephone number, consumers can now purchase and pay for products easily and conveniently.

Although there are doubtless other factors, these five have really spawned the growth of direct marketing over the past ten years or so.

In spite of the incredible growth of direct marketing and direct marketing investments, there is still considerable confusion as to what direct marketing really is, how it works, and most of all, how direct marketing can be used by what are perceived to be mass marketers, i.e., companies that sell widely used products through self-service outlets. This chapter will look at direct marketing from their point of view.

WHAT IS DIRECT MARKETING?

The Direct Marketing Association's official definition is

> Direct marketing is an interactive system of marketing which uses one or more advertising media to effect a measurable response and/or transaction at any location.[1]

As an illustration of the total concept of direct marketing, the following schematic (Exhibit 14–1) was developed by several industry experts and published in *Direct Marketing* magazine. This flowchart shows the many areas, elements, and techniques that can be used in direct marketing. It has been adopted as the formal flowchart of direct marketing.

After studying the DMA definition and the flowchart, it becomes clear why there is and will continue to be some confusion about direct marketing, particularly among some advertising people. To most advertisers and marketers, direct marketing is equated with direct mail. Therefore, when a package goods marketer talks of direct marketing, he or she usually has in mind mailing information or material or coupons to a list of customers or prospects. Conversely, direct marketers think of and use direct marketing in a totally different way. Therein may lie much of the confusion.

---

[1]Attributed to the Direct Marketing Association in Bob Stone, *Successful Direct Marketing Methods,* 4th ed. (Lincolnwood, Ill.: NTC Business Books, 1988): 3.

Exhibit 14–1   Direct Marketing Flowchart

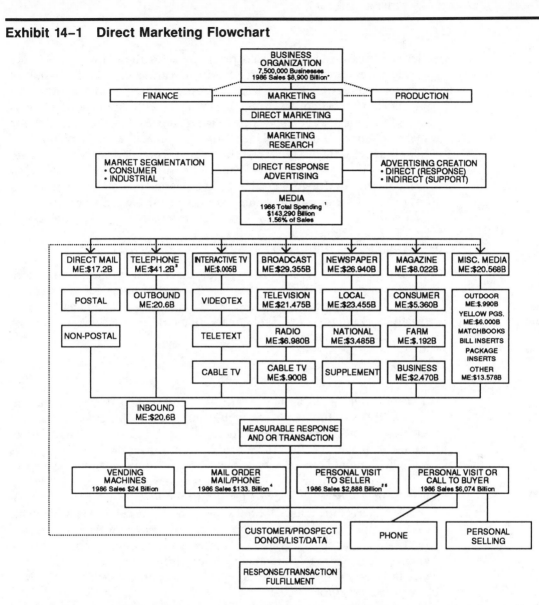

[1]Source: Arnold Fishman, U.S. Census, Robert Coen, McCann Erickson (Media Figures).

[2]Personal visit to seller includes $1.204 billion of Consumer Product Sales at retail plus 90% of Consumer Services Sales. 10% of Consumer Services Sales are conducted by salespeople visiting the buyer.

[3]Rudy Oetting, Telephone Marketing Resources, New York City, working with AT&T figures, says that roughly half of Telemarketing Expenditures are for Outbound Calls; 50% for inbound.

[4]The Mail Order Sales Figure includes roughly $33 billion of charitable contributions which are not included in the $9,300 billion of U.S. Aggregate Sales.

[5]This total does not include $870 billion in investment spending minus $75 billion in Net Exports.

*Dollars in Billions

ME: Media Expenditures

SOURCE: Martin Baier, Henry R. Hoke, Jr., and Bob Stone, "Direct Marketing—What Is It?" *Direct Marketing*, January, 1988. Reprinted by permission of *Direct Marketing* magazine.

Because this text is concerned primarily with the planning, development, and implementation of an advertising campaign, the discussion of direct marketing has been restricted to those areas directly related to such a campaign. In other words, although catalogs, continuity programs, negative option clubs, direct response television, and the like are critical to the direct marketing community in developing the areas, elements, and techniques illustrated by the flowchart, our discussion will deal primarily with those direct marketing activities that can be used to support, enhance, or assist a planner in developing a total and complete marketing communications program for a package goods product or for a widely available consumer service.

FORMS OF DIRECT MARKETING

We can categorize all the many forms of direct marketing into three convenient groups for discussion. These are direct response, data base marketing, and direct mail. Each is discussed separately because each could logically be used as part of a total marketing communications program or advertising campaign.

Direct Response

No matter how the sales or communication message is delivered through the mail, through broadcast, through print media—direct response seeks to achieve a direct, measurable response from the target audience. Direct response can range from a mail-order house's magazine advertisements seeking to generate catalog requests and in-home purchases from prospective customers (Exhibit 14–2), to business-to-business companies placing ads in trade publications seeking leads for their sales force (Exhibit 14–3), to book clubs selling a line of books directly to magazine readers (Exhibit 14–4), to a magazine's direct mail package soliciting new subscribers (Exhibit 14–5). Generally, customers and prospects respond or reply either by calling a toll-free 800 telephone number or through a return form or order blank through the mail. In addition, direct response offers can be made through the broadcast media.

Further, we can classify direct response into one-step or two-step programs. A one-step program is one such as the Better Homes and Gardens Book Club offer (Exhibit 14–4) or the *Advertising Age* subscription offer (Exhibit 14–5). In these examples, supposedly all the information a respondent would need to know to make a purchase decision can be found in the advertisement or direct mail package. The prospect responds directly to the advertiser—a one-step process from solicitation to purchase.

In a two-step program, the prospect normally requests additional information or material. This material usually takes the form of a brochure,

Exhibit 14–2 Lands' End Magazine Advertisement

Oh, the warmth, ah, the comfort

of Lands' End Cotton Flannel Sheets

(imported from Portugal)

In Portugal, they weave cotton flannel sheets for Europe's coldest countries, from Germany on up to Sweden.

But even these near-legendary sheets didn't quite pass muster with our finicky Domestics Buyer. The materials she riffled through her fingers and held up to the light were too thin, too transparent. They pilled. They shrank.

So she went to work with her supplier. Specified an increase in construction to 40 picks of yarn per square inch (others use 32 to 34), for more loft and durability. And, while she was at it, sized our sheets generously to avoid any shrinkage problems.

Voila! Or whatever they say in Portuguese.

The result of all this is sheets replete with soft, napped comfort. Sheets that don't ice up in cold rooms like synthetics do, but greet your wary toes with night after night of cozy warmth. And even earn their keep in warm weather, warm climates as soft, breathable lightweight blankets.

To all the inherent natural attractions of our cotton flannel sheets we add a few typical Lands' End extras. A selection that includes both solid colors and printed patterns (as well as New Zealand wool bed pads, Irish wool throws, plump goosedown comforters, and other bedtime delights). And the kind of value you've come to expect from Lands' End (seriously, you could pay up to three times as much elsewhere for sheets of this quality).

This, of course, is always the Lands' End idea.

In whatever you buy from us, <u>quality</u> comes first. Then, a struggle with price points until we achieve a ratio that assures you value. <u>Our</u> kind of value, which we've found over the years is also <u>your</u> kind of value. Not only in sheets, but in sweaters, shirts, skirts and shoes; in soft luggage, and parkas, and all manner of useful accessories.

Of course, your entree to all this wondrous value—and the Lands' End experience of being served with it—begins with the drop of the coupon below, or a toll-free phone call anytime day or night to 800-356-4444.

Remember, everything you buy from us wears our iron-clad guarantee, a guarantee so unconditional we can and do express it in just two words: GUARANTEED. PERIOD.

Before you go to bed tonight, give us a call. There's always somebody up at our house, even though we sell flannel sheets.

© *1988, Lands' End, Inc.*

GOURMET / NOVEMBER 1988

Please send free catalog.
Lands' End, Inc. Dept. O-43
Dodgeville, WI 53595

Name _____

Address _____

City _____

State _____ Zip _____

Or call Toll-free:
800-356-4444

Exhibit 14–3   Hewlett-Packard Ad

Order the HP 8673G with an HP 437B Power Meter and HP 8485A Power Sensor, and the power meter is FREE.

HP's 8673G Synthesized CW Generator delivers high signal quality and HP reliability at a truly affordable ($29,000) price.

Why pay thousands of dollars more than you need for a synthesizer? The HP 8673G provides a high-performance 2 to 26 GHz CW signal you can utilize in a wide range of applications. And its HP-IB programming is fully compatible with all HP 8673 family synthesizers, making it a perfect fit for ATE systems that utilize existing software.

This is *the* synthesizer for your 26 GHz bench—especially now, when you can purchase it together with our HP 8485A Power Sensor and HP 437B Power Meter—and get the $2,500 power meter at no cost!*

A powerful incentive.

The new HP 437B is HP's highest performance, single-channel power meter. It provides automatic calibration, HP-IB programmability, and outstanding reliability. It's easy to use, too, with powerful features such as frequency entry, selectable resolution, offset, and duty cycle.

For offer details and technical data, call our toll-free number today, or use the convenient Business Reply Card. And get the story on the 26 GHz synthesizer and power meter that also generate big savings.

1-800-752-0900
ext. 697B

Offer good through March 31, 1989

Exhibit 14–4   Better Homes and Gardens Book Club Ad

Exhibit 14–5 *Advertising Age*'s Direct Mail Piece

ALL THE CREATIVITY YOU'LL EVER NEED!

see inside...

"Marketing Genius Award" Mug awaits SCHULTZ --Advertising Age editors await reply--

Good news--you are now eligible to receive Advertising Age hot off the press and fresh on your desk...every week for a full 39% off the news stand price! Now, you'll stay right on top of the most comprehensive and authoritative advertising and marketing news available anywhere in the world...at any price. News that'll help you keep strategies focused...creative efforts meaningful...and products moving.

But, that's not all. You'll also get the handsome personalized "Marketing Genius Award" mug--like the one pictured above--absolutely free with your paid subscription.

This is the famous mug that touts you as a marketing wizard...and announces it to the rest of the world. Whether or not you drink coffee, it's guaranteed to pick you up. Remember, the mug is free...and you don't have to send any money with your reply. Please read the enclosed letter for complete details on this important free offer.

OFFICIAL NOTIFICATION FOR:

Don Schultz
Northwestern University
101 Fisk Hall
Evanston, IL 60208

NON-TRANSFERABLE

folder, or catalog. It might identify a local dealer or representative who can provide more information or take an actual order. Another alternative might be to request the advertiser company to send a sales representative to discuss the purchase. The Hewlett-Packard example (Exhibit 14–3) has both a one-step and a two-step process. The two-step process is used when additional information is needed by the prospect to make a decision.

In direct response, the goal is an immediate response from the target audience that results in a direct sale or a solid lead for follow-up action by the direct marketing organization.

Data Base Marketing

Data base marketing involves more than just a single direct response. It is an integrated system; companies and organizations build a historical file on each individual customer, account, or prospect. Commonly these files contain name, address, household or organization information, past purchase history, record of contacts with the individual customer or account, and so on.

The program that has been developed by American Express for their various levels of Travel and Entertainment Cards is an example of this type of data base marketing. Because the American Express Card is essentially a charge card, the cardholder must furnish the company with a fairly extensive credit record to receive a card and the card priviledges. Over time, American Express records all purchases made with the card. By using this data base information, American Express has been able to develop additional products and services, such as publications, products sold through direct mail, insurance, and credit card loss protection, which can be offered to cardholders. From their data base on each customer, American Express is able to target these additional products to those customers whose data base profile fits those of the best prospect for these products. This is true "data base marketing." In addition, American Express has an extensive program of "relationship" contacts which they use to thank customers for using the card, for purchasing the other services, and so on. In essence, data base marketing is a method of developing semipersonal relationships with customers and prospects through various media forms. Other companies that practice data base marketing include Spiegel (catalogs), United Airlines ("Mileage Plus" frequent flyer program), and Colonial Penn or Allstate (insurance companies).

Direct Mail

We classify all forms of direct contact with customers and prospects through the United States Postal Service as direct mail. This would include mass cooperative mailings of coupons, products, and other offers, such as the Carol Wright cooperative couponing program, developed by Donnelley Marketing (see Exhibit 14–6); local, regional, and national publication subscription solicitations, such as that used by *Chicago* magazine (see Exhibit 14–7); and highly selective, short-term offers, such as the three-day sale illustrated in the direct mail folder sent by a Chicago-area automobile dealer to Saab and Volvo owners (see Exhibit 14–8).

Direct mail can be highly selective, for example, a mailing to a list of specific college alumni, or on a broader scale, such as a mailing to all automobile-owning households in the western half of the U.S. In addition, direct mail need not require a specific response from the target audience. It may be used to build the image or impression of the organization, as are other forms of media, with the hope of later purchasing activity. In other words, direct mail can be used in the same way as any other advertising medium to send sales messages to customers and prospects. In most cases, the advantage of direct mail is that it can be highly targeted to predetermined and selected groups of people or companies.

With these basic definitions in mind, we now look at the structure of the direct marketing business.

STRUCTURE OF THE DIRECT MARKETING BUSINESS

As is the case with the advertising or sales promotion fields, an infrastructure of suppliers has developed in direct marketing. Knowing the players and what they do can be very helpful to the advertising campaign planner.

Direct Marketing Agencies

As with general advertising, a group of specialized agencies have developed in the direct marketing area. Although many are broad-based direct marketing agencies, serving a broad range of clients, others are much more specialized. For example, there are direct marketing agencies that specialize in such areas as financial, health care, pharmaceutical, not-for-profit, and television direct response. Direct marketing agencies are usually structured in the same manner as traditional general advertising agencies. The major differences are that most direct marketing agencies work on some sort of project basis with their clients, and are commonly paid through fee or commission compensation systems.

List Suppliers and List Enhancers

Most direct marketing practitioners believe the "list," or the names, addresses, titles, and so on to which direct marketing offers are made, is the key ingredient of the discipline. Some have gone so far as to say the list is approximately 50 percent of the value of any direct marketing program.

Exhibit 14–6 Carol Wright Mailer

SOURCE: Reprinted with permission of Donnelley Marketing Information Service, Stamford, Connecticut.

Exhibit 14–7   *Chicago* Magazine Direct Mail Piece

**Mail back the token on the enclosed card
for the best deal in town.**

Dear Neighbor:

For you, only the best.

Best restaurants -- top tables in town. Best entertainment -- tickets to
the top shows, concerts, special events ... seats at Chicago's best clubs.
Best <u>information</u> -- advance word on what's playing, who's performing,
what's opening ... where the good times to be had are in and around Chicago.

> For you, CHICAGO magazine, now at the best deal in town.
> You save over half off the cover cost. Get a money-back
> guarantee.

Your timing is perfect.

See the calendar? Summer's flying by. Only a few weeks until Fall.
The start of a season. A full concert and cultural calendar. The city's
nightlife will be getting into high gear.

New fashions are arriving. Shops are being stocked with new merchandise.
New restaurants will be opening, some of them near you. Nightspots where
you can hear some good jazz, blues, country, folk, whatever your choice.

> The connection between you and all this activity? The
> link between you and the rest of the best of Chicago?
> CHICAGO magazine. Your kind of town. Now your kind of
> magazine -- more than ever before!

If you've seen our covers lately, you'll know something's different. New
editor. New look. New design throughout. More features. All of which
makes CHICAGO magazine even more interesting, more vital, more useful
than before. It's time you had a look inside!

See CHICAGO before you make your dining plans. Over 180 restaurants
listed, rated, described every month ... with menu suggestions! Which
restaurants are superb? Unusual? Which dining places are fun?
Pretentious? A bargain? New listings and updates every month.

What's on for the weekend? What can you do with the kids? Where can you
take your out-of-town guests? What's the program for tonight? The phone
number of the box office? See CHICAGO's listing of Events.

Where can you sign up for some courses? Get into fitness? Where can

(over, please)

414 North Orleans • Suite 800 • Chicago, Illinois 60610

Exhibit 14–8   Saab/Volvo Direct Mail Piece

SAAB SAAB SAAB   **DIRECT FACTORY LIQUIDATION**   **VOLVO VOLVO VOLVO**

Dear Luxury Import Owner, Through Special pooling arrangements & joint cooperation, all factory incentive programs have been combined and expanded for the year's most extensive DIRECT SWEDISH CAR SALES OPPORTUNITY.

Held for the first time ever, you are part of a select hand picked customer group invited to take part in this unprecedented FIRST TIME JOINT VENTURE.

★★

THREE DAYS ONLY

The SAAB & VOLVO Midwest Distribution Centers have shipped sale preferenced cars to a centralized 2½ acre suburban warehouse for a final dispersal.

★★

TIL MIDNIGHT EVERY SALE NIGHT

350 factory tagged Volvos & Saabs have now been priority shipped to the Midwest's largest volume joint outlet for FINAL LIQUIDATION.

★★

FACTORY DIRECT PRICING

This will be the only sale opportunity of this magnitude in Wisconsin, Illinois & Indiana this year. Please make note of sale days & location shown below.

THREE DAY SALE INCENTIVES include:

1. Bank Financing from **0.0%**

2. Genuine cash discounts from **$1000** Minimum to **$8000** Maximum **Guaranteed**

3. **$3500** Guaranteed value for your trade-in'

4. Professional wholesale buyers on hand to insure top market appraisal value

---

NOTE:
Every car sold & delivered will include 3 watt Audiovox Cellular Car Phone as standard equipment **FREE**
OFFER ENDS MIDNIGHT OF FINAL SALE

SALE DATE: May 19, 20 & 22
SALE HOURS: 9AM until MIDNIGHT
SALE LOCATION: PATRICK VOLVO/SAAB
526 Mall Drive • Schaumburg
1 block South of Woodfield Mall
SALES HOTLINE: dial P•A•T•R•I•C•K

PLEASE USE THIS ATTACHED CHECK FOR ADDITIONAL SAVINGS OR DOWNPAYMENT IT'S YOUR CHOICE!

PROMOTIONAL MARKETING DRAFT   Valid only on May 19-22, 1989

PAY   THE SUM OF **2000** DOLS **00** CTS   DOLLARS $ 2000.00

PAY TO THE ORDER OF

Check good on select new Volvo's in stock to qual buyers. Must buy & take delivery by 5/22/89. Not valid on prior sales or with any other offer. See dealer for details.

(The balance: offer = 25%, format or package = 15%, and copy = 10%.)

There are a number of organizations involved with list and list rentals. They include:

List owners.   List owners are the organizations that own a list of names, addresses, and additional customer or purchase information that they generate and maintain. Often, these lists are lists of the organization's customers. For example, Spiegel might make available a list of persons who have ordered from their catalog, *Reader's Digest* might offer a list of their subscribers, or VISA might furnish a list of their card members. In any case, the list is owned and maintained by the organization which, in turn, is willing to rent the list for direct marketing purposes.

There is another group of companies that do what is called "list enhancement." A list enhancer might take a list of the names and addresses of persons who subscribe to a certain magazine and add or "overlay" additional information about each household to the original list. For example, National Demographics & Lifestyles processes warranty cards for a number of electronics products. When given a direct marketer's list, they can then add household file information—whether and when certain products were purchased or used by the household—to it. Thus a marketer of 35mm film could enhance a customer list by adding or identifying persons who have recently purchased new 35mm cameras. This enhancement process has become very sophisticated. As a result, marketers can build very complex consumer behavior models that are used to target and predict the response of the list.

List brokers and managers.   List brokers and managers act as the agents for the list owners. Generally, they are independent companies that arrange the rental of the list of names for the company developing a direct marketing campaign. Brokers receive a commission for each list they rent.

It should be noted that, in general, lists are rented, not sold. In other words, the list broker contacts a company that is interested in developing a direct marketing program. The broker works with the marketer to find the best list available from the group of companies whose lists the broker represents. The list is then rented to the direct marketing organization for a one-time-only use. The list owner has the right of approval of (a) the copy the direct marketer will use, (b) the timing of the list use and delivery dates, and (c) any selections the direct marketer might want to make from the list. For example, the marketer might want to rent only names in certain zip codes, or names of persons who have made purchases in the past six months. Under this agreement, the direct marketer rents the list on a cost-per-thousand-names basis (the going rate today is $60 to $100 per thousand names). The list broker receives a commission on the rental, usually 10 to 20 percent of the total order paid by the list owner.

Service bureaus and letter shops.   Service bureaus are organizations that deal primarily with lists, list maintenance (e.g., changes and corrections), and merge-purge operations. (*Merge-purge* is a computer process by which two lists are combined and duplications of names and households or companies are noted and removed.) Service bureaus also print a list of the names on a set of labels or prepare the list of names on a magnetic tape to be sent to the direct marketing organization that rented the list for their mailing use.

Letter shops are organizations that print the direct mail materials, attach the labels to the mailing envelopes or pieces, assemble the entire direct marketing package, and deliver it to the post office for mailing.

Co-ops.   A cooperative arrangement allows several direct marketing organizations to mail packages with multiple direct response offers, manufacturer or retailer coupons, and the like together. Some of the most common co-ops include:

1.   Mail order co-ops. Direct marketers join forces and make combined mailings to their buyer lists.
2.   In-house co-ops. One marketer gathers several products that the company sells and combines them in one mailing package.
3.   Vertical co-ops. A group of noncompetitive direct marketing companies interested in selling to the same general group, such as lawyers, college students, and engineers, do a mailing together.
4.   Magazine co-ops. Magazines sometimes put together mailings that they make to their subscriber list.[2]

Of perhaps most interest to the campaign planner is the mail order co-op, such as the Carol Wright Program developed by Donnelley Marketing. Donnelley has developed a list of the names of some 70 million households in the U.S. This list has been classified and categorized according to variables, such as product use, income level, and zip code. Donnelley plans and prepares large mailings to selected groups of those homes on a regular schedule. Advertisers can insert their advertising, merchandising, or promotional materials in the mailing at a shared cost. Usually, this is much less expensive than an individual mailing. These types of co-op mailings are broadly used by package goods companies to distribute coupons, rebate offers, or even product samples.

Fulfillment houses.   In many cases, direct response organizations do not physically package and ship products for delivery. Packaging and shipping are done by outside organizations, which provide this service for a

---

[2]Bob Stone, *Successful Direct Marketing Methods,* 4th ed.: 268–69.

fee. For example, a direct marketing organization might be selling stuffed bears through direct mail. The direct marketer buys the bears in bulk and has them shipped to the fulfillment organization. Orders are sent to the direct marketer who handles billing and collection. The direct marketer then sends the orders to the fulfillment organization. This group packages and ships the bears. Fulfillment service is also provided for magazine subscriptions, coupon redemptions, rebate offers, and so on.

Creative services. A number of companies and individuals provide outside creative services—usually specialized—for direct marketers. For example, there are persons who specialize in preparing direct mail letters, catalog copy, or material for specific businesses, such as those in insurance or finance or health care.

Having considered the direct marketing structure, we are ready to move on to how direct marketing programs are planned and implemented.

HOW DIRECT MARKETING WORKS

Information Is the Key Element

The basic premise of direct marketing is that the individual is the key element in making a sale. Many mass marketers, because they use several channels for distribution, such as retailers and wholesalers, have only vague ideas of who their customers or users really are. Direct marketers, however, believe that customer identification and purchasing data are really the key elements in successfully selling a product. Although direct marketers may not always have specific information about the household they want to sell to, usually they do have information that allows them to categorize or segment prospects and select the very best available. This information often comes from specialized lists, enhanced data bases, and known direct marketing respondents. To understand direct marketing, we must understand how direct marketers categorize or segment markets.

Direct marketing segmentation. Most direct marketers separate their data bases into internal and external files. The internal file is the list of actual customers or solidly qualified prospects that has been developed over time. The external file consists of those persons or organizations about which the direct marketer knows enough to believe they would be good prospects.

If we use what is known about the household, person, or organization as the basis for a segmentation approach, it might look something like this:

Customers. "Customers" include persons or organizations who have purchased from the direct marketer at some time in the past. Obviously, this group could be further segmented into one-time customers, regular customers, lapsed customers, and so on. The key point is that the direct marketer knows something about the purchase history of these people or organizations.

Prospects. The second group consists of those persons or organizations that have evidenced some interest in the direct marketer's product or service in the past. For example, they may have asked for a brochure, or made an inquiry by 800 number, or returned a coupon. In other words, these people have "held their hand up" in some way to signify their interest in the product or service being offered. They might also be people who are known users of competitive products. For example, for Ford, the owner of a Chevrolet might be a prospect. Also, people who share certain characteristics with existing customers might be prospects, for example, people who have purchased fishing equipment might be good prospects for a fishing magazine.

We can take the idea of prospects somewhat further by considering mothers of babies to be prospects for disposable diapers. Although we may have no evidence that the mother is even using disposable diapers, simply having a six-month-old baby would qualify her as a prospect. Most marketers use a number of ways to identify or categorize people, households, and organizations as prospects.

Suspects. The final group is composed of "suspects." This group might include persons living in a geographic area—people in Duluth are suspects for Florida winter vacations—or businesses of a certain size—suspects for example, for office copying machines. The direct marketer may know very little about these groups and has to surmise that logically they might be suspects, prospects, for the product or service being offered. In most cases, all most marketers know about mass media audiences is some basic demographic information and some media usage information. That is about it. For the most part, mass media audiences are really suspects—not prospects or customers—for many products or services.

By creating a hierarchy based on the information known about the person, household, or organization, a segmentation scheme can be created. It might look something like this:

Best Potential	Customers
Some Potential	Prospects
Hoped for Potential	Suspects

The goal of any direct marketing activity (or any advertising effort, for that matter) is to move more and more people or organizations up this hierarchical ladder so that prospects become customers and suspects become prospects. In truth, this is what all types of marketing communication really attempt to do. The major difference is that, in general, the direct marketer is working with a great deal more information about each of the three groups than is the general advertiser, who often relies on the retailer or other distribution channel member to develop a classification scheme.

Using this target market classification approach, specific direct marketing objectives can be developed.

Setting Direct Marketing Objectives

There are four basic objectives for most direct marketing campaigns, or for direct marketing techniques used in support of an overall advertising campaign: building a marketer–customer relationship, including a trial or brand switch, developing a market through direct response, and building volume and usage of a brand.

Retain current customers.   Most direct marketing is based on the concept of building relationships between the marketer and the customer. The direct marketer believes that the on-going relationship and continual purchases really make direct marketing different from traditional marketing. Therefore, the direct marketer is willing to invest heavily to gain a new customer, often in excess of the first year's sales returns, because he or she is building for these repeat or future purchases.

Generally, consumer package goods companies try to build this sort of relationship, but because they have little information on their customers, it is very difficult to do. As a result, because the mass marketer doesn't know the customer and relies on other channel members to build that relationship, brand switching is simply an acceptable part of the mass market businessplace. Alternatively, the direct marketer, because he or she can maintain continuous contact with a known list of customers and prospects, is in a better position to maintain the customer loyalty.

In most business organizations, the 80–20 rule holds, that is, about 80 percent of the company's sales are made to 20 percent of the customer base. Although the figures may vary somewhat, the relationship seems to hold in most every category. In a marketplace where there is little economic or population growth, one of the key elements of success is holding onto present customers and building sales or volume over time. That is what direct marketers are teaching the mass marketers today.

Induce trial or switching.   Direct marketing is an excellent marketing tool to generate trial of a product or to encourage brand switching. Assuming something is known about the customer or prospect, then specific direct marketing programs can be developed to build trial of the brand. For example, assume a list of persons known to have vegetable gardens is available. It would then be a simple task for a marketer of a new type of fertilizer to mail a letter, a coupon, or even a sample to this group. One would naturally expect high response from prospects who are known to have a garden. This is just one example of how direct marketers deal with prospects, not just suspects. Alternatively, if a list of known users of competitive brands of facial bar soap were available, some type of trial offer could be made by a marketer of a competitive product to try to get the consumer to switch to the marketer's brand, and so on.

Sell through direct response.   The third objective might be to attempt to sell the product through direct response. For example, General Foods tried first to get their premium Swedish coffee, Gevalia, distributed through traditional retail food store outlets. Because the market was small, the price of the product high, and the cost of building awareness and trial through mass media advertising was high, the product was introduced through direct response. It has been a solid success. (Exhibit 14–9 is an example of one of the advertisements that has been used to sell Gevalia through direct response.)

Increase volume.   The final objective is to build volume or usage of the brand. By using various direct marketing techniques, such as newsletters, a user club, continuity programs, and premiums, Friskies cat food has not only built a relationship with their customers but has encouraged them to use more of the product as well. (An example of the Friskie's "Lost Pet" program is illustrated as Exhibit 14–10.)

The key task for the advertising planner is to relate the possible direct marketing objectives to the overall goals of the brand, product, or service for which the campaign is being developed. Based on an analysis of what the brand needs to accomplish with the advertising campaign, the direct marketing objectives can then be identified. This is how integrated marketing communications programs are developed using direct marketing.

The easiest way to understand how direct marketing might be used in an overall advertising campaign is through example. On the following pages, a step-by-step approach that an advertising planner might use in developing an integrated marketing communications program for a product or service is illustrated.

Inbound or Outbound?

All direct marketing activities can be classified as either outbound or inbound. *Outbound* activities are messages sent to customers or prospects through the mail, by telephone, and through various mass media. An example of an "outbound" direct marketing program is the mail solicitation program that AT&T has developed for their Reach Out® America long-distance calling program (Exhibit 14–11). In this case, AT&T, because they have an individual customer record of long-distance usage for each cus-

Exhibit 14–9 Direct Response Piece

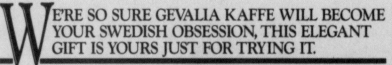

WE'RE SO SURE GEVALIA KAFFE WILL BECOME YOUR SWEDISH OBSESSION, THIS ELEGANT GIFT IS YOURS JUST FOR TRYING IT.

Over a century ago, in the port of Gävle, Sweden, Victor Theodor Engwall was seized by an obsession to produce a perfect cup of coffee.

Today, we invite you to share his obsession, starting with a gift: the European-style automatic drip coffee-maker. It's an ideal way to enjoy the full, rich flavor of Gevalia® Kaffe quickly, simply and at its finest.

Victor Theodor Engwall would have wanted nothing less. For he spent years tirelessly roasting and blending and tasting and testing the finest beans from the world's great coffee plantations. Kenyan AA, Costa Rican, Colombian, Guatemalan—up to six variet-ies of premium Arabica beans.

His efforts were rewarded when Gevalia was appointed coffee purveyor to the Swedish Royal court, an honor we have proudly held for generations.

MAKE GEVALIA YOUR OBSESSION.

Gevalia Kaffe is not sold in stores in the U.S. But now you can enjoy it in your home or office via the Gevalia Kaffe Import Service.

You may order Gevalia whole bean or ground. And if you prefer decaffeinated, prepare for a pleasant surprise.

Gevalia naturally decaffeinated coffee is made using a patented process, with the same ingre-dients found in sparkling water. So caffeine is re-moved naturally while the magnificent flavor of Gevalia remains intact.

For fresh-ness, each batch of Gevalia is vacuum-sealed in half-pound pouches of golden foil, within seconds of roasting. Whether you order Traditional or Decaffeinated, you'll always enjoy Gevalia Kaffe at its peak of flavor.

YOUR GIFT: THE EUROPEAN-STYLE COFFEEMAKER. RETAIL VALUE $39.95

With your Trial Shipment of Gevalia Kaffe you will receive the high-quality automatic drip coffeemaker shown. It's our way of ensuring that you enjoy Gevalia at its best.

The coffeemaker makes up to four cups at a time, and has a European-style filter cone to ensure full flavor even when making a single cup.

The retail value of this coffeemaker is $39.95. But it is yours as our gift with your Trial Ship-ment (one pound) of Gevalia Kaffe, with the under-standing that if after trying it you want more, you will get further shipments through our Import Service. That's how sure we are that one taste will make Gevalia your Swedish obsession.

To order, simply complete and return the coupon or, for credit card orders, call toll-free: **1-800-678-2687.**

Complete and mail this coupon to:

GEVALIA KAFFE IMPORT SERVICE, P.O. BOX 11424, DES MOINES, IA 50336

☐ **YES,** I would like to try one pound of Gevalia Kaffe for $10.00, including shipping and handling, and receive with it the European-style Automatic Drip Coffeemaker (retail value $39.95) as a free gift. Send me Gevalia Kaffe—two ½ pound packages of the types I indicated below, with the understanding that if after trying it I want more, I will get further shipments through the Gevalia Kaffe Import Service.

Check One: A ☐ Traditional Roast Regular
B ☐ Traditional Roast Decaffeinated
C ☐ ½ lb. Traditional Roast Regular, ½ lb. Decaf

Check One: 1 ☐ Whole Bean
2 ☐ Ground

How many coffee drinkers are there in your household? **Check:** ☐ 1 ☐ 2 ☐ 3 or more

Charge my: ☐ VISA ☐ MASTERCARD ☐ AMERICAN EXPRESS

Card Number_____ Exp. Date_____

☐ My check is enclosed, payable to Gevalia Kaffe for $10.00.

CODE: 140533

Please sign here_____

Name_____

Address_____

City_____ State_____ Zip_____

Telephone Number (_____)_____

G·E·V·A·L·I·A ✦ K·A·F·F·E

A SWEDISH OBSESSION

HOW THIS SERVICE WORKS: 1. You must find Gevalia Kaffe pleasing to your taste or you may send a postcard within 10 days after you receive your introductory supply telling us to cancel, and we will send you nothing further. The Regal Gevalia Kaffe Canister is yours to keep in any case. 2. Otherwise about one month after you receive your introductory package, you will receive your first standard shipment containing four packages (1 lb. each) of the type(s) you have indicated. Your standard shipment of 4 packages will be sent to you thereafter once every 6 weeks. 3. You will be billed only $4.25 for each package of regular Gevalia Kaffe and $4.75 for each package of Decaffeinated. A shipping and handling charge will be added. 4. You agree to pay as soon as you receive each shipment. For those using credit cards, subsequent shipments will also be conveniently billed to your card. 5. The above prices are guaranteed not to rise through May 31, 1990. 6. You may change the quantities and types of Gevalia you want at any time or cancel the arrangement and receive no further shipments simply by notifying us. 7. Limit one membership per household. 8. Offer is open only to residents of Continental U.S. 1990 Vict. Th. Engwall & Co.

Exhibit 14–10 Friskies' "Lost Pet" Program

tomer household, can identify and segment those customers who might be the best prospects for the service. They can then mail these best prospects the material describing the program. Customers may not have necessarily required the information on "Reach Out America," but AT&T believes they are good enough prospects that they are worth soliciting directly. Thus, this type of direct marketing is considered to be "outbound."

Inbound direct marketing relies on the customer's identifying themselves in some way as prospects for a product or service. The most common examples of "inbound" direct marketing are orders taken via a toll-free 800 number, or on an order form or coupon. In some instances, customers or prospects simply request more information or ask that a salesperson contact them. On occasion, inbound direct marketing is the only way in which a customer can receive a product not offered in a retail store or through another distribution channel. Companies that use television commercials and toll-free 800 numbers to sell records, tapes, household gadgets, and the like are prime examples of this type of direct marketing. (Another example is illustrated by the advertisement for Strong Funds, Exhibit 14–12.)

With these concepts of inbound and outbound direct marketing in mind, we can review the ways in which an advertising planner considers various direct marketing activities in the development of an overall advertising campaign.

It All Starts with the Objective

The first step for the advertising planner in considering various direct marketing activities is to review the advertising objectives. Only after achieving a thorough understanding of the objectives of the advertising campaign, can the planner determine whether direct marketing—direct mail, data base or direct response—might be useful in the campaign development process. Assuming that direct marketing is a viable method of communicating with and getting responses from customers and prospects, the next step is to develop the direct mail, direct response, or data base marketing campaign.

The List Is the Key Element

The first step in most direct marketing/direct mail campaigns is to locate or identify the list of customers/prospects that will be used. For most package goods companies, a list of current customers is not available. Because many consumer products are sold through some sort of distribution channel, such as a wholesaler, distributor, or retail store, or because the product or service is used by such a large number of people, developing a specific list of customers, prospects, and suspects is not really economically practical, or in some cases, possible.

Exhibit 14–11   AT&T "Reach Out" America Ad

How AT&T's <u>REACH OUT</u> AMERICA billing plan works:

"Reach Out" America is an innovative long distance billing plan, and is preferred by many AT&T customers. We have included this pamphlet to let you know how it works and why we are suggesting it for you.

A full hour of AT&T weekend and night calls for just $7.20 a month.

"Reach Out" America gives you an hour of out-of-state, direct-dialed AT&T Long Distance calls* each month. Only calls made during the plan's specified hours (shown on the accompanying chart) are credited to this hour.

Whether you make one 60-minute call, three 20-minute calls or a dozen 5-minute calls, you still pay the same low price.

You pay by the hour, not by the mile.

Unlike the charges on your present long distance bill, "Reach Out" America calls cost the same regardless of distance. You can make out-of-state calls to the farthest corners of the country, including Alaska and Hawaii, as well as to Puerto Rico and the U.S. Virgin Islands, and they will be included in the plan. Naturally, the farther you call, the more you could save.

Additional hours cost even less than the first.

If you make more than one hour of calls with the "Reach Out" America plan, you will enjoy an even greater value. Additional hours of these calls cost just $6.90 each.

And this additional calling time is "prorated," so you will be charged only for the additional minutes you use.

You can save 15% on evening calls.

Most people who decide to switch their billing plan to "Reach Out" America also choose the 15% Evening Discount option.

If you make evening calls, you can enjoy 15% off AT&T's already-reduced evening prices, on direct-dialed, out-of-state AT&T Long Distance calls, Sunday through Friday, from 5 PM to 10 PM. This option costs only an additional $1.00 per month.

Save on daytime calls, too!

If you make daytime calls, you can also enjoy 5% off direct-dialed, out-of-state AT&T Long Distance calls during weekdays, Monday through Friday, 8 AM to 5 PM. This 5% Daytime Discount option costs an

*"Reach Out" America applies only to AT&T Long Distance calls. Any calls made outside your state that do not appear on the AT&T portion of your telephone bill will not apply to the plan. "Reach Out" America prices are subject to change.

If you choose AT&T'S REACH OUT° AMERICA plan, please indicate your decision below.
Check the blue box for the recommended plan.
To save $5, respond by June 30, 1989.
Or call toll free: 1 800 REACH OUT°, ext. 3057
(1 800 732-2468, ext. 3057)

☐ **I wish to change my long distance billing to AT&T's <u>Reach Out</u> America plan.** Every month I will be billed $7.20. This gives me one hour of out-of-state AT&T Long Distance calls dialed direct from my home during the "Reach Out" America plan's weekend and night calling hours. Each additional weekend and night hour I use will cost just $6.90 (prorated, so I pay only for the minutes I use). I understand that the usual one-time $10 order-processing charge will be reduced to $5 if I respond by June 30, 1989, and will appear on my first month's bill.

☐ **I wish to add the 15% Evening Discount Option to my <u>Reach Out</u> America plan.** In addition to $7.20 a month for the plan, I will be billed an extra $1.00 a month (a total of $8.20). This will give me a 15% discount off AT&T's already-reduced prices, Sunday through Friday between 5 PM and 10 PM.

☐ **Along with my Evening Discount Option, I wish to add the 5% Daytime Discount Option to my <u>Reach Out</u> America plan.** In addition to $8.20 a month for the plan, I will be billed an extra 50 cents a month (a total of $8.70). This will give me a 5% discount off daytime out-of-state AT&T Long Distance calls made between 8 AM and 5 PM, Monday through Friday. I understand that I can only get this option along with the Evening Discount option.

Your order cannot be processed without completing the area below:

Signature_____ Date_____

Home Phone ( )_____ Daytime Phone ( )_____

Note: A 3% Federal Excise Tax will be added to your monthly bill and, where applicable, a state surcharge.

Tear here and fold in half.

Exhibit 14–12   Inbound Direct Marketing Ad

Higher Rates Than Money Funds.

Are you looking for higher rates than fixed-price money market funds? The no-load **Strong Short-Term Bond Fund** strives for the highest level of interest income consistent with high principal stability. You also get:

- Free check writing
- No sales charges
- No withdrawal penalties
- 24-hour service

Call For Latest Yield!

1 800 368-3863   CALL 24 HOURS!

For more complete information, including charges and expenses, call or write for a free prospectus. Please read it carefully before you invest or send money.

I am also interested in:
☐ IRAs
☐ Pension/Profit Sharing Plans

MMB0689

name _____

address _____

city _____   state ___   zip ___

STRONG SHORT-TERM BOND FUND
P.O. Box 2920, Milwaukee, WI 53201

STRONG

SOURCE: Reprinted with permission of Strongs Funds.

Customer lists, which generally include names, addresses, some demographics, purchase histories, and perhaps some psychographic information, are commonly called "house lists" or "internal lists" because they have been developed and are maintained by the marketer. Assuming that the list is updated regularly, this is the best possible list. Using this customer list, some direct marketers have been able to develop specific customer profiles. These profiles identify common traits among consumers, allowing the development of models of future customers; they single out factors that allow the selection of the best prospects from the general marketplace.

If a customer list is not available, or if the marketer is seeking to expand trial or usage or to encourage a brand switch among a new group of prospects, then "outside lists" are commonly used. Outside lists are names and addresses of persons who have some trait in common. For example, the list might be composed of magazine subscribers, members of the local opera guild, dog owners, or even purchasers of automobile hobby kits. Only about fifty percent of the general population responds to direct marketing offers or sales efforts. Many direct marketers are willing to use this common trait, direct responsiveness, as the criterion for selecting names from the general population. (Note that Standard Rate & Data Service publishes a directory of available lists. It gives a general indication of the list membership, cost, and so on.)

Understanding the List Business

Earlier in this chapter, we described the basic structure of the list business. For the most part, the advertising planner will be involved only with the list broker, not the list owner or manager. With that fact in mind, we'll turn to the process of list selection.

The broadest category of segmentation and list purchase is based on geographics, geodemographics, or zip codes. Organizations using U.S. Census data, such as Claritas, Donnelley Marketing, and Geographic Data Technology, have developed demographic profiles of all neighborhoods in the U.S., down to the census tract level (about 200 homes per tract). Income levels, basic demographics, value of home, purchasing power, and so on can be identified for various areas of the country from this type of segmentation analysis. By tying this data to zip codes, marketers can target specific areas of the country that contain the best prospects for their product or service. Segmented lists based on these geodemographics can be purchased for mailing by the marketing organization, or they can be developed through solo or cooperative programs with the list supplier. (An example of the type of lists and data available from Donnelley Marketing is illustrated in their advertisement in Exhibit 14–13.)

Today, several organizations have taken basic geodemographic data a step further. Through surveys, these list companies have identified users of specific product categories and even brands. Therefore, the marketer is now able to purchase lists of category users or even users of competitive brands. Although these types of lists are just starting to become available from groups including National Demographics & Lifestyles, Behaviorbank, and others, they offer the marketer a much more refined list of prospects than do those lists based on geographics or demographics alone. (An example of the type of list or data available from National Demographics & Lifestyles is illustrated in their advertisement in Exhibit 14–14.)

The next category of list segmentation is based on some trait or attribute that households or individuals share. Lists of these types include:

1. Compiled lists. These lists contain names identified with some common characteristic or interest. They are developed by organizations

Exhibit 14–13 Geodemographic Information—Donnelley Marketing

"To the winner belongs the rewards of CONQUEST."
Socrademos, 1989 A.D.

WINNING THE AD GAME

...depends on knowing the right moves.
Depend on Donnelley Marketing Information Services for the strategic advantage of CONQUEST®/Advertising — vital marketing and demographic information for every neighborhood and market area in the U.S.A. — all on your PC.

You'll win with sophisticated targeting built on CONQUEST's integrated information sources: our geo-demographics and ClusterPLUS lifestyles, Nielsen Media, Dun's BusinessLINE, SMRB and MRI product usage information, to name just a few.

With CONQUEST on your desk, you can zero in on the right media mix, sales promotions, cross selling and direct mail — to reach the right people, at the right time.

You get the picture at a glance with CONQUEST's maps and information graphics. Capture new business. Gain credibility. Achieve accountability.

Put CONQUEST/Advertising on your PC. You'll get today's most advanced CD-ROM driven desk-top market analysis and planning system.

You'll be a master strategist.

The Single Source for Marketing Success

Donnelley Marketing Information Services

a company of
The Dun & Bradstreet Corporation

Sales Office — East: (203) 353-7474 • Central: (312) 495-1211 • West: (714) 978-1122

SOURCE: Reprinted with permission of Donnelley Marketing Information Service, Stamford, Connecticut.

Exhibit 14–14   Refined Geodemographic Information—NDL

SOURCE: Client: National Demographics and Lifestyles. Agency: Vennillion Design, Boulder, Colorado. Reprinted by permission.

who gather the names, maintain the list, and offer it for sale to marketers. An example is the R.L. Polk list of automobile registrations. Leaders in this type of list development and rental are Metromail, R.L. Polk, and Donnelley Marketing.

2.   Inquiries or customer lists. These are lists of other organizations' customers, users, responders, and so on. These lists include persons, such as magazine subscribers or catalog users, who have signified interest in the organization or its products or services. There are literally thousands of such lists available to the advertising planner.

If an outside list is to be used, the rental of the list is usually negotiated through a list broker. There are rules about the use of the rented list. Bob Stone has listed six of them.[3]

> Lists can be ordered directly from a list owner, but most list rental orders are placed through list brokers. The broker handles all the details with the list owner: clearances, order placement, follow up for order completion, billing, collecting, and payment to the list owner, less the usual 20 percent commission that accrues to the list broker.
>
> The rental of lists involves certain conditions:
>
> 1. The names are rented for *one time use* only. No copy of the list is to be retained for any purpose whatsoever.
> 2. Usage must be cleared with the list owner in advance. The mailing piece which is approved is the only one that can be used.
> 3. The mail date approved by the list owner must be adhered to.
> 4. List rentals are charged on a per-thousand-name basis.
> 5. Net name arrangements vary, but most list owners will specify the percentage (of the names supplied) for which the full list rental charge per M must be paid plus a specific running cost for the names not used.
> 6. Most list owners charge extra for selections such as: sex, recency, ZIP, state, unit of sale, or any segmentation available on the particular list. Prices vary.

Most lists are rented on the basis of a cost-per-thousand (CPM) names for one time use. In the late 1980s, customer list costs were approximately $60 to $100 per thousand, plus selections, label costs, and other charges. Compiled lists rent for considerably less.

In making list selections for mailings, brokers usually develop "data cards" on each available list. These cards give the prospective list renter information and details of the list, its cost, who is included on it, how it was developed, and so on. (See Exhibit 14–15 for an example of a data card.)

In most cases, direct marketing planners make use of some form of list test response—a mailing or solicitation of a segment or portion of the list to see the response rate that is achieved—prior to using the entire list. Most of these list tests consist of mailings of 5,000 to 10,000 names, considered an adequate sample.

If the marketer has a customer list, in order to avoid duplication or resolicitation of existing customers, most direct marketing experts recommend the use of a computer technique—merge-purge. This technique involves comparing by computer-matching the names on the proposed outside list against the company's current customer list, and is designed to remove duplicated names. The list renter then pays only for those unduplicated

---

[3]Bob Stone, *Successful Direct Marketing Methods,* 4th ed.: 173.

Exhibit 14–15   Data Card

House & Garden (Condé Nast)

454,016 Subscribers	@ $85/M	Feb. 1987	K01 Y02
13,308 Canadian Subscribers	@ $85/M		D01
10,162 Address Changes (Quarterly)	@ $95/M		
71,259 Expires (Last 4 Months)	@ $55/M	Minimum:	

(Hotline Selection not available at this time.)

(Add $15 per reel for nonreturnable magtape.)

Minimum:

10,000 (Actives)
5,000 (Expires)

Data   Published monthly by Condé Nast Publications, *House & Garden* is the magazine of creative living, international, interior decoration, art, architecture and gardens, travel, dealers, and collectors.

Magtape or Cheshire from:

Neodata Services
Att: Larry Cline
833 W.S. Boulder Road
Louisville, CO 80027

Unit $24.00/year

Profile   Median Age: 43.4.
Median Household Income: $65,200.
Median Net Worth of Household: $494,500.
93% own their own home.
Median value of home is $156,100.
21% own a weekend/vacation home or condominium.
45% are professional or managerial.
93% are married.
70% attended/graduated from college.

Two complete samples required in advance for all new tests and continuations.

No phone clearances.

Sex   Mostly women. Can select @ $5/M: 256,678 women Subscribers; 71,823 men Subscribers; balance unidentified.

Allow 3 weeks to process orders.

Media   100% Direct Response. No source select.

Signed agreement form from Mailer required for initial test order.

Filed   ZIP sequence / 4-up Cheshire / 9T/1600 Magtape. DMA Mail Preference Service Names suppressed.

Selections   Nth name @ N/C.
State / SCF / ZIP @ $3.50/M. Can use ZIP tape.
Pressure sensitive lavels @ $8/M.

Net Name Arrangement (100,000 minimum): 85% + $6/M with computer verification.

Keying $2.00/M (up to 4 digits).

Note: List owner requires payment 30 days after mail date.

Note: List owner will not rent to sweepstakes offers.

Note: For Canadian Subscribers, see Kleid data card no. 20806 (Condé Nast Master Canadian Active file).

Note: Orders cancelled five days prior to or after original mail date will require full payment.

names or a previously agreed upon percentage of names from the outside list supplier.

The Offer

The selling proposition made to customers and prospects through direct marketing is called the *offer.* Like the promise or competitive customer benefit made in general advertising, the offer sums up in a few words or sentences the value the product or service brings to the prospective purchaser. In most cases, however, the direct marketing offer goes beyond the simple presentation of product or service benefits and is combined with an incentive to generate action. For example, a price reduction, a cents-off coupon, a rebate offer, or a sweepstakes are all considered methods of increasing or improving response to the basic product offer made in the direct marketing program.

Here, the differences between sales promotion and direct marketing begin to blur. Is a coupon mailed to the home sales promotion or is it direct marketing? The best way to differentiate is through the list. If the customer or prospect is known, it's direct marketing. If not, and the offer is to a general target market, it's most likely sales promotion. Even this differentiation is becoming more and more difficult to support.

The major difference between general advertising themes or benefits and direct marketing offers is the opportunity, in direct marketing, to provide multiple support points. Most general advertisements or commercials offer one clear customer benefit and one or two support points or product features; direct marketing offers generally list and/or illustrate a number of product features and support points. Because there is really no limit to the amount of copy or material that can be included in a direct mail package, folder, or brochure, there is a tendency for these offers to contain much more information, product and feature descriptions, and sales copy than does a general advertisement. The assumption is that the direct marketing offer is the only information the customer or prospect will have available when making a purchasing decision. Therefore the offer, the direct mail package and the supporting material must be as complete as possible so that the recipient can make a fully informed decision. For example, AT&T, in an effort to generate more usage of their toll-free 800 number telephone service, sent a direct mail folder to all customers who had requested the *AT&T Toll-Free 800 Directory.* In the brochure, several offers were made to customers and prospects, most of which involved some form of discount when the customer ordered the item by calling any of the category companies listed in the 800-number directory. (The full brochure is illustrated as Exhibit 14–16. One of the offers within the brochure is illustrated as Exhibit 14–17.)

Exhibit 14–16   AT&T 800-Number Brochure

Exhibit 14–17   AT&T 800-Number Offer

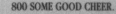

800 SOME GOOD CHEER.

SAVE 15% on any gift selection of wine, champagne, or spirits from 800-Cheers!

Whatever the celebration or the occasion, let 800-Cheers! send your message of good will. Choose from sparkling champagnes, vintage and imported wines, or warming spirits and liquors. And because 800-Cheers! features over 5,000 selections, you're virtually guaranteed to find anyone's favorite refreshment. Whether it's "Congratulations," "Good luck," or "Thank you," 800-Cheers! is bound to lift their spirits.

Look for 800-Cheers! under Wine and Spirits in the AT&T 800 Consumer Directory. Tell them you saw their ad in the AT&T 800 Directory...and save!

In each case, the offer made by AT&T has been enhanced with a reduced price or free offer of some sort to generate an immediate response by the customer.

Distributing the Direct Marketing Offer

To this point, it might seem that all direct marketing offers go through the postal service. Although mail is by far the largest method of distributing direct marketing offers and materials, other media sources are important too. Direct marketers call the distribution of their messages and offers *circulation*. This should not be confused with the same term as used by magazines and newspapers. In essence, when direct marketers talk of circulation, they are talking about how to get the direct marketing offers in front of customers and prospects.

In addition to mail, direct marketing offers can be distributed through newspapers, magazines, radio, television, and other forms of electronic media—computers and even facsimile machines.

There are three key ingredients in the selection of distribution methods of direct marketing support programs.

1. Cost per thousand (CPM). The cost of distributing direct marketing offers is usually based on the cost of distributing 1,000 copies or the CPM rate. The CPM may range from a few dollars in the mass media to well into the hundreds of dollars for direct mail sent to very specific target markets, such as physicians and CEOs.
2. Response rate. Response rates are usually calculated as a percentage of the number of replies received based on the total number distributed. Some forms of direct marketing media traditionally generate greater response rates than do others. As a rule of thumb, the more targeted the mailing list, the greater the response. Thus, some business-to-business direct marketing programs generate a 40 percent response or more. Generally, mass media direct mail or marketing offers made through newspapers and magazines and even FSIs have response rates in the 3 percent to 6 percent range.
3. Cost per order (CPO). Although knowing the cost per thousand to distribute the direct marketing offer is helpful, and estimating the response rate is a closer measure of the value of the media, the calculation that is important to direct marketers is that of cost per order (CPO). This calculation takes the total cost of the direct marketing or mail program and divides it by the number of responses received from that media distribution system. Thus, for example, a direct-mail-delivered package might have a cost per order of $6.50, while a

newspaper-delivered offer might have a CPO of $15.00. In this case, even though the newspaper might have a lower CPM and a higher response rate than direct mail, it is the actual cost per order, cost per lead, cost per redemption, or whatever the goal of the direct marketing campaign is rather than the gross cost of media or the response rate that is important to the planner in a direct marketing program.

A Quick Look at Telemarketing

Although the use of toll-free 800 numbers and telemarketing are growing at a rapid rate, space does not allow a full discussion of the advantages and opportunities of these forms of direct marketing as support for or as an integral part of the development of an overall advertising campaign. The following, however, are some of the more common uses of the telephone and telemarketing that might be used for a package goods product.

1. Direct ordering. Through the use of inbound 800-number telephone programs, the customer can usually order products and services twenty-four hours a day, seven days a week, from major catalog houses and other direct marketing organizations. With the growth and acceptance of nationwide credit cards and those of individual organizations, this system has become more attractive to consumers.
2. Additional information or customer service. Through the use of a toll-free 800 number, questions about the product, repair services, product add-ons, and the like can be handled easily and quickly by a manufacturer. A good example of this is the General Electric AnswerCenter, the telemarketing service that GE provides to answer customer questions and provide customer service for all GE products.
3. Lead qualification. Often telemarketing is used to qualify leads for the sales force on either an in-bound or out-bound basis.
4. Outbound telemarketing. In some instances, particularly in business-to-business areas, telemarketing is used as a sales call on customers who cannot be visited regularly by the sales force, or as a way to take orders for products that are repurchased regularly. In these instances, the calls are generated by the telemarketer on a regular basis to a list of prospects or customers.

No matter how telemarketing is used, there are certain costs associated with any program. The chief cost is that of personnel and training. Telemarketing is very labor intensive and turnover among telemarketing representatives is high. In addition, there is the cost of telephone equipment and service and office facilities.

Developing a Direct Mail Package

There is an almost unlimited choice of what can or should be included in a direct mail package. The primary decision points are as follows:

1. What is the objective of the package? If its goal is to generate an order for a product by immediate direct response, more information, material, and other elements will be required than if the objective is simply to deliver a cents-off coupon to a known customer.
2. What is the manner of distribution? The package's format will differ depending on how the direct marketing message will be delivered. For example, first-class mail generally takes a different form than that used for third-class mail, UPS, or Federal Express.
3. How complex is the product or service or idea? If the product is relatively well known and well accepted, fewer selling materials are required than for products that are new or hard to explain.
4. What is the available budget? Obviously, the more materials you include, the more personalization involved, the more color or die-cuts or involvement devices included, the higher the cost of the overall package. For the advertising planner, the key questions to ask are, What additional response will I get from the additional elements or art or involvement devices? Will the increased costs be justified by results?

Direct mail packages can be categorized in three ways:

1. The classic format. This format consists of a separate outside envelope, an order form, a letter of some type, and some additional brochure, folder, or description of the product or service.
2. The self-mailer. The self-mailer can vary from a single sheet of paper, folded and stapled, to a very colorful table-size sheet folded and prepared for mailing.
3. The catalog. The catalog is a series of pages that are folded, stapled, or glued together to form a booklet which can be sent through the mail.

Inherent in most direct mail packages are various forms of involvement devices or items included to get the recipient to pay additional attention to the mailing. Some of the more popular ones are stamps, tokens, rub-offs, puzzles, and insert letters. Although much can be said about the value of these involvement devices, the real test of the direct mail package is still the list and the offer being made. They are what really determines the response rate to a mailing.

A unique element of a direct mail promotion is the inclusion of an order form, or directions on how to order or purchase the product or service.

For package goods sold through retail outlets, the order form may simply be a directive to see the local dealer, or a list of dealers. For products that are offered through the mail or that require a response—such as a lead for the sales force or the dealers—the order form is vital. It should be clear, concise, easy to read, and complete, with enough space to allow the printing of name, address, and so on. Often, the "order form" is simply the opportunity to use an 800 number to call in orders. Many marketers have found it is best to offer both an order form and a toll-free number to maximize results. In some cases, however, the addition of the 800 number has been shown to depress results.

The Final Phase—Fulfillment

Filling customers' orders, delivering product information, and providing leads for the sales force all fall under the heading of direct marketing fulfillment. These activities often determine the success of a direct marketing program. Not being able to deliver the product, having distribution delays that cause the customer to cancel the order, bad order handling, and simply not handling the financial operations of the direct marketing operation are all problem areas in terms of fulfillment. In direct marketing terminology, such follow-up to the initial order is often called the *back end* of operations. This is a very specialized area of direct marketing; the advertising planner should be aware of it, and should know how to contact and engage experts in this area to assure the success of the overall marketing communications program.

EVALUATING DIRECT MARKETING PROGRAMS

What really separates direct marketing or direct mail from other areas of general advertising and sales promotion is the evaluation systems that are used. Because direct marketers know their costs in advance and can estimate their response rates, based on previous efforts or on test mailings or programs, it is much easier for the advertising planner to evaluate direct marketing programs than it is to evaluate general advertising or even sales promotion plans and proposals. Program evaluation can be quite accurate on an after-the-fact basis when all costs are known and the specific response rate to the program has been determined.

Some of the more common ways that direct marketing or direct mail is evaluated is on cost per order, return on selling or inventory investment, and general return on investment. Perhaps the most unique element of direct marketing is the ability to calculate what is called the lifetime value of a customer. If the customer is known, and the costs to solicit that customer can be calculated, these factors can be measured against that customer's continuing purchases. Thus, the marketer can actually calculate the exact profit on each purchase the customer makes. It is then possible to estimate the length of time the person will be a customer based on experience with other customers, and, therefore, determine, with a fair degree of accuracy, what the value of each customer will be to the company. Using this information, the marketer can then decide how much he or she is willing to invest to obtain a new customer, and maintain a relationship with that customer over a period of time. This sort of calculation, which is becoming more popular among all types of direct marketers, is really the key to the evaluation of all forms of advertising and promotion in the future.

Case Studies

Stearns Food Market

Stearns Food Market was one of three major supermarket chains serving the Washington, D.C. area. Stores were located throughout the District of Columbia and suburban Maryland and Virginia. All of the Stearns stores had undergone extensive remodeling in the early 1980s in order to become more competitive in the market and to respond to changing consumer needs.

Stearns stores now featured stores-within-a-store—each store had a full-service deli, bakery, butcher shop, gourmet shop, cheese counter, and seafood market in addition to traditional grocery and health and beauty products. Additionally, all checkouts in all Stearns stores were equipped with scanners, speeding up checkout lines and improving store inventory management.

The store enhancements seemed to be working—although Stearns had fewer stores than the other two major chains in the market, Stearns was only a few share points behind the number two chain and had maintained that position for the past several years. Annual customer satisfaction surveys showed that Stearns attracted a loyal following of relatively upscale customers. Most of the regular customers for an individual store lived within a five-mile radius of the store; occasional customers were drawn from a slightly larger area.

While Stearns's manager Heidi Dickens was very happy with Stearns's current strength, she believed there was cause for concern. Stearns and the other two chains were engaging in more and more price fighting. Stearns's ads immediately after the remodeling had highlighted the changes in the store and tried to create an image of a new, modern supermarket. However, within two years the other chains had matched many of Stearns's enhancements. Current promotion for all three chains was almost completely price oriented. All three stocked the same brands and none of the three chains had well-established store brands.

Although Dickens felt Stearns could continue to fight it out with the other two chains on a price basis, she was concerned about the long-term impact of such an approach on Stearns's image. Also, it looked like a major "warehouse" supermarket retailer would be entering the Washington market in the next year and a half. Warehouse stores typically offer customers fewer services in exchange for consistently lower product prices. Dickens worried that the actions of the three chains were turning many Washington-area shoppers into price shoppers. If that was true, the warehouse store chain would probably appeal to many of those people, taking customers away from all three chains.

In looking for options to both get away from constant price-oriented advertising and prepare to compete with the warehouse store chain, Dickens had been paying close attention to recent articles in the supermarket trade journals about "frequent purchaser programs." Supermarket chains in several cities had been testing such programs. The frequent purchaser program involved monitoring individual customer purchases and rewarding customers with discounts or free merchandise when they reached particular spending points. For example, a customer might receive a $25 gift certificate after buying $500 worth of merchandise.

Although the mechanics of the program varied from chain to chain, most programs involved recordkeeping through the supermarket's scanner system. Customers participating in the program would be given a membership card with a UPC code keyed to that customer. Each time the customer made a purchase, they would first hand the cashier their membership card. The card would be scanned, followed by the customer's purchases. In this way, the store would have a record not only of how much the customer had bought, but also of which specific items had been purchased.

Dickens had some experience in direct marketing from a previous job with a food products catalog company. She thought it might be possible to use the basics of a frequent purchaser program to create a data base for the Stearns stores. Stearns could collect basic demographic data, such as name, address, age, family size, and occupation, from customers interested in joining the frequent purchaser program. In addition to offering purchase level awards, such as those used by other stores, Stearns could use the new customer data base to send promotional material and other store information directly to the purchaser-program members.

Dickens felt that by beginning to build a data base of Stearns's customers, she might be able to get an advantage over the other two chains. She doubted that either would be in a position to start their own program very soon. The number one store had such a large customer base that such a program might be unmanageable, or would at least take quite a while to get going. The number two store was having some cash problems because of its own remodeling program, and would have trouble committing funds to a frequent purchaser program anytime soon. Although Dickens doubted that the frequent purchaser program would bring many new customers into Stearns (stores with frequent purchaser programs had not reported any sizable increase in shoppers), she did think it would be a way to hold on to current customers. And, if it added some value to shopping at Stearns, it might help hold on to customers once the warehouse store chain came into the market.

Given those positives, Dickens decided to proceed with planning for the introduction of the "Stearns's Shoppers Club."

Questions

1. How would you begin to build a mailing list of suspects for the "Stearns's Shoppers Club"? (This would be for the initial promotional mailing to get people to send for a membership card.)
2. What other options can you think of in addition to the prizes tied to purchase levels that might be offered as part of Stearns's frequent purchaser program?
3. Dickens's main objective is to maintain/retain current customers. How might a frequent purchaser program be used to get (a) consumer trial or switching, and (b) increased purchase volume by current customers?
4. What should Dickens look at to evaluate the effectiveness of the Stearns's Shoppers Club program?

The Plush Company

The Plush Company is a small, family-owned manufacturer of stuffed animal toys. No two animals are exactly alike, and each is hand finished. The Plush Company's quality control standards are very strict, and in the company's thirty-year history, no toy has ever been returned because of defects in workmanship. In keeping with the quality of the product, Plush Company toys generally retail for 40–50 percent above competitive toys.

The Plush Company has always distributed its toys through a limited number of department stores and specialty toy stores in the Pacific Northwest region of the United States. Because of the high quality of the product, above-average margins for the retailer, and high customer satisfaction, the Plush Company has been able to choose the retailers it wishes to work with, and maintains fairly tight control over the way its toys are displayed in the stores.

The Plush Company relies primarily on word of mouth to promote its products, and many purchasers are people who already own one or more Plush Company toys. The company is beginning to get sales from people who were given a Plush Company toy when they were children and are now buying the toys for their own children. The company has a fair amount of information on the people who purchase the toys, because each toy is packaged with a registration card. The idea of registering ownership complements the individuality of the toys and their premium price. The registration card asks for the purchaser's name, address, age, reason for buying the toy, and where the toy was purchased.

Plush Company sales have remained flat for the past several years. Because overall toy sales have been dropping in line with the declining U.S. birth rate, the company's sales performance is relatively good. About half of the Plush Company's annual volume is sold during the Christmas season, with the other half spread evenly throughout the year. (May and June sales are slightly above those of other months. Registration cards from toys bought in those months show that the toys are being given as graduation presents for female college and high school seniors.)

The Plush Company runs print advertisements in regional magazines during October and November and has done some co-op print advertising with its department store retailers. The ads are very image oriented, and talk about the joy of giving someone you love a Plush Company toy. (The company relies on the salespeople in the retail stores to educate potential purchasers about the craftsmanship that goes into making the toys, justifying the higher price.)

Melody Lind, a daughter of the Plush Company founder, has recently been appointed marketing director. Melody went to college in Virginia, and worked in the marketing department of a major East Coast department store before coming home to join the family business. Her former employer had an active catalog program, and Melody had seen first hand how much that program had added to overall sales. The catalog had not only offered current customers a new way of purchasing the store's products, but had also expanded the store's customer base, because it could be mailed into areas outside the store's trading area.

Melody felt that direct marketing might be a way to increase Plush Company sales. However, the program would have to be carefully constructed. For example, the apparently simple solution of getting Plush Company toys included in the catalog of one or more of the stores that already carried the line wouldn't work because the company might not be able to keep up with the volume of orders. In fact, several retailers had approached the company with that idea in the past and had been turned down. The feeling throughout the company was that catalog distribution suggested a mass-produced product, not one that was hand crafted.

Melody also felt that any direct marketing efforts would have to exclude the Pacific Northwest. The company's relationships with its retailers had been built up over time, and direct marketing in the Pacific Northwest would almost certainly be viewed as competition for the retailers' customers. Melody didn't want to hurt those relationships, and viewed direct marketing as a way of getting new customers, not giving current buyers a different way of getting the product.

Melody arranged a meeting with the president, vice president, and production manager of the company (her mother, father, and older brother, respectively) to get their approval to start work on a direct marketing program. The questions and concerns they raised were similar to her own, but she assured them that any program she developed would not hurt their retail relationships and would not generate more orders than the company could handle. Her brother estimated that the company could make up to thirty more toys a month from December through August, but was already at capacity for September–November.

Obviously, Melody would want to develop a very targeted program. She wondered if there was some way to use the information in the registration cards to start to define the best prospects for her program. She remembered that the department store she had worked for had used information from National Demographics & Lifestyles to identify which of their customers had bought particular types of products from other sources. Those people had then been sent particular catalogs featuring similar products. Maybe she could find out what other products the people who had bought Plush Company toys used. That might tell her more about them, and help her identify prospects in other parts of the country. Or, perhaps she could get a zip-code analysis of Plush Company toys buyers to see if they tended to live in similar neighborhoods. Also, she might be able to rent lists of toy purchasers.

Whatever she ended up doing, Melody's chief goal was to increase the Plush Company's sales to capacity without damaging the company's current image.

Questions

1. Do you agree with Melody that the Plush Company is a good candidate for a direct marketing program? Why or why not?
2. What vehicle do you recommend Melody use for her message—direct mail, direct response television, telemarketing, direct response magazine advertising, and so on? Why?
3. What sort of information would you look for in generating/renting a list for Melody's program? What characteristics would be important?
4. Given the medium you recommended in Question 2, what information would you include in your package/ad/telemarketing script?
5. Assuming Melody were able to get the information from National Demographics & Lifestyles described earlier, how might she use that in developing her program?

Evaluating the Advertising Campaign

Throughout this text, there has been a recurring theme: Set measurable objectives for the various stages and elements in the advertising campaign. Objective setting was stressed when the overall objectives of the campaign were determined, when the budget was established, when the creative strategy was finalized, when the media plan was prepared, even when the extra steps of sales promotion and direct marketing were added to the campaign. The time has now come to take those measurements—to evaluate the advertising campaign. The planner needs to know whether or not the advertising campaign achieved the goals that were set.

In some companies, the advertising evaluation process is called *accountability*. Management wants the advertising planners and managers to identify exactly what results were obtained for the advertising investment and to provide evidence of the return on investment. And this is reasonable and logical. After all, advertising uses the scarce resources of the firm, resources that could be invested in a number of ways. Therefore, the real question management poses is, "Is advertising the best way to use those funds?" And it is the job of the advertising campaign planner to be able to answer that question. To do so usually requires some form of advertising evaluation.

Although advertising campaign evaluation is a form of research, it is often quite different from other forms. Most advertising research is used to pretest or predict what might occur in the real-world marketplace. Evaluation research, on the other hand, is used to determine exactly what did happen. Although this information might be used as a basis for future actions, its basic purpose is to measure what occurred as a result of the advertising campaign and, therefore, what return was received on the investment made.

In summary, the three primary reasons to evaluate the advertising campaign are as follows:

1. To determine if the overall objectives set for the advertising campaign were met. If those overall objectives were not met, determine which of the individual objectives for the various elements of the campaign were met. Based on these evaluations, it can be determined where the failure may have occurred.
2. To quantify and justify the return on the campaign investment. By knowing what was achieved, management can relate that information to other potential uses for the funds and determine cost effectiveness of the advertising campaign.
3. To use the measurement information to make changes, additions, or corrections for future campaigns. No advertising campaign is ever totally successful in and of itself. It can always be improved. Evaluations of previous campaigns are a great help in improving and refining the elements and makeup of future campaigns.

In most organizations, the question is not whether to measure the results of the campaign, it is how to do so.

WHAT TO MEASURE AND WHY

If the campaign planner has built measurable objectives into the campaign plan, the evaluation is greatly simplified. There are, however, some rather traditional steps in campaign evaluation and some problems, too. Each is discussed in turn.

Evaluating the Results against the Objectives

In spite of some management's pleas that advertising must always produce sales, the advertising campaign must be evaluated against the objectives of the advertising plan. Thus, if the objective of the campaign was to generate direct sales, then the measurement of success of the campaign must be sales. If the goals established for a business-to-business campaign involved obtaining qualified leads for the sales force, then leads obtained as a direct result of the campaign should be the measuring stick. It is all too easy for the advertising campaign planner to fall into the trap of attempting to measure the total marketing efforts of the organization and relate them to the advertising campaign, rather than to measure the actual effects of the advertising that appeared. The rule is simple: Measure and evaluate the advertising campaign on the basis of the objectives contained in the advertising plan. Nothing more, nothing less. The importance of setting specific measurable advertising objectives for the advertising campaign is critical.

Some Problems in Campaign Measurement

No matter what objectives were set for the campaign, whether sales, market share, communication effects, or some other, there are some problems inherent in the measurement process. The campaign planner should be aware of these problems and try to minimize them while developing the plan.

Most advertising results must have soft objectives.   Unlike the hard physical measurement that can be made of the number of cans of peas processed on a packing line, the objectives of most advertising campaigns are much softer and subject to interpretation. Interpretation presents an inherent problem when any measurement is being made on people, particularly when the objectives are communication effects, such as awareness, knowledge, liking, or even past purchase recall. Although measurements for advertising often can't be as precise as those for sales promotion and direct marketing, objectives can be set and effects measured.

Measurement over time.   Because most advertising campaigns run over several months or even a year, it is often difficult to pinpoint the exact results of the campaign. In many instances, the campaign effects may build over time. In addition, there is the lagged effect of advertising.

Multiple advertising and marketing variables.   Even when measuring the communication effects of the advertising campaign, there is a problem in differentiating between what is advertising and what is not. For example, if the advertising sales message is carried on the product package and the consumer sees the package and remembers it but not the actual media advertising itself, should that then be credited to the advertising campaign? Questions such as this one make the identification of actual advertising effects very difficult. Often they really can't be separated from the other marketing efforts on behalf of the brand. Of course, in an integrated promotional effort, you may be more interested in the effects of the combined marketing elements, and so such separation may not be wanted.

The problems of human memory.   Human beings simply don't remember everything. And they certainly don't remember all the advertising they have seen or been exposed to. Although more and more is being learned about how the human mind works, it still is almost impossible to say whether advertising goes into short-term memory, long-term memory, is dismissed, is stored, or what happens to advertising impressions. Until there is a better understanding of how human memory and information storage works, it is difficult to say exactly what should be measured, and even if the use of recall and memory is the best way to evaluate advertising impressions.

In spite of these problems, the results of the advertising campaign must be measured. The measurement of sales messages and communication effects is one sound and accepted way.

Measuring Communication Effects

Because communication of a sales message is the usual goal of advertising, the measurement of some form of communication effect is quite natural. And because the goal of most consumer package goods advertising is either to keep present customers purchasing the particular brand or to influence other purchasers who have the brand in their evoked set to give the brand greater preference in future buying decisions, such measurement also seems satisfactory. Thus, although it is difficult indeed to measure the absolute effects of advertising in terms of sales, surrogate measures, such as brand awareness, sales messages delivered, and information about the brand transferred, can be used as methods of evaluating the effects of the campaign.

What to measure and why. The first step in measuring communication effects is to determine what those effects are and what evaluation tool will be used. Earlier, the use of the Lavidge and Steiner "hierarchy of effects" model was suggested as a sound, consistent method. Lavidge and Steiner see the movement from "unawareness" to the "purchase" of a product as a series of six distinct steps. The first step is *awareness* and the second, *knowledge,* both of which relate directly to information or ideas about the product or service. The third step, *liking,* and the fourth step, *preference,* are the "feeling" steps that deal with attitudes about the product. The fifth step, *conviction,* and the sixth step, *purchase,* are "action" or behavioral steps that result in the actual purchase of the product.

The six specific steps in the Lavidge and Steiner model are usually collapsed into the four used in the evaluation model for advertising campaigns: (a) awareness/knowledge (recall), (b) liking (attitude change), (c) preference, and (d) conviction/brand to be purchased or brand bought last.

Translating these four concepts into the more traditional form of a model, advertising really is intended to move people along a continuum from no information or sales messages to the final purchase behavior as shown in Exhibit 15–1. And, advertising constantly is having some effect on purchasers in either moving them forward or backward toward purchase or helping them to remain where they are.

Awareness and knowledge. The lowest level of the communication effect of advertising or the first objective of a sales message is the awareness or knowledge of either the brand being advertised or the advertising message itself. When the product is new or unknown, the objective of the campaign may be simply to make the consumer aware that the brand ex-

Exhibit 15–1   From Awareness to Purchase

Lack of information or awareness	———————— **Communication effects** ————————	Purchase
	Awareness/knowledge ◗ Liking ◗ Preference ◗ Conviction	

ists. Awareness of either the brand or the sales message is the simplest measure and, therefore, is the most widely used.

For an existing or known brand, the advertising task usually is to develop awareness or knowledge within the target market about a specific benefit the brand provides or the consumer problem it may solve. These measures do not necessarily attempt to determine whether the message has a communication effect. The assumption is made that if the consumer is aware of the message or has gained knowledge about the brand, the advertising has achieved its basic objective.

Under the assumption that the advertising message for the brand was unknown prior to the start of the campaign, the awareness measure can be made at any time after the campaign starts. The usual quantification is a determination of how many persons are aware of or recognize the product, the campaign theme, the benefit of the promises made, or some other identification of the sales message.

Recall.   The second level of advertising effectiveness is recall. Persons exposed to the advertising campaign can repeat or play back certain portions or ideas they may have seen or heard. They "recall" the advertising message. Again, no measure is made of the value of the advertising message or the impact it may have had on the target market.

Two types of recall are used in advertising evaluation, unaided and aided.

1. In *unaided recall,* respondents are asked if they remember having seen or heard advertising recently for any brand in a certain product category. No further clues are given to help identify the sponsor, the brand, or the message.

2. In *aided recall,* certain clues are given to help the respondent remember the advertising. For example, rather than asking only if the advertising for a certain product category has been seen or heard, the question might be phrased in such a way as to see if the respondent is able to recall which brand or what advertiser used a certain graphic device or made a certain claim in his or her advertising. Thus, the hints or suggestions "aid" in recalling the advertising.

Both aided and unaided recall are used in evaluating an advertising campaign. Unaided recall is believed to be the stronger, however, because the respondent is asked only about the product category and is expected to spontaneously recall or remember the advertising. The assumption is that a longer-lasting impression has been made.

The strongest effect of the campaign at this level is specific information about the brand. If consumers learn from advertising that only one brand of cough drop has the advantage of dual action—for example, it's both antiseptic and anesthetic—and that the product with these properties is Brand Z, then the assumption is made that knowledge has been communicated. It is assumed this sales message will have some effect on the future purchase behavior of the consumer, although that relationship is somewhat tenuous. Measures of awareness, recall, and knowledge of the brand, the message, or the benefits probably make up the bulk of all campaign evaluation.

Liking and attitude change.   The third level of advertising effect is liking the brand. Liking assumes the consumer is aware of the brand and has some knowledge of it either from the advertising or from actual use. Often, it is difficult to separate advertising knowledge from experience, which makes taking its measure more difficult.

In the liking measure, it is assumed the advertising has had an effect on the consumer's mental condition or that some sort of attitude change has occurred. The consumer has moved beyond the awareness or knowledge stage and has formed a positive opinion about the product. Liking does not mean that the consumer will purchase the product. It simply means that positive feelings or impressions exist.

An example of the "liking" measure is having a consumer name several acceptable brands of products in a category. The assumption is made that if the products are acceptable, they are liked (the "evoked set"). Although liking is an important step in evaluating the results of an advertising campaign, the measure still does not assume a purchase action. A consumer may like many products but only purchase a few.

Preference.   The final communication effect to be considered is preference, that is, that among a certain number of brands within a category one is preferred over the others. In terms of campaign evaluation, an assumption is made that the advertising message has created a level of acceptance for a specific brand, so that among available alternatives the advertised brand is preferred and would likely be purchased.

Because preference indicates that, all things being equal, certain brands will probably be purchased over others, preference is one of the stronger measures of the effect of advertising. If advertising is the major decision-making factor in creating product preference, the campaign is usually considered successful whether or not any actual sales result.

Preference is the final communication stage in which the actual effects of the advertising campaign can be measured. Once preference has been developed, there is little more that the advertising or the sales messages can do to trigger the purchase decision. From this point on, the consumer may or may not purchase the product based on many market factors, such as price, availability, and sales promotion.

Purchasing behavior.   If the advertising message that has been communicated is successful and market conditions and other marketing variables are favorable, the final step in the purchasing process is behavior or actual purchase of the brand. Lavidge and Steiner believe that conviction and purchase are behavioral. There is some question as to whether the concept of conviction is or is not a behavioral variable.

Conviction and behavior are the most difficult concepts to measure because of the many variables involved. There are some instances, though, in which purchase behavior can be traced directly to the advertising message, such as in direct response advertising (see Chapter 14).

In the conviction measure, as in all others, it is assumed that members of the target market have seen and reacted to the advertising message. The consumer has become aware of the brand advertised, has developed a liking, has moved up through the preference stage, and is now prepared to take or has taken the final step of conviction—making a purchase of the brand.

In the Lavidge and Steiner model, conviction and purchase behavior are in the cognitive or motivational area of behavior. Because a person often cannot accurately describe a conviction, some of the measures in this evaluation require questions of purchase intention or past purchase behavior. Thus, attempts are made to identify advertising as the force that created a switch of brands or stimulated the purchase of a brand in the past or the consideration of a purchase in the future. Intent to purchase is assumed to be a strong indicator of advertising success.

Most evaluation questions in the area of conviction deal with what was purchased. A given purchase is compared with past or usual behavior to determine if a change occurred. If change, such as a brand switch, did occur or if there is an indication that a brand switch might occur on the next purchase, an attempt is made to link that behavioral change to the advertising. Although the link is often questionable, it is used as a form of evaluation, especially if the reason given for the brand switch is implicit in the advertising message.

Many behavioral or psychological models can be used to evaluate advertising. The Lavidge and Steiner hierarchy of effects model, in whole or in part, has gained widespread industry acceptance. The model provides a practical and useful, if somewhat arbitrary, method of advertising campaign evaluation.

MEASURING THE ADVERTISING CAMPAIGN

With this review of the measurement of communication effects of the advertising campaign, the actual methods used to evaluate an advertising campaign can be examined. There are two basic approaches: (a) concurrent measurement (while the campaign is in progress), or (b) the more traditional method of evaluating the campaign after its completion.

Concurrent Evaluation

Today, because of high media costs, varying marketing conditions, and the need to react to competition, more and more advertisers are measuring, evaluating, and adjusting their campaigns while they are in progress. This form of evaluation is not a form of pretesting as was discussed in Chapter 11. It is simply a matter of measuring the campaign as it unfolds in the marketplace and then making adjustments and fine tuning it to maximize the results. There are two methods of measuring the communication effects of the campaign while it is in progress.

Coincidental studies.   Coincidental studies attempt to measure and evaluate consumer exposure and reaction to the advertising as it appears. It is particularly effective with broadcast advertising.

The most common type of coincidental study is the telephone interview. For example, an advertiser may want to determine if the advertising message is reaching the correct target market and to learn how and what information is being conveyed. Telephone calls are made to members of the target market while the advertising is being broadcast on either radio or television. By learning what stations or shows are being watched or heard, the advertiser then knows whether or not the target audience is receiving the message, and, if so, what information or meaning is attached to it. Because coincidental surveys are designed to furnish only very basic data, little information about the campaign can be obtained other than a quick reading of message distribution and general information content.

Tracking studies.   Studies of this type usually consist of a series of interviews during the course of the campaign. The purpose is to determine the levels of exposure and effect that are being achieved by the advertising campaign. Because it is commonly agreed that advertising effects build over time, tracking studies are usually conducted in "waves" on a predetermined schedule. An example may help:

Assume that on March 1 a new advertising campaign for Millie's Peanuts is started. The campaign is to run through November 1. Tracking studies using a telephone survey format are planned for April 1 and June 1.

On April 1, a series of telephone calls are made to randomly selected customers. The sample size is sufficiently large so that reasonable assumptions may be made about the results. Questions are asked such as:

Question 1:   Have you seen or heard any advertising for the peanut category?

If the consumer has seen or heard any advertising for peanuts, he or she is asked:

Question 2:   What brand was it for?

Follow-up questions include:

Question 3:   Where did you see or hear the advertising?

Question 4:   What did the advertising say?

Question 5:   What brand of peanuts do you normally buy?

This first study establishes a benchmark for the campaign. In addition, it spotlights problems, such as a lack of exposure with prospects, misunderstanding of the message, and misidentification of the sponsor, that might be occurring. Based on this first "wave," the advertiser can then make any necessary adjustments.

On June 1, another series of random calls is made and the same questions are asked. It is assumed that the two samples are comparable. The second "wave" is compared with the first to see if a change in consumer response has occurred and to determine if the changes made after the first study have corrected the problems they were aimed at.

Tracking studies of this kind can be conducted at any time during the campaign at normal intervals of about sixty days. For some product categories, a shorter or longer time period may be required.

Telephone studies are the most common form of tracking, although they may be done through personal interview or diaries or by other means.

The major advantage of concurrent testing is the rapid accumulation of information. Based on this information, any problems can be spotted and corrections can be made quickly and efficiently. The major disadvantage is the limited amount of information that can be obtained. In addition, because concurrent testing takes place during the campaign, a quick reading may not accurately reflect what the final results might be.

The coincidental and tracking studies work very well as long as the objectives of the advertising campaign are communication effects. In some cases, however, the goal of the campaign may be to generate actual sales, such as through direct response, or to persuade present users to purchase more of the brand or to use it in additional ways or simply to attempt to develop a brand switch. When one of these is the objective, a different type of concurrent study is undertaken. There are two basic types: the consumer diary, and the consumer pantry check.

1. Consumer diaries. These diaries are used by some advertisers to record the behavior of persons in their target market during the campaign. For example, customers or prospects may keep diaries of such activities as brands purchased, brands used for various activities, brand switches, media usage, exposure to competitive promotions, and use of coupons. By reviewing the diaries, an advertiser may determine if the advertising message is being exposed to the target market and what effect this exposure is having. If the respondents are exposed to the advertising message and no attitude or behavioral changes occur, the advertiser may determine the message is not effective. There are obvious limitations on the amount of information that can be obtained through a consumer diary, but the methodology often serves as an early warning system spotting potential strengths or weaknesses in an advertising campaign and allowing the planner to make changes.

2. Pantry checks. An alternative to the diary is the pantry check. A research person physically goes to target market homes and asks consumers what brands of products have been purchased or used recently. In some cases, a physical count of products or brands in the home is taken and recorded. This may be done on several occasions over time; changes in purchasing habits are noted. A variation called the "dust bin" approach is also used. Consumers are asked to save empty packages of products they have used. These packages are then picked up, counted, and evaluated by the research team. In both cases, the object is to determine what if any changes in purchasing habits may have occurred while a particular advertising campaign was in progress.

The Posttest

The traditional campaign evaluation methodology is the posttest, which is conducted at the conclusion of the campaign. Although data gathering through panels, diaries, personal interviews, telephone surveys, or other means is common to both the concurrent evaluation and the posttest, the primary purpose of the latter is to evaluate the final results of the campaign against predetermined advertising goals or objectives.

In a standard posttest, consumers in the target market or area in which the campaign was conducted are questioned about the advertising and the effects of the message on their opinions, attitudes, and behavior. These results are then weighted against the objectives and goals of the advertising campaign to determine if satisfactory results were achieved for the advertising investment.

The major problem in a simple posttest is lack of information on changes that may have been caused by the advertising campaign. Unless concurrent testing has been done, little may be known about consumer attitudes toward and opinions about the brand prior to the time the advertising messages were placed in the media. It is difficult to determine, therefore, if the advertising had the desired effect or if the attitude and opinions found in the posttest were already present or were caused by other factors. A better approach, one using a pre–posttest, can solve this problem.

In the pre–posttesting technique, advertisers conduct a pretest in the market before launching the advertising campaign. This test provides a benchmark for later evaluation. By knowing what attitudes and opinions were held by consumers prior to the start of the campaign, a comparison can be made with posttest findings after the campaign has run.

For example, assume the advertising objective for a specific campaign was to raise the awareness level about a particular product benefit within the target market population by 25 percent. Without a pretest, it would be difficult to determine if the objective had been achieved at the end of the campaign or if that level was already present. If, however, a pretest were used, it might have been found that an awareness level of 16 percent already existed among the target group. Thus, to achieve the goal of a 25 percent increase, awareness of the product benefit at the end of the campaign would have to measure at least 20 percent (a 25 percent increase over the 16 percent base). If, after the campaign had been run, it was found that the awareness level of the specific product benefit was 32 percent among the target population, the campaign could be judged very successful; the advertising goal was only a 25 percent increase in awareness and a 50 percent increase was achieved.

The posttest and pre-post techniques can be used to evaluate almost any campaign objective. The chief distinction of the methodology is that the study is conducted after the campaign has been run and there is no opportunity for change or revision. This inability to change or revise is also the chief disadvantage.

RESEARCH METHODS FOR EVALUATING THE ADVERTISING CAMPAIGN

Although it is usually not the task of the planner to physically conduct the evaluation of the campaign (that usually falls to the research department or an outside research organization), often, the planner is required to specify the particular way in which the campaign should be evaluated. Therefore, whether the evaluation is the task of the planner or a research person, the planner should have an understanding of the various research tools available. That understanding will help the planner build an evaluation system into the plan. A brief review of the various tools and techniques used to evaluate a campaign follows.

Individual Methods of Measuring the Results of the Campaign

In general, the evaluation of the campaign is conducted with consumers in the marketplace. Of course, some campaigns are directed at dealers, distributors, or others, but for the most part, in package goods advertising, the concern is with how the campaign performed with the ultimate consumer. The most common method of gathering information is through some form of survey research. Although the actual structure and development of an evaluation survey is beyond the scope of this text, some general suggestions may be helpful in developing or evaluating a questionnaire to be used in this type of study.

Measuring awareness. Awareness is generally regarded as a measure of knowledge without reference to source. Although the primary interest in advertising evaluation is knowing if there is a relationship between the advertising and consumer awareness, establishing this relationship is not usually possible. There are four primary methods of measuring awareness:

1. Yes-or-no questions. Example: "Have you ever heard of Fred's Flour?" Yes _____ No _____. Although the yes–no questions are simple to administer and tabulate, no information is gained beyond the direct answer.
2. Open-end questions. Example: "What companies can you name that package flour?" In this instance, more information is obtained than in a yes–no situation, but no relationship to the advertising campaign can be inferred.
3. Checklist questions. Example: "Which of the following products does Fred's Company manufacture?" Flour _____ Rolling pins _____ Automobiles _____ Electronic computers _____. Here the answers are easily obtained, although the range of answers is restricted. As in the open-end and yes–no questions, no connection with the advertising campaign can be developed.
4. Rating scales. Examples: "How would you rate Fred's Flour in comparison with other brands of flour you have used?" Better _____ About the same as _____ Not as good as _____. With this approach, a measure of familiarity is achieved, but differences among the persons doing the rating make it difficult to combine answers or interpret the exact results. Additional scales or other approaches are sometimes used to make this form of measurement more reliable.

Measurement of awareness through these techniques is quick and fairly low in cost because it can be done through the mail or by telephone interview. The results are easy to tabulate and generally straightforward. These advantages are balanced by the lack of knowledge of a significant change in awareness; that is, awareness may have been higher before the campaign than after. This change is not measurable with a straight awareness approach. In addition, it is difficult to determine the source of the awareness. Awareness may or may not have come from the advertising campaign; as discussed in Chapter 3, consumers get product information from many sources. Although measurement of awareness is important to the evaluation of the campaign, it is the simplest of all measures and does not, in most cases, provide a direct relationship.

Measuring recall.   In advertising evaluation, recall can be determined by the amount of knowledge among consumers directly related to the advertising. The campaign should be identifiable as the source of that knowledge. Recall is normally used to determine to what extent advertising messages have been retained by consumers. Although it is a tenuous one, the assumption is made that recall of an advertising message and purchase behavior are somehow related. Thus, recall is believed to be an important measure for the advertising campaign.

As outlined in the previous section, two types of recall can be measured, aided and unaided.

1. Unaided recall. Example: "Can you recall any brands of flour being advertised in the last few weeks?" The respondent is given no clue as to what brand is being investigated or what additional questions might be asked. He or she must recall any or all advertising messages seen in the past and relate them to the question. The assumption is made that advertising remembered without any clue from the interviewer is stronger than that remembered with some direction.
2. Aided recall. Example: "Do you remember seeing or hearing any advertising for Fred's Flour recently?" The respondent's reply is aided by the brand name. Rather than trying to remember all flour advertising, the respondent can concentrate on the particular brand. Care must be taken that not too much aid is given or the respondent may resort to guessing rather than recalling.

The major advantage of measuring recall is that it allows measurement of at least one aspect of the advertising campaign. If the respondent remembers the campaign message or portions of the actual advertising, a direct correlation can be made. The main problem is that recall and purchase behavior may not be directly connected. In other words, the person may recall the message, but that message may not influence the purchase decision. In addition, because over the years many campaigns appear quite similar, the respondent may actually recall a previous advertising message and put it into the context of the present campaign. It is often difficult to identify or isolate specific campaign features.

Measuring attitudes.   Recall and attitude tests are often combined in an attempt to determine if there are major differences between consumers who remember the advertising message and those who don't. Attitude tests are also used to measure changes in consumer perceptions of a brand, or degrees of acceptance of various claims made in the advertising.

Five basic techniques are used to measure attitudes:

1. Direct questions. Example: "How would you describe the use of Fred's Flour for baking?" Only a favorable or unfavorable attitude toward the product is measured. The level or degree of feeling is not possible. As a result, this approach may be combined with a rating scale.

2. Rating scales. Example: "How would you describe the self-measuring spout on Fred's Flour packages?" Very easy to use _____ Easy to use _____ Neither easy nor hard to use _____ Hard to use _____ Very hard to use _____ . Although scales are easy to apply and tabulate, the main problem is correlating the views of the respondents. A "Very easy to use" answer by one person may be the same as an "Easy to use" response from another. A rating scale does not discriminate sufficiently to permit a precise line to be drawn between the various attitudes.

3. Checklists. Example: "Which of the following is most important to you when you purchase flour?" Price _____ Package _____ Presifted _____ Reputation of manufacturer _____ . The attributes can be easily ranked by the respondents and easily tabulated by the advertiser. The primary problem, however, is that there is no assurance that the most important factors have been isolated and listed on the questionnaire. In addition, the meaning of each question is not always totally clear. For example, does "Reputation of manufacturer" mean the same thing to all respondents?

4. Semantic differential tests. Example: "Would you say the user of Fred's Flour is":

   A good cook _____ _____ _____ _____ _____ A poor cook

   Extravagant _____ _____ _____ _____ _____ Price-conscious

   Paired opposite descriptive words or phrases are separated on a scale. The respondent is allowed to check the place on the scale where the product would be rated. Thus, the respondent's attitude toward the product can be determined. The scale is easy to use and the results are simple to tabulate. The major problem with this type of measure is that the scale may not be interpreted by all respondents in the same manner.

5. Partially structured interviews. Example: "I'd like you to tell me some of your feelings about baking and the ingredients you use, such as flour, butter, and eggs." In this approach, an attempt is made to allow the respondent to discuss the general topic area and reveal attitudes about the brand without using a specific set of questions. Although

the interviewer knows the general areas about which information and attitudes will be sought, the use of the unstructured interview allows the respondent an opportunity to indicate areas of interest that might not have been previously considered.

Attitudinal tests are viewed as an important element in advertising campaign evaluation. A favorable attitude is considered to be an indication that the person is more likely to purchase a brand than if he or she has an unfavorable attitude. As a result, changes in attitudes are regarded as more important in advertising evaluation than awareness or recall. Unfortunately, there is little evidence that a favorable attitude will always result in behavioral change, such as purchase of a brand. The use of attitude measurements is also open to question because it is very difficult to obtain an accurate measure of people's attitudes about any subject.

Measuring brand usage.   Brand usage is the ultimate measure of the effectiveness of an advertising campaign. Although it has been stressed that, for the most part, advertising should be considered only on the basis of communication effects, in some instances, advertisers want to trace sales results. This is done by measuring such things as movement of goods through store audits, pantry audits, and consumer panels. When consumer interviews are used, they consist primarily of a series of questions about past, present, and future brand usage. For example:

1. "What brand of flour do you normally purchase?"
    Fred's _____ Harry's _____ Aunt Ethel's _____ Brand X _____
2. "What brand of flour did you buy last?"
    Fred's _____ Harry's _____ Aunt Ethel's _____ Brand X _____
3. "What brand of flour do you think you will buy next?"
    Fred's _____ Harry's _____ Aunt Ethel's _____ Brand X _____

By using this type of consumer questionnaire, primarily on a pretest–posttest basis, changes in purchasing habits can be measured. When these usage changes are combined with tests of awareness, recall, and attitudes, determination of the effects of an advertising campaign is sometimes possible. The attempt to relate advertising to sales is sometimes fruitful when all variables can be controlled, although the relationship is somewhat tenuous. (Note that *actual* purchase behavior can be observed through in-store scanner data. However, as in the survey methodology described earlier, changes in purchase patterns cannot usually be attributed to advertising.)

Syndicated and Custom Research Techniques

A number of syndicated research services specialize in the evaluation of individual advertisements and, on occasion, advertising campaigns. Because these services vary so greatly in methodology, we are only covering the major organizations. Those who wish to investigate specific techniques should consult the individual organization offering the services.

Syndicated print techniques. The most common technique for evaluating print advertisements or campaigns is that employed by Daniel Starch and Staff. Although Starch studies are designed primarily to evaluate individual advertisements in magazines, the techniques can be adapted to other forms of print.

The Starch technique consists of a recognition-and-recall test. First, a list of magazines that respondents believe they have seen before is developed. Based on their acknowledged exposure to the publication, respondents are taken through the magazine page by page and are asked questions about each advertisement recognized. Every advertisement in the issue is scored. Advertisers may then compare the score of their advertisement to the scores of others in the same product category or to all advertisements in the magazine.

Other organizations, such as Gallup & Robinson, offer evaluations of print advertisements, and nearly all follow some form of the recognition-and-recall technique. Most industrial publications conduct some form of readership study whereby individual readership scores are computed for each advertisement appearing in the issue.

Starch and Gallup & Robinson syndicated services are widely used by many advertisers. However, some advertisers and agencies have reservations about this form of measurement. They cite the fact that these techniques measure only the recall of the advertisement by the reader and not the selling effectiveness or the persuasive ability of the ad as a whole. They further argue that in some cases the very devices used to gain memorability and recall in a Starch or Gallup & Robinson study may work against developing a strong sales message; that is, an advertisement may be remembered for itself because of its unusual nature, but the brand or sales message forgotten. At best, Starch and Gallup & Robinson scores measure only one aspect of a print advertisement—the ability to be recalled.

Broadcast evaluation techniques. There are few if any individual commercial or campaign evaluation techniques used to rate broadcast commercials specifically. Having used a pretest on the commercials, most advertisers are content to use one of the other forms of advertising evaluation to determine the success or failure of the commercials used.

One additional evaluative measure commonly taken by many advertising agencies is the "postbuy media analysis." Because all time purchases on radio and television are based on estimates of the audience that might be exposed to the individual commercial, the real question concerns the number of people who were actually in the audience. Therefore, the media department, commonly using Nielsen or Arbitron figures, takes the estimated audience and compares it with the measured audience for each of the commercials on the schedule. Those figures are then compared against the media campaign objectives and estimates. This evaluation tells whether or not the commercials received the expected exposures and how well the media buy was made. Some service organizations provide this type of service to the advertisers and the agency. Although these are not technically syndicated services, they do offer another form of campaign evaluation, particularly with regard to the media buy.

Sales results.   Our primary emphasis has been on the communication effects of the campaign; nonetheless, advertisers often use sales or marketing information for evaluation. Their chief sources are internal sales data and syndicated or custom research.

Internal sales data are used to learn whether or not product sales are a response to the advertising campaign. This cause-and-effect relationship can be measured either by comparing current sales data with those of previous periods, or against sales goals that have been set for the brand. Broker or sales force reports are widely used sources of information.

Syndicated or custom research usually consists of subscription to one of the auditing services such as the Nielsen Retail Index, SAMI (Selling Areas-Marketing, Inc.), National Retail Tracking Index (NRTI), National Total Market Index, or various scanner-based systems, such as National Scantrack, BehaviorScan, and Supermarket Product Movement Data. These services monitor product movement out of wholesalers' warehouses or retail food outlets and drugstores to obtain information on distribution levels, penetration of the product into different types of stores, share of national case volume, share of in-store distribution, product movement, and activities of competitors.

Although many marketing variables are involved in the sale of the product, if sales measurement techniques such as those already discussed are used, one can sometimes determine if the failure or success of the product can be related to the advertising campaign.

Other methods of advertising campaign evaluation, such as personal observation and expert opinion, are sometimes used. The methods listed earlier, however, make up the bulk of the data gathering and evaluation techniques.

Custom research techniques.   Although many forms of data gathering may be used, the four that follow are most commonly used in campaign evaluation.

1.   Personal interviews. These are usually considered the most accurate of all advertising campaign evaluation techniques. Whether the evaluation centers on past purchase behavior, understanding of present campaign messages, or questions about competitive activity, the personal interview is usually able to elicit the necessary information from the respondent.

Personal interviews may take many forms, from traditional door-to-door to mall intercepts. The major advantage is the opportunity for face-to-face discussion and clarification of answers to the questions asked. The major disadvantages are the extremely high cost of personal data gathering, and the inability of interviewers to make contact with people not at home or to contact respondents in certain urban areas.

2. Consumer panels. These panels are widely used to gather all types of advertising information. They consist of respondents who agree either to keep records or to answer inquiries on an ongoing basis. Questions asked each panel may take almost any form. The major advantage of the panel is the high rate of return from respondents who are usually committed to the techniques. The major disadvantage is the lack of selectivity among respondents. In addition, the panel response technique consists of polling those who have agreed to participate. This group may or may not be representative of the whole population.

3. Mailed questionnaires. Sending questionnaires by mail is a relatively low-cost method of obtaining an evaluation of an advertising campaign. The mail questionnaire offers many advantages, from selection of the sample to wide geographic distribution for response. Usually, more detailed questions can be asked in a mail survey than any other form. The major disadvantage is the length of time needed to carry out the study and the often low return response rate. Mail surveys are widely used to evaluate industrial advertising studies.

4. Telephone interviewing. This is an increasingly popular form of data gathering for advertising evaluation. The telephone call has many of the advantages of the personal interview, yet it is much less expensive. It can be used in areas where personal interviews cannot be made. Often respondents will answer questions by telephone that they will not answer any other way. The obvious disadvantages of telephoning are inability to show advertising materials or to ask very complex questions. The innovation of WATS (Wide Area Telephone Service) has enabled advertisers and researchers to poll people on advertising campaigns all over the country from one central location.

Some research organizations offer a syndicated form of custom research for campaign evaluation. Usually, this methodology requires the advertisers to submit one, two, or more questions about the campaign to the research organization. The organization gathers several noncompetitive advertisers who have done the same. The questions are then combined into a usable format, and a certain number of consumers are contacted and asked these questions. Because several advertisers have participated, the price is usually much lower than that for an individual study. (In another form of evaluation study, the research organization investigates several product categories through consumer studies, compiles the data, and then offers this information on a syndicated basis to various companies at a flat rate.)

The methodology used for campaign evaluation varies according to factors including available funds, type of campaign to be evaluated, geographic area, type of product, and advertising media used. Thus, there is no one best way or predetermined methodology that should be used for any given campaign or any type of advertiser. The evaluation should be developed to fit the needs of the advertiser and the marketplace.

The major point in the choice of a technique or methodology to evaluate the campaign is to be sure the technique measures the objectives stated in the campaign strategy. If the intent is to measure advertising awareness, the methodology used should be keyed to fit that goal. If, on the other hand, the goal of the campaign is to increase product preference, the evaluation methodology may be vastly different. As is the case with the development of an advertising campaign, there is no hard-and-fast rule for evaluation. It all depends on the campaign.

EVALUATING THE EVALUATION

For purposes of "evaluating" the evaluation, certain questions should be asked about the research itself. Although numerous considerations can be cited for any research study, Simon Broadbent has suggested four.

Is the Sample Representative?

Obviously, the respondents in the evaluation sample should be members of the target market to whom the advertising campaign is directed. The advertising may do an excellent job of communicating the sales message to women 35 to 49 years of age. But that's of little value if the target group for whom the advertising is intended is young men 18 to 24. The groups simply aren't that much alike.

Does the Respondent Understand the Questions Being Asked?

Too many times, in follow-up interviews, it has been found that the respondents didn't actually understand the questions they were asked. As a result of this misunderstanding, garbled—or even worse—misleading or incorrect information was obtained. To be able to reply with the information sought, the respondent must understand the question being asked.

Are the Conclusions Drawn from the Advertising Campaign Evaluation Substantiated?

Leaping to conclusions is prevalent in advertising evaluation. Because so much time and effort have gone into the campaign, the creators are sometimes inclined to explain away problems or assume as accepted things that might not be true. The research conclusions reached in the campaign must be based solely on the information gathered and reported with a minimum of explanation required.

Was the Sample Large Enough?

A frequent problem in advertising evaluation is finding enough respondents who have seen or are familiar with the advertising to make an adequate evaluation of it. The problem becomes crucial for products that have a small market share, are purchased infrequently, or have a limited media schedule. Yet, for meaningful conclusions to be drawn, the sample base must be of a sufficient size to be statistically accurate.[1]

TEST MARKETING

Most of the concern in the preceding sections has been with measuring the effects of advertising for existing or established products. Although these types of evaluations are satisfactory, they assume that the campaign is being used in a widespread area. In some instances, for both established and new products, test markets are used to evaluate advertising campaigns before large sums of money are invested in either national media or national markets.

Why Use Test Markets?

Although many reasons exist for using a test market, the following three are predominant.

A trial of the compaign.   With marketers attempting to take more and more of the risk out of advertising, the test market offers an excellent opportunity to try out the campaign. By testing the campaign in a smaller market or on a reduced scale, the advertiser has the opportunity to see how it might work and to make any needed adjustments before moving the campaign into the larger, more expensive broad-scale market.

---

[1]Simon Broadbent, *Spending Advertising Money* (London: Business Books, 1975): 210–43.

An opportunity to try variations.   When alternative campaigns have been developed, test markets allow an advertiser to try the variations in an actual market setting to determine which of the campaigns is the best choice. For example, two or more campaign themes have been developed, and each has performed about the same in a pretest format. The test market allows the measurement to be made and the results evaluated in a "real-world" setting.

A way to reduce the financial risk.   With the increasing cost of media and the need to stretch advertising investments as much as possible, the test market gives the advertiser an opportunity to try a campaign in a controlled-risk situation. A failure in a test market is not nearly as costly as one on a national scale.

Types of Test Markets

Although test markets may be developed for many reasons, three essential purposes predominate.

Product test.   The product test is an opportunity to learn how the product or service is accepted by consumers prior to a national or broad-scale introduction. Although the preliminary laboratory test may have proved successful, the acid test for a new product is the response or results in the actual marketplace.

Advertising test.   Like the product test, the advertising test is an opportunity to try the advertising campaign on a reduced scale prior to a rollout. As mentioned previously, the advertising program may be fine tuned or alternatives evaluated based on success or failure in the test market.

Media weight tests/spending level tests.   Advertisers often use test markets to evaluate various levels of media weight or various levels of advertising spending. These tests give the advertiser the opportunity to determine the most effective and efficient spending level for achieving the advertising goals.

How to Develop a Test Market

Two basic steps are required in developing a test market plan. First, the broad-scale or national plan must be developed. This is the advertising campaign that will be used, provided the test market is successful. In other words, all parts of the major program must first be developed in detail. The second step is to reproduce this broad-scale program in miniature; that is, the major plan is then scaled down to fit the test market or markets selected. This is usually accomplished by means of a translation of the broad-scale program in the form of a percentage of expenditure or investment. For example, if the proposed national advertising investment for the campaign is planned at $5 million, the test market expenditure would then be determined based on the test market size as a percentage of the national program. For example, if Terre Haute, Indiana was determined to be 1 percent of the planned size of the national campaign, then the investment in Terre Haute for a $5,000,000 campaign would be $50,000 ($5,000,000 × .01 = $50,000). Other relationships may be used, but population, size of the test market as part of the broad-scale plan, and percentage of media costs are the most common methods of determining the amount to be invested in the test market. In addition to the estimated advertising campaign costs, other investments, such as sales promotion programs and consumer incentives, are scaled to fit the test market. In short, the entire broad-scale plan is miniaturized to fit the test market.

Developing a Test Market Plan

Several major factors should be considered in developing a test market plan.

Test market size and location.   The proposed test market must be large enough to be reasonably representative of the broad-scale market. While test markets should be small enough to control and evaluate, they must be large enough and have enough pertinent market variables for the campaign to get a fair test. The test market should be of sufficient size to represent the national competitive climate. The same competitors with approximately the same competitive weight found in the national market should be present in the test market.

While the test market must be large enough to give the campaign a fair test, it must be small enough to reduce the financial risk to worthwhile proportions. For example, New York City might represent the national program exactly, but it would make a poor test market simply because of the amount of investment required to conduct the program.

Test market media.   The test market must also be capable of satisfactorily reproducing the national media plan. For example, if the national plan calls for the use of newspaper supplements, the test market must provide adequate newspaper supplements for the test. Attempting to test a media plan on a reduced scale with other media forms as substitutes can often be misleading with regard to possible national results.

Duration of test.   The length of time in a test market, another major factor in planning, is usually based on the minimum amount of time required to accurately measure the results. Thus, there is no hard-and-fast rule on how long a test market should run. The two major factors that are usually considered are

1. The test should run long enough to permit checking the initial levels of product distribution, trade stocking, and displays. With some products, the test might run for a matter of days, and with others, weeks or even months may be required to take the product through the distribution channels.
2. There should be sufficient time to allow for a clear assessment of the level of consumer trial and the proportion of repeat purchases achieved. In other words, a short test might be misleading because consumers try the product initially but fail to make repeat purchases. Advertisers frequently have read the results of a test market incorrectly because their interpretation was based on initial purchases. The lack of repeat purchases after the first trial was not evaluated and, as a result, what appeared to be a successful product was, in reality, a failure. The same is true of the advertising campaign. Although initial awareness might be very high, knowledge and preference might not develop. Unless sufficient time is allowed for the test market to show the full results of the campaign, the results could be misleading.

Measurement and control of results.   The final factor in the determination of the relative success of a test market is the ability to measure the results. Closely allied with measurement is the control the advertiser has over obtaining or gathering the results of the test market. It does little good to develop a test market and then not be able to obtain the necessary test results or control the factors in the market that prevent an accurate appraisal. For example, if you attempt to use a test market in which obtaining sales figures for the product is very difficult, your problem is compounded. If you are to use a test market, the measurement and control of the results of the test are vital.

Test Market Problems

Although test marketing is widely used by advertisers in many categories, two major problems exist.

Competition reading the test.   In most good test markets, it is as easy for the competition as it is for the advertiser to obtain information about the test market. Because all marketers use many of the same techniques and often the same syndicated information sources, it is a simple matter for a competitor to watch a test market while it is in progress. When this occurs, the competitor often knows about the success or failure of the campaign as quickly as the advertiser. With this knowledge, a competitor may be able to react and generate a campaign that will offset an advertiser's success. He or she might, for example, run a sales promotion program to load consumers up with his or her brand, taking them out of the market for the test product. It is almost impossible to hide the results of a test market from competition.

Competition destroys the test market. Competitors may also take market actions that will give a false reading in the test market. For example, if a campaign is developed with a strong competitive price story, a competitor might lower his price in the test market to make the results inconclusive. A competitor often prefers to destroy the test market with competitive activities rather than risk facing the results of the successful test.

In spite of the cost of development and the risks involved, test markets are an excellent way to learn how an advertising campaign would perform in a real-world setting at a reasonable cost.

Test Areas and Control Groups

A useful way to evaluate a specific advertising campaign on a limited basis is through test areas and control groups. This technique is widely used to evaluate the advertising campaign for new products. It is usually conducted prior to a widespread use of the campaign or a national rollout.

Cities or areas are selected for the test and matched as closely as possible. For example, three different areas might be selected to test an advertising campaign. A similar group of three areas matching as nearly as possible the geographic, demographic, and product-usage patterns of the test cities would then be identified. The advertising campaign to be evaluated would be conducted in the three test areas. The three matching markets would receive no advertising and would serve as controls. At the end of the test campaign, studies and comparisons of advertising effects would be made between the test and control markets to determine differences. Because the areas were matched as closely as possible, it could be assumed that the advertising campaign in the advertised markets was the reason for any differences found.

The major advantage of the test-and-control approach is the comparatively low cost of placing and evaluating the campaign in a few limited areas as opposed to widespread use without testing. In addition, if necessary, changes can be made in the materials after the test results are obtained. The major disadvantage of this evaluation method is the difficulty of matching the control and test areas and the possibility that competition may "read" the test and learn what is planned for the future.

Evaluating a Test Market

In the preceding sections, it was assumed that in most cases the test market is simply a test of a new advertising program for an existing product. Indeed, that is often the case. Measuring the results of that type of test market is often quite different from measuring a test for a new product or a new brand. A brief review of test market evaluation for a new product or brand follows.

Awareness.   Advertising awareness of the brand or the product is often the major measurement in a test market. Because the product is new, and in some cases it may be the first of its kind in the market, just making consumers aware of the product and the brand may be the key ingredient for success. In a test market, advertising often has the double task of making consumers aware not only of the new product type but also of the brand. Evaluating the advertising against these two objectives is often sufficient.

Obtaining distribution.   Distribution of the brand may also be an advertising goal in a test market. Because new products have no track record, retailers are sometimes hesitant to stock them until they are in demand. Thus, the use of consumer advertising to "pull" the product through distribution channels is often stated as an advertising objective.

When advertising is powerful enough to have consumers ask for the product, particularly to such an extent that retailers feel it necessary to stock it, the campaign is usually considered effective. Similarly, if advertising in a test market fails to sufficiently convince customers to go to the store and purchase the product after distribution has been achieved, then retailers may discontinue the product. Although distribution was obtained, the advertising was not powerful enough to generate a consumer behavioral change.

Sales.   Sales may be a logical evaluative basis for an advertising campaign in a test market, all other factors being equal. Many test products are unknown and rely almost entirely on advertising to achieve awareness and, ultimately, sales. In these cases, the traditional marketing variables that impinge on an existing product may not be present for a test product. Thus, it may be possible to gauge the strength of the advertising campaign on the basis of sales in a test situation. This seems to be particularly true for a product that is the first entry in a new category or is the newest brand in an existing product category.

SUMMARY

One of the most important elements of good advertising and marketing is the ability to measure results—and that comes from measuring the results produced by the campaign. As in the case of pretesting, the first issue is, "What will be measured?" That issue, of course, involves determining objectives. Whether the planner is evaluating the results of a pretest or the results of a campaign, many of the same problems present themselves—multiple marketing effects, communication effects, and sales, for example.

Case Studies

Fleur de Lis Cognac

Final plans were being made for the national introduction of Fleur de Lis Importers' new cognac. This would be Fleur de Lis's first nationally distributed product. Due to some processing innovations, Fleur de Lis would be able to sell its premium French cognac at a price well below that of most imports on the market.

During a corporate planning session, Jordan Uland, brand manager for the cognac, reviewed the promotional plan for the national introduction.

As you'll recall, we've established the following objectives for the Fleur de Lis Cognac campaign:

- Achieve 90 percent awareness of Fleur de Lis cognac among brandy and cognac drinkers (17,136,000 adults in the U.S.)
- Among those aware, achieve 70 percent knowledge of Fleur de Lis as a low-price, premium imported cognac
- Among those with knowledge, achieve 60 percent preference for Fleur de Lis over other cognacs
- Achieve 20 percent purchase among those preferring Fleur de Lis

This should result in Year 1 market share of approximately 12.6 percent. Approximate market shares (%) for the top five competitors are

Courvoisier	30.1
Hennessey	24.7
Remy Martin	17.9
Martell	6.8
Armagnac	3.4

We have defined the primary target market as young adults, aged 25–34, both single and recently married (1–2 person households). They work full time in professional or managerial positions and have an annual household income above $40,000.*

Several renowned experts have pronounced Fleur de Lis equal to or better than other cognacs, including other imports. Their endorsement will be a chief component in the advertising campaign. Our theme is that "Fleur de Lis is premium cognac at a pleasing price."

We will advertise in two national weekly news magazines, three monthly business publications, one business weekly, and three monthly food-enthusiast magazines. The planned schedule for the first two months is as follows:

Time	1 page, four color, 8 insertions
Newsweek	1 page, four color, 8 insertions

Mediamark Research Study (Spring 1986): Volume P-4.

Business Week	1 page, four color, 6 insertions
Fortune	1 page, four color, 2 insertions
Forbes	1 page, four color, 2 insertions
Barron's	1 page, four color, 2 insertions
Gourmet	1 page, four color, 2 insertions
Cuisine	1 page, four color, 2 insertions
Bon Appétit	1 page, four color, 2 insertions

This will give us national reach of approximately 40 percent (95 percent among our target market).

In addition, we will run a full page, four-color advertisement in the following publications to provide localized heavy-up in major markets:

Chicago	*Los Angeles*
Washingtonian	*Boston*
New York	*Philadelphia*
Minneapolis-St. Paul	*San Francisco*
San Diego	*Atlanta*
Denver	*D* (Dallas)
Houston City	*Cleveland*
Pittsburgh	

We have two alternative advertising executions. Both have scored well in localized pretesting. One places primary emphasis on premium quality, one on low price. The first is headlined, "A truly excellent cognac," and pictures a gentleman holding a snifter of Fleur de Lis. He is identified in the caption as a cognac expert. Body copy points include the product's premium quality, French origin, and low price. A tag line, positioned beside a photograph of the Fleur de Lis bottle, reads, "Premium cognac at a pleasing price." We have three separate executions in this campaign, each featuring a different expert.

The alternative campaign depicts a young couple relaxing at home, enjoying Fleur de Lis cognac. The headline reads "Fleur de Lis: Premium Cognac at a Pleasing Price." The copy reads, "Fleur de Lis is a premium French import. And with a price that's well within our budget, we can afford to indulge ourselves regularly."

Fleur de Lis cognac will be distributed through an established wholesaler we've dealt with in the past. Response from retailers has been very favorable and we are projecting a national distribution level of approximately 75 percent.

Because Fleur de Lis is already low priced, we do not plan on any consumer sales promotion at this time.

Before we launch the full-scale campaign, and prior to implementing a final import schedule, we'd like to try the product in a test market situation. We will be able to approximate the national media level through use of regional editions of the publications we've identified. In addition, we will use daily newspaper ads during the first two weeks of the test. This test will give us a chance to calculate import quantities based on demand,

and test the two advertising campaigns to see which is more effective in an actual market situation.

We have selected two pairs of markets: Boston–Dallas and Philadelphia–San Diego. We will run the "expert" campaign in the first pair of markets and the "couple" campaign in the second pair. Test duration will be six weeks. Assuming that all is well, the national introduction should begin on November 1.

Questions

1. Do you agree that Fleur de Lis is a good candidate for a test market?
2. Do you foresee any problems with the test market developed by Uland?
3. At the end of the staff meeting, Uland was told to develop an evaluation plan that would be able to measure the effectiveness of the national campaign.

   a. Would you advocate a concurrent evaluation or posttest?
   b. Should a pre-post test be used?
   c. Uland decided that telephone surveys might be helpful in the evaluation. Develop some questions that would test achievement of the knowledge objective.
   d. Uland was contacted by a syndicated research service that uses an established base sample in their studies. Before contracting with this service, what questions should be answered?

Carson Publications

Zaundra Pruett, a marketing analyst at Carson Publications, had just received the assignment of putting together a recommendation for an evaluation plan for Carson's upcoming corporate advertising campaign. Her recommendation would have to cover both the viability of using a test market for the campaign before going national, and an evaluation plan for the eventual national campaign.

Carson Publications publishes magazines and books aimed at a "total-family" audience. The Carson line includes book clubs for toddlers, preteens, teen boys, teen girls, and several special-interest book clubs for adults. Additionally, Carson publishes a series of weekly magazines that are used in and distributed through school classrooms. This magazine line is Carson's oldest product, and its best known.

The book clubs are Carson's newest venture. Several years ago, a thorough analysis of the book publishing and distribution industry revealed that most existing book clubs were general interest, offering a wide variety of titles and book types. Members of these clubs selected far fewer books than they rejected. Carson decided there might be an opportunity to develop a line of book clubs that would be more targeted, both in terms of the titles offered and the market they appealed to. Because there were very few nonadult book clubs, and because Carson had a great deal of expertise with the school-age segment, several book clubs for children were included in the line. Carson's book clubs have been quite successful, and there are plans to introduce two additional clubs in the next few years.

Like the in-school magazines, sales and distribution of the book clubs is done through direct marketing. Carson regularly buys mailing lines from other publications and list compilers. Response rates from these mailings, which include a brochure describing the club and a reply device, typically average 4 percent, though the response is higher (around 6%) for the children's clubs. Carson also runs 90-second direct response television advertisements for specific clubs. Those ads include an 800 number consumers can call to join the club. The ads are evaluated based on the number of calls generated per airing, which varies greatly depending on which club is being advertised.

As mentioned earlier, Carson's clubs are doing quite well from a profitability standpoint. But, like all direct marketers, Carson would like to increase response rates. The corporate advertising campaign is an attempt to do that.

Some consumer research conducted last year revealed that although awareness for the Carson in-school magazine was very high among all of Carson's targets (children, teens, adults), awareness for the various book clubs was much lower. And, even those people aware of the book clubs didn't associate them with the magazine. Awareness of the Carson name and knowledge of Carson's publishing activities was extremely low. At the same time, attitudes toward the Carson magazine were very positive.

Carson's advertising agency suggested that a corporate campaign that would increase awareness for the Carson name, and firmly link Carson, the magazine, with the book clubs in the consumer's mind might also help in increasing response rates. The agency argued that improving consumer's perceptions of Carson by tying the company name to the well-known, well-liked magazine could decrease the risk consumers associated with joining a book club. The basic message would boil down to, "You really like this magazine. We're the people who publish it. Look what else we do." Although the corporate ads would not ask for club memberships, increased response to the direct marketing efforts for the individual clubs should be the result. The agency was recommending a national television and magazine campaign that would cost about $8 million for the first year.

Although Carson's management welcomed any idea that might increase response rates, they were a bit leery of a corporate advertising campaign.

Image-oriented advertising, advertising that wasn't designed to generate an immediate response, that couldn't be measured in actual orders, was a real unknown. Like all direct response companies, Carson was big on evaluating advertising based on sales results. Although they understood that such an evaluation would not be appropriate for the corporate campaign, they still felt that the effectiveness of any advertising investment should and could be evaluated. Hence Zaundra's assignment.

As Zaundra viewed it, the objectives for the corporate campaign were twofold: communications objectives in the form of increased awareness, knowledge, and liking of Carson Publications; and sales objectives in the form of a "lift" in the response rates for the book club offers. She felt that any evaluation plan would have to address both.

There was also the question of whether the corporate campaign should be test marketed rather than immediately implemented nationally. The agency had drawn up a plan for a test market in the northeastern U.S. at a monthly cost of $200,000. The test market campaign would use spot television ads in the same type of programs as those recommended for the national campaign and regional editions of the magazines included in the national plan. The agency had not made a recommendation on the duration of the test market, for the most part, because they were opposed to the idea of doing the corporate campaign on anything other than a national basis. The agency's reasoning was that any corporate advertising campaign was a long-term proposition rather than something that would produce immediately obvious effects. The time needed to run a test market would delay the national implementation of the campaign for an unnecessarily long time. The $8 million budgeted for the corporate campaign was very little money compared to the amount Carson was spending on direct response advertising, and the agency felt that Carson should go ahead and commit the resources to a national corporate campaign.

Questions

1. You've heard the agency's reasons for not doing a test market. What are some reasons that a test market *would* make sense in this situation?
2. Is it necessary to develop evaluation measures for the communication effects objectives in this campaign? Why or why not?
3. What factors would you look at to develop specific numerical objectives for the response "lift" Carson would like the campaign to generate?
4. How would you recommend that Carson evaluate the campaign's communication objectives? Who would you include in your sample?
5. Evaluate the regional test market program described in the case. How long should such a test last?

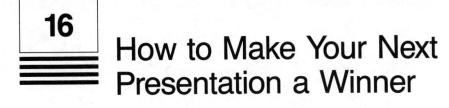

16

How to Make Your Next Presentation a Winner

Recently, while having dinner with a long-time friend in the advertising agency business, he made an observation I'd like to share:

> You know, Ron, you can have excellent content with good presentation technique and win the business. You can have good content with excellent presentation technique and win. But I've never heard of a poor presentation—with any set of redeeming factors—winning anything.

That's an observation worth tucking into your notebook. Poor presentations are among the world's most consistent losers. And that simple observation applies to all kinds of business, not just the advertising business.

In this chapter, we'll investigate the underlying causes of pathetic presentations as well as the recurring components of brilliantly successful presentations. We'll relate good and bad to the preparation of your next presentation. That's really what this chapter is all about: your next presentation and how you can make it a winner.

PRESENTATIONS: A TRANSCENDENT MEDIUM

First, what's all the fuss about? What makes presentations so pervasive and so all-fired important?

Presentations have become the preferred medium for clarifying issues and making crucial decisions in advertising. Got a campaign that's run amuck? Either fix it fast, or create a new one, and get back to the client with an impeccably organized presentation that is *bullet-proof*. Got a new

This chapter was written by Ron Hoff, the head of Ron Hoff & Associates, and a presentation consultant. He was Executive Creative Director of Foote, Cone & Belding in New York and Chicago, and Creative Director of Ogilvy & Mather in New York.

product to get off the ground? Launch it with a presentation that leaves the sales force chomping to clobber the competition. Want to introduce a key member of your staff in the best possible light? Give her or him a presentation to make. Got a crisis? Give a presentation!

If anybody ever asks you why advertising people devote such an inordinate amount of time to presentations, here's an answer that seldom fails to elicit a certain awe:

> Presentations? That's how we in advertising win our business—how we keep our business—and how we lose our business.

George Lazarus, marketing columnist of the *Chicago Tribune,* reported on how a $25-million advertising account (Sheraton hotels worldwide) landed in the laps of a large Manhattan-based agency, somewhat to the astonishment of industry observers. The gist of the story: *"Wells Rich came up with a presentation that blew their minds."*

Minds are blown, minds are benumbed, and minds are occasionally alienated forever by presentations—but presentations, for good or evil, have become indispensable. Blame it on television if you want (we are so used to *watching* people talk to us on TV). Blame it on the fact that prospective clients now expect to *see* the people who will tend to their accounts. ("We want to see how they think, how they handle themselves under pressure. We want to sense the interaction of a 'live' presentation. We want to feel the chemistry.")

So be it. Presentations have arrived. And they carry a ton of baggage.

Presentations are often expensive ($500,000 is not an unusual production cost for a major new business presentation); longwinded (a recent presentation for a $75,000,000 account went on and on, interminably, for over six hours); and painfully boring (you've seen the look—the eyes of the audience take on the glaze of highly polished marble).

No one has ever had the guts to figure how many dollars the advertising business spends on presentations every year, but *Business Week* has had the temerity to say that U.S. business conducts over 33,000,000 presentations every business day. That's not only a lot of time and money, that's a lot of competition for any presenter.

It boils down to this: If you want to make it big in advertising (or any business), you'd better put "presentations" somewhere near the top of your list of required courses.

WHAT IT ISN'T. WHAT IT IS

One of the ways that you can compete more effectively, as a presenter, is to understand that a business presentation isn't what most people think it is. It isn't a "pitch." It isn't a "sales talk." It isn't really about "us." It's about "them." Here's a definition that will help you to get a workable "handle" on presentations and what they're really about:

> A *presentation* is a commitment by the presenter to help the audience *do* something. Solve a problem. Make a market. Revive a brand share. At the very same time, the audience is making a minute-by-minute judgment on the real worth of that commitment.

"I can help you reverse the declining brand share of your product in Duluth," promises the presenter.

"Well, maybe you can—maybe you can't," muses the audience, sitting back—arms folded, legs crossed, eyes narrowing.

Commitment by the presenter. *Judgment* by the audience. Simultaneously. That's the way it goes in presentations. The presenter advocates. The audience evaluates. And renders its verdict.

In point of fact, an interesting way to think of your next presentation is to *visualize* it as a courtroom trial. You are one of the attorneys—presenting your case—and your mission is to win the vote of every single member of that jury (your jury will be your client or your prospective client).

Your evidence (case histories) must be relevant. Your documentation (research) must be solid. Your point of view (theme) must be clear. You must know the answers to tough questions before they are even asked. And the more pictorial your presentation, the more easily it will be remembered.

So, there you stand, ready to present your case (campaign). The audience looks at you expectantly. The room settles down. The presentation is about to begin.

Let's step right into it . . . with eight real-life principles of presentation that can make a measurable, meaningful difference in the success of your next presentation.

EIGHT PRINCIPLES TO PIN TO YOUR WALL

1. In Preparing Your Presentation, Maybe You Should Start about Halfway Through

Recently, I was interviewing a man named Tom Theobold, head of the Continental Bank in Chicago and, previously, a top executive with Citicorp in New York. He made a statement that really stuck in my memory. "You know," he said, "you advertising people should start most of your presentations about half-way through because that's when you stop talking about yourself and you start talking about *me.*" After watching and being involved in literally thousands of advertising agency presentations, I had to admit that Tom Theobold had uttered one of the gigantic truisms of all times. There isn't an audience in the world that hasn't said to itself, "When is that presenter going to stop yakking about his business and start talking about mine?" So instead of "Opening Remarks," why not structure your outline to begin with, "An Issue of Direct Concern to My Audience."

If the client's product is dying on the shelves in Detroit, your audience doesn't want to hear about your agency's latest triumph at the Cannes Film Festival. The sooner you can stop being *self*-conscious and start being *audience*-conscious, the better your chances of winning a positive verdict. Don't do anything rash, but consider Tom Theobold's theory before you make your next presentation. Maybe half of it should go.

2. Content Is Always the First Requirement of Any Presentation. Once Content Breaks Down, Delivery Is Never Far Behind

If you don't know your subject, your voice is going to tighten. If you don't believe what you're saying, your gestures are going to be halfhearted. If you get a question that catches you unprepared, your body language is going to answer for you. (Most of us squirm, shift from one foot to the other, and do a lot of leaning.)

Great presentations are a seamless combination of substance and style, but always—always—in that order. How much substance do you need in order to feel supremely confident about your next presentation? I have an answer for you, based upon twenty-six years of making presentations to clients and prospects:

> Have in your head about *seven* times as much information as you are likely to use in your presentation.

I tried to abide by that principle for many years, and it worked most of the time. It saw me through many prolonged audiovisual breakdowns, hundreds of probing question and answer sessions, and quite a few times when my entire organizational structure simply collapsed in my mind.

By knowing far more than your presentation will probably cover, you'll never be surprised. Well, *hardly* ever. At the very least, you'll have the feeling that you can't be "blindsided"—and that will quell a lot of uneasiness.

If you're not crazy about principles with numbers in them (or you simply have an aversion to "7"), here's a more general guideline that never, ever fails.

> Know your subject better than anybody in the room and your delivery may not be magnificent, but it will carry conviction—and that's better than empty theatrics any day.

3. It's Impossible to Be Too Clear

When was the last time you heard someone in an audience say, "Not a bad presentation but it was just too clear." Doesn't happen very often, does it?

Many presentations are so muddled that members of the audience say to themselves, "What in the world is that person talking about?" or, more to the point, "What on earth am I doing here?"

Here's a simple but effective exercise: Ask yourself, "If I were going to put a fifteen-word headline on my presentation, what would it say?" Isolate the meat of what you want to communicate and make sure you say it—clearly, prominently. Once you've got that headline inscribed indelibly in your mind, ask yourself, "What do I really want my audience to do as a result of this presentation?" If your answer is, "Know more about my business," you're going to join that great army of folks who lose presentations.

The headline should be something specific that goes right to the audience's self-interest. For example: "Let us fix your Detroit market. If market share isn't up in six months, fire us." The audience knows what to do. It's in their interest. You've given them something actionable. Clarity is absolutely vital. The minute you amble off into some dark thicket of confusion or contradiction, your audience is gone. If not physically gone, mentally gone. They're daydreaming their own giddy thoughts—about the weekend, the weather, the upcoming football game, whatever. Daydreams may not be compelling, but most of them are clear.

4. Keep in Mind That Your Audience Is Going to Remember about One Quarter of What You Say

A surprising number of presenters will assume that once a statement is made, the audience retains it—soaking up every delectable word. This impression is widely held in advertising—even though repetition is preached to every client as a bedrock necessity of every campaign.

The truth is this: The average audience retains approximately 25 percent of a presentation if the verbal content is given visual reinforcement (slides, charts, videotapes, whatever). If the presenter is simply standing there, plowing through a manuscript, flooding the atmosphere with words, he or she will be lucky to have one tenth of the total message retained by the audience.

Turning it around, nine out of ten "verbal only" points are going to be quickly forgotten. They just disappear, blotted out by boredom before ever reaching a brain cell. Audience participation will bolster the dozing memory, but most business presentations will do well to register 25 percent of their content.

Realizing that daunting fact, what do you do about it? One thing: Make sure your audience remembers the right 25 percent.

Maybe the old public speaking pronouncement, "tell them what you're going to tell them—tell them—then tell them what you told them," wasn't such bad advice after all. It, at least, recognizes reality.

Put your proposition up.   The *best* advice is this: Put your proposition in big type on a big display board, introduce it early, and then leave it in plain view throughout your presentation. Keep referring to it, relating supplementary points to it—then bring it back to center stage at your conclusion. Make sure your proposition and "the next step" are clearly part of the 25 percent that will stick in the minds of your audience.

It's not that audiences have poor memories, it's simply that presenters assume that audiences have perfect memories. They don't, but they do like to participate (under certain circumstances), and that can give their imperfect memories an enormous boost. Read on.

5. Participation by Your Audience Will Help Them Remember You and Your Message, but "Handle with Care." Participation Can Backfire

Research tells us that active participation by an audience will push retention of your message up around the 90 percent market. That is, providing you also have good verbal and visual techniques.

You know, from your own experience, that the second a presenter calls upon you to answer a question or make a comment, your adrenalin flow quickens, your blood pressure jumps, and you may feel your palms sweat a bit. There's good reason. You are being projected, physically as well as mentally, into the presentation. The mind flashes all kinds of warning signals. The nervous system is activated. Most importantly, the memory comes to full alert. It is a basic truth of audience dynamics: We recall most vividly what we actively participate in.

You, the presenter, can ask your audience to do almost anything. Stand up. Sit down. Sing. Work out a puzzle. Play a role. Most audiences are surprisingly agreeable. They'll do almost anything. Church audiences are doing something almost all the time.

So maybe, you ask a member of your audience to play a part in your commercial, or taste a new product, or critique an ad. This is all good stuff, good memory helpers. Nonetheless, a few words of caution may be in order.

- Study your audience carefully before you get up to present. If their attitude is essentially positive, you'll receive a good-natured response to your calls for participation. If your audience is looking at the clock and eyelids are beginning to droop, better postpone your plans for their participation.
- Look for the most animated people in your audience to be your participators. Facial language can tell you a lot. Look for eyes that are alive, bright, and follow the proceedings carefully. Avoid the scowlers and frowners. Stay away from the people who look like they've wandered into the room by mistake.

- Never force anybody to participate if you detect even a hint of reluctance. Cajolery is not advisable.
- Don't allow your presentation to depend on the abilities of one person. Have three or four candidates in mind. If one begs off, move on.
- Never allow anybody to look bad. Even the worst singer in the world is worth a rousing round of applause if he or she sang your new jingle.

Participation by your audience can make you unforgettable. Just make sure the dynamics in the room are right for group activities. If in doubt, seek out a few volunteers before you get up to present. Test the atmosphere. The secret of successful audience participation is that you know, insofar as humanly possible, what's going to happen before the games begin.

6. Nervousness Isn't All Bad, but It Can Become Serious When Your Audience Becomes More Concerned about Your Nerves Than Your Subject

Nervousness is an almost nondefinable malaise. It changes people—as if a mystical spell were cast over them. I have seen big, strapping account executives march up to make a major presentation and watched them diminish physically before my eyes. Their shoulders seem to shrink—horizontally. Trumpeting voices become squeaky falsettos. Legs, sturdy as redwoods, shake like sea grass. Hands twitch merely because there's nothing else to do with them.

> Nervousness is the number one problem of people who make important presentations in advertising.

Just to compound matters, "speaking before a group" has been repeatedly identified by researcher R.H. Bruskin & Associates as the most fearsome experience in life—about 2½ times as awful as *dying*!

Now, that's fearsome!

When I ask people why they are so vulnerable to nervousness, the old "R" word is usually rolled out. "Rejection" is an almost unbearable human experience, and presentation virtually invites it to drop by.

"Well, here I am . . . what do you think?"   You stand up there, open yourself to instant evaluation (ninety seconds, according to the most reliable research), and communicate—without saying *anything*—"Well, here I am, this is how I turned out. This is the sum total of my years on this planet. What do you think?" Self-presentation does have its awesome aspects.

But nervousness isn't all bad, and it is often reassuring to realize that people like Maureen Stapleton, Laurence Olivier, Williard Scott, and other performers have openly admitted to it (sometimes known as "stage fright").

Let's take this mind-numbing problem and cut it down to size. There are ways to deal with it and some of them can actually be fun. For example: I have noticed that Olympic athletes, ballet dancers, opera singers, and other professionals who are susceptible to nervousness invariably have a small "ritual" they follow just before presenting themselves. No two rituals are ever the same. The ritual is always unique to the person. And, whatever the ritual, it is always done in exactly the same way—right down to the smallest detail.

Included in the "ritual" are some physiological things that really do reduce nervousness. But, usually, there are some exercises that border on superstition. Never mind. Rituals *work*. Ask any professinal athlete, actor, or presenter. I swear by mine, and would never consider making a presentation without meticulously going through the following steps:

My "antinervousness ritual."

- Take a brisk 2-minute walk. It can be around the block, through the halls, or anywhere you want to walk. Exercise of any kind breaks the strain that creates nervousness. It gets the body chemistry going.
- Look at yourself in a mirror and check your appearance. All buttons buttoned. Nothing's out of place. You look like you want to look. That reduces anxiety.
- Next, I take *five* deep breaths (never four, never six), so that I feel my stomach pushing out against my belt—exhaling so that my stomach retreats toward my backbone. Deep breathing always calms the nervous system. Ask anybody who has hypertension.
- I say two words out loud, "*Let go.*" There's something about those two words that is almost magical. It's like the moment that you ease into a nice tub of warm water after a particularly hectic day. Your muscles melt.
- I tell myself that my presentation has one goal and one goal only: to genuinely *help* the people in my audience. That uncomplicates my mind and keeps the focus clear.
- I take out a St. Patrick's Day card that was given to me by a dear friend. It shows an elf floating over the Irish countryside holding onto a four-leaf clover. I see myself. I pat it once and put it away. It brings me luck!
- I tell myself to have a good time, and I really mean it. Life is too short to anticipate bad times.

The entire seven-step "ritual" has taken four minutes, more or less, and it has worked on my physical system as well as my psyche. Most importantly, it has created a kind of self-protecting mystique around me. I suspect it has a few touches that are derived from religious ritual. Whatever it is, it works.

Once you've created your own personal "antinervousness ritual," the following suggestions will help you to stay cool as you ease into your presentation:

- At the very start, say something to get your vocal chords going, but don't say anything that will be calamitous if it comes out sounding like a bullhorn. "Good morning" isn't a bad way to wake up your vocal chords. It's a nice thing to do, but your presentation isn't going down in flames if you sound like a frog. The important thing is—you've started. You've spoken. You're functioning. You haven't lost anything—and you've probably made friends with a few people, at least.
- Smile. Not just because you're friendly (which you are), but because smiling breaks up the planes in your face and proves you're not a statue. Roger Ailes, in his first-rate book, *You Are the Message,* says, "Smiling originates first in the brain, then on the face." You visualize something that makes you smile. Maybe it's your kid putting his dinner plate on his head. Maybe it's your mother blowing out all seventy candles. The mind remembers, the face reacts. Don't give us a "cheese" smile. Give us a smile that comes from a cheery reality.
- Don't cross your legs before you get up to speak. Chances are, they'll go to sleep and you'll approach the platform like a sailor on shore leave. Here's the way (if you're sitting down before speaking): Both feet are flat on the floor—arms are at your sides—and you're telling yourself, "I can feel the nervousness draining out of my fingertips, out of my toes, and disappearing into the carpet." Sounds silly, doesn't it? Try it.
- As you're sitting there, waiting to go on, pretend you just bought a very heavy overcoat and you're wearing it. It looks great. Let the weight of the coat relax your shoulders. Tense shoulders do more to encourage nervousness than almost anything else. Think of cold weather, when your shoulders are all scrunched up. You're miserably cold. When you tell your shoulders to "let go," the cold goes with them. The same thing happens with nervousness.
- When you stand up to present, keep your hands at your sides, or give them meaningful work to do (such as maneuvering your flipchart so that everybody can see it). If you don't have work for your hands to do, touch the index finger against the thumb on both hands. The very fact that you feel your own body heat will be reassuring and reduce your nervousness.

A final word on nervousness: A little bit of nervousness shows your audience that you're up for them, that you think they're pretty important. That's a compliment to them which works in your favor. But never tell your audience that you're nervous. That will just make them worry about you. And you want their confidence, not their concern.

7. Eye Contact Is the Strongest Force in Your Favor during a "Live" Presentation

When Tom Brokaw delivers the news, he may think he's making eye contact wih me—but I may be reading a book, washing the dishes, or scolding the cat. Tom doesn't know.

When you make your next presentation, you'll know whether you're making eye contact or not because you can see your audience. You can look into their eyes. Do you realize the enormous power that gives you?

- You can impose a kind of obligation upon an audience to actually listen to your message. Most audiences feel a certain responsibility to listen to a speaker. When you look directly at a person in your audience, you increase that responsibility by tenfold. The person in the audience says, "Hey, he or she is talking to me. I'd better pay attention." Eye-to-eye contact is the most direct form of communication in the world. Maybe that's why lovers are constantly looking into each other's eyes. Maybe that's why eyes have been called (mostly by poets) "windows of the soul."
- You can alter your message in response to the eye contact you're making. Mike Vance, a superb professional speaker, says, "I'm talking to what I see in your eyes." If the eyes are dull, you're not connecting. If the eyes are blinking, you're confusing the listener. If the eyes are shut, you've put the poor devil to sleep.
- You can listen with your eyes. Most people think eye contact is valuable only to the speaker. If you're presenting to a small group where the audience is constantly interacting with you, you can establish your interest in them by listening with your eyes. Eyes prove that you're listening. Ears don't prove anything.

Eye contact has very few absolutes. It tends to be instinctive. Self-confident presenters find eye contact to be easy. Uneasy presenters have problems with it. If you're insecure, you may feel that eye contact reveals your insecurities (and you're probably right).

Here are three fundamentals on eye contact that will benefit your next presentation:

- Don't set any specific length of time to maintain eye contact with one person. Stay only as long as it's comfortable for both people.
- Eye contact should be broken by natural pauses in meaning—between phrases—or thoughts. Eye contact usually breaks most comfortably at punctuation points.

- There's a big difference between staring at people and eye contact. Staring is intimidating, confrontational. Eye contact reduces the distance between people. It reaches out, asks for understanding on a one-to-one basis. If there is any question about the feeling that eye contact is creating between you and someone in your audience, give way and move on. You can always return.

8. "People May Lie, but Body Language Never Does"

That quote, anonymous in origin, has a terribly conclusive sound to it—but I know of no research to document it. Nevertheless, it's helpful. Body language, once you've learned how to read it, is going to tell you more than what your audience will say.

A word of caution: Don't read a lot of significance into isolated signals of body language. For example, if a member of your audience is sitting there with his fingers interlaced across his belly, it doesn't always mean that he is putting up a barrier to your message. This may be the customary meeting posture of this particular person.

But if the fingers are interlaced, the legs are crossed, the person has slithered down into his or her seat and is looking out the window—it's safe to say that you've got a problem. The body language, en toto, is issuing a stern rejection of your message. You've got to do something. Anything. In all probability, your point of view on your subject is clashing horribly with the viewpoint of the person who obviously isn't buying your act. You may want to get him or her involved in a bit of Q&A, or call a break, or call an audible. "Change" is the immediate and obvious answer.

Idea: Rate by body language.   You can rate people by their body language, and use your ratings to apportion the amount of time you spend with each member of your audience. Obviously, you'll want to work a little harder—with eye contact and participation techniques—on the person who's scoring low on your body language scale. Next time you're presenting, look at your audience in terms of numbers:

A solid ten: Head up, face agreeable, body leaning forward slightly, arms and legs composed, uncrossed; a contributor of good comments. A ready volunteer.

A seven: Attentive, but easily distracted. Abbreviated eye contact. Makes a few notes, asks some questions, but tends to be argumentative.

A five: Avoids eye contact, sits in back of room, never volunteers, may whisper while you're talking, keeps body turned away.

A three: Keeps one hand (or both) in front of face most of the time, shakes head (No! Disagree!) from time to time, maintains a general cynical expression.

A one: Spends the whole time doing something else—clipping finger-nails, doodling, checking contents of wallet. Total disinterest. Re-cently, when I was conducting a seminar in St. Cloud, Minnesota, I was told of a local CEO who invariably enters a meeting with an arm-ful of mail and proceeds to go through it, piece by piece, during the presentation! This executive surely deserves a zero.

Now, there are some very interesting things about all of these people:

- You like all of them. They're yours—just as the jury belongs to the at-torney. It is your job to convert them all, and that means being patient—reminding yourself, constantly, that your one objective is to make a genuine contribution to the life of each and every person (and that includes the hapless 3's, 2's and zeros).
- They all came. They all have a reason to be there. They all made an ef-fort to see your presentation. Unless you're speaking to a group of pris-oners at Sing Sing, your audience volunteered to attend (and the convicts probably did too). So, you've got to tap into the reason that brought them there. Note: For the CEO from St. Cloud, I'd suggest do-ing some intensive intelligence. Find out the one thing in life that is most compelling to that person and center your presentation on that subject. If mail, for example, has some kind of obsessive hold on this person, give your direct mail expert a big (and early) part in your presentation.
- Invariably, the people who don't participate have the worst body lan-guage. They also evaluate the presenter most poorly. So, you must resist the temptation to ignore the people who don't show a whole lot of in-terest in you. Involve the people who seem bored. Ask for their opin-ions. Listen carefully. Don't be afraid to acknowledge and appreciate their comments.

The point is—ignored people seldom get back into things on their own. Bring them back. They are your audience.

Sensitivity is vital.   This whole subject of body language depends, for its value, on the ability of the presenter to *observe* what's happening in the audience. Extreme sensitivity to the audience is an absolute necessity of presentation effectiveness.

And that suggests two jottings for your presentation notebook:

- Keep the lights up high enough so that you can read the body language of everybody in your audience.
- Don't hesitate to get close enough to your audience so that you can see how they're responding to you, and so that you can establish a strong presence with them.

Body language is fascinating. And you can practice just about anywhere. Try a cocktail lounge after 5 P.M. Or, if you'd rather go in another direction, watch the body language at a meeting of a board of trustees, or the city council, or the "People's Court" on television. Lots of talk in these places, but you'll be the only one who knows what's really being said.

PRESENTER: DEFINE THYSELF

Now that you understand some of the principles and techniques of presentation, let's get personal.

What kind of a presenter are you anyway? What kind of a presenter would you like to be? Where do you fit into a presentation team that's been formed to sell an important campaign to a major client?" What's your role? And does all of this self-analysis really matter?

It does if you plan to win in advertising. Most presenters have absolutely no conception of how they are perceived by their audiences. They haven't really visualized themselves as presenters. They like to say, "Oh, I'll just be myself." If you ask, "What does *that* mean?" you're likely to get a look of consternation and a casual, "Oh, you know . . . ."

The truth is, they don't know. Nobody knows. Without definition, they are gray blobs. And gray blobs are not in great demand. At least not in the advertising business. Gray blobs have trouble getting their own work approved, because—in a very real sense—clients perceive presenters as being part of the product they're buying.

Here are some questions to ask yourself about yourself. They won't require much more than ten minutes to answer—but you'll use the information for the rest of your career—maybe the rest of your life!

1. What do you consider to be your greatest strength as a presenter? When are you at your best? What is working hardest for you?
    Sample answer: "I'm an analyst. I can take the world's driest, most complex data and make sense out of it—so that it comes out clear and interesting."
2. What is the presentation weakness that you'd like to fix first?
    Sample answer: "I often go blank. My mind just turns to mush. It takes me a few moments to refocus and get going again. The situation is embarrassing."
3. Are you a red, blue, or gray presenter?
    Note that all presenters fit into the red, blue, or gray zones—at least basically. Red presenters speak from their emotions. They can be fiery, inspirational, entrepreneurial. Jesse Jackson is a perfect example.
    Blue presenters are pragmatic, logical, informational. They move through a subject deliberately, logically. Think of Henry Kissinger.
    Gray presenters are dull, bland, boring. They are usually neutral

and eminently forgettable. You can think of plenty of examples. The advertising business is full of them.

Red presenters may have a dash of blue in them. And blue presenters may flare up occasionally and show a little red. (Gray presenters are usually just that.) But most presenters will fit into one of those three zones. The question: Where are you?

4. How would you like to be perceived by your audience? What are the precise words you would like to hear the members of your audience saying about you and your presentation after you're finished?

Sample answer: "You know, that presentation really made me feel good about our product. I'm excited about it. I feel like I've got the support I need. That speaker was out-and-out inspirational."

Maybe you'll grab a blank sheet and answer these questions right now. Just putting the answers into writing—making them *tangible*—will crystallize a lot of things that may have been only foggy suspicions before. Acknowledging strengths as well as weaknesses, and writing them down, is the first step in self-analysis.

The second step is to determine whether or not your self-analysis matches up with reality. Are you the presenter you think you are? There's only one way to answer that question accurately. Make a presentation to a group of business colleagues, or a few neighbors, or a friend or two—and ask for candid comments. Compare these "outside" comments with your self-analysis. If there's a sizable gap, you have some bridgework to do. If your analysis of yourself is consistent with the observations of your audience, there are three things you should be doing as you prepare your next presentation.

*   Be more of your greatest strength. Be more of what you like best about yourself. Don't worry—you won't overdo it. And you'll be remembered for something that comes easily to you. You'll also find that focusing on one strength brings other strengths to the fore.
*   Take some positive steps regarding that weakness you've described and then don't worry about it anymore. It's history.
*   Run off a dozen copies of the words you'd like your audience to say about you. Keep a copy handy and read it just before your next presentation. Knowing how you want your audience to perceive you, and keeping it firmly in mind, will help you turn it into reality. You'll have a positive self-image that's solidly based on something you've developed. That's far better than "just being yourself" without having a clue as to what that's all about.

QUESTIONS ON YOUR MIND

Almost every major presentation in advertising ends with a question and answer period. If you don't get any questions, it's a bad sign. "No questions" generally means "no interest." Or, it can mean that you've run so hopelessly overtime that there's no time left for questions. Whatever the reason, it's trouble.

Questions are to be cherished, not feared. Questions not only indicate an interest in you and your presentation, they usually reveal a lot about your audience—and that's always valuable, particularly if you will meet with them again.

So, being an optimist, I'm assuming that you've got a few questions about presentations in general—and your next presentation in particular.

Let's see if I can get inside your mind and ask a few of the questions that may be brewing there. We'll concentrate on frank questions, short answers.

1. *What's the best structure for preparing a presentation? How do you go about it?*

Most presentation structures are way too complicated. They get tangled up in their own underwear. Here's a nice simple structure, and it may be the best of all time:

A. Understanding the problem (defining it, demonstrating your knowledge of it).

B. Resolving the problem (offering solutions, weighing alternatives, making a selection, citing benefits).

C. "The Next Step" (how to implement the solution—a specific bid for action).

If you've got *seven* times as much information as you'll actually use, you'll find it's relatively easy to organize your material into this three-part structure. Of course, it needn't be a problem. It could be an "opportunity"—or a "situation." But in most advertising presentations, it's a "problem."

2. *What audiovisual aids should I use? What about all of the new electronic and computer-driven AV equipment?*

There have been major improvements in two areas of AV that you should know about and use if the situation permits. One is the wireless equipment that eliminates cords (and all the tripping and stumbling that cords inevitably cause). A remote for changing slides can be invaluable. An FM transmitter microphone (about two inches wide) clipped to your collar can project your voice throughout an auditorium with nary a wire—and you won't have to be rooted to a stationary microphone stand.

The second major development is computer-produced slides, transparencies, and "hard copy" for flipcharts and leave-behinds. Anything that can be seen on a computer screen can now be made into a slide. And the slides are brighter and infinitely more imaginative than the old slides from predesktop days.

What to avoid: AV that overwhelms you or baffles you with its endless possibilities for screwing up.

Advertising presentations need AV for memorability and drama. But I've never heard of a major account being awarded to an agency because of its AV equipment. You're the star. Your brains are what the audience wants to see. The rest is "supporting cast."

3. *How long should an effective presentation last?*

    Most presentations have preset time allotments. One hour, thirty minutes, whatever. Generally, anything over two hours is too long, no matter what the subject.

    The most important thing about time is this: never go over. Most presenters do, and most audiences fidget and fume.

    Do this: Close your presentation *under*time. How much? Give your audience a "gift" of five minutes for every 30-minute segment. If it's a 30-minute presentation, end five minutes early. If it's a 60-minute presentation, take a five minute break *and* end five minutes early. Ninety minutes—give your audience fifteen minutes to "break" or get away a bit early.

    Staying *under*time, while your competition is running *over*time, will win you more points than anything else you can do.

    P.S. Don't look at your watch while you're presenting. The body language indicates that you're bored with your own presentation. Rig up a clock in the back of the room (if there isn't one already there, and there usually isn't). This way, you can keep track of your time without sending bad signals to your audience.

4. *What happens if people doze off while I'm presenting?*

    Usually, falling asleep isn't a probem. Eyelids fluttering and glazed eyeballs are frequent problems. Consider them as signals. What are they telling you? It could be that our audience is dreadfully hung over. More likely, your audience isn't interested in what you're presenting. Either shift gears and get into the next part of your presentation—or start moving around more. It's strange how motion by the speaker tends to bestir people and make them think something's going on. Also, if you've got the lights down, make sure they get back up (never show slides or films after lunch). Once the lights are up, try a little eye contact on the droopers and dozers.

    Note that the worst thing you can do is call attention to their condition and embarrass them. (I've seen presenters bang their fists on a table or chair to awaken dozers and nodders.) *Not* a good idea. Make your wake-up technique as subtle as possible.

5. *What about memorizing a presentation—good idea or bad?*

    Bad. Memorizing a script instills the fear of forgetting it. Also, audiences sense when a script has been memorized—and they'll be worried about you too. Some presenters memorize the first paragraph and the last paragraph of their presentations so they can be sure of opening and closing strong. If that sounds good to you, try it. But memorizing is basically risky.

6. *Where do most presenters go wrong? What should I guard against?*

   More presentations are lost in the question and answer section than anywhere else. The reason—presenters don't prepare for questions. They should—at least one day before the presentation is scheduled to go on. Two things to remember:

   - Anticipate the questions you're likely to get. Write them down. It's easy if you know your audience. Members of an audience always ask questions that are closest to their individual responsibilities. The marketing director, for instance, is going to want to know how much of your advertising budget could be redirected to sales promotion. The corporate communications director will ask about "image" and possible implications for Wall Street. Just study the titles of those attending and you can, with a little imagination and empathy, anticipate their questions 70 percent of the time.

   - Rehearse the answers. Hone your answers into short, simple statements. Cut long sentences down to one point. Eliminate ambiguities. Use a microcassette recorder to help you. If you're part of a presentation team, make sure you know what questions you're supposed to answer. There's nothing worse than five members of a team answering the same question simultaneously—and everybody saying something different. It's chaos. Then someone invariably says, "What I really think Tom (or whoever) was trying to say . . . ." Make sure you know *who's* going to say *what*.

7. *Is there one piece of advice that will help me overcome all my fears and be absolutely brilliant?*

   No, not one—but will you settle for two?

   First, prepare yourself so thoroughly that you feel like you own the subject. You should be able to say (and mean), "I've got a lock on this subject." Command of the subject goes a long way toward giving you command of your audience.

   Second, tell yourself that this presentation is an opportunity for you to show what you're all about. *Newsweek,* in an article about Bruce Springstein said, "He makes a complete commitment to the immediacy of the moment." Think about that. That's just got to be a terrific feeling. Reach for it in your next presentation and you'll have a good shot at brilliance.

Presentations? Sure. That's how we in advertising win our business—how we keep our business—and how we lose our business. I wish you many winners and keepers. We won't fret about the rest.

Appendix
W.K. Kellogg Company

One of the best ways to understand the development and implementation of an advertising campaign is to see an example of one. On the following pages, you will find an excellent advertising campaign plans book developed by a student group from Baruch College.* It's for a new cereal product being considered by the W.K. Kellogg Company.

Note that the terminology and format found in the Baruch College plans book sometimes doesn't coincide exactly with the format recommended in this edition of *Strategic Advertising Campaigns*. However, the basic advertising campaign development principles are the same, and the content and direction will fit with almost any campaign planning process. What is perhaps most important, the Baruch College team illustrated one of this text's basic principles, the development of an integrated marketing communications program. You'll see that their recommendations to Kellogg include

advertising, trade and consumer sales promotion, trade advertising, and even a sales representative program. Overall, it is a well-conceived, well-developed advertising campaign program. We recommend it to you as a planning aid for the advertising campaigns you will be developing.

SITUATION ANALYSIS

The Battle Creek Toasted Corn Flake Company was formed in 1906 by W.K. Kellogg who saw opportunity in the aggressive marketing of cold cereal. He believed strong production, advertising, and promotion programs were key to business growth. He was right.

New Product Definition

Kellogg is currently developing a new product to be introduced in January of 1990. The

---

*This plans book, developed by students at Baruch College, was judged the best of fifteen regional entries in the 1989 National Student Advertising Competition conducted by the American Advertising Federation. The competition gives advertising students from around the world an opportunity to compete in a professional setting using a real-world product or product concept.

The student team consisted of Ivette Alvarez, Maria Antonopoulos, Ariella Bernstien, David Bushnell, Thomas Davis, Eric Dell, Christopher Demers, Lina Garcia, Marianna Lokis, Jennifer Lynch, Johnny Ng, Henry Lau Pong, Deblyn Seeley, Janice Sileo, Debbie Wally, and Francis Wu. Their AAF faculty advisor was Professor Carol Finn Meyer.

product, code named Alpha, is a whole wheat and wheat bran cereal in the shape of elongated strands or "shreds". It was originally conceived as a wholesome, natural cereal targeted more toward adults/all-family than to kids.

Kellogg Sales and Market Share

The Kellogg Company is the leading ready-to-eat (RTE) cereal manufacturer worldwide with a 42 percent share of the U.S. market and a 50 percent share of the global market. Though the company competes well in several food categories—toaster pastries, frozen waffles, frozen pies, and yogurt—it has been particularly successful in the RTE cereal market.

Decline 1970–1983.   Through the second half of the 1970s and into the early 1980s, Kellogg steadily lost market share. Kellogg was underspending its competition in marketing and new product development and by 1983 its U.S. market share hit a final low of 36.7 percent. One Wall Street analyst described Kellogg as "a fine company that's past its prime."

Revitalization 1983–1987.   Under the leadership of Chairman William E. LaMothe, Kellogg changed its marketing strategy by focusing on consumers and developing products tailored to their wants and needs. This strategy helped Kellogg tap into underexploited segments, like the baby-boom segment, and to spot other niches in the category.

The success of Kellogg's Mueslix brand, which created an entirely new "gourmet segment" of cereals, is one example of how the strategy has paid off. Matching products with consumer wants and needs is the key.

Future growth potential.   Kellogg currently markets over thirty-five different RTE cereals, five of which are among the top ten cereals. As part of the revitalization of the marketing program, annual spending has tripled to an

estimated $865 million or 20 percent of sales since 1983. The number two cereal marketer, General Mills (GM), has also increased ad expenditures for its cereals and market analysts predict that the combined force of Kellogg and GM could force smaller marketers out of the segment.

Considering the intensity of Kellogg's recent marketing efforts, a 50 percent U.S. market share in 1990 is well within reach.

Category Volume and Growth

The RTE cereal market has a sales volume of $5.3 billion; it is the largest dry goods category in the supermarket. Sales volume has increased an average of 8 percent over the last three years, and is expected to rise at least another 9 percent in 1989. The following graph shows volume growth from 1983 to 1987:

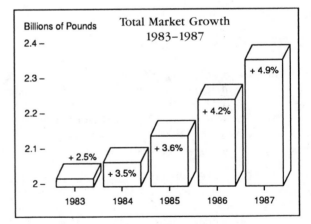

Market Shares

Kellogg has gained market share steadily over the last five years to the detriment of its competitors, notably, General Mills, General Foods (Post), and Ralston Purina. These manufacturers have not been as tuned in to consumer trends and opportunities in the marketplace, particularly in the adult cereal segment.

Market Shares

Company	1983	1984	1985	1986	1987
Kellogg	38.5	40.5	42.4	42.6	42.5
General Mills	20.8	20.7	20.9	21.2	20.7
General Foods Post	16.6	14.3	13.3	12.8	12.8
Quaker Oats	8.9	8.3	7.3	7.1	7.8
Ralston Purina	5.9	5.9	5.8	5.9	5.5
Nabisco	4.9	4.9	4.9	5.0	5.3

SOURCE: Wheat First Securities/*Advertising Age.*

As the competition plays catch-up by launching new cereals, Kellogg can expect tougher competition for its adult cereals. With increasing competition, the success of a new brand will depend even more on the effective communication of a consumer-valued point of difference.

Major Players in the Category

General Mills. GM is the second largest cereal manufacturer with a 20.7 percent share of the market in pounds. Major brands include Cheerios, Total, Wheaties, Raisin Nut Bran, Crispy Wheats and Raisins, and Fiber One. GM also manufactures many children's cereals.

General Foods Post. Post is the third largest manufacturer, with a market share of 12.8 percent—about half that of General Mills. Major brands include Grape Nuts, Raisin Bran, Fruit & Fibre, 40% Bran Flakes, along with a good many children's cereals.

Quaker Oats. Quaker holds a 7.8 percent market share. A full 3.2 percent of that share can be attributed to the Cap'n Crunch brand. The Life brand accounts for another 1.5 percent. Other major brands are 100% Natural, Oh's, Quaker Oat Squares, and Crunchy Bran.

Ralston Purina. Market share for Ralston is 5.5 percent with the Chex line of cereals accounting for 3.6 percent of that figure. Other major brands are Almond Delight, Sun Flakes, Bran News, and Muesli. Muesli is the Ralston Purina entry into the premium niche Kellogg created with Mueslix.

Nabisco. Market share for Nabisco is 5.4 percent with the Shredded Wheat line accounting for nearly three-quarters of the company's sales. Other major brands are Fruit Wheats, 100% Bran, and Apple Raisin Squares.

Characteristics of the RTE Cereal Market

- Low brand loyalty
- Frequent new product introductions
- High rate of new product failures
- No seasonal sales fluctuations
- No significant regional consumption skews
- Price insensitivity

New product performance. The following table shows typical market share gained by successful new products over a range of five years. (Note that each one-tenth of a percentage point represents about $5.3 million in sales.)

Sample New Product Market Shares

Brands	1982	1983	1984	1985	1986	1987
Kellogg Nutri Grain Wheat & Raisin	.2	.4	.5	.5	.5	.4
Kellogg Fruitful Bran		0	.7	.6	.5	.4
Kellogg Crispix		.5	1.0	1.0	1.0	1.0
Ralston Crispy Oatmeal & Raisin Chex		0	.4	.1	—	—
Quaker Raisin Life		0	.2	.2	—	—
General Mills Toasted Wheat 'n Raisins		.3	.3	.3	.2	.1
Post Fruit & Fibre Tropical Fruit			0	.5	.4	.3
Kellogg Apple Raisin Crisp			.4	.5	.5	.4
Kellogg Just Right				.1	.8	.8
Nabisco Shredded Wheat & Bran				0	.6	.8
General Mills Fiber One				.2	.5	.4

Product segments. The RTE category is broken down into six major product segments: all-family, presweetened, healthy halo presweets, nutritional/natural, fiber, and fruit added. Market shares for each product segment are shown in the following graph:

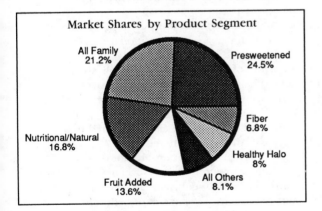

Market Shares by Product Segment

All Family 21.2%
Presweetened 24.5%
Fiber 6.8%
Nutritional/Natural 16.8%
Healthy Halo 8%
Fruit Added 13.6%
All Others 8.1%

Individual product positionings. It is important to note that the top twelve brands in the cereal category account for nearly *half of all cereal sales*. Market share for these major brands, however, is diminishing as manufacturers introduce cereals that appeal to specific consumer wants and needs. As a result, the cereal category has been filled with a profusion of niche brands. Opportunities for growth through niche marketing continue to be the focus of cereal manufacturers as the battle for market share goes on.

With over thirty-five different varieties of ready to eat cereal, Kellogg brands occupy a multitude of these niches. Although Alpha's product attributes preclude competing in most of these niches, there are several that should be avoided in positioning Alpha, so as not to cannibalize existing Kellogg brands:

- A strictly* high-fiber appeal (All-Bran/All-Bran Extra Fiber)
- A high-protein, low-fat appeal (Special K)
- A strictly "for the athlete" appeal (Pro Grain)
- A strictly "feel young again" appeal (Product 19)
- A "perfectly balanced nutrition" appeal (Just Right)

Market Trends

- The RTE cereal market is expected to expand in 1990 with 3–4 percent volume growth in lbs.

---

*"Strictly" means that this is the primary appeal.

- The major trend in the category is marketing "healthy" cereals to health-conscious adult consumers.
- The adult cereal segment will be the fastest growing segment in the RTE cereal category due to the movement of the baby-boom population to a more family-oriented stage of life associated with their increased consumption of cold cereal.
- Competition is intensifying as manufacturers begin to redirect marketing efforts with new products that will compete directly with Kellogg brands.
- Consumer awareness of dietary fiber is widespread. The bran/fiber segment has seen fantastic growth and will continue to grow as consumer demand continues to increase. (See chart that follows.)
- The fiber segment is currently being dominated by oatbased cereals touting the extremely popular oat bran fiber.

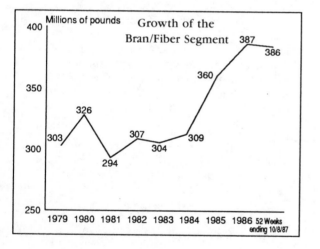

PRODUCT ANALYSIS

Physical Product

Alpha is a unique cereal form consisting of loose, elongated strands (shreds) made primarily of whole wheat. Alpha ingredients

are whole wheat, wheat bran, sugar, malt flavoring, and salt. Kellogg has provided the following nutritional information:

Serving size: 1 ounce	
Carbohydrate	23 grams
Protein	3 grams
Calories	90
Fat	0 grams
Cholesterol	0 grams
Fiber	5 grams
Sodium	250 mg
Potassium	120 mg

Taste Tests

Product test results for Alpha provided in the Kellogg case study yielded the following information:

- Alpha scored *below* the Kellogg product norm for overall taste.
- Alpha scored *above* the Kellogg product norm for overall texture both with milk and without.
- Alpha scored *above* the Kellogg product norm for perceived nutritional value.

Analysis of taste tests. Although Alpha scored below the product norm in overall taste, we must consider that presweetened cereals are factored into the Kellogg product norm and so Alpha is being compared out of its class. All this considered then, Alpha's below-average taste scores are not dramatic. In the same respect, the above-average perceived nutritional value scores are also not surprising; Alpha's shape and texture make it easily identified as a "healthy" cereal.

Of greater significance is the overall texture score recorded for Alpha. The definition of "overall texture," as it relates to the Kellogg taste tests, is "how crispy or soggy the product is when eaten." Alpha is a wholesome, relatively nutritious cereal; for such a cereal to score above the Kellogg product norm, where presweetened cereals are a factor, indicates a high degree of "crispiness" for Alpha.

An Ideal Cereal—How Alpha Stacks Up

A *Consumer Reports'* October 1986 article on breakfast cereals provides a useful listing of the components of an ideal cereal. From this guide we can see how Alpha compares.

Fiber—The National Cancer Institute recommends 20–35 grams of dietary fiber daily from a variety of foods. Cereal grains can provide both soluble and insoluble fiber and each provides distinct health benefits. An ideal cereal should be high in fiber, whether soluble or insoluble.

Alpha—Alpha is high in fiber, with 5 grams of insoluble fiber per ounce. The average for unsweetened cereals is 2.7 grams per ounce.

Protein—The protein in grain is good but not complete; it lacks certain essential amino acids that are protein's building blocks. Cereals borrow nutrients from the milk added to complete the protein. An ideal cereal should be a good source of protein.

Alpha—Alpha has 3 grams of protein, most regular (unsweetened) brands have between 2 and 4 grams of protein with the majority at 2 grams. Alpha can be considered above average in protein content.

Sugar—Three grams of added sugar per ounce or less was considered low by *Consumer Reports;* that's less than a teaspoon. An ideal cereal is low in sugar.

Alpha—Alpha is low in added sugar with only 3 grams per ounce.

Sodium—Cereal grains contain little sodium but manufacturers often add sodium to improve a cereal's taste. Because sodium can increase blood pressure and affect hypertension levels it is a negative factor. An ideal cereal should be low in sodium.

Alpha—Alpha has a relatively high sodium content at 250 milligrams. Of the eighty-six unsweetened cereals our team examined, the average sodium level was 186 mg, however, some cereals contain as much as 370 mg.

Fat—Most RTE cereals are low in fat although using whole milk in cereal increases fat levels. An ideal cereal should have little or no fat content.

Alpha—Alpha has zero fat content and zero cholesterol. Comparing caloric levels, Alpha is lower than average at 90 calories per ounce. The average level for the eighty-six cereals we examined was 102 calories.

Vitamins—*Consumer Reports* did not favor fortification in its ratings because theoretically vitamin supplements are unnecessary with a balanced diet. Furthermore, fortification can add 25 percent to the cost of a cereal. Added vitamins are not required in an ideal cereal.

Alpha—Alpha has average vitamin content, with the exception of iron, which is at 45 percent of the U.S. recommended daily allowance.

Flavor and Texture—Taste is the most important aspect of a cereal to most people. An ideal cereal should have a rich, often nutlike grain flavor. There should be no excessive sweetness or "off flavors." The texture should be moderately firm and crispy/crunchy with little "toothpacking" or residual particles noticeable.

Alpha—Taste tests show Alpha to be below average in taste appeal when compared with *all other cereals.* As discussed previously, this low rating must be offset in consideration of the influence of presweetened cereals on the results of these taste tests.

Statement of Assumptions

To effectively explore the marketplace for opportunities for Alpha, we established preliminary assumptions about the cereal. These assumptions were then used to measure the cereal's appeal to consumers through concept testing. Two sources of information were used in formulating preliminary assumptions about Alpha.

1. The described attributes and perceptions provided in the Kellogg case study:
   - Alpha is a wholesome wheat and wheat bran cereal.
   - It has above average insoluble fiber content.
   - It has standard fortification levels.
   - It has fewer calories than most cereals (90 per oz.).
   - It is neither dramatically good or bad tasting.
   - It has a high degree of crispiness both with and without milk.
   - It is lighter in density than most cereals (1 oz. per cup), so it doesn't leave you with a heavy feeling.

2. Consumer perceptions of the product based on the color photograph of Alpha:
   - Alpha looks healthy and nutritious.
   - It looks crispy/crunchy.
   - It looks dry.
   - It looks like a "fiber cereal."

Defining a New Product Segment

There is a group of cereals on the market that appeal mostly to adults. These cereals are often referred to in the trade papers as "adult cereals." This segment, by our definition, would include cereals that are not presweetened, and that are perceived by consumers to be good for you. This segment, as defined, best represents the competitive field Alpha will face.

We have identified the following subsegments in the adult cereal category:

Bran/Fiber—Some of the cereals in this group have an especially high fiber content and include cereals such as All Bran with 10 grams of fiber and All Bran/Extra Fiber with 13 grams—both are Kellogg cereals. General Mills's Fiber One has 12 grams of fiber. The majority of the brands in this subsegment have much lower levels, averaging around 3 grams per ounce. Some brands that make high fiber claims have as little as 2 grams of fiber per ounce.

Fortified—These cereals provide uncommonly high vitamin and/or mineral content. This group includes cereals like Kellogg's Just Right, Product 19, and General Mills Total.

Nutritional—This category includes cereals that are considered to be healthy based on the inclusion of some healthy ingredients or the exclusion of unhealthy ingredients. Some examples are Shredded Wheat, Post Bran Flakes, and Special K.

Fruit Added—These provide some added fruits or fruit-nut combination to improve taste and offer convenience to consumers who don't want to bother with fresh fruit. The added fruits/nuts give a health appeal to these cereals. Examples are Raisin Squares, Fruitful Bran, and Raisin Bran types.

Oat Bran—These cereals offer some form of oat bran. Cracklin' Oat Bran, Common Sense Oat Bran, and Oat Squares are examples.

Traditional—These are the old favorites that are generally simple grains cereals. Corn Flakes, Chex, and Rice Krispies are examples. These cereals are also eaten by children whose parents do not allow presweetened cereals.

These subsegments define the broad competitive field that Alpha will be facing.

Obviously, with so many cereal types competing for the attention of adult cereal eaters, Alpha will need a selling appeal that is both unique and important to these consumers.

Population trends factor in significantly to the future growth of the adult cereal segment.

- In 1990, baby boomers will range from about 25 to 44 years old, this age group currently accounts for 47.1 percent of all households.
- Over the next decade the 25–34 age group as a whole will grow 12 percent, the 35–44 age group will grow 23 percent, and the 45–54 age group will grow 45 percent.

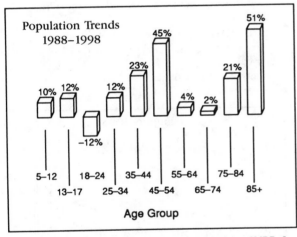

Population Trends
1988–1998

Age Group

SOURCE: U.S. Census, *American Demographics; * SMRB, Inc.

☐ = % Change.

The adult cereal segment will grow more than any other segment over the next decade. Alpha will have the greatest potential for growth competing in this segment.

CONSUMER ANALYSIS

Secondary Research

Consumer mindset: Health centeredness.   *American Health* magazine

in association with the Daniel Yankelovich Group and the Gallup organization have studied Americans' attitudes and perceptions relating to health. Their research reveals changing attitudes toward the notion of healthful living that are characterized by "health-centeredness"; a feeling that health is the center of an energetic, balanced life.

The *American Health* study points to six major trends that will shape American's concept of health in the 1990s.

1. **Getting older—thinking younger.**
    Two-thirds of people over 40 years of age feel much younger than that, an average of thirteen years younger than they really are. Looking good is an important part of feeling young; concerns about appearance are growing steadily, particularly with baby boomers. A recent Gallup survey of 800 adults found that weight control is the aspect of appearance felt to be most central to health.

2. **Time—devoting more to ourselves.**
    The time crunch is very real; Americans average only eighteen hours of leisure time a week—fully one-third less than we had in the 1970s. Average work hours have increased by 20 percent to nearly fifty weekly hours. The people who have the least time are professional high-achievers, especially women who may have heavy responsibilities at work and at home. Americans will be looking for ways to deal with the problem of too little time.

3. **Families—strong but stressed.**
    Nine-tenths of young adults say that family is the most important thing to them. Contrary to popular belief, the divorce rate is actually falling and the marriage rate is climbing; this contributes to a rising birth rate. But family life has changed, with most households needing two incomes to survive. Fully half of women with children under one year old are

working—twice as many as did in 1970. The new stresses on the family will require special attention to nutritional dilemmas that result from time constraints on proper meal planning.

4. **The Environment—getting back to nature.** Two-thirds of Americans feel that the environment is so important that "requirements and standards cannot be too high," and cost is not an issue. Outdoor leisure activities are bringing Americans into closer contact with the environment as bicycling, walking, hiking, and swimming become more and more popular. There is an increased interest in getting back to nature with the foods we eat too, as consumers worry about pesticides, additives, and unhealthy ingredients.

5. **Emphasis on the mind.** Americans are not observers, they're participants. Participation in a wide variety of artistic hobbies including music, photography, singing, modern dance, and pottery has roughly doubled since 1975. Forty million Americans, for example, now write stories and poems in their spare time. The focus is no longer on physical exercise solely to improve the body; exercise is important to mental fitness as well—it makes us more calm, more alert. It's the union of sound body and mind that is important.

6. **Fun and adventure.** Americans are looking for excitement and adventure to escape the treadmill of life once in a while. Exotic vacations, white water rafting, a new interest in ethnic foods and exotic fruits and vegetables, it's all part of what's been called the "experiential" approach to living. But we're less willing to choose between pleasure and health, and so we may choose to cut calories during the day and still have dessert at night. We're looking for new ways to exercise in more entertaining ways, with soft aerobics, fun sports, walking, and hiking.

In summary, feeling in control of your health is essential to well being. People who are confident that they can take care of their health are twice as likely to be very satisfied with their lives. No other factor, age, sex, education, exercise level or even salary, affects our happiness so dramatically.

Cereal consumption patterns. The following list contains results of a readers' survey conducted by *Consumer Reports* for its October 1986 article on breakfast cereals:

- Cereal is served as breakfast in nine out of ten households.
- Two-thirds of *Consumer Reports'* readers eat cereal at least once a week.
- About 40 percent eat cereal three mornings a week.
- Sixty percent prefer cereals low in sugar.
- Few sprinkle sugar or honey on their cereal.
- Many add fresh fruit.
- Most pour on low fat milk.

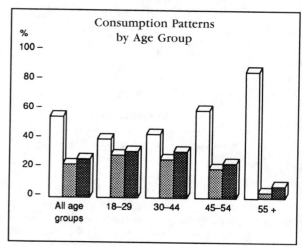

SOURCE: U.S. Department of Health.

Eat Breakfast:
- ☐ = Almost everyday.
- ▦ = Sometimes.
- ■ = Rarely or never.

Grocery shopping habits. Lieberman Research, Inc., conducted research on food shopping that included both men and women.

The method used was in-home depth interview. Highlights of their findings follow:

- Seventy-seven percent of men do major food shopping in a four-week period as compared with 98 percent of women. (Major food shopping defined as trips where people spend a lot of money and buy a lot of food.)
- Both men and women do major food shopping about equally often—an average of 3.6 major food shopping trips for men versus an average of 3.2 major food shopping trips for women in a four-week period.
- Seventy-two percent of both men and women use a shopping list. Women are *primarily responsible* for preparing the shopping list. Cereal is one of the most likely items to appear on a shopping list.
- Shoppers are apt to know which brand of cereal they will buy before going to the store.
- Nonworking women are more likely to do their major food shopping on weekdays (Monday–Thursday) and during morning and afternoon hours.
- When men or women do major food shopping there is a 50/50 chance they will be accompanied by someone else. Women are more likely to do their major food shopping alone. However 41 percent of women do shop with other people. Men and women are most likely to shop together on Fridays and weekends. Women are almost as likely to do shopping with friends/relatives as with a spouse.
- When married persons shop with their spouse, 89 percent say they stay together in the store rather than shop apart.
- Thirty-three percent of shoppers spend over an hour in the store; 32 percent spend less than an hour, 35 percent spend about an hour in the store.
- Seventy-six percent of women and 64 percent of men reported using coupons in the last four weeks. Men and women redeemed about the same number of coupons in a four-week period—twelve. In the 80 percent of households that clip coupons women do most of the coupon clipping.
- Check prices: 90 percent.
- Look for special sales: 87 percent.
- Check ingredients between brands: 40 percent.
- Check number of servings per package: 42 percent.
- Check serving size: 44 percent.
- Check salt content: 41 percent.
- Check calories per serving: 38 percent.

Original Research

Because actual samples of Alpha were unavailable, the problem of measuring consumer reaction to the cereal was made a great deal more difficult. We devised research that would reveal opportunities for Alpha in the marketplace and provide answers to questions that were not obtainable from secondary sources.

Original research provided a more full understanding of the consumer in relation to breakfast, health consciousness, cereal consumption and cereal purchase behavior. From this analysis, opportunities for Alpha emerged.

Summary of Key Findings

Focus groups.

- Health-conscious adults see healthy living as a long term investment as well as a present-day asset.
- Eating healthy helps you feel good about yourself.
- Eating too much in the morning makes you feel sluggish; this is a detriment when you have to get moving.
- People don't always make time for breakfast in the morning.
- Consumers are aware that the nutritional information based on 1-ounce servings is misleading and in some cases deceptive.

Concept test.

- Alpha's strongest appeals are good taste, high fiber, crispiness, low calories, and high quality.
- The most likely prospects for Alpha are females, current users of fiber, or low-calorie cereals.

The cereal purchase decision process.

- Good taste, high fiber, natural ingredients, low fat/cholesterol, low calories, and crispy/crunchiness are what adult consumers are looking for in new cereals.
- Advertising and word of mouth are the major builders of new-cereal awareness levels.
- Coupons are also important in creating awareness among consumers who actively clip coupons.
- Seventy-two percent of respondents use coupons at least sometimes; 32.7 percent always look for coupons before shopping.
- The decision to select a particular brand of cereal is often made in the store rather than beforehand.

Research objectives, methodology, and results follow.

Focus Group Highlights

Why eating healthy is important.

- To stay healthy and live longer; to stay healthy as I get older.
- When you eat healthy, you feel better about yourself.
- Eating healthy is very important to staying healthy; so many of the major illnesses are directly related to a poor diet.

How to eat healthy.

- Avoid cholesterol, salt, fat, food additives, too much sugar.
- Eat a lot of bran.
- Eat more fish, chicken, steamed vegetables; less red meats and fatty foods.
- Overeating is bad.

The morning.

- The morning can be a quiet time or a hectic time.
- There's a certain "fresh" feeling you get in the morning.
- Sometimes it's very hard to get out of bed in the morning.
- Once up and fully awake, it feels good to have the whole day ahead of you.

Research Objective 1: To explore consumer feelings/perceptions/attitudes with regard to health consciousness, the morning, breakfast, and cold cereal in order to gain insights into consumer mindset.

Methodology: Three focus groups were conducted with from eight to twelve male and female, adult cereal eaters. Moderators discussed the following topics:

- Is eating healthy important to you? Why?
- What kinds of things do you eat in order to eat healthy?
- What are your thoughts about breakfast?
- What is breakfast like in your home?
- How do you feel about the morning in general (likes and dislikes)?
- How do you feel about cold cereal for breakfast?
- What kinds of cereal do you like? Why?
- Describe the perfect cereal.

- The weather can affect your mood in the morning.
- Some people are "morning people"; some are not.

Breakfast.

- Breakfast is the most important meal of the day.
- Breakfast can be leisurely or hurried or even skipped altogether.
- Sometimes its too hard to wake up early enough to eat breakfast.
- You feel guilty when you don't eat breakfast.
- Breakfast should hold me over until lunch.
- You feel good when you have eaten a healthy breakfast; your outlook is more positive; you're ready to meet the day.
- Breakfast symbolizes the start of a new day.
- Eating too much at breakfast makes you feel sluggish.

Cold cereal.

- Cold cereal is quick and it tastes good.
- Cold cereal is a good supplier of nutrition and fiber; cereal companies have become more conscious of consumer's nutritional concerns.
- Cereal is good because it doesn't weigh you down the way heavier breakfast foods will.

- The nutritional information based on 1-ounce servings is misleading; every cereal is different; some are more filling than others; you don't always eat an ounce.
- It's good that there are so many varieties of cereal.
- You can add whatever you want to cold cereal according to taste.
- You can snack on cold cereal.
- Some people keep cereal at work and eat breakfast there.
- Cereal is an easy meal to fix for the kids.
- Crispy is to flakes; crunchy is to more substantial cereals like Cheerios.

Cereal preferences.

- Taste is most important.
- Cereal should stay crispy in milk.
- Cereal should be nutritious.

The perfect cereal.

- Tastes good
- Crispy/crunchy
- Low calorie
- High fiber
- Good nutrition

Verbatims.

- "I would like to stay healthy and live longer, and if I'm going to live longer I want to stay healthy."

Research Objective 2: To measure consumer perceptions and attitudes toward Alpha in order to match Alpha's attributes and benefits with consumer wants and needs.

Methodology: We distributed a descriptive concept test to 106 male and female, adult cereal eaters. Respondents were asked to read a detailed description of Alpha's attributes and benefits and then to answer a series of probing questions. We then analyzed responses and performed extensive correlation analysis on variables in relation to the respondent's *declared likeliness to purchase.* From this analysis we were able to key in on Alpha's strongest appeals and to identify likely prospects for the cereal.

- "Sometimes I don't eat breakfast because I don't want to lose those few extra minutes of sleep."
- "Bran is good for the colon; elimination and all that."
- "I think psychologically you just feel better because if you've had—not too much—and it's good nutrition even your mental attitude is better; eating more healthy gives you a more positive outlook."
- "Every once in a while we have bacon and eggs, but when we have to get moving in the morning, we like to have a lighter breakfast that lets you keep moving."
- "Too many Grape Nuts make you feel uncomfortable; you feel sluggish and it's hard to get moving; you feel more energetic if you're not real stuffed."

Concept test highlights.

Respondents were initially broken down into two groups: likely to purchase and unlikely to purchase.

- Likely to purchase—47.2 percent
- Unlikely to purchase—52.8 percent

Variables *positively correlated* with intent to purchase follow:

Very strong correlations.

- Good tasting—respondents who rated Alpha to be potentially good tasting on the semantic differential scale
- Fiber—respondents who valued fiber content in a cereal
- Crispiness—valued Alpha's crispiness
- Lively/exciting—respondents who rated Alpha as lively and/or exciting on the semantic differential scale
- Likely to try new products—respondents who considered themselves likely to try new products
- Favoring bananas—respondents who said they would eat Alpha with bananas

Strong correlations.

- Low calorie—respondents who valued low calorie content
- Filling—respondents who perceived Alpha as "filling" on the semantic differential scale
- Fiber cereal users—respondents who currently eat a fiber cereal
- Quality—respondents who perceived Alpha to be high quality on the semantic differential scale
- Females—likeliness to purchase was strongly correlated with the sex of respondent
- Age—as age increases

Other significant correlations. The following variables were strongly correlated with female respondents:

- Good tasting—perceived Alpha as potentially good tasting
- Fiber—value a cereal's fiber content or currently eat a fiber cereal
- Low calorie—value a cereal's low calorie content or currently eat a low calorie cereal
- Lively and exciting—perceived Alpha as lively and/or exciting
- Filling—perceived Alpha as filling

Likely to purchase group.

- 57.1 percent use lowfat milk on their cereal.
- 60.7 percent said they would eat Alpha with bananas.
- Respondents are not price conscious.

Questionnaire Highlights

To identify some of the reasons consumers are trying new cereals, we asked respondents to identify a brand of cereal they recently tasted for the first time and then asked why they decided to try that particular cereal.

- 35.5 percent tried the new cereal because they thought it would *taste good*.

Semantic Differential

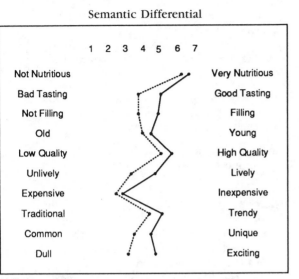

Unlikely to purchase ·····················.

Likely to purchase ——————— .

- 28.3 percent were enticed by *fiber content.*
- 17.0 percent were enticed by *natural ingredients.*
- 15.3 percent were enticed by *low calories.*
- 15.1 percent were enticed by *added fruits/nuts.*
- 11.3 percent were enticed by *crispy/crunchiness.*
- 10.8 percent tried the cereal because it was *in the house.*

The brands most frequently mentioned were

- Post Natural Bran Flakes
- Kellogg's Nut & Honey Crunch
- Kellogg's Mueslix
- Post Fruit & Fibre
- Kellogg's Cracklin' Oat Bran

When asked how they became aware of this cereal,

- 43.4 percent became aware of the brand through an *advertisement.*
- 24.5 percent said the brand was *recommended by someone* they knew.
- 9.4 percent became aware through a *coupon.*
- 5.7 percent became aware via the *cereal's box.*
- 4.0 percent became aware through an *in-store display.*
- 3.8 percent became aware through a *supermarket circular.*

The response frequencies that follow relate to the actual purchase of cereals.

Boxes purchased per month.

- 43 percent buy 1–2 boxes of cereal in a given month.
- 44 percent buy between 3–6 boxes in a month.
- —The number of boxes bought per month was strongly correlated with number of children living at home.

Research Objective 3: Examine the cereal purchase decision process in general and more specifically in relation to new product trial—from initial awareness of a new cereal to the actual purchase. Identify common practices and key influencers.

Methodology: A questionnaire was delivered to 124 adult female cereal users. The questionnaire was delivered only to females because secondary research indicates that females are primarily responsible for preparing grocery lists and collecting coupons and can therefore be considered gatekeepers with regard to cereal purchase decisions. (Cereal is one of the most likely items to appear on a grocery list—see section on grocery shopping habits.)

Boxes purchased per shopping trip.

- 45 percent average one box per shopping trip.
- 28.3 percent average two per shopping trip.
- 18.8 percent average three or more.
- —Again this was strongly correlated with presence of children.

Influencers.

- 37.7 percent of married respondents said their husband request a specific brand of cereal at least sometimes.
- 41.5 percent said their children request a specific brand of cereal often or always.

Shopping lists.

- 88.6 percent use a shopping list.
- 37.7 percent write the specific brand of cereal they want on their list.
- 50.9 percent write a generic "cereal" on their list.

Coupons.

- 32.7 percent always look for cereal coupons before shopping.
- 72 percent use coupons for cereal at least sometimes.

In-store decision making.

- 66 percent wait until they're in the store to decide on a brand at least sometimes.
- 28 percent wait until they're in the store to decide on a brand often or always.

Finding the Right Name for Alpha

With such an enormous number of brands competing for the consumer's attention, one of the greatest factors in building a successful, long-term franchise for a brand is the product name.

Taking a look at successful brands on the market, we see two common characteristics in brand names:

- They communicate key product attributes or benefits.
- They are easy to remember.

In short, a brand must shout out its identity to shoppers or risk being passed over.

Name testing. Our creative team came up with over 300 names during brainstorming sessions, and then began to narrow the field. In the end, a list containing nine of the most appealing names was used to test with members of the target market. The names tested were

> Kellogg's Fiber Crisp
>
> Kellogg's Select
>
> Kellogg's Nothin' but Fiber
>
> Kellogg's Choice Bran
>
> Kellogg's Bran Shreds
>
> Kellogg's Fiber Lite
>
> Kellogg's Lo Cal Fiber
>
> Kellogg's Fiber Free
>
> Kellogg's Rise n' Shine

Participants were given a list of these names along with a color photograph of the cereal and asked to choose the name they liked best or the name they thought best fit the product.

Kellogg's Choice Bran, Fiber Crisp, and Fiber Lite were the names that received the most positive responses. Of these choices, given the positioning opportunities for Alpha, the name that made the most marketing sense to our team was Kellogg's *Fiber Lite*. This name was well liked among respondents and conforms to the two most important criteria for choosing a successful brand name: it communicates the key attributes/benefits of the cereal, and it is easy to remember. *Fiber Lite* is a new cereal from Kellogg.

New Product Concept Statement

Fiber Lite gives the health-conscious consumer an easy and sure way to eat healthy and light by offering a high fiber bran cereal that is low in calories, fat, and cholesterol free, and is less dense than other fiber cereals on the market, so it doesn't leave you with a heavy feeling. In addition, *Fiber Lite* is packaged in single-serving stay-fresh packs that facilitate healthy and light eating by providing regulated portion size, but with an ample supply of cereal in each pack. Other benefits to the packaging are product portability and product freshness. *Fiber Lite* will come packaged in a box of ten 1.2 ounce packs and will cost the consumer $3.19.

From a marketing point of view, the unique packaging for *Fiber Lite* projects the product positioning by embodying the concept of dietary control. The consumers will benefit by achieving a sense of control over what they are eating. An article that appeared in the January 1989 issue of *Glamour* magazine best illustrates the need for this type of control. The title of the article, "Power Breakfast in a Bowl," begins with the following subtitle:

Calorie Counts, Hidden Fat:
How to Read the Label

The first paragraph reads as follows:

Box-panel calorie counts can mislead. Take granolas: Most list a harmless 130 cals/serving, but look closer. A 1-oz. "serving" is only 4 tablespoons! Most of us eat much more (resembling the bowlful on the front of the box). See chart for a more realistic tally.

The chart next to the article shows some disturbing tallies for some of the cereals *Fiber Lite* will be competing with including Fiber One, 100% Bran, Post Natural Bran Flakes,

Bran Chex, Fruit & Fibre, and Shredded Wheat. The *Glamour* article would have considered a 1-ounce serving of *Fiber Lite* to be a full bowl as they did Kellogg's Special K which is the same density as *Fiber Lite*.

The article goes on to discuss the fat content in some cereals:

Another watchword: *fat*. A cupful of some cereals—especially those with nuts and coconut—can be as high-fat as 5 bacon slices. It's often the most unhealthy kind of fat—coconut or hydrogenated oils that can clog arteries. Best bets: airy-light "puffed" cereals or flakes like corn or bran; all keep fat to a minimum.

We couldn't have said it better ourselves. Each package of *Fiber Lite* will come has only 108 calories, and contains zero fat, zero cholesterol, and *6 grams* of dietary fiber to boot. The *Glamour* article recommends cereals with at least 5 grams of fiber per cup.

How we arrived at a price for Fiber Lite.

1. Price per ounce for two, individually packaged, instant oatmeals was calculated.
2. Price per ounce for each of these brands of oatmeal in their regular bulk packaging was calculated.
3. The ratio of respective costs was recorded and the two figures were averaged to arrive at a packaging cost factor of $1.98.
4. This factor was applied to the cost per ounce of Post Natural Bran Flakes; this cereal most closely resembles *Fiber Lite* in composition.
5. The resulting price of $3.32 was reduced slightly because each pack of *Fiber Lite* will contain 20 percent more cereal than the 1-ounce oatmeal packs, thus reducing the number of individual packs required by 20 percent, or two packages per box.

TARGET MARKET SELECTION

Target Market Rationale

The target market was chosen using the following data and methods:

- Analysis of heavy and medium user data from Simmons Research (SMRB Inc.)
- Analysis of SMRB Inc. profile of regular* cereal users
- Analysis of SMRB, Inc., data on existing adult cereal brands
- Correlation analysis of concept test responses
- Evaluation of life-style/psychographic data
- An examination of health consciousness in the U.S.

Women. Both primary and secondary research indicate that women are the most likely prospects for *Fiber Lite*. In addition, the woman as the chief coupon clipper and shopping list preparer (i.e., gatekeeper), is the key individual in the cereal-purchase decision process.

Twenty-five–fifty-four year olds. SMRB, Inc., usage data and primary research show women in the upper half of this age group to be the heavy users of fiber cereals, and the lower half to be heavy users of light-eating cereals. The two halves, however, are not mutually exclusive; both are interested in dietary fiber and eating light, but no other cereal has ever offered both. The combination of the fiber and light benefits in *Fiber Lite* will appeal to the entire age group.

Health conscious. Because *Fiber Lite* is a light-eating, high-fiber cereal, it will appeal primarily to health-conscious consumers.

Achievers. *Fiber Lite* prospects are achievement oriented, whether that means

rising up the corporate ladder or simply an involvement with the community or both; the key word is *involvement. Fiber Lite* consumers are involved in keeping themselves healthy and fit.

A large segment of the target audience is comprised of the baby-boom population. These consumers are between ages 25 and 44 and are good prospects for healthful cereals. Overall cereal consumption for this age group is increasing as life-styles become more family oriented, and as adults grow more aware of the value of cereal grains in a healthy eating program. Cereal manufacturers have only recently begun to tap into this market, following a strong lead from Kellogg. The baby-boom market currently offers very high growth potential for new cereal entries that stress good health.

The 45–54 age group also represents high potential sales in the adult cereal segment, and especially the bran/fiber segment. This age group was included in the target market after consideration was given to the relative homogeneity of the two age groups. Our team found no significant differences in *attitudes or life-styles* that might influence brand preference within the *bran/fiber segment*. The target market as defined includes the best prospects for *Fiber Lite*.

Target Market Psychographics/Life-styles

The following characteristics apply to the 25–54 age group and help us to better understand the consumer as an individual.

- Active and energetic
- Health conscious
- Achievement oriented
- Enjoy a host of leisure-time activities
- Hold values that are a blend of traditional, liberal, and conservative
- Interest in family and community

*Simmons's research differentiates between regular, presweetened, and all-natural cereals.

- Enjoy buying for themselves, their homes, and for others
- Like to have choices and variety
- Wish they had the time to do all the things they want to do

COMPETITIVE ANALYSIS

Secondary Competitive Forces

- All breakfast foods eaten in the home
- All breakfast foods purchased out of the home
- All adult breakfast cereals

Primary Competitors

A brand was considered a primary competitor if it met each of the following criteria:

- The brand makes high-fiber claims on its box or in advertising.
- The brand is backed by substantial advertising expenditures.

A competitive spending analysis was made using *Adcomp* computer analysis of BAR/LNA data from 1985–87. The analysis included all primary competitors with media expenditure listings in BAR/LNA.

Analysis of Competitive Brands

Brand name	Price/oz.	Calories/oz.	Cups/oz.	Fiber	Fat	Sugar	Protein	Price/box
Post Grape Nuts Flakes	18¢	100	.88	2	1	5	3	$2.15
GM Raisin Nut Bran	19¢	110	.5	3	3	8	3	$2.59
GM Clusters	21¢	100	.5	3	3	7	3	$2.75
Post Natural Bran Flakes	14¢	90	.66	5	0	NA	3	$2.25
GM Fiber One	15¢	60	.5	13	1	1	2	$2.05
Post Fruit & Fibre	19¢	90	.5	5	1	4	3	$2.69
Post Oat Flakes	20¢	110	.66	2	1	6	5	$2.45
Ralston Bran News	18¢	100	.75	3	1	9	2	$2.65
Kellogg All Bran	14¢	70	.33	10	1	5	4	$2.49
Nabisco Shredded Wheat	15¢	110	.66	3	1	0	2	$2.29
Nabisco 100% Bran	14¢	70	.5	10	2	6	3	$2.25
Quaker Crunchy Bran	17¢	90	NA	5	1	6	2	$2.75
Kellogg Fiber Lite	**26¢**	**90**	**1**	**5**	**0**	**3**	**3**	**$3.19**
Fiber Lite/1.2 oz. packs	32¢	108	1.2	6	0	3.6	3.6	$3.19

Profile of Top Spenders

Post Fruit & Fibre*

Total Media Budget		Media Mix 1987	
1985	$17.2 (million)	Network TV	65.1%
1986	$15.3	Spot TV	3.1%
1987	$14.5	Cable TV	3.1%
		Magazines	21.9%
Share of Voice		Net Radio	6.8%
Network TV	24.4%		
Spot TV	9.7%		
Cable TV	34.9%		
Magazines	80.4%		
Total SOV:	29.2%		

Fruit & Fibre has decreased total spending by 20 percent over the last two years. The media budget supports four Fruit & Fibre varieties. Magazines, Network TV, and Cable TV have been receiving increased weight, while Spot TV spending has decreased from 13.6 percent of total budget in 1986 to 3.1 percent in 1987. In 1988, the brand had magazine insertions in *Cooking Light, Country Living, Food & Wine, Good Food, Good Housekeeping, Health, Ladies Home Journal, McCalls,* and *People.* Only *Good Food* carried full-page ads (three insertions). Judging from magazine selection, the media strategy seems to be less good-health oriented and more good-eating oriented.

General Mills Raisin Nut Bran

Total Media Budget		Media Mix 1987	
1985	NA	Network TV	69.0%
1986	$8.8 (million)	Spot TV	26.8%
1987	$8.2	Cable TV	4.2

Share of Voice	
Network TV	14.5%
Spot TV	47.1%
Cable TV	27.0%
Total SOV:	16.5%

*SOV versus seven competitors analyzed.

As a new product, Raisin Nut Bran has dropped print and decreased Spot in 1987, while increasing both Network and Cable TV spending.

General Mills Clusters

Total Media Budget		Media Mix 1987	
1985	NA	Network TV	85.5%
1986	NA	Spot TV	13.7%
1987	$4.8 (million)	Cable TV	0.8%

Share of Voice	
Network TV	10.5%
Spot TV	14.0%
Cable TV	2.9%
Total SOV:	9.6%

General Mills Fiber One

Total Media Budget		Media Mix 1987	
1985	$6.8 (million)	Network TV	76.8%
1986	$5.1	Spot TV	2.9%
1987	$4.4	Cable TV	2.9%
		Magazines	17.4%

Share of Voice	
Network TV	8.8%
Spot TV	2.8%
Cable TV	9.9%
Magazines	19.6%
Total SOV:	17.4%

In 1986, Fiber One kicked almost its entire Spot TV and Magazine budget into Network TV. In 1987 the Magazine budget was restored, while the Spot budget remained low. Fiber One had Magazine insertions in *Modern Maturity, Prevention,* and *Reader's Digest. Reader's Digest* received the most weight (ten insertions). *Modern Maturity* was second with four insertions. Magazine strategy reflects the older market such extra high fiber cereals appeal to.

Post Natural Bran Flakes

Total Media Budget	Media Mix 1987	
1985 $2.0 (million)	Network TV	92.1%
1986 $2.7	Spot TV	4.8%
1987 $4.2	Cable TV	3.1%

Share of Voice

Network TV	10.0%
Spot TV	4.3%
Cable TV	10.1%
Total SOV:	8.4%

In 1987, Post Bran Flakes threw almost its entire budget into Network TV. In 1985 and 1986, the brand spent 88 percent of its budget in print vehicles, including, in 1985, Newspaper Supplements (11%). In 1987, the brand began advertising on Cable TV.

Kellogg's All-Bran

Total Media Budget	Media Mix 1987	
1985 $11.2 (million)	Network TV	92.2%
1986 $14.9	Spot TV	6.4%
1987 $9.4	Cable TV	1.4%

Share of Voice

Network TV	22.2%
Spot TV	12.9%
Cable TV	10.2%
Total SOV:	18.8%

Spending for All-Bran has remained consistent over the last three years with the bulk (90%) going to Network TV in each year.

PROBLEMS AND RECOMMENDATIONS

Problem: The RTE cereal category is highly competitive; new products must have a unique and meaningful positioning to be successful.

Recommendation: Do not position *Fiber Lite* head to head with established brands; position *Fiber Lite* to meet a currently unmet consumer need.

Problem: Brand loyalty in the RTE cereal market is very low.

Recommendation: Establish *Fiber Lite* as an *integral* part of a healthy life-style.

Problem: Oat bran cereals currently dominate the bran cereal market.

Recommendation: Promise the consumer a benefit that oat bran cereals either cannot offer or do not currently offer, to differentiate *Fiber Lite* from these cereals.

Problem: Myriad brands in the cereal category and frequent new product introductions limit the impact of new product introductions in general.

Recommendation: Back the launching of *Fiber Lite* with a strong, single-minded selling message and a marketing program that creates excitement for the product.

Problem: Store shelves overcrowded with cereals confuse and overwhelm consumers and may obscure a new product.

Recommendation: Create a unique and distinctive package that will turn consumer confusion to our advantage.

OPPORTUNITIES

Opportunity: Take advantage of consumer interest in dietary fiber and light eating as two important components of healthy eating.

Recommendation: Position *Fiber Lite* as a cereal for people who want to eat lightly and get more fiber in their diet.

Opportunity: *Fiber Lite* is a perfect cereal for dieters who worry about healthy eating while dieting.

Recommendation: Present *Fiber Lite* as a way to eat lightly without sacrificing good nutrition.

Opportunity: *Fiber Lite* is an especially crispy cereal, a strong consumer benefit.

Recommendation: Use crispiness to enhance *Fiber Lite's* taste appeal.

Opportunity: Take advantage of special packaging opportunities that will complement and enhance *Fiber Lite's* selling message.

Recommendation: Package *Fiber Lite* in individual serving, stay-fresh packs which help the consumer by regulating portion size, providing portability, and preserving product freshness.

Opportunity: Capitalize on Kellogg's high-quality image and good-health reputation.

Recommendation: Articulate the Kellogg name and quality image in all promotional activity, and reinforce the association of Kellogg with healthy eating.

MARKETING RECOMMENDATIONS

Marketing Objectives

Introductory year.

- To gain a .5 percent share of the RTE cereal market (lbs./volume) by the end of the introductory year
- To differentiate *Fiber Lite* from all other cereals on the market
- To concentrate all marketing efforts on a strong, single-minded selling message
- To combat low brand loyalty
- To present *Fiber Lite* as a high-quality, tasty product for health-conscious consumers

Long-term objectives.

- To continue building market share for *Fiber Lite* with a share goal of .8 percent at the end of the second year
- To encourage brand loyalty among users
- To generate trial among prospects who have not yet sampled *Fiber Lite*

Marketing Strategies

Introductory year.

- Use advertising, sales, and trade promotion techniques to present the target consumer with a strong, single-minded selling message which will drive them to a trial purchase.
- Position *Fiber Lite* as a high-fiber, light cereal for people who are health conscious.
- Package *Fiber Lite* in ten individual serving packets to facilitate a healthy eating program.
- Present *Fiber Lite* as an integral part of a healthy eating program to encourage brand loyalty.
- Always present *Fiber Lite* in an appetizing way, with colorful fruits and/or as part of a balanced breakfast.

Long-Term Strategies

- Continue to emphasize *Fiber Lite's* role in a healthy eating *program* as a means of encouraging brand loyalty.
- Consider new varieties of *Fiber Lite* to entice both current users and prospects.
- Consider tie-ins or with complimentary organizations, such as *Jack La Lanne, Weight Watchers,* and the *National Cancer Institute,* which are associated with the healthy life-styles of our target audience.

ADVERTISING RECOMMENDATIONS

Understanding the Brand

Attributes:

- Tasty wheat bran
- High fiber
- Low in calories—90 per ounce
- Zero fat
- Zero cholesterol
- Less dense than most cereals, so you get more for less
- Low sugar
- Stays crisp in milk
- Comes in single serving, stay fresh packs

Benefits:
Fiber Lite will help me to eat light and to get a good supply of dietary fiber; eating *Fiber Lite* will help me feel good about myself.

Values:
I want to stay healthy and look better; I want to feel good about myself—emotionally and physically.

Product Personality:
Smart, successful, busy, confident, physically fit, naturally healthy—not fanatically healthy.

Brand Essence:
Fiber Lite helps you feel good about yourself.

Communication objective.

- To build awareness among our target audience of *Fiber Lite's* unique offering of high fiber in a light cereal that is packaged to facilitate a healthy eating program.

Communication strategy.

- To convince the target audience that *Fiber Lite* is the only high-fiber, light-eating cereal, packaged in individual packs that offer regulation of portion size, while providing an ample amount of cereal.

Copy Platform

Positioning:

Fiber Lite is a high-fiber, light cereal for adults who know that good health is essential to feeling good about yourself.

Objective:

To introduce a new cereal for health-conscious consumers

Source of Business:

Competitors in the bran/fiber segment

Target Audience:

- Women
- Age 25–54
- Health conscious
- Achievers

U.S.P.:

Fiber Lite gives you high fiber in a lower-calorie, no-fat/cholesterol cereal that is packaged to facilitate a healthy eating program.

Strategic Support:

- *Fiber Lite* has 5 grams of dietary fiber per ounce.
- *Fiber Lite* has only 90 calories per ounce.
- *Fiber Lite* has no fat/cholesterol content.

- *Fiber Lite* is less dense than most cereals— 1 cup per ounce.
- *Fiber Lite* is packaged in single serving packs that regulate portion size, but also supply an ample amount of cereal.

Other Features:

- Packs are stay-fresh.
- Packs provide product portability.
- *Fiber Lite* is low in sugar.
- *Fiber Lite* stays crisp in milk.

Tonality:
Introductory, light, sincere

Brand Essence:
Fiber Lite helps you feel good about yourself.

SALES PROMOTION

Primary Research: Interviews with Store Managers

We conducted interviews with three grocery store managers to better understand the relationship sales rep and store manager, and to identify any problems or opportunities with regard to sales promotion activities. The participating chains were A & P, Grand Union, and Food Emporium.

Key Findings

- Shelf location and number of facings can often be negotiated through store managers. In many of the chains, however, this negotiation takes place only through the chain's headquarters.
- Sales reps can negotiate with store managers to gain cooperation for certain in-store promotional activities, such as end aisle displays or in-store sampling.
- Successful negotiation with sales managers requires that a good rapport be established

BUDGET RECOMMENDATIONS · Three-Year Payout Plan

	1990	1991	1992	Totals
Size of total mkt.	2,620,000,000	2,700,000,000	2,790,000,000	
Year-end mkt. share for				
Fiber Lite	0.5%	0.8%	1.0%	
Units sold (12 oz. boxes)	17,466,667	28,800,000	37,200,000	
Total income	$47,750,897	$78,734,304	$101,698,476	$228,183,677
Less cost of goods*				
Fixed	$6,159,866	$10,156,725	$13,119,103	$29,435,694
Variable	$17,620,081	$29,052,958	$37,526,738	$84,199,777
Total	$23,779,947	$39,209,683	$50,645,841	$113,635,471
Administrative expenses				
Dist. & delivery	$2,578,548	$4,251,652	$5,491,718	$12,321,919
General administrative	$1,910,036	$3,149,372	$4,067,939	$9,127,347
Sales force	$1,671,281	$2,755,701	$3,559,447	$7,986,429
Market research	$238,754	$393,672	$508,492	$1,140,918
Total	$6,398,620	$10,550,397	$13,627,596	$30,576,613
$ avail. for promotion & profit	$17,572,330	$28,974,224	$37,425,039	$83,971,593
Reallocation of budget weight	$36,107,785	$28,550,342	$19,313,466	
% of reallocated budget	43%	34%	23%	100%
Advertising	$15,165,270	$11,991,144	$8,111,656	$35,268,069
Consumer promotion	$10,471,258	$8,279,599	$5,600,905	$24,351,762
Trade promotion	$10,471,258	$8,279,599	$5,600,905	$24,351,762
Total	$36,107,785	$28,550,342	$19,313,466	$83,971,593
Profit or loss	($18,535,455)	$423,882	$18,111,573	
Cumulative investment	($18,535,455)	($18,111,573)	($0)	
Advertising/sales ratio	76%	36%	19%	

Payout plan variables

Allocation to media	42%
Allocation to consumer promotion	29%
Allocation to trade promotion	29%
Retail price/12 oz. box	$3.19
Gross margin at retail	14.3%
Cost/box wholesale	$2.73

SOURCE (for cost of goods and operating expense percentages): Phillip Kotler, *Marketing Management,* 6th ed. (New York: Prentice Hall, 1988); (for retail gross profit margin for cereals): *Supermarket Business,* September 1988. Note: Of the $9 million plus to be spent on trade promotion, $8,835,212 is for case allowances alone—20 percent of case cost; these are standard introductory allowances.

between rep and manager. This translates into a "one hand washes the other" situation. For example, a rep may offer a store manager "1 on 10" in exchange for a special display; meaning that one case for every ten ordered will be free goods in exchange for cooperation in setting up a display. The display moves more product and the free goods increases the store manager's profit margin.

- End-aisle displays require extra promotional activity by the manufacturer. The store manager must be convinced that consumers will be looking for the product. A substantive couponing effort in conjunction with heavy advertising support is usually sufficient.

- New products are usually cased with twelve boxes. Large chains do not keep cereal in inventory, so cases move directly from truck to shelf. Only through special negotiation will a store take a twenty-four-box cases of a new product. *Fiber Lite* will be shipped in 12-box cases to make sell-in as easy as possible.

Assumption. To provide reasonable cost estimates for the sales promotion plan, eleven sales districts have been assumed, each with 100 sales reps.

Trade promotion

Objectives.
- Obtain 80 percent All Commodity Volume (ACV) by end of the introductory year.
- Motivate the sales force to sell *Fiber Lite* as a priority over other brands.

Strategies.
- Provide incentives for retailers to order and stock *Fiber Lite*.
- Provide comprehensive, informative, and interesting sales kits to effectively communicate the sales potential of *Fiber Lite*.
- Sponsor a sales rep contest.

Tactics.
- A standard new listing case allowance of 20 percent per case will be provided to retailers as an initial incentive to stock *Fiber Lite*. Retailers will be asked to cooperate in the Kellogg Special Participation Program, providing in exchange for this liberal allowance *at least* one of the following considerations:
  - Take shipment of two 12-box cases and provide a double-shelf facing.
  - Provide an eye level shelf location with a shelf talker.
  - Maintain an end-aisle display.
  - Maintain a floor stand display.

Implementation of any of these options would provide *Fiber Lite* with an impressive and attention-getting in-store presence.

- Special sales kits will be created resembling an actual *Fiber Lite* cereal box, hinged to open forward like a cigar box. Inside the box will be ten actual packets of *Fiber Lite* cereal—each printed with an exiting reason why *Fiber Lite* will increase profits, and be *the* most talked-about product of 1990. The sales kit will also include a complete promotional flowchart emphasizing the support Kellogg will be providing to keep the product moving fast.
- Recognizing the importance of personal selling in achieving our target ACV levels, Kellogg will sponsor contest for sales reps to keep them focused on *Fiber Lite* in the introductory year. In each of the eleven sales districts Kellogg will sponsor a holiday week for two in a resort area, total trip valued at $5,000. Winners will be selected based upon points accrued under the following sample rating system:
  - For each major retailer adding *Fiber Lite* to its Plan-O-Gram, 50–100 points, depending on All Commodity Volume (ACV) of retailer.
  - *Fiber Lite* sold in to a wholesaler, 10–20 points, depending on ACV.
  - All points awards subject to bonuses based upon retailer/wholesaler

cooperation with the Kellogg Special Participation Program.

Consumer promotion

Objectives.
- Gain awareness among target market within the first twelve weeks of the product shelf life.
- Encourage product trial among target consumers.
- Reenforce product positioning among target consumers.
- Encourage repurchase.

Strategies/Rationales.
- Initiate and maintain a strong brand presence at the point of purchase.
- Use a combination of coupons and discount vehicles to reduce the cost of trial.
- Develop a series of cross-ruff promotions with other products that directly reinforce *Fiber Lite*, a leading part of a healthy breakfast.
- Print a cents-off coupon for the next purchase of *Fiber Lite* on one of the ten inside packets.

Tactics.
1. *Point-of-Purchase.* One of the most positive ways of encouraging brand trial at the store level is through an organized sampling effort. Some of the key reasons for this technique's success are

- Immediate product velocity—Sales of product in sampling targeted stores have been known to increase up to 38 percent.
- Reaches key consumers—Research shows that 43 percent of redemptions of sampling-distributed coupons are by brand switcher or trial users.
- Store manager support—Personal interviews with store managers showed they considered the "event" atmosphere of a sampling program to help business throughout the store.

2. *Coupon Efforts*

- A substantial "free box" coupon will be placed in the May edition of selected national women's magazines, specially chosen to target innovators and opinion leaders in the target market.
- Seventy-five cents off introductory offer to be dropped once in Quad/Marketing Sunday supplements in the thirteenth week of the year.
- In-pack coupon printed on one of the ten *Fiber Lite* individual packets throughout the introductory period.
- Fifty cents off coupon in Quad/Marketing Sunday supplements as a continuing effort to encourage purchase.

3. *Trade Budget*

Case allowances
$9,536,800

Trade promotion kits
11 Sales Districts
100 Reps/District

1100 Kits
+ 200 contingency

1300 Kits
× $9.00

$11,700

Sales rep contest
$5,000/District
× 11 Districts

$55,000

Special Participation Program
Shelf talkers
2000 @ $3.50 = $7,000
Free-standing displays
1000 @ $9.00 = $9,000

$16,000

Media budget/trade magazines
$852,658

Total trade budget
$9,618,600

4. *Consumer Promotion*

Free box promotion
Total coupons circulated
16,220,000
Coupon value = 1 free box
$3.19
Redemption rate = 6%
973,200
× $3.19
$3,104,508

1st FSI drop 75¢
Cost of placement
$341,604
Fulfillment
50,000,000 × 5% redemption = $1,875,000
$2.216,604

In-store sampling
Top 100 stores/11 districts
2 days of sampling @ $250
$550,000
Supplies for sampling
$168,960
$718,960

2nd FSI drop 50¢
Cost of placement
$341,604
Fulfillment
50,000,000 × 5% redemption
$1,250,000
$1,591,604

3rd FSI 35¢
Cost of placement
$341,604
Fulfillment
50,000,000 × 5% redemption
$875,000
$1,216,604

In-pack coupon 35¢
18,000,000 coupons circulated
25% redemption rate
$1,575,000

MEDIA RECOMMENDATIONS

Business Goal
To gain a .5% share of the ready to eat market in the introductory year.

Competitive Situation
Fiber Lite will be competing in the bran/fiber segment, specifically, and in the adult cereal segment, in general. The vast number of brands in the cereal category create advertising clutter that *Fiber Lite* must compete against.

Media Budget
The 1990 *Fiber Lite* media plan budget is $15,165,270.

Target Audience
Objective.

- To reach women age 25–54 who are health conscious and achievement oriented.

Strategy/Rationale.

- Use media that will efficiently provide high coverage of the target audience.

Geographics
Objective.

- Support the *national* roll-out of *Fiber Lite*.

Strategy/Rationale.

- Utilize only national media.

With no regional skews and no BDI/CDI information, the focus will be on national media until brand and market information is available.

Scheduling/Communication
Objectives.

- Schedule media to begin after reaching 50 percent All Commodity Volume (ACV); the start-ship date is January 1, 1990.
- Front-load the media plan to create early awareness and trial.
- Reach and continuity are priorities.
- Support key promotions.
- Evaluate plan at the 3+ frequency level.

Strategy/Rationale.

- Schedule media beginning April 1, 1990.
- Generate high-reach levels early by heavying up in the first twenty-six weeks with heaviest spending in the first twelve weeks.
- Maintain continuity using a pulsing schedule.

We are assuming that ACV will have reached 50 percent three months after the start-ship date (target distribution levels provided by Kellogg are 80% ACV). Getting high-trial levels early will encourage retailers to feature *Fiber Lite* in their stores. A pulsing schedule will provide continuity and allow heavying-up in the key introductory period.

Creative
:30s Spots
1 page, 4/c print

Media Plan Highlights

With a budget of $15,165,270 the plan uses the following media:

- National Primetime
  - 28 weeks/31–44 W25–54 GRPs per week
- National Daytime
  - 29 weeks/29–40 W25–54 GRPs per week
- Cable TV
  - 30 weeks/5–6 GRPs per week—Lifetime Network Programming
- National Magazines
  - 39 weeks/376 GRPs (total schedule)

MARKETING ACTIVITY FLOWCHART

	JAN	FEB	MAR	APR	MAY	JUN	JUL	AUG	SEPT	OCT	NOV	DEC
Advertising												
Supermarket Business												
Food & Beverage Marketing												
Progressive Grocer												
Supermarket News												
Consumer Promotion												
Sampling												
Free Box												
50¢ FSI												
35¢ FSI												
35¢ In-Pack												
Package Promotion												
Rep Contest												
Rep Kits												
S.P. Program												

TOTAL COST

Tactics/Rationale

National Prime

       28 weeks   – Builds reach
    $10,336,648   – Quality programming
  68% of budget   – Showcase for new creative
                        – Low clutter

Primetime extends reach levels beyond that of any other daypart and reaches a different type of viewer, one that cannot be reached through Daytime TV. Prime generates unparalleled impact through a quality environment that attracts highly attentive viewers. Finally, Prime is a highly effective trade tool for the Kellogg sales force.

National Day

      29 weeks   – High composition of target
                          audience
   $2,584,162   – Cost efficient
  17% of budget   – Builds frequency and continuity
                        – Good reminder medium

Cable TV

      30 weeks   – Reach selective audiences
    $409,462   – Programming compliments
                         product
 2.7% of budget

The specific programming offered on the *Lifetime Network* makes cable a highly targeted medium and a great opportunity for *Fiber Lite*.

Vehicles

                       Woman Watch
                       It Figures
                       Attitudes
                       Cagney & Lacey
                       Regis Philbin
                       Mothers Day

National Magazines

      39 weeks   – Reach selective audiences
   $1,828,925   – Complimentary editorial
 12.1% of budget   – Long life

Magazines provide heavy-up support in the key introductory period and continuity throughout the year.

Vehicles

Family oriented	*Health oriented*	*Image oriented*
Family Circle	Prevention	Self
Parents	American Health	Working Woman
Working Mother	Shape	New Woman
	Cooking Light	Redbook
	Health	People
	Weight Watchers	

Specific magazines were selected on the basis of delivery versus the target audience and with consideration given to editorial environment. The editorial styles of the chosen magazines reflect the "achiever" qualities of the target audience for both working and nonworking women. A special emphasis was placed on health and fitness magazines. Care was taken not to place simultaneous insertions in magazines where duplication is likely to be high.

1. How likely would you be to buy this cereal if it were on the market?
   Very unlikely   1   2   3   4   5   6   Very likely

2. How confident are you about your answer in question 1?
   Unsure   1   2   3   4   5   6   Confident

3. How different is this cereal from other cereals on the market?

Very different	Somewhat different	Not too different	Not at all different
____	____	____	____

4. Why do you say that?
   _____

5. What, if anything, do you particularly like about the cereal you just read about?
   _____

6 What else?
   _____

7. What, if anything, do you particularly dislike about it?
   _____

8. What, if anything, would you like to see changed?
   _____

9. If you decided to try this cereal, how would you eat it?

with low fat milk ☐		with strawberries ☐	
with whole milk ☐		with banana ☐	
without milk ☐		with raisins ☐	
plain ☐		with dates ☐	
with sugar ☐		with prunes ☐	
with blueberries ☐		Other _____	

10. Based on what you read, please indicate your feelings about this cereal.
    (Mark appropriate box with an "x.")

Not nutritious	☐	☐	☐	☐	☐	☐	☐	Nutritious
Good tasting	☐	☐	☐	☐	☐	☐	☐	Bad tasting
Filling	☐	☐	☐	☐	☐	☐	☐	Not filling
Young	☐	☐	☐	☐	☐	☐	☐	Old
Low quality	☐	☐	☐	☐	☐	☐	☐	High quality
Lively	☐	☐	☐	☐	☐	☐	☐	Unlively
Expensive	☐	☐	☐	☐	☐	☐	☐	Inexpensive
Traditional	☐	☐	☐	☐	☐	☐	☐	Trendy
Common	☐	☐	☐	☐	☐	☐	☐	Unique
Exciting	☐	☐	☐	☐	☐	☐	☐	Dull

11. Why do you eat cold cereal for breakfast? Please rate each of the following reasons on a scale of 1 to 5, with "5" being very important and "1" being not important at all. You may use any number between 1 and 5.

    Taste . . . . ———
    Fiber . . . . ———
    Low in Calories . . . . ———
    Nutrition
      (Apart from calories or fiber) . . . . ———
    Low cost . . . . ———
    Ease of preparation . . . . ———
    Satisfies hunger . . . . ———

12. Which cold cereal do you eat most often for breakfast? (If you eat two or more brands equally, select the brand you ate most recently.)

    _____

13. Why do you usually eat *that cereal?* Again on a scale of 1 to 5, with 5 being very important and 1 being not important at all, please rate each of the following:

    Taste . . . . ———
    Fiber . . . . ———
    Low in Calories . . . . ———
    Nutrition
      (Apart from calories or fiber) . . . . ———
    Other members of household like it . . . . ———
    Low cost . . . . ———
    Says crisp . . . . ———
    Satisfies hunger . . . . ———

14. Is there any other cold breakfast cereal you eat regularly?

    _____

15. Why do you eat *this cereal?* Again, rate each of the following on a scale of 1–5.

    Taste . . . . ———
    Fiber . . . . ———
    Low in Calories . . . . ———
    Nutrition
      (Apart from calories or fiber) . . . . ———

Other members of household like it . . . . ____
Low cost. . . . . ____
Stays crisp . . . . ____
Satisfies hunger . . . . ____

16. How likely are you to try new products? (Circle one)
    Very likely   5   4   3   2   1   Very unlikely

17. Are you
    ☐ Male ☐ Female
    ☐ Married   ☐ Single   ☐ Divorced/Widowed/Separated

18. How many children, if any, do you have living at home?
    ☐ None ☐ 1 ☐ 2 ☐ 3 ☐ 4 ☐ 5 or more

19. Are you employed
    ☐ Full-time   ☐ Part-time   ☐ Not employed

20. What is your total household income?
    ☐ Under $20,000   ☐ $20,000–$29,999   ☐ $30,000–$39,999
    ☐ $40,000–$49,999   ☐ $50,000 or more

21. What is your age range?
    ☐ 18–24 ☐ 25–34 ☐ 35–44 ☐ 45–54 ☐ 55–64 ☐ 65+

22. About how many bowls of cereal were eaten by your household in the last 7 days?
    ☐ 15 or more ☐ 10–14 ☐ 5–9 ☐ 3–4 ☐ 1–2 ☐ None

Thank you very much for your time!

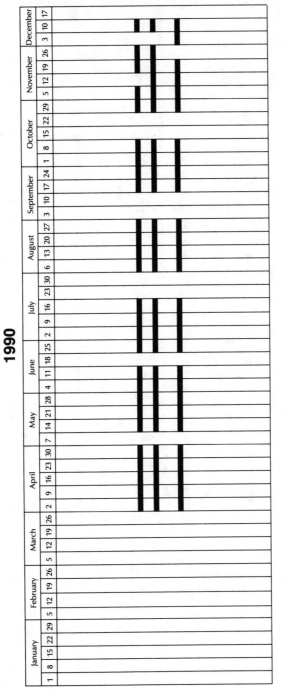

Kellogg's
TELEVISION

1990

	January				February				March				April				May				June				July				August				September				October				November				December		
	1	8	15	22	29	5	12	19	26	5	12	19	26	2	9	16	23	30	7	14	21	28	4	11	18	25	2	9	16	23	30	6	13	20	27	3	10	17	24	1	8	15	22	29	5	12	19	26	3	10	17

NETWORK TV

Primetime

Daytime

CABLE TV

Summary Evaluation	**Unweighted**	**Weighted**
Reach (1+)	99.20%	97.32%
Effective Reach (3+)	95.65%	89.93%
Average Frequency	18.30	14.92
Gross Rating Points	1,815.00	1,452.00
Gross Impressions (000)	875,211.14	700,168.90
CPM/Gross Impressions	$12.10	$15.12
Cost Per Rating Point	$5,833.95	$7,292.44

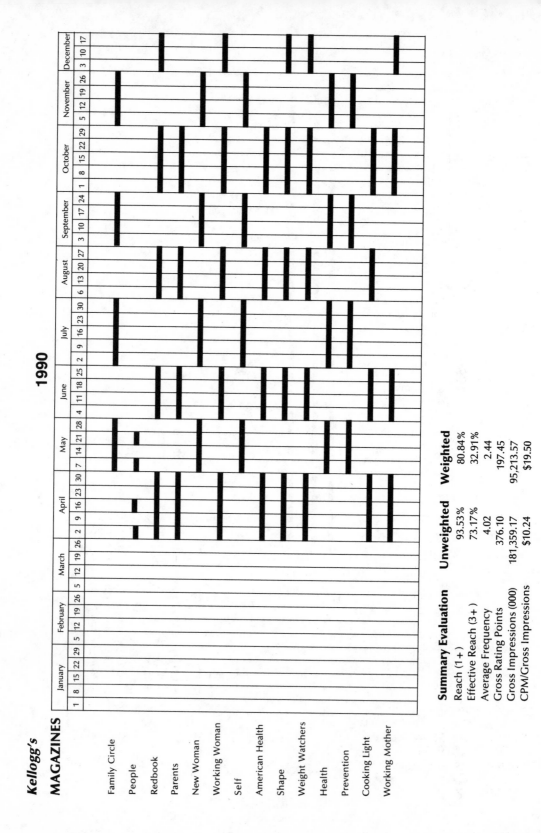

Kellogg's

MAGAZINES

1990

	January				February				March			April				May				June				July				August			September				October				November				December		

Magazines (rows): Family Circle, People, Redbook, Parents, New Woman, Working Woman, Self, American Health, Shape, Weight Watchers, Health, Prevention, Cooking Light, Working Mother

Summary Evaluation	**Unweighted**	**Weighted**
Reach (1+)	93.53%	80.84%
Effective Reach (3+)	73.17%	32.91%
Average Frequency	4.02	2.44
Gross Rating Points	376.10	197.45
Gross Impressions (000)	181,359.17	95,213.57
CPM/Gross Impressions	$10.24	$19.50

BIBLIOGRAPHY

Food & Beverage Marketing, January 1988, "Bringing mail-order to cereal boxes," p. 22

Food & Beverage Marketing, November 1987, "Cereal bears adult image," p. 47

Supermarket Business, September 1987, "Consumer expenditures study; CEREAL," pp. 155, 156

Supermarket Business, June 1987, "New cold cereal products continue to play up the 'fruit' connection," p. 75

Chilton's Food Engineering, June 1987, "Breakfast cereals," p. 85

"Cereals put snap crackle pop into battle," *Grocery Marketing,* July 1988, p. 27

International Journal of Advertising, V. 4, No. 4, 1985, pp. 305–18

"Manufacturer tries new category" (Mueslix), *Marketing News,* September 1987

"Creativity in advertising," *Journal of Advertising,* 1986, V.15 (4), pp. 43–50

"Sugar shame" (marketing cereals to adults), *American Demographics,* December 1987, p. 25

"Fancy is as Fancy does" (packaging), *Time,* July 27, 1987, p. 70

"Brand perception and preference," *Journal of Consumer Research,* December 1986, p. 382ff.

"Regulating health claims," *Currents,* January–February, 1987, p. 7ff.

Fortune, August 29, 1988, "How King Kellogg beat the blahs," pp. 54–64

Prepared Foods, July 1988, "General Foods," p. 26

Marketing & Media Decisions, March 1988, "Crunching the competition," pp. 70–75

Marketing & Media Decisions, April 1987, "Brand report: BRANTASTIC," pp. 93–109

Supermarket News, February 1, 1988, "Bran cereal's healthy boom," pp. 15, 16

Supermarket News, June 29, 1987, "High-fiber types swelling sales of cold cereal," pp. 22, 28

Progressive Grocer, September 1987, "Breakfast foods," p. 122

Progressive Grocer, July 1987, "A cereal for every bowl," pp. 65, 66

Progressive Grocer, September 1987, "Product usage profiles" (1987 Guide), p. 96ff.

Business Week Industrial Edition, March 30, 1987, "The health craze has Kellogg feeling G-R-R-Reat," pp. 52, 53

Crain's Chicago Business, March 15, 1987, "Quaker puts familiar face on new cold cereal," p. 8

Milling & Baking News, March 3, 1987, "Fiber Pack contains six high-fiber cereals from Kellogg," p. 56

Marketing Communications, December 1986, "State of the market: Breakfast foods," p. 40, 42ff.

Food Engineering, June 1988, "Kellogg kicks off cholesterol-screening campaign for consumers," pp. 13–14

Advertising Age Articles

7/25/88: "Kellogg pours out more new cereals," pp. 2, 66

5/9/88: "Cereal giants X-cited," p. 8

5/2/88: "Reveille for raisins," p. 78

2/1/88: "Ralston aims Dinersaurs at children's cereal market," p. 66

1/26/88: "Kellogg exercises health claims," p. 72

9/7/87: "Kellogg opens superpremium niche for cereal," pp. 3, 55

7/6/87: "General Mills adds Clusters," pp. 3, 30

4/27/87: "Nabisco warms to cold cereals," p. 3

4/6/87: "Other late news: General Foods," p. 8

3/16/87: "General Mills raises adult cereal stakes," p. 4

7/17/86: "Adults lead cereal boom," p. 54

7/7/86: "Kelloggs bran-ching out with new cereal," p. 40

Index